CRIMINAL LAW

FIFTH EDITION

Other books in the *Essentials of Canadian Law* Series
Immigration Law
International Trade Law
Family Law
Copyright Law
The Law of Equitable Remedies
The Law of Sentencing
Administrative Law
Ethics and Canadian Criminal Law
Securities Law
Computer Law 2/e
Maritime Law
Insurance Law
International Human Rights Law
The Law of Trusts 2/e
Franchise Law
Personal Property Security Law
The Law of Contracts
Pension Law
Constitutional Law 3/e
Legal Ethics and Professional Responsibility 2/e
Refugee Law
Bank and Customer Law in Canada
Statutory Interpretation 2/e
National Security Law: Canadian Practice in International Perspective
Remedies: The Law of Damages 2/e
Public International Law 2/e
Individual Employment Law 2/e
Environmental Law 3/e
Bankruptcy and Insolvency Law
The Law of Partnerships and Corporations 3/e
The Charter of Rights and Freedoms 4/e
Youth Criminal Justice Law 2/e
Civil Litigation
International and Transnational Criminal Law
Conflict of Laws
Detention and Arrest
Canadian Telecommunications Law
The Law of Torts 4/e
Intellectual Property Law 2/e
The Law of Evidence 6/e
Animals and the Law
Income Tax Law 2/e
Fundamental Justice
Mergers, Acquisitions, and Other Measures of Corporate Control 2/e
Criminal Procedure 2/e

ESSENTIALS OF
CANADIAN LAW

CRIMINAL LAW

FIFTH EDITION

KENT ROACH

Faculty of Law and Centre of Criminology
University of Toronto

Criminal Law, fifth edition
© Irwin Law Inc., 2012

Published in 2012 by

Irwin Law Inc.
14 Duncan Street
Suite 206
Toronto, ON
M5H 3G8

www.irwinlaw.com

ISBN: 978-1-55221-301-8
e-book ISBN: 978-1-55221-302-5

Cataloguing in Publication data available from Library and Archives Canada

The publisher acknowledges the financial support of the Government of Canada through the Canada Book Fund for its publishing activities.

We acknowledge the assistance of the OMDC Book Fund, an initiative of Ontario Media Development Corporation.

Printed and bound in Canada.

2 3 4 5   16 15 14 13

SUMMARY
TABLE OF CONTENTS

FOREWORD   *xxi*

PREFACE   *xxiii*

CHAPTER   1:   Overview   *1*

CHAPTER   2:   The Criminal Law and the Constitution   *24*

CHAPTER   3:   The Prohibited Act, Or *Actus Reus*   *81*

CHAPTER   4:   Unfulfilled Crimes and Participation in Crimes   *124*

CHAPTER   5:   The Fault Element, or *Mens Rea*   *163*

CHAPTER   6:   Regulatory Offences and Corporate Crime   *213*

CHAPTER   7:   Intoxication   *246*

CHAPTER   8:   Mental Disorder and Automatism   *279*

CHAPTER   9:   Self-Defence, Necessity, and Duress   *317*

CHAPTER   10:   The Special Part: Homicide, Sexual, Property, and Terrorism Offences   *382*

CHAPTER   11:   Sentencing   *469*

CHAPTER   12:   Conclusion   *496*

GLOSSARY   *517*

TABLE OF CASES   *523*

INDEX   *555*

ABOUT THE AUTHOR   *561*

DETAILED
TABLE OF CONTENTS

FOREWORD *xxi*

PREFACE *xxiii*

CHAPTER 1:
OVERVIEW *1*

A. Crime in Canada *1*

B. The Criminal Process *3*

C. Sources of Criminal Law *5*

D. Criminal Offences *5*

E. Regulatory Offences *6*

F. The Criminal Law and the Constitution *6*

G. Substantive Fairness *7*

H. Procedural Fairness *8*

I. The Elements of Criminal Offences *9*

J. The Prohibited Act, or *Actus Reus* *10*

K. Attempts and Other Unfulfilled Crimes *11*

L. Participation in Crimes *12*

M. The Fault Element, or *Mens Rea* *13*

N. Regulatory Offences and Corporate Crime *15*

O. Defences *17*

P. The Special Part: Some Selected Offences   *20*

Q. Sentencing   *21*

Conclusion   *22*

Further Readings   *23*

CHAPTER 2:

THE CRIMINAL LAW AND THE CONSTITUTION   *24*

A. Criminal Justice And The Division Of Powers   *25*

1) Federal Jurisdiction over Criminal Law   *25*
2) Provincial Jurisdiction to Enact Regulatory Offences   *27*
3) Prosecutors, Police, and Prisons   *28*
4) Trials and Trial Courts   *28*
5) Appeals and Appellate Courts   *30*

B. Criminal Law And The *Charter Of Rights*   *31*

1) Division of Powers and the *Charter* Compared   *32*
2) The *Charter* and the Investigation of Crime   *33*
   a) Search and Seizure   *33*
   b) Arbitrary Detention and Imprisonment   *36*
   c) Right to Counsel   *39*
   d) Entrapment   *42*
3) The *Charter* and the Criminal Trial Process   *44*
   a) Disclosure   *45*
   b) Right to Full Answer and Defence   *46*
   c) Trial in a Reasonable Time   *47*
   d) Pre-Trial Publicity   *48*
   e) Right to a Jury Trial   *48*
   f) Right to Be Presumed Innocent   *50*
      i)   Quantum of Proof   *50*
      ii) Persuasive Burdens   *51*
      iii) Presumption Applies to Elements of Offences, Collateral Factors, and Defences   *52*
      iv) Evidential Burdens and Mandatory Presumptions   *55*
      v)   Threshold "Air of Reality" Tests   *56*
      vi) Summary   *58*
   g) Other Trial Rights   *58*
4) The *Charter* and Substantive Criminal Offences and Defences   *59*
   a) Fundamental Freedoms   *60*
   b) Principles of Fundamental Justice   *62*
   c) Vagueness and Overbreadth   *64*
   d) Arbitrariness and Gross Disproportionality   *64*
   e) Fault Requirements   *66*
      i)   Moral Innocence and Absolute Liability   *67*

      ii) Negligence As a Sufficient Fault Element under the *Charter* for
           Most Offences *68*
      iii) Negligence Standards: Marked Departure from the Standards
           of a Non-Individuated Reasonable Person *70*
      iv) No Requirement of Correspondence or Symmetry between
           Prohibited Act and Fault Element *71*
      v) Subjective Fault Required in Relation to the Prohibited Act for
           a Few Offences with Special Stigma *71*
   f) Criminal Defences *75*
   g) Moral Involuntariness *76*
  5) The *Charter* and Punishment *77*

Conclusion *78*

Further Readings *80*

CHAPTER 3:
THE PROHIBITED ACT, OR *ACTUS REUS* *81*

A. **Codification of the Criminal Act** *82*

  1) Strict and Purposive Construction of the Criminal Law *84*
  2) Requirements for Marked Departure and the *De Minimis* Defence *89*
  3) Unconstitutionally Vague and Overbroad Laws *91*
  4) Ignorance of the Law *94*
   a) Distinguishing Mistakes of Law and Fact *95*
   b) Preclusion of Mistake of Law As the Only Defence Making an
      Offence One of Absolute Liability *97*
   c) Non-Publication *97*
   d) *Mens Rea*, Colour of Right and Mistake of Law *98*
   e) Officially Induced Error *99*
  5) Application of the *Criminal Code*: Territorial and
     Age-Based Restrictions *100*
  6) Policy Elements in the Definition of the *Actus Reus*: The Case of
     Consent *101*

B. **The Role Of The *Actus Reus* In Criminal Liability** *106*

  1) The Coincidence of the *Actus Reus* and *Mens Rea* *106*
  2) Causing Prohibited Consequences *108*
   a) Statutory Provisions Concerning Causation *108*
   b) General Principles of Causation *109*
   c) Concurrent Causes and New Acts That Sever the Chain
      of Causation *111*
   d) Causation in Non-Homicide Cases *113*
   e) Attempts and Accomplice Liability as Alternative Forms
      of Liability in Cases of Reasonable Doubt About Factual
      Causation *114*

3) Omissions 115
4) Voluntariness of the Act 117

Conclusion 119

Further Readings 122

CHAPTER 4:
UNFULFILLED CRIMES AND PARTICIPATION IN CRIMES 124

A. **Attempts** 127

    1) *Mens Rea* for Attempts 128
       a) Constitutional Fault Element for Attempted Murder 129
       b) Mens Rea for Other Attempted Offences 130
    2) The *Actus Reus* of Attempts 131
    3) Impossibility and Attempts 134

B. **Conspiracy** 136

    1) The *Actus Reus* of Conspiracy 137
       a) Attempted Conspiracies and Other Attempts to Combine Inchoate Forms of Liability 138
    2) The *Mens Rea* for Conspiracy 139
    3) Impossibility and Conspiracy 140

C. **Counselling A Crime That Is Not Committed** 141

    1) The *Actus Reus* of Counselling a Crime That Is Not Committed 141
    2) The *Mens Rea* for Counselling a Crime That Is Not Committed 142
    3) Impossibility and Counselling 144

D. **Counselling a Crime that Is Committed** 145

    1) The *Actus Reus* of Counselling a Crime That Is Committed 146
    2) The *Mens Rea* for Counselling a Crime That Is Committed 146

E. **Aiding and Abetting** 147

    1) The *Actus Reus* of Aiding and Abetting 148
    2) The *Mens Rea* for Aiding and Abetting 150

F. **Common Intention To Commit An Unlawful Purpose And Section 21(2)** 154

    1) The *Actus Reus* of Section 21(2) 154
    2) The *Mens Rea* for Section 21(2) 155
       a) Common Unlawful Purpose 155
       b) Knew or Ought to Have Known That the Crime Would Be Committed 156

G. **Accessory After The Fact** 158

1) The *Actus Reus* of Being an Accessory after the Fact   *158*
2) The *Mens Rea* for Being an Accessory after the Fact   *158*

Conclusion   *159*

Further Readings   *161*

CHAPTER 5:
THE FAULT ELEMENT, OR *MENS REA*   *163*

A. **Conceptual Considerations**   *164*

    1) The Relation of the Fault Element to the Prohibited Act   *164*
    2) Subjective and Objective Fault Elements   *166*
    3) Common Law Presumptions of *Mens Rea*   *169*
    4) Constitutional Requirements of *Mens Rea*   *171*
        a) Requirements of Subjective Fault in Relation to Prohibited Act for Special Stigma Crimes: Murder, Attempted Murder, and War Crimes   *171*
        b) Principles of Fundamental Justice as Outlined in *Creighton*   *174*
        c) Constitutional Requirements with Respect to Criminal Negligence   *176*
        d) Substituted Elements for Constitutionally Required Elements   *177*
    5) Fault Elements in Relation to the Defences of Mistake of Fact and Intoxication   *179*

B. **The Degrees Of Subjective *Mens Rea***   *180*

    1) Intent, Purpose, or Wilfulness   *180*
    2) Intent, Purpose, or Wilfulness Distinguished from Motive   *184*
    3) Knowledge   *187*
    4) Wilful Blindness   *189*
    5) Recklessness   *191*
    6) Transferred Subjective *Mens Rea*   *192*

C. **The Degrees Of Objective *Mens Rea***   *193*

    1) Who Is the Reasonable Person?   *193*
    2) Degree of Negligence   *196*
    3) The Relevance of Subjective Perceptions and Exculpatory Factors to Objective Fault   *198*

D. **Mistake Of Fact**   *202*

    1) Early Cases   *202*
    2) Mistake Related to the Degree of Fault   *203*
    3) Mistake of Fact and Drug Offences   *204*
    4) Mistake of Fact and Sexual Assault   *204*

E. **Mixed Subjective and Objective Fault Elements**   *208*

Conclusion *209*

Further Readings *212*

CHAPTER 6:

REGULATORY OFFENCES AND CORPORATE CRIME *213*

A. **Absolute Liability Offences** *215*

1) The Common Law Presumption against Absolute Liability *217*
2) The *Charter* and Absolute Liability *219*
3) Corporations and the *Charter* *221*
4) Corporate Liability for Absolute Liability Offences *221*
5) Defences to Absolute Liability Offences *222*

B. **Strict Liability Offences** *222*

1) Simple Negligence *223*
2) Negligence and the *Charter* *224*
3) The Defence of Due Diligence *224*
4) The Defence of Due Diligence and the *Charter* *226*
5) Corporate Liability for Strict Liability Offences *227*
6) Requirements of Fault beyond Negligence in Regulatory Offences *228*

C. **Vicarious Liability** *229*

1) Vicarious Liability and the *Charter* *229*

D. **Corporations And *Mens Rea* Offences** *230*

1) The Common Law Directing Mind Approach *230*
2) New Statutory Provisions for Corporate Criminal Liability *233*
   a) Organizational Liability *234*
   b) Representatives of an Organization *235*
   c) Senior Officers of an Organization *235*
   d) Section 22.1 of the *Criminal Code* and Organizational Fault for Negligence Offences *236*
      i) The Commission of the Prohibited Act by the Organization's Representative(s) *237*
      ii) Marked Departure from Reasonable Standards by the Organization's Senior Officer(s) *237*
   e) Section 22.2 of the *Criminal Code* and Organizational Fault for Subjective Intent Offences *239*
      i) Senior Officers Being a Party to the Offence *240*
      ii) Senior Officers Directing Representatives to Commit the Offence *240*
      iii) Senior Officers Failing to Prevent Representatives from Committing the Offence *242*

Conclusion *243*

Further Readings   *244*

CHAPTER 7:
INTOXICATION   *246*

A. **Beard's Case**   *247*

B. **The Distinction between General And Specific Intent Offences**   *248*

C. **The Intoxication Defence for Specific Intent Offences**   *250*

  1) Intent Not Capacity to Commit the Offence   *251*
  2) Threshold Air of Reality Tests   *252*

D. **Liability for the Intoxicated Commission of General Intent Offences**   *253*

E. **Extreme Intoxication and General Intent Offences**   *255*

  1) The Development of the *Daviault* Defence   *255*
  2) The Legislative Response to *Daviault*: Section 33.1   *261*
  3) The Constitutionality of Section 33.1   *264*

G. **Involuntary Intoxication**   *272*

  1) Involuntary Intoxication as an Independent Defence   *272*
  2) Involuntary Intoxication and Section 33.1   *273*

Conclusion   *275*

Further Readings   *277*

CHAPTER 8:
MENTAL DISORDER AND AUTOMATISM   *279*

A. **Procedural Considerations In The Mental Disorder Defence**   *280*

  1) Unfitness to Stand Trial   *280*
  2) Who Can Raise the Mental Disorder Defence?   *282*
  3) Burden of Proof   *283*
  4) Disposition of an Accused Acquitted by Reason of Mental Disorder   *285*

B. **The *M'Naghten* Rules And Their Codification**   *287*

C. **Mental Disorder or Disease of the Mind**   *289*

  1) Policy Considerations   *289*
  2) Continuing Danger and Internal Causes   *290*
  3) The *Cooper* Definition   *292*
  4) Mental Disorder and Transitory States   *293*

5) Mental Disorder and Organic Conditions *294*

D. **Capacity to Appreciate the Nature and Quality of the Act** *296*

E. **Capacity to Know that the Act Is Wrong** *297*

F. **Irresistible Impulse** *300*

G. **Effect of a Mental Disturbance Short of Insanity on *Mens Rea*** *301*

H. **Automatism** *302*

1) Relation to Mental Disorder and Consequences of an Automatism Defence *302*
2) Air of Reality and Persuasive Burdens of Proof *304*
3) Automatism and Sleepwalking *307*
4) Automatism and Emotional Blows *309*
5) Automatism and Organic Conditions *311*
6) Automatism and Intoxication *312*
7) Automatism and Other Defences *313*

Conclusion *314*

Further Readings *316*

CHAPTER 9:

SELF-DEFENCE, NECESSITY, AND DURESS *317*

A. **Conceptual Considerations** *319*

1) Excuses and Justifications *319*
2) Relation to Fault Element *321*
3) Subjective and Objective Components *321*
4) Burden of Proof *323*
5) Air of Reality *324*

B. **Self-Defence** *324*

1) Self-Defence and Defence of Others in the New Section 34 *327*
   a) Self-Defence Applies to a Broad and Expanded Range of Offences *327*
   b) No Specific Reference to Self-Defence as a Justification *328*
   c) First Requirement: Belief on Reasonable Grounds that Force or Threat of Force Is Being Used under Section 34(1)(a) *329*
   d) The Protection of Others *332*
   e) Second Requirement: Subjective Purpose of Defending Oneself or Others under Section 34(1)(b) *333*
   f) Third Requirement: Acts Done in Self-Defence Must Be Reasonable in the Circumstances under Section 34(1)(c) *333*
   g) Contextual Objective Standard and the History of the Relationship between the Parties to the Incident *334*

h)   Retreat from Homes and Other Situations   337
i)   The Proportionality of the Act Done in Self-Defence   338
j)   The Accused's Role in the Incident   339
k)   Excessive Self-Defence   340
l)   Section 34(3): Self-Defence against Law Enforcement Actions   341
m) Summary   341
2) Defence of Property in the New Section 35   342
a)   Defence of Property Applies to a Broad and Expanded Range of Offences   343
b)   No Specific Reference to Defence of Property as a Justification   343
c)   No Deeming of Assault but Continued Overlap between Defence of Property and Self-Defence   344
d)   The Contextual and Modified Objective Standard   344
e)   First Requirement: Reasonable Belief in Peaceable Possession and Claim of Right under Section 35(1)(a)   344
f)   Second Requirement: Reasonable Belief That Property Is Being Threatened under Section 35(1)(b)   345
g)   Third Requirement: Subjective Purpose of Protecting Property under Section 35(1)(c)   346
h)   Fourth Requirement: Act Must be Reasonable in the Circumstances under Section 35(1)(d)   347
i)   Section 35(3): Defence of Property against Law Enforcement Actions   349
j)   Summary   349
3) Related Defences   351

C. Necessity   353

1) Necessity an Excuse and Not a Justification   354
2) First Requirement: Reasonable Belief in Imminent Peril and Danger   357
3) Second Requirement: Reasonable Belief in No Legal Way Out or Safe Avenue of Escape   358
4) Third Requirement: Proportionality between Harm Inflicted and Harm Avoided   360
5) Modified and Contextual Objective Standard for Imminence and No Legal Way Out but Not Proportionality   361

D. Duress   362

1) Section 17 as Applied to Principal Offenders   363
a)   First Requirement: Threats of Death or Bodily Harm against the Accused or a Third Party   364
b)   Second Requirement: Subjective Belief That Threats Will Be Carried Out   367
c)   No Section 17 Defence if Offences are Excluded   368
d)   No Section 17 Defence If Accused Is Party to a Conspiracy or Criminal Association   368

e) Summary *369*

2) The Common Law Defence of Duress as It Applies to Parties to the Offence *370*
   a) First Requirement: Reasonable Belief in Threats of Death or Bodily Harm *371*
   b) Second Requirement: Reasonable Belief in No Legal Way Out or Safe Avenue of Escape *372*
   c) Third Requirement: Proportionality Between Harm Inflicted and Harm Avoided *373*
   d) Modified and Contextual Objective Standard *374*
3) Duress and *Mens Rea* *375*
4) Summary *377*

Conclusion *377*

Further Readings *380*

CHAPTER 10:

THE SPECIAL PART: HOMICIDE, SEXUAL, PROPERTY, AND TERRORISM OFFENCES *382*

A. **Homicide Offences** *383*

1) The *Actus Reus* of Causing Death *383*
   a) Statutory Provisions in Homicide Cases *384*
   b) General Principles of Causation in Homicide Cases *385*
   c) Substantial Cause Requirements for Some Forms of First-Degree Murder *388*
   d) Concurrent Causes of Death and New Acts That Break the Chain of Causation *389*
2) Murder *391*
   a) The Constitutionally Required Fault for Murder *392*
   b) Section 229(a)(i) *394*
   c) Section 229(a)(ii) *395*
   d) Section 229(b) and Transferred Intent *396*
   e) Section 229(c) *397*
   f) Parties to Murder Offences *399*
3) First-Degree Murder *401*
   a) Planned and Deliberate Murder under Sections 231(2) and (3) *401*
   b) Killing Police Officers and Other Officials in the Execution of Their Duties *402*
   c) Killing While Committing Other Serious Crimes *403*
4) Provocation *405*
   a) A Wrongful Act or Insult that Is Not Incited by the Accused or the Result of the Victim Exercising a Legal Right *407*
   b) Sudden Provocation *410*

       c) Subjective Provocation *411*

       d) Objective Standard That the Wrongful Act or Insult Is Capable of Depriving an Ordinary Person of Self-Control *412*

           i)   The Modified Objective and Contextual Standard *416*

           ii) Factors Not Relevant to an Ordinary Person *418*

           iii) Cultural Background of the Accused *419*

       e) Proportionality Not Required *422*

       f) Provocation and the *Charter* *423*

       g) Relation of Provocation to the Fault Element *425*

       h) Relation of Provocation to Other Defences *426*

  5) Infanticide *427*

  6) Manslaughter *428*

       a) Unlawful Act Manslaughter under Section 222(5)(a) *428*

       b) Criminal Negligence Manslaughter under Sections 222(5)(b) and 220 *431*

       c) Manslaughter under Sections 222(5)(c) and (d) *432*

       d) Parties to a Manslaughter Offence *433*

  7) Suicide and Assisted Suicide *433*

B. **Sexual Offences** *434*

  1) Sexual Assault Offences *434*

  2) The *Actus Reus* of Sexual Assault *435*

       a) Assaults under Section 265 *435*

       b) Sexual Assaults Distinguished from Other Assaults and Sexual Offences *436*

       c) Consent under Section 273.1 *436*

       d) Consent in *Ewanchuk* *437*

       e) Specific Instances Where Consent Is Not Valid *438*

  3) The *Mens Rea* of Sexual Assault *442*

       a) Mistaken Belief in Consent *442*

       b) Establishing an Air of Reality for a Mistake of Fact Defence *443*

       c) Wilful Blindness in Relation to Consent *444*

       d) Restrictions on the *Pappajohn* Mistake of Fact Defence under Section 273.2 *445*

       e) The Requirement of Reasonable Steps in Section 273.2(b) *447*

       f) Mistake of Fact Precluded if Based on a Mistake of Law *450*

       g) The Constitutionality of Section 273.2(b) *450*

       h) Sexual Assault and Intoxication *452*

C. **Property Offences** *453*

  1) Theft *453*

  2) Fraud *454*

D. **Terrorism Offences** *457*

  1) The Offence of Participation in a Terrorist Group *458*

  2) Definition of a Terrorist Group *459*

3) Definition of Terrorist Activities 459
4) The Requirement of Political or Religious Motive 462
5) Fault Elements in Other Terrorism Offences 463

Conclusion 465

Further Readings 468

CHAPTER 11:
SENTENCING 469

A. Procedural Considerations 472

1) The Guilty Plea 472
2) The Sentencing Hearing 473
3) Sentencing Appeals 474

B. The Principles and Purposes of Sentencing 475

1) The Fundamental Principle of Proportionality 476
2) The Fundamental Purpose of Sentencing 478
3) Denouncing Unlawful Conduct 479
4) Deterring and Incapacitating Offenders 479
   a) General Deterrence 480
   b) Specific Deterrence 480
5) Rehabilitating Offenders 482
6) Providing Reparations and Promoting a Sense of Responsibility 483
7) Sentencing Aboriginal Offenders 484

C. Aggravating and Mitigating Factors in Sentencing 485

D. Constitutional Considerations 486

E. Sentences Other Than Imprisonment 489

1) Alternative Measures 489
2) Absolute and Conditional Discharges 489
3) Suspended Sentences and Probation 489
4) Conditional Sentences of Imprisonment 490
5) Fines 492
6) Restitution 493
7) Forfeiture 493

Conclusion 494

Further Readings 494

CHAPTER 12:
CONCLUSION 496

A. The *Charter* and the Criminal Law 498

1) The *Charter* and the Due Process Model *498*
2) The *Charter* and the Crime Control Model *500*
3) The *Charter* and the Punitive Model of Victims' Rights *502*
4) The Non-Punitive Model of Victims' Rights *503*

B. **Trends in the Criminal Law** *505*

1) Definition of Crimes *505*
2) Subjective and Objective Fault Elements *506*
3) Regulatory Offences and Corporate Crime *508*
4) Intoxication, Mental Disorder, and Other Defences *510*

Conclusion *512*

Further Readings *513*

GLOSSARY *517*

TABLE OF CASES *523*

INDEX *555*

ABOUT THE AUTHOR *561*

FOREWORD

It is a great pleasure to write this foreword to the fifth edition of my colleague Kent Roach's book, *Criminal Law*. There is no Canadian book like it and all those studying criminal law will be indebted to Professor Roach for his very readable and careful analysis of Canadian criminal law. This book will be an excellent companion for students in criminal law courses both in the law schools and criminology and criminal justice departments. As is demonstrated by its citation by the Supreme Court and other courts, even judges and seasoned criminal lawyers will benefit from reading the thoughtful views on the basic principles of criminal law articulated in this book. In addition, it deals with many new developments in criminal law, such as new provisions relating to self-defence and defence of property. The fact that Professor Roach has acted as counsel in a number of important *Charter* and sentencing cases discussed in the book provides an added dimension to this work. This thoroughly revised fifth edition, like the first, second, third and fourth, is destined to be widely used and praised. I look forward to many future editions of this valuable book.

Martin L. Friedland, C.C., Q.C.
Professor of Law and University Professor Emeritus
University of Toronto

PREFACE
TO THE FIFTH EDITION

This book is designed to provide a concise and current discussion of the basic principles of Canadian criminal law. To this end, the heart of this book examines the principles of the general part of the criminal law: the elements of offences and the relevant defences. It follows the traditional conceptualization of the general part, but it examines unfulfilled crimes and participation in crimes earlier than other works because of their great practical importance and their effective expansion of the prohibited act. Regulatory offences and corporate criminal liability are examined together because of their functional and contextual similarities.

A few chapters attempt to place the general principles of the criminal law in context. Chapter 1 provides an overview of all the topics examined in the book. Chapter 2 examines the constitutional principles that affect the investigation of crime, the criminal trial process, and the substantive criminal law as they relate to fault requirements and defences. Chapter 10 examines selected offences including homicide, sexual offences, property, and terrorism offences. Provocation is also examined in this chapter. Other contextual chapters include chapter 11, which examines the principles of sentencing, and chapter 12, which outlines models of the criminal process and trends in the criminal law. These chapters are not intended to be comprehensive, and each deserves a book in its own right, but it is hoped they will provide readers with a fuller sense of the criminal law than would be provided if the book were restricted to the general part of the criminal law.

I have avoided the temptation to engage in extended criticisms of decided cases in order to focus on how each case fits into the overall structure of the criminal law. Unfortunately, the fit is not always natural and my impression after nearly twenty five years of teaching is that Canadian criminal law is complex, challenging, and at times incoherent, even for the brightest of students. Fortunately, Parliament has addressed and considerably simplified the law of both self-defence and defence of property and chapter 9 contains an extensive examination of these provisions..

This fifth edition comes at an opportune time. The Supreme Court has issued a number of important decisions especially in relation to the provocation defence and its use of a modified and contextual objective standard that has implications for other defences. Moreover, Parliament has repealed the old, multiple and complex provisions relating to self defence, defence of others and defence of property and replaced them with new and radically simplified defences in sections 34 and 35 of the *Criminal Code*. The Supreme Court in *Roy* has unanimously confirmed the importance of *Beatty* in ensuring that accused are only held to be criminally at fault for marked departures from standards of reasonable conduct. The Supreme Court has recently in the *Ipeelee* case confirmed the need for restraint in the use of imprisonment and for a different approach to the sentencing of Aboriginal offenders, but Parliament continues to restrict the use of conditional sentences and enact new mandatory minimum sentences.

I am grateful to many colleagues and students who have read the book and made encouraging comments or helpful suggestions for improvement. Don Stuart deserves particular credit for his generous yet challenging and helpful review of the first edition. I have benefited greatly from discussions with Sanjeev Anand, Benjamin Berger, Alan Brudner, Michael Code, Markus Dubber, Marty Friedland, Patrick Healy, Ken Jull, Anil Kapoor, Martha Shaffer, Hamish Stewart, Simon Stern, James Stribopoulos, and Gary Trotter about many of the issues discussed in this book.

K.R.
May 2012

OVERVIEW

Criminal law is enacted and applied in Canada in an increasingly complex constitutional framework that is examined in chapter 2. The basic elements of criminal and regulatory offences are the prohibited act and the required fault element, which are examined in chapters 3 and 5, respectively. Chapter 4 examines how criminal offences are expanded by various provisions prohibiting attempted and unfulfilled crimes and participation as an accomplice in crimes. Special provisions governing regulatory offences and corporate crime are examined in chapter 6. Various defences to crimes are examined in subsequent chapters, including intoxication (chapter 7), mental disorder and automatism (chapter 8), and self-defence, necessity, and duress (chapter 9). Chapter 10 examines the application of general principles of criminal liability in the context of some selected specific offences including the various forms of homicide, sexual, property, and terrorism offences. Punishment depends on the exercise of sentencing discretion, which is examined in chapter 11. A final chapter examines models of the criminal justice system and trends in the criminal law.

A. CRIME IN CANADA

Victimization studies suggest that about 25 percent of all Canadians are victims of crime in a year. Most of these crimes are theft of personal or household property. Most who suffer both property and violent crimes do not report them to the police. In only 31 percent of cases in a 2009 survey did victims report the crime to the police. The reasons for not reporting vary but often relate to a perception that reporting would not be useful for the crime victim or that the incident was not serious enough or that the victim would deal with the crime in another way. The perpetrator of most violent crime is often someone known to the victim, and the site of most violence is the home.

In 2010, there were just over 2.1 million crimes reported to the police. This represented the lowest level of reported crime since 1973. There were 554 homicides reported to the police, the lowest number since 1996. The majority (79 percent) of crimes reported to the police are non-violent. The majority of crimes reported to the police do not result in charges. The majority of cases in which charges are laid are resolved without a trial, and end in a finding of guilt. In a process commonly known as plea bargaining, the prosecutor may withdraw some charges or take certain positions on sentence if the accused agrees to plead guilty. The accused may receive a more lenient sentence because he or she has pled guilty. Less than 10 percent of cases go to trial and about 40 percent of these trials result in acquittals, but acquittals account for only 3 percent of all criminal cases. Only a very small minority of either convictions or acquittals are ever appealed. Nevertheless, appeal cases are crucial to the development of the criminal law. Appeal courts, most notably the Supreme Court of Canada, interpret the *Criminal Code*. They also develop judge-made common law, so long as this law is not inconsistent with the *Code* and does not create new offences. Appeal courts also apply the *Canadian Charter of Rights and Freedoms* (the *Charter*) to the activities of police and prosecutors, as well as to laws enacted by legislatures.

In 2008/09, adult criminal courts disposed of 392,907 cases involving more than 1.1 million charges. The accused were found guilty in 66 percent of cases and acquitted in 3 percent. The remaining cases were generally stayed or withdrawn by the prosecutor. The most frequently occurring offences were impaired driving (11 percent), theft (10 percent), and common assault (9 percent).

Although its rate of incarceration is much lower than in the United States, Canada has one of the highest rates in the developed democracies. On any given day in 2008/09, there were 37,200 adults imprisoned in Canada. Men represent the majority of prisoners, but women account for about 1 in 10 offenders admitted to custody, with Aboriginal women being 37 percent of women admitted to sentenced custody. Prisoners have significantly less education and employment history than other Canadians. Aboriginal people represent 27 percent of admissions to provincial institutions for those serving less than two years' imprisonment and 18 percent of admissions to federal penitentiaries for those serving two or more years' imprisonment, but are only 3 percent of the population according to the 2006 Canadian census. Aboriginal people are also three times more likely than non-Aboriginal people to experience a violent victimization. The chart that follows illustrates how the criminal law affects only a small percentage of crime committed.

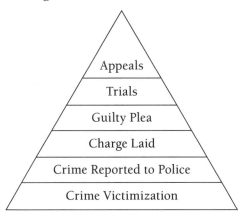

B. THE CRIMINAL PROCESS

The criminal law assumes concrete meaning when it is administered through the criminal justice system or the criminal process. The process starts with a decision of a legislature to make certain conduct illegal. The criminal law is then enforced by the police who respond to the decisions of crime victims to report crime and sometimes, especially in drug and prostitution cases, proactively investigate the crime themselves. As examined in chapter 2, the investigative activities of the police are restricted by various rights under the *Charter*, such as the right to counsel and the right against unreasonable search and seizure.

If the accused is charged, then the trial process begins. A prosecutor (sometimes called the Crown) will decide what of any charges are warranted and can make a decision to divert the charges out of court to alternative-measure programs. If charges proceed, the accused will have to make a decision whether to hire a lawyer or, if a lawyer cannot be afforded, to apply for legal aid to have a lawyer paid by the state. The trial process may include pre-trial detention by the denial of bail and in the most serious cases may include the holding of a preliminary inquiry and trial by jury. The vast majority of cases in Canada are decided by a judge without a jury. As noted above, most cases do not result in full trials, and the judge only has to engage in sentencing after the accused has pled guilty to some offence. The trial process is affected by various *Charter* rights, such as the right not to be denied reasonable bail without just cause and the right to be tried in a reasonable time. If the accused is convicted, the judge must then sentence the accused and the accused may appeal. Jails and penitentiaries are the end of the criminal process, and parole boards have powers to determine if a prisoner will be released from custody before the expiry of his or her sentence.

Each year, governments spend about $10 billion on the criminal process with 60 percent of this money going to the police, 25 percent to corrections, 9 percent to courts, and 6 percent to legal aid for those who cannot afford a defence lawyer. The chart that follows outlines the major steps in the criminal process.

The Major Steps in the Criminal Process

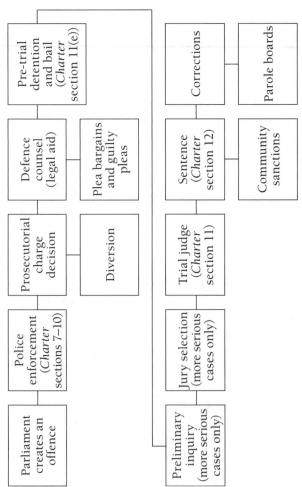

C. SOURCES OF CRIMINAL LAW

There are three main sources of criminal law in Canada: 1) the Constitution, including both the division of powers and the *Canadian Charter of Rights and Freedoms*; 2) statutes enacted by legislatures, including the *Criminal Code* and other statutes creating offences; and 3) judge-made common law in the form of defences that have not been codified in the *Criminal Code* and common law presumptions of fault.

Not all sources of the criminal law are equal. The Constitution is the supreme law and prevails over both statutes and common law. Thus a criminal offence that is enacted by Parliament can be struck down by the courts on the grounds that it violates the Constitution. Statutes prevail over judge-made common law. Thus, Parliament could abolish a common law defence to a crime through clear legislation and they can also displace judge-made common law presumptions of fault. At the same time, however, the result must accord with the Constitution and statutory abolition of some defences or abolition of fault requirements might be held to be unconstitutional because it would result in convictions that violate the *Charter.* Thus the courts play the prime role both in interpreting the Constitution and shaping the common law. At the same time, differences remain because common law can be displaced by the enactment of a clear statute whereas any limit on a constitutional right protected under the *Canadian Charter of Rights and Freedoms* must be either demonstrably justified under section 1 of the *Charter* or enacted notwithstanding the fundamental freedoms, legal rights, or equality rights of the *Charter.*

An emerging source of criminal law may be international law. Parliament has created statutory offences such as crimes of terrorism, war crimes, hate propaganda, and torture in order to fulfill its obligations under international law. The courts also make increasing reference to various forms of international law to guide their interpretation of the *Charter*, statutes, and the common law.

D. CRIMINAL OFFENCES

Criminal law in Canada is enacted only by the federal Parliament. The *Criminal Code* contains many offences, ranging from traditional crimes such as murder, assault, robbery, and theft to newer crimes such as driving with a blood alcohol level over 80. Some offences such as assault or sexual assault protect bodily integrity, while others such as theft protect property. Crimes such as firearms and drunk-driving offences attempt to prevent conduct that presents a significant risk of harm to others. Crimes against the possession and sale of illegal drugs or obscene material may prevent harm, but they also proclaim standards of socially acceptable behaviour. Criminal laws are primarily designed to denounce and to punish inherently wrongful behaviour, and to deter people from committing crimes or engaging in behaviour that presents a serious risk of harm. Courts consider these purposes when sentencing offenders, but they are also concerned with the incapacitation and rehabilitation of the particular offender and with providing reparation to the victim and the community for the crime committed.

E. REGULATORY OFFENCES

The *Criminal Code* contains many crimes, but they constitute only a small number of all the offences in Canada. Most offences are regulatory offences that can be defined in legislation enacted by the federal Parliament, provinces, or municipalities. Regulatory offences include traffic offences such as speeding, environmental offences, offences for engaging in a regulated activity without a licence or proper records, and offences relating to harmful commercial practices, such as misleading advertising or not complying with health and safety regulations. The punishment for regulatory offences is usually a fine, but may include imprisonment. In any event, the accused is frequently a corporation that cannot be imprisoned. The primary purpose of regulatory offences is to deter risky behaviour and prevent harm before it happens, rather than to punish intrinsically wrongful and harmful behaviour. The standards used to govern the investigation of regulatory offences and to impose convictions for such offences are more favourable to the state than the standards used for criminal offences.

F. THE CRIMINAL LAW AND THE CONSTITUTION

Criminal offences must be consistent with the supreme law of the Constitution. In Canada, this means that only the federal Parliament can enact criminal laws. The provinces (and their delegates, the municipalities) can, however, enact regulatory offences and such offences can even be punished by imprisonment. In addition, a criminal law may be unconstitutional if it infringes a right or a freedom protected under the *Canadian Charter of Rights and Freedoms,* and if it cannot be justified under section 1 as a reasonable and demonstrably justified limit on a right.

Sections 7 and 11(d) of the *Charter* are particularly important to the criminal law. Section 7 provides that people cannot be deprived of life, liberty, and security of the person except in accordance with the principles of fundamental justice. Imprisonment most definitely affects the liberty or security of the person. Thus, it is necessary that the criminal law be in accord with the principles of fundamental justice. These principles have been defined as the fundamental tenets of the legal system. They address the substantive fairness of criminal laws to ensure that the morally innocent are not convicted and that people who could not have reasonably been expected to obey the law are not punished for conduct committed in a morally involuntary fashion. As well, the principles of fundamental justice support the procedural fairness of the criminal law to ensure that the accused is treated fairly. Section 11(d) protects the accused's right to be presumed innocent and to receive a fair and public hearing by an independent and impartial court.

G. SUBSTANTIVE FAIRNESS

A criminal law or a regulatory offence can be declared invalid by the courts if it results in an unjustified violation of a *Charter* right, such as freedom of expression. Expression has been interpreted broadly to include non-violent attempts to convey meaning. Thus, offences prohibiting hate literature, communication for the purposes of prostitution, defamatory libel, or pornography must be justified by the government under section 1 of the *Charter* as a reasonable limit on the *Charter* right.

The principles of fundamental justice in section 7 of the *Charter* have been interpreted as prohibiting the use of vague, aribtrary, overbroad, or grossly disproportionate laws. Section 7 of the *Charter* also prohibits the punishment of the morally innocent who are not at fault, as well as those who act in a morally involuntary manner in dire circumstances where there was no other realistic choice but to commit the crime. The question of what constitutes moral innocence is quite complex and depends very much on the particular context. What is required under section 7 of the *Charter* to sustain a conviction for murder or war crimes is quite different from what is required to sustain a manslaughter conviction. It is also quite different from what is required for a conviction of a regulatory offence, such as misleading advertising.

Fault requirements should generally increase with the seriousness of the offence and intentional crimes should be punished more severely than those committed negligently.

A denial or a restriction on a defence, such as the defences of intoxication, mental disorder, or duress, may also violate section 7 of the *Charter* if it results in a deprivation of liberty in a manner that is not in accordance with the principles of fundamental justice. For example, it would be fundamentally unjust to convict a person for involuntary conduct or for committing a crime where threats or dire circumstances meant that there was no other realistic choice but to commit the crime. Section 7 jurisprudence, as it affects criminal and regulatory offences, will be examined at various junctures of this book.

H. PROCEDURAL FAIRNESS

Both the police and the prosecutor must comply with the accused's *Charter* rights, or risk having the trial process diverted from the issue of guilt or innocence by the accused seeking a *Charter* remedy for the violation of his or her legal rights. Sections 8 and 9 of the *Charter* provide individuals with the rights to be free from unreasonable searches and seizures and from arbitrary detentions during the investigative process. Section 10 ensures that people will know why they have been arrested or detained, and that they can obtain legal advice from a lawyer. Sections 7 and 11 of the *Charter* protect an accused's right to a fair trial. These rights include the right to a trial in a reasonable time, and the right to a trial by jury when the accused faces five years' imprisonment or more. The prosecutor, often known as the Crown, has special obligations of fairness and must disclose relevant evidence in its possession to the accused.

An important procedural protection is the presumption of innocence protected under section 11(d) of the *Charter*. The Crown must bear the burden of proving that the accused is guilty beyond a reasonable doubt. A reasonable doubt is not imaginary or frivolous, but is based on reason and common sense derived from the evidence or absence of evidence. The Crown must go well beyond demonstrating that it is probable or likely that the accused is guilty, but does not have to establish guilt as an absolute certainty. The accused is entitled to the benefit of any reasonable doubt about any matter essential to conviction. The matters essential to conviction include the elements of the offence, as well as the existence of any defence that would excuse or justify the commission of the offence. The presumption of innocence is offended if an accused is required to prove that he or she did not have one of the elements of the offence or even if he or she did not have a defence to the crime. The presumption of innocence is designed to ensure that the accused always receives the benefit of any reasonable doubt as to guilt and that the judge and jury are never forced by the law to convict the accused even though there might be a reasonable doubt. At the same time, violations of the presumption of innocence may be justified under section 1 of the *Charter* on the basis that they are necessary to protect social interests.

I. THE ELEMENTS OF CRIMINAL OFFENCES

The basic elements of a criminal offence are the act or omission that is prohibited by the legislation, or the *actus reus*, and the fault element, or *mens rea*, with which the accused must commit the prohibited act or omission. The Crown must prove beyond a reasonable doubt that the accused committed the prohibited act, and did so with the required fault element. There is also a general requirement that the accused have the necessary fault or *mens rea* at the same time as the prohibited act or *actus reus* occurred. For murder, the Crown would have to prove that the accused committed the prohibited act of causing another person's death, and at the same time had the fault element of knowing that the victim's death was likely to occur. It is possible that the accused could commit a criminal act without the required fault, and in such a case, the accused would not be convicted.

The Crown must, subject to exceptions justified under section 1 of the *Charter*, also prove beyond a reasonable doubt that the accused did not have a relevant defence. An accused will, for example, be acquitted of murder if there is a reasonable doubt that he or she acted in self-defence as defined by the *Criminal Code*, or if there is a reasonable doubt that intoxication prevented him or her from knowing that the victim was likely to die. A few defences, most notably mental disorder and automatism, must be established by the accused on a balance of probabilities even though this violates the presumption of innocence by allowing a conviction even if there is a reasonable doubt about the existence of a defence. If the Crown proves the prohibited act and fault element beyond a reasonable doubt, and there is no defence, then the accused will be convicted.

J. THE PROHIBITED ACT, OR *ACTUS REUS*

Every criminal or regulatory offence will have a prohibited act or omission, or *actus reus*. The prohibited act depends on how the legislature has worded the offence. For example, the prohibited act of theft is defined by Parliament in section 322(1) of the *Criminal Code* as the taking and conversion of anything. The prohibited act also depends on how the courts interpret the words of an offence. Sometimes the courts interpret these words restrictively to benefit the accused, but they may not do so if a restrictive interpretation defeats the clear purpose of the offence. The Supreme Court has interpreted the word *anything* in the offence of theft not to include the taking of confidential information from a computer screen, even though taking a piece of paper with confidential information on it would be theft. Parliament could always amend the criminal law to state clearly that confidential information constitutes a thing that can be stolen, or it could create a new offence of stealing confidential information from a computer. The definition of the prohibited act is perhaps the most important policy component of the criminal law. The trend is towards expansive legislative definitions of the prohibited act, with the most obvious example being the replacement of the offence of rape with sexual assault.

The *actus reus* is usually defined as an overt act, such as the taking of another person's property. The legislature can, however, define the prohibited conduct as an omission or a failure to take action. For example, a parent can be guilty of the criminal offence of failing to provide the necessities of life to his or her child. Regulatory offences may often prohibit the failure to take action, such as keeping proper business records or taking health and safety precautions. The definition of the criminal act must not be so vague or broad that it fails to give fair notice to the accused or to limit law enforcement discretion. Although each offence must have an *actus reus* that is not excessively vague or overbroad, it is generally no excuse that the accused did not know that his or her conduct was illegal.

Whether the accused has committed the prohibited act is usually a distinct issue from whether the accused had the required fault element. For example, a person commits the prohibited act of theft if he or she mistakenly takes another person's jacket at a party. If the person honestly believes that it is his or her jacket, however, then the person may not have committed the crime with the fault element required for theft. The person would have taken another's property, but not with the required moral fault, or *mens rea*. There is some blurring of the concepts of *actus reus* and *mens rea* when a person acts in an involuntary manner because, for example, he or she is sleepwalking or having a seizure. In such cases, it may not be fair to say even that the accused has committed the criminal act.

K. ATTEMPTS AND OTHER UNFULFILLED CRIMES

The criminal law intervenes even before the accused has committed the criminal act required for a complete crime. Thus, a person who attempts to steal an object but fails can be charged with attempted theft. Section 24 of the *Criminal Code* states that anyone, having an intent to commit an offence, who does or omits to do anything beyond mere preparation to commit a criminal offence is guilty of attempting to commit the offence regardless of whether or not it was possible to commit an offence. A person who had just entered a backyard to steal a barbecue, but had not started to remove it, could be guilty of attempted theft. The Crown would have to prove beyond a reasonable doubt that the accused had gone beyond mere preparation to commit the offence and had the intent to steal the barbecue. A person punished for an attempted crime is punished more for his or her intent to commit the crime than for the harm caused.

Sometimes activity that is preparatory to completing a crime is defined by Parliament as a completed crime. Section 322(2) of the *Criminal Code* provides that a person commits theft when, with the intent to steal, he or she moves an item or even begins to cause it to become movable. A person who has cut a chain on a backyard barbecue to make it movable with the intent to steal could be guilty of theft as opposed to attempted theft. Similarly terrorism offences relating to the financing or facilitation of terrorism generally apply to conduct done in preparation to commit an actual act of terrorism.

In addition to attempts, a person could be guilty of conspiracy to commit a theft if he or she had agreed with others to commit the theft. This offence would apply even though they had done nothing more than agree to commit a crime. A person could also be guilty of counselling a crime if he or she had procured, solicited, or incited another person to commit an offence, even though that second person never committed the offence. For example, Jane could be guilty of counselling theft if she attempted to persuade Sam to steal a barbecue, even though Sam never stole the item, and never intended to do so. If Sam did go on to steal the barbecue, Jane could be guilty of theft as a party or accomplice to the offence. Finally, a person who knowingly assists another person to escape after a crime can be guilty of the separate crime of being an accessory after the fact.

As can be seen, the criminal law prohibits and punishes not only complete crimes such as theft or murder, but also attempts to commit crimes, conspiracies to commit crimes, counselling other people to commit crimes, and assisting known criminals to escape. All of these offences, with the exception of conspiracies, are not subject to as severe punishment as the commission of the complete crime, but they are crimes nevertheless.

L. PARTICIPATION IN CRIMES

Often a crime is committed by more than one person. A person who assists in the commission of an offence can be convicted of the same offence as the person who actually commits the offence. Section 21 of the *Criminal Code* provides that people are parties to an offence and guilty of that offence not only if they commit the offence, but also if they aid or abet the commission of the offence. A person would aid a theft if he or she acted as a lookout or caused a distraction for the purpose of allowing another person time to take the property without being caught. A person would abet a crime if he or she encouraged or procured the commission of a crime. A store clerk might, for example, encourage and knowingly allow a customer to shoplift. The clerk could also be guilty of the crime under section 22 of the *Criminal Code* if she counselled or incited someone to commit a crime even though she did not actually commit the offence herself.

Section 21(2) provides that once two or more people have formed a common intent to carry out an unlawful purpose, they are guilty of every offence that each of them commits provided they knew or ought to have known that the commission of the crime would be a probable consequence of carrying out the unlawful purpose. If Jane and Sam agreed to assault a person and, in carrying out that assault, Jane also steals the victim's wristwatch, then Sam would be guilty of theft if he knew or ought to have known that it was probable that Jane would also steal when assaulting the victim. If Jane murdered the victim during the assault, Sam would not be guilty of murder, because of the special stigma and penalty that accompany a murder conviction, unless he subjectively knew that it was probable that Jane would also murder the victim they had planned to assault.

The parties' provisions in section 21 mean that people who had different levels of involvement in a crime may be found guilty of the same offence. Because section 21 makes those who actually commit an offence, as well as those who aid or abet the offence, a party to the offence, a jury can convict a person of the crime without necessarily agreeing on whether the person actually committed the crime or aided or abetted the crime. Both the person who performs the actual theft and a person who assists in the theft can be convicted of theft. The extent of an offender's participation in a crime will be considered by the judge when determining the appropriate sentence.

Expansive definitions of the criminal act are found in the above criminal prohibitions that apply to those who have attempted or planned to commit a crime, and to those who have assisted others in committing a crime. In order to convict a person of an attempted crime or for being a party to an offence, however, the Crown must also prove that the person had the fault or mental element of intending to commit the full offence or intending to assist the other person in the commission of the crime. In other words, the commission of a broadly worded prohibited act, or *actus reus*, is not enough; the accused must also have acted with the required fault element, or *mens rea*.

M. THE FAULT ELEMENT, OR *MENS REA*

A great variety of fault elements are used in criminal and regulatory offences. Sometimes the fault element is specified in the wording of an offence by words such as *intentionally, knowingly, recklessly,* or *negligently*. Frequently, however, the courts will have to infer what type of fault element is required. Often a distinction between subjective and objective fault elements is drawn. A subjective fault or mental element depends on what was in the particular accused's mind at the time that the criminal act was committed. In determining this condition, the judge or jury must consider all the evidence presented, even if it reveals factors, such as the accused's diminished intelligence, that are peculiar to the accused. On the other hand, an objective fault element does not depend on the accused's own state of mind, but on what a reasonable person in the circumstances would have known or done.

The criminal law has over the past two decades increasingly accepted objective negligence as a legitimate form of criminal fault. That said, negligence for the purpose of imposing criminal liability and punishment is different than negligence used in private law to require one party to compensate the other. Under the criminal law, the prosecutor must establish beyond a reasonable doubt that the accused engaged in a marked departure from what a reasonable person would have done in order to distinguish criminal from civil negligence. Criminal negligence, of course, can result in the accused going to jail whereas civil negligence established in a lawsuit between two individuals will only result in damages being awarded against the negligent person. Personal characteristics of the accused such as age are generally not relevant in applying objective fault standards of negligence, but they may be relevant if they render the accused incapable of appreciating the relevant risk. The courts have also stressed that negligence liability cannot be determined in the abstract or deduced from the commission of the prohibited act. The judge or jury must consider all the circumstances and all the evidence, including any explanation offered by the accused and the accused's state of mind. That said, the purpose of this process is not, as it is with respect to subjective fault, to determine what was in the accused's state of mind, but only to determine whether the accused engaged in a marked departure from reasonable standards.

Courts will often presume that a criminal offence requires proof of a subjective fault element unless the offence clearly or by implication only requires proof of objective fault. There are significant gradations among subjective mental elements. To be convicted of theft, for example, an accused must act with a fraudulent purpose or intent. A person who mistakenly takes another's coat at a party does not act with the fraudulent purpose of taking and keeping that person's coat. Other forms of subjective *mens rea* require less elaborate thought processes. As will be seen, it is enough in a murder case to prove that the accused knew that death was likely to occur, even though he or she may not have had the purpose or intent to kill. In many other cases, some subjective awareness of the prohibited conduct or consequence will be enough. In Canada, this is called recklessness. It is distinct from negligence because it requires some awareness of the prohibited risk by the accused, and it is not sufficient to conclude that a reasonable person would have been aware of the risk. Sam would recklessly commit theft if the thought crossed his mind that the coat he took might not belong to him. He would negligently commit theft if his conduct was a marked departure from what a reasonable person in his situation would have done to determine the proper ownership of the coat. The actual offence of theft, however, requires more than negligence or even recklessness.

The Supreme Court has found that sometimes the principles of fundamental justice under section 7 of the *Charter* require that the Crown prove that the accused subjectively knew that the prohibited act was likely to occur. This principle has only been applied with respect to a few serious crimes—murder, attempted murder, and war crimes—that because of their stigma and penalty have a constitutionally required form of subjective *mens rea*. Thus, in order to obtain a conviction for murder, the Crown must prove that the particular accused knew that the victim was likely to die, not simply that a reasonable person in the accused's position would have recognized the likelihood of death. Note, however, that knowledge is not the highest form of subjective *mens rea* and it is not necessary under section 7 of the *Charter* to prove that an accused's intent or purpose was to kill the victim. The *Charter* only provides minimum standards and Parliament could require such higher forms of *mens rea*. The courts have only constitutionalized subjective *mens rea* for a few serious crimes.

Another important consideration is the relation between the fault element and the prohibited act. As discussed earlier in this chapter, the fault element must generally occur at the same time as the commission of the prohibited act, though the latter may be defined in a broad manner, for example, to include the whole process of causing death. In addition, there is a general principle that the fault element relate to all parts of the prohibited act. In the case of murder, the fault element of knowledge must relate to the prohibited act of causing death. In other cases, however, such a matching or symmetry between the *actus reus* and the *mens rea* is not required. Thus, the fault element for unlawful act manslaughter relates to negligence with respect to the risk of causing non-trivial bodily harm, whereas the prohibited act requires that the accused have caused the victim's death. A number of other crimes, such as dangerous or impaired driving causing death or bodily harm, recognize the consequences of the accused's actions, but do not require proof of fault with respect to these consequences. Other crimes such as attempts may require a fault element that extends beyond the *actus reus* and contemplates the commission of a complete crime. In other words, the *mens rea* or fault element does not always relate to the *actus reus* or prohibited act.

N. REGULATORY OFFENCES AND CORPORATE CRIME

Regulatory offences are an important feature of penal law in Canada and may be enacted by Parliament, the provincial legislatures, or municipalities. Traditionally, courts were in a dilemma of interpreting a regulatory offence to require either absolute liability, for which a conviction follows from the commission of the prohibited act, or subjective fault, as is presumed for criminal offences. As will be seen, both of these options were problematic.

An absolute liability offence could punish a person who was morally innocent or without fault. The Supreme Court invalidated an absolute liability offence under section 7 of the *Charter* on the basis that it could send a person to jail for driving with a suspended licence when that person did not have subjective fault (that is, she did not know or was not aware of the risk that her licence was suspended) and did not have objective fault (that is, a reasonable person in her circumstances would not have known that the licence was suspended). Although absolute liability offences offend the principles of fundamental justice by punishing the morally innocent, they will not violate section 7 of the *Charter* unless they threaten the accused's right to life, liberty, and security of the person. The courts have upheld absolute liability offences that could not result in imprisonment.

Requiring proof of subjective fault for a regulatory offence would mean that the Crown would have to prove some form of subjective fault beyond a reasonable doubt even if the conduct was risky and harmful and could have been avoided by reasonable precautions. A compromise between absolute liability and subjective fault has now been adopted for most regulatory offences. In Canada, this halfway house is called a strict liability offence. Because it is based on the fault element of negligence, strict liability offences, unlike absolute liability offences, cannot be criticized for punishing without fault and they would generally not violate section 7 of the *Charter* even if they imposed imprisonment. Unlike criminal offences, however, the prosecutor does not have to prove the existence of the fault element beyond a reasonable doubt and the prosecutor does not have to establish that the negligence constitutes a marked departure from reasonable standards as required for criminal offences requiring criminal negligence. The fault of negligence for a regulatory offence is presumed to exist once the commission of the prohibited act has been proven beyond a reasonable doubt. The accused must demonstrate that it was not negligent by establishing a defence of due diligence on a balance of probabilities. A corporation, for example, would have to establish that it took reasonable precautions to prevent pollution.

Requiring the accused to prove a defence or lack of fault to escape a conviction violates the presumption of innocence, which requires the state to prove all aspects of guilt beyond a reasonable doubt. It would, however, generally be justified under section 1 of the *Charter* because of the difficulty that the Crown might have in establishing beyond a reasonable doubt that a person or corporation accused of a regulatory offence was negligent. Placing the onus on the accused to establish the due diligence defence to a regulatory offence also creates incentives on those individuals and corporations who enter a regulated field to take reasonable precautions to prevent harms.

Corporations may be charged not only with regulatory offences, but also with more serious criminal offences that require some form of *mens rea*. Until recently, only a directing mind of a corporation, namely a senior official with responsibility for creating corporate policy, could have his or her fault or *mens rea* attributed to the corporation for the purpose of determining the corporation's liability for criminal offences. In 2003, Parliament amended the *Criminal Code* to make it somewhat easier to convict corporations and other organizations of criminal offences. The fault of senior officers in the corporation is now attributed to the corporation and senior officers are defined in the *Criminal Code* to include not only those who play an important role in the establishment of the organization's policies, but also those who are responsible for managing an important aspect of the organization's activities. A corporation can be held liable for a subjective fault crime if the responsible senior officer commits the offence or intentionally directs the work of any representative of the corporation (including contractors and agents of the corporation) so that they commit the offence. In addition, the corporation may be liable if the senior officer knows that any representative is committing or is about to commit an offence but fails to take all reasonable measures to stop the representative from committing the offence. A corporation can be liable for a negligence-based crime if the responsible senior officer(s) depart markedly from the standard of care that, in the circumstances, could reasonably be expected to prevent representatives from committing the offence.

O. DEFENCES

Even if the Crown proves that the accused committed the prohibited act and had the required fault element, the accused may still avoid conviction by raising a relevant defence. Some common defences, such as mistake of fact and intoxication, are not really defences, but conditions that prevent the Crown from proving the required mental or fault element beyond a reasonable doubt. A person accused of murder could be so intoxicated that he or she did not know that the victim was likely to die. Likewise, a hunter accused of murder could commit the prohibited act of causing another hunter's death but have had the mistaken impression that he or she was shooting a deer. In such instances, the Crown can prove the commission of the prohibited act, but will be unable to prove that the accused had the mental element required for murder. The defences of intoxication and mistake of fact are derived from the fault element of the particular crime. For example, an offence requiring objective negligence will allow a defence of mistake of fact only if the mistake was a reasonable one. It will also generally not allow any intoxication defence because the reasonable person is sober.

Other defences may excuse or justify conduct, even though the accused committed the offence with the required fault element. Those who defend themselves may have a defence of self-defence, even if they intentionally kill or harm the attacker. Self-defence is usually considered a defence that justifies conduct, and it leads to a full acquittal. Those who commit a crime in reasonable response to serious threats of harm by third parties may have a defence of duress, even if they commit the crime with the required fault element. An example would be the person who goes along with a robbery with a gun at his or her head. Similarly, a person who commits a crime in response to circumstances of dire peril may have a defence of necessity. This would apply to a lost hiker who intentionally breaks into a cabin because he or she desperately needs food and water. Those who have valid defences of duress and necessity act in a morally involuntary manner because in the dire circumstances it was impossible for them to comply with the law and there was no safe and lawful avenue of escape. The defences of necessity and duress are usually thought to excuse conduct, but they also lead to a full acquittal.

Defences are related to the appropriate disposition of the accused. The defence of intoxication has traditionally been available only as a defence to some offences, known as specific intent offences, but not to others, known as general intent offences. A specific intent offence, such as robbery, requires more complicated mental processes that require some thought beyond the immediate commission of the act while a general intent offence, such as assault, only requires that the accused has fault in relation to the commission of the immediate act. Traditionally, an accused so intoxicated as to be unable to have the subjective foresight of death would be acquitted of murder, a specific intent offence, but almost always convicted of manslaughter, a general intent offence. Manslaughter is a less serious offence than murder, and it generally allows for the exercise of sentencing discretion.

The defence of extreme intoxication to a general intent offence is controversial in no small part because it may lead to the complete acquittal of an accused who commits a crime after voluntarily becoming intoxicated. The defence proclaimed by the Court under the *Charter* requires the accused to establish extreme intoxication that produces involuntary behaviour on a balance of probabilities. In response, Parliament enacted sections 33.1 to 33.3 of the *Criminal Code*. These provisions deem that becoming extremely intoxicated is not a defence to general intent offences that involve assaults or other interferences with bodily integrity. Parliament's rationale was that the fault of voluntarily becoming so intoxicated is sufficient to convict a person of a general intent offence that involves violence. The Supreme Court has yet to determine whether this legislative restriction on the extreme intoxication defence can be justified under the *Charter*.

Defences related to mental disorders are also influenced by concerns about the appropriate disposition of the accused. The insanity or mental disorder defence applies to those who, because of a mental disorder, cannot appreciate the physical consequences of the prohibited act they commit or know that it is legally or morally wrong. Such a person, although not convicted, would be detained and examined to determine if further detention was required to protect the public from a significant threat of danger. Automatism refers to involuntary behaviour that may prevent the Crown from proving the fault element or even the prohibited act of a crime. An accused found to be in such a state will not be convicted. If the automatism is caused by a mental disorder, however, the accused can be subject to detention as a person held not criminally responsible by reason of mental disorder. If the automatism is caused by a factor that is not a mental disorder, such as a blow on the head, the accused is simply acquitted. The accused now has the burden of establishing both the mental disorder and non-insane automatism defences on a balance of probabilities.

Many defences require that the accused act in a reasonable fashion. To be able to claim self-defence, the accused must not only subjectively believe that force or threat of force is being used against them or others, but there must also be a reasonable basis for such beliefs. In addition, the new section 34(1)(c) of the *Code* requires that acts of self-defence be reasonable in the circumstances. The criminal law generally excuses crimes committed in response to threats and dire circumstances only if a reasonable person in the accused's circumstances would have committed the crime. The use of objective standards in defences raises the question of who is the reasonable person. Unlike in the case of objective fault elements, the trend in Canada is to consider the particular accused's own experiences and characteristics when applying objective standards relating to defences such as provocation, self-defence, duress, and necessity. In the self-defence context, the Supreme Court has indicated that what is reasonable to expect of a man in a bar-room brawl may not be reasonable to expect of a woman who has been previously battered by the person she kills. In judging whether an ordinary person would have lost self-control when provoked, the courts consider the accused's characteristics and experiences, as they affect the gravity or meaning of the insult. This provides a more generous defence that is sensitive to the particular experiences and frailties of the accused, but it also risks blurring the conceptual distinction between objective and subjective standards. The courts attempt to contextualize the reasonable person while maintaining common standards of reasonable behaviour that apply to all.

Restrictions on a defence may violate the principles of fundamental justice protected under section 7 of the *Charter*. The Supreme Court has held that the complete denial of an intoxication defence when a person is charged with a general intent offence, such as an assault, or sexual assault, violates the principles of fundamental justice. It could result in the conviction of a person who acted in an involuntary manner because of extreme intoxication. Statutory restrictions on the defence of duress also offend the principles of fundamental justice because they allow a person to be convicted even though he or she acted in a morally involuntary manner in response to threats. A person acts in a morally involuntary manner if any reasonable person in the same circumstances with the same characteristics would have committed the offence. A conviction of a person who acts in a morally involuntary manner because of external pressures offends section 7 of the *Charter* because it would deprive a person of liberty in a manner that is not in accordance with the principles of fundamental justice.

P. THE SPECIAL PART: SOME SELECTED OFFENCES

The focus of this book is on general principles that define criminal liability and provide excuses or justifications for the commission of all crimes. Nevertheless, it is useful to have a sense of some of the most serious or important offences and how they are informed by contextual considerations that are specific to the particular crime. Although homicide offences are statistically rare, they are the place where much criminal law is developed. There are three homicide offences: murder, manslaughter, and infanticide. In addition, the most serious murders are classified as first-degree murder, which requires the proof of additional fault such as planning and deliberation or the commission of another serious crime during the killing. Provocation is a controversial defence available only to accused charged with murder. It applies when an accused kills in a rage produced by a sudden and wrongful act or insult that would have caused an ordinary person to lose self-control. This defence does not lead to a complete acquittal, but reduces murder to manslaughter. This avoids the mandatory penalty of life imprisonment that follows a murder conviction.

Sexual assault has been a particularly controversial offence and the subject of much law reform. In 1982, the offence of rape was replaced with offences of sexual assault that were designed to stress the violence in sexual crimes and to expand the prohibited act. There are three forms of sexual assault that mimic the offences of assault, assault with a weapon or causing bodily harm, and aggravated assault. In 1992, new provisions were enacted that addressed both the prohibited act and fault element for sexual assault offences. These reforms were designed to reflect the particular circumstances of sexual violence. They were called the "no means no" reforms and provided concrete examples of circumstances where consent to sexual activity would not be valid. They also modified the controversial defence that the accused had a mistaken belief that the victim consented, in part by providing that the defence would not apply if the accused did not take reasonable steps in the circumstances known to him to ascertain whether the complainant was consenting. In this way, Parliament combined subjective and objective fault elements in a creative and innovative manner.

Q. SENTENCING

Most accused plead guilty to some charge and proceed directly to sentencing without a criminal trial. A majority of those who do go to trial are convicted of some offence and are subject to sentencing. In Canada, judges have traditionally had significant sentencing discretion guided only by general principles in the *Criminal Code* and high maximum penalties. Robbery, for example, is subject only to a maximum punishment of life imprisonment, with no minimum sentence. Committing a robbery with a firearm, however, does have a mandatory minimum sentence of four years' imprisonment. Mandatory penalties can be challenged as violating the right against cruel and unusual punishment, but most mandatory penalties have been upheld from such challenges and judges cannot craft exemptions under the *Charter* from mandatory sentences.

The fundamental principle of sentencing is that a sentence must be proportionate to the gravity of the offence and the degree of responsibility of the offender. This is an important principle, given the various types of conduct that can be caught under broad legislative definitions of the prohibited act, and the provisions that make parties to an offence guilty of the same offence as those who actually pull the trigger. This principle also suggests that the punishment should fit the crime and that an offender should not be treated more harshly than the crime warrants, in order to deter others or to incapacitate or even rehabilitate the offender.

Despite the fundamental principle that a sentence must fit the crime, there are other legitimate purposes of sentencing, including deterring others from committing crimes; deterring the particular offender from reoffending; incapacitating the particular offender from committing more crimes; rehabilitating the particular offender; and providing reparation for harm done to victims or the community. In fulfilling these multiple purposes, judges can impose punishments other than actual imprisonment, including community service orders, discharges with conditions in the form of probation orders, fines, and restitution orders. Conditional sentences allow offenders to serve sentences of imprisonment in the community so long as they satisfy prescribed conditions. They cannot be used if the accused is subject to any mandatory term of imprisonment and Parliament has in recent years imposed other restrictions on their use. If a person is imprisoned, he or she can usually apply to a parole board before the end of the sentence for various forms of supervised release into the community. There are also provisions that allow repeat offenders to be declared dangerous and subject to indeterminate detention.

CONCLUSION

The criminal law is the result of a complex process that starts with the decision of a legislature to define something as a prohibited act. The next steps are usually the investigation by the police and the prosecution by the Crown. These phases of the criminal process must be procedurally fair, or the accused will be able to seek a remedy for the violation of his or her rights under the *Charter*. The offence and the available defences must ensure that the morally innocent are not punished and that people are also not punished if they act in a morally involuntary manner. The Crown must also prove beyond a reasonable doubt to the judge or jury that the accused committed the prohibited act with the required fault element. The accused has available various defences, most of which will apply if there is a reasonable doubt as to their existence. Some defences such as self-defence lead to a complete acquittal, whereas others such as intoxication and provocation may result in the accused being acquitted of a serious offence such as murder but still convicted of a less serious offence such as manslaughter. The mental disorder defence leads to a special disposition in which the accused, although not convicted, may be subject to further detention or treatment if he or she presents a significant threat to public safety. The judge can, subject to statutory restrictions, exercise sentencing discretion to tailor punishment to the offender's degree of responsibility, but also to consider what punishment will best deter, rehabilitate, or incapacitate the particular offender, deter others from committing the same crime, and provide reparation to the victims and the community for the crime.

FURTHER READINGS

BRENNAN, S., & M. DAUVERGNE, "Police-reported Crime Statistics in Canada, 2010" (2011) Juristat article available at www.statcan.gc.ca/pub/85-002-x/2011001/article/11523-eng.pdf.

CALVERY, D., "Adult Correctional Services in Canada 2007–2008" (2010) 30:3 Juristat article available at www.statcan.gc.ca/pub/85-002-x/2010003/article/11353-eng.pdf.

PERREAULT, S., & S. BRENNAN, "Criminal Victimization in Canada, 2009" (2010) Juristat article available at www.statcan.gc.ca/pub/85-002-x/2010002/article/11340-eng.htm.

THOMAS, J., "Adult Criminal Court Statistics, 2008-2009" (2010) 30:2 Juristat article available at www.statcan.gc.ca/pub/85-002-x/2010002/article/11293-eng.pdf.

THE CRIMINAL LAW AND THE CONSTITUTION

In order to understand criminal law in Canada, it is increasingly necessary to understand constitutional law. The Constitution, which is the supreme law of the land, has always played a role in the criminal law. The constitutional division of powers between the federal and provincial governments, created in 1867, allows only the federal Parliament to enact laws concerning criminal law and procedure. The provinces can, however, enact regulatory offences to help them govern matters within their jurisdiction, such as liquor licensing. The federal government can also enact regulatory offences to help it govern matters such as navigation and shipping that are within federal jurisdiction. In deciding whether an offence is within federal or provincial jurisdiction, the courts are concerned with the law's primary purpose.

In 1982 the *Canadian Charter of Rights and Freedoms* was added to the Constitution, and it places new restraints on the state's ability to enact and apply criminal laws. It does so by recognizing various rights, such as the right to be free of unreasonable searches and seizures, the right to counsel, and the right to a fair trial. In most cases, people will only have the incentive to invoke their *Charter* rights when they are charged with an offence. Hence, most *Charter* litigation arises in criminal cases. Many of the rights in the *Charter* require procedural fairness or due process in the investigation and prosecution of crime. Other rights are concerned that the substance of the law is fair, and does not punish a person who is morally innocent, responds to threats in a morally involuntary manner that a reasonable person could not resist, or is only exercising constitutional rights such as freedom of expression. A law or practice can infringe a *Charter* right because it has the effect of violating an individual's right, even if it was enacted for a valid and legitimate purpose.

If a criminal or regulatory offence or procedural provision violates a right protected under the *Charter*, the government will have an opportunity to justify the law under section 1 of the *Charter* as a reasonable limit that is demonstrably justifiable in a free and democratic society. The government must demonstrate not only that the law has been enacted for an important purpose, but also that there is no other reasonable manner to fulfill that purpose except by violating the accused's rights and the good that the law achieves in advancing its objective outweighs the harm to the *Charter* right. If the accused's rights have been violated and the violation is not justified under section 1, the courts can order a range of constitutional remedies. For example, they can strike down an unconstitutional offence, terminate a prosecution through a stay of proceedings, or exclude relevant evidence because it was obtained through a *Charter* violation such as an unconstitutional search or interrogation.

The new emphasis on the accused's rights in Canadian criminal law has diverted some trials away from their traditional focus on whether the accused was factually guilty. The *Charter* protects the rights of the accused to due process or fair treatment, but section 1 allows the government to justify some restrictions on the accused's rights as necessary for crime control or some other important objective. Other people affected by a criminal law, including victims, witnesses, or the media, may also have *Charter* rights such as the rights to privacy and the equal protection and benefit of the law. The *Charter* does not eliminate the need to balance competing interests in criminal laws and prosecutions, but it provides a new framework for reconciling these interests.

A. CRIMINAL JUSTICE AND THE DIVISION OF POWERS

1) Federal Jurisdiction over Criminal Law

Under section 91(27) of the *Constitution Act, 1867*, only the federal Parliament can enact laws concerning criminal law and procedure. Most criminal law is contained in the *Criminal Code*[1] although the *Controlled*

---

1   R.S.C. 1985, c. C-46 [*Code*].

Drugs and Substances Act[2] and the *Youth Criminal Justice Act*[3] are often considered criminal law. Not all laws enacted by the federal government fall under its power to enact criminal law and procedure. For example, a federal law prohibiting the sale of margarine or establishing the alcohol content of light beer would not be a valid criminal law.[4] Courts have, however, been quite generous in allowing the federal government to enact laws that facilitate the administration of the criminal law. For example, federal laws regulating the detention of the criminally insane or those found unfit to stand trial because of a mental disorder[5] and enabling judges to order the accused to make restitution to the victims of crime[6] have been upheld as valid criminal law. Parliament's criminal law power has also been interpreted broadly to allow laws restricting the advertising of tobacco,[7] prohibiting pollution,[8] and prohibiting the possession of marijuana.[9] When the federal government relies on its criminal law power, it must emphasize the use of prohibitions and punishments, as opposed to other forms of regulation such as licensing and inspections.

Unlike in the United States and Australia, the provinces (or states) cannot make laws that are classified by the courts as having the dominant purpose of prohibiting acts by the criminal sanction. Provincial and municipal attempts to prohibit the propagation of ideas,[10] the use of streets for prostitution,[11] or abortions,[12] have all been struck down as infringing the federal government's exclusive jurisdiction over criminal law. A provincial offence or a municipal by-law will be unconstitutional if its prime purpose is to punish behaviour as criminal. Before the enactment of the *Charter*, these restrictions acted as an indirect but important protection of civil liberties.

Provincial or municipal laws have also been upheld if found to have the primary purpose of responding to the conditions that cause

---

2   S.C. 1996, c. 19.
3   S.C. 2002, c. 1.
4   *Canadian Federation of Agriculture v. Quebec (A.G.)*, [1951] A.C. 179 (P.C.); *Labatt Breweries of Canada Ltd. v. Canada (A.G.)*, [1980] 1 S.C.R. 914.
5   *R. v. Swain* (1991), 63 C.C.C. (3d) 481 (S.C.C.); *R. v. Demers*, [2004] 2 S.C.R. 489.
6   *R. v. Zelensky* (1978), 41 C.C.C. (2d) 97 (S.C.C.).
7   *RJR-MacDonald Inc. v. Canada (A.G.)* (1995), 100 C.C.C (3d) 449 (S.C.C.). The advertising restrictions were, however, struck down under the *Charter* as an unjustified restriction on freedom of expression.
8   *R. v. Hydro–Quebec* (1997), 118 C.C.C. (3d) 97 (S.C.C.).
9   *R. v. Malmo-Levine* (2003), 179 C.C.C. (3d) 417 (S.C.C.) [*Malmo-Levine*].
10 *Switzman v. Elbling* (1957), 117 C.C.C. 129 (S.C.C.).
11 *R. v. Westendorp* (1983), 2 C.C.C. (3d) 330 (S.C.C.).
12 *R. v. Morgentaler* (1993), 85 C.C.C. (3d) 118 (S.C.C.) [*Morgentaler*].

crime as part of provincial jurisdiction over local matters.[13] The courts have recently upheld various provincial laws designed to prevent and respond to crimes by various preventive and remedial measures even though there were already provisions in the federal criminal law addressing the same mischief.[14]

2) Provincial Jurisdiction to Enact Regulatory Offences

Under section 92(15) of the *Constitution Act, 1867*, the provinces (and their delegates, the municipalities) can create offences punishable by fine, penalty, or imprisonment for matters within their jurisdiction. The provinces have been allowed to enact highway traffic offences[15] and to make provisions for the classification and censorship of films[16] and even the compulsory treatment of heroin addicts.[17] Provincial offences will be constitutional provided that their dominant purpose is to regulate some matter within areas of provincial jurisdiction, such as property and civil rights and matters of a local and private nature.

Provincial offences are often classified as regulatory or public welfare offences. They can be tried in the same courts as criminal offences and can even result in imprisonment. The standards for investigation and conviction of regulatory offences are generally less protective of the accused than those for criminal offences.[18] The federal government can also enact regulatory offences under other areas of its jurisdiction, such as its power over fisheries. In terms of offences and prosecutions, regulatory offences far outnumber criminal offences. Individuals are more likely to be charged with speeding or performing an act without a licence than with crimes such as murder, theft, or break and enter.

---

13   *Bedard v. Dawson*, [1923] S.C.R. 681; *Canada (Attorney General) v. Dupond*, [1978] 2 S.C.R. 770.

14   See *Chatterjee v. Ontario*, [2009] 1 S.C.R. 624 upholding provincial laws for forfeiture of proceeds and instruments of crime; *R. v. Banks* (2007), 216 C.C.C. (3d) 19 (Ont. C.A.) upholding provincial law against soliciting from people in a parked vehicle; *R. v. Dyck*, 2008 ONCA 309 upholding a provincial requirement that all sexual offenders register with the police; and *Baril v. Obnecki* (2007), 279 D.L.R. (4th) 304 (Man. C.A.) upholding provincial protection orders targeting domestic violence. In all four cases, the laws were also held to be consistent with the *Charter*.

15   *O'Grady v. Sparling* (1960), 128 C.C.C. 1 (S.C.C.).

16   *McNeil v. Nova Scotia (Board of Censors)* (1978), 44 C.C.C. (2d) 128 (S.C.C.).

17   *R. v. Schneider* (1982), 68 C.C.C. (2d) 449 (S.C.C.).

18   See ch. 6, "Regulatory Offences and Corporate Crime."

3) Prosecutors, Police, and Prisons

The Attorney General of a province will generally prosecute offences under the *Criminal Code*,[19] but the federal Attorney General may prosecute drug offences.[20] The same division of labour is true of policing, with the provinces being able to establish police forces to enforce the *Criminal Code* (this power in turn often being delegated to a municipality or a region) and the federal government being able to create police to investigate other offences under federal law. Many provinces, however, purchase policing services from the Royal Canadian Mounted Police, the federal police force. Peace officers (including the public police, customs officials, and jail guards, but not usually private police or security guards) have special powers, duties, and protections under the *Criminal Code*.[21] A fundamental feature of the rule of law is that peace officers are bound by the law including the *Criminal Code* and the *Charter*. Ordinary individuals have legal powers to arrest a person fleeing from the commission of a serious offence[22] and to go before a judicial official to establish reasonable and probable grounds that a criminal offence has been committed.[23]

The provinces have jurisdiction over those sentenced to less than two years' imprisonment, while the federal government administers penitentiaries for those sentenced to longer periods.[24] The provinces generally administer probation orders, while provincial and federal parole boards administer gradual release or parole from imprisonment before an offender's sentence has expired.

4) Trials and Trial Courts

The majority of criminal cases are resolved in provincial courts formally known as magistrates' courts. Provincial court judges are appointed by the provinces and they cannot sit with a jury. They can, however,

---

19   *Code*, above note 1, s. 2. The Attorney General of Canada through the Public Prosecution Service of Canada is the prosecutor for the Northwest and Yukon Territories and Nunavut. The Attorney General of Canada can also prosecute certain *Criminal Code* crimes with extraterritorial effect and crimes involving terrorism or otherwise affecting the security of Canada, United Nations personnel, or capital market frauds.

20   *R. v. Hauser* (1979), 46 C.C.C. (2d) 481 (S.C.C.).

21   *Code*, above note 1, ss. 25, 129, 270, 495, and 503. Peace officers are defined in s. 2.

22   *Ibid.*, s. 494(1).

23   *Ibid.*, ss. 504 and 507.

24   *Constitution Act, 1867* (U.K.), 30 & 31 Vict., c. 3, ss. 91(28) and 92(6) [*CA 1867*]; *Code*, above note 1, s. 743.1.

hear most serious indictable offences,[25] provided that the accused decides or elects to be tried in provincial court without a jury or a preliminary inquiry to determine whether there is enough evidence to put the accused on trial. The least serious indictable offences can only be tried in provincial court,[26] and provincial courts or justices of the peace also hear the least serious criminal offences, known as summary conviction offences, as well as provincial regulatory offences enacted under section 92(15) of the *Constitution Act, 1867*. Both summary conviction and provincial offences can generally only be punished by up to six months' imprisonment and $2000 in fines.[27] A growing number of offences, such as sexual assault, if prosecuted by way of summary conviction can be punished by up to eighteen months' imprisonment.

In "hybrid" offences the Crown has the discretion to prosecute the offence by indictment or as a less serious summary conviction offence. If the prosecutor elects to prosecute the offence as a summary conviction offence, the accused is not entitled to a preliminary inquiry or a trial by jury but the maximum punishment is limited. The prosecutor's election to prosecute by summary conviction or indictment may also determine what maximum and minimum penalty will apply if the accused is convicted.

Those under eighteen years of age are generally tried in youth court, which in most provinces is the provincial court. Youth sentences are lower from those available upon conviction of the same offence in adult court. In some cases, however, adult sentences can be imposed on young offenders; but the Supreme Court has held that a presumption that a young person would receive an adult sentence for specified offences violates a principle of fundamental justice, which presumes that young people are less blameworthy for crimes because of their age, vulnerability, and reduced capacity for moral judgment.[28]

Only federally appointed superior court judges can sit with a jury in what is known in different provinces as the Superior Court, Supreme Court, or Queen's Bench.[29] Murder charges must be tried by a superior court judge, usually with a jury.[30] Superior court judges may also try most other indictable offences, provided the accused elects to be tried in this higher level of trial court. The accused can elect to be tried in the superior court with a preliminary inquiry (heard by a provincial

---

25 But not those, such as murder, listed in the *Code, ibid.*, s. 469.
26 Including theft and other offences listed in the *Code, ibid.*, s. 553.
27 *Ibid.*, s. 787.
28 *R. v. D.B.*, 2008 SCC 25 [*D.B.*].
29 *CA 1867*, above note 24, s. 96.
30 *Code*, above note 1, s. 469.

court judge or justice of the peace) and with or without a jury. The appearance of a superior court trial can be impressive (for example, the lawyers are gowned), but it should be remembered that most criminal cases are resolved in the less formal and more hectic atmosphere of the provincial courts.

Trial judges have to provide reasons for their decisions and these reasons should set out all the elements of an offence for a conviction. Such reasons, however, can be briefer in cases of an acquittal based on the fact that the Crown has not proven one of the elements of the offence.[31] This also reflects a fundamental asymmetry in the criminal law in which the state has to establish guilt beyond a reasonable doubt and the accused is given the benefit of reasonable doubts about guilt.

5) Appeals and Appellate Courts

Canada has a generous appellate structure that allows both the accused and the Crown wide rights of appeal. Appeals in summary conviction offences can be made by either the accused or the prosecutor and are heard by a superior court judge with further appeals on questions of law to the Court of Appeal.[32] Appeals for indictable offences go directly to the provincial Court of Appeal, which has federally appointed judges and hears appeals in panels of three and sometimes five judges. The accused has broad rights of appeal and can appeal matters of fact or law, as well as the fitness of his or her sentence.[33] The accused's appeal can be allowed on three grounds: 1) that the conviction is unreasonable or cannot be supported by the evidence; 2) that the conviction entails a miscarriage of justice; or 3) that the trial judge made an error of law. In the last case, the appeal can be denied if the appeal court concludes that notwithstanding the legal error, "no substantial wrong or miscarriage of justice has occurred."[34] If the accused's appeal is successful, a new trial will usually be ordered, but in some cases an acquittal may be entered. In addition, the Minister of Justice can order a new trial, or direct an appeal to a provincial Court of Appeal when he or she is "satisfied that there is a reasonable basis to conclude that a miscarriage of justice likely occurred" after having inquired into an application by a person convicted of an offence whose appeal rights have been

---

31   R. v. Sheppard, [2002] 1 S.C.R. 869; R. v. Walker, 2008 SCC 34.
32   Code, above note 1, ss. 813, 830, and 839.
33   Ibid., s. 675.
34   Ibid., s. 686(1)(b)(iii).

exhausted.[35] A similar power was used to order new appeals in cases involving miscarriages of justice, such as the wrongful convictions of Donald Marshall, Jr., David Milgaard, and William Mullins-Johnson.

The prosecutor may appeal questions of law and the fitness of sentence to the Court of Appeal.[36] If the appeal is allowed and the prosecutor can show that the outcome would not have been the same without the legal error, a new trial will be ordered. In rare cases, the appeal court might enter a conviction instead of ordering a new trial, but this cannot be done if the accused was acquitted at trial by a jury. The right of the prosecutor to appeal acquittals and to have new trials ordered is broader in Canada than in either the United States or the United Kingdom.

Either the accused or the prosecutor can appeal to the highest court, the Supreme Court of Canada, with nine federally appointed judges. Appeals to that Court are of right on any question of law from which a judge in the provincial Court of Appeal dissents, and by leave on any matter of law of national importance.[37]

B. CRIMINAL LAW AND THE *CHARTER OF RIGHTS*

In 1982 the *Canadian Charter of Rights and Freedoms* was added to the Canadian Constitution. The *Charter*'s greatest impact has been on the criminal justice system, and it provides constitutional standards that affect the criminal process from the investigation of crime to the punishment of offenders. A violation of the *Charter* may occur if police, prosecutorial, or correctional practices or some law has the effect of violating the accused's rights. Under section 24 of the *Charter*, courts can provide a range of remedies if police, prosecutors, or prison officials violate the *Charter* rights of the accused. These remedies can include the termination of a prosecution through a stay of proceedings, the release of a person, and the exclusion of unconstitutionally obtained evidence. Criminal laws passed by Parliament can also be struck down by the courts under section 52 of the *Constitution Act, 1982,* if they are found to violate one of the rights in the *Charter* and the government cannot justify the violation under section 1 of the *Charter* as a proportionate and reasonable means to fulfill an important purpose. Parlia-

---

35   *Ibid.,* s. 696.3(3). Pardons may also be granted under s. 748 of the *Code* and pursuant to the royal prerogative of mercy.

36   *Ibid.,* s. 676.

37   *Ibid.,* ss. 691 and 693; *Supreme Court Act,* R.S.C. 1985, c. S-26, s. 40.

ment and the provincial legislatures retain the final, but very rarely exercised, option to declare that a law will operate notwithstanding the fundamental freedoms, legal rights, or equality rights otherwise guaranteed under the *Charter*.[38]

1) Division of Powers and the *Charter* Compared

The division of powers in the *Constitution Act, 1867* and the *Charter* provide a complex constitutional framework that governs the enactment of criminal and regulatory offences in Canada. The history of legislation requiring Sunday observance provides a good illustration. At the turn of the twentieth century, provincial legislation requiring Sunday observance was struck down on the grounds that it was criminal law that only Parliament could enact.[39] The federal *Lord's Day Act*[40] was subsequently upheld as valid criminal law because it was designed with the religious purpose of requiring the observance of the Christian Sabbath.[41] By that time, however, the *Charter* had been enacted, and the Supreme Court decided that a law enacted with the religious purpose of compelling observance of a common Sabbath was a direct violation of freedom of conscience and religion as protected under section 2(a) of the *Charter*.[42] Since the law was based on a purpose contrary to *Charter* values, it could not be justified by the government under section 1 and was declared to be invalid.

A year later, the Supreme Court had to decide the constitutionality of a provincial law requiring Sunday closing. The Court found that the law had been enacted for the secular purpose of establishing a common rest day, a matter of civil and property rights within provincial jurisdiction. At the same time, however, the Court found that the law violated the right to freedom of religion and conscience because it had the effect (but not the purpose) of placing burdens on those who, because of their religious beliefs, could not open their stores on either Sunday or their own religious Sabbath.[43] That conclusion did not end

---

38   *Canadian Charter of Rights and Freedoms*, Part I of the *Constitution Act, 1982*, being Schedule B to the *Canada Act 1982* (U.K.), 1982, c. 11, s. 33 [*Charter*].

39   *Ontario (A.G.) v. Hamilton Street Railway Co.*, [1903] A.C. 524 (P.C.). Subsequent provincial attempts to compel observance of religious holidays were struck down as invasions of federal jurisdiction over criminal law. *Henry Birks & Sons v. (Montreal) Ltd. (City)* (1955), 113 C.C.C. 135 (S.C.C.).

40   R.S.C. 1970, c. L-13.

41   *R. v. Big M Drug Mart Ltd.* (1985), 18 C.C.C. (3d) 385 (S.C.C.).

42   *Ibid.*

43   *R. v. Edwards Books & Art Ltd.* (1986), 30 C.C.C. (3d) 385 (S.C.C.).

the constitutional analysis, however, because the Court held that the government had justified the law under section 1 of the *Charter* as a reasonable limit that was necessary to ensure a common rest day. The legislatures in many Canadian jurisdictions had the last word when they repealed Sunday closing laws in response to public opinion.

2) The *Charter* and the Investigation of Crime

Before the enactment of the *Charter*, courts conducting a criminal trial were generally not concerned with the manner in which the police investigated crime. The failure of the police to warn suspects that their statements might be used against them did not affect the admissibility of their statements[44] and evidence could not be excluded because it was unfairly obtained.[45] The only real restraint was that confessions had to be proven to be voluntary in the sense that they were not obtained through fear or hope of advantage. This was done to ensure the reliability of confessions more than their fairness. The *Charter* has changed this exclusive emphasis on crime control by recognizing rights to be secure against unreasonable search and seizures (section 8); rights not to be arbitrarily detained or imprisoned (section 9); and rights to be informed of the reason for arrest or detention and to retain and instruct counsel without delay (sections 10(a) & (b)). A violation of any of these rights can result in the exclusion of relevant evidence from the criminal trial if its admission will bring the administration of justice into disrepute (section 24(2)).

a) Search and Seizure

Section 8 of the *Charter* provides that everyone has a right to be secure against unreasonable search and seizure. This provision protects all reasonable expectations of privacy, and such expectations are not sacrificed simply because an accused was committing a criminal offence or risked that the state would discover his or her illegal activities.[46] What constitutes a reasonable expectation of privacy, however, depends on the context. In divided decisions, the Court has held that students enjoy a reasonable expectation of privacy that is violated when sniffer dogs are used to examine their backpacks or when such dogs are used with respect to bus station lockers. The dogs have the ability to detect the

---

44   *R. v. Boudreau* (1949), 94 C.C.C. 1 (S.C.C.).

45   *R. v. Wray*, [1970] 4 C.C.C. 1 (S.C.C.).

46   *R. v. Duarte* (1990), 53 C.C.C. (3d) 1 (S.C.C.) [*Duarte*]; *R. v. Wong* (1990), 60 C.C.C. (3d) 460 (S.C.C.) [*Wong*].

use being made of the backpack or locker.[47] In contrast, the Court has held that the use of technology to detect heat arising from homes for drug enforcement purposes does not invade a reasonable expectation of privacy because the technology does not permit inferences about the precise activity causing the heat.[48] Searches of garbage put out for collection do not invade reasonable expectations of privacy.[49]

Individuals and businesses operating in a regulated field have diminished expectation of privacy over their business records.[50] Regulatory inspections, like regulatory offences, are thought to carry with them less stigma and for this reason the state is given greater scope in its activities. Similarly, a demand by government investigators for the production of documents is seen as less intrusive than an actual search.[51] The Supreme Court has made clear, however, that warrant requirements apply when regulators "cross the Rubicon" from regulation to prosecution. This occurs when the predominant purpose of their inquiries is the determination of penal liability.[52] Complex issues are raised when regulatory search and seizure powers are intertwined with searches for evidence of crime.[53]

It is not only those who operate in a regulatory context that have diminished or no expectations of privacy. An individual who occasionally stays at an intimate friend's home may have no reasonable expectation of privacy when that friend's home is searched,[54] and passengers may not have a reasonable expectation of privacy when the car they are driving in is searched.[55] Students in schools also have diminished expectations of privacy from searches,[56] as do prisoners,[57] drivers asked to produce their licences,[58] individuals who pass customs,[59] and those whose power consumption can be determined by access to commercial records.[60]

---

[47] R. v. A.M., 2008 SCC 19; R. v. Kang-Brown, 2008 SCC 18.

[48] R. v. Tessling, [2004] 3 S.C.R. 432.

[49] R. v. Patrick, [2009] 1 S.C.R. 579.

[50] R. v. Potash (1994), 91 C.C.C. (3d) 315 (S.C.C.).

[51] Thomson Newspapers Ltd. v. Canada (Director of Investigation & Research) (1990), 54 C.C.C. (3d) 417 (S.C.C.); R. v. McKinlay Transport Ltd. (1990), 55 C.C.C. (3d) 530 (S.C.C.).

[52] R. v. Jarvis (2002), 169 C.C.C. (3d) 1 (S.C.C.) [Jarvis].

[53] R. v. Nolet, [2010] 1 S.C.R. 851.

[54] R. v. Edwards (1996), 104 C.C.C. (3d) 136 (S.C.C.).

[55] R. v. Belnavis (1997), 118 C.C.C. (3d) 405 (S.C.C.).

[56] R. v. M.(M.R.) (1998), 129 C.C.C. (3d) 361 (S.C.C.).

[57] Weatherall v. Canada (A.G.) (1993), 83 C.C.C. (3d) 1 (S.C.C.).

[58] R. v. Hufsky (1988), 40 C.C.C. (3d) 398 (S.C.C.) [Hufsky].

[59] R. v. Simmons (1988), 45 C.C.C. (3d) 296 (S.C.C.); R. v. Jacques (1996), 110 C.C.C. (3d) 1 (S.C.C.).

[60] R. v. Plant (1993), 84 C.C.C. (3d) 203 (S.C.C.); R. v. Gomboc, [2010] 3 S.C.R. 211.

If there is a reasonable expectation of privacy, the state must generally obtain prior judicial authorization to authorize a search and seizure, except if there are exigent circumstances that make it impossible to obtain a warrant.[61] The police need not wait to obtain a warrant if there is imminent danger that evidence of a crime will be destroyed or that someone will be harmed. At the same time, s.8 requires some form of accountability for searches even in such exigent circumstances and the Court has struck down a scheme of warrantless electronic surveillance in exigent circumstances on the basis that the scheme did not even require notification after the fact of those who had their conversations electronically recorded.[62]

The police also do not need to obtain a warrant if the person consents to a search or if they are conducting a reasonable search incident to arrest.[63] Searches incident to arrest must not be conducted in an abusive fashion and do not include the power to seize bodily samples for DNA testing[64] or to take body impressions.[65] The power to conduct a strip search does not follow automatically from the power to conduct a less intrusive search incident to arrest. There must be reasonable and probable grounds for concluding that a strip search is necessary in the particular circumstances of the arrest in order to discover weapons or evidence.[66]

When prior judicial authorization for a search and seizure is sought, it should generally be granted only if there are reasonable and probable grounds established on oath to believe that an offence has been committed and that the search will reveal evidence of the offence.[67] Searches must also be authorized by law, and the law must be reasonable.[68] In response to numerous decisions holding warrantless and illegal searches to be unreasonable, Parliament has enacted new laws to grant warrants and authorizing warrantless searches in exigent circumstances. For example, the Court's decision that wearing a wire without a warrant violated section 8 of the *Charter* was followed

---

61 *R. v. Grant* (1993), 84 C.C.C. (3d) 173 (S.C.C.).
62 *R. v. Tse*, 2012 SCC 16.
63 *Cloutier v. Langlois* (1990), 53 C.C.C. (3d) 257 (S.C.C.); *R. v. Caslake* (1998), 121 C.C.C. (3d) 97 (S.C.C.).
64 *R. v. Stillman* (1997), 113 C.C.C. (3d) 321 (S.C.C.) [*Stillman*]. Warrants can be issued for obtaining DNA samples. See *Code*, above note 1, ss. 487.04–487.091. These warrant provisions have been upheld under the *Charter*: *R. v. S.A.B.*, [2003] 2 S.C.R. 678.
65 *Stillman, ibid.* But see *Code, ibid.*, s. 487.092 for warrants to obtain body impressions.
66 *R. v. Golden*, [2001] 3 S.C.R. 679 at 733.
67 *Canada (Director of Investigation & Research, Combines Investigation Branch) v. Southam Inc.* (1984), 14 C.C.C. (3d) 97 (S.C.C.).
68 *R. v. Collins* (1987), 33 C.C.C. (3d) 1 (S.C.C.).

by the enactment of new provisions allowing judges to issue such warrants and also authorizing the use of wires without warrants in urgent circumstances and to prevent bodily harm.[69] The Court's decision declaring the warrantless use of videotaping to be a violation of section 8 of the *Charter* led to the enactment of a new general warrant provision that allows a judge to grant a warrant authorizing any investigative technique that, if not authorized, would constitute an unreasonable search and seizure.[70] When the Supreme Court declared the common law rule that allowed a warrantless search of a dwelling house in order to make an arrest violated section 8 of the *Charter*, Parliament enacted new provisions that allowed such warrants to be granted and also authorized warrantless entries into dwelling houses to make arrests in exigent circumstances.[71]

Evidence obtained in violation of section 8 of the *Charter* will not automatically be excluded under section 24(2) of the *Charter*. Judges will apply a three-part test that examines [1] the seriousness of the *Charter* violation, [2] the impact of the *Charter* violation on the accused's *Charter*-protected interests, and [3] society's interests in an adjudication on the merits.[72] The courts have been reluctant to exclude evidence that was unreasonably seized if the police have acted in good faith and have not committed flagrant improprieties. They will balance the seriousness of the *Charter* violation and the impact of the *Charter* violation on the accused's *Charter*-protected interests against the harm to the repute of the administration of justice caused by the exclusion of evidence.

b) Arbitrary Detention and Imprisonment

Section 9 of the *Charter* provides that everyone has the right not to be arbitrarily detained or imprisoned. Detention has been defined broadly under both sections 9 and 10 of the *Charter* to include detention with respect to a demand or direction that may have legal consequences, such as a demand for a breath sample, physical restraint, and psycho-

---

69   *Duarte*, above note 46. See *Code*, above note 1, ss. 184.1–184.4. See now *R. v. Tse*, above note 62.

70   *Wong*, above note 46. See now *Code, ibid.*, ss. 184.1–184.4 and 487.01. This general warrant provision does not authorize interference with bodily integrity. Parliament, however, has enacted other provisions that allow warrants to be obtained to seize DNA samples and take body impressions. See *Code, ibid.*, ss. 487.04–487.09 and 487.091.

71   *R. v. Feeney* (1997), 115 C.C.C. (3d) 129 (S.C.C.). See *Code, ibid.*, ss. 487.04–487.09, 487.091, and 529. Exigent circumstances are defined to include the need to prevent imminent bodily harm or death and the imminent loss or destruction of evidence. *Code, ibid.*, s. 529.3.

72   *R. v. Grant*, [2009] 2 S.C.R. 353 [*Grant*].

logical compulsion that leaves individuals with the reasonable belief that they have no choice but to comply with the police.[73] People are detained when pulled over to the side of the road by the police, and laws authorizing random vehicle stops violate section 9 because they provide no objective criteria to govern who is detained. Nevertheless, these laws have been upheld under section 1 as reasonable limits necessary to prevent drunk driving and to ensure traffic safety[74] despite a strong dissent that argued that the Court was allowing "any individual officer to stop any vehicle, at any time, at any place. The decision may be based on any whim. Individual officers will have different reasons."[75] Random stops are permissible when undertaken for reasons of traffic safety.

The Supreme Court has held that a person will not be detained under section 9 if questioned by the police in a non-adversarial manner, for example, with respect to emergency calls or accidents. Other relevant factors include the nature of the police conduct and the characteristics of the individual, including age and minority status. In *Grant*, the accused was not detained when a police officer asked him his name and address but was detained when the police officer told him to keep his hands in front of him.[76]

Section 9 only provides protection against arbitrary detention not all detention. A detention will be arbitrary if it is not authorized by law or if the law that authorizes the detention is itself arbitrary.[77] A detention may also be arbitrary if the officer "was biased towards a person of a different race, nationality or colour" or had "a personal enmity"[78] towards a particular detainee.

The Supreme Court has recognized and effectively created powers of investigative detention that allow a person to be briefly detained if there are reasonable grounds to suspect that he or she is connected to a particular crime and the detention is reasonably necessary. In such cases, a person is detained, but the detention is not arbitrary. Reasonable suspicion will generally require individualized suspicion.[79] If a stop goes beyond a brief detention, however, it may be characterized as an arbitrary detention.[80] There is some evidence in Canada that un-

---

73   *Ibid.* at para. 31.
74   *Hufsky*, above note 58; *R. v. Ladouceur* (1990), 56 C.C.C. (3d) 22 (S.C.C.).
75   *Ladouceur, ibid.* at 29.
76   *Grant*, above note 72 at paras. 36–37, 44, and 48–52.
77   *Ibid.* at para. 54.
78   *R. v. Storrey*, [1990] 1 S.C.R. 241 at 251–52.
79   *R. v. Mann*, [2004] 3 S.C.R. 59.
80   *R. v. Clayton*, 2007 SCC 32 at para. 19.

popular minorities are disproportionately targeted for investigative stops by the police.[81]

If the accused has been arbitrarily detained, there is a limit to what the criminal court can do. If evidence was obtained, it can be excluded under section 24(2). In *Grant*,[82] however, the Court was unwilling to exclude drugs and a gun discovered as a result of an arbitrary detention of a young African-Canadian man. A criminal court cannot award damages, but courts can reduce the accused's sentence if convicted in response to Charter violations and other abuses of power.[83] Halting the prosecution by a stay of proceedings may be an option if the violation is very serious.

[handwritten margin note: what a criminal court can do in response to breach]

A detained person has the right under section 10(c) of the *Charter* to seek *habeas corpus* and to be released if the detention is not lawful. Under section 11(e) of the *Charter*, a detainee has a right not to be denied reasonable bail without just cause. A person can be detained for valid reasons such as ensuring his or her appearance in court or preventing the commission of a crime. Despite recognizing the difficulty of predicting future danger, the Supreme Court has upheld denial of bail to prevent the substantial likelihood of future crime or interference with the administration of justice on the basis that "the bail system . . . does not function properly if individuals commit crimes while on bail."[84] The Court also upheld a reverse onus that required those charged with drug trafficking to establish why they should not be detained.[85] The Court did strike down pre-trial detention in the public interest as excessively vague on the basis that "a standardless sweep does not become acceptable simply because it results from the whims of judges and justices of the peace rather than the whims of law enforcement officials. Cloaking whims in judicial robes is not sufficient to satisfy the principles of fundamental justice.[86] In 1997, Parliament responded by authorizing the denial of bail for

> any other just cause . . . and, without limiting the generality of the foregoing, where detention is necessary in order to maintain confidence in

---

81   *Report of the Manitoba Aboriginal Justice Inquiry* (Winnipeg: Queen's Printer, 1991); *Report of the Commission on Systemic Racism in the Ontario Criminal Justice System* (Toronto: Queen's Printer, 1995); Ontario Human Rights Commission, *Paying the Price: The Human Cost of Racial Profiling* (Toronto: Ontario Human Rights Commission, 2004).

82   *Grant*, above note 72.

83   *R. v. Nasogaluak*, [2010] 1 S.C.R. 206.

84   *R. v. Morales* (1992), 77 C.C.C. (3d) 91 at 107 (S.C.C.) [*Morales*].

85   *R. v. Pearson* (1992), 77 C.C.C. (3d) 124 (S.C.C.).

86   *Morales*, above note 84 at 101.

the administration of justice, having regard to all the circumstances, including the apparent strength of the prosecution's case, the gravity of the nature of the offence, the circumstances surrounding its commission and the potential for a lengthy term of imprisonment.[87]

The Supreme Court held that this provision, with the exception of the vague phrase "any other just cause" did not violate section 11(e) of the *Charter* because the maintenance of confidence in the administration of justice was a legitimate object of the bail system. Four judges dissented and argued that the new section was not fundamentally different from the prior and vague public interest ground and that it could allow an accused's liberty to be deprived on the basis of subjective and irrational fears by the public.[88]

c) Right to Counsel

Section 10(b) of the *Charter* provides those who are subject to arrest or detention with both a right to retain and instruct counsel without delay and a right to be informed of that right. Detention has been interpreted broadly to include not only deprivation of liberty by physical constraint, but also the assumption of control over a person by a demand with significant legal consequences that would otherwise impede access to counsel and psychological compulsion in the form of a reasonable perception of a lack of freedom of choice. Even a brief five-minute detention in the back of a police car may require a right to counsel warning, if the police ask questions.[89] A person is detained when required to provide a breath sample, either at the roadside or at a police station. However, the denial of the right to counsel for a person who must give a breath sample into a roadside screening device has been held to be justified under section 1 of the *Charter* as a reasonable limit required to combat drunk driving.[90] This section 1 limit has also been extended to requests by the police that the driver answer questions about his or her drinking and perform roadside sobriety tests even though these actions were not specifically authorized by legislation.[91] Nevertheless, a person facing a demand for a breath sample at the police station must be informed of his or her right to retain and instruct counsel without

---

87 *Code*, above note 1, s. 515(10) as am. by S.C. 1997, c. 18, s. 59.
88 *R. v. Hall* (2002), 167 C.C.C. (3d) 449 (S.C.C.).
89 *R. v. Elshaw* (1991), 67 C.C.C. (3d) 97 (S.C.C.).
90 *R. v. Thomsen* (1988), 40 C.C.C. (3d) 411 (S.C.C.).
91 *R. v. Orbanski*, [2005] 2 S.C.R. 3.

delay[92] and the limitations under section 1 that apply to *Charter* rights at the roadside only apply for a limited time.[93]

Upon arrest or detention, the police must inform detainees not only that they can consult a lawyer, but also about the availability of publicly funded legal aid for those who cannot afford a lawyer and duty counsel who can provide temporary legal advice regardless of the suspect's financial status.[94] Most provinces have established toll-free telephone numbers that allow detainees to contact duty counsel on a twenty-four-hour basis. The police must generally inform detainees of available services, including the toll-free telephone number, but the Supreme Court has refused to require governments to establish such services despite evidence that they are efficient and practical.[95] The courts have also not required the police to videotape or audiotape interrogations.[96]

Once a detainee asks to speak to a lawyer, the police must facilitate access to counsel by offering the use of a telephone.[97] The police must hold off eliciting evidence until the suspect has had a reasonable opportunity to contact counsel. The detainee should be allowed, within reason, to consult a lawyer of his or her own choice and to consult with that lawyer in privacy. The detainee must, however, exercise the right to contact counsel with reasonable diligence and the police do not have to hold off in cases where detainees wish to speak to a particular lawyer who is likely to be unavailable.[98]

Once an accused has been given a reasonable opportunity to consult counsel, questioning may resume without again informing the accused of the right to counsel or providing another reasonable opportunity to consult counsel.[99] There is no right to have a lawyer present during police questioning as there is in the United States, but the police may have to give the detainee another opportunity to speak to counsel before asking the detainee to engage in non-routine procedures such as participating in a line-up or a polygraph. The ability of the police to continue to interrogate applies even in cases where the accused and/or counsel have indicated a desire not to talk and the interrogation is lengthy and involves confronting the accused with actual or fake evi-

---

92   R. v. *Therens* (1985), 18 C.C.C. (3d) 481 (S.C.C.).

93   R. v. *Woods*, [2005] 2 S.C.R. 205.

94   R. v. *Brydges* (1990), 53 C.C.C. (3d) 330 (S.C.C.) [*Brydges*].

95   R. v. *Prosper* (1994), 92 C.C.C. (3d) 353 (S.C.C.).

96   R. v. *Barrett* (1995), 96 C.C.C. (3d) 319 (S.C.C.).

97   R. v. *Manninen* (1987), 34 C.C.C. (3d) 385 (S.C.C.) [*Manninen*].

98   R. v. *Smith* (1989), 50 C.C.C. (3d) 308 (S.C.C.); R. v. *Willier*, [2010] 2 S.C.R. 429; R. v. *McCrimmon*, [2010] 2 S.C.R. 402.

99   R. v. *Hebert* (1990), 57 C.C.C. (3d) 1 (S.C.C.) [*Hebert*].

dence.[100] The right to counsel may, however, be violated by prolonged questioning without counsel being present, police denigration of counsel, or the offer of a plea bargain without counsel being present.[101]

The accused's right to counsel can be subject to informed and voluntary waiver. A murder suspect who was too drunk to be aware of the consequences cannot waive her rights to counsel.[102] Accused persons who answered baiting questions or participated in a line-up before being given a reasonable opportunity to consult counsel have not waived their right to counsel.[103] An accused who asked about legal aid, but was not informed about its availability, did not waive the right to counsel when he subsequently answered questions.[104] An accused who confessed after the police had insulted his counsel of choice also did not waive the right to counsel.[105]

Statements taken in violation of the right to counsel will presumptively be excluded because of the importance of the police respecting the right to counsel, the adverse effect of such statements on Charter-protected interests such as the right to silence, and concerns about the reliability of statements taken in violation of the Charter. Nevertheless, exclusion of evidence taken in violation of section 10(b) is not automatic especially in cases of minor violations.[106]

Section 10(a) of the Charter also requires a person to be informed promptly of the reason for detention or arrest. This does not require an explicit warning if the matter being investigated was obvious.[107] The right was violated, however, when an accused was not aware that he was also held for a second more serious sexual assault[108] or when he believed he was being held for drug offences, not murder.[109] If an attempted murder becomes a murder after the victim dies, the accused should be so informed and have another opportunity to consult counsel.[110] There is no constitutional obligation to inform detainees of their right to silence, but such a warning is customary. An independent right to silence under section 7 of the Charter may also be violated where the state tricks an accused under detention into making a statement by having

---

100 R. v. Sinclair, [2010] 2 S.C.R. 310.
101 R. v. Burlingham (1995), 97 C.C.C. (3d) 385 (S.C.C.) [Burlingham].
102 R. v. Clarkson (1986), 25 C.C.C. (3d) 207 (S.C.C.).
103 Manninen, above note 97; R. v. Ross (1989), 46 C.C.C. (3d) 129 (S.C.C.).
104 Brydges, above note 94.
105 Burlingham, above note 101.
106 Grant, above note 72 at paras. 89–98.
107 R. v. Evans (1991), 63 C.C.C. (3d) 289 (S.C.C.) [Evans].
108 R. v. Borden (1994), 92 C.C.C. (3d) 404 (S.C.C.).
109 Evans, above note 107.
110 R. v. Black (1989), 50 C.C.C. (3d) 1 (S.C.C.).

an undercover officer or informant elicit a statement from him or her. Listening to an incriminating statement that was volunteered would not violate the right to silence.[11] In most cases, a voluntary statement will be found not to violate the right to silence and the right to silence is not violated just because a person in custody initially refuses to speak to the police.[112]

voluntary statements

The division between regulatory and criminal contexts is also relevant to the right to silence. A person who enters into a regulated environment may have to answer questions from state regulators, but such co-operation cannot be required when the Rubicon from regulation to prosecution has been crossed and the dominant purpose of the inquiry is the determination of criminal liability.[113] A person can be required by law to provide incriminating answers and materials as part of a terrorism investigation, provided that the state is not allowed to use such answers or materials or any other evidence derived from such material or answers.[114]

regulatory / criminal offences

terrorism

d) Entrapment

Before the advent of the *Charter*, Canadian courts were reluctant to recognize a defence of entrapment. In the 1982 case of *R. v. Amato*,[115] the Supreme Court affirmed a conviction for trafficking in narcotics even though an undercover police officer had persistently solicited the accused to sell him cocaine and made implied threats of violence. In a strong dissent, Estey J. concluded that entrapment should be recognized as a common law defence designed to ensure that the administration of justice is not brought into disrepute. He would have stayed proceedings because of the police conduct in the case. Six years later in *R. v. Mack*,[116] the Supreme Court recognized the defence of entrapment. The Court stressed that the defence could be available even though the accused committed the *actus reus* with the requisite degree of fault. A finding of entrapment results in a permanent stay of proceedings rather than an acquittal. Because it is a matter independent of guilt or innocence, entrapment must be established by the accused on a balance of probabilities, and the determination of entrapment can be left until after the accused's guilt has been established. The judge, rather

---

111 *Hebert*, above note 99; *R. v. Broyles* (1991), 68 C.C.C. (3d) 308 (S.C.C.); *R. v. Liew* (1999), 137 C.C.C. (3d) 353 (S.C.C.).

112 *R. v. Singh*, 2007 SCC 48.

113 *Jarvis*, above note 52 at para. 88.

114 *Re Section 83.28 of the Criminal Code*, [2004] 2 S.C.R. 248.

115 (1982), 69 C.C.C. (2d) 31 (S.C.C.).

116 *R. v. Mack* (1988), 44 C.C.C. (3d) 513 (S.C.C.) [*Mack*].

than the jury, decides whether entrapment has been made out because the judge is the best person to determine whether the state's activities would bring the administration of justice into disrepute.

Entrapment occurs if the state offers a person an opportunity to commit a crime without reasonable suspicion that the person was engaged in criminal activity or while not engaged in a *bona fide* inquiry into crime in a high-crime area. The state must provide an opportunity to commit a crime and a simple drug buy may not even constitute offering an opportunity.[117] Even if there is a reasonable suspicion or a *bona fide* inquiry, entrapment will also occur if the state goes beyond providing the accused with an opportunity to commit a crime and actually induces its commission.

A reasonable suspicion is less than reasonable and probable grounds to believe a person has committed a specific crime. In *Mack*, the Court determined that the police acted with reasonable suspicion in conducting a six-month drug sting because the accused was a former drug user with several drug convictions and even though the accused told the police informer he was only interested in real estate. On the other hand, the police officer in *Barnes* who had a (correct) hunch that a scruffily dressed male who looked around a lot was selling marijuana did not have a reasonable suspicion because her impressions of the suspect were too general and subjective.[118]

Even though the police did not have a reasonable suspicion and engaged in random virtue testing in *Barnes*, the Supreme Court held there was no entrapment because the police were acting pursuant to a *bona fide* inquiry into criminal activity by offering a person an opportunity to commit the crime because he was present in a place (the Granville Street Mall in Vancouver) associated with the particular criminal activity. McLachlin J. dissented on the basis that the high-crime area was described very broadly and that insufficient attention had been paid to the likelihood of the crime at the location targeted, its seriousness, the number of innocent people affected, and the availability of less intrusive investigative techniques. In any event, the majority's approach would allow random virtue testing of those found in areas associated with drugs or prostitution. In other words, the police can offer someone an opportunity to sell drugs or solicit prostitution simply because that person is in an area associated with that crime and even if they do not have a reasonable suspicion that the person is engaged in the particular crime.

---

117 *R. v. Imoro*, 2010 ONCA 122, aff'd [2010] 3 S.C.R. 62 [*Imoro*].

118 *R. v. Barnes* (1991), 63 C.C.C. (3d) 1 (S.C.C.) [*Barnes*].

inducing commission of crime

Even if they have reasonable suspicion or are acting on a *bona fide* inquiry, the police should never go beyond providing the suspect an opportunity to commit a crime and actually induce the commission of a crime. The police will go over this line if their conduct is so objectionable that it brings the administration of justice into disrepute and would have induced an average person to have committed the crime. A few phone calls to an old friend to set up a drug buy do not go over the line, but persistent solicitation accompanied with veiled threats does.[119] A brief conversation between an undercover officer and a person selling drugs will also not constitute entrapment.[120] The courts will also examine the proportionality between the conduct of the state and the accused and whether the state had instigated the crime and exploited the accused. The fact that the police may have acted illegally in selling the accused narcotics does not automatically merit a stay unless the activity would shock the conscience of the community and be so detrimental to the proper administration of justice that it warrants judicial intervention.[121] When determining whether the state has gone beyond providing an opportunity, the focus is on the propriety of the conduct of police and their agents. There may still be entrapment even though the accused was predisposed to commit the crime and had the intent to commit the crime.[122] At the same time, the fact that the police or a state informant violated the law does not automatically result in entrapment and a stay of proceedings.[123] There will not be an entrapment defence, when the accused is entrapped into committing a crime by private individuals not acting for the state. Depending on the threats used, such an accused may nevertheless have a defence of duress. That defence is examined in chapter 9.

3) The *Charter* and the Criminal Trial Process

The *Charter* also plays an important role in the criminal trial process by ensuring that the trial is conducted in a fair manner. Section 7 of the *Charter* provides the basic guarantee that everyone has the right to life, liberty, and security of the person and that these rights can only be taken away "in accordance with the principles of fundamental justice." This broad guarantee affects all aspects of the criminal process, with

---

119 *Mack*, above note 116; *R. v. Showman* (1988), 45 C.C.C. (3d) 289 (S.C.C.).

120 *Imoro*, above note 117.

121 *R. v. Campbell* (1999), 133 C.C.C. (3d) 257 (S.C.C.) [*Campbell*].

122 *R. v. S.(J.)* (2001), 152 C.C.C. (3d) 317 (Ont. C.A.).

123 *Campbell*, above note 121. See now s. 25.1 of the *Criminal Code* authorizing the police to do acts that would otherwise constitute an offence.

section 11 of the *Charter* articulating specific rights possessed by any person charged with an offence. Section 11 includes the right to be tried within a reasonable time (11(b)); not to be compelled to be a witness in proceedings against that person in respect of the offence (11(c)); to be presumed innocent until proven guilty according to law in a fair and public hearing by an independent and impartial tribunal (11(d)); to trial by jury where the maximum punishment for the offence is imprisonment for five years or more (11(f)); and protection from double jeopardy (11(h)).

a) Disclosure

One of the most important rights in the criminal trial process is the Crown's obligation to disclose to the accused all relevant evidence in its possession. Disclosure is considered necessary to protect the accused's right to make full answer and defence under section 7 of the *Charter*. The Crown has a special obligation within an adversarial system of criminal justice to treat the accused fairly. The Supreme Court has explained:

> [T]he fruits of the investigation which are in the possession of counsel for the Crown are not the property of the Crown for use in securing a conviction but the property of the public to be used to ensure that justice is done. In contrast, the defence has no obligation to assist the prosecution and is entitled to assume a purely adversarial role toward the prosecution.[124]

In general, all relevant evidence in the Crown's possession should be disclosed to the accused and there is no distinction between inculpatory and exculpatory evidence. The investigating police force also has a duty to participate in this disclosure, including disclosing misconduct relating to the investigation or that could reasonably impact the case against the accused.[125] Evidence disclosed to the defence will usually include statements that witnesses made to the police and physical evidence seized at the crime scene. The Crown can decide what evidence is relevant and can delay disclosure for legitimate reasons, such as protecting informers. In controversial decisions, the Supreme Court has ruled that the Crown must disclose to the accused all medical and therapeutic records in its possession without regard to the privacy and equality interests of complainants in sexual assault trials[126] and stayed proceedings because a rape crisis centre had shredded its records of

---

124 R. v. *Stinchcombe* (1991), 68 C.C.C. (3d) 1 at 7 (S.C.C.).
125 R. v. *McNeil*, [2009] 1 S.C.R. 66.
126 R. v. *O'Connor* (1995), 103 C.C.C. (3d) 1 (S.C.C.).

an interview with a complainant.[127] Parliament responded to these decisions with new legislation restricting the accused's access to the personal records of complainants in sexual assault cases including material in the Crown's possession. The legislation has been upheld as a reasonable balance of the accused's and complainant's rights.[128] Criminal courts may also award costs and order new trials as remedies for disclosure violations.[129]

b) Right to Full Answer and Defence

Section 7 of the *Charter* also has been interpreted to provide the accused with a right to make a full answer and defence in response to criminal charges. In general, the prejudice of evidence must substantially outweigh its probative value before the accused is prevented from calling evidence. In *R. v. Seaboyer*,[130] the Supreme Court held that section 277, which bans evidence about sexual reputation to challenge or support the credibility of the complainant in a sexual assault trial, did not violate section 7 because there was no logical link between one's sexual reputation and one's truthfulness. The Court did, however, find that a "rape shield" provision that restricted the admissibility of the complainant's prior sexual conduct with people other than the accused did violate the accused's right to make full answer and defence in part because such conduct might be relevant to the controversial defence that the accused honestly but perhaps not reasonably had a mistaken belief that the complainant consented. Parliament responded to this ruling by modifying the mistaken belief in consent defence and by establishing a new procedure that requires judges to balance the accused's right to make full answer and defence against other factors, including society's interest in encouraging the reporting of sexual assaults, the need to remove discriminatory bias from fact-finding and potential prejudice to the complainant's rights of privacy, personal security, and the full protection and benefit of the law.[131] This new provision has been held to be consistent with the accused's rights.[132] The right to full answer and defence also requires that the accused be able

---

127 *R. v. Carosella* (1997), 112 C.C.C. (3d) 289 (S.C.C.).

128 *Code*, above note 1, ss. 278.1–278.89. Upheld in *R. v. Mills*, [1999] 3 S.C.R. 668.

129 *R. v. 974649 Ontario Inc.* (2001), 159 C.C.C. (3d) 321 (S.C.C.); *R. v. Taillefer*, [2003] 3 S.C.R. 307.

130 (1991), 66 C.C.C. (3d) 321 (S.C.C.).

131 *Code*, above note 1, s. 276.

132 *R. v. Darrach* (2000), 148 C.C.C. (3d) 97 (S.C.C.) [*Darrach*].

to conduct a thorough cross-examination of the Crown's witnesses,[133] as well as call his or her own witnesses.

c) Trial in a Reasonable Time

An important right in the pre-trial process is the Crown's obligation under section 11(b) of the *Charter* to provide a trial in a reasonable time. If the accused's section 11(b) right is violated, the accused is entitled to a stay of proceedings.[134] This right does not usually apply to delay before a charge is laid, and there is no statute of limitations that prevents the prosecution of indictable offences committed long ago.[135] Courts have allowed charges to proceed even though the allegations relate to matters that occurred decades ago.[136] A stay of proceedings might be entered if the passage of time has made it impossible for the accused to exercise the right to full answer and defence because of the unavailability of crucial evidence.[137]

Whether the accused's right to a trial in a reasonable time has been violated depends on the length of the delay (delays of more than eight to ten months can be suspect) and the explanation for the delay (some delays may be attributable to the accused, but systemic delay caused by a backlog of cases and unavailability of judges is charged to the Crown). It also depends on whether the accused has waived his or her rights by consenting to the delay, and whether the accused has suffered prejudice. This latter factor has been stressed more in cases after the 1990 *Askov* decision, indicating that delays beyond six to eight months were unreasonable, led to the stay of more than 50,000 charges.[138] Even under this more deferential approach there are limits to how much delay will be tolerated. A thirty-month delay in a case where the defence did not contribute to the delay led to the stay of proceedings of a sexual assault case.[139]

---

133 *R. v. Lyttle*, [2004] 1 S.C.R. 193.

134 *R. v. Askov* (1990), 59 C.C.C. (3d) 449 (S.C.C.).

135 There is a six-month statute of limitations on less serious summary conviction offences but this can be waived with the agreement of the prosecutor and the accused. The accused might agree to waive the limitation in cases in which the prosecutor has the discretion to lay the charge as a more serious indictable offence. *Code*, above note 1, s. 786(2).

136 *R. v. L.(W.K.)* (1991), 64 C.C.C. (3d) 321 (S.C.C.).

137 *R. v. MacDonnell* (1997), 114 C.C.C. (3d) 145 (S.C.C.).

138 *R. v. Morin* (1992), 71 C.C.C. (3d) 1 (S.C.C.).

139 *R. v. Godin*, [2009] 2 S.C.R. 3.

d) Pre-Trial Publicity

The *Criminal Code* provides for mandatory publication bans at the accused's request on evidence heard at bail hearings or at preliminary inquiries.[140] The Supreme Court has upheld the former as a reasonable limit on freedom of expression in large part because of the importance of ensuring a fair trial and an expeditious bail process.[141] Trial proceedings when the jury is not present, such as a voir dire to determine the admissibility of evidence, also cannot be published until the jury retires to consider its verdict.[142].

A discretionary publication ban must be justified on the basis that it is necessary to prevent a real and substantial risk to the fairness of the trial because alternative measures will not prevent the risks. Courts should attempt to harmonize the public's right to freedom of expression with the accused's right to a fair trial by devising, where possible, alternatives short of publication bans.[143] Alternatives include adjournments of trials; changing the location or venue of the trial to where there has been less publicity; allowing the accused to question prospective jurors more closely; sequestering juries and instructing them to disregard matters that they heard outside the courtroom. Even if a publication ban is the only way to protect the accused's right to a fair trial, it must be as limited in scope and time as possible, and the Court must determine that the good achieved by the ban in protecting a fair trial or other important interests outweighs the harm the ban causes to freedom of expression.

e) Right to a Jury Trial

An accused who faces five years of imprisonment or more has a right to trial by jury under section 11(f). If the accused fails to appear for trial, however, he or she can subsequently be denied trial by jury.[144] If the accused is charged with an indictable offence that is not listed in section 553 of the *Criminal Code*, he or she may elect or select a trial by jury. A jury is composed of twelve citizens who should represent a fair cross-sample of the public in the place where the case is tried. It is possible, however, to have a jury trial moved to another location within the province.[145]

---

140 *Code*, above note 1, ss. 517, 539,
141 *Toronto Star Newspapers Ltd. v. Canada*, [2010] 1 S.C.R. 721.
142 *Code*, above note 1, s. 648.
143 *Dagenais v. Canadian Broadcasting Corp.* (1994), 94 C.C.C. (3d) 289 (S.C.C.); *R. v. Mentuck*, [2001] 3 S.C.R. 442.
144 *R. v. Lee* (1989) 52 C.C.C. (3d) 289 (S.C.C.).
145 *Code*, above note 1, s. 599.

In selecting the jury, the Crown and the accused can challenge prospective jurors for cause, with the most important ground being that the person is not indifferent between the Crown and the accused. They can ask prospective jurors questions provided a judge has decided that the questions respond to a realistic potential for partiality.[146] These questions may be aimed at the possibility of racial bias against the accused but need not include the interracial nature of an alleged crime or possible partiality with respect to the complainant[147] or bias based on the nature of the charge faced by the accused.[148] The last two jurors called, as opposed to the judge, determine whether the next juror is impartial. The accused and the Crown each have the same limited number of peremptory challenges they can use to remove prospective jurors without giving any reasons.[149] The jury deliberates in secret and they must agree unanimously to a verdict of guilt or innocence. If they cannot agree, they are a "hung jury" and a new trial may be held. An instruction from the judge that the jury must convict violates the right to a trial by jury under section 11(f).[150] Except in limited circumstances, it is a criminal offence for a juror to disclose information about the jury's deliberations.[151]

Section 11(d) protects the right to a fair and public hearing by an independent and impartial tribunal. Judges must have security of tenure, and can only be removed for cause related to their capacity to perform judicial functions. They must also have financial security and independence over their administration as it bears directly upon the exercise of their judicial function. Provincial court judges and even part-time judges have been held to be sufficiently independent, but military officers acting as court martial judges have not.

The accused's right to a fair trial will in more complex cases include a right to have a lawyer if the accused cannot afford one. In such cases, courts can stay proceedings until a lawyer is appointed or order that counsel be provided. The accused also has a right to effective assistance of counsel. To violate that right, however, it is necessary that the accused

146 R. v. Williams (1998), 124 C.C.C. (3d) 481 (S.C.C.).

147 R. v. Spence, [2005] 3 S.C.R. 458.

148 R. v. Find, [2001] 1 S.C.R. 863.

149 Code, above note 1, s. 634. The accused's right to a fair trial was violated by previous provisions that effectively gave the Crown over four times as many peremptory challenges as the accused. R. v. Bain (1992), 69 C.C.C. (3d) 481 (S.C.C.).

150 R. v. Krieger, [2006] 2 S.C.R. 501.

151 Code, above note 1, s. 649.

establish both that the performance by the lawyer was unreasonable and that it caused prejudice in the form of a miscarriage of justice.[152]

f) Right to Be Presumed Innocent

Section 11(d) also provides that the accused has the right "to be presumed innocent until proven guilty according to law in a fair and public hearing by an independent and impartial tribunal." The first part of the right embraces the presumption of innocence, which has been referred to as the "one golden thread" running "throughout the web of the English common law."[153] The presumption of innocence refers to the burden placed on the Crown to prove the accused's guilt. It also includes the requirement that the Crown prove guilt by a high degree or quantum of proof. Chief Justice Dickson has stated that "[t]he presumption of innocence confirms our faith in humankind; it reflects our belief that individuals are decent and law-abiding members of the community until proven otherwise."[154]

i)   Quantum of Proof

Proof beyond a reasonable doubt is not easily defined, but it requires the Crown to go beyond the burden used in private law cases of proving that something is more probable than not. If proof on a balance of probabilities as required in civil cases (and when an accused in a criminal trial bears a reverse onus) represents something like a "51 percent rule," then proof beyond a reasonable doubt requires the Crown to establish a significantly higher likelihood that the crime was committed. This mathematical analogy is quite rough and ready and should not be used by judges in their directions to juries.

In *R. v. Lifchus*,[155] the Supreme Court held that the meaning of reasonable doubt must be explained to a jury and undertook that difficult task. The Court indicated that the jury should be told that the reasonable doubt standard is related to the presumption of innocence. It requires more than proof that the accused is probably guilty, but does not require proof to an absolute certainty. A reasonable doubt is not a frivolous or imaginary doubt, but rather a doubt based on reason and common sense that must logically be derived from evidence or absence of evidence. The Supreme Court approved of the following suggested charge to the jury, which explains the meaning of a reasonable doubt and relates it to the presumption of innocence.

---

152 *R. v. B.(G.D.)* (2000), 143 C.C.C. (3d) 289 (S.C.C.).
153 *Woolmington v. D.P.P.*, [1935] A.C. 462 at 481 (H.L.).
154 *R. v. Oakes* (1986), 24 C.C.C. (3d) 321 at 333–34 (S.C.C.) [*Oakes*].
155 (1997), 118 C.C.C. (3d) 1 (S.C.C.).

The accused enters these proceedings presumed to be innocent. That presumption of innocence remains throughout the case until such time as the Crown has on the evidence put before you satisfied you beyond a reasonable doubt that the accused is guilty.

What does the expression "beyond a reasonable doubt" mean?

The term "beyond a reasonable doubt" has been used for a very long time and is a part of our history and traditions of justice. It is so engrained in our criminal law that some think it needs no explanation, yet something must be said regarding its meaning.

A reasonable doubt is not an imaginary or frivolous doubt. It must not be based upon sympathy or prejudice. Rather, it is based on reason and common sense. It is logically derived from the evidence or absence of evidence.

Even if you believe the accused is probably guilty or likely guilty, that is not sufficient. In those circumstances you must give the benefit of the doubt to the accused and acquit because the Crown has failed to satisfy you of the guilt of the accused beyond a reasonable doubt.

On the other hand you must remember that it is virtually impossible to prove anything to an absolute certainty and the Crown is not required to do so. Such a standard of proof is impossibly high.

In short if, based upon the evidence before the Court, you are sure that the accused committed the offence you should convict since this demonstrates that you are satisfied of his guilt beyond a reasonable doubt.[156]

In *R. v. Starr*,[157] a majority of the Supreme Court held that trial judges would err if they did not make clear to the jury that the reasonable doubt standard was much closer to absolute certainty than the balance of probabilities standard used in civil trials and everyday life.

ii) Persuasive Burdens

The presumption of innocence is infringed whenever the accused is liable to be convicted despite the existence of a reasonable doubt about a factor essential for conviction. In *Oakes*, section 11(d) was violated by a statutory provision that required, once the Crown had proven beyond a reasonable doubt the possession of narcotics, that the accused establish on a balance of probabilities that he or she did not have the intent to traffic in order to escape a conviction for the offence of possession

---

156 *Ibid.* at 14.
157 (2000), 147 C.C.C. (3d) 449 (S.C.C.).

of narcotics with the intent to traffic. Dickson C.J. explained how the provision could allow a conviction despite a reasonable doubt:

> If an accused bears the burden of disproving on a balance of probabilities an essential element of an offence, it would be possible for a conviction to occur despite the existence of a reasonable doubt. This would arise if the accused adduced sufficient evidence to raise a reasonable doubt as to his or her innocence but did not convince the jury on a balance of probabilities that the presumed fact was untrue.[158]

Another approach is to examine the relationship between the element that the Crown proves (in this case, possession of narcotics) and the element that is presumed (in this case, the intent to traffic in the narcotics) unless the accused satisfies the burden placed upon him or her. The substitution of one element for an essential element of an offence violates section 11(d) unless "if upon proof beyond reasonable doubt of the substituted element it would be unreasonable for the trier of fact not to be satisfied beyond a reasonable doubt of the essential element."[159] In *Oakes*, there was not this extremely close or inexorable link between what was proved (possession of narcotics) and what was presumed (intent to traffic), and the provision violated section 11(d). In many cases, the jury may have been satisfied beyond a reasonable doubt that the accused had the intent to traffic upon proof of possession of a large quantity of narcotics. The problem was that the provision stated that the jury must draw such a conclusion in all cases. This would include those where the accused failed to provide enough evidence to prove on a balance of probabilities that there was no intent to traffic, but the jury still had a reasonable doubt about the intent to traffic. An important purpose of the presumption of innocence is to ensure that the jury always has the ability to find a reasonable doubt on the basis of any evidence in the case.

iii) Presumption Applies to Elements of Offences, Collateral Factors, and Defences

The presumption of innocence applies not only to essential elements of an offence but also to defences and collateral factors. This makes sense once it is recognized that whether something is an element of an offence, a defence, or a collateral matter is a simple matter of legislative drafting. For example, murder could be redrafted to include all killings, with the accused then having the ability to establish on a balance of

---

158 *Oakes*, above note 154 at 343.
159 *R. v. Vaillancourt* (1987), 39 C.C.C. (3d) 118 at 136 (S.C.C.) [*Vaillancourt*].

probabilities a defence of a lack of intent to kill. Similarly, Parliament could provide that the intent to kill be presumed unless the accused established a collateral factor such as the victim's death was unavoidable. If the presumption of innocence was not applied to these defences and factors, the accused could still be convicted despite a reasonable doubt as to his or her guilt. As Dickson C.J. has explained:

> The exact characterization of a factor as an essential element, a collateral factor, an excuse, or a defence should not affect the analysis of the presumption of innocence. It is the final effect of a provision on the verdict that is decisive. If an accused is required to prove some fact on the balance of probabilities to avoid conviction, the provision violates the presumption of innocence because it permits a conviction in spite of a reasonable doubt in the mind of the trier of fact as to the guilt of the accused.[160]

In *Whyte*, the Court examined a provision that required an accused found in the driver's seat while intoxicated to prove an absence of intent to put the vehicle in motion in order to escape a presumption that the accused was in care and control of the vehicle. This provision violated section 11(d) because it required the accused to be convicted even if he or she was able to raise a reasonable doubt about the intent to put the vehicle in motion but was unable to prove on a balance of probabilities that there was no such intent. This, in turn, triggered a mandatory presumption that the accused was in care and control of the vehicle, which was an essential element of the offence of care and control of a vehicle while impaired. Looked at another way, proof of the substituted fact (being in the driver's seat), plus the accused's inability to prove on a balance of probabilities that there was no intent to drive the car, did not lead inexorably to the conclusion that the presumed fact (care and control) exists. The accused could be convicted even though there was a reasonable doubt about whether he was guilty.

Subsequent to *Whyte*, the Court has held that requiring an accused to prove a defence on a balance of probabilities violates section 11(d) because it allows a conviction despite a reasonable doubt about a factor essential for a conviction. For example, section 319(3) of the *Criminal Code* violates section 11(d) because it requires the accused to prove on a balance of probabilities the defence of truth when charged with a hate propaganda offence. The accused could be convicted even though there was a reasonable doubt that his or her statements were true.[161] Require-

---

160 *R. v. Whyte* (1988), 42 C.C.C. (3d) 97 at 109 (S.C.C.).
161 *R. v. Keegstra* (1990), 61 C.C.C. (3d) 1 (S.C.C.) [*Keegstra*].

ments that an accused prove a defence of due diligence when charged with a regulatory offence violate section 11(d), because the accused could be convicted even though there was a reasonable doubt that he or she was negligent.[162] Similarly, a requirement that the accused establish the mental disorder defence on a balance of probabilities also violates section 11(d), because the accused could be convicted despite a reasonable doubt about his or her sanity.[163] In all these cases, however, the Court found that the legislation was justified under section 1 of the *Charter* as a reasonable limit on section 11(d), because of the difficulties of requiring the Crown to prove beyond a reasonable doubt that the accused did not have the respective defences.

To justify an infringement of section 11(d) or any *Charter* right under section 1 of the *Charter*, the Crown must demonstrate that the objective of the limit is a compelling objective. Moreover, the Crown must then show that there is a rational connection between the violation and the objective. In *R. v. Laba*,[164] the Supreme Court held that it is not necessary for there to be a rational connection between the proven and the presumed factors for a reverse onus to be justified under section 1 of the *Charter*. The Court did note, however, that the lack of a rational connection between the proven and presumed factors would increase the danger of convicting the innocent.[165] Even if the section 11(d) violation is rationally connected with a compelling objective, it must also be the least restrictive means of advancing the objective, and there must be proportionality between the objective and the rights violation. In *Laba*, the Court held that a reverse onus requiring a seller of precious metals to prove legal ownership was not a proportionate limitation on the presumption of innocence because the objective of deterring the theft of such metals could be as effectively advanced by the less restrictive alternative of requiring the accused to meet an evidential burden as to the presence of legal authorization. Once the accused pointed to some evidence of legal authorization, the Crown would still

---

162 *R. v. Wholesale Travel Group Inc.* (1991), 67 C.C.C. (3d) 193 (S.C.C.) [*Wholesale Travel Group*].

163 *R. v. Chaulk* (1990), 62 C.C.C. (3d) 193 (S.C.C.).

164 *R. v. Laba* (1994), 94 C.C.C. (3d) 385 at 417 (S.C.C.) [*Laba*].

165 A rational connection between the proven and the presumed fact would not be sufficient under section 11(d) of the *Charter*, above note 38, because it means only that upon proof of the proven fact, it is probable that the presumed fact was present. Section 11(d) contemplates that the Crown prove its case beyond a reasonable doubt, not on a simple balance of probabilities. In other words, s. 11(d) requires an inexorable connection between the proven element and the presumed element, a condition that would make it unreasonable for the jury to have even a reasonable doubt about the presumed factor.

have to prove beyond a reasonable doubt that the accused did not have such authorization. An evidential burden is a less restrictive alternative to a persuasive burden, even though, as will be seen, it also violates section 11(d) if accompanied by a mandatory presumption.

The courts have on their own initiative imposed persuasive burdens on the accused. In the pre-*Charter* case of *R. v. Sault Ste. Marie (City)*,[166] the Supreme Court imposed a persuasive burden on the accused to establish a new defence of due diligence to strict liability offences. If the accused did not establish this defence, it would be presumed to have been negligent in allowing the *actus reus* to have occurred. The Court also reasoned that the accused was in a good position to prove due diligence. The Court has upheld such reverse onuses under the *Charter* as a reasonable limit on the presumption of innocence.[167]

Even after the *Charter* entrenched the presumption of innocence, courts have imposed burdens on the accused. In *R. v. Daviault*,[168] the Supreme Court imposed a persuasive burden on the accused to prove a defence of extreme intoxication to a general intent offence such as manslaughter or assault, even though the traditional defence of intoxication applies whenever there was a reasonable doubt that the accused had the intent for a specific intent offence such as murder or robbery. In *R. v. Stone*,[169] the Court again on its own initiative held that the accused must establish the defence of non-mental disorder automatism on a balance of probabilities. Thus, an accused no longer will have the benefit of a reasonable doubt that he or she acted in an involuntary manner because of a condition such as sleepwalking or a severe physical or emotional blow. The Court was concerned about consistency in the law and noted that the accused already had to establish the mental disorder and extreme intoxication defences on a balance of probabilities.

In many recent cases, the presumption of innocence seems to be honoured more in its breach. This makes it easier for the Crown to obtain a conviction, but it also opens the possibility for a conviction even though there may be a reasonable doubt that the accused was not guilty.

iv) Evidential Burdens and Mandatory Presumptions

The Supreme Court has held that section 11(d) is violated not only by persuasive burdens that require an accused to prove some factor on a balance of probabilities, but also by evidential burdens that only re-

---

166 (1978), 40 C.C.C. (3d) 353 (S.C.C.).

167 *Wholesale Travel Group Inc.*, above note 162; *R. v. Ellis-Don Ltd.*, [1992] 1 S.C.R. 840.

168 *R. v. Daviault* (1994), 93 C.C.C. (3d) 21 (S.C.C.) [*Daviault*].

169 *R. v. Stone* (1999), 134 C.C.C. (3d) 353 (S.C.C.) [*Stone*].

quire the accused to point to evidence to raise a reasonable doubt about a mandatory presumption. In *R. v. Downey*,[170] the Court held that a provision violated section 11(d) when it required the trier of fact to conclude "in the absence of evidence to the contrary" that an accused was guilty of the offence of living off the avails of prostitution once the prosecution had proven that the accused was habitually in the company of prostitutes. Cory J. stressed: "the fact that someone lives with a prostitute does not lead inexorably to the conclusion that the person is living off the avails."[171] This mandatory presumption violated section 11(d), even though it could be displaced by an accused pointing to some evidence in either the Crown's or the accused's case to raise a reasonable doubt as to the presumed fact and did not require the accused to establish on a balance of probabilities that he did not live off the avails of prostitution. The Court, however, held that the mandatory presumption that could be displaced by satisfying an evidential burden was justified under section 1 of the *Charter* because of the difficulties of requiring prostitutes to testify against their pimps and the ease that a person in a lawful relationship with a prostitute would have in pointing to some evidence that could raise a reasonable doubt about the presumption.[172]

v) Threshold "Air of Reality" Tests

The above combination of an evidential burden with a mandatory presumption should be distinguished from the requirement that there be an air of reality to justify the judge in instructing the jury about a particular issue or defence. These sorts of burdens of establishing an air of reality are quite common. They do not require the accused to prove anything and they make no mandatory presumptions about the commission of the crime. They have generally been seen as a matter of efficient and orderly trial administration and not as raising any presumption of innocence problems.

At the same time, air of reality tests can be quite important and determine the practical meaning of a particular defence. For example, the administration of the defence of mistaken belief in the complainant's consent in sexual assault cases often depends on whether there is

---

170 (1992), 72 C.C.C. (3d) 1 (S.C.C.).

171 *Ibid.* at 14.

172 Three judges dissented on the basis that there was not only no inexorable but also no rational connection between the proven fact (living with a prostitute) and the presumed fact (living off the avails). The requirement of such a connection under s. 1 has now been rejected in *Laba*, above note 164.

an air of reality to justify instructing the jury about the controversial defence.[173]

The air of reality test may also be influenced by whether the accused bears a persuasive burden on the issue. In both *Daviault*[174] and *Stone*,[175] the Court indicated that in order to establish an air of reality about the extreme intoxication and automatism defences respectively, the accused must point to evidence upon which a properly instructed jury will find that the defence has been established on a balance of probabilities. The holding in *Stone* has been qualified in the subsequent case of *Fontaine*[176] in which the Court stressed that the judge should not determine whether evidence is credible or will support proof by the accused on a balance of probabilities of a defence such as extreme intoxication or automatism. Fish J. stated that the threshold air of reality test is not "intended to assess whether the defence is likely, unlikely, somewhat unlikely or very likely to succeed at the end of the day. The question for the trial judge is whether the evidence discloses a real issue to be decided by the jury and not how the jury should ultimately decide the issue. The 'air of reality' test . . . should not be used to . . . introduce a persuasive requirement."[177] The Court also noted that "the cost of risking a wrongful conviction and possibly violating the accused's constitutionally protected rights by inadvisably withdrawing a defence from the jury is a high one."[178]

In *R. v. Cinous*,[179] a majority of the Supreme Court indicated that a consistent air of reality test should be applied throughout the criminal law. The test justifies not instructing the jury about a particular defence if there was no evidence that a properly instructed jury acting reasonably could use to acquit on the basis of the evidence. There must be an air of reality on every requirement of a defence to justify instructing the jury about the defence, but the judge should not determine the credibility of the evidence when assessing whether it has an air of reality. In *Fontaine*,[180] a unanimous Court similarly stated: "In determining whether the evidential burden has been discharged on any

---

173 See ch. 5(D)(4), "Mistake of Fact and Sexual Assault," and ch. 10(B)(3)(b), "Establishing an Air of Reality for a Mistake of Fact Defence."
174 *Daviault*, above note 168.
175 *Stone*, above note 169 at 430.
176 *R. v. Fontaine*, 2004 SCC 27 [*Fontaine*].
177 *Ibid.* at paras. 68 and 70.
178 *Ibid.* at para. 61, quoting Arbour J. in dissent in *R. v. Cinous* (2002), 162 C.C.C. (3d) 129 at para. 200 (S.C.C.).
179 (2002), 162 C.C.C. (3d) 129 (S.C.C.).
180 Above note 176 at para. 57.

defence, trial judges, as a matter of judicial policy, should therefore always ask the very same question: "Is there in the record any evidence upon which a reasonable trier of fact, properly instructed and acting judicially, could conclude that the defence succeeds?" Although the Court in both cases stressed that the accused did not have a persuasive burden to overcome the air of reality test and that the credibility of evidence should be left to the jury, decisions about whether there is an air of reality about a particular defence can be very important in a criminal trial. The air of reality test for each defence depends on the necessary elements of the particular defence and will be discussed in subsequent chapters in relation to various defences.

vi) Summary

Section 11(d) of the *Charter* has been interpreted broadly, so that it is violated any time a statutory provision allows an accused to be convicted in the face of a reasonable doubt as to any factor essential to conviction, including any applicable defences. It also has been interpreted to apply to evidential burdens that only require the accused to point to some evidence to raise a reasonable doubt about a mandatory presumption. At the same time, however, the courts frequently uphold violations of section 11(d) under section 1 of the *Charter* and have on their own initiative imposed a persuasive burden on the accused to establish the defences of extreme intoxication and automatism. Statutory requirements that the accused prove the defence of due diligence in regulatory offences or the defences of mental disorder have also been upheld on the basis that it would be too difficult for the Crown to prove beyond a reasonable doubt that the defence did not apply. There need not be a rational connection between the proven and presumed factors for a presumption to be upheld under section 1 of the *Charter*. Even though an evidential burden with a mandatory presumption itself violates section 11(d), it can be a less drastic alternative to a persuasive burden.

g) Other Trial Rights

Accused have the right in section 14 of the *Charter* to continuous, competent, and contemporaneous interpretation at trial if they are deaf or do not understand or speak the language in which the proceedings are conducted.[181] Under section 11(c), accused cannot be compelled to testify in their own trials. This protection does not extend to corporations and an officer of a corporation can be compelled to testify against his or

---

181 *R. v. Tran* (1994), 92 C.C.C. (3d) 218 (S.C.C.).

her corporation.[182] It also generally does not require judges to instruct juries that they should not draw adverse inferences from the accused's failure to testify.[183] It is not violated by requirements that the accused apply and provide detailed particulars when he wishes to introduce evidence of a complainant's prior sexual conduct in a sexual offence trial.[184]

Under section 13, evidence that an accused gave as a witness in a prior proceeding cannot be used to incriminate him or her "except in a prosecution for perjury or for the giving of contradictory evidence." A person can generally be forced to testify in other proceedings such as the trial of another person or at a public inquiry, but evidence derived from such testimony cannot be admitted in a subsequent trial against that person unless the Crown can demonstrate that it could have been discovered without forcing the accused to participate in his or her own self-incrimination.

Other *Charter* rights are designed to protect the principle of legality by requiring that a person charged with an offence has the right "to be informed without unreasonable delay of the specific offence" (section 11(a)). Section 11(i) protects the accused against the burden of retroactive criminal laws, as does section 11(g), which provides that the accused has the right not to be found guilty unless the act or omission at the time it was committed was an offence under Canadian law or international law, or was criminal according to the general principles of law recognized by the community of nations. The latter phrase was included to allow for the prosecution of war crimes committed in other nations, and such legislation has been upheld under the *Charter*.[185] At the same time, the Court indicated that because of the special stigma of such crimes, the Crown must prove the accused knew or was wilfully blind to facts and circumstances that would bring his acts within the definition of war crimes or crimes against humanity.[186]

4) The *Charter* and Substantive Criminal Offences and Defences

Although they have been primarily concerned with the procedural fairness of investigations and prosecutions, courts under the *Charter* have also evaluated the substance of offences and defences. An accused cannot be convicted if the criminal offence itself results in an unjusti-

---

182 *R. v. Amway Corp.*, [1989] 1 S.C.R. 21.
183 *R. v. Boss* (1988), 46 C.C.C. (3d) 523 (S.C.C.).
184 *Darrach*, above note 132.
185 *R. v. Finta* (1994), 88 C.C.C. (3d) 417 (S.C.C.) [*Finta*].
186 *Ibid.* at 503.

fied violation of one of the rights guaranteed by the *Charter*. Criminal offences have generally been challenged on the grounds that they violated fundamental freedoms, such as freedom of expression, or the principles of fundamental justice.

a) Fundamental Freedoms

Section 2(b) of the *Charter* has been interpreted broadly to include protection for all forms of expression short of violence or threats of violence. At the same time, however, the courts have recognized that criminal prohibitions on some types of expression can be justified as a reasonable limit under section 1 of the *Charter*.

A criminal offence prohibiting solicitation in a public place for the purpose of prostitution has been held to violate freedom of expression, but to be justified as a reasonable response to "the social nuisance of street solicitation."[187] The restriction in section 163 of the *Criminal Code* on the making and distribution of obscene materials also has been found to violate freedom of expression. This restriction, however, is a reasonable limit on freedom of expression provided it is interpreted not to "proscribe sexually explicit erotica without violence that is not degrading or dehumanizing."[188] The Supreme Court has indicated that the criminal law cannot be used to enforce morality *per se,* but that it can act to respond to Parliament's "reasoned apprehension of harm" even if the causal links between the expression and the harm of violence against women and children are not conclusive. The Court also approved of the use of the criminal law "to enhance respect for all members of society, and non-violence and equality in their relations with each other," especially as this relates to the enforcement of "*Charter* values" such as equality.[189]

The crime of possession of child pornography that depicts a person under eighteen years of age in explicit sexual activity or which encourages unlawful sexual activity with those under eighteen years of age has also been held to be a reasonable limit on freedom of expression. The Supreme Court, however, indicated that defences of artistic merit, educational, scientific, or medical purpose or the public good should be liberally interpreted to protect freedom of expression. In addition, exceptions for expressive material created and held privately and for consensual visual recordings of lawful sexual activity that are held pri-

---

187   *Reference re ss. 193 & 195.1(1)(c) of the Criminal Code (Canada)* (1990), 56 C.C.C. (3d) 65 at 77 (S.C.C.).

188   *R. v. Butler* (1992), 70 C.C.C. (3d) 129 at 165 (S.C.C.).

189   *Ibid.* at 168.

vately and not distributed publicly were read into the offence by the Court in order to protect freedom of expression and privacy.[190]

A provision prohibiting the wilful promotion of hatred against an identifiable group has been held to be a reasonable limit on freedom of expression. Dickson C.J. stressed that the requirements that the accused have the intent of wilfully promoting hatred and that the Attorney General approve any prosecution restrict the reach of the provision. He also argued that Parliament can act to prevent the serious harms caused by racial and religious hatred and to respond to "the severe psychological trauma suffered by members of those identifiable groups targeted by hate propaganda."[191]

Two years later, the Supreme Court struck down a provision prohibiting wilfully spreading false news that is likely to injure the public interest. McLachlin J. argued that although the provision could be used to prohibit statements, such as the accused's denial of the Holocaust, which denigrate vulnerable groups:

> Its danger, however, lies in the fact that by its broad reach it criminalizes a vast penumbra of other statements merely because they might be thought to constitute a mischief to some public interest, however successive prosecutors and courts may wish to define these terms. The danger is magnified because the prohibition affects not only those caught and prosecuted, but those who may refrain from saying what they would like to because of the fear that they will be caught.[192]

This provision was struck down because it was broader and less narrowly tailored than the hate propaganda provision examined above. The crime of defamatory libel was also upheld as a justified restriction on freedom of expression, given the need to protect reputations and to establish that the accused intended to make defamatory statements.[193]

In summary, an offence that prohibits any form of expression short of violence will likely violate freedom of expression. Depending on the objective and reach of the offence, however, the courts may find it to be a reasonable limit on expression that can be justified under section 1 of the *Charter.*

---

190 *R. v. Sharpe*, [2001] 1 S.C.R. 45.
191 *Keegstra*, above note 161 at 58.
192 *R. v. Zundel* (1992), 75 C.C.C. (3d) 449 at 521 (S.C.C.).
193 *R. v. Lucas* (1998), 123 C.C.C. (3d) 97 (S.C.C.).

b) Principles of Fundamental Justice

Section 7 of the *Charter* provides that "everyone has the right to life, liberty, and security of the person and the right not to be deprived thereof except in accordance with the principles of fundamental justice." Corporations are not entities that enjoy rights to life, liberty, and security of the person.[194] Nevertheless, courts have allowed corporations to challenge offences that they are charged with on the basis that the offence can also apply to natural persons who enjoy rights under section 7 of the *Charter.*[195] A corporation should be precluded from bringing a section 7 challenge to provisions that only apply to corporations,[196] because section 7 of the *Charter* does not protect the principles of fundamental justice in the abstract, but only in cases where a human being is deprived of the right to life, liberty, and security of the person.

Criminal offences have been struck down under section 7 of the *Charter* as deprivations of liberty and security of the person that are not in accordance with the principles of fundamental justice. The most famous case is *R. v. Morgentaler (No. 2),*[197] in which the Supreme Court found that a law that made it a criminal offence to obtain or provide an abortion without the approval of a hospital committee violated section 7 of the *Charter* and could not be justified under section 1 of the *Charter.* The majority stressed that the law was procedurally unfair to women because of geographic variations in the availability of committees and delays in the process of committee approval. This unfairness was especially significant because committee approval was necessary if a person was to avoid conviction of a criminal offence for either performing or having an abortion. Dickson C.J. stressed the vagueness of the requirement that the committee conclude that the continuation of the pregnancy would likely endanger the woman's life or health. Beetz J. did not think this was too vague, but believed that the provision violated section 7 of the *Charter* because it required delays that were not rationally connected to either the protection of the fetus or the life and health of the pregnant woman. Wilson J. took a more substantive approach and argued that it was a matter of a woman's conscience whether or not to have an abortion and that the state could regulate this decision only in the later stages of the pregnancy. Two judges dissented on the grounds that the law did not violate constitutional rights and the availability of abortions was a matter of policy for the elected legislature.

---

194 *Irwin Toy Ltd. v. Quebec (A.G.),* [1989] 1 S.C.R. 927.

195 *Wholesale Travel Group,* above note 162.

196 See, e.g., *Code,* above note 1, ss. 22.1–22.2 on organizational liability, which is discussed in ch. 6, "Regulatory Offences and Corporate Crime."

197 *R. v. Morgentaler (No. 2)* (1988), 37 C.C.C. (3d) 449 (S.C.C.) [*Morgentaler (No. 2)*].

In *Rodriguez v. British Columbia (A.G.)*,[198] a 5:4 majority of the Supreme Court upheld section 241(b) of the *Criminal Code*, which prohibits a person from assisting a suicide. The majority concluded that the provision affected the applicant's security of the person because it prevented her from receiving assistance in taking her life. However, it did not violate the principles of fundamental justice because of a consensus about the value of protecting human life. In dissent, two judges argued that, following the principles of *Morgentaler*, Sue Rodriguez should be able to make the decision to terminate her own life, while two others argued that the law discriminated against her because of a physical disability that would eventually prevent her from committing suicide without assistance from another person. The Supreme Court has held that smoking marijuana does not engage either protected liberty[199] or privacy[200] interests under section 7 of the *Charter*.

The test for whether a rule or principle constitutes a principle of fundamental justice is that the proposition must be 1) a legal principle; 2) there must be a consensus that the rule or principle is fundamental to the way the legal system ought fairly to operate; and 3) the rule or principle must be identified with sufficient precision to constitute a manageable standard to measure deprivations of life, liberty, or security of the person.[201]

The Court has held that the principle that the criminal law only be used to respond to harm is not a principle of fundamental justice because of a lack of consensus that the criminal law should only be used to respond to harms to others and a lack of precision in the meaning of harm.[202] The Court has also found that the principle that the law should pursue the best interests of children was not a principle of fundamental justice because there was no consensus that it was vital or fundamental to justice and it fails to produce manageable standards.[203] In contrast, the Court held that the presumption that young people are less blameworthy for offences is a principle of fundamental justice with a majority holding that the principle was violated by a presumption that young

---

198 (1993), 85 C.C.C. (3d) 15 (S.C.C.). In *Carter v. Canada (Attorney General)*, 2012 BCSC 886, the prohibition on assisted suicide was struck down as an unjustified violation of the equality rights of the physically disabled and on the basis that it was overbroad and grossly disproportionate as applied to those physically unable to take their own lives.

199 *Malmo-Levine*, above note 9.

200 *R. v. Clay* (2003), 179 C.C.C. (3d) 540 (S.C.C.).

201 *Malmo-Levine*, above note 9 at para. 113; *D.B.*, above note 28 at paras. 46 and 125.

202 *Malmo-Levine*, ibid.

203 *Canadian Foundation for Children, Youth and the Law v. Canada (A.G.)*, [2004] 1 S.C.R. 76 at paras. 11–12 [*Canadian Foundation for Children*].

offenders convicted of certain serious offences should receive an adult sentence.[204] The Court's caution in accepting even well-established legal principles such as the harm and best interests of the child standard as principles of fundamental justice may in part be related by its position that "violations of s. 7 are seldom salvageable by s. 1."[205]

c) Vagueness and Overbreadth

The principles of fundamental justice in section 7 of the *Charter* are offended by offences that are so vague or overbroad that they fail to give fair notice to citizens and provide no limit for law enforcement discretion. As this doctrine relates to the manner in which the courts have defined the criminal act, it will be discussed in chapter 3, which examines the definition and interpretation of the criminal act. It should be noted, however, that courts are very reluctant to hold that criminal offences or defences are unconstitutionally vague and they make allowances for the ability of courts to add an interpretative gloss on vague words such as "undue" or "reasonable."

A law's vagueness may also be a consideration in determining if the law violates a *Charter* right or can be justified under section 1 of the *Charter*. A limitation on a *Charter* right under section 1 must be "prescribed by law" and provide an intelligible standard to determine the manner in which the legislature has limited a *Charter* right.

d) Arbitrariness and Gross Disproportionality

In *R. v. Malmo-Levine*,[206] the Supreme Court considered whether section 7 of the *Charter* restricted Parliament to criminalizing conduct that harmed others. The accused challenged the criminal offence that prohibited the possession of marijuana. The majority of the Court rejected the idea that the harm principle was a principle of fundamental justice or that Parliament could only criminalize conduct that harmed others. It held that there was no consensus that the criminal law should only be used to respond to harms to others and that there was little agreement about what constituted harm. The Court's subsequent finding that there was a reasonable apprehension of harm for

---

204 *D.B.*, above note 28.
205 *Ibid.* at para. 89, quoting Lamer in *Reference Re Motor Vehicle Act (British Columbia) S. 94(2)*, [1985] 2 S.C.R. 486 at 518, 23 C.C.C. (3d) 289 [*B.C. Motor Vehicle Reference*], stating: "[s]ection 1 may, for reasons of administrative expediency, successfully come to the rescue of an otherwise violation of s. 7, but only in cases arising out of exceptional conditions, such as natural disasters, the outbreak of war, epidemics, and the like."
206 (2003), 179 C.C.C. (3d) 417 (S.C.C.).

criminalizing marijuana suggests that even the constitutionalization of the harm principle would not have been a robust tool for demanding parliamentary restraint in the use of the criminal sanction. The courts below, which unlike the Supreme Court had applied the harm principle as a principle of fundamental justice, also found that there was sufficient harm to justify criminalizing the possession of marijuana.[207]

The Supreme Court indicated that a criminal law that was arbitrary, irrational, overbroad, or grossly disproportionate to the state interest being protected would violate section 7 of the *Charter*. In this case, a majority of the Court upheld the marijuana possession offence, concluding that criminalization was not grossly disproportionate to the state interest. The new section 7 standard that criminal laws not be arbitrary or grossly disproportionate seems no more certain than the harm principle that the Court criticized and rejected under section 7 of the *Charter*. The Court held that the availability of imprisonment for the offence of marijuana possession did not violate section 7 of the *Charter* even though it also indicated that imprisonment would ordinarily not be a fit sentence for possession of small amounts of marijuana. The Court seemed to have relied on the availability of sentencing discretion to uphold the criminalization of marijuana under section 7 of the *Charter*. Two judges dissented on the basis that the criminalization of marijuana possession was disproportionate to the harms of marijuana consumption. A third judge dissented on the basis that Parliament could only use the criminal sanction to prevent harm or a risk of harm to others and there was not sufficient harm to others to justify criminalizing the possession of marijuana.

In the Insite safe injection site case,[208] the Supreme Court held that the Minister of Health's refusal to continue to grant a statutory exemption from drug laws was both arbitrary and grossly disproportionate given evidence that removing the use of dirty needles potentially infected with HIV saved lives and the absence of evidence that it increased crime in Vancouver's Downtown Eastside. The Court's decision was important, but was also based on the particular facts established in the case. Similar claims of gross disproportionality and arbitrariness have been made to challenge prostitution laws. The Ontario Court of Appeal concluded that "bawdy house" and "living off the avails of prostitution" were overbroad and grossly disproportionate in imposing costs on the safety of prostitutes that were not necessary to the objectives of the law and clearly outweighed the benefits of the offences.

---

207 See also *R. v. Murdoch* (2003), 11 C.R. (6th) 43 (Ont. C.A.).
208 *Canada (Attorney General) v. PHS Community Services*, 2011 SCC 44.

In both cases, however, the Court of Appeal did not find that the offences were arbitrary or inconsistent with the objectives of controlling nuisances and protecting prostitutes from exploitation. The Court of Appeal read in a restriction that the living off the avails offence would only apply to exploitative relationships and struck the bawdy house offence down while also making it clear that Parliament might enact a new offence that struck a different balance by, for example, only prohibiting large-scale brothels. In a divided decision, the majority of the Court of Appeal also held that the soliciting offence was not arbitrary, overbroad, or grossly disproportionate in addressing the nuisance and neighborhood harms of public solicitation for the purpose of prostitution. It stressed that the trial judge had underemphasized the importance of the legislative objective and overestimated the harms that the solicitation offence could cause to the safety of street prostitutes. Two judges in dissent accepted that the soliciting offence was not arbitrary or overbroad to the legislative objective, but concluded that the balance between achieving the objective and allowing street prostitutes to take steps to protect themselves were grossly disproportionate. This case affirms the willingness of courts to balance the benefits and costs of criminal law when deciding whether a criminal law is grossly disproportionate.[209] At the same time, the offence of polygamy has been held not to be grossly disproportionate or arbitrary given Parliament's reasoned apprehension of harms caused by plural marriages. The Court, however, did hold that the offence was overbroad as it could be applied to minors between twelve and seventeen years of age who could be married, because of the harms that would be caused to them by prosecution.[210] These claims demonstrate the potential of substantive section 7 review on the basis of arbitrariness, gross disproportionality, and overbreadth to be potentially more searching than section 7 review based on vagueness, harm, or required fault elements. It remains to be seen how willing courts will be to strike down democratically enacted criminal laws on the basis that social science evidence suggests that they cause far more harm than they prevent.

e) Fault Requirements

Fault requirements will be discussed in greater detail in chapters 5 and 6. Nevertheless, at this juncture it will be helpful to provide a somewhat less detailed overview of how section 7 of the *Charter* requires certain minimal fault requirements.

---

209 *Canada (Atttorney General) v. Bedford,* 2012 ONCA 186.
210 *Reference re Section 293,* 2011 BCSC 1588 at paras. 1202–5 and 1226.

i)   Moral Innocence and Absolute Liability

In the *B.C. Motor Vehicle Reference*,[211] the Supreme Court indicated that a "law enacting an absolute liability offence will violate section 7 of the *Charter* only if and to the extent that it has the potential of depriving of life, liberty, and security of the person." In that case, there was no doubt that the regulatory offence would deprive an accused of liberty, because it set a minimum penalty of seven days' imprisonment. The law specifically stated that the offence was one of absolute liability so that an accused would be convicted of driving with a suspended licence regardless of whether the accused knew that his or her licence was suspended or was negligent in respect to whether it was suspended. The Supreme Court concluded that the offence could allow the morally innocent to be punished and suggested that a better alternative would have been to allow the accused a defence of due diligence or lack of negligence once the Crown proved the prohibited act of driving with a suspended licence. A strict liability offence, as opposed to one of absolute liability, would do "nothing more than let those few who did nothing wrong remain free."[212]

In *R. v. Pontes*,[213] the Supreme Court subsequently upheld an absolute liability offence but only on the basis that an accused could not be imprisoned for violating it. The rationale would seem to be that while absolute liability offends the principles of fundamental justice by allowing the morally innocent to be punished, it does not violate section 7 of the *Charter* because a sentence other than imprisonment does not affect the accused's rights to life, liberty, or security of the person. At the same time, the Court has not yet decided whether a fine that may result in imprisonment if the accused defaults on payment also affects the accused's right to liberty and security of the person. The Court has also invalidated as absolute liability offences part of a misleading advertising offence punishable by imprisonment that required the accused to make forthwith corrections regardless of whether the accused knew or ought to have known that the advertisement was misleading. The Court stressed that such mandatory retraction requirements were considerably more onerous than the due diligence defence that is generally available to those charged with regulatory offences and could apply in situations where the accused could not reasonably know that there was any misleading advertising requiring correction.[214]

---

211 *B.C. Motor Vehicle Reference*, above note 205 at 311 (C.C.C.). See ch. 6(A), "Absolute Liability Offences," for further discussion.

212 *Ibid.* at 316.

213 (1995), 100 C.C.C. (3d) 353 (S.C.C.).

214 *Wholesale Travel Group Inc.*, above note 167.

The Supreme Court has held that absolute liability criminal offences also violate section 7 of the *Charter*. In *R. v. Hess*,[215] the Court held that a "statutory rape" offence that made sex with a girl under fourteen years of age a crime regardless of whether the accused had an honest belief that she was older constituted an absolute liability offence. The Court held that "a person who is mentally innocent of the offence—who has no *mens rea* with respect to an essential element of the offence—may be convicted and sent to prison."[216] The majority also held that the violation of the accused's section 7 rights could not be justified under section 1 of the *Charter* because a person who honestly believed a girl was over fourteen could not be deterred from committing the crime and, in any event, it would be unjust to punish a morally innocent person in order to deter others. The Court also noted that Parliament had already replaced the unconstitutional offence with one that allowed the accused a defence that he had taken "all reasonable steps to ascertain the age of the complainant."[217] This new provision violated the accused's rights less because it allowed an honest and reasonable mistake that the child was older than fourteen years of age to be a defence. In other words, the new offence imposed fault on the basis of negligence and not simply on the basis that the accused committed the criminal act.

ii) Negligence As a Sufficient Fault Element under the Charter for Most Offences

The above cases indicate that absolute liability offences, where a conviction follows from proof of the prohibited act, will violate section 7 of the *Charter* whenever the offence has the potential to deprive the accused of life, liberty, or security of the person.[218] In these circumstances, section 7 of the *Charter* requires a fault element of at least negligence.[219]

The courts have been more cautious about striking down offences because they do not have fault elements higher than negligence. Criminal offences prohibiting unlawfully causing bodily harm,[220] danger-

---

215 (1990), 59 C.C.C. (3d) 161 (S.C.C.).
216 *Ibid.* at 168.
217 *Code*, above note 1, s. 150.1(4).
218 Corporations do not enjoy life, liberty, or security of the person. Section 7 of the *Charter*, above note 38, would not apply if the offence was drafted to apply only to corporations, but corporations are allowed to argue that an offence is unconstitutional because of its effects on natural persons. *Wholesale Travel Group*, above note 162.
219 Negligence can be defined in various ways. See ch. 5, "The Fault Element, or *Mens Rea.*"
220 *R. v. DeSousa* (1992), 76 C.C.C. (3d) 124 (S.C.C.).

ous driving,[221] careless use of a firearm,[222] and failing to provide the necessities of life[223] have all been upheld on the basis that they require proof of a marked departure from the standard of care that a reasonable person would take in the circumstances. In addition, <u>subjective fault or subjective knowledge of the prohibited consequences is not required to convict an accused of "unlawful act manslaughter"[224] or of misleading advertising.</u>[225] In other words, "an objective fault requirement is constitutionally sufficient for a broad range of offences other than those falling within the relatively small group of offences"[226] so far including only murder, attempted murder, and war crimes.

Objective fault is sufficient even for serious crime such as manslaughter that may be punished by up to life imprisonment. An objective fault element of reasonable foresight of non-trivial bodily harm was held in *Creighton* not to violate section 7 of the *Charter* because

> by the very act of calling the killing *manslaughter* the law indicates that the killing is less blameworthy than murder. It may arise from negligence, or it may arise as the unintended result of a lesser unlawful act. The conduct is blameworthy and must be punished, but its stigma does not approach that of murder.[227]

Section 7 of the *Charter* will not be violated so long as 1) the *mens rea* and the available penalties reflect the particular nature of the crime and its stigma; 2) the punishment is proportionate to the moral blameworthiness of the offender; and 3) those who cause harm intentionally are punished more severely than those who cause harm unintentionally. As will be seen, the courts have held that murder, attempted murder, and war crimes have a special stigma that requires subjective fault in relation to the prohibited act. Although the third standard could affect that ability of Parliament to combine objective and subjective forms of liability, the preceding three principles listed above have so far made a minimal impact on the substantive criminal law.

---

221 R. v. *Hundal* (1993), 79 C.C.C. (3d) 97 (S.C.C.) [*Hundal*].
222 R. v. *Gosset* (1993), 83 C.C.C. (3d) 494 (S.C.C.); R. v. *Finlay* (1993), 83 C.C.C. (3d) 513 (S.C.C.) [*Finlay*].
223 R. v. *Naglik* (1993), 83 C.C.C. (3d) 526 (S.C.C.).
224 R. v. *Creighton* (1993), 83 C.C.C. (3d) 346 (S.C.C.) [*Creighton*].
225 *Wholesale Travel Group*, above note 162.
226 *Creighton*, above note 224 at 354–55, Lamer C.J. in dissent, but not on this issue.
227 *Ibid.* at 374 [emphasis added].

iii) Negligence Standards: Marked Departure from the Standards of a Non-Individuated Reasonable Person

Section 7 of the *Charter* has been interpreted to require more than simple or civil negligence, but rather "a marked departure from the standards of a reasonable person,"[228] in order to convict a person of a criminal offence based on objective fault. This applies even if the offence seems to contemplate a lower standard of negligence such as carelessness, because "the law does not lightly brand a person as a criminal."[229] In *R. v. Beatty*,[230] the Court explained:

> if every departure from the civil norm is to be criminalized, regardless of the degree, we risk casting the net too widely and branding as criminals persons who are in reality not morally blameworthy. Such an approach risks violating the principle of fundamental justice that the morally innocent not be deprived of liberty.

Negligence as a criminal form of fault that can result in the deprivation of liberty requires the prosecutor to prove that the accused's conduct was a marked departure from the standard of care that would be used in the circumstances by the reasonable person.

The question remains, however, who is the reasonable person who is used for the purpose of determining negligence as a form of criminal fault? A majority of the Court in *Creighton* held that when applying an objective standard, personal characteristics of the accused are only relevant if they establish incapacity to appreciate the nature and quality of one's conduct or incapacity to appreciate the risk involved in one's conduct.[231] Four judges dissented and argued that the accused's personal characteristics should be factored into the objective standard to the extent that they indicate either enhanced or reduced foresight from that of a reasonable person.[232] Section 7 is thus not offended by applying objective standards without consideration of the accused's own characteristics, at least when those characteristics do not render the accused incapable of appreciating the relevant risk.

In *R. v. Beatty*,[233] the Court affirmed that a modified objective approach that takes into account the personal characteristics of the ac-

---

228 *Ibid.* at 371–72, quoting *Hundal*, above note 221. See ch. 5(C), "The Degrees of Objective *Mens Rea*," for further discussion.

229 *Finlay*, above note 222 at 521.

230 2008 SCC 5 at para. 34 [*Beatty*].

231 Above note 224 at 384–85, McLachlin J. For further discussion, see ch. 5, "The Fault Element, or *Mens Rea*."

232 *Ibid.*, Lamer C.J.

233 *Beatty*, above note 230 at paras. 37–40.

cused is not required when applying standards of criminal negligence. At the same time, the Court affirmed that all negligence used for criminal liability must be a marked departure in order to distinguish criminal from civil negligence. It also suggested that judges examine the accused's state of mind, but only to determine if there is a reasonable doubt about whether a reasonable person in the accused's position would have been aware of the risk created by this conduct.[234] It is not clear whether this latter requirement is based on section 7 of the *Charter* as is the requirement for a marked departure of standards of reasonable care. It could simply be a reminder for judges and juries to consider all the circumstances of the case in determining whether the accused was criminally negligent.

iv) No Requirement of Correspondence or Symmetry between Prohibited Act and Fault Element

A majority of the Court in *Creighton* held that section 7 of the *Charter* does not require that objective fault relate to all the prohibited consequences in the offence, so that proof of objective foresight of bodily harm (as opposed to death) is sufficient to convict a person of manslaughter.[235] Four judges dissented and argued that the fault element of objective foresight should be related to the prohibited consequences of the offence. Section 7 is thus not offended by offences that punish a person for causing certain harm even though the accused may not have subjectively or objectively been at fault for causing the harm that forms part of the *actus reus*.

v) Subjective Fault Required in Relation to the Prohibited Act for a Few Offences with Special Stigma

The Supreme Court has held that section 7 of the *Charter* requires proof of subjective fault for only a limited number of offences. *R. v. Vaillancourt*[236] and *R. v. Martineau*[237] established that because of its stigma and mandatory life imprisonment, the offence of murder requires proof

---

234 *Ibid.* at para. 49.

235 McLachlin J. stated: "It is important to distinguish between criminal law theory, which seeks the ideal of absolute symmetry between *actus reus* [the prohibited act] and *mens rea* [the required fault requirement], and the constitutional requirements of the *Charter*. Provided an element of mental fault or moral culpability is present, and provided that it is proportionate to the seriousness and consequences of the offence charged, the principles of fundamental justice are satisfied." *Creighton*, above note 224 at 378–79. For further discussion, see ch. 5(A), "Conceptual Considerations."

236 *Vaillancourt*, above note 159.

237 *R. v. Martineau* (1990), 58 C.C.C. (3d) 353 (S.C.C.) [*Martineau*].

that the accused either intended to cause death or knew that death was likely to occur. In those cases, the Court struck down "felony" or constructive murder provisions that allowed an accused committing some other serious offence such as robbery or sexual assault to be convicted of murder "whether or not the person means to cause death to any human being and whether or not he knows that death is likely to be caused."[238] In *Vaillancourt*, the section provided that a person committing a serious offence such as robbery was guilty of murder if death resulted from the use or possession of a weapon. In *Martineau*, the section provided that a person was guilty of murder if he or she meant to cause bodily harm for the purpose of facilitating a serious offence. The Court also suggested that it was unconstitutional to convict a person of murder under section 229(c) of the *Criminal Code* on the basis that while pursuing an unlawful object, he or she ought to have known that death was likely to result. Under section 7 of the *Charter*, the Crown must at least prove that an accused has subjective knowledge that death is likely to result before that person can be convicted of murder.[239]

The Supreme Court has also stated that section 7 is violated by provisions that allowed an accused to be convicted as a party to attempted murder on the basis that he or she ought to have known death was likely to result.[240] Even though the penalty was not mandatory life imprisonment, the Court stressed that a person convicted of attempted murder would suffer the same stigma as a murderer. Hence, the Crown must establish as a constitutional minimum that the accused subjectively knew that death was likely to occur. The *Charter*, however, only establishes minimum standards and, as will be seen, the courts have gone above the minimum constitutional standards by requiring proof of an intent to commit murder as the fault requirement for attempted murder.[241]

In *Finta*,[242] the Court indicated that the "stigma and opprobrium" that would accompany conviction of crimes against humanity or war crimes required the Crown to prove that the accused knew, was aware of, or was wilfully blind to the aggravating facts and circumstances that would make crimes such as robbery or manslaughter a war crime or a crime against humanity. In the subsequent *Mugesera v. Canada (Min-*

---

238 *Code*, above note 1, s. 230.

239 At the same time, the Court has defined manslaughter quite broadly to apply to an accused who causes death when a reasonable person would have foreseen the likelihood of bodily harm, provided that the accused had the capacity to see such a risk. *Creighton*, above note 224.

240 *R. v. Logan* (1990), 58 C.C.C. (3d) 391 (S.C.C.).

241 *R. v. Ancio*, [1984] 1 S.C.R. 225 discussed in ch. 4.

242 *Finta*, above note 185 at 499–503.

ister of Citizenship and Immigration) case,[243] the Court recognized that in international criminal law "it is now well settled that in addition to the *mens rea* for the underlying act, the accused must have knowledge of the attack and must know that his or her acts comprise part of it or take the risk that his or her acts will compromise part of it."[244] The Court has reformulated the *Finta* holding as requiring that "the accused must have knowledge of the attack and must know that his or her acts are part of the attack [constituting a crime against humanity], or at least take the risk that they are part of the attack."[245] The Court did not advert to the requirements of section 7 of the *Charter*, but this reformulated fault requirement would allow recklessness with respect to the conditions that make a crime a war crime or a crime against humanity. Although recklessness is a subjective form of fault that requires proof that the accused adverted to the prohibited risk, it is a lower and lesser form of fault than knowledge or even wilful blindness, which was previously the lowest constitutionally required fault element for war crimes. Knowledge remains the minimal fault requirement under section 7 of the *Charter* with respect to murder and attempted murder.

Beyond the limited context of murder, attempted murder, and war crimes, the Supreme Court has refused to require subjective fault under section 7 of the *Charter*. The Court has held that the stigma attached to offences such as unlawfully causing bodily harm, dangerous driving, misleading advertising, careless use of a firearm, failure to provide the necessities of life, and unlawful act manslaughter is not sufficient to require proof of subjective as opposed to objective fault. It could, however, be argued that new crimes based on the commission of terrorist activities should require subjective fault in relation to the prohibited act and the circumstances that elevate a crime to an act of terrorism because of the stigma and enhanced penalties attached to crimes of terrorism. An analogy could be drawn to war crimes. If terrorism is seen as a stigma offence, some of the new crimes enacted by Parliament after the terrorist attacks of September 11, 2001, may be found not to satisfy constitutional requirements of subjective fault.[246] The stigma concept

---

243 [2005] 2 S.C.R. 100.

244 *Ibid.* at para. 173 [emphasis in the original].

245 *Ibid.* at para. 176.

246 In general the new terrorism offences in ss. 83.01–83.23 appropriately require proof of subjective fault in the form of knowledge or purpose. Section 83.19 prohibits the knowing facilitation of a terrorist activity, but may be vulnerable because it states that it is not necessary that "any particular terrorist activity was foreseen or planned at the time it was facilitated." See ch. 10(D)(5), "Fault Elements in Other Terrorism Offences."

has often been criticized as circular and tautological, but there is no consensus that the Court should constitutionalize subjective fault beyond the offence of murder and attempted murder.

Even if subjective fault is required as an essential element of an offence under section 7 of the *Charter*, it is theoretically possible that another fault element could be substituted for that essential element. Following the section 11(d) jurisprudence outlined above, Parliament can substitute proof of another element for an essential element if proof of the substituted element leads inexorably to proof of the essential element, so that the trier of fact could not have a reasonable doubt about the essential element. In *Martineau*, the majority held that proof of the *mens rea* for the underlying offence and the intent to cause bodily harm did not lead inexorably to the conclusion that the accused had the essential element of subjective foresight of death.[247] Proving under section 230(c) of the *Criminal Code* that the accused "wilfully stops, by any means, the breath of a human being" also does not lead inexorably to proof that the accused had subjective foresight of death.[248] In cases of suffocation, it is now necessary to charge the accused with murder under section 229 of the *Criminal Code* and prove that he or she had subjective foresight that death was likely to result. The jury could infer from the attempt at suffocation that the accused knew that death was likely, but it cannot be required by the wording of the offence to draw this inference. Following the presumption of innocence, the jury would be obliged to acquit the accused of murder if it had a reasonable doubt about his or her subjective foresight of death for any reason, including intoxication or diminished intelligence.

In both *Vaillancourt* and *Martineau*, the Supreme Court considered whether the violation of sections 7 and 11(d) of the *Charter* could be justified under section 1 of the *Charter*. The Court stated that the goals of the "felony murder" provisions—namely, deterring the carrying of weapons and the use of force when committing serious crimes such as robbery—were important enough to justify overriding a constitutional right. The Court also conceded that there was a rational connection between the objective of deterrence and convicting those who caused

---

247   In dissent, L'Heureux-Dubé J. argued that proof of the substituted element would lead to the "inexorable conclusion" that there was objective foreseeability of death which, in her view, should be the constitutionally required minimal mental element for murder. *Martineau*, above note 237 at 375.

248   *R. v. Sit* (1991), 66 C.C.C. (3d) 449 at 453 (S.C.C.). Similar reasoning would apply to *Code*, above note 1, s. 230(b), providing that a person who "administers a stupefying or overpowering thing" in order to facilitate an offence was guilty of murder if death ensues.

death but did not have subjective knowledge that death would result. However, in both cases the Court concluded that the restrictions on sections 7 and 11(d) were not reasonable because there were other ways Parliament could achieve its objectives. Parliament could punish for the possession of a weapon while committing an offence as a separate offence.[249] In cases where death results from the possession of a weapon or the infliction of harm, "very stiff" sentences for manslaughter would be available. The Court concluded that

> [t]o label and punish a person as a murderer who did not intend or foresee death unnecessarily stigmatizes and punishes those whose moral blameworthiness is not that of a murderer, and thereby unnecessarily impairs the rights guaranteed by ss. 7 and 11(d) of the *Charter.*[250]

In other words, departures from constitutional requirements of subjective fault could not be justified under section 1 of the *Charter* because of the availability of other means more respectful of *Charter* rights to pursue the state's legitimate objective of deterring the use of weapons and violence in the commission of crimes.

f) Criminal Defences

As will be examined in greater depth in chapters 7 through 9, statutory or common law restrictions on defences may also violate the *Charter.* One exception is if a defence would be inconsistent with the very purpose of an offence. For example, intoxication is not recognized as a defence for impaired driving.[251] At the same time, however, the courts have been most active with respect to the defence of intoxication and have held that various common law restrictions on that defence violate section 7 of the *Charter.* They have expressed concern that not considering evidence of extreme intoxication when an accused is charged with a general intent offence such as assault or sexual assault could result in the conviction of the morally innocent, at least in cases where the accused is so extremely intoxicated that he or she is in a state akin to automatism and acts in an involuntary manner.[252] The Court has also changed traditional common law rules which focus on whether

---

249 The use of a firearm while committing an offence is punishable as a separate offence with a mandatory minimum sentence of one year imprisonment. *Code, ibid.,* s. 85. The commission of certain offences with a firearm such as robbery now has a mandatory minimum sentence of four years. *Code, ibid.,* s. 344.

250 *Martineau,* above note 237 at 362.

251 *R. v. Penno* (1990), 59 C.C.C. (3d) 344 (S.C.C.).

252 *Daviault,* above note 168. But see now *Code,* above note 1, s. 33.1, both discussed in ch. 7(E)(2), "The Legislative Response to *Daviault:* Section 33.1."

[margin note: because of the drum, the accused could have the intent, but actually didn't b/c of intoxication]

evidence of intoxication raises a reasonable doubt about the accused's capacity to commit a specific intent crime such as murder because they could allow the conviction of an accused who may have been capable of having the required intent, but did not actually have the intent.[253]

The Supreme Court has held that section 43 of the *Criminal Code*, which authorizes parents and teachers to use reasonable force to correct a child or pupil, does not violate sections 7, 12, or 15 of the *Charter*. The Court acknowledged that the defence affected the security of the person of children, but held that it was not so vague or overbroad as to violate section 7 of the *Charter*. The Court also indicated that the "best interests of the child" was not a principle of fundamental justice; that the application of reasonable force was not cruel and unusual; and that the offence did not demean the equal dignity of children. The later holding was related to the adverse effects that striking down section 43 would have on families and ultimately on children because it would criminalize all applications of force without the child's consent. The Court also indicated that restrictions or denials of defences could violate the *Charter* with the exception of cases in which the defence would be inconsistent with the nature of the offence. For example, the purpose of the offence of intoxicated driving would be defeated if the *Charter* was interpreted to allow an accused to raise the defence of intoxication.[254]

[margin note: holding took into account effect of striking down the provision.]

g) Moral Involuntariness

As discussed above, cases such as *B.C. Motor Vehicle Reference* and *R. v. Hess* indicated that the principles of fundamental justice will be violated if a morally innocent person who is not at fault will be imprisoned as a result of a criminal offence. In the context of defences, the Supreme Court in *R. v. Ruzic* indicated that the appropriate focus under section 7 of the *Charter* is not on whether restrictions or denial of a defence will result in the conviction of the morally innocent, but rather whether they will result in the conviction of a person who has acted in a "morally involuntary" manner. A person acts in a morally involuntary manner if he or she did not have "any realistic choice" in the circumstances but to commit the crime. "In the case of morally involuntary conduct, criminal attribution points not to the accused but to exigent circumstances facing him, or to threats of someone else . . . . Depriving a person of liberty and branding her with the stigma of criminal liability would infringe the principles of fundamental justice if the accused

---

253 *R. v. Robinson* (1996), 105 C.C.C. (3d) 97 (S.C.C.).
254 *Canadian Foundation for Children*, above note 203.

did not have any realistic choice."[255] A person who commits a crime in such exigent circumstances acts in a morally involuntary manner even though he or she committed the crime with a physically voluntary act and with the required fault element and even if he or she cannot be said to be morally innocent.

Applying the principle of fundamental justice that a person should not be punished for morally involuntary actions, the Supreme Court has held that severe statutory restrictions under section 17 of the *Criminal Code* on the defence of duress violate section 7 of the *Charter* because they would allow the conviction of a person who had no realistic choice but to commit the crime in response to threats. The Court struck down the requirement under section 17 of the *Criminal Code* that threats must be of immediate death or bodily harm from a person who is present when the offence is committed.[256] It left open the question of whether the categorical restrictions in section 17 on the commission of a long list of offences in response to threats would also violate section 7 of the *Charter*. The decision in *Ruzic* points in the direction of striking down such offence-based exclusion on the defence of duress if the accused committed such offences when he or she had no realistic choice but to do so. If the accused acted in a morally involuntary manner then a conviction should violate section 7 of the *Charter*. Moreover, the Court in *Ruzic* indicated that violations of section 7 of the *Charter* can only be justified in "exceptional circumstances, such as the outbreak of war or a national emergency."[257]

5) The *Charter* and Punishment

The *Charter* places restrictions on the state's ability to punish people for criminal offences. Section 12 provides that everyone has the right not to be subjected to cruel and unusual treatment or punishment and the Court's jurisprudence on this issue will be examined in chapter 11. In general, however, section 12 of the *Charter* prohibits grossly disproportionate punishments.[258] A judge who concludes that a mandatory sentence imposes cruel and unusual punishment must strike down the sentence and is not allowed to craft a constitutional exception or exemption from the mandatory sentence.[259]

---

255 *R. v. Ruzic* (2001), 153 C.C.C. (3d) 1 at paras. 46 & 47 (S.C.C.).
256 *Ibid.*
257 *Ibid.* at para. 92.
258 *R. v. Smith* (1987), 34 C.C.C. (3d) 97 (S.C.C.); *R. v. Latimer* (2001), 150 C.C.C. (3d) 129 (S.C.C.).
259 *R. v. Ferguson*, 2008 SCC 6.

In a landmark case, the Supreme Court has interpreted section 7 of the *Charter* generally to preclude the extradition of a fugitive to face trial in another country unless assurances are received that the death penalty will not be applied. The Court stressed both an emerging international consensus on this issue and the risk of wrongful convictions.[260] This decision reviews a number of wrongful convictions that have occurred in Canada, the United Kingdom, and the United States and stands as an important reminder of the inherent fallibility of the criminal process.

Section 11(h) provides protection against double jeopardy, which is being tried or punished twice for the same offence. This does not preclude criminal trials after a person has been tried on disciplinary charges at work or in prison.[261] In Canada, protection against double jeopardy applies only if a person has been "finally acquitted of the offence." This right accommodates the generous rights of appeal that the prosecutor enjoys in Canada, which allow an appeal even after a jury has acquitted the accused.[262] The section is violated, however, if the accused is retried for the same offence after an acquittal, as opposed to having the Crown take a more limited appeal on specific grounds that the trial court had made errors of law.[263] The principle of double jeopardy also prohibits conviction for multiple offences if there are no additional or distinguishing elements among the offences.[264] Thus, an accused could not be convicted of using a firearm while committing an indictable offence and of pointing a firearm, because there is no distinguishing element between these two offences.[265]

CONCLUSION

Constitutional law has a pervasive and foundational influence on criminal law and it is relevant at all stages of the criminal process. The division of powers limits the enactment of criminal law to Parliament

---

260 *United States of America v. Burns and Rafay* (2001), 151 C.C.C. (3d) 97 (S.C.C.), effectively reversing *Kindler v. Canada (Minister of Justice)* (1991), 67 C.C.C. (3d) 1 (S.C.C.).

261 *R. v. Wigglesworth* (1987), 37 C.C.C. (3d) 385 (S.C.C.); *R. v. Shubley* (1990), 52 C.C.C. (3d) 481 (S.C.C.).

262 *Morgentaler (No. 2)*, above note 197.

263 *Corp. professionelles des médecins (Québec) v. Thibault* (1988), 42 C.C.C. (3d) 1 (S.C.C.).

264 See also *Code*, above note 1, s. 12.

265 *R. v. Krug* (1985), 21 C.C.C. (3d) 193 (S.C.C.). See also *R. v. Kienapple* (1974), 15 C.C.C. (2d) 524 (S.C.C.).

but allows provinces and municipalities to enact regulatory offences. Sections 7 to 10 of the *Charter* restrain the investigative activities of the police. These rights are enforced primarily by the decisions of courts under section 24(2) of the *Charter* to exclude unconstitutionally obtained evidence if its admission would bring the administration of justice into disrepute. In the *Charter* era, Canadian courts are also prepared to stay proceedings if the accused has been entrapped into committing a crime. At the same time, the entrapment defence allows police to offer people an opportunity to commit a crime so long as they have a reasonable suspicion that the suspect is engaged in criminal activity or the suspect is present in a high-crime area. Even if they have a reasonable suspicion or are acting on a *bona fide* inquiry into crime, the police cannot actually induce the commission of a crime by shocking activity that would bring the administration of justice into disrepute.

The *Charter* affects the trial process by giving the accused various rights including the right to make full answer and defence and the right to be presumed innocent. The presumption of innocence is violated whenever the accused has to establish an element of an offence or a defence on a balance of probabilities because this allows a conviction to occur despite a reasonable doubt. Even mandatory presumptions that can be displaced by satisfying an evidential burden violate the presumption of innocence. At the same time, the courts have frequently accepted limitations on the presumption of innocence as reasonable limits and have, on their own initiative, required the accused to establish the defences of extreme intoxication and automatism on a balance of probabilities.

The *Charter* also affects substantive criminal offences that infringe freedom of expression, are excessively vague, overbroad, arbitrary, grossly disproportionate, or allow the punishment of the morally innocent. These matters will be discussed in greater depth in subsequent chapters, it should be noted that section 7 of the *Charter* is offended by imprisonment of the morally innocent who have committed a prohibited act but through no fault of their own. The courts have found that because of their penalty and stigma, a few crimes—murder, attempted murder, and war crimes—require proof of subjective fault in relation to their *actus reus*. The Court has not, however, extended such requirements to the vast majority of crimes. For crimes such as manslaughter, objective fault is constitutionally sufficient and does not have to extend to all aspects of the *actus reus* or require that the reasonable person be endowed with the same characteristics as the accused.

Section 7 of the *Charter* may also be violated by restrictions on defences. As examined in greater depth in chapters 7 and 9, restrictions on the intoxication and duress defences have been struck down under section 7 of the *Charter*. The Court has recognized a general principle under section 7 of the *Charter* that people should not be punished for crimes that are committed in a morally involuntary manner in the sense that they have no realistic choice but to commit the crime. Although many of these matters will be revisited in subsequent chapters, it is important to have a sense of how the *Charter* affects the entire criminal process and how constitutional law has become fundamental to the criminal law in Canada.

FURTHER READINGS

CAMERON, J., & J. STRIBOPOULOS, eds., *The Charter and Criminal Justice: Twenty-Five Years Later* (Markham, ON: LexisNexis, 2008)

COUGHLAN, S., *Criminal Procedure,* 2d ed. (Toronto: Irwin Law, 2012)

HOGG, P.W., *Constitutional Law of Canada*, 5th ed. (Toronto: Carswell, 2007), chs. 18–19, 33–41, and 44–52

LASKIN, J., ET AL., eds., *The Canadian Charter of Rights and Freedoms Annotated* (Aurora, ON: Canada Law Book, as updated)

PENNEY, S., V. RONDINELLI, & J. STRIBOPOULOS, *Criminal Procedure in Canada* (Markham, ON: LexisNexis, 2011)

QUIGLEY, T., *Procedure in Canadian Criminal Law*, 2d ed. (Toronto: Carswell, 2005)

ROACH, K., *Constitutional Remedies in Canada* (Aurora, ON: Canada Law Book, as updated) chs. 9 & 10

————, *Due Process and Victims' Rights: The New Law and Politics of Criminal Justice* (Toronto: University of Toronto Press, 1999) chs. 2–5

SHARPE, R.J., & K. ROACH, *The Charter of Rights and Freedoms*, 4th ed. (Toronto: Irwin Law, 2009)

STEWART, H., *Fundamental Justice: Section 7 of the Charter* (Toronto: Irwin Law, 2012)

STUART, D., *Charter Justice in Canadian Criminal Law*, 5th ed. (Toronto: Carswell, 2010)

CHAPTER 3

THE PROHIBITED ACT, OR *ACTUS REUS*

The *actus reus* or prohibited act of any offence has important policy elements. For example, in 1983 the offence of rape, which was defined as non-consensual sexual intercourse by a man with a woman who was not his wife, was replaced with the broader, gender neutral offence of sexual assault which applied to all persons. In 1992 the law of sexual assault was again changed, with Parliament defining consent and stating specific instances in which consent did not exist. The Supreme Court subsequently decided that for purposes of determining the *actus reus*, consent should be based on the subjective views of the complainant. Although much of the controversy over sexual assault has concerned the appropriate fault or mental element,[1] the expansion of the prohibited act in this and other crimes plays an important role in determining the extent of criminal liability. The broad nature of many of the prohibited acts in the *Criminal Code*[2] requires the judge to distinguish at sentencing among the relative culpability of various levels of participation in crimes.

Almost all crimes in Canada are defined in the *Criminal Code*. In order to ensure that there is fixed predetermined law, the courts cannot create crimes on their own except in the case of contempt of court. At the same time, however, courts play an important role in interpreting

---

1   See the discussion of mistake of fact in ch. 5, "The Fault Element, or *Mens Rea*."
2   Including the provisions governing liability as a party or accomplice to an offence, and prohibiting attempts to commit crimes. See ch. 4, "Unfulfilled Crimes and Participation in Crimes."

the words used to define crimes. Sometimes, courts interpret words in an offence restrictively in order to benefit the accused, but not in all cases. Laws may be struck down under section 7 of the *Charter* if they are so vague or overbroad that they do not provide fair notice of what is prohibited, or any limitation on law enforcement discretion. The ideal of a fixed, predetermined law should in theory allow citizens to determine beforehand whether conduct is illegal. If citizens do not determine what is illegal, or if they mistakenly think something is legal when it is not, ignorance of the law is not an excuse.

In order to obtain a conviction for a criminal or a regulatory offence, the Crown must always prove beyond a reasonable doubt that the accused committed the prohibited act (*actus reus*). The *actus reus* is only one element of a criminal offence, and it must in theory coincide with the fault element, or *mens rea*, that is required for the crime. It will be seen in this chapter that the courts have sometimes finessed this requirement, often by defining the criminal act in a broad fashion so that it overlaps with a time in which the accused had the required fault element. Sometimes when determining whether the accused has committed the *actus reus*, it is necessary to determine if he or she caused some prohibited result. As will be seen, causation is defined broadly in homicide cases so that an accused may be held to have caused another's death even though other factors, such as lack of medical treatment or the victim's "thin skull," contributed to the death. This approach fits into the trend towards expansive definitions of the criminal act.

The criminal law has traditionally been reluctant to punish an omission or a failure to act, but this attitude seems to be changing as criminal and regulatory offences punish people for failing to act or to fulfill specific legal duties. Although the criminal law generally keeps the physical and mental elements of crimes distinct, an emerging line of authority suggests that an accused who acts involuntarily may not have committed an *actus reus*. This interpretation effectively builds a minimal fault or mental element into the *actus reus*. As a practical matter, it could prevent the Crown from convicting an accused who acted in an involuntary and unconscious manner even though the offence may have no fault element or one based on negligence.

A. CODIFICATION OF THE CRIMINAL ACT

The prohibited act, or *actus reus*, of an offence is a matter of statutory interpretation. Since 1953, section 9 of the *Criminal Code* has provided that no person shall be convicted of an offence at common law (judge-made law) except contempt of court. To be convicted of a criminal or regulatory offence in Canada, a person must do something that is prohibited by a valid statute or regulation. This requirement accords with the ideal that one should not be punished except in accordance with fixed, predetermined law.

The value of certainty and having a predefined criminal law is now supported by some *Charter* rights. As discussed in chapter 2, section 11(a) gives an accused the right to be informed without unreasonable delay of the specific offence charged; section 11(i) protects the accused against the burden of retroactive laws; and section 11(g) provides that the act or omission must, at the time it was committed, have been illegal under Canadian or international law. As will be discussed below, section 7 of the *Charter* has also been interpreted to prohibit criminal sanctions that are so vague or overbroad that they do not provide fair notice to the citizen or limit law enforcement discretion.

Even before the enactment of section 9 of the *Criminal Code* and the *Charter*, Canadian courts were reluctant to create common law or judge-made crimes on the basis that they

> would introduce great uncertainty into the administration of the criminal law, leaving it to the judicial officer trying any particular charge to decide that the acts proved constituted a crime or otherwise, not by reference to any defined standard to be found in the *Code* or in reported decisions, but according to his individual view as to whether such acts were a disturbance of the tranquillity of people tending to provoke physical reprisal.[3]

The Court thus held that a common law charge of acting in a manner likely to cause a breach of the peace by being a "peeping tom" was not sustainable.[4] In contrast, courts in England continue to exercise "a residual power, where no statute has yet intervened to supersede the common law, to superintend those offenses which are prejudicial to the public welfare."[5] Crimes such as conspiracy to corrupt public morals or to outrage public decency have been created under this common law

---

3   *Frey v. Fedoruk* (1950), 97 C.C.C. 1 at 14 (S.C.C.). The Supreme Court interpreted a previous offence against conspiring to effect an unlawful purpose to require a purpose contrary to federal and provincial legislation as opposed to the common law. *R. v. Gralewicz* (1980), 54 C.C.C. (3d) 289 (S.C.C.).

4   Parliament subsequently enacted a new crime of loitering and prowling at night on the property of another person near a dwelling house. See *Criminal Code*, R.S.C. 1985, c. C-46, s. 177 [*Code*].

5   *Shaw v. D.P.P.*, [1962] A.C. 220 at 268 (H.L.).

power. In Canada, a person can only be convicted for conspiring to commit an offence created by a legislature and defined in law.

The only remaining judge-made crime in Canada, contempt of court, has been upheld under the *Charter* on the basis that codification is not required as a principle of fundamental justice and that uncodified crimes can still be consistent with the principle of fixed, predetermined law. The Court stressed that an accused could predict in advance if conduct constituted contempt of court and that a prohibited act and fault must be proven beyond a reasonable doubt to result in a conviction for contempt of court.[6] Thus, there is no constitutional requirement under section 7 of the *Charter* that all crimes be codified by legislation. This does not, however, mean that the *Charter* cannot be applied to the exercise of the contempt power. Some attempts by judges to punish people for contempt of court have been found to violate *Charter* rights, such as the right to an impartial tribunal and to freedom of expression.[7] At the same time, the very concept of a judge-made or common law offence does not offend the principles of fundamental justice.

1) Strict and Purposive Construction of the Criminal Law

Another means of ensuring that the criminal law is fixed and predetermined is to apply the doctrine that it should be interpreted or construed strictly to the benefit of the accused. This doctrine has been defined by the Supreme Court as follows:

> It is unnecessary to emphasize the importance of clarity and certainty when freedom is at stake . . . . [I]f real ambiguities are found, or doubts of substance arise, in the construction and application of a statute affecting the liberty of a subject, then that statute should be applied in such a manner as to favour the person against whom it is sought to be enforced. If one is to be incarcerated, one should at least know that some Act of Parliament requires it in express terms, and not, at most, by implication.[8]

---

6   *U.N.A. v. Alberta (A.G.)* (1992), 71 C.C.C. (3d) 225 at 253–54 (S.C.C.).
7   *R. v. Martin* (1985), 19 C.C.C. (3d) 248 (Ont. C.A.); *R. v. Kopyto* (1987), 39 C.C.C. (3d) 1 (Ont. C.A.). Before determining whether a person is guilty of contempt of court, judges should give the person notice and an opportunity to be represented by counsel and to make representations. The judge should avoid making determinations that will taint the fairness of the trial. *R. v. K.(B.)* (1995), 102 C.C.C. (3d) 18 (S.C.C.); *R. v. Arradi*, [2003] 1 S.C.R. 280.
8   *Marcotte v. Canada (Deputy A.G.)* (1976), 19 C.C.C. (2d) 257 at 262 (S.C.C.).

This doctrine was used most extensively three hundred years ago when even comparatively minor criminal offences, such as theft, were subject to capital punishment. The Supreme Court has stated that "while the original justification for the doctrine has been substantially eroded, the seriousness of imposing criminal penalties of any sort demands that reasonable doubts be resolved in favour of the accused."[9] For example, the word "conceals" in the criminal offence of removing, concealing, or disposing of property with the intent to defraud creditors has been interpreted as requiring "a positive act done for the purpose of secreting the debtor's property."[10] The accused would have concealed property if he had hidden it in a remote warehouse, but he did not conceal it simply because he failed to tell bankruptcy officials about its existence. Similarly, people would only be guilty of causing a public disturbance if their shouting, swearing, or singing caused a foreseeable interference with the use of a public place, not mere mental annoyance.[11]

Strict construction in favour of the liberty of the accused suggests that offences, but not defences, should be given a restrictive reading. In *R. v. McIntosh*,[12] the Court invoked strict construction as a rationale for giving the statutory defence of self-defence a reading that favoured the liberty of the accused, as opposed to one that expanded the scope of criminal liability. Defences can also be expanded to favour the accused by giving them a broad and purposive reading.[13]

Strict construction of offences in the criminal law is in some tension with modern purposive approaches to statutory interpretation. Purposive approaches acknowledge the limits of grammatical or dictionary-based interpretation of words and instruct courts to look at the broader purposes of a particular statute. For example, section 12 of the *Interpretation Act*,[14] which applies to all federal law including the *Criminal Code*,[15] states:

---

9   *R. v. Paré* (1987), 38 C.C.C. (3d) 97 at 106 (S.C.C.) [*Paré*].
10 *R. v. Goulis* (1981), 60 C.C.C. (2d) 347 (Ont. C.A.). The accused was acquitted of the criminal offence, but at the same time convicted of regulatory offences under the *Bankruptcy Act*, R.S.C. 1985, c. B-3, which required him to divulge such information.
11 *R. v. Lohnes* (1992), 69 C.C.C. (3d) 289 (S.C.C.).
12 (1995), 95 C.C.C. (3d) 481 at 493 (S.C.C.).
13 *R. v. Cooper* (1979), 51 C.C.C. (2d) 129 (S.C.C.) [*Cooper*].
14 R.S.C. 1985, c. I-21.
15 *R. v. Robinson* (1951), 100 C.C.C. 1 (S.C.C.); *R. v. Hasselwander* (1993), 81 C.C.C. (3d) 471 (S.C.C.) [*Hasselwander*]; *R. v. Gladue* (1999), 133 C.C.C. (3d) 385 (S.C.C.). The *Canadian Charter of Rights and Freedoms*, Part I of the *Constitution Act, 1982*, being Schedule B to the *Canada Act 1982* (U.K.), 1982, c. 11 [*Charter*] is also accorded a broad and purposive interpretation by courts. See *Canada*

> Every enactment is deemed remedial, and shall be given such fair, large and liberal construction and interpretation as best ensures the attainment of its objects.

The purposive approach to statutory interpretation has been reconciled with the doctrine of strict construction by holding that the preference for the interpretation that most favours the accused applies only if, after consulting the purposes of a statute, reasonable ambiguities remain in its meaning. Thus, a criminal law should first be given a purposive reading and the doctrine of strict construction only applied if there are still reasonable ambiguities after such a broad interpretation.

There are several recent examples of courts interpreting criminal laws in a purposive manner, even though more restrictive interpretations were grammatically possible. For example, in *Paré*,[16] the Supreme Court recognized that while "it is clearly grammatically possible to construe the words 'while committing' . . . as requiring murder to be classified as first degree only if it is exactly coincidental" with the offences listed in section 231(5) of the *Criminal Code*, it was not reasonable to attribute such a restrictive meaning to the provision. The Court held that the purpose of section 231(5) is to punish, as more severe, murders that were committed while the victim was being unlawfully dominated by the commission of an underlying offence. In the result, the Court held that a murder committed two minutes after the accused had indecently assaulted the victim was indeed committed while the indecent assault took place. The murder was part of the same transaction and the same continuous sequence of events involving the illegal domination of the young victim. There was no resort to the doctrine of strict construction because, considering the purpose of the provision, there was no reasonable ambiguity in the provision. Similar purposive reasoning has been applied to hold that an accused murders a person "while committing" a sexual assault, even if the sexual assault takes place after the victim has died,[17] that a police officer is murdered "acting in the course of his duties" when on duty, but not actually enforcing the law;[18] and that a firearm is a prohibited weapon "capable of firing bullets in rapid succession" if it can readily be converted to do so.[19]

(*Director of Investigation & Research Combines Investigation Branch*) v. *Southam Inc.* (1984), 14 C.C.C. (3d) 97 (S.C.C.).

16 Above note 9.
17 *R. v. Richer* (1993), 82 C.C.C. (3d) 385 (Alta. C.A.).
18 *R. v. Prevost* (1988), 42 C.C.C. (3d) 314 (Ont. C.A.).
19 *Hasselwander*, above note 15.

In *R. v. Russell*,[20] the Supreme Court went beyond *Paré* to hold that first-degree murder can be committed even if the underlying offence was committed against a third party and not the person murdered. The Court stressed that strict construction was not relevant because the ordinary words of section 231(5) of the *Criminal Code* did not require that the underlying offence be committed against the victim. It dismissed the idea in *Paré* that first-degree murders were united by the unlawful domination of the murder victim as too narrow and restrictive given the wording of the statute. All that was necessary under section 231(5) was that the killing was "closely connected, temporally and causally, with an enumerated offence. As long as the connection exists, however, it is immaterial that the victim of the killing and the victim of the enumerated offence are not the same."[21] This case underlines that courts will not lightly resort to the doctrine of strict construction and will often give even the most serious criminal offences a generous reading if supported by the language of the enactment.

Resort is only made to the doctrine of strict construction if there are reasonable ambiguities in a law after it has been interpreted in a purposive manner consistent with its intent.[22] As the *Criminal Code* is federal legislation enacted in both French and English, both officially authoritative versions of the *Code* should be consulted to see if one of them resolves an ambiguity that may be present in the other version.[23] If, however, the English and French versions of the *Criminal Code* are not consistent, the Court should select the more restrictive provision.[24] Such an approach is consistent with the doctrine of the strict construction of the criminal law and its concerns that there be fair notice about criminal liability and that reasonable doubts be resolved in favour of the accused.

Although the Court has not made reference to the doctrine of strict construction, it has interpreted some indecency offences quite narrowly

---

20 [2001] 2 S.C.R. 804.

21 *Ibid.* at para. 43.

22 *CanadianOxy Chemical v. Canada*, [1999] 1 S.C.R. 743 at para. 14; *Bell Express Vu v. Canada* (2002), 212 D.L.R. (4th) 1 at para. 21.

23 *R. v. Mac* (2002), 163 C.C.C. (3d) 1 (S.C.C.) (ambiguity in English version resolved by French version); *R. v. Lamy* (2002), 162 C.C.C. (3d) 353 (S.C.C.) (ambiguity in French version resolved by English version).

24 "It would not be fair to propose an interpretation whereby in one language the elements of the *actus reus* would be met, but not in the other. If we adopted the English version, which is broader than the French one, this Court would be making an undue judicial amendment of the statute. For these reasons, the Court must favour the French version." *R. v. Daoust* (2004), 180 C.C.C. (3d) 449 at para. 37 (S.C.C.).

so as to maximize privacy and autonomy interests. In *R. v. Labaye*,[25] the Court overturned a conviction of keeping a common bawdy house with respect to a private and locked floor of a club that was used as a place for members and their guests to engage in group sex. A common bawdy house is defined as a place resorted to for the purpose of prostitution or acts of indecency. The Court interpreted acts of indecency to require conduct that by its nature

> causes harm or presents a significant risk of harm to individuals or society in a way that undermines or threatens to undermine a value reflected in and thus formally endorsed through the Constitution or similar fundamental laws by, for example: (a) confronting members of the public with conduct that significantly interferes with their autonomy and liberty; or (b) predisposing others to anti-social behaviour; or (c) physically or psychologically harming persons involved in the conduct, and that the harm or risk of harm is of a *degree* that is incompatible with the proper functioning of society.[26]

On the facts of the case, there was no evidence of harm or anti-social conduct in this case that involved consenting adults behind closed doors. Two judges dissented on the basis that the Court was substituting a new harm-based test for the traditional test of community tolerance that had been used to measure indecency. They concluded that the actions, even if consensual, breached community standards of tolerance.[27] In another case, the Court acquitted a man, who was observed masturbating in his house, of committing an indecent act in a public place on the basis that his home was not a public place; a public place was interpreted as a place to which the public has physical as opposed to visual access.[28] The Court did not rely on strict construction to reach this conclusion but rather contextual interpretation based on the fact that, in other parts of the *Criminal Code*, Parliament had extended offences to apply not only to public places but also to places on private property that were exposed to public view.[29] In both cases, however, the Court opted for the interpretation of an offence that was most consistent with the liberty of the accused.

---

25   [2005] 3 S.C.R. 728.
26   *Ibid.* at para. 62 [emphasis in original].
27   *Ibid.* at paras. 73–76.
28   *R. v. Clark*, [2005] 1 S.C.R. 6.
29   See, e.g., s. 174(1)(b) defining the offence of nudity on private property while "exposed to public view."

2) Requirements for Marked Departure and the *De Minimis* Defence

The criminal law is society's most severe sanction and should be applied with restraint so that the "law does not lightly brand a person as a criminal."[30] In *R. v. Gunning*,[31] the Supreme Court suggested that the offence of careless use of a firearm required that "the conduct in question" constitute a "marked departure" from the standard of care expected of a reasonable person. In *R. v. Boulanger*,[32] the Supreme Court similarly interpreted the *actus reus* of the offence of breach of trust by a public officer to require a marked departure from the standards of conduct required by public officials so as to ensure that the prohibited act of the criminal offence would be distinguished from ethical breaches that could be dealt with by internal discipline within the public service. The accused, the director of public security, had asked a police officer to fill out a supplementary report about an accident involving his daughter, but he did not ask that the report be falsified. Although it would have been better to have the insurance company communicate directly with the officer, the accused's conduct was characterized as "an error in judgment" and not a marked departure from the standards that would be expected from a person in a position of public authority.[33] In many cases, the need for restraint in the criminal law would be better served by imposing "marked departure" requirements as part of the fault requirement. Interpreting the *actus reus* should be a matter of statutory interpretation and reading marked departure standards into prohibited acts may strain legislative intent.

In *R. v. Beatty*,[34] a majority of the Court did not read in a requirement of marked departure into the *actus reus* of dangerous driving. The majority focused on interpreting the words used by Parliament to define the *actus reus* while at the same time reading in the marked departure requirement into the fault element of negligence that applied to that offence. Although this approach is at odds with that taken in *Boulanger*, it recognizes the traditionally dominant role accorded to the

---

30 *R. v. Creighton*, [1993] 3 S.C.R. 3 at 59.
31 [2005] 1 S.C.R. 627 at para. 21.
32 [2006] 2 S.C.R. 49 [*Boulanger*].
33 *Ibid.* at para. 67.
34 *R. v. Beatty*, 2008 SCC 5 at para. 45 [*Beatty*]. McLachlin C.J.C. (Binnie and LeBel JJ. concurring) dissented on this point and held that the marked departure should be read into the act of dangerous driving as well as its fault requirement and that this approach was supported by concerns about both restraint in the use of criminal law and the need for symmetry between the fault and act requirements. *Ibid.* at paras. 57–67.

legislature in defining the criminal act. There is a danger that reading in a requirement of a marked departure into every criminal act will alter the clear intent of the legislature in defining the criminal act.

Another way to articulate the concern with restraint in the use of the criminal law is the application of an old common law concept of "*de minimis non curat lex.*" This concept recognizes that the law should not punish a "mere trifle."[35] It would allow for an acquittal of a person even if he or she were technically guilty of the *actus reus* and *mens rea*. For example, it could apply in a case where the accused possessed a minute amount of drugs, stole something of limited value, or engaged in a trivial assault. Given the breadth of many prohibited acts as they are defined by Parliament and the rejection of the idea that it is a principle of fundamental justice that the criminal law must always respond to proven harms,[36] the doctrine of *de minimis non curat lex* should be recognized as a common law defence designed to ensure that the criminal law does not lightly brand someone with a stigma of a criminal offence.[37] Such a defence would not distort Parliament's intent for the offence and could be shaped and limited by the courts.

The *de minimus* doctrine has not yet been adopted by a majority of the Supreme Court even in the context of acceptance of a benefit by a public servant.[38] The Court has strongly rejected the *de minimis* defence in the context of sexual assault as it might be applied to kissing or cuddling a sleeping partner who is not capable of providing contemporaneous consent to the sexual activity. Chief Justice McLachlin rejected the *de minimus* defence on the basis that "even mild non-consensual touching of a sexual nature can have profound implications for the complainant"[39]. Justice Fish in dissent similarly stated: "I do not view sexual assault of any kind as a trifling matter."[40] The *de minimus* defence has also been rejected by Courts of Appeal in relation to assaults[41] and the possession of small or trace amounts of drugs.[42] At the same

---

35   *"The Reward"* (1818), 165 E.R. 1482 at 1484.

36   *R. v. Malmo-Levine*, [2003] 3 S.C.R. 571, discussed in ch. 2.

37   For an argument that the doctrine exists under s. 8(3) of the *Criminal Code*, see *Canadian Foundation for Children, Youth and the Law v. Canada (A.G.)*, [2004] 1 S.C.R. 76 at paras. 200–7 [*Canadian Foundation for Children*], Arbour J. in dissent but not on this point.

38   *R. v. Hinchey*, [1996] 3 S.C.R.1128 at para. 69. But see *Ontario v. Canadian Pacific*, [1995] 2 S.C.R. 1031 at para. 65 approving of the *de minimus* and absurdity provisions when interpreting a regulatory offence of impairing the environment.

39   *R. v. J.A.*, [2011] 2 S.C.R. 440 at para. 63.

40   *Ibid.* at para. 121.

41   *R. v. Kubassek* (2004), 188 C.C.C. (3d) 307 (Ont. C.A.); *R. v. R.H.L.*, 2008 NSCA 100.

42   *R. v. Quigley* (1954), 111 C.C.C. 81 (Alta. C.A.).

time, the possession of a minute and old trace of a drug may lead to a conclusion that the accused did not actually have the *actus reus* of present possession.[43]

Although not yet definitely recognized, a *de minimus* defence could provide more narrowly tailored relief from potentially overbroad criminal offences than either reading in a marked departure requirement to the definition of all criminal acts or holding that the overbreadth of the law violates section 7 of the *Charter*. A *de minimus* defence could also recognize that courts now make less frequent resort to strict construction of the criminal law and that Parliament often errs on the side of defining criminal acts too broadly rather than too narrowly. It could also be a more candid alternative to strained reading down of the *actus reus* of an offence. Section 8(3) of the *Criminal Code* contemplates that courts can as a matter of judge-made law develop new common law defences. Although a *de minimus* doctrine could be abused, courts would have to justify its use and they could be corrected on appeal.

3) Unconstitutionally Vague and Overbroad Laws

A law that is excessively vague or overbroad because it does not give fair notice to citizens of what is prohibited, or place any limits on law enforcement discretion, violates section 7 of the *Charter*. This is sometimes known as the void for vagueness doctrine. Although the words used in statutes to define criminal acts cannot provide certainty, they should provide some boundaries of permissible and non-permissible conduct. When determining whether an offence is excessively vague, the courts examine not only the words used by Parliament, but also the cases in which courts have interpreted those words. In many cases, these interpretations add more certainty about what is prohibited, and limit the extent of the criminal prohibition. For example, the Supreme Court has held that statutory prohibitions against "bawdy houses," or commercial behaviour that "lessens, unduly, competition," are not vague, in large part because courts have been able to give these statutory phrases ascertainable meanings.[44] As McLachlin J. has stated:

> Laws must of necessity cover a variety of situations. Given the infinite variability of conduct, it is impossible to draft laws that precisely foresee each case that might arise. It is the task of judges, aided by

---

43   *R. v. McBurney* (1975), 24 C.C.C.(2d) 44 (B.C.C.A.).

44   *Reference re ss. 193 & 195(1)(c) of the Criminal Code (Canada)* (1990), 56 C.C.C. (3d) 65 (S.C.C.); *R. v. Nova Scotia Pharmaceutical Society* (1992), 74 C.C.C. (3d) 289 (S.C.C.).

precedent and considerations like the text and purpose of a statute, to interpret laws of general application and decide whether they apply to the facts before the court in a particular case. This process is not in breach of the principles of fundamental justice; rather, it is in the best tradition of our system of justice.[45]

Most challenges to criminal laws as excessively vague have failed. The Supreme Court has upheld a regulatory offence against impairing the quality of the natural environment for any use that can be made of it, on the basis that the legislature should be able to use broadly worded offences to protect the environment.[46] Statutes that allow people to be detained in order to protect public safety have also been found not to be excessively vague.[47] Section 43 of the *Criminal Code* was held by a majority of the Court not to be unduly vague or overbroad in authorizing the use of force to correct children that is "reasonable under the circumstances." McLachlin C.J. noted that "the criminal law often uses the concept of reasonableness to accommodate evolving mores and avoid successive 'fine-tuning' amendments. It is implicit in this technique that current social consensus on what is reasonable may be considered." The fact that the defence had been subject to varying interpretations in the past was not fatal because it could still be given "a core meaning in tune with contemporary standards" and because it "sets real boundaries and a risk zone for criminal sanction."[48] In this case, the Court placed several new restrictions on the ambit of the defence that clarified its availability. For example, the Court indicated that it would not be reasonable to use force on children under two or over twelve years of age or to use objects or blows to the head. This case affirms that the key question in "void for vagueness" challenges is not the vagueness of the language used by Parliament or even the variety of interpretations placed on the law in the past but rather the Court's ability to interpret the law in an intelligible manner that establishes a "risk zone" for the use of the criminal law. One consequence of the Court's approach is that the public and law enforcement officials can be misled by simply reading the terms Parliament has employed in the *Criminal Code* and that they will have to consult the Court's jurisprudence to understand the full extent of the criminal law.

---

45 *Winko v. British Columbia (Forensic Psychiatric Institute)* (1999), 135 C.C.C. (3d) 129 at 166–67 (S.C.C.) [*Winko*].

46 *R. v. Canadian Pacific Ltd.* (1995), 99 C.C.C. (3d) 97 (S.C.C.).

47 *R. v. Morales* (1992), 77 C.C.C. (3d) 91 (S.C.C.); *Winko*, above note 45.

48 *Canadian Foundation for Children*, above note 37 at paras. 36, 39, and 42.

One exception to the Supreme Court's unwillingness to strike down criminal laws as excessively vague or overbroad is its 5:4 decision in *R. v. Heywood*[49] to strike down a vagrancy provision that made it illegal for a person convicted of a sexual offence to be "found loitering in or near a school ground, playground, public park or bathing area."[50] The Court held that the provision was too broad in defining the prohibited conduct, and that it did not give the accused fair notice of what was prohibited. Overbreadth, like vagueness, was related to "a lack of sufficient precision by a legislature in the means used to accomplish an objective. In the case of vagueness, the means are not clearly defined. In the case of overbreadth the means are too sweeping in relation to the objective."[51] The law was struck down by the Court. Parliament, however, enacted a new law that allowed those convicted of sexual offences involving children to be prohibited from attending public parks or public swimming areas where children under fourteen years of age could reasonably be expected to attend. This included daycare centres, school grounds, playgrounds, or community centres. This less broad and more carefully tailored law was held not to violate section 7 of the *Charter* except to the extent that it prohibited attendance at community centres in which children might not be present.[52] The Supreme Court has subsequently reinterpreted *Heywood* as a case based on gross disproportionality between the state interest and the rights infringed upon.[53] The problem with such an interpretation of *Heywood* is that the state's interests in protecting children from sexual abuse were particularly compelling compared to the restrictions that the vagrancy offence struck down in *Heywood* placed on the liberties of those convicted of sexual offences. The best rationale for the decision in *Heywood* is not gross disproportionality but rather the original rationales for the void for vagueness doctrine: the lack of fair notice to the offender and the unfettered discretion that the old vagrancy offence gave to the police.

---

49 (1994), 94 C.C.C. (3d) 481 (S.C.C.) [*Heywood*]. See also *R. v. Demers*, [2004] 2 S.C.R. 489 at para. 37 stating that "it is a well-established principle of fundamental justice that criminal legislation must not be overbroad" and holding that a law that denied the ability to grant an absolute discharge to a person found not fit to stand trial was an unjustified violation of s. 7 of the *Charter*.

50 *Code*, above note 4, s. 179(1)(b). See now s. 161.

51 *Heywood*, above note 49 at 516. The dissenters would have saved the legislation on the basis that it should be interpreted only to apply to those who loitered in the named areas for malevolent purposes related to the predicate sexual offences.

52 *R. v. Budreo* (2000), 142 C.C.C. (3d) 225 (Ont. C.A.).

53 *R. v. Clay* (2003), 179 C.C.C. (3d) 540 at para. 38 (S.C.C.).

4) Ignorance of the Law

Codification, and the doctrines of strict construction of the criminal law and void for vagueness, help promote the principle that people should only be punished by fixed, predetermined laws. These doctrines are especially important because the criminal law has historically not allowed ignorance of the law to be an excuse to a criminal offence. Early cases held that people were guilty even if they committed an act they could not have known had recently been made illegal or was not illegal in their home country.[54] Since the *Criminal Code* was enacted in 1892, it has provided that "ignorance of the law by a person who commits an offence is not an excuse for committing that offence."[55] This provision is uncontroversial when applied to offences that a person should know are crimes. It can, however, have harsh results when applied to matters that one may reasonably believe to be legal, especially if competent authorities have contributed to that belief.

In *R. v. Molis*,[56] the Supreme Court held that the principle that ignorance of the law is no excuse precluded an accused from arguing that he had a defence of reasonable mistake in believing that drugs he manufactured were not prohibited under the *Food and Drug Act*. The accused had tried to determine if the drugs were legal, and the drugs in question had only recently been added to the prohibited list. Given his efforts, the accused would have most likely had a valid defence of due diligence if he had made a factual mistake about the nature of the drugs,[57] as opposed to a legal mistake as to whether the drugs had been prohibited under the relevant law. Courts have also rejected as an excuse the accused's reliance on a lower-court judgment, which wrongly held that the activity in question was legal.[58] People rely on their own knowledge of the law, or even a lawyer's advice, at their peril. The ignorance of the law is no excuse principle can have harsh effects on a person who has made genuine and reasonable attempts to ascertain what the law is and to comply with it.

Nevertheless, the Supreme Court has affirmed that ignorance of the law is no excuse in the post-*Charter* era by stating that "it is a prin-

---

54   *R. v. Bailey* (1800), 168 E.R. 651 (C.C.R.); *R. v. Esop* (1836), 173 E.R. 203.

55   *Code*, above note 4, s. 19.

56   (1980), 55 C.C.C. (2d) 558 (S.C.C.).

57   In *R. v. Beaver* (1957), 118 C.C.C. 129 (S.C.C.), the Supreme Court held that those in possession of a prohibited drug had a defence because they believed it was a harmless substance. See ch. 5, "The Fault Element, or *Mens Rea*" for discussion of the mistake of fact defence.

58   *R. v. Campbell* (1972), 10 C.C.C. (2d) 26 (Alta. Dist. Ct.); *R. v. MacIntyre* (1983), 24 M.V.R. 67 (Ont. C.A.).

ciple of our criminal law that an honest but mistaken belief in respect of the legal consequences of one's deliberate actions does not furnish a defence to a criminal charge, even when the mistake cannot be attributed to the negligence of the accused.[59] An accused who makes reasonable mistakes about the law will generally not have a defence, even though reasonable mistakes about the facts will provide a defence to most criminal and regulatory offences.[60]

a) Distinguishing Mistakes of Law and Fact

The refusal to recognize a mistake of law as a defence means that an accused could be convicted of selling obscene material even though the accused relied reasonably on a newspaper report, a case, or a lawyer's advice that the material was not obscene. On the other hand, if the accused made a mistake about the facts, as opposed to the law, then he or she would have a defence.[61] This would apply, for example, to a vendor who believed a magazine contained pictures of consenting adults, not children, engaged in sexual activity. Thus, the Supreme Court has acquitted a vendor on the basis that he had no knowledge of the features of videotapes that made them obscene while at the same time indicating that the vendor's belief that the videotapes were not legally obscene was not relevant. Even the fact that the videos had been approved by a provincial film board was not a defence because it only supported the accused's claim to have made a mistake about the law of obscenity.[62]

In *R. v. Jones*,[63] the Supreme Court held that the accused did not have a defence because they believed they were not legally required to have a provincial licence to operate a bingo on an Aboriginal reserve. The Court stressed that the mistake was not a defence because it related

---

59   R. v. Forster (1992), 70 C.C.C. (3d) 59 at 64 (S.C.C.).

60   A person accused of a strict liability offence would have a defence if he or she "reasonably believed in a mistaken set of facts which, if true, would render the act or omission innocent." R. v. Sault Ste. Marie (City) (1978), 40 C.C.C. (2d) 353 at 374 (S.C.C.). See ch. 6, "Regulatory Offences and Corporate Crime."

61   R. v. Metro News Ltd. (1986), 29 C.C.C. (3d) 35 (Ont. C.A.).

62   R. v. Jorgensen (1995), 102 C.C.C. (3d) 97 (S.C.C.) [Jorgensen]. But the decision of Chief Justice Lamer, who would have held that the board's approval of the films provided a defence of officially induced error, was subsequently approved by the Supreme Court in Lévis (City) v. Tétreault, [2006] 1 S.C.R. 420 [Lévis] so that now the accused might be entitled to a stay of proceedings if he reasonably relied on erroneous legal advice from an official responsible for the administration of the law. Reliance by the accused on his own legal research or his own lawyer's advice would still not be a defence under the ignorance of the law is not an excuse principle.

63   (1991), 66 C.C.C. (3d) 512 (S.C.C.) [Jones].

not "to those facts here . . . [but] in believing that the law does not apply because it is inoperative on the reserves."[64] The accused might have had a defence if they, for example, had mistakenly believed that the Band had obtained a provincial licence for the bingo. The ignorance of the law is no excuse principle seems to punish those who have formed a mistaken belief about the legality of their actions more than a person who has made a mistake about the facts This may seem unjust, but, as will be examined in chapter 5, it is consistent with the general tendency of focusing on the accused's immediate intent in relation to the prohibited act as opposed to the accused's underlying motive or rationale for intentionally committing an act that in law constitutes an offence. The ignorance of the law principle as articulated in *Jones* means that Aboriginal people who conclude that they are exercising an Aboriginal or treaty right are often put in the difficult position of having to violate a regulatory law and then defend the violation on the basis of their rights. If the court accepts the validity of their claim of right, they will not be convicted. If, however, the court rejects their claim of right, their honest and perhaps reasonable mistake of law will not be an excuse to criminal or regulatory liability.

The distinction between a mistake of law, which is no excuse, and a mistake of fact, which may be an excuse, can be slippery and difficult. In 1979, a majority of the Supreme Court stated that a driver's knowledge of whether his licence was suspended was a matter of fact. As such, a driver who believed his licence was not suspended could have a defence of a lack of *mens rea* to a *Criminal Code* offence of driving while disqualified.[65] Three years later, the Court distinguished this finding and stated that while knowledge of a licence suspension was still a matter of fact when the accused was charged with a *Criminal Code* offence, it was a matter of law when the accused was charged with a provincial offence.[66] The Supreme Court subsequently recognized in *R. v. Pontes*[67] that such arbitrary distinctions cannot be maintained, with Cory J. stating that it "cannot be that a mistake as to the law under the *Criminal Code* constitutes a mistake of fact, whereas a mistake as to the provisions of the provincial statute constitutes a mistake of law." Unfortunately, the Court was not clear on what precedent should be maintained. As will

---

64   *Ibid.* at 517. The Court did note that the accused had not formally challenged the validity of the law as inconsistent with Aboriginal or treaty rights protected under s. 35 of the *Constitution Act, 1982*, being Schedule B to the *Canada Act 1982* (U.K.), 1982, c. 11.

65   *R. v. Prue* (1979), 46 C.C.C. (2d) 257 (S.C.C.).

66   *R. v. MacDougall* (1982), 1 C.C.C. (3d) 65 (S.C.C.).

67   *R. v. Pontes* (1995), 100 C.C.C. (3d) 353 at para. 40 (S.C.C.) [*Pontes*].

be seen, the Court held in that case that the offence of driving with a suspended licence should be classified as an absolute liability offence because section 19 deprived the accused of any possible defence based on the automatic suspension of a driver's licence.

b) Preclusion of Mistake of Law As the Only Defence Making an Offence One of Absolute Liability

In *Pontes*, Cory J. suggested for the majority that where section 19 operates to deny the accused his only possible defence, then the offence should be classified as one of absolute liability for which imprisonment cannot be imposed.[68] In the case, he held that the accused's lack of knowledge that his licence was suspended was the only possible defence to the offence of driving without a valid licence. Because the licence was automatically and without notice suspended upon the accumulation of a certain amount of demerit points, the defence that the accused did not know that his licence was suspended must amount to a mistake of law and as such be prohibited. An example given by the Court was those who as a result of a *Criminal Code* conviction received a licence suspension and who honestly and reasonably believed that they could drive after the *Criminal Code* suspension because they did not recognize that their licence was automatically suspended for a longer period under provincial law. This preclusion of the only available defence led the majority of the Court to characterize the offence as one of absolute liability with a minority arguing in dissent that the conviction of the accused because of ignorance and mistake of the law might be harsh, but has long been accepted in the criminal law. *Pontes* preserves the ignorance of the law is no excuse principle, but somewhat mitigates its harshness by, in this one limited context, taking imprisonment away as a sentencing option.

c) Non-Publication

There are some exceptions to the principle that ignorance of the law is not an excuse. A person may not be convicted of violating a law or regulation that has not been officially promulgated or published.[69] The rationale would be that it would be impossible for a person to ascertain and comply with a law that was not available to the public.

---

68 *Ibid.* at 368.

69 *R. v. Ross* (1944), 84 C.C.C. 107 (B.C. Co. Ct.); *Lim Chin Aik v. R.*, [1963] A.C. 160 (P.C.); *R. v. Catholique* (1980), 49 C.C.C. (2d) 65 (N.W.T.S.C.). See also *Statutory Instruments Act*, R.S.C. 1985, c. S-22, s. 11(2).

d) *Mens Rea*, Colour of Right and Mistake of Law

Sometimes the *mens rea* or fault element of specific offences will be defined in a manner that can make the accused's mistake of law a matter that will negate proof of *mens rea*. In other words, a person may not be convicted if the fault element required for a particular offence includes some knowledge of the relevant law. Thus, an accused has been acquitted of wilfully breaching his probation order because he wrongly believed that he had not committed the offence of care and control of a vehicle while impaired because the car was not moving.[70] If the accused thought he was doing something perfectly legal, it could not be said that he was wilfully breaching his parole. This was tied to the complex or high fault element implicit in the offence of wilfully breaching parole.[71] Similarly, a mistake about the extent of one's legal obligations to pay taxes can prevent proof of the high *mens rea* that one has wilfully evaded income tax. That said, the court held that there was no defence when a person did not pay taxes because he did not believe that the federal government had the constitutional power to impose taxes.[72]

A legal error about who owns property may afford a defence to theft and other property offences because the fault element of the crime itself contemplates that an accused act "without colour of right."[73] Theft has a particularly complex and high fault element and this makes some mistakes of law relevant to proof of *mens rea*. A colour of right based on

---

70 *R. v. Docherty* (1989), 51 C.C.C. (3d) 1 (S.C.C.) [*Docherty*].

71 Parliament subsequently amended the offence to provide that an accused was guilty when a probation order was breached "without reasonable excuse." *Code*, above note 4, s. 733.1. It is possible that a court might find that the accused's genuine belief that he was not acting illegally and in breach of a probation order constituted a reasonable excuse, but the Supreme Court's decision in *Docherty*, *ibid.*, was based on the high level of *mens rea* employed in the previous offence.

72 *R. v. Klundert* (2004), 187 C.C.C. (3d) 417 (Ont. C.A.).

73 The fault element of theft requires that the accused act "fraudulently and without colour of right." *Code*, above note 4, s. 322(1). A person "who is honestly asserting what he believes to be an honest claim cannot be said to act 'without colour of right,' even though it may be unfounded in law or in fact." *R. v. De-Marco* (1973), 13 C.C.C. (2d) 369 at 372 (Ont. C.A.). See also *R. v. Shymkowich* (1954), 110 C.C.C. 97 (S.C.C.); *R. v. Howson*, [1966] 3 C.C.C. 348 (Ont. C.A.); *R. v. Spot Supermarket Inc.* (1979), 50 C.C.C. (2d) 239 (Que. C.A.); *R. v. Lilly* (1983), 5 C.C.C. (3d) 1 (S.C.C.). Section 429 provides that no person shall be convicted of property offences under ss. 439–46 including mischief, arson, and cruelty to animals if she acted with colour of right. This phrase has been interpreted as requiring an honest belief in facts and law that would support the accused's property or possessory rights. It does not include the accused's belief that she was outside of the jurisdiction of Canadian criminal law. *R. v. Watson* (1999), 137 C.C.C. (3d) 422 (Nfld. C.A.).

a mistaken belief by the accused about his or her legal entitlement to property can prevent the Crown from establishing the particular fault element of theft beyond a reasonable doubt.[74] The issue is the accused's belief and not the actual legal entitlement.[75] These exceptions to the ignorance of the law principle depend on the particular fault element of the particular offence and the presence of a specific defence of colour of right.[76] They are limited exceptions that would not exonerate an accused who simply argued that he or she did not think that theft or care and control of a vehicle while impaired was illegal. The colour of right defence has been denied to Aboriginal protesters on the basis that they believed they had a moral and not a legal right to occupy land.[77] Colour of right defences are a limited incursion on the principle that ignorance of the law is not an excuse. They generally relate to mistaken beliefs by the accused that they have a personal right or entitlement to property as opposed to more global beliefs that the criminal law is invalid or beyond constitutional limits.

e) Officially Induced Error

The Supreme Court has recently recognized a defence of officially induced error for all criminal and regulatory offences. The Court affirmed its commitment to the principle that ignorance of the law is not an excuse, but recognized that an inflexible approach to this rule could cause injustice "where the error in law of the accused arises out of an error of an authorized representative of the state" while at the same time the state prosecutes the accused. The accused must establish the defence of officially induced error on a balance of probabilities and it results in a stay of proceedings. The defence applies to errors of law or mixed law and fact where the accused "considered the legal consequences of his or her actions" and obtained erroneous legal advice "from an appropriate official" and "relied on the advice in committing the act." The Court stressed the need for both the legal advice and the reliance placed on the advice to be reasonable. Hence, it "is not sufficient in such cases to conduct a purely subjective analysis of the reasonableness of the information."[78] The defence did not apply in the case because the accused relied on an "administrative practice" that they

---

74   *R. v. Dorosh* (2003), 183 C.C.C. (3d) 224 (Sask. C.A.).

75   *R. v. Lilly*, [1983] 1 S.C.R. 794 at 798–99.

76   Colour of right does not apply to offences such as the illegal operation of a bingo: *Jones*, above note 63.

77   *R. v. Billy* (2004), 191 C.C.C. (3d) 410 (B.C.S.C.).

78   *Lévis*, above note 62 at paras. 26–27 following the approach taken by Lamer C.J. in *Jorgensen*, above note 62 at paras. 28–35.

would receive a renewal notice when their licences expired and they did not obtain a specific legal opinion from responsible officials about the consequences of their actions or rely on that opinion.[79] This novel defence responds to the injustice of the state with one hand approving of conduct that it on the other hand prosecutes. It has been accepted in a case in which custom officials appeared to accept documentation offered at the border by protesting farmers as they left Canada to sell their wheat in the United States on the basis that they relied on legal advice from appropriate customs officials.[80]

Officially induced error is a fairly limited defence that leaves intact the general principle that ignorance of the law is no excuse. For example, it would not assimilate the manner in which the law treats mistakes of law and mistakes of fact. It would also not apply in cases where the accused relied on an error about the law made as a result of his or her own research or that of a lawyer.[81] The advice has to come from an appropriate governmental official responsible for administering the law and it cannot be based on tacit non-enforcement of the law in the past.[82] Even in cases where there has been advice from an appropriate governmental official, reliance on the advice must be objectively reasonable. The defence has been recognized, but restrictively circumscribed.

Will the courts recognize a more general defence based on honest and reasonable mistakes of laws in general? It is not likely that the courts would recognize the idea that reasonable mistakes about the law should prevent a conviction as a principle of fundamental justice under section 7 of the *Charter* given that such a legal principle has never been recognized, there is no consensus that it should be recognized, and it could be difficult to apply.[83]

5) Application of the *Criminal Code*: Territorial and Age-Based Restrictions

The basic rule in section 6(2) of the *Criminal Code* is that no person can be convicted for offences committed outside Canada.[84] This rule is sub-

---

79   *Jorgensen, ibid.* at para. 34.

80   *R. v. Charles* (2005), 197 C.C.C. (3d) 42 (Sask. C.A.).

81   See for example *R. v. Beierl*, 2007 ONCJ 267.

82   *Canada (Attorney General) v. Shiner*, 2007 NLCA 18; *R. v. Marsland*, 2011 SKQB 207.

83   On the test for recognizing a legal rule or principle as a principle of fundamental justice, see *R. v. D.B.*, 2008 SCC 25, discussed in ch. 2.

84   A person in Canada who has committed a crime elsewhere can, subject to *Charter* standards, above note 15, be sent back or extradited to that country.

ject to various exceptions including for war crimes, crimes committed on aircrafts, crimes in relation to dangerous nuclear materials, sexual offences committed against children by Canadians while abroad, and crimes of terrorism.[85] The conspiracy provisions in section 465 are also worded broadly to apply to those who conspire outside Canada to commit a crime within Canada, and to those who conspire inside Canada to commit a crime outside Canada. Other crimes including treason and torture are defined so that they can apply to conduct outside Canada.

Section 13 of the *Criminal Code* provides that no person shall be convicted of an offence committed while that person was under twelve years of age.[86] Before 1983, only those under seven were deemed incapable of committing a crime, and those between seven and fourteen years of age could only be convicted if they "were competent to know the nature and consequence of their conduct and to appreciate that it was wrong."[87]

6) Policy Elements in the Definition of the *Actus Reus*: The Case of Consent

The definition of the prohibited act is an important policy component of the criminal law. The legislative definition of the *actus reus* indicates what conduct will be prohibited and criminalized in our society. Sexual offences provide an important example. Rape used to be defined in the *Criminal Code* as sexual intercourse with a female person who is not the accused's wife.[88] In 1983, the offence of rape was replaced with offences of sexual assault, sexual assault with a weapon or threats, and aggravated sexual assault. In an attempt to emphasize the violence in sexual offences, Parliament broadened the prohibited act to include all intentional applications of force without consent in circumstances that were objectively sexual.[89] The marital rape exception was also repealed.

In a further attempt to protect the sexual integrity of women and spell out that "no means no," Parliament in 1992 further defined con-

---

Extradition Act, R.S.C. 1985, c. E-23.

85 *Code*, above note 4, s. 7. See also s. 46(3) (treason); s. 57 (forging a passport); s. 58 (fraudulent use of citizenship certificate); s. 74 (piracy); s. 290 (bigamy); s. 462.3 (enterprise crime).

86 Those who are twelve years of age but under eighteen may be convicted of *Criminal Code* offences, but they are tried and punished under the provisions of the *Youth Criminal Justice Act*, S.C. 2002, c. 1.

87 *Criminal Code*, R.S.C. 1970, c. C-34, s. 13.

88 *Ibid.*, s. 135.

89 *R. v. Chase* (1987), 37 C.C.C. (3d) 97 (S.C.C.).

sent for the purpose of sexual assault as "the voluntary agreement of the complainant to engage in the sexual activity in question." Moreover, it provided that no consent is obtained where

(a) the agreement is expressed by the words or conduct of a person other than the complainant;
(b) the complainant is incapable of consenting to the activity;
(c) the accused induces the complainant to engage in the activity by abusing a position of trust, power or authority;
(d) the complainant expresses, by words or conduct, a lack of agreement to engage in the activity; or
(e) the complainant, having consented to engage in sexual activity, expresses, by words or conduct, a lack of agreement to engage in the activity.[90]

This provision defines certain examples where the accused will be precluded from arguing that the prohibited act of sexual assault did not occur because the complainant consented. It establishes as an objective statement of law that consent is a voluntary agreement to engage in the particular sexual activity and that there cannot be consent if (a) agreement is given by a third party, (b) the complainant is incapable of consenting,[91] (c) the complainant is induced to participate by abuse of a position of trust, power, and authority, or (d, e) the complainant expresses a lack of agreement, by either words or comments, to engage or continue to engage in sexual activity. The accused can still argue that although there was no consent in these situations and the *actus reus* was committed, he still did not have the *mens rea* to commit sexual assault. This topic will be discussed in chapter 10. The above examples of deemed non-consent are not exhaustive and the Ontario Court of Appeal has held that there was no consent or voluntary agreement when a man threatened to distribute nude photographs of his ex-girlfriend if she did not have sex with him.[92]

The Supreme Court has rejected the defence of either advance[93] or implied[94] consent to sexual assault. As a matter of determining the *actus reus* of consent "[t]he absence of consent . . . is subjective and de-

---

90   *Code*, above note 4, s. 273.1, introduced in *An Act to Amend the Criminal Code (Sexual Assault)*, S.C. 1992, c. 38, s. 1.

91   For cases rejecting the idea that an unconscious complainant could have given prior consent, see *R. v. Humphrey* (2001), 143 O.A.C. 151 (C.A.); *R. v. Ashlee* (2006), 212 C.C.C. (3d) 477 (Alta. C.A.).

92   *R. v. D.S.* (2004), 72 O.R. (3d) 223 (C.A.), aff'd [2005] 1 S.C.R. 914.

93   *R. v. J.A.*, [2011] 2 S.C.R. 440.

94   *R. v. Ewanchuk* (1999), 131 C.C.C. (3d) 481 (S.C.C.) [*Ewanchuk*].

termined by reference to the complainant's subjective internal state of mind toward the touching, at the time it occurred.[95] This requires that the complainant be conscious at the time of the sexual activity in question and prevents the use of advance consent.[96] The trier of fact "may only come to one of two conclusions: the complainant either consented or not. There is no third option. If the trier of fact accepts the complainant's testimony that she did not consent, no matter how strongly her conduct may contradict that claim, the absence of consent is established.[97] The existence of consent for the purpose of defining the *actus reus* of sexual assault thus depends on the subjective perceptions of the victims as opposed to external and objective standards of law. Similarly, consent will be negated by the complainant's fear of the application of force regardless of the reasonableness of the fear or whether it was communicated to the accused. A statement by the victim that she did not consent or did so because of fear will be determinative unless it is found not to be a credible statement of her state of mind at the time the offence occurred. The Court is understandably concerned about maximizing the physical and sexual integrity of women and rejecting the rape myths that women implicitly consent to sexual activity unless they protest or resist or clearly express fear. The Court's vehicle for rejecting these myths is to make the issue of consent for the purpose of defining *actus reus* dependent on the subjective perceptions of the complainant even if they are uncommunicated and unreasonable.

The Court took a different approach in *R. v. Cuerrier*,[98] which dealt with the issue of whether a person's non-disclosure of his positive HIV status constituted fraud vitiating his partner's consent to unprotected sexual intercourse. Cory J. stated that in determining whether consent was obtained fraudulently "[t]he actions of the accused must be assessed objectively to determine whether a reasonable person would find them to be dishonest."[99] A person only had a duty to disclose if the failure

---

95   *Ibid.* at 494.
96   Above note 93.
97   *Ewanchuk*, above note 94 at 495.
? 98   (1998), 127 C.C.C. (3d) 1 (S.C.C.) [*Cuerrier*]. In *R. v. Esau* (1997), 116 C.C.C. (3d) 289 at 312 (S.C.C.) McLachlin J. also stated that "[a]t issue, as elsewhere in dealing with consent, is the social act of communicating consent, not the internal state of mind of the complainant. The accused is not expected to look into the complainant's mind and make judgments about her uncommunicated thoughts. But neither is he entitled to presume consent in the absence of communicative ability." It is possible, however, that both the above statements might be characterized as relating to the *mens rea* as opposed to the *actus reus* of the offence.
99   *Cuerrier, ibid.* at 49.

to disclose presented a significant risk of serious bodily harm. Thus, a person must disclose HIV-positive status, but not the existence of a common cold. Finally, it must be proven that the complainant would have refused to have unprotected sex if the accused's HIV status was disclosed. The rest of the Court rejected Justice L'Heureux-Dubé's view *dissent in Lueme* that any fraud designed to induce the complainant to consent would nullify the consent. There was a concern that her view would trivialize the criminal process by allowing consent to be nullified because, for example, the accused lied about his age or his job. Although requiring objective dishonesty, Justice L'Heureux-Dubé's approach seems more consistent with the approach in *Ewanchuk*, which ties consent not to objective and external legal standards of what society will accept as consent, but to the complainant's subjective and perhaps idiosyncratic perceptions.

Parliament has defined what is meant by consent for policy reasons in other sections of the *Criminal Code*. For example, section 14 provides that people cannot consent to their death, and section 286 provides that consent is no defence to the abduction of a child. Section 150.1(1) provides that the complainant's consent is no defence to various sexual offences involving those under the age of sixteen.[100] This provision defines consent for the purpose of determining the *actus reus*. Section 150.1(4) addresses the accused's fault or mental element by providing that a subjective belief that the complainant was sixteen or older is not a defence "unless the accused took all reasonable steps to ascertain the age of the complainant."[101]

In *R. v. Jobidon*,[102] the Supreme Court held that a person could not consent to an assault that intentionally causes "serious hurt or non-trivial bodily harm . . . in the course of a fist fight or brawl," and that a minor could not consent to an adult's intentional application of force in a fight. Gonthier J. recognized that "some may see limiting the freedom of an adult to consent to applications of force in a fist fight as unduly paternalistic and a violation of self-rule," but he argued:

> All criminal law is "paternalistic" to some degree—top-down guid-
> ance is inherent in any prohibitive rule. That the common law has
> developed a strong resistance to recognizing the validity of consent
> to intentional applications of force in fist fights and brawls is merely

---

100 Some exceptions are made if the accused is under sixteen years of age, less than two years older than the complainant, and not in a position of trust, authority, or dependency with the complainant. *Code*, above note 4, s. 151.1(2).

101 See ch. 5, "The Fault Element, or *Mens Rea*."

102 (1991), 66 C.C.C. (3d) 454 at 494 (S.C.C.) [*Jobidon*].

one instance of the criminal law's concern that Canadian citizens treat each other humanely and with respect.[103]

The Court did indicate that consent would not be negated if the bodily harm was trivial or an accepted part of socially valued activity such as sports. Subsequent cases have made clear that "*Jobidon* requires serious harm both intended and caused for consent to be vitiated.["][104]

In dissent in *Jobidon*, Sopinka J. argued that the above rule interfered with Parliament's decision to make lack of consent a requirement for an assault and allowed judges to use the common law to expand the breadth of the offence of assault. On the facts of the case, however, even Sopinka J. found no consent, because what had started as a consensual fist fight had become a severe beating resulting in death. Subsequent cases have found that minors cannot consent to fights where serious harm is intended and caused, but they can consent to schoolyard scuffles where serious harm is not intended or caused.[105] Whether by statutory words or judicial interpretation, the definition of the prohibited act is an important policy element of the criminal law.

Other terms in the criminal law are defined broadly. Assault is defined in section 265 to include not only the non-consensual and intentional application of direct or indirect force on another person, but also attempts or threats "by an act or a gesture, to apply force to another person" if the accused causes the complainant to believe on reasonable grounds that he or she has the present ability to effect his purpose. In addition, section 264.1 creates the separate offence of uttering threats.

Section 4(3) defines possession broadly to include not only personal possession, but also knowingly having something in the actual possession or custody of another person or in another place. Joint possession is deemed where "one of two or more persons, with the knowledge and consent of the rest, has anything in his custody or possession." Courts have interpreted a person's knowledge and consent to require that the person deemed to be in possession must have a measure of control over the matter.[106]

Section 322 defines theft as the taking or conversion of anything. Despite this apparently broad definition of the *actus reus* of theft, the

---

103 *Ibid.*

104 *R. v. Paice*, [2005] 1 S.C.R. 339 at para. 18.

105 *R. v. W.(G.)* (1994), 90 C.C.C. (3d) 139 (Ont. C.A.); *R. v. M.(S.)* (1995), 97 C.C.C. (3d) 281 (Ont. C.A.). Consent will not be vitiated so long as non-trivial bodily harm is not intended even though it may be caused. *R. v. B.(T.B.)* (1994), 93 C.C.C. (3d) 191 (P.E.I.C.A.); *R. v. McIlwaine* (1996), 111 C.C.C. (3d) 426 (Que. C.A.).

106 *R. v. Terrence* (1983), 4 C.C.C. (3d) 193 (S.C.C.).

Supreme Court has excluded the taking of confidential information from the offence of theft on the basis that information alone does not constitute property as protected under the criminal law, and its theft does not deprive the possessor of the use or possession of the confidential information.[107] The Court's interpretation of the *actus reus* of theft means that taking confidential information alone is not presently theft, but taking a piece of paper that contains confidential information may be theft. This definition seems anachronistic in the computer age. Parliament can, of course, always amend the crime of theft to make clear that taking confidential information does indeed constitute theft, or it can enact a new offence.[108]

B. THE ROLE OF THE *ACTUS REUS* IN CRIMINAL LIABILITY

1) The Coincidence of the *Actus Reus* and *Mens Rea*

A traditional principle of criminal law has been that the accused must commit the criminal act at the same time that he or she has the fault element required for the particular crime.[109] This requirement, sometimes called the simultaneous principle, has frequently been finessed. In *Fagan v. Metropolitan Police Commissioner*,[110] the accused accidentally drove his car on a police officer's foot. After being informed of this fact, the accused switched off the ignition and swore at the officer, before eventually moving the car. The accused was convicted of assaulting a police officer and the conviction upheld on appeal. In his dissent, Bridge J. noted the theoretical dilemma that when the accused committed the initial act of assault, he did not know what he was doing, while when the accused did know that he was assaulting the officer, he did not act. The majority, however, took a more practical approach and held that the *actus reus* was not complete when the accused first drove onto the officer's foot, but continued while the force of the car was applied and the accused became aware of his actions. Thus, the mental

---

107 R. v. *Stewart* (1988), 41 C.C.C. (3d) 481 at 494–95 (S.C.C.).

108 For example, see *Code*, above note 4, ss. 326 and 342.1, prohibiting the taking of electricity, gas, or telecommunication services and unauthorized use of a computer.

109 The Latin phrase is *actus non facit reum, nisi mens sit rea* or "the intent and the act must both concur to constitute the crime." *Fowler v. Padget* (1798), 101 E.R. 1103 at 1106 (K.B.).

110 (1968), [1969] 1 Q.B. 439.

element of knowledge coincided with this expanded definition of the act of assault. An alternative to the continuous act approach would be to hold that the accused, having created a danger by driving onto the officer's foot, was under a duty to take reasonable steps to rectify the situation.[111] This would make the failure to act a sufficient criminal act even though it might not technically fit the definition of the crime of assaulting a police officer.

In murder cases, courts have also been prepared to hold the accused guilty if the mental element was present at any point of time during the transaction that culminated in death. In *R. v. Meli*,[112] the accused struck the victim with the intent to kill, and then threw him over a cliff. The victim survived those events, but died some time later of exposure. The Privy Council upheld the murder conviction, stating that the accused had formed the intent to kill and it was impossible to divide the transaction that resulted in the victim's death. In *R. v. Cooper*,[113] the Supreme Court of Canada adopted *Meli* and upheld a murder conviction, on the basis that at some point during two minutes of strangulation the accused formed the intent to kill. The accused need not have had the intent throughout the entire transaction and the possibility that he may have "blacked out" because of intoxication did not excuse so long as the accused had the fault at some time during the strangulation. Cory J. concluded: "It was sufficient that the intent and the act of strangulation coincided at some point. It was not necessary that the requisite intent continue throughout the entire two minutes required to cause the death of the victim."[114]

Another departure from the requirement that the fault element and the prohibited act occur at the same time has been the traditional rule with respect to intoxication for general intent offences such as assault or sexual assault. If the accused was so intoxicated at the time the assault was committed that he did not have the minimal mental element required, then the fault in becoming so intoxicated would be sufficient to convict the person of the general intent offence.[115] The fault in becoming extremely intoxicated would be formed long before the prohibited act was committed, but would be sufficient. This departure from the simultaneous principle has been held by the Supreme Court to violate sections 7 and 11(d) of the *Charter* by substituting the fault

---

111 *R. v. Miller*, [1983] 2 A.C. 161 (H.L.) [*Miller*].
112 [1954] 1 W.L.R. 228 (P.C.) [*Meli*].
113 (1993), 78 C.C.C. (3d) 289 (S.C.C.) [*Cooper*].
114 *Ibid.* at 298.
115 *R. v. Majewski* (1976), 62 Cr. App. Rep. 262 (H.L.); *R. v. Leary* (1977), 33 C.C.C. (2d) 473 (S.C.C.). See ch. 7, "Intoxication."

of becoming drunk for the mental element of a general intent offence, when the former does not lead inexorably to the latter.[116] Parliament has, however, responded by deeming the fault of becoming extremely intoxicated to be sufficient for a conviction of violent offences.[117]

Criminal and regulatory offences based on negligence may also constitute a departure from the principle that fault occurs at the same time as the prohibited act. An accused can be found to be negligent for failing to take precautionary measures long before the prohibited act was committed. For example, an oil tanker may spill its content and the shipping company be negligent because the tanker was not inspected and repaired the last time it was in harbour. The purpose of regulatory and negligence-based offences, of course, is to prevent harm before it occurs, and some departure from the simultaneous principle may be necessary to achieve this end.

2) Causing Prohibited Consequences

When the criminal act prohibits a consequence or a result, it is necessary to determine if the accused's actions have actually caused the prohibited consequence or result. Canadian criminal law does not take an overly strict approach to causation and allows a person to be held liable for causing consequences even if the consequences are caused in part by the victim's peculiar and perhaps unforeseeable vulnerabilities. This is often called the "thin skull" rule, or the principle that accused take their victims as they find them. In addition, it is not necessary that the accused's acts be the sole operative cause of the prohibited consequences. This fits into the general trend towards expansive definitions of the criminal act but may have some harsh results in particular cases. The unanticipated harm caused by actions may be a mitigating factor in sentencing, particularly in manslaughter, which has no minimum penalty.

a) Statutory Provisions Concerning Causation

Parliament remains free to impose its own statutory rules to define the test for when a person will be held responsible for causing a prohibited consequence or result as part of its ability to define the prohibited act. As will be examined in greater detail in chapter 10, Parliament has generally defined causation broadly for the purpose of homicide offences. For example, section 222(1) provides that a person commits homicide when, directly or indirectly, by any means, he or she causes the death

---

116   R. v. Daviault (1994), 93 C.C.C. (3d) 21 (S.C.C.) [Daviault].
117   Code, above note 4, s. 33.1. See ch. 7(E).

of a human being. This is a broad definition that has been satisfied in a case where an accused abducted a child who subsequently died of hypothermia when left in a car.[118] There are also specific and more restrictive causation rules under the first-degree murder provisions in section 231(5) that require that the death be caused while the accused is committing or attempting to commit a list of enumerated offences, including sexual assault, kidnapping, and hostage-taking.[119] Finally, Parliament has enacted specific causation rules in sections 224 to 226 of the *Criminal Code* to deal with certain issues of remoteness between the accused's actions and the victim's actual death and some intervening causes such as treatment. The Supreme Court has Court noted that "ss. 224 and 225 of the *Criminal Code* provide that the chain of causation is not broken if death could otherwise have been prevented by resorting to proper means (s. 224), or if the immediate cause of death is proper or improper treatment that is applied in good faith (s. 225).[120]

b) General Principles of Causation

The *Criminal Code* does not comprehensively codify all causation issues. As the Supreme Court has stated, "[w]here the factual situation does not fall within one of the statutory rules of causation in the *Code*, the common law general principles of criminal law apply to resolve any causation issues that may arise."[121] In *R. v. Smithers*,[122] the Supreme Court upheld a manslaughter conviction on the basis that the accused's action of kicking the deceased in the stomach "was at least a contributing cause of death, outside the *de minimis* range," even though the death was in part caused by the victim's malfunctioning epiglottis, which caused him to choke to death on his own vomit. Dickson J. upheld the applicability of the thin skull principle in the criminal law of homicide by stating:

> Death may have been unexpected, and the physical reactions of the victim unforeseen, but that does not relieve the [accused] . . . .
>
> It is a well-recognized principle that one who assaults another must take his victim as he finds him.[123]

---

118   *R. v. Younger* (2004), 186 C.C.C. (3d) 454 (Man. C.A.).
119   *R. v. Harbottle*, [1993] 3 S.C.R. 306, discussed in ch. 10(A)(1)(c), "Substantial Cause Requirements for Some Forms of First-Degree Murder."
120   *R. v. Maybin*, 2012 SCC 24 at para. 52.
121   *Ibid.*
122   (1977), 34 C.C.C. (2d) 427 (S.C.C.) [*Smithers*].
123   *Ibid.* at 437.

One Court of Appeal has stated that the contributing cause and thin skull principles set out in *Smithers* establish "a test of sweeping accountability" for causing death that might be vulnerable to challenge under section 7 of the *Charter* as infringing the principles of fundamental justice.[124]

Nevertheless, the *Smithers* approach to causation in homicide cases has survived under the *Charter*. In *R. v. Cribbin*,[125] the Ontario Court of Appeal concluded that the *de minimis* causation test and thin skull principles approved in *Smithers* and *Creighton* are consistent with the principles of fundamental justice that forbid the punishment of the morally innocent. Arbour J.A. stated that the requirement for proof of fault in addition to the criminal act removed any risk that the broad causation test would punish the morally innocent.[126] A manslaughter conviction was upheld in *Cribbin* because the accused's assault had contributed to the victim's death, even though the victim had been subject to more serious assaults by another person and had died because he drowned in his own blood.

In *R. v. Nette*,[127] the Supreme Court revisited *Smithers*. Although the Court did not overrule *Smithers*, it reformulated and arguably elevated the test for causation in homicide cases. Arbour J. for a majority of the Court concluded that "the causation standard expressed in *Smithers* is still valid and applicable to all forms of homicide" (that is, murder, manslaughter, and infanticide). Nevertheless, she added:

> In order to explain the standard as clearly as possible to the jury, it may be preferable to phrase the standard of causation in positive terms using a phrase such as "significant contributing cause" rather than using expressions phrased in the negative such as "not a trivial cause" or "not insignificant." Latin terms such as *de minimis* are rarely helpful.[128]

L'Heureux-Dubé J. with three other judges dissented and would have maintained the negative formulation contemplated under *Smithers*. She argued that "[t]here is a meaningful difference between expressing the standard as 'a contributing cause that is not trivial or insignificant' and expressing it as a 'significant contributing cause.'"[129] All the judges were agreed, however, that the accused had caused the death of a nine-

---

124 *R. v. F.(D.L.)* (1989), 52 C.C.C. (3d) 357 at 365 (Alta. C.A.).
125 (1994), 89 C.C.C. (3d) 67 (Ont. C.A.) [*Cribbin*].
126 *Ibid.* at 88.
127 [2001] 3 S.C.R. 488 [*Nette*].
128 *Ibid.* at para. 71.
129 *Ibid.* at para. 6.

ty-five-year-old widow he had left hog-tied and alone after robbing her home. The victim died of asphyxiation some twenty-four to forty-eight hours later. Medical evidence showed that a number of factors contributed to the death, including the hog-tied position, a moderately tight ligature that the accused had left around the victim's neck, as well as the victim's age, asthma, and congestive heart failure. Arbour J. concluded that "the fact that the appellant's actions might not have caused death in a different person, or that death might have taken longer to occur in the case of a younger victim, does not transform this case into one involving multiple causes."[130] Courts now describe causation in the positive terms of whether the accused's actions were a significant contributing cause as opposed to the older formulation of a cause that is not trivial or insignificant.[131] They have indicated that "evidence that an act was possibly a cause of death cannot provide the evidentiary basis for a finding beyond a reasonable doubt that the act significantly contributed to the death."[132] The causation requirement, like other elements of the prohibited act, must be established beyond a reasonable doubt.

c) Concurrent Causes and New Acts That Sever the Chain
    of Causation

Courts have concluded that an accused caused death when he or she set off a chain of events that ended in a person's death, even though the immediate cause of death had not been at the accused's hands. In *R. v. Kitching*,[133] an accused who had assaulted the victim, causing his "brain death," was held responsible, even though the immediate cause of death was the medical withdrawal of life support. The accused's conduct "need not be shown to be the sole or 'effective' cause of a crime . . . there may be two or more independent operative causes of death."

In *Maybin*,[134] the Supreme Court stressed that the ultimate issue was whether the accused's actions still constituted a significant cause of death. It indicated that the test of whether the intervening act was reasonably foreseeable from the accused's actions and whether the intervening act was independent of the accused's actions were only analytical aids and not new legal tests of causation in determining whether a particular intervening act was sufficient to break the chain

---

130 *Ibid.* at para. 81. See also *R. v. Knight*, [2003] 1 S.C.R. 156.
131 *R. v. Pangowish* (2003), 171 C.C.C. (3d) 506 (B.C.C.A.), leave to appeal to S.C.C.
     refused (2003), 176 C.C.C. (3d) vi (S.C.C.).
132 *R. v. Talbot* (2007), 217 C.C.C. (3d) 415 at para. 82 (Ont. C.A.).
133 (1976), 32 C.C.C. (2d) 159 at 175 (Man. C.A.).
134 2012 SCC 24.

of causation so that the accused's actions were no longer a significant cause of the victim's death. In holding that brothers who assaulted another patron in a bar were still responsible for the patron's death even though a bouncer also punched the victim (who died of bleeding in the brain) in the back of the head, the Court stressed that it was reasonably foreseeable that either bouncers or other patrons would join in the fight.[135] The Court also held that the bouncer's assault on the victim was not so independent an act that it rendered the accused's initial assault so remote to suggest that the accused "were morally innocent of the death."[136] The approach to causation taken in this case is broad, but it also based on statutory interpretation of the relevant prohibited act, in this case the test that requires that the accused's actions be a significant but not necessarily the only cause of a death.

Although an accused may still be held responsible for causing death when there are concurrent causes of the death, it will be necessary in some cases for the jury to be instructed about whether an intervening event has "severed the chain of causation" in such a manner that the accused's actions are no longer a significant contributing cause of the victim's death. A person engaged in illegal drag racing may be held responsible for causing the death of a fellow racer, a passenger, other vehicles and pedestrians, but only so far as the accused's actions constitute a significant cause of the death.[137] A racer has been held not responsible for a fatal crash of a fellow racer because of a reasonable doubt that the deceased would have recognized that the accused "was backing away and had given up the race before the fatal crash."[138] In other words, the Crown failed to prove beyond a reasonable doubt that the accused's actions in racing constituted a significant contributing cause of the death.

A new trial was ordered in another case in which the accused caused the victim to become unconscious because of a headlock, but the victim died when his friends' attempts at resuscitation had the unfortunate effect of causing the victim to choke to death on his own vomit. The Nova Scotia Court of Appeal concluded that the jury should be asked whether it was "satisfied beyond a reasonable doubt that the actions [of the accused] are so connected to the death . . . that they can be said to have had a significant causal effect which continued up to the time of his death, without having been interrupted" by the intervening act of the botched resuscitation. The Court of Appeal added that the jury must not be convinced that the accused's actions were "the sole cause" of the

---

135 *Ibid.* at para 41.
136 *Ibid.* at para 59.
137 *R. v. Menzies* (2002), 50 C.R. (5th) 343 at para. 105 (Ont. S.C.J.).
138 *Ibid.* at para. 125.

death but rather, consistent with *Nette*, that they were "a significant contributing cause."[139] At the same time, however, the Court of Appeal indicated that it was not sufficient to instruct the jury on the *Nette* test of causation; the jury must also be instructed about the intervening event and asked to determine if the accused's actions remained a significant contributing cause of death. In another case, an impaired driver was acquitted of impaired driving causing death because the victim was jaywalking and the accused's impaired driving did not cause death.[140]

The Supreme Court in a 4:3 decision reversed a murder conviction and ordered a new trial in a case where the victim who was shot in the stomach and barely survived died as a result of a blood clot a few days after being released from hospital. A new trial that would include the possible verdict of attempted murder was required because the pathologist would not rule out the possibility that while the blood clot was probably related to the shooting, it could have been caused by cocaine ingested by the victim shortly before his death.[141]

These cases indicate that while the accused's actions do not have to be the sole cause of death, there may be situations where the chain of causation will be broken so that the accused's actions are no longer the significant cause of death. For example, the accused would not be responsible for causing a person's death if he or she assaulted a victim, leaving the victim unconscious, but the victim was then killed by a subsequent and independent fire or building collapse. A reasonable doubt about whether the accused caused the prohibited consequences may leave the accused vulnerable to charges that he nevertheless attempted to commit the crime because he had the required intent for the crime and did an act that even if did not cause the prohibited result, nevertheless constituted an attempt.

d) Causation in Non-Homicide Cases

Causation issues sometimes arise in non-homicide cases. In *R. v. Winning*,[142] a conviction of obtaining credit by false pretences was overturned because even though the accused made false statements in her application for a credit card, the company did not rely on these statements when issuing the credit card. If the accused had the necessary intent, however, it might be possible to convict him or her of attempting to obtain credit by false pretences because the *actus reus* for attempts only requires some step beyond mere preparation to commit

---

139 *R. v. Reid and Stratton* (2003), 180 C.C.C. (3d) 151 at para. 89 (N.S.C.A.).

140 *R. v. Horton* (2003), 20 C.R. (6th) 161 (Sask. Q.B.).

141 *R. v. Sarrazin* 2011 SCC 54 at paras 6, 20, 42

142 (1973), 12 C.C.C. (3d) 449 (Ont. C.A.).

the offence. When a person is charged with impaired driving causing bodily harm or death, the Crown must show that the accused's impairment was a contributing cause outside the *de minimis* range to the bodily harm or death. It cannot simply rely on the fact that the driver was impaired with alcohol.[143]

A distinction is sometimes drawn between legal and factual causation with factual causation referring to whether the accused is the "but for" cause of a prohibited consequences and legal causation referring to whether the accused should be held criminally responsible for the prohibited consequences. In *R. v. Williams*[144] a man was charged with aggravated assault on the basis that he had sex with a woman, knowing he was HIV-positive. The man learned he was HIV-positive in November and failed to inform the victim, but the sexual relationship had begun in June. The woman became HIV-positive, but there was no certainty about exactly when she became so infected. The Supreme Court held that the man should be acquitted of aggravated assault because it was possible that the woman was already infected at the point in time at which the accused had sex with her knowing he was HIV-positive. This case suggests that the accused will have the benefit of any reasonable doubt about factual causation. It also illustrates the continued need for a coincidence between the *actus reus* and *mens rea*. When the accused had the required fault of knowingly risking HIV transmission, he could not commit the *actus reus* because the woman was already infected. When the accused may have committed the act of infecting the victim, he did not have the guilty knowledge

e)   Attempts and Accomplice Liability as Alternative Forms of Liability in Cases of Reasonable Doubt About Factual Causation

Although Williams was acquitted of aggravated assault on the basis of a reasonable doubt that he was the factual cause of the victim's HIV infection at the time he knew he was HIV-positive, the Court held that he was guilty of attempted aggravated assault. Liability for attempts as well as accomplice or party liability will be examined in chapter 4, but it should be noted that both can provide alternative forms of legal liability in cases where doubts about whether the accused caused the prohibited consequences may prevent the accused from being held responsible as the principal offender who caused the prohibited con-

---

143   *R. v. Ewart* (1989), 53 C.C.C. (3d) 153 (Alta. C.A.); *R. v. Powell* (1989), 52 C.C.C. (3d) 403 (Sask. C.A.); *R. v. Stephens* (1991), 27 M.V.R. (2d) 24 (Ont. C.A.); *R. v. Fisher* (1992), 13 C.R. (4th) 222 (B.C.C.A.); *R. v. Laprise* (1996), 113 C.C.C. (3d) 87 (Que. C.A.).

144   *R. v. Williams*, 2003 SCC 41 [*Williams*].

sequences. The accused in *Williams* was convicted of attempted aggravated sexual assault because at the time he had the necessary fault of knowing he was HIV-positive and not telling the woman, he committed an act that was sufficient to constitute the very broadly defined *actus reus* of attempt. A person can be guilty of an attempted crime even though the commission of the completed offence may be impossible.[145] Similarly, accomplice or party liability as an aider or abetter may also be an alternative form of legal liability in cases where there may be doubts as to whether a particular accused was the factual cause of a prohibited consequence.[146] This would apply in a case where there was a reasonable doubt about whom of multiple accused actually killed the victim, but it is clear that all the accused assisted in the killing through aiding or abetting the killing.[147]

3) Omissions

One possible exception to the trend to wide definitions of the criminal act is the traditional reluctance to use a failure to act as an *actus reus*. Traditionally, the criminal law has prohibited harmful conduct; it has not required socially desirable conduct. An omission or failure to act will generally only form the *actus reus* of a criminal offence when an individual has a specific legal duty to act.

Legal duties to act can be found throughout the *Criminal Code* and other statutes. Section 215 of the *Criminal Code* provides that a parent, spouse, or guardian has a legal duty to provide the necessaries of life for his or her child, spouse, or charge, and makes it an offence to fail to do so without lawful excuse. If a person commits this offence[148] or is criminally negligent in omitting to perform another duty imposed by law,[149] he or she can be convicted of manslaughter by means of an

---

145 As examined in chapter 4, accused under s. 24 of the Code may be guilty of an attempted crime if they do or omit to do "anything" beyond mere preparation to commit the crime with the intent to commit the crime and it is no defence that the commission of the complete crime was impossible.

146 As explained by Lebel J., in dissent in *R. v. Pickton*, [2010] 2 S.C.R. 198 at paras. 60–61 where he states "party liability as codified in s. 21 of the *Criminal Code* often bridges the gap which might otherwise exist between factual and legal causation" and may apply in a case where there is reasonable doubt whether an accused factually caused a prohibited consequence such as causing death.

147 As examined in chapter 4, accused under s. 21(1) of the Code may be guilty of committing an offence if they purposefully aided or abetted the offence as well as if they actually committed it.

148 *R. v. Naglik* (1993), 83 C.C.C. (3d) 526 (S.C.C.).

149 *Code*, above note 4, s. 219.

unlawful act, or criminal negligence.[15] Those who undertake to do an act have a legal duty to perform the act, if an omission to do the act is or may be dangerous to life.[151] This duty could apply to a person who agreed to be a lifeguard, but who did not make reasonable efforts to save a drowning person. On the other hand, a person who had not agreed to be a lifeguard would be under no such duty. He or she legally could walk away from a drowning person. The Ontario Court of Appeal has stressed that only binding and intentional commitments will suffice to expose an accused to criminal liability for failing to act. A mere expression of words will not normally be enough to create a duty under section 217.[152]

There is a duty to use reasonable care when providing medical treatment or other lawful acts that may endanger the life of others.[153] This duty was breached by a person who donated blood that he knew was infected with HIV.[154] It is also an offence not to use reasonable care in handling explosives,[155] to disobey a court order;[156] to fail to assist a peace officer when requested;[157] to abandon a child;[158] not to obtain assistance in child-birth;[159] to fail to stop when your vehicle is involved in an accident;[160] to neglect animals;[161] and to fail to take steps to protect holes in ice or open excavations.[162] A new duty provides that those who direct others to perform tasks or how to work have "a legal duty to take reasonable steps to prevent bodily harm to that person, or any other person, arising from that work or task."[163] Regulatory offences even more frequently penalize the failure to act, by, for example, mandating safety measures or keeping proper records. As criminal and regulatory offences are used to regulate conduct, there seems to be a trend away from the traditional reluctance to penalize omissions.

---

150 *Ibid.*, ss. 222(5)(a)–(b).
151 *Ibid.*, s. 217.
152 *R. v. Browne* (1997), 116 C.C.C. (3d) 183 (Ont. C.A.), leave to appeal to S.C.C. refused, [1997] S.C.C.A. No. 398.
153 *Code*, above note 4, s. 216.
154 *R. v. Thornton* (1993), 82 C.C.C. (3d) 530 (S.C.C.) [*Thornton*].
155 *Code*, above note 4, ss. 79–80.
156 *Ibid.*, s. 127.
157 *Ibid.*, s. 129(b).
158 *Ibid.*, s. 218.
159 *Ibid.*, s. 242.
160 *Ibid.*, s. 252.
161 *Ibid.*, s. 446.
162 *Ibid.*, s. 263.
163 *Ibid.*, s. 217.1.

Duties may also be implicit in particular crimes. In *R. v. Colucci*,[164] the accused was convicted of publishing a false statement with intent to deceive shareholders when he failed to inform them about an engineer's report, which stated that there were no prospects for development of a particular mine. A refusal to identify yourself to a police officer who saw you commit a crime has been held to be an obstruction of a police officer under section 129 of the *Criminal Code*.[165] In that case, however, Dickson J. wrote a strong dissent warning that "the criminal law is no place within which to introduce implied duties, unknown to statute and common law, breach of which subjects a person to arrest and punishment."[166]

There is also the possibility of courts creating common law duties on their own. In *Miller*,[167] the House of Lords held that a person who accidentally set a house on fire had a duty to take reasonable steps to extinguish the fire or to call the fire department. In the Canadian context, however, such common law duties come precariously close to creating common law crimes contrary to section 9 of the *Criminal Code*. Common law duties challenge the principle of legality because they are created and applied retroactively by courts. In Canada, the preferred approach to *Miller* is found in the Court of Appeal's decision, which did not create a free-standing common law duty but instead found that the accused had adopted the act of setting the fire when he awoke and did not take steps to put out the fire.[168] The controlling principle is not that society is not justified in imposing duties on people to take reasonable steps to respond to dangers, but that this should be done by the democratic enactment of general, accessible, and prospective duties in the *Criminal Code* and not by judges imposing retroactive common law duties on a case-by-case basis.

4) Voluntariness of the Act

The criminal law has traditionally kept distinct the issue of whether the accused has committed the *actus reus* from whether he or she had the required fault element. In many cases, this does not create a practical problem because a person who commits a prohibited act while asleep or having an involuntary seizure will not have the required fault element. Problems emerge in those cases in which the Crown is not required

---

164 [1965] 4 C.C.C. 56 (Ont. C.A.).
165 *R. v. Moore* (1978), 43 C.C.C. (2d) 83 (S.C.C.).
166 *Ibid.* at 96.
167 Above note 111.
168 *R. v. Miller*, [1982] 2 All E.R. 386 (C.A.).

to prove some fault element or perhaps fault based on objective negligence. For example, a person brought into the country under custody has been convicted of the regulatory offence of being an illegal alien even though the jury believed she was guilty through circumstances beyond her control.[169]

The Supreme Court of Canada has been a pioneer in building a voluntariness requirement into the *actus reus*.[170] In the 1962 case of *King*, the Supreme Court refused to convict a person of impaired driving when the impairment was caused by involuntarily consuming a drug at the dentist's office. One judge argued that "there can be no *actus reus* unless it is the result of a willing mind at liberty to make a definite choice or decision."[171] This approach builds a minimal mental or fault element into the *actus reus* and suggests that an accused who acts involuntarily may not have committed the *actus reus* of an offence.

In *Théroux*,[172] McLachlin J. stated that the *mens rea* of an offence "does not encompass all of the mental elements of a crime" because "the *actus reus* has its own mental element"—namely, that "the act must be the voluntary act of the accused for the *actus reus* to exist." McLachlin J. and Lamer C.J. have also stated that the involuntary conduct that would accompany a heart attack, an epileptic seizure, a detached retina, or a bee sting would prevent the Crown from proving the *actus reus* of dangerous driving.[173] La Forest J. has indicated that the unconscious and involuntary behaviour that results in a defence of automatism "is conceptually a subset of the voluntariness requirement which in turn is part of the *actus reus* component of criminal liability."[174] In *Daviault*,[175] Lamer C.J. stated that extreme intoxication that produced involuntary or unconscious behaviour should be seen as negating the *actus reus* of the offence. The majority of the Court held that extreme intoxication would negate the mental element of the assault but seemed to concede

---

169   *R. v. Larsonneur* (1933), 24 Cr. App. Rep. 74 (C.C.A.).

170   See also the statement of New Zealand judges that the commission of the *actus reus* cannot be involuntary or unconscious. *Kilbride v. Lake*, [1962] N.Z.L.R. 590 (S.C.).

171   *R. v. King* (1962), 133 C.C.C. 1 at 3 (S.C.C.) [*King*]. In England, however, an accused was convicted despite the involuntary consumption of drugs. *R. v. Kingston*, [1994] 3 W.L.R. 519 (H.L.).

172   *R. v. Théroux* (1993), 79 C.C.C. (3d) 449 at 458 (S.C.C.) [*Théroux*].

173   *R. v. Hundal* (1993), 79 C.C.C. (3d) 97 (S.C.C.). But see *R v. Beatty*, [2008] 1 S.C.R. 49 at para. 43 where it is suggested that such a sudden occurrence may also be relevant to determining even objective *mens rea* or fault requirements.

174   *R. v. Parks* (1992), 75 C.C.C. (3d) 287 at 302 (S.C.C.). See ch. 8, "Mental Disorder and Automatism."

175   *Daviault*, above note 116 at 25.

that such a condition could also prevent the voluntary formation of the *actus reus.* In *R. v. Stone*,[176] the Court also acknowledged that, subject to the mental disorder defence, an accused should be acquitted if he or she acted in an involuntary manner. In *R. v. Ruzic*,[177] the Court again referred to the requirement of voluntariness as a fundamental principle of criminal law and a fundamental principle of justice under section 7 of the *Charter*. It related the principle of voluntariness to the requirement that people only be punished if they acted as "autonomous and freely choosing agents."

Courts seem increasingly willing to consider a lack of voluntary or conscious conduct as something that prevents the commission of the criminal act, or *actus reus*. This means a lack of voluntariness may be a defence to all criminal and regulatory offences, regardless of the fault element required. In practice, this will be most important in cases with no fault element or one based on negligence because involuntary conduct should usually be inconsistent with subjective forms of fault.

CONCLUSION

Legislative reform could clarify some of the ambiguities in determining the *actus reus* or prohibited act of offences. Although the common law crime of contempt of court survives and codification of all crimes is not required under section 7 of the *Charter*, Parliament could provide that federal laws are the sole source of criminal offences. Even this reform, however, would not truly make the criminal law accessible to most people who understandably do not have the time or inclination to read thick books of statutes. In order to provide fair notice to the accused and prevent unlimited law enforcement discretion, legislatures should ensure that every criminal act is defined in a manner that is neither excessively vague or overbroad. In reality, however, courts have been very reluctant to strike laws down under section 7 of the *Charter* on the basis that they are excessively vague.[178] They have also added interpretative glosses on offences and defences so that they diverge in significant ways from the words of the statute. The result is that even a conscientious citizen who reads the many pages of the *Criminal Code* will be unable to determine the extent of criminal liability.

---

176 *R. v. Stone* (1999), 134 C.C.C. (3d) 353 (S.C.C.).

177 (2001), 153 C.C.C. (3d) 1 (S.C.C.) at paras. 42 and 46.

178 *Heywood*, above note 49.

The present trend is towards broad legislative definitions of the prohibited act. There will always be a need for judicial interpretation, but controversial policy issues such as whether a person can consent to non-trivial bodily harm[179] and whether consent should be based on the subjective views of the complainant in a sexual assault case[180] should probably be specifically addressed by Parliament. A related issue is whether Parliament should provide new offences to deal with new problems such as accused who give blood or have sex without disclosing that they are HIV-positive or whether we should continue to rely on existing offences subject to judicial interpretation.[181]

There is an emerging principle that involuntary actions may not constitute the prohibited act and this constitutes an important restraint on criminal law, particularly in those cases where there is no fault element. The courts have not always been consistent about whether the prohibited act should be interpreted subject to a marked departure standard.[182] The interpretation of the prohibited act should largely depend on the words used in the offence interpreted in a purposive manner. The doctrine of strict construction, which requires judges to give the criminal law a reasonable interpretation that favours the accused, only applies if there are reasonable ambiguities after the law has been given a purposive interpretation designed to achieve its objects. This approach recognizes both the accused's claim to clear and fair notice and society's claim not to have criminal laws trivialized by stunted interpretations that are not designed to achieve Parliament's objectives.

There may also be a role for official recognition by the courts of the doctrine of *de minimus non curat lex* to ensure that the criminal law is used with restraint and does not apply to trifles even if the prohibited act and fault element are present. An application of such a common law defence in trivial cases may be a more tailored response to overbreadth in the criminal law than either striking a law down under section 7 of the *Charter* because it is overbroad or vague or reading in a requirement that the prohibited act be a marked departure from reasonable conduct in every case.

The blunt rule that ignorance of the law is no excuse seems unstable and requires some reform. The Supreme Court has now recognized that reasonable reliance on mistaken legal advice from an official who administers the law will provide a defence of officially induced

---

179 *Jobidon*, above note 102.
180 *Ewanchuk*, above note 94.
181 *Thornton*, above note 154; *Cuerrier*, above note 98; *Williams*, above note 144.
182 Compare *Boulanger*, above note 32 and *Beatty*, above note 34, discussed above in this chapter.

error. This defence must be established by the accused on a balance of probabilities and it will result in a stay of proceedings. The recognition of the new defence of officially induced error is a positive development that should prevent the state from encouraging and prosecuting conduct at the same time.[183] Nevertheless, the defence is a limited qualification of the ignorance of the law is not an excuse principle. For example, it would not be available to accused who reasonably relied on their own legal research or even that of their lawyer. The fault elements of some crimes such as theft allow the accused to argue that a belief that he or she was acting legally raises a reasonable doubt concerning *mens rea*. In addition, courts may continue to be tempted to interpret some matters as mistakes of fact in order to avoid the harshness of holding that they are mistakes of law that offer no excuse.[184] The Supreme Court has also suggested that the operation of section 19 can in some cases turn what might otherwise be a strict liability offence that allows a defence of due diligence into an absolute liability offence.[185] This somewhat mitigates the harshness of the ignorance of the law is no excuse principle because as will be discussed in chapter 6, an accused cannot be imprisoned for an absolute liability offence. At the same time, it does not fundamentally challenge the ignorance of the law is no excuse principle. In general, only prosecutorial or sentencing discretion can mitigate the harshness of convicting a person who acted under a reasonable mistake of law.

Although the present law provides different rules of causation with respect to different offences, there have been many proposals to have a general test of causation in the *Criminal Code*. Different tests based on a substantial contribution, a significant contribution, and more than a negligible contribution have been proposed at various times. The Supreme Court has indicated that the general test in homicide cases is one of a significant contributing cause.[186] The accused's actions need not be the sole cause of the prohibited consequences, but the possibility that intervening events will break the chain of causation should be considered. Causation like other elements of the prohibited act should be proven beyond a reasonable doubt.

It would be helpful if Parliament addressed the issue of criminalizing omissions or failure to act in a principled and comprehensive fashion. Specific duties to act will likely still be imposed on parents and those undertaking dangerous activities, but general duties, such as tak-

---

183 *Lévis*, above note 62.
184 *Jorgensen*, above note 62.
185 *Pontes*, above note 67.
186 *Nette*, above note 127.

ing reasonable steps to rescue and taking reasonable steps to rectify a danger that one has created, could be clearly codified. It would be very important that these duties be accessible and well-known to the public. It would also be best if it was specifically recognized that the *mens rea* only need coincide with the *actus reus* at some point during the *actus reus*[187] and that the *actus reus* does not occur if the accused acts in an involuntary manner. These are important principles of criminal liability that should be clearly articulated in the *Criminal Code*.

FURTHER READINGS

ASHWORTH, A., "The Scope of Criminal Liability for Omissions" (1989) 105 L.Q. Rev. 424

BOYLE, C., & S. DE GROOT, "The Responsible Citizen in the *City of Levis*: Due Diligence and Officially Induced Error" (2006) 36 C.R. (6th) 249

COLVIN, E., & S. ANAND, *Principles of Criminal Law*, 3d ed. (Toronto: Thomson Carswell, 2007) chs. 3 & 4

COMISKEY, M., & M. SULLIVAN, "Avoidance, Deception and Mistake of Law: The *Mens Rea* of Tax Evasion" (2006) 51 Crim. L.Q. 303

GALLOWAY, D., "Causation in Criminal Law: Interventions, Thin Skulls and Lost Chances" (1989) 14 Queen's L.J. 71

GRANT, I., D. CHUNN, & C. BOYLE, *The Law of Homicide* (Toronto: Carswell, 1994) ch. 3

HART, H.L.A., & T. HONORE, *Causation in the Law*, 2d ed. (Oxford: Oxford University Press, 1985) chs. 12–14

HOLLAND, W., "HIV/AIDS and the Criminal Law" (1994) 36 Crim. L.Q. 279

MANNING, M., & P. SANKOFF, *Criminal Law*, 4th ed. (Markham: LexisNexis, 2009) ch. 4

MANSON, A., "Rethinking Causation: The Implications of Harbottle" (1994) 24 C.R. (4th) 153

STEWART, H., "Mistake of Law under the *Charter*" (1998) 40 Crim. L.Q. 279

---

187 *Cooper*, above note 113.

STUART, D., *Canadian Criminal Law: A Treatise*, 5th ed. (Toronto: Carswell, 2007) chs. 2, 4, and 5

WILLIAMS, G., "Criminal Omissions: The Conventional View" (1991) 107 L.Q. Rev. 86

CHAPTER 4

UNFULFILLED CRIMES AND PARTICIPATION IN CRIMES

The trend towards broad definitions of the criminal act examined in the last chapter is a means of expanding the breadth of the criminal sanction. The provisions examined in this chapter also cast the net of criminal liability broadly to include those who attempt but fail to complete a crime; those who encourage or plan the commission of a crime; and those who assist others to commit a crime.

A person who goes beyond mere preparation to rob a bank, with the intent to commit the robbery, can be convicted of attempted robbery, even though no robbery took place and it may have been impossible for the complete crime to ever occur. An attempted robbery is, however, subject to less punishment than a robbery. On the other hand, a person who assists in the robbery by driving the getaway car can be convicted of being a party to the robbery by aiding the robbery, even though he or she never took the property with force. Similarly, a bank teller who helped the robber plan the heist might also be guilty of the robbery as a person who abets the crime. The provisions governing attempts and parties to a crime will be considered separately, but they are united in imposing the criminal sanction on those who do not actually commit the complete crime. The relatively high level of *mens rea* required for attempts and parties, however, generally limits these provisions to those who act with guilty intent or knowledge. Sentencing discretion also plays an important role in distinguishing the various degrees of culpability caught by the broad definitions of criminal attempts and parties to a crime.

In section 24 of the *Criminal Code*, Parliament has prohibited attempts to commit criminal offences. Any act beyond mere preparation may be a sufficient *actus reus* for an attempted crime, even if the act does not amount to a moral wrong or a social mischief. The counterbalance to this broad definition of the *actus reus* is that the Crown must prove beyond a reasonable doubt that the accused acted with the intent to commit the complete offence. In addition to attempts, a person who counsels or solicits the commission of a crime or is part of an agreement to commit a crime may also be guilty of the separate crimes of counselling or conspiracy, even though the complete crime was never committed. These unfulfilled crimes are designed to discourage the commission of the complete offence and to recognize that the accused had the intent to commit the complete crime. They are, however, separate offences and, with the exception of conspiracy, subject to less punishment than the complete crime.

The law concerning parties to a crime is in some respects even broader and harsher than the law relating to inchoate crimes such as attempts, counselling, and conspiracy. Parliament has provided in section 21(1)(b) and (c) of the *Criminal Code* that those who assist the person committing the actual criminal offence through aiding or abetting are guilty as parties of the same criminal offence as the person who actually commits the crime. The person who acts as lookout or drives the getaway car can be convicted of robbery just as the person who actually takes the money by force. The *actus reus* is defined to include acts of assistance and acts of encouragement but not mere presence. At the same time, however, the Crown must prove the *mens rea* that the accused intentionally and knowingly aided or abetted the offence. A person who unwittingly delivers a package containing a bomb assists in the bombing, but would not have the intent required to be guilty as an aider or abettor to the bombing.

Section 21(2) makes an accused who has formed an unlawful purpose with an accomplice responsible for crimes that the accused knew or ought to have known would be a probable consequence of carrying out their common purpose. This section requires the formation of an unlawful purpose and either subjective or objective foresight of the additional crimes. The fault element of objective foresight has been found to be unconstitutional when applied to parties charged with murder and attempted murder. Thus, an accused who agreed with an accomplice to assault a person could not be convicted of murder unless he knew that it was likely that the accomplice would actually kill the victim. A requirement for a high level of *mens rea* may counterbalance the broad definition of the prohibited act. At the same time, the courts have indicated that the accused who forms an unlawful purpose does not necessarily have to desire that unlawful purpose. In addition, objective foresight of the further crime is all that is required under section 21(2) for crimes other than murder and attempted murder.

The provisions for attempted crimes and participation in crimes examined in this chapter apply to all criminal offences in the *Code* and constitute important extensions of criminal liability. For example, the September 11 terrorists could have been charged with attempted murder or conspiracy to commit murder if they were apprehended before they boarded the planes. Similarly, those who knowingly and intentionally assisted them in carrying out their plots could be charged as parties to their offences. At the same time, however, Parliament may create new crimes that may apply to conduct that might or might not constitute an attempt to commit to a crime or a form of participation in the commission of the crime.

New crimes can serve as a functional substitute for attempted crimes. For example, charges of attempted sexual assault or attempted sexual interference may not be necessary if a person is guilty of the crime of inviting a person under sixteen years of age to engage in sexual touching or new offences relating to luring children over the Internet.[1] New crimes such as financing, facilitating, or instructing a person to carry out activities for the benefit of a terrorist group may be alternatives to establishing that a person is guilty of attempting or conspiracy to commit the crime intended to be committed by the terrorists.[2] Crimes based on participation in the activities of a terrorist group[3] or a criminal organization[4] can be used instead of charging a person as a party to a crime committed by the group or with an attempt to commit the crime or with a conspiracy to commit the crime. The Supreme Court has called a new computer luring offence under section 172.1 of the *Code* an "incipient or 'inchoate' offence, that is, a preparatory crime that captures otherwise legal conduct meant to culminate in the commission of a completed crime."[5] It has stressed that it was appropriate to require subjective fault in relation to all the elements of the offence including the age of the child and the purpose of facilitating a sexual offence given the remoteness of the offence to actual harm.[6] Nevertheless, the Court also indicated that a person may be guilty under

---

1   *Criminal Code*, R.S.C. 1985, c. C-46, ss. 152 and 172.1 [*Code*].
2   *Ibid.*, ss. 83.02, 83.03, 83.04, 83.19, 83.21, & 83.22.
3   *Ibid.*, s. 83.18.
4   *Ibid.*, s. 467.11.
5   *R. v. Legare*, 2009 SCC 56 at para. 25.
6   *Ibid.* at para. 33.

such offences even if the secondary crime was not likely to have been committed in a case involving a man luring a thirteen-year-old girl in a different province over the computer.[7] It will be important that such crimes have a high level of fault given their expansion of criminal liability. It is also possible that such broadly defined completed crimes may go beyond the traditional inchoate crimes. The courts, for example, have refused to combine inchoate forms of liability and have refused to create a crime of attempted conspiracy on the basis that the criminal law should not expand so far as to criminalize a "risk that a risk"[8] of a completed crime will occur. Statutory offences such as computer luring or terrorist financing may, however, criminalize conduct that presents a risk that a particularly dangerous risk may occur.

A. ATTEMPTS

Section 24 of the *Criminal Code* provides:

(1) Every one who, having an intent to commit an offence, does or omits to do anything for the purpose of carrying out his intention is guilty of an attempt to commit the offence whether or not it was possible under the circumstances to commit the offence.

(2) The question whether an act or omission by a person who has an intent to commit an offence is or is not mere preparation to commit the offence, and too remote to constitute an attempt to commit the offence, is a question of law.

Section 463 sets out the punishment for attempted crimes. A person guilty of an attempted crime is generally subject to one-half of the longest term to which a person guilty of the completed offence is liable.[9] A few substantive offences, including bribery and obstructing justice, include attempts as part of the completed offence and, as such, punish them in the same fashion as the completed offence.[10] A broadly defined offence may also be a substitute for charging a person with an attempted crime. For example, many acts that may have been attempted rapes before 1983 could now constitute sexual assaults. Similarly, some

---

7   *Ibid.* at para. 44.

8   *R. v. Déry*, [2006] 2 S.C.R. 669 at para. 50.

9   An attempt to commit an offence punishable on summary conviction is itself punishable on summary conviction: *Code*, above note 1, s. 463(c). Attempted murder is subject to life imprisonment: *Code*, *ibid.*, s. 239.

10 *Code*, *ibid.*, ss. 119(1)(a)(iii), 123(2), and 139(1).

unsuccessful thefts could still qualify as thefts if the accused, with the intent to steal, begins to move the object to be stolen.[11] The crime of assault is also defined broadly by Parliament to include not only the striking of another person, but also attempts or threats, by act or gesture, to apply force. Thus, there would be no need to charge a person with attempted assault if he or she threatened a person in a manner that made that person reasonably believe that he or she could be assaulted.[12]

1) *Mens Rea* for Attempts

The *mens rea*, or fault element, is the most important element of attempted crimes because the *actus reus* will, by definition, not include the completed crime. As the Ontario Court of Appeal has observed, "whereas in most crimes it is the *actus reus* which the law endeavours to prevent, and the *mens rea* is only a necessary element of the offence, in a criminal attempt, the *mens rea* is of primary importance and the *actus reus* is the necessary element."[13] Similarly, the Supreme Court has recognized that "the criminal element of the offence of attempt may lie solely in the intent."[14]

After having initially interpreted "the intent to commit an offence" in section 24(1) to include any intent provided in the *Criminal Code* to commit the completed offence,[15] the Supreme Court now interprets the intent to commit an offence as the specific intent to commit the completed offence. In the context of murder, McIntyre J. reasoned as follows:

> The completed offence of murder involves a killing. The intention to commit the complete offence must therefore include an intention to kill . . . . I am then of the view that the *mens rea* for an attempted murder cannot be less than the specific intent to kill . . . .
>
> . . . Section 24 defines an attempt as "having an intent to commit an offence." Because s. 24 is a general section it is necessary to "read in" the offence in question. The offence of attempted murder then is defined as "having an intent to commit murder." . . .
>
> . . . The fact that certain mental elements, other than an intent to kill, may lead to a conviction for murder where there has been a kill-

---

11   *Ibid.*, s. 322(2).
12   *Ibid.*, s. 265(b)(ii).
13   *R. v. Cline* (1956), 115 C.C.C. 18 at 27 (Ont. C.A.).
14   *R. v. Ancio* (1984), 10 C.C.C. (3d) 385 at 402 (S.C.C.) [*Ancio*].
15   *R. v. Lajoie* (1973), 10 C.C.C. (2d) 313 (S.C.C.).

ing does not mean that anything less than an intent to kill will suffice for an attempt at murder.[16]

The intent that is "read in" for attempted murder is the intent to kill in section 229(a)(i), even though it is constitutionally permissible to convict a person of the completed offence of murder on the basis of a lesser intent.[17] It should be noted that *Ancio* was a decision made without any reference to the *Charter*.

a) Constitutional Fault Element for Attempted Murder

In *R. v. Logan*,[18] the Supreme Court considered the fault element required under section 7 of the *Charter* for a conviction of attempted murder. Lamer C.J. held that the minimal fault element for attempted murder should be the same as for the commission of murder, on the grounds that the stigma of being convicted of the two offences was the same. He reasoned:

> The stigma associated with a conviction for attempted murder is the same as it is for murder. Such a conviction reveals that, although no death ensued from the actions of the accused, the intent to kill was still present in his or her mind. The attempted murderer is no less a killer than a murderer: he may be lucky—the ambulance arrived early, or some other fortuitous circumstance—but he still has the same killer instinct.[19]

In determining whether subjective foresight of death was constitutionally required, "the crucial consideration is whether there is a continuing serious social stigma which will be imposed on the accused upon conviction"[20] and not the existence of sentencing discretion that is available for attempted murder but not murder.[21] *Logan* suggests that the minimum fault requirement for attempted murder is the knowledge that death will result and that Parliament could lower the *mens rea* of attempted murder to that point but not below. Nevertheless, it does not overtake the higher standard of an intent to kill that is required by *Ancio*. It is an error to instruct the jury that knowledge that the victim

---

16 *Ancio*, above note 14 at 402–3.
17 Namely, subjective foresight of death as required in *R. v. Martineau* (1990), 58 C.C.C. (3d) 353 (S.C.C.) [*Martineau*], discussed in ch. 2(B)(4)(e), "Fault Requirements."
18 (1990), 58 C.C.C. (3d) 391 (S.C.C.) [*Logan*].
19 *Ibid.* at 399.
20 *Ibid.* at 400.
21 Attempted murder is punishable by up to life imprisonment, whereas murder has a mandatory sentence of life imprisonment.

is likely to die is a sufficient *mens rea* for attempted murder: the Crown must rather prove the *Ancio* standard of an intent to kill.[22] The *Charter* provides minimum standards of fairness towards the accused, not maximum standards.

b) *Mens Rea* for Other Attempted Offences

On the basis of *Ancio*, in principle, nothing less than the specific intent to obtain the prohibited result will suffice, even if a conviction for the completed offence could be based on some lesser form of intent. In *R. v. Colburne*,[23] the Quebec Court of Appeal stated that an attempt requires a specific intent to carry out the crime, even if the completed offence requires a lesser intent. On this basis, it could be argued that an attempted sexual assault must be based on the subjective intent to engage in non-consensual sexual activity, even though a person could now be convicted of the completed offence of sexual assault on the basis of recklessness, wilful blindness, or a failure to "take reasonable steps, in the circumstances known to the accused at the time, to ascertain that the complainant was consenting."[24] A discussion of the requirements of the crime of attempted sexual assault may, in many cases, be academic, given the wide definition of the *actus reus* of the completed crime of sexual assault.[25] That said, Canadian courts should not follow other jurisdictions that allow attempts to be punished on the basis of recklessness or knowledge with respect to the completed offence.[26] The essence of an attempt crime is the accused's clear intent to commit the completed offence. This is particularly the case when it is considered that the *actus reus* of the attempt may not in itself be a crime or even a social mischief. It is unclear whether courts will accept crimes such

---

22   *R. v. Latoski* (2005), 77 O.R. (3d) 505 at paras. 11–12 (C.A.).

23   (1991), 66 C.C.C. (3d) 235 at 240 and 248–49 (Que. C.A.).

24   *Code*, above note 1, s. 273.2.

25   Section 265(b) of the *Code* defines the *actus reus* of assaults to include attempts or threats to apply force, provided the accused causes the complainant to believe on reasonable grounds that he has the present ability to effect his purpose.

26   See E. Colvin & S. Anand, *Principles of Criminal Law*, 3d ed. (Toronto: Thomson Carswell, 2007) at 528–30. The authors examine the Australian and British law and argue in favour of recognizing conditional intent or knowledge, but not recklessness, as a sufficient *mens rea* for attempts, in part because knowledge is a sufficient form of fault for most completed offences including murder. As suggested above, however, the fact that knowledge is sufficient for serious completed offences does not justify its use for attempted crime, which may not have involved even the commission of a harmful act, let alone the completed offence. For similar criticisms but with some suggestion that wilful blindness might suffice for an attempt, see M. Manning & P. Sankoff, *Criminal Law*, 4th ed. (Markham: LexisNexis, 2009) at 292.

as attempted manslaughter or an attempt to commit a strict liability offence as offences because of the difficulties of reconciling such crimes with the idea that attempts require a specific intent to carry out the complete crime.

In *R. v. Williams*,[27] the Supreme Court recognized the relevance of the high-intent standard contemplated in *Ancio* outside the context of attempted murder. In this case, the Court convicted a man of attempted aggravated assault for having unprotected sex when he knew he was HIV-positive. As discussed in chapter 3, an attempt conviction was entered because there was at least a reasonable doubt that the accused's partner was already infected with HIV when the accused had sex with her, knowing that he was infected. This *actus reus* of aggravated assault was not proven beyond a reasonable doubt, but there was a sufficient *actus reus* for attempted aggravated assault. On the *mens rea* issue, Binnie J. stated for the Court:

> The crime of attempt, as with any offence, requires the Crown to establish that the accused *intended* to commit the crime in question: *R. v. Ancio* [1984] 1 S.C.R. 225 at pp. 247–48. The requisite intent is established here . . . . The respondent, knowing . . . he was HIV-positive, engaged in unprotected sex with the complainant intending her thereby to be exposed to the lethal consequences of HIV.[28]

Attempted crimes, by their very nature of not resulting in the prohibited consequences of a completed crime, are characterized by the intent of the accused to carry out the completed crime. Attempts are, in the words of the Supreme Court, crimes where "the *mens rea* of the completed offence is present entirely."[29] Attempts to commit crimes will often require proof of a higher form of *mens rea* than the completed crime because of their very nature as inchoate offences. An intent to commit the complete crime is required for attempt, whereas knowledge or even recklessness will be a sufficient *mens rea* for most complete crimes.

2) The *Actus Reus* of Attempts

Although section 24(2) of the *Criminal Code* states that it is a question of law whether an act or omission "is not mere preparation to commit

---

27   2003 SCC 41 [*Williams*].

28   *Ibid.* at para. 62 [emphasis in original].

29   *Ibid.* at para. 65, quoting *United States of America v. Dynar*, [1997] 2 S.C.R. 462 at para. 74 [*Dynar*].

the offence, and too remote to constitute an attempt to commit the offence," Canadian courts have not been able to provide a universal definition of the prohibited act in criminal attempts. In *Cline*,[30] the Ontario Court of Appeal stated that "a precise and satisfactory definition of the *actus reus* is perhaps impossible," while concluding that "each case must be determined on its own facts, having due regard to the nature of the offence and the particular acts in question." The Court of Appeal added that the *actus reus* for an attempt need not "be a crime or a tort or even a moral wrong or social mischief," nor demonstrate by its nature an unequivocal intent.[31] The *actus reus* must not be mere preparation to commit a crime, but it can be the next step done with the intent to commit the crime after preparation is complete. On the facts, the Court of Appeal held that the accused had gone beyond mere preparation when, following his pattern of past indecent assaults, he approached and offered a young boy money to help carry his suitcases. By donning large sunglasses and selecting a secluded alley, the accused had finished preparing to commit the crime, and his approach to the young boy was a sufficient *actus reus*.

In *R. v. Deutsch*,[32] the Supreme Court took a fact and offence specific approach to determine when preparation has ended and the *actus reus* for a criminal attempt has begun. Le Dain J. stated:

> [T]he distinction between preparation and attempt is essentially a qualitative one, involving the relationship between the nature and quality of the act in question and the nature of the complete offence, although consideration must necessarily be given, in making that qualitative distinction, to the relative proximity of the act in question to what would have been the completed offence, in terms of time, location, and acts under the control of the accused remaining to be accomplished.[33]

The Supreme Court held that the accused had gone beyond mere preparation for the crime of attempted procurement of prostitution when he indicated to job applicants that they could earn up to $100,000 a year and might be required to have sex with clients in order to secure business contracts. By holding out large financial awards in the course of the job interviews, the Court concluded that the accused had gone beyond mere preparation, even though no formal job offer was made

---

30   Above note 13 at 26 and 28.
31   *Ibid.* at 28. See also *R. v. Sorrell* (1978), 41 C.C.C. (2d) 9 (Ont. C.A.) [*Sorrell*].
32   (1986), 27 C.C.C. (3d) 385 (S.C.C.) [*Deutsch*].
33   *Ibid.* at 401.

and any prostitution would happen "a considerable period of time" in the future.

Determining whether the accused has gone beyond mere preparation and committed an *actus reus* for an attempted crime is difficult to predict. In a subsequent case, the Supreme Court has observed that "the distinction between preparation and attempt is essentially a qualitative one, involving the relationship between the nature and quality of the act in question and the nature of the complete offence." It indicated that "consideration must necessarily be given, in making that qualitative distinction, to the relative proximity of the act in question to what would have been the completed offence, in terms of time, location, and acts under the control of the accused remaining to be accomplished." The Court found that the accused had gone beyond preparation and there was "sufficient proximity" to the completed offence of selling illegally obtained fish when the accused had brought a sample of illegally obtained fish to a store and asked the owner if he was "interested."[34]

In a practical sense, the determination of whether the act has gone beyond mere preparation may depend in part on the strength of the evidence of wrongful intent. Going through the glove compartment of a car has been held to be the *actus reus* for its attempted theft when the accused indicated that he was searching for keys to steal the car.[35] The accused's actions in pointing a loaded gun at and following his ex-wife have been held sufficient for an attempted murder, even if the accused did not fire the gun.[36] On the other hand, making a plasticine impression of a car key has been held to be only preparation to steal the car.[37] Approaching a store with balaclavas and a gun could be a sufficient *actus reus* for attempted robbery, but retreat when informed that the store was closed may reveal a reasonable doubt about the intent to commit the robbery.[38] In practice, a more remote *actus reus* will be accepted if the intent is clear. Another factor may well be the magnitude of the planned crime. In a case in which the accused intends to commit murder or even mass murder, the approach in *Deutsch* of holding that the accused has gone beyond mere preparation and committed the *actus reus* of an attempt even though the completed crime may still be months away makes eminent sense.

Some countries recognize abandonment or desistance as a defence to attempt. The Canadian authorities have rejected abandonment as an

---

34   *R. v. Gladstone* (1996), 109 C.C.C. (3d) 193 at 202 (S.C.C.).
35   *R. v. James* (1971), 2 C.C.C. (2d) 141 (Ont. C.A.).
36   *R. v. Boudreau* (2005), 193 C.C.C. (3d) 449 (N.S.C.A.).
37   *R. v. Lobreau* (1988), 67 C.R. (3d) 74 (Alta. C.A.).
38   *Sorrell*, above note 31.

independent defence that is not contemplated in section 24,[39] while at the same time recognizing that it may create a reasonable doubt about whether the accused had the intent to commit the crime in the first place.[40] Although an act beyond mere preparation is required, the emphasis throughout the law of attempts should be on the accused's intent to commit the completed offence. Abandonment may raise a reasonable doubt about whether the accused had the intent to commit the complete offence in the first place, but in Canada it is not an independent defence to an attempted crime.

Something that goes beyond mere preparation may still constitute the *actus reus* of attempt in cases where the complete crime does not and even cannot occur. In *Detering*,[41] the accused had gone well beyond mere preparation in their attempt to commit fraud, but were convicted of attempted fraud as opposed to fraud because the intended victims were not deceived. In *Williams*,[42] unprotected acts of sexual intercourse by an accused who knew he was HIV-positive constituted the *actus reus* of attempted aggravated assault. The accused "took more than preparatory steps. He did everything he could to achieve the infection of the complainant." The fact that it may have been impossible to infect the complainant because she was already infected with HIV did not prevent the conviction of the accused for attempt.

3) Impossibility and Attempts

The theoretical issue of whether an accused should be held liable for attempts when it was impossible to commit the completed offence has been settled by section 24(1) of the *Criminal Code*, which states that a person can be guilty of attempt "whether or not it was possible under the circumstances to commit the offence." This provision precludes either legal or factual impossibility as a possible defence to an attempted crime. Factual impossibility would include a case in which an accused attempted to pick a pocket that contained no money[43] and the

---

39   *R. v. Kosh*, [1965] 1 C.C.C. 230 at 235 (Sask. C.A.), stating that "once the essential element of intent is established, together with overt acts towards the commission of the intended crime, the reason why the offence was not committed becomes immaterial. Once these elements are established, it makes no difference whether non-commission was due to interruption, frustration or a change of mind."

40   *Sorrell*, above note 31.

41   *R. v. Detering* (1982), 70 C.C.C. (2d) 321 (S.C.C.) [*Detering*].

42   *Williams*, above note 27 at para. 64.

43   *R. v. Scott*, [1964] 2 C.C.C. 257 (Alta. C.A.).

case of a person who tried to infect someone with HIV even though she was already infected.[44] Legal impossibility would include attempting to receive goods believed to be stolen, but which were in law not stolen.[45] The distinction between factual and legal impossibility has been rejected on the basis that under section 24 "[t]here is no legally relevant difference between the pickpocket who reaches into the empty pocket [that is, factual impossibility] and the man who takes his own umbrella from a stand believing it to be some other person's umbrella [legal impossibility]."[46] In both cases, the accused had the *mens rea* of a thief, had taken steps beyond preparation to consummate the crime, and was thwarted by circumstances over which he had no control.

On several occasions, the Supreme Court has indicated that impossibility is not a defence to attempted crimes in Canada.[47] In *Dynar*,[48] the Court again affirmed that impossibility was not a defence to an attempt. Thus, an accused who believed he was engaged in laundering drug money could be convicted of attempted money-laundering even though the money was government money provided by the police in a sting operation and not drug money. Similarly, a person who stabs a corpse with the intent to murder a real person would be guilty of attempted murder.[49] A person who accepts a package believing it to contain a large amount of drugs would be guilty of attempting to possess drugs for the purpose of trafficking even if the package did not contain any drugs.[50] A person who comes to a hotel hoping to have sex with an eleven year old is still guilty of attempting to procure the sexual services of a child even though no child was involved in the police sting operation.[51]

The only time impossibility could be a defence would be if a person intended to commit an "imaginary crime." Thus, a person who believed that the possession of $100 bills was illegal would be innocent because

---

44   *Williams*, above note 27.

45   For an acquittal in this scenario, see *Anderton v. Ryan*, [1985] A.C. 560 (H.L.). This case was overruled a year later in *R. v. Shivpuri*, [1986] 2 All E.R. 334 (H.L.).

46   *Dynar*, above note 29 at para. 62.

47   *Detering*, above note 41; *R. v. Kundeus* (1975), 24 C.C.C. (2d) 276 (S.C.C.).

48   *Dynar*, above note 29 at para. 67. In any event, the offence was subsequently amended to criminalize laundering money either knowing or believing that it was the proceeds of crime. *Code*, above note 1, s. 462.31(1).

49   In dissent, Major J. pointed out that this approach could lead to what he saw as the absurdity of convicting someone of attempted murder who placed a voodoo stick in a doll thinking that this would cause the death of a person. *Dynar, ibid.* at para. 173.

50   *R. v. Chan* (2003), 178 C.C.C. (3d) 269 at paras. 63–64 (Ont. C.A.) (*obiter* ruling) [*Chan*].

51   *R. v. Kerster* (2003), 175 C.C.C. (3d) 28 (B.C.C.A.).

that person has "no *mens rea* known to law" and "has not displayed any propensity to commit crimes in the future." It is highly unlikely that a person would ever be charged with the commission of an imaginary crime and it is best simply to conclude that factual or legal impossibility is not a defence to an attempted crime. What matters is whether the accused had the intent to commit the crime and went beyond mere preparation to commit the crime.

B. CONSPIRACY

A conspiracy, like an attempt, is something that occurs before a completed offence is committed. The Supreme Court has indicated that "conspiracy is in fact a more 'preliminary' crime than attempt, since the offence is considered to be complete before any acts are taken that go beyond mere preparation to put the common design into effect. The Crown is simply required to prove a meeting of the minds with regard to a common design to do something unlawful, specifically the commission of an indictable offence."[52] Unlike attempts, however, conspiracies are generally punished as severely as the completed offence.

Section 465(1)(c) establishes the general offence of conspiracy by providing that "every one who conspires with any one to commit an indictable offence . . . is guilty of an indictable offence and liable to the same punishment as that to which an accused who is guilty of that offence would, on conviction, be liable."[53] A general provision for conspiracies to effect an unlawful purpose was repealed after the Supreme Court indicated a reluctance to recognize conspiracies to commit common law as opposed to statutory crimes.[54] There are specific provisions relating to conspiracy to commit murder;[55] conspiracy to prosecute a person known to be innocent;[56] conspiracy with extraterritorial effects;[57] and conspiracy in restraint of trade.[58] The agreement of more than one person to commit a crime is seen as a particular menace

---

52 *Dynar*, above note 29 at para. 87.
53 *Code*, above note 1, s. 465(1)(d), now provides that everyone who conspires to commit a summary conviction offence is guilty of an offence punishable on summary conviction and it is not yet clear whether this includes provincial and regulatory offences that can be prosecuted as summary conviction offences.
54 *R. v. Gralewicz* (1980), 54 C.C.C. (2d) 289 (S.C.C.).
55 *Code*, above note 1, s. 465(1)(a).
56 *Ibid.*, s. 465(1)(b).
57 *Ibid.*, ss. 465(3) & (4).
58 *Ibid.*, ss. 466 & 467.

to society that deserves punishment even before the conspirators have taken steps beyond preparation and attempted to commit the crime. In practice, conspiracy charges are most often brought in cases involving organized crime and drug trafficking. Other offences such as participation in the activities in a terrorist organization or a criminal organization may be functional substitutes for conspiracy charges.

1) The *Actus Reus* of Conspiracy

The *actus reus* of conspiracy is an agreement to carry out the completed offence. "The essence of criminal conspiracy is proof of agreement. On a charge of conspiracy the agreement is the gist of the offence. The *actus reus* is the fact of agreement."[59] The commission of acts in furtherance of the scheme does not constitute the *actus reus*; there must be an agreement and meeting of minds to commit the offence.[60] Once an agreement to commit an offence is reached, it is not necessary to do anything else. A criminal plot may be a conspiracy long before it has gone beyond the preparation necessary for a criminal attempt. Thus, "[c]onspiracy is in fact a more 'preliminary' crime than attempt, since the offence is considered to be complete before any acts are taken that go beyond mere preparation to put the common design into effect. The Crown is simply required to prove a meeting of the minds with regard to a common design to do something unlawful, specifically the commission of an indictable offence."[61] An agreement to launder money could be a conspiracy even though the money was not yet transferred between the parties and there would not be a sufficient *actus reus* for an attempt.

Although an agreement must be between two or more people, a person can be convicted of conspiracy even if, for some other reason, the co-conspirators are not convicted.[62] As discussed in the next section, however, the conspirators must not only intend to agree, but also intend to carry out their common design. There must be communication for an agreement to be reached, but an implicit or tacit agreement to commit an offence is enough to prove the act of conspiracy:[63] "So long as there is a continuing overall, dominant plan there may be changes

---

59   R. v. *Cotroni* (1979), 45 C.C.C. (2d) 1 at 17 (S.C.C) [*Cotroni*]. See also R. v. *Douglas* (1991), 63 C.C.C. (3d) 29 (S.C.C.).

60   R. v. *H.A.* (2005), 206 C.C.C. (3d) 233 at paras. 46–48 (Ont. C.A.).

61   *Dynar*, above note 29 at para. 87.

62   R. v. *Murphy* (1981), 60 C.C.C. (2d) 1 (Alta. C.A.); *Cotroni*, above note 59.

63   *Atlantic Sugar Refineries Co. v. Canada (A.G.)* (1980), 54 C.C.C. (2d) 373 at 381 (S.C.C.).

in methods of operation, personnel, or victims, without bringing the conspiracy to an end. The important inquiry is not as to the acts done in pursuance of the agreement, but whether there was, in fact, a common agreement."[64] The *actus reus* of conspiracy is thus an agreement, but the agreement itself need not be etched in stone or carried out.

a) Attempted Conspiracies and Other Attempts to Combine Inchoate Forms of Liability

The courts have refused to recognize an offence of attempted conspiracy when an agreement is not reached between the parties. In R. v. *Déry*,[65] the Supreme Court set aside a conviction of an attempt to conspire on the basis that it would extend the criminal law too far and criminalize "bad thoughts of this sort that were abandoned before an agreement was reached, or an attempt made, to act upon them." The Court distinguished an attempt to conspire, which it characterized as "a risk that a risk will materialize,"[66] from both conspiracies and attempts that pose more direct risks.

At the same time, the Court noted that "unilateral conspiracies," in which there was no agreement, "will in any event normally be caught under our law by the offence of 'counselling an offence not committed'"[67] under section 464 of the *Code*.[68] A person who unsuccessfully attempts to enter a conspiracy may nevertheless be guilty of the independent offence of counselling a crime that is not committed. In addition, a person who abets or encourages any of the conspirators to pursue the object of the conspiracy can be guilty of being a party to the conspiracy even though he or she did not actually agree to the conspiracy.[69] A person who pursues a unilateral conspiracy beyond the point of mere preparation would also be guilty of an attempt to commit the crime. Given all these other offences, there is no need for an offence of attempted conspiracy.

The Court in *Déry* left open the question of whether one could attempt to commit an offence such as treason that is defined to include a conspiracy to commit the offence.[70] It could be argued that the dangers

---

64 *Cotroni*, above note 59 at 17–18.

65 [2006] 2 S.C.R. 669 at para. 51 [*Déry*].

66 *Ibid.* at para. 50.

67 *Ibid.* at para. 36.

68 See also R. v. *Dungey* (1979), 51 C.C.C. (2d) 86 (Ont. C.A.); *Chan*, above note 50.

69 R. v. *McNamara (No. 1)* (1981), 56 C.C.C. (2d) 193 (Ont. C.A.); R. v. *Vucetic* (1998), 129 C.C.C. (3d) 178 (Ont. C.A.).

70 *Déry*, above note 65 at para. 20. The completed offence of treason is defined in s. 46(2)(c) of the *Code*, above note 1, to include a conspiracy to use force or

of these specified offences justify punishment of attempts to commit them and that the form of the offence allows cases such as *Déry* to be distinguished.[71] Nevertheless, the courts should not be overly influenced by form because cases such as *Déry* are based on sound principles about the need for restraint in the criminal law and the dangers of punishing people simply for bad thoughts and reckless talk.

A similar issue could arise under the definition of terrorist activities in section 83.01 of the *Criminal Code*, which includes attempts, counselling, threats, and conspiracies to commit terrorist activities. In turn, terrorist activities are included in the definition of offences such as facilitation and instruction of terrorist activities, which in substance function as inchoate offences that are completed long before any actual terrorist act. Here the question is perhaps more difficult because Parliament has clearly indicated an intent to criminalize not only what are in substance but not form inchoate offences, but also attempts, threats, counselling, and conspiring to commit terrorist activities. In other words, Parliament has clearly enacted offences that target a risk that a risk that actual acts of terrorism will occur. In particular, a person might be charged with facilitating a terrorist activity that is defined as a threat or a conspiracy or perhaps even an attempted conspiracy to commit a terrorist act. The courts seem to have little choice but to stack or pile these concepts together, at least in the absence of a finding that the result violated section 7 of the *Charter* because of the vagueness, overbreadth, arbitrariness, or gross disproportionality. As criminal prohibitions are extended to include conduct that is very remote from the ultimate harms punished, it will be especially important for courts to insist on the need for the proof of high levels of *mens rea*.

2) The *Mens Rea* for Conspiracy

The *mens rea* for conspiracy includes both the "intention to agree" and the "intention to put the common design into effect." Taschereau J. explained:

> Although it is not necessary that there should be an overt act in furtherance of the conspiracy to complete the crime, I have no doubt that there must exist an intention to put the common design into effect . . . . The intention cannot be anything else but the will to attain the object of the agreement. I cannot imagine several conspirators

---

violence for the purpose of overthrowing the government. See also s. 466, *ibid.*, providing a complete offence of conspiracy in restraint of trade.

71   Colvin & Anand, above note 26 at 526.

agreeing to defraud, to restrain trade, or to commit any indictable offence, without having the intention to reach the common goal.[72]

In that case, no conspiracy was found because only one of the parties to the agreement actually had the intent to carry out the kidnapping. An agreement between one person and an undercover officer could not be a conspiracy because the officer would not intend to carry out the offence.[73] An agreement between two people and an undercover officer could, however, be a conspiracy because in that case two or more people would intend to commit the crime.

In *R. v. Sokoloski*,[74] the Supreme Court convicted two people of conspiracy to traffic in a controlled drug on the basis that the seller of the large quantity of the drugs must have known that the purchaser would in turn sell the drugs. A minority criticized this decision as an unwarranted extension of conspiracy, because the seller and the buyer had not agreed to carry out the trafficking enterprise in common. To support a conspiracy, there should be something more than mere knowledge that drugs will be sold, but rather an agreement on a common design and an intent to implement that agreement.

In *R. v. Nova Scotia Pharmaceutical Society*,[75] the Supreme Court indicated that to be convicted of conspiracy to lessen competition unduly, it was necessary to prove that the accused had a subjective intent to enter into an agreement, and knowledge of its terms. An objective fault element, however, was sufficient in relation to the aims of the agreement, so that the accused would be guilty if reasonable business-people in their position would have known that the agreement would unduly lessen competition. An accused who deliberately entered into an agreement could be guilty even if he or she did not intend or know the agreement would unduly lessen competition.

3) Impossibility and Conspiracy

Given the rejection of impossibility as a defence to an attempted crime, it is not surprising that impossibility is also not a defence to the related crime of conspiracy. Thus, two accused[76] could conspire to laun-

---

72   *R. v. O'Brien* (1954), 110 C.C.C. 1 at 3 (S.C.C.).

73   As examined in the next section, the suspect might be guilty of the separate crime of counselling a crime that was not committed.

74   (1977), 33 C.C.C. (2d) 496 (S.C.C.).

75   (1992), 74 C.C.C. (3d) 289 at 326 (S.C.C.).

76   The two accused would have to both intend to agree and intend to carry out the agreement so that an agreement between one person and an undercover officer

der drug money even though it was impossible to launder the money because the money was government money provided in a sting operation. The accused still reached an agreement (the *actus reus*) and their intention to agree and launder drug money (the *mens rea*) remained the same "regardless of the absence of the circumstance that would make the realization of that intention possible . . . . The essential element of conspiracy is the existence of the agreement to put the intention of the conspirators into effect."[77] As with attempts, impossibility would only prevent a conspiracy conviction if two or more people agree to commit what they may think is a crime, but what is actually only an imaginary crime. There is no possible social interest in punishing an agreement to do something that is not a crime.

C. COUNSELLING A CRIME THAT IS NOT COMMITTED

As discussed above, a person could not be convicted of conspiracy for agreeing with an undercover police officer to commit a crime because one party to the agreement would not have the intent to put the common design into effect. In that case, or in any case, where a person attempts to solicit another to commit a crime and the second person is unwilling to do so, the appropriate charge will be counselling a crime that is not committed. This is a separate offence under section 464 of the *Criminal Code* and it is subject to the same reduced punishment as an attempt. It is distinct from counselling an offence that is committed, which under section 22 of the *Code* is a method by which a person becomes a party to an offence and is punished as if he or she had committed the complete offence.

1) The *Actus Reus* of Counselling a Crime That Is Not Committed

Section 22(3) provides that for the purposes of the *Criminal Code* "counsel" includes procure, solicit, or incite. It does not matter whether the person counselled acts on the solicitation or has any intention of doing so.[78] This means that a person can be guilty of counselling an undercover officer to commit a crime, even if the person so solicited

---

would not be sufficient.

77   *Dynar*, above note 29 at para. 108.

78   *R. v. Glubisz (No. 2)* (1979), 47 C.C.C. (2d) 232 (B.C.C.A.).

would never commit the offence. The Supreme Court has indicated that "the *actus reus* for counselling will be established where the materials or statements made or transmitted by the accused *actively induce or advocate*—and do not merely *describe*—the commission of an offence."[79] The Ontario Court of Appeal has stated that a person can be guilty of counselling, even if the person solicited immediately rejects the idea of going through with the offence.[80] Of course, if the person counselled does carry out the crime, then the person who counselled the crime is guilty as a party to the offence that is eventually committed.[81]

2) The *Mens Rea* for Counselling a Crime That Is Not Committed

The *mens rea* in section 464 is not spelled out, but given the possible breadth of the *actus reus*, it will be important to require subjective knowledge of the crime counselled and an actual intent by the accused (but not necessarily the person counselled) that the crime be performed. In *R. v. McLeod*,[82] Georgia Strait Publishing Ltd. was convicted of counselling the illegal cultivation of marijuana by publishing an article explaining how to grow marijuana. The Court of Appeal concluded that the paper was deliberately counselling readers of the paper to cultivate marijuana, but held that the evidence was insufficient to prove that the editor of the paper had this intent. If this case arose today, the protection of freedom of expression in section 2(b) of the *Charter* would also be a factor.[83]

In *R. v. Janeteas*,[84] the Ontario Court of Appeal issued a comprehensive judgment that stressed the importance of *mens rea* in a counselling offence. Moldaver J.A. stated that, as with the other inchoate crimes of attempts and conspiracy, the accused must intend the commission of the offence in order to be guilty of the crime of counselling an offence that is not committed. Recklessness was not a sufficient form of

---

79   *R. v. Hamilton*, [2005] 2 S.C.R. 432 at para. 15 [emphasis in original] [*Hamilton*]. See also *Mugesera v. Canada (Minister of Citizenship and Immigration)*, [2005] 2 S.C.R. 100 at para. 64, stating: "[T]he offence of counselling requires that the statements, viewed objectively, actively promote, advocate or encourage the commission of the offence described in them."

80   *R. v. Gonzague* (1983), 4 C.C.C. (3d) 505 (Ont. C.A.).

81   *Code*, above note 1, s. 22, discussed later in this chapter.

82   (1970), 1 C.C.C. (2d) 5 at 8 (B.C.C.A.).

83   *Iorfida v. MacIntyre* (1994), 93 C.C.C. (3d) 395 (Ont. Gen. Div.) (law restricting sale or promotion of drug literature an unjustified violation of freedom of expression).

84   (2003), 172 C.C.C. (3d) 97 (Ont. C.A.).

fault because it could result in the conviction of a person who made only casual comments about the possibility of a crime being committed. The Court of Appeal rejected the policy argument that a person should be convicted simply because he may have placed a dangerous thought about the commission of a crime into another's mind. The Alberta Court of Appeal has likewise stressed the requirement of intent as opposed to lesser forms of subjective *mens rea* such as recklessness or wilful blindness for the section 464 offence. It has related this high *mens rea* standard to the fact that the offence relates to counselling a crime that is not committed.[85] The decisions are helpful in their recognition that counselling a crime that is not committed is, like an attempt or a conspiracy, a form of inchoate liability. As such, it should require an intent to commit the complete offence.

Unfortunately, the Supreme Court of Canada in a 6:3 decision held that the *mens rea* of counselling an offence included not only an intent to commit the substantive crime, but also a lesser form of *mens rea* in the form of knowingly counselling a crime while aware of an unjustified risk that the offence was likely to be committed as a result of the accused's conduct.[86] Although described as a "relatively demanding standard," the majority of the Court has lowered the fault element to something perhaps less than knowledge by its reference of knowledge of an unjustified risk that the offence will likely be committed as a result of the accused's conduct. Charron J. in a strong dissent contemplated a *mens rea* requirement that was both higher, simpler, and easier to explain to the jury when she stated that "the counsellor must intend that the counselled offence be committed for the offence to be made out."[87]

The majority's judgment in R. v. *Hamilton* should not be interpreted as encompassing recklessness as a sufficient fault for the offence of counselling a crime not committed. Although the majority does refer to a risk of an offence being committed, it requires that the risk be that the offence is likely to be committed, which is a higher standard than a reckless awareness of the possibility that an offence would be committed.[88]

---

85   R. v. *Hamilton* (2003), 178 C.C.C. (3d) 434 at paras. 5 and 27 (Alta. C.A.).

86   *Hamilton*, above note 79 at para. 29.

87   *Ibid.* at para. 82.

88   Professors Colvin and Anand, however, interpret *Hamilton* as including recklessness liability, above note 26 at 570, as does Professor Don Stuart in *Canadian Criminal Law*, 5th ed. (Scarborough, ON: Thomson Carswell, 2007) at 712. See also Manning & Sankoff, above note 26 at 227. Although Justice Fish's reference to "risk" suggests recklessness, his statement about the need for the accused to know that the offence will "likely" be committed and his reference

In *Mugesera*,[89] the Court also considered section 464, albeit in the context of immigration law. The Court indicated that the accused's knowledge that a speech given during the Rwandan genocide would be understood as incitement to commit murder demonstrated that "Mr. Mugesera not only intentionally gave the speech, but also intended that it result in the commission of murders." Thus this case is consistent with the requirement that an accused intend or at least have knowledge of the complete crime to be guilty of the offence of counselling an offence. A requirement that the Crown only have to prove recklessness as opposed to intent or knowledge could result in a counselling offence that would be a disproportionate restriction on intemperate speech. As Charron J. recognized, "[I]f mere recklessness as to the communication's potential power of persuasion were to suffice, some may argue that the publication of Shakespeare's *Henry VI*, with its famous phrase 'let's kill all the lawyers', should be subject to state scrutiny!"[90] Recklessness would also raise other constitutional issues, at least as applied to the offence of counselling a murder that was not committed.[91] That said, it would have been more principled for the Court in *Hamilton* to have recognized that a common feature of all inchoate offences, at least in the absence of a clear legislative intent to the contrary, is that they require proof of an intent to commit the completed offence. If the accused is being punished primarily for his or her intent, then it makes sense to require proof of a clear intent to commit the completed offence.

3) Impossibility and Counselling

Given the willingness to convict an accused for impossible attempts and conspiracies and for counselling crimes that are immediately rejected by the person solicited, it would be expected that impossibility would not be a defence to the crime of counselling a crime that is not committed. In *R. v. Richard*,[92] however, the Manitoba Court of Appeal held that an adult accused could not be convicted of counselling the

---

to the "demanding" nature of the fault requirement suggest that he did not intend to include recklessness as the lowest form of subjective fault as a sufficient fault element for an inchoate crime.

89   Above note 79 at para. 79.

90   *Hamilton*, above note 79 at para. 76.

91   It could be argued that such an offence would have the same stigma as attempted murder and should require knowledge as a constitutional minimum form of *mens rea*. See *Logan*, above note 18.

92   (1986), 30 C.C.C. (3d) 127 (Man. C.A.). It is also surprising that the Crown did not charge the accused with an attempt to commit indecent assault.

commission of an indecent assault because the child he attempted to procure was incapable of committing the completed offence because she was under twelve years of age.[93] This strange and impractical result helps to explain Parliament's enactment of a separate offence of inviting a child under sixteen to engage in sexual touching.[94] A broadly worded offence may be a substitute for an inchoate crime such as an attempt or counselling a crime that is not committed.

Parliament has now provided in section 23.1 of the *Criminal Code* that a person could be guilty of being a party to an offence even though the person aided or abetted, counselled or assisted, cannot be convicted of the offence. Strangely, this provision may not change the result in *Richard*, because it applies only to offences that are committed, not to the separate offence in section 464 of counselling a crime that is not committed. Nevertheless, an accused in Richard's position could be charged with the separate crime of inviting a child to engage in sexual touching or attempted sexual interference. For these crimes, as well as for crimes in sections 21 to 23 of the *Code*, it does not matter that the other person involved could not be convicted of an offence. Thus, adults who counsel young children under twelve years to commit drug offences can be convicted even though the child they tried to recruit could not be prosecuted.

D. COUNSELLING A CRIME THAT IS COMMITTED

Section 22(1) provides that a person who counsels a crime that is committed becomes a party to that offence and, as such, is subject to the same punishment as if he or she had actually committed the offence. This provision applies "notwithstanding that the offence was committed in a way different from that which was counselled." An accused who counsels a person to kill another with a bomb would still be guilty of murder if the person counselled used a gun instead. In addition, section 22(2) expands liability further by providing that a counsellor becomes a party "to every offence that the other commits in consequence of the counselling that the person who counselled knew or ought to

---

93   As examined in ch. 3(A)(5), "Application of the *Criminal Code*: Territorial and Age-Based Restrictions," s. 13 of the *Code*, above note 1, deems those under twelve years of age incapable of committing any criminal offence.

94   *Code, ibid.*, s. 152.

have known was likely to be committed in consequence of the counselling."

1) The *Actus Reus* of Counselling a Crime That Is Committed

The *actus reus* of counselling remains the act of procuring, soliciting, or inciting a crime. In addition, a crime must then be committed by the person counselled. The crime need not be committed in the same way as was counselled or even be the same crime that was counselled. It must, however, be a crime that was reasonably foreseeable from the counselling. Under section 23.1, an accused could be convicted of counselling even though the person who actually committed the offence could not. For example, an adult who involved children under twelve years of age in the drug trade could be convicted even though the children could not. Similarly, a person who procured a reluctant person to commit an offence could be guilty even though the reluctant person might have a valid defence such as duress.

2) The *Mens Rea* for Counselling a Crime That Is Committed

The accused must intentionally counsel a criminal offence under section 22(1). It would not be fair to hold that an accused is a party to an offence for comments that were not intended to solicit or incite a crime, but which had that effect. Under section 22(2), an accused who intentionally counsels an offence is also a party "to every offence that the other commits in consequence of the counselling that the person who counselled knew or ought to have known was likely to be committed in consequence of the counselling." This extends liability not only to the offence intentionally counselled but any other offence that the person knew or ought to have known would be committed as a result of the counselling. The latter fault element of objective foreseeability would violate section 7 of the *Charter* when applied to murder or attempted murder, which has a minimum fault element of subjective foresight of death.[95] Nevertheless, objective foreseeability would be a constitutionally sufficient fault element for most other crimes. For example, an accused who counselled a severe beating could be convicted of manslaughter because he or she ought to have known that manslaughter

---

95   *Martineau*, above note 17; *Logan*, above note 18; *R. v. Chenier* (2006), 205 C.C.C. (3d) 333 at para. 62 (Ont. C.A.).

could result.[96] The accused would, however, only be guilty of murder if he or she actually knew that death was likely to result.

Section 22(2) incorporates objective forms of fault while section 464 always requires subjective fault even though both offences are based on the counselling of a crime. A rationale for the different approaches is that counselling under section 22 constitutes a form of participation in a completed crime whereas counselling under section 464 is a form of inchoate liability that applies when the crime counselled has not been committed.

E. AIDING AND ABETTING

Section 21(1) of the *Criminal Code* provides that everyone is a party to an offence who "actually commits it; or does or omits to do anything for the purpose of aiding any person to commit it; or abets any person in committing it." A person who either aids or abets an offence is a party to that offence and guilty of the same offence as the person who actually commits the offence, often known as the principal. It is not necessary for the Crown to specify whether a person is guilty as the principal offender or as an aider or abettor of the offence. In the famous Colin Thatcher case, the Crown was able to argue that the accused was guilty of murder on the alternative theories that he actually killed his ex-wife or he assisted others to do the killing.[97] In the Robert Pickton serial murder case, the jury was initially instructed according to the Crown's theory of the case that Pickton personally shot his multiple victims. The Supreme Court, however, upheld a subsequent jury instruction that left open the possibility that Pickton would be guilty if he was "otherwise an active participant" in the killings and indicated that it was not necessary that he be the actual shooter to be guilty of murder. Relying on the *Thatcher* case, the Court stressed that section 21(1) was designed to put the aider or abettor on the same footing as the person who actually committed the crime.[98] A number of accused

---

96   Because of the fault element required for manslaughter, this conviction requires only objective foreseeability that bodily harm would result. *R. v. Jackson* (1993), 86 C.C.C. (3d) 385 at 391 (S.C.C.) [*Jackson*].

97   *R. v. Thatcher* (1987), 32 C.C.C. (3d) 481 (S.C.C.).

98   *R. v. Pickton*, [2010] 2 S.C.R. 198 at para. 33. Charron J. for the majority indicated that it would have been preferable had the jury been instructed specifically about aiding and abetting but that the omission of such an instruction could only have benefited the accused; *ibid.* at para. 12. The dissenters in the case agreed that the alternatives of aiding and abetting could be put to the jury,

could be convicted of murder if they all knowingly assisted in causing the victim's death even though it was unclear which one of the accused actually killed the victim.[99] Imposing the same liability and maximum penalty on a person who has knowingly assisted an offence as on the person who actually committed the offence may seem harsh in some cases. Limited participation in a crime may, however, be a mitigating factor in sentencing though the mitigating factor may be limited by the existence of a mandatory minimum penalty.

1) The *Actus Reus* of Aiding and Abetting

It is common to speak of aiding and abetting together, but the two concepts are distinct, and liability can flow from either one. Broadly speaking, "[t]o aid under s. 21(1)(b) means to assist or help the actor. . . . To abet within the meaning of s. 21(1)(c) includes encouraging, instigating, promoting or procuring the crime to be committed."[100] Abetting has been held to include intentional encouragement whether by acts or words.[101] A person who distracts a security guard so that his or her friend can shoplift may aid a theft, whereas a salesclerk who encourages or allows a customer to shoplift would abet the theft. Both people would be guilty of theft, even though they did not themselves steal the merchandise. The terms aiding and abetting are generally used together, but they remain distinct forms of liability for being a party to an offence.

In *Dunlop v. R.*,[102] Dickson J. stated that a person is not guilty of aiding or abetting a rape

> merely because he is present at the scene of a crime and does nothing to prevent it . . . . If there is no evidence of encouragement by him, a man's presence at the scene of the crime will not suffice to render him

---

but stated that "the phrases 'active participation,' 'acting in concert,' or 'joint venture' do not in and of themselves adequately convey the law of party liability to a trier of fact"; *ibid.* at para. 38.

99 *Chow Bew v. The Queen*, [1956] S.C.R. 124; *R. v. Issac*, [1984] 1 S.C.R. 74 at 80–81; *R. v. McMaster*, [1996] 1 S.C.R. 740 at para. 33; *R. v. McQuaid*, [1998] 1 S.C.R. 244; *R. v. Biniaris*, [2000] 1 S.C.R. 381; *R. v. Suzack* (2000), 141 C.C.C. (3d) 449 (Ont. C.A.); *R. v. H.(L.I.)* (2003), 17 C.R. (6th) 338 at para. 60 (Man. C.A.); *R. v. Portillo* (2003), 17 C.R. (6th) 362 at para. 71 (Ont. C.A.); *R. v. J.F.D.* (2005), 196 C.C.C. (3d) 316 at para. 14 (B.C.C.A.); *R. v. Rojos* (2006), 208 C.C.C. (3d) 13 (B.C.C.A.).

100 *R. v. Briscoe*, [2010] 1 S.C.R. 411 at para. 14 [*Briscoe*], citing *R. v. Greyeyes*, [1997] 2 S.C.R. 825, at para. 26 [*Greyeyes*].

101 *R. v. Wobbes*, 2008 ONCA 567; *R. v. Hennessey*, 2010 ABCA 274 at para. 39.

102 (1979), 47 C.C.C. (2d) 93 at 111 (S.C.C.).

liable as aider and abettor. A person who, aware of a rape taking place in his presence, looks on and does nothing is not, as a matter of law, an accomplice. The classic case is the hardened urbanite who stands around in a subway station when an individual is murdered.

In the case, the accused were acquitted of rape on the basis that there was no evidence that they "rendered aid, assistance, or encouragement" to the gang rape of a young woman. Dickson J. did indicate, however, that presence at the commission of an offence can be evidence of aiding and abetting if accompanied by other factors such as prior knowledge that the crime was going to be committed. Similarly, presence at a crime that prevents the victim's escape or prevents the victim receiving assistance is a sufficient *actus reus*.[103] Some members of the Supreme Court have disapproved of a case in which an accused was found not to be a party to a rape, despite having witnessed the crime with his pants down.[104] At the same time, the Court has recently affirmed as sound the proposition in *Dunlop* that "an accused's mere presence at the scene of a crime in circumstances consistent with innocence will not support a conviction."[105] In that case it upheld a conviction of a man producing marijuana, on the basis that there was evidence beyond his mere presence to convict him because he was found sleeping in a camouflaged tent with fertilizer at a remote marijuana plantation. Two judges dissented, however, on the basis that there was no evidence of anything beyond the accused's presence at the site.

The position that mere presence and passive acquiescence in a crime is not sufficient to make a person an aider or abettor mirrors the criminal law's traditional reluctance to penalize omissions. As with omissions, however, courts recognize exceptions to this principle in cases where the person who stands by is under a specific legal duty to act. Owners of cars who do nothing while others engage in dangerous driving have been held to have abetted the dangerous driving because they did not exercise their power to control the use of their vehicle.[106] A senior officer in charge of a police lock-up has also been found to have aided and abetted an assault on a prisoner by failing to exercise

---

103 *R. v. Black*, [1970] 4 C.C.C. 251 (B.C.C.A.); *R. v. Stevenson* (1984), 11 C.C.C. (3d) 443 (N.S.C.A.).

104 *R. v. Salajko*, [1970] 1 C.C.C. 352 (Ont. C.A.), disapproved of in *R. v. Kirkness* (1990), 60 C.C.C. (3d) 97 at 106 (S.C.C.), Wilson J. (L' Heureux-Dubé J. concurring) [*Kirkness*].

105 *R. v. Jackson*, 2007 SCC 52 at paras. 3 and 9.

106 *R. v. Halmo* (1941), 76 C.C.C. 116 (Ont. C.A.); *R. v. Kulbacki*, [1966] 1 C.C.C. 167 (Man. C.A.).

his statutory duty to protect a prisoner in his charge.[107] The conclusion in these cases that a failure to act can amount to aiding and abetting is strengthened by the fact that section 21(1)(b) provides that one who *omits* to do anything for the purpose of aiding any person to commit an offence may be charged as a party to that offence.

2) The *Mens Rea* for Aiding and Abetting

The broad definition of the *actus reus* of aiding and abetting is balanced with a requirement that the act or omission of assistance be committed for the purpose of assisting in the commission of the offence. To be convicted as an aider or abettor, the accused must not only knowingly assist the principal, but also intend to assist the principal.[108] There are thus two different *mens rea* requirements for aiding and abetting: 1) the intent to assist the principal offender and 2) knowledge of the type but not the exact nature of the crime committed.

Section 21(1)(b) requires that the accused act or omit to do anything for the purpose of aiding any person to commit an offence. A person who unwittingly delivers a bomb or administers a poison would not be guilty as a party to an offence, even though he or she may have committed the *actus reus* of assisting the commission of the offence.[109] Such a person would not have acted for the purpose or with the intent of aiding the offence. The requirement that the accused act with the purpose of aiding the offence does not mean that the accused must desire that the offence be committed or even share the exact same *mens rea* as the principal offender. A person who assists in a robbery by driving the getaway car will have acted with the purpose of aiding the offence, even though he or she participated only because of death threats. Chief Justice Lamer has concluded that "the expression 'for the purpose of aiding' in section 21(1)(b), properly understood, does not require that the accused actively view the commission of the offence he or she is aiding as desirable in and of itself. As a result, the *mens rea* for aiding under section 21(1)(b) is not susceptible of being 'negated' by duress."[110] The issue should be whether the accused intended to assist the principal offender. The jury should not be confused by being asked to consider duress both in relation to *mens rea* and in relation to the separate defence of

---

107 R. v. *Nixon* (1990), 57 C.C.C. (3d) 97 (B.C.C.A.).

108 R. v. *Morgan* (1993), 80 C.C.C. (3d) 16 at 21 (Ont. C.A.).

109 R. v. *Berryman* (1990), 57 C.C.C. (3d) 375 (B.C.C.A.).

110 R. v. *Hibbert* (1995), 99 C.C.C. (3d) 193 at 214 (S.C.C.) [*Hibbert*]. Such a person could be acquitted on the basis of the common law defence of duress if there was no safe avenue of escape from the threats. See ch. 9(D), "Duress."

duress. A person who arranges a drug buy may intend to aid or abet in trafficking even though his or her motivation may have only been to assist the purchaser.[111] This follows the traditional position that motive is not normally relevant to subjective fault.[112] Similarly, a person may intentionally assist others to commit a planned and deliberate murder without necessarily planning and deliberating as the principal offenders did.[113]

The Ontario Court of Appeal has concluded with respect to section 21(1)(b) that "purpose is synonymous with intent and does not include recklessness."[114] It has also indicated that the high level of *mens rea* for section 21(1)(b) is justified not only by the specific purpose requirement in the section, but also by the need to ensure that a person who assists in the commission of an offence has a sufficient level of fault to justify convicting that person of the same offence as the person who actually committed the offence. The high subjective *mens rea* of aiding and abetting applies even in cases where the principal offender may be convicted on the basis of an objective fault requirement.[115] Recklessness is not a sufficient form of fault to convict a person as a party to an offence under section 21(1)(b).[116] This is appropriate because an aider and abetter's involvement with the crime will be more peripheral than that of the principal offender(s) and this lesser form of physical involvement should be counterbalanced by higher fault requirements.

In addition to the intent or purpose to assist the principal offender, an aider or abettor must also know that the principal offender will commit the crime, but not necessarily precisely how the crime will be committed.[117] In other words, it is not necessary that the aider or abettor know all the details of the crime committed; it is sufficient that he or she

---

111 *Greyeyes*, above note 100 at 349.

112 See ch. 5(B)(2), "Intent, Purpose, or Wilfulness Distinguished from Motive."

113 The Court has stated: "[T]he aider to a murder must 'have known that the perpetrator had the intent required for murder.' … The perpetrator's intention to kill the victim must be known to the aider or abettor; it need not be shared. *Kirkness* should not be interpreted as requiring that the aider and abettor of a murder have the same *mens rea* as the actual killer. It is sufficient that he or she, armed with *knowledge* of the perpetrator's intention to commit the crime, acts with the intention of assisting the perpetrator in its commission. It is only in this sense that it can be said that the aider and abettor must intend that the principal offence be committed." *Briscoe*, above note 100 at para. 18.

114 *R. v. Roach* (2004), 192 C.C.C. (3d) 557 at para. 36 (Ont. C.A.); *R. v. Helsdon*, 2007 ONCA 54 at paras. 32–33 [*Helsdon*].

115 *Helsdon*, *ibid.* at paras. 36–38.

116 *Hibbert*, above note 110 at para. 26; *R. v. L.* (2003), 172 C.C.C. (3d) 44 at para. 48 (B.C.C.A.).

117 *Ibid.* at para. 17.

was "aware of the type of crime to be committed"[118] and knew "the circumstances necessary to constitute the offence he is accused of aiding."[119] In *R. v. Briscoe*,[120] the Supreme Court held that in an appropriate case wilful blindness could be substituted for this knowledge requirement and distinguished wilful blindness as a form of "deliberate ignorance" that is distinct from recklessness. This suggests that the mens rea requirements for s.21(1)(b) are quite high and that recklessness will not suffice either for the intent to assist requirement or the knowledge of the crime that is being assisted.

An accused's actions in abandoning a crime may in some cases be evidence of a lack of intent as is the case with respect to attempts. The Supreme Court has, for example, upheld the acquittal of a man for murder who participated in a break-in in a home, but who told the principal offender to stop strangling the victim because he was going to kill her. The Court held that the accused had given "timely notice" to the accused that he was acting on his own.[121] The idea that there must be timely notice to ground a defence of abandonment of an intent to aid or abet is well established, but in principle the matter is best viewed, as it is with respect to attempts, as a matter that can raise a reasonable doubt about *mens rea*. In any event, abandonment will inevitably depend on the quality of any particular withdrawal or abandonment and the accused's particular form and degree of participation. For example, the notice must be "timely" because if it occurs too late, the accused will already have committed the relevant *actus reus* and *mens rea*. An accused's remorse after the commission of a crime is not an act of abandonment relevant to criminal liability.

The courts are reluctant to find purchasers of drugs guilty of aiding and abetting trafficking on the basis of the purchase alone.[122] They are concerned that such people do not deserve the stigma of a trafficking conviction and are more appropriately convicted of possession of narcotics or possession with the intent to traffic, either as a principal offender or an aider or abettor. Assisting a person to purchase drugs is

---

118   *R. v. Yanover* (1985), 20 C.C.C. (3d) 300 at 329 (Ont. C.A.).
119   *R. v. F.W. Woolworth Co.* (1974), 18 C.C.C. (2d) 23 at 32 (Ont. C.A.).
120   *Briscoe*, above note 100 at paras. 22–25.
121   *R. v. Kirkness*, [1990] 3 S.C.R. 74 citing *R. v. Whitehouse*, [1941] 1 D.L.R. 683 (B.C.C.A.), quoted with approval in *Miller v. The Queen*, [1977] 2 S.C.R. 680.
122   *R. v. Poitras* (1974), 12 C.C.C. (3d) 337 (S.C.C.); *R. v. Meston* (1975), 28 C.C.C. (2d) 497 (Ont. C.A.). As Justice L'Heureux-Dubé has stated, "despite his or her crucial assistance in helping to complete the sale of narcotics, the purchaser cannot *by this action alone* be found guilty of the offence of aiding and abetting the offence of trafficking." *Greyeyes*, above note 100 at 340 [emphasis in original].

another matter. In *Greyeyes*, the Supreme Court upheld the trafficking conviction of a person who located a seller for a purchaser, negotiated the purchase price, and accepted $10 for his efforts.[123] The Court reasoned that these were not the acts of a mere purchaser, but rather the acts of one who offered crucial assistance to the trafficking. The accused had the dual *mens rea* of intending to assist the trafficking and knowledge that trafficking was being assisted. The accused, who acted as a go-between between the purchaser and the seller and assisted the trafficking transaction, was convicted and sentenced as a drug trafficker. Hopefully, his rather peripheral involvement in the trafficking enterprise would be considered at sentencing.

What is the relevance of impossibility to a charge of aiding and abetting? In *R. v. Chan*,[124] the Ontario Court of Appeal applied the Supreme Court's reasoning in *Dynar*[125] to a case where an accused was convicted of possessing drugs when he thought he was participating in the purchase of a large quantity of heroin. The drugs had been previously intercepted by the police and only contained a very small amount of heroin. The Court of Appeal held that what mattered in determining the *mens rea* was the accused's belief that he was dealing with heroin and not the truth of the matter.[126] This suggests that the accused might have had the *mens rea* even if there were no drugs in the package that was received. The question then would be whether the accused had the necessary *actus reus* to be guilty of aiding or abetting the offence. If there were no drugs present, then it would be difficult to conclude that the accused had aided and abetted a drug offence. The accused would not necessarily be acquitted because he or she could be guilty of the separate offence of attempting to possess the heroin. As in the Supreme Court's *Williams*[127] case, the accused would have the *mens rea* both for the complete and attempted offence, and would have the *actus reus* for the attempt offence, because he would have done an act beyond mere preparation to commit the crime.[128]

---

123 *Greyeyes, ibid.*
124 *Chan*, above note 50.
125 Above note 29.
126 *Chan*, above note 50 at para. 40.
127 Above note 27.
128 *Chan*, above note 50 at para. 64.

F. COMMON INTENTION TO COMMIT AN UNLAWFUL PURPOSE AND SECTION 21(2)

Section 21(2) enlarges the scope of who is a party to an offence beyond those who knowingly aid or abet an offence by providing that those who "form an intention in common to carry out an unlawful purpose and to assist each other therein" are parties to any consequential offence committed by one of them provided that the accused "knew or ought to have known that the commission of the offence would be a probable consequence of carrying out the common purpose." Thus, a person who forms a common unlawful intent (for example, to engage in a robbery) is a party to other offences that he or she knew or ought to know would probably occur (such as forcible confinement or manslaughter). In practice, section 21(2) applies when the principal has committed crimes beyond which the parties have intended to aid and abet.[129]

1) The *Actus Reus* of Section 21(2)

Under section 21(2) there must be a formation of a common intent to assist each other in carrying out an unlawful purpose, but not necessarily any act of assistance.[130] It could be argued that this requires an agreement akin to conspiracy, although most cases do not dwell on the issue. In addition, it is assumed that the unlawful purpose means a purpose contrary to the *Criminal Code*. The subsequent offence committed has to be one that the accused either knows or ought to have known would be a probable consequence of carrying out the common purpose. In *Jackson*,[131] the Supreme Court held that the offence is not confined to that which the principal was convicted, but encompasses any included offence. For example, a party to an unlawful purpose could be convicted of manslaughter, even though the principal was convicted of murder. This would happen when the party did not have the subjective foresight of death required for a murder conviction, but did have objective foresight of bodily harm necessary for a manslaughter conviction. Less clear is whether a party with the *mens rea* for murder can be convicted of murder even though the principal offender was only convicted of manslaughter. There is some authority that the party

---

129 *R. v. Simpson* (1988), 38 C.C.C. (3d) 481 (S.C.C.).
130 *R. v. Moore* (1984), 15 C.C.C. (3d) 541 at 555 (Ont. C.A.).
131 Above note 105.

could only be convicted of the same offence as the principal offender,[132] but general principles as well as section 23.1 suggest that a party with the required *mens rea* could be convicted of a more serious offence than a principal offender. For example, a sober or unprovoked accomplice might have the *mens rea* for murder even though the actual drunken or provoked killer might only have the *mens rea* for manslaughter.[133]

2) The *Mens Rea* for Section 21(2)

There are two distinct mental or fault elements for section 21(2): the first is the formation of the common unlawful purpose and the second is either subjective knowledge or objective foresight that the actual offence would be a probable consequence of carrying out the unlawful purpose.

a) Common Unlawful Purpose

In *R. v. Paquette*,[134] the Supreme Court held that a person who drove others to a robbery had not formed a common unlawful purpose to assist them in the robbery because he had been forced at gun point to co-operate. Martland J. stated:

> A person whose actions have been dictated by fear of death or of grievous bodily injury cannot be said to have formed a genuine common intent to carry out an unlawful purpose with the person who has threatened him with those consequences if he fails to co-operate.[135]

In *Hibbert*, the Supreme Court subsequently rejected this interpretation on the basis that section 21(2) requires only a common intent to commit the offence and not "a mutuality of motives and desires between the party and the principal."[136] On this reasoning, Paquette would have had the required mental element because he intended to commit a robbery even though he did not truly desire to commit the robbery. The fact that he wanted to commit a robbery only because his life was threatened would be a matter of motive that is not relevant to the mental element. It would, however, be relevant to whether Paquette had a

---

132 *R. v. Hébert* (1986), 51 C.R. (3d) 264 (N.B.C.A.).

133 *R. v. Rémillard* (1921), 62 S.C.R. 21.

134 (1976), 30 C.C.C. (2d) 417 (S.C.C.).

135 *Ibid.* at 423.

136 *Hibbert*, above note 110 at 216. See *Dunbar v. R.* (1936), 67 C.C.C. 20 (S.C.C.), also drawing a distinction between intention and motive when an accused was threatened if he did not assist in a robbery.

common law defence of duress that would prevent his conviction.[137] As with section 21(1)(b), the Court has rejected the idea that intent requires proof of desire even though section 21(2) requires the formation of an intention in common to assist in the commission of an offence. It was concerned that cases such as *Paquette* would complicate the task of the jury by considering duress as both a matter relevant to *mens rea* and as a separate defence and that it would not fulfill Parliament's purpose in widening the net of criminal liability to catch those who assist in the commission of crimes.

As with aiding and abetting, it is possible that an accused might abandon the common unlawful purpose through timely notice. The Court's decision in *Hibbert*, however, suggests that reluctance to engage in the common unlawful purpose will not be inconsistent with the *mens rea*. In addition, abandonment including surrender to the authorities or remorse after the commission of the relevant *actus reus* and *mens rea* should not relieve accused of responsibility for having committed the crime. That said, an accused who forms a common unlawful purpose is not automatically responsible for all the crimes that his or her accomplice commits while pursuing that purpose. As will be seen later in this chapter, the accused is only liable for crimes that he or she knows or in most cases ought to have known would be a probable consequence of carrying out the common unlawful purpose.

b) Knew or Ought to Have Known That the Crime Would Be Committed

In most cases the accused will be liable if he or she either knew or ought to have known that the commission of the offence was a probable consequence of the common unlawful purpose. In *Logan*,[138] however, the Supreme Court declared the phrase "ought to have known" to be an unjustified violation of the *Charter* when the accused is charged with murder or attempted murder. Section 7 of the *Charter* requires subjective as opposed to objective foresight of death for a conviction of murder or attempted murder. As Lamer C.J. explained:

> When the principles of fundamental justice require subjective foresight in order to convict a principal of attempted murder, that same minimum degree of *mens rea* is constitutionally required to convict a party to the offence of attempted murder. Any conviction for attempted murder, whether of the principal directly or of a party

---

137 See ch. 9(2), "The Common Law Defence of Duress as It Applies to Parties to the Offence."
138 Above note 18.

pursuant to s. 21(2), will carry enough stigma to trigger the constitutional requirement. To the extent that s. 21(2) would allow for the conviction of a party to the offence of attempted murder on the basis of objective foresight, its operation restricts s. 7 of the *Charter*.[139]

In cases of murder and attempted murder, the objective arm of section 21(2) should not be left to the jury and the jury should only convict if a party has actual foresight or knowledge that the principal offender would attempt to kill a person while carrying out their common unlawful purpose.[140]

Logan is a case of limited application. The Court stated that "because of the importance of the legislative purpose, the objective component of section 21(2) can be justified with respect to most offenses."[141] Lamer C.J. concluded that it was not a principle of fundamental justice that a person convicted as a party to an offence have as high a *mens rea* as the principal offender. This means that a party could be convicted under the objective arm of section 21(2) even though subjective *mens rea* was required to convict the principal. For example, an accused who formed an unlawful purpose to rob a bank could be convicted of assault on the basis that he or she ought to have known an assault would occur, whereas the person who actually assaulted one of the guards or tellers would be convicted on the basis of a subjective intent to apply force. In upholding the objective arm of section 21(2) as constitutional in most cases, the Court emphasized the importance of recognizing different degrees of involvement when exercising sentencing discretion.[142] A fundamental principle of sentencing is that the punishment be proportionate to the degree of the offender's responsibility.

---

139 *Ibid.* at 401.
140 *R. v. Rodney* (1990), 58 C.C.C. (3d) 408 (S.C.C.); *R. v. Laliberty* (1997), 117 C.C.C. (3d) 97 at 108 (Ont. C.A.); *R. v. Portillo* (2003), 17 C.R. (6th) 362 at paras. 72–73 (Ont. C.A.).
141 Above note 18 at 403.
142 Lamer C.J. stated: "It must be remembered that within many offences there are varying degrees of guilt and it remains the function of the sentencing process to adjust the punishment for each individual offender accordingly. The argument that the principles of fundamental justice prohibit the conviction of a party to an offence on the basis of a lesser degree of *mens rea* than that required to convict the principal could only be supported, if at all, in a situation where the sentence for a particular offence is fixed. However, currently in Canada, the sentencing scheme is flexible enough to accommodate the varying degrees of culpability resulting from the operation of ss. 21 and 22." *Ibid.* at 398.

G. ACCESSORY AFTER THE FACT

Section 23 provides a separate offence for receiving, comforting, or assisting a person that one knows has been a party to an offence for the purpose of enabling that person to escape. An accessory after the fact is not a party to an offence but is punished under section 463 as if he or she had been guilty of an attempt of the crime that the person assisted committed.

1) The *Actus Reus* of Being an Accessory after the Fact

The *actus reus* for this provision requires a person to receive, comfort, or assist a person who has committed a crime. This requires more than the mere failure to inform authorities about the fugitive's whereabouts.[143] At the same time, advising fugitives that the police had their names and licence numbers is enough.[144] This again mirrors the traditional reluctance in the criminal law to punish an omission or failure to act.

Section 23(2) used to provide that a married person cannot be guilty of assisting his or her spouse after the commission of a crime, but it was repealed in 2000. Section 23.1 allows a person to be convicted of being an accessory after the fact even though the person assisted has not been convicted of an offence. The Supreme Court has upheld the conviction of an accused for being an accessory after the fact by assisting her brother by transporting him from a killing and orchestrating a false alibi even though her brother was eventually acquitted of the murder.[145]

2) The *Mens Rea* for Being an Accessory after the Fact

Section 23(2) requires two distinct mental elements: 1) subjective knowledge that the person assisted has been a party to an offence, and 2) assisting the fugitive for the purpose of assisting him or her to escape.

The accused must know or be wilfully blind to the fact that the other accused has committed a specific offence such as murder; knowledge that the accused may have committed some general crime is not

---

143   R. v. *Dumont* (1921), 37 C.C.C. 166 (Ont. C.A.).
144   *Young v. R.* (1950), 98 C.C.C. 195 (Que. C.A.).
145   R. v. *S.(F.J.)* (1997), 115 C.C.C. (3d) 450 (N.S.C.A.), aff'd (1998), 121 C.C.C. (3d) 223 (S.C.C.).

sufficient.[146] It is not sufficient that the acts of assistance have the effect of helping the person escape[147] or that they be undertaken for the purpose of not being suspected for the crime itself.[148] The requirement that the accused act with the purpose of assisting a known criminal to escape is a high form of subjective *mens rea* that may be more difficult for the Crown to prove than lower forms of subjective mental elements such as knowledge or recklessness. It should also be noted that some specific crimes such as obstruction of justice or harbouring a terrorist may in some circumstances be functional alternatives to the general crime under section 23 of being an accessory after the fact.

CONCLUSION

The following chart summarizes how various provisions of the *Criminal Code* expand the net of criminal liability to apply to those who did not themselves perform the complete crime. The underlying rationale seems to be that society is justified in intervening and punishing people for their criminal intent or fault and participation in crimes even if they do not commit the complete criminal act.

Counselling a crime that is not committed s. 464	Conspiracy s. 465	Attempts s. 24	Counselling a crime that is committed s. 22	Unlawful purpose and commission of further offence s. 21(2)	Aiding or abetting s. 21(1)(b) & (c)	Accessory after the fact s. 23
			Party to the offence	Party to the offence	Party to the offence	

An accused could be convicted of counselling murder under section 464 simply for asking an undercover officer to kill someone. The same person could be convicted under section 465 of conspiracy to commit murder if he or she agreed with another person that they would kill someone and both intended to carry out the agreement. That person could not be convicted of attempted conspiracy because the courts have refused to recognize such a crime because of concerns about extending criminal liability too far. If an accused acted alone with respect to a murder, he or she could be convicted of attempted murder under

---

146 R. v. *Duong* (1998), 124 C.C.C. (3d) 392 (Ont. C.A.).
147 R. v. *McVay* (1982), 66 C.C.C. (2d) 512 (Ont. C.A.).
148 R. v. *Morris* (1979), 47 C.C.C. (2d) 257 (S.C.C.).

section 24 if he or she did anything beyond mere preparation for the purpose of carrying out the intent to kill. The accused may be held to have gone beyond mere preparation to commit an offence by for example purchasing a weapon even though the murder would not happen until sometime in the future. The fact that it was impossible to kill the intended victim because he was already dead would not be a defence. The accused would be punished more for having the intent to kill than the harm that was caused or could have been caused.

An accused could be guilty of murder under section 22 if he or she counselled another person to commit a murder and that person went on to actually commit the murder. The accused would be guilty of murder under section 21(2) if he or she formed an unlawful purpose with another person and he or she knew that it was likely that his accomplice would kill the victim while carrying out the unlawful purpose. For crimes other than murder and attempted murder,[149] all that would have to be proven under section 21(2) would be the formation of the unlawful purpose and that the accused ought to have known that his accomplice would commit the further crime. If the accused aided or abetted the murder with the fault required for murder[150] (the minimum fault is subjective foresight of death), the accused would also be guilty of murder under section 21(1). Knowingly assisting a person to escape after a crime can be punished as a separate offence under section 23. There is also the possibility that some complete offences such as participation in a terrorist organization could also apply to those who prepare for or have assisted in the commission of murders. Although these offences are not inchoate forms of liability, they do extend criminal liability in a manner similar to both the inchoate and parties provisions examined in this chapter. In all cases, the fact that the accused is liable for actions that may be remote from the actual commission of harm makes it important that high levels of subjective fault be proven to justify criminal liability.

Although there is a consensus that participation in crime should be criminal, the law could be made clearer and less complex. Any distinctions among counselling, aiding, and abetting under sections 21(1) and 22 are quite fine and could be eliminated by a generic provision criminalizing the intentional assistance and encouragement of crime. There is less agreement about whether criminal liability should be extended under section 21(2). The existing law is complex because the objective fault element provided under section 21(2) is unconstitutional as ap-

---

149 *Logan*, above note 18; *Jackson*, above note 96.
150 *Kirkness*, above note 104.

plied to murder and attempted murder but continues to apply to other crimes.[151] One reform option would to eliminate section 21(2) altogether while another would be to require subjective foresight for all crimes that are committed in furtherance of an unlawful objective. A requirement of subjective foresight, however, would blur the practical distinction between section 21(2) and aiding and abetting under section 21(1)(b) and (c). The Supreme Court has simplified the law somewhat by holding that duress cannot negate the *mens rea* requirements under either section 21(1)(b) and 21(2). The requirements in those sections that the accused act with the purpose of aiding and form an intention in common to carry out an unlawful purpose should not be equated with either desire or motive.[152]

The law concerning attempts is relatively settled, but there remains uncertainty in determining exactly when an accused's actions will have gone beyond mere preparation[153] and whether an intent to commit the complete offence is required for all crimes.[154] Given that attempts are driven by concerns about intent and not social harm, the intent to commit the complete offence should be established for all attempted crimes, not just murder. There is a case for keeping the *actus reus* flexible and in practice more remote forms of *actus reus* may be accepted if the *mens rea* is clear or if the magnitude of the attempted crime is great. It should now be crystal clear that impossibility will not be a defence to either an attempt or conspiracy. This also makes sense when it is recognized that society is intervening primarily to punish criminal intent, not the complete crime.

FURTHER READINGS

COLVIN, E., & S. ANAND, *Principles of Criminal Law*, 3d ed. (Toronto: Thomson Carswell, 2007) chs. 9 & 10

GRANT, I., D. CHUNN, & C. BOYLE, *The Law of Homicide* (Toronto: Carswell, 1994) ch. 5

MACKINNON, P., "Making Sense of Attempts" (1982) 7 Queen's L.J. 253

MANSON, A., "Re-Codifying Attempts, Parties, and Abandoned Intentions" (1989) 14 Queen's L.J. 85

---

151 *Jackson*, above note 96.
152 *Hibbert*, above note 110.
153 *Deutsch*, above note 32.
154 *Ancio*, above note 14; *Williams*, above note 27.

MEEHAN, E., & J. CURRIE, *The Law of Criminal Attempt*, 2d ed. (Toronto: Carswell, 2000)

MANNING, M., & P. SANKOFF, *Criminal Law*, 4th ed. (Markham: LexisNexis, 2009) chs. 6 & 7

RAINVILLE, P., "Le Verbe Fait Crime" (2007) 11 Can. Crim. L. Rev. 177

ROSE, G., *Parties to an Offence* (Toronto: Carswell, 1982)

STUART, D., *Canadian Criminal Law: A Treatise*, 5th ed. (Toronto: Thomson Carswell, 2007) chs. 9 & 10

CHAPTER 5

THE FAULT ELEMENT, OR *MENS REA*

Generic references to *mens rea* are confusing because each different crime has a specific fault element that must be related to the *actus reus* of the specific crime. In 1889 Stephen J. indicated that *mens rea* exists only in relation to particular definitions of crime, so that,

> "*Mens rea*" means in the case of murder, malice aforethought; in the case of theft, an intention to steal; in the case of rape, an intention to have forcible connection with a woman without her consent; and in the case of receiving stolen goods, knowledge that the goods were stolen. In some cases it denotes mere inattention. For instance, in the case of manslaughter by negligence it may mean forgetting to notice a signal. It appears confusing to call so many dissimilar states of mind by one name.[1]

In Canada, confusion about *mens rea* continues because Parliament has not clearly and consistently defined fault elements such as "purposely," "knowingly," "recklessly," or "negligently" or specified what particular fault element applies for each offence.[2] As a result, the fault element must often be inferred by the courts from the legislative definition of each separate offence. This means that criminal offences that may appear at first reading to have no fault element, may actually be inter-

---

1   *R. v. Tolson* (1889), 23 Q.B.D. 168 at 185 (C.C.R.) [*Tolson*].
2   But see *Criminal Code*, R.S.C. 1985, c. C-46, ss. 433 and 436 [*Code*], for clear definitions of separate offences of intentional and negligent arson.

preted as requiring fault. In some cases, courts will require the proof of fault in relation to all aspects of the prohibited act and in some cases they will not. References in the *Criminal Code* to carelessness, dangerousness, or negligence are misleading because the courts now require proof of a marked departure from standards of reasonable care in order to distinguish criminal from civil negligence. The fault element for crimes is often uncertain and complex in part because Parliament has long resisted reform proposals to define fault elements and provide for residual fault rules.

A. CONCEPTUAL CONSIDERATIONS

In order to explain the fault element of any criminal offence accurately, it is necessary to specify 1) the circumstances and consequences to which the fault element is directed, including its relation to the *actus reus* of the offence; and 2) the precise fault element required. It is not very helpful to say the *mens* rea for murder is subjective. A more precise approach would be to say the *mens rea* for murder requires at least subjective knowledge that the victim would die. Similarly, stating that the *mens rea* of manslaughter is objective tells only part of the story. The fault is objective foreseeability of bodily harm. The degree of negligence should also be explained, as should who is the reasonable person used to apply the objective fault or negligence standard.

It is also important to understand the differences between constitutional requirements and common law presumptions of particular forms of *mens rea* and how the so-called defences of intoxication and mistake of fact are really conditions that prevent the prosecutor from establishing the fault element beyond a reasonable doubt.

1) The Relation of the Fault Element to the Prohibited Act

The fault element does not exist in the air or in the abstract but must be related to certain consequences or circumstances. As McLachlin J. has stated,

> Typically, *mens rea* is concerned with the consequences of the prohibited *actus reus*. Thus, in the crimes of homicide, we speak of the consequences of the voluntary act—intention to cause death, or

reckless and wilfully blind persistence in conduct which one knows is likely to cause death.[3]

On this principle, a person is not guilty of assaulting a peace officer in the execution of his or her duties unless the accused has the *mens rea* for assault and subjective knowledge that the person is a peace officer. Similarly, the Court classified the old offence of statutory rape as absolute liability because Parliament had excluded fault in relation to a crucial aspect of the *actus reus*, namely the age of the girl.[4] The fault element should generally extend to all the elements of the prohibited act.

The Supreme Court has recognized that the criminal law "has traditionally aimed at symmetry between the *mens rea* and the prohibited consequence of the offence" as discussed above. Nevertheless, a majority in *Creighton* concluded:

> It is important to distinguish between criminal law theory, which seeks the ideal of absolute symmetry between the *actus reus* and *mens rea* and the constitutional requirements of the *Charter* . . . .
>
> I know of no authority for the proposition that the *mens rea* of an offence must always attach to the precise consequence which is prohibited as a matter of constitutional necessity.[5]

In the result, McLachlin J. held that objective foresight of the risk of bodily harm was a sufficient fault element for the crime of unlawful act manslaughter, even though the *actus reus* of the crime was causing death as opposed to causing bodily harm. Offences that do not require a fault element in relation to all aspects of the *actus reus* are sometimes

---

3   R. v. *Théroux* (1993), 79 C.C.C. (3d) 449 at 458 (S.C.C.) [*Théroux*]. This is not an absolute rule, as seen in her own majority judgment in R. v. *Creighton* (1993), 83 C.C.C. (3d) 346 (S.C.C.) [*Creighton*] and discussed below, note 5.

4   R. v. *Hess* (1990), 59 C.C.C. (3d) 161 (S.C.C.), discussed in chs. 2 and 6.

5   Above note 3 at 378–79. In R. v. *DeSousa* (1992), 76 C.C.C. (3d) 124 at 141 (S.C.C.) [*DeSousa*], the Court noted a number of offences punish a person more severely because of the consequences of his or her actions even though there is no fault requirement with regards to those aggravating consequences. Examples cited included "manslaughter (s. 222(5)), criminal negligence causing bodily harm (s. 221), criminal negligence causing death (s. 220), dangerous operation causing bodily harm (s. 249(3)), dangerous operation causing death (s. 249(4)), impaired driving causing bodily harm (s. 255(2)), impaired driving causing death (s. 255(3)), assault causing bodily harm (s. 267(1)(b)), aggravated assault (s. 268), sexual assault causing bodily harm (s. 272(c)), aggravated sexual assault (s. 273), mischief causing danger to life (s. 430(2)), and arson causing bodily harm (s. 433(b)). As noted by Professor Colvin, "[i]t would, however, be an error to suppose that *actus reus* and *mens rea* always match in this neat way."

called offences of partial intent, constructive crimes, or crimes based on predicate offences.

Constructive murder violates section 7 of the *Charter* because while it required the fault of a predicate offence (such as robbery) and the fault of causing bodily harm, it did not require fault with respect to the prohibited act of killing and did not satisfy the constitutional requirement that a murderer at least have subjective foresight of death.[6] The Supreme Court pulled back, however, from declaring as a general constitutional principle that people could not be punished for the consequences of their actions in the absence of some fault or responsibility for those consequences. Thus, a person can be punished for causing death in a manslaughter case even though his or her fault only related to the objective risk of causing bodily harm.

Other offences require a *mens rea* that extends beyond the commission of the *actus reus*. Any attempted crime is a good example because it requires a *mens rea* that goes farther than the *actus reus* committed by the accused. Similarly, a person who assists a crime does something, such as acting as a lookout, for the further purpose of assisting the commission of the crime. Discharging a firearm with the intent to wound also requires proof of an intent to wound, even though an actual wounding is not part of the *actus reus*. Such offences are sometimes called ulterior intent offences, because they require an intent beyond the *actus reus* that is committed.

2) Subjective and Objective Fault Elements

A broad distinction is often drawn between subjective and objective fault elements. A subjective fault or mental element requires the Crown to establish that the accused subjectively had the required guilty knowledge in relation to the specified circumstances or consequences, whereas an objective fault element requires only that a reasonable person in the accused's position would have had the required guilty knowledge or would have acted differently.

A distinction should be made between the subjective mental elements that the Crown must prove and the means used to establish such guilty knowledge. The judge or jury who must determine what was in an accused's mind must rely on inferences from the evidence presented in the case. In deciding whether to draw these inferences, the trier of fact will almost inevitably consider what a reasonable person in the

---

6   *R. v. Martineau*, [1990] 2 S.C.R. 633.

accused's place would have thought or recognized. As Martin J.A. has explained,

> Since people are usually able to foresee the consequences of their acts, if a person does an act likely to produce certain consequences it is, in general, reasonable to assume that the accused also foresaw the probable consequences of his act and if he, nevertheless, acted so as to produce those consequences, that he intended them. The greater the likelihood of the relevant consequences ensuing from the accused's act, the easier it is to draw the inference that he intended those consequences. *The purpose of this process, however, is to determine what the particular accused intended, not to fix him with the intention that a reasonable person might be assumed to have in the circumstances, where doubt exists as to the actual intention of the accused.*[7]

In other words, what the reasonable person would have known may provide the basis for the jury to conclude that the accused had a particular subjective mental element, but it never requires the jury to make such a determination.[8] The trier of fact must remain open to all the evidence presented in the case (especially evidence relating to peculiarities about the accused) and acquit the accused if any evidence raises a reasonable doubt as to whether that particular person, with all of his or her frailties and experiences, had the required subjective mental element.

Subjective *mens rea* operates as a doctrine that prevents the conviction of an accused who, for whatever reason, does not have the knowledge and foresight that a reasonable person would have. It operates to protect those who because of impaired reasoning or lack of thought do not recognize or intend what may be obvious to the reasonable observer. The function of subjective *mens rea* is "to prevent the conviction of the morally innocent—those who do not understand or intend the consequences of their acts."[9]

---

7   *R. v. Buzzanga* (1979), 49 C.C.C. (2d) 369 at 387 (Ont. C.A.) [emphasis added] [*Buzzanga*]. "Where liability is imposed on a subjective basis, what a reasonable man ought to have anticipated is merely evidence from which a conclusion may be drawn that the accused anticipated the same consequences. On the other hand, where the test is objective, what a reasonable man should have anticipated constitutes the basis of liability." *R. v. Tennant* (1975), 23 C.C.C. (2d) 80 at 91 (Ont. C.A.).

8   This formulation also accords with the presumption of innocence. See ch. 2(B)(3)(f), "Right to Be Presumed Innocent."

9   *Théroux*, above note 3 at 458.

The Supreme Court has kept clear the distinctions between subjective and objective fault elements, but it has been increasingly willing to see the latter as an appropriate form of fault. In *Wholesale Travel Group*,[10] Cory J. stated:

> It should not be forgotten that *mens rea* and negligence are both fault elements. . . . *Mens rea* focuses on the mental state of the accused and requires proof of a positive state of mind such as intent, recklessness or wilful blindness. Negligence, on the other hand, measures the conduct of the accused on the basis of an objective standard, irrespective of the accused's subjective mental state. Where negligence is the basis of liability, the question is not what the accused intended but rather whether the accused exercised reasonable care.

The preceding statement was made in the context of regulatory offences outside of the *Criminal Code*, but the Court has also accepted that negligence, albeit modified for the purposes of imposing criminal as opposed to civil liability, can be a sufficient fault level for most criminal offences.

In the context of *Criminal Code* offences based on negligence, the Supreme Court has indicated that there must be "a marked departure from the standard of care that a reasonable person would observe in the accused's situation."[11] In *R. v. Beatty*, the Court arguably elevated the marked departure standard to a constitutional requirement when it warned:

> If every departure from the civil norm is to be criminalized, regardless of the degree, we risk casting the net too widely and branding as criminals persons who are in reality not morally blameworthy. Such an approach risks violating the principle of fundamental justice that the morally innocent not be deprived of liberty.[12]

---

10   *R. v. Wholesale Travel Group Inc.* (1991), 67 C.C.C. (3d) 193 (S.C.C.) at 252 [*Wholesale Travel Group*].

11   *R. v. Hundal*, [1993] 1 S.C.R. 867 at para. 43 [*Hundal*]; *Creighton*, above note 3 at 361 (Lamer C.J.), and 383 (McLachlin J.). In *R. v. Tutton* (1989), 48 C.C.C. (3d) 129 at 140 (S.C.C.) [*Tutton*], McIntyre J. (L'Heureux-Dubé J. concurring) stated in relation to criminal negligence: "The test is that of reasonableness, and proof of conduct which reveals a marked and significant departure from the standard which could be expected of a reasonably prudent person in the circumstances will justify a conviction of criminal negligence." Other means of adapting negligence as a principle of criminal liability will be discussed later in this chapter.

12   *R .v. Beatty*, [2008] 1 S.C.R. 49 at para. 34 [*Beatty*].

In addition to the requirement of a marked departure from reasonable standards, the Court in *Beatty* also held that courts should examine the actual mental state of the driver to determine whether it might raise a reasonable doubt about whether the accused was criminally negligent. The Court called this approach a modified objective approach which is potentially confusing because it does not modify the standards demanded by the reasonable person standard to reflect matters such as the accused's age or gender. Rather, the focus is on administering the objective standard in a contextual manner that is sensitive to the possibility that "a reasonable person in the position of the accused would not have been aware of the risk or, alternatively, would not have been able to avoid creating the danger."[13] In *Beatty*, the Court upheld an acquittal for dangerous driving on the basis that the accused had only engaged in a momentary lapse when his vehicle went over the centre line and killed three people. This decision suggests that objective fault will not always follow from the commission of an act that is in itself negligent and that in all cases the prosecutor must prove a marked departure from reasonable standards considering all the evidence in the case.

The exact differences between subjective and objective fault elements may be quite small and will depend on what level of subjective or objective *mens rea* is required, and how the objective standard of negligence is applied.

3) Common Law Presumptions of *Mens Rea*

It is important to keep distinct the issues of what is required under section 7 of the *Charter* to prevent the conviction of the morally innocent and what the courts will presume as a matter of judge-made common law in the absence of a clear legislative intent or design to the contrary. The Supreme Court has been reluctant to constitutionalize subjective *mens rea* for all but the most serious crimes, but it has long relied on common law presumptions in favour of subjective *mens rea* in relation to all aspects of the *actus reus*.[14]

Long before the enactment of the *Charter*, the Supreme Court presumed that criminal offences would require subjective *mens rea*.[15] Thus,

---

13   *Ibid.* at para. 37. See also R. v. Roy, 2012 SCC 26.
14   As will be examined in the next chapter, the Court has also relied on a common law presumption in R. v. Sault Ste. Marie (City) (1978), 40 C.C.C. (2d) 353 (S.C.C.) [Sault Ste. Marie] that regulatory offences will be crimes of strict as opposed to absolute liability.
15   R. v. Watts (1953), 105 C.C.C. 193 (S.C.C.); R. v. Rees (1956), 115 C.C.C. 1 (S.C.C.) [Rees]; R. v. Beaver (1957), 118 C.C.C. 129 (S.C.C.) [Beaver]; R. v. Prue

an offence of possession of narcotics was interpreted in 1957 to require proof that the accused had knowledge of the substance that in law constituted the illegal drugs even though Parliament did not specifically require that the offence be the "knowing" possession of drugs. The Court recognized that "[i]t would, of course, be within the power of Parliament to enact that a person who, without any guilty knowledge, had in his physical possession a package which he honestly believed to contain a harmless substance such as baking soda but which in fact contained heroin, must on proof of such facts be convicted of a crime and sentenced to at least 6 months' imprisonment." Nevertheless, the Court would not adopt an interpretation with the "monstrous consequences" of allowing the conviction of the morally innocent unless "the words of the statute were clear and admitted of no other interpretation."[16] Similarly, when interpreting an offence of knowingly or wilfully contributing to the delinquency of a child, the Court concluded that the fault element should be established with regards to all the elements of the *actus reus*, including whether the accused had subjective knowledge that the girl he had sexual intercourse with was actually under eighteen years of age. It was always open for Parliament to provide that the accused's belief about the age of the child was not relevant, but in this case Parliament had not made such a clear statement. Hence a requirement of subjective knowledge would be presumed in relation to all aspects of the *actus reus*.

The leading statement of the common law presumption of *mens rea* is contained in *Sault Ste. Marie.*[17] In that case, Dickson J. stated:

> Where the offence is criminal, the Crown must establish a mental element, namely, that the accused who committed the prohibited act did so intentionally or recklessly, with knowledge of the facts constituting the offence, or with wilful blindness toward them. Mere negligence is excluded from the concept of the mental element required for conviction. Within the context of a criminal prosecution a person who fails to make such inquiries as a reasonable and prudent person would make, or who fails to know facts he should have known, is innocent in the eyes of the law.

This means that the courts should presume that criminal offences require some form of subjective *mens rea*—intent, knowledge, reckless-

---

(1979), 46 C.C.C. (2d) 257 (S.C.C.).

16   *Beaver, ibid.* at 141.

17   *Sault Ste. Marie*, above note 14 at 362.

ness, or wilful blindness—in relation to all aspects of the *actus reus* unless Parliament clearly indicates otherwise.

Common law presumptions concerning *mens rea* remain valid. A reluctance to impose criminal liability on the basis of negligence explains why recklessness in Canadian law requires proof that the accused subjectively was aware of the prohibited risk.[18] Common law presumptions remain quite important given the frequency with which Parliament enacts criminal offences without specifying any fault element. Common law presumptions will, however, be overcome once Parliament has clearly indicated, through either the words or design of the offence, that it has intended some other result. Common law presumptions require Parliament to clearly state when it does not desire subjective *mens rea* when enacting a criminal offence.[19]

4) Constitutional Requirements of *Mens Rea*

The topic of *mens rea* has become more complex in part because there are a number of different principles of fundamental justice that govern the fault element. Some of these principles require proof of subjective fault, some of them require a proportionality between the moral blameworthiness of an offence and its punishment, including maintaining distinctions between the seriousness of subjective and objective fault offences, and some of them modify objective fault standards to ensure that they can be used to impose criminal liability.

a) Requirements of Subjective Fault in Relation to Prohibited Act for Special Stigma Crimes: Murder, Attempted Murder, and War Crimes

As seen earlier in this chapter, there are common law presumptions that require proof of subjective *mens rea*—at least recklessness—in relation to all elements of the prohibited act, but these can be displaced by clear legislation. A constitutional requirement of subjective *mens rea* under section 7 of the *Charter* would leave Parliament far fewer options than a common law presumption. Violations of section 7 of the

---

18   *R. v. Sansregret* (1985), 18 C.C.C. (3d) 223 (S.C.C.) [*Sansregret*]. In some parts of English law, however, recklessness was an objective form of liability that only requires the accused's failure to advert to an obvious risk. *Metropolitan Police Commissioner v. Caldwell* (1981), [1982] A.C. 341 (H.L.).

19   As examined in the next chapter, the common law presumption in *Sault Ste. Marie*, above note 14, that regulatory offences will be strict liability, requires legislatures to clearly state if they desire a regulatory offence to be an absolute liability offence.

Charter are almost never upheld under section 1 of the *Charter*[20] and the substitution of elements for essential elements are also almost never accepted under section 11(d) of the *Charter*. The remaining legislative option would be the rather draconian use of the section 33 override to allow the legislation to operate for at least five years notwithstanding the legal rights in the *Charter*. The finality of constitutional requirements of *mens rea* may help explain the Supreme Court's caution about constitutionalizing subjective *mens rea* in relation to the prohibited act under section 7 of the *Charter*.

In *R. v. Vaillancourt*,[21] Lamer J. expressed preference for a general constitutional principle of subjective *mens rea* in relation to all aspects of the prohibited act, while recognizing that many crimes were based on objective fault. He stated:

> It may well be that, as a general rule, the principles of fundamental justice require proof of a subjective *mens rea* with respect to the prohibited act, in order to avoid punishing the "morally innocent."
> . . . There are many provisions in the *Code* requiring only objective foreseeability of the result or even only a causal link between the act and the result. As I would prefer not to cast doubt on the validity of such provisions *in this case*, I will assume, but only for the purposes of this appeal, that something less than subjective foresight of the result may, sometimes, suffice for the imposition of criminal liability for causing that result through intentional criminal conduct.[22]

Subsequent cases have made it clear that subjective foresight of the prohibited consequences is not required for all crimes. Indeed, subjective *mens rea* so far has only been required under section 7 of the *Charter* for murder,[23] attempted murder,[24] and war crimes.[25] The Supreme Court has ruled that it is not required for many other crimes, including unlawfully causing bodily harm,[26] dangerous driving,[27] unlawful act

---

20 *Reference re Motor Vehicle Act (British Columbia) S. 94(2)*, [1985] 2 S.C.R. 486 at 518 [*B.C. Motor Vehicle Reference*]; *R. v. D.B.*, 2008 SCC 25 at para. 89.

21 (1987), 39 C.C.C. (3d) 118 (S.C.C.).

22 *Ibid.* at 133–34 [emphasis in original].

23 *Martineau*, above note 6.

24 *R. v. Logan* (1990), 58 C.C.C. (3d) 391 (S.C.C.) [*Logan*].

25 *R. v. Finta* (1994), 88 C.C.C. (3d) 417 (S.C.C.) [*Finta*].

26 *DeSousa*, above note 5.

27 *Hundal*, above note 11.

manslaughter,[28] careless use of a firearm,[29] and failing to provide the necessities of life.[30] As will be discussed in chapter 6, the *Charter* also does not require proof of subjective *mens rea* for regulatory offences found outside of the *Criminal Code* in various provincial and federal statutes.[31]

What then distinguishes murder, attempted murder, and war crimes as crimes that require subjective *mens rea* in relation to the prohibited act? Murder is the easiest to explain because "a conviction for murder carries with it the most severe stigma and punishment of any crime in our society."[32] Attempted murder only has a maximum penalty of life imprisonment and not a mandatory penalty of life imprisonment as does murder. Nevertheless, the Court has stressed that it carries with it the same stigma as murder because one who commits attempted murder has the same intent or "killer instinct" as a murderer but was "lucky—the ambulance arrived early, or some other fortuitous circumstance."[33] With respect to both murder and attempted murder, the constitutionally required *mens rea* is knowledge of the probability that death will be caused.

The Court was more divided on whether war crimes and crimes against humanity also were special stigma crimes that required proof of subjective knowledge in relation to all aspects of the prohibited act. The majority of the Court in *Finta*[34] stressed that a person convicted of war crimes would be subject to "additional stigma and opprobrium" associated with war crimes that would not normally be associated with the underlying crimes charged in that case: unlawful confinement, robbery, kidnapping, and manslaughter of Jews during the Holocaust. The minority relied on the general principle that section 7 of the *Charter* does not require proof of fault in relation to all aspects of the prohibited result and that any additional stigma attached to a war crimes conviction would be caused by the surrounding circumstances as opposed to the nature of the offence.

The theory behind special stigma offences appears to be that fair labelling is required, albeit only for the most serious of crimes. It is difficult to see what other crimes might be added to this short list of spe-

---

28   *Creighton*, above note 3.
29   *R. v. Finlay* (1993), 83 C.C.C. (3d) 513 (S.C.C.) [*Finlay*]; *R. v. Gosset* (1993), 83 C.C.C. (3d) 494 (S.C.C.) [*Gosset*].
30   *R. v. Naglik* (1993), 83 C.C.C. (3d) 526 (S.C.C.) [*Naglik*].
31   *Hundal*, above note 11.
32   *Martineau*, above note 6 at 645.
33   *R. v. Logan*, [1990] 2 S.C.R. 731 at 743.
34   [1994] 1 S.C.R. 701.

cial stigma crimes, although terrorist offences may qualify given the stigma and enhanced penalties associated with them. In such a result, the offences would have to require at least subjective knowledge of the prohibited result. Although most of the new terrorism offences created at the end of 2001 require subjective knowledge of terrorist activities and a subjective purpose to assist terrorists, the requirements of subjective fault are diluted with respect to some terrorism offences. In particular, the offence under section 83.19(1) of the *Code* requires knowing facilitation of a terrorist activity but then provides in section 83.19(2) that it is not necessary to establish that "any particular terrorist activity was foreseen or planned at the time it was facilitated." This provision may be vulnerable under section 7 of the *Charter* should terrorism be found to be one of the few stigma offences that requires a subjective *mens rea* that reflects the particular nature of the crime.

b) Principles of Fundamental Justice as Outlined in *Creighton*

Constitutional requirements of subjective knowledge in relation to the prohibited result for crimes of special stigma do not exhaust constitutional requirements of fault. In *Creighton*,[35] Justice McLachlin indicated that the following considerations were relevant in determining constitutional requirements of *mens rea*:

1. the stigma attached to the offence, and the available penalties requiring a *mens rea* reflecting the particular nature of the crime;
2. whether the punishment is proportionate to the moral blameworthiness of the offender; and
3. the idea that those causing harm intentionally must be punished more severely than those causing harm unintentionally.

This articulates constitutional requirements of *mens rea* at a greater level of generality than often circular conclusions about whether the stigma, penalty, or moral blameworthiness of particular crimes demand a greater degree of *mens rea*.

The first *Creighton* proposition builds on a line of cases culminating in *Martineau* and *Logan* that indicated that murder and attempted murder because of their nature and labelling effects will require a subjective *mens rea* in relation to the *actus reus* of the crime. As discussed earlier, the Supreme Court in its first war crimes case concluded, albeit in a 4:3 decision, that the prosecutor must establish not only the fault of

---

35 *Creighton*, above note 3 at 374.

the underlying offence but also subjective fault, including wilful blindness, of the circumstances that elevated the crime from an ordinary crime into a war crime.[36] The first *Creighton* proposition will only be relevant with respect to a small number of crimes with a special stigma.

The second *Creighton* proposition relates to proportionality between the moral blameworthiness of the offender and the punishment. The Court has not elaborated on this particular concept, but subsequent to *Creighton* it has indicated that a law that is grossly disproportionate to a state interest would also violate section 7 of the *Charter*.[37] The Court refused to strike down either the offence of possession of marijuana in *Malmo-Levine* or the offence of manslaughter in *Creighton* under section 7 of the *Charter* and in both cases relied on the notion that sentencing discretion, including the option of alternatives to imprisonment, would allow judges to tailor punishment to moral blameworthiness. At the time of both decisions, there were no mandatory minimum sentences for either crime. This raises the question of whether the Court's analysis would be different if there were a mandatory sentence of imprisonment as there is now with respect to manslaughter committed with a firearm. The Court has been quite reluctant to strike down mandatory sentences as cruel or unusual punishment under section 12 of the *Charter*. For example, it upheld a mandatory four-year sentence of imprisonment that was enacted subsequent to *Creighton* and would now apply to manslaughter committed with a firearm.[38] At the same time, the question under section 7 would be whether the existence of a mandatory sentence meant that the punishment was no longer proportionate to the moral blameworthiness of the offence. The existence of safety valves such as sentencing discretion may be quite important to maintaining proportionality between punishment and moral blameworthiness required by section 7 of the *Charter*.

The idea expressed in the third *Creighton* proposition that the intentional causing of harm should be punished more severely than the unintentional causing of harm was easily satisfied because of the important distinction between murder and manslaughter. Nevertheless, this principle creates the possibility that section 7 might be violated by some broadly defined crimes such as sexual assault,[39] the new organizational criminal liability provisions for subjective intent offences,[40] and

---

36   *Finta*, above note 25.
37   *R. v. Malmo-Levine* (2003), 179 C.C.C. (3d) 417 (S.C.C.).
38   *R. v. Morrisey*, [2002] 2 S.C.R. 90 discussed in ch. 11.
39   *Code*, above note 2, s. 273.2(b) discussed in ch. 10.
40   *Code, ibid.*, s. 22.2(c) discussed in ch. 6.

the new restrictions on the defence of extreme intoxication,[41] which combine objective and subjective fault elements. This approach, however, would require courts to scrutinize the policy reasons that Parliament may have for broadly defining crimes to include a range of culpable conduct. Courts may very well retreat to the notion, firmly established in the cases, that the stigma, penalty, and blameworthiness of only a few crimes demand a *mens rea* that reflects the particular nature of the crime. Thus, courts may well conclude that the stigma and penalty that accompany a sexual assault conviction,[42] or most subjective offences committed by organizations, do not require proof of subjective fault for every element of the offence or the creation of a separate less serious offence of negligent sexual assault. In addition, the third *Creighton* proposition may discount that sometimes it may be quite appropriate for Parliament to combine subjective and objective fault elements and that this may not result in disproportionate punishment that punishes those who cause harm unintentionally more than those who cause harm intentionally. Rather, the result may be to punish those who had elements of both subjective and objective fault.

c) Constitutional Requirements with Respect to Criminal Negligence

Section 7 of the *Charter* also plays a role in shaping negligence standards when they are used to determine criminal liability resulting in imprisonment. There is a requirement that negligent conduct constitute a marked departure from reasonable conduct so as to distinguish criminal from civil negligence. Charron J. explained:

> If every departure from the civil norm is to be criminalized, regardless of the degree, we risk casting the net too widely and branding as criminals persons who are in reality not morally blameworthy. Such an approach risks violating the principle of fundamental justice that the morally innocent not be deprived of liberty.[43]

The constitutional requirement that criminal uses of negligence be distinguished from civil uses of negligence by proof of a marked departure explains why the Court has interpreted crimes such as careless use of a firearm and dangerous driving to require proof of a marked departure from reasonable standards of care despite statu-

---

41   *Code*, above note 2, s. 33.1 discussed in ch. 7.
42   See *R. v. Daviault*, [1994] 3 S.C.R. 63 per Sopinka J. in dissent.
43   *Beatty*, above note 12 at para. 34.

tory language that suggests an intent to punish mere carelessness that would ordinarily only be sufficient for imposing civil liability.[44]

A second modification in the criminal context is the need to consider the actual mental state of the accused along with all the evidence to determine if it raises a reasonable doubt about whether a reasonable person in similar circumstances would have been aware of the risk created by the conduct.[45] This contextual approach would, for example, take into account whether the driver charged suffered an unexpected heart attack, seizure, or detached retina or loss of consciousness. It does not, however, require that the reasonable person have the same characteristics of the accused or that the accused has subjectively adverted to the prohibited risk. Although the Court has upheld the constitutionality of using objective fault for most offences other than those which have special stigma, it has stressed that section 7 of the *Charter* requires 1) proof of a marked departure from a reasonable standard of care and 2) that all the evidence, including the accused's actual mental state, be examined in determining whether the accused has engaged in such a marked departure from standards of reasonable care.

d) Substituted Elements for Constitutionally Required Elements

As discussed earlier, constitutional requirements concerning fault elements will be less easily overcome than common law presumptions. The Supreme Court has concluded that because of the stigma and penalty of a murder conviction, section 7 of the *Charter* requires proof that the accused knew that the victim was likely to die. Thus, subjective knowledge of the *actus reus* is a constitutional requirement for the offence of murder.

It is theoretically possible to substitute another fault element for the fault element required under section 7 of the *Charter*. As examined in chapter 2, however, the Court has been quite stringent and held that another element could only be substituted for a required element if proof of the substituted element would lead inexorably, or prove beyond a reasonable doubt, that the required element was present.[46] In *Martineau*,[47] the Supreme Court held that proof that the accused means to cause bodily harm for the purpose of facilitating a serious offence—the *mens rea* required for constructive murder under section

---

44   *Hundal*, above note 11; *R. v. Finlay*, [1993] 3 S.C.R. 103; *Beatty, ibid.*

45   *Beatty, ibid.* at para. 49.

46   *R. v. Whyte* (1988), 42 C.C.C. (3d) 97 (S.C.C.) as discussed in ch. 2(B)(3)(f), "Right to Be Presumed Innocent."

47   *Martineau*, above note 6.

230(a)—could not be substituted for proof of the essential element of murder required for a murder conviction under section 7 of the *Charter*—namely, proof of subjective knowledge that the victim was likely to die. Similarly, proof under section 230(c) that the accused wilfully stops the breath of a human being for the purpose of facilitating a serious offence could not be substituted for the essential element under section 7 of the *Charter* of knowledge of death. Proof of the substituted element in section 230 did not lead inexorably to a conclusion that the state had proven beyond a reasonable doubt the existence of the essential element required under section 7 of the *Charter*.[48]

Another possibility would be to justify the violation of section 7 caused by providing some other fault element as a reasonable limit under section 1 of the *Charter*. The Supreme Court has, however, been extremely reluctant to hold that violations of section 7 of the *Charter* are justified under section 1 of the *Charter*. In both *Vaillancourt* and *Martineau*, the Court held that it was not necessary or proportionate for the Court to use a lesser fault element than knowledge of death in order to advance the important objective of deterring the use of weapons and violence in the commission of serious offences. The Court noted that Parliament could and does punish the use of weapons in the commission of offences and that the accused could always receive a stiff sentence for manslaughter. In other cases, the Court seems even more categorical, even suggesting that a section 7 violation could only be justified under section 1 in exceptional circumstances such as war and other emergencies.[49] A final means to overcome a constitutional requirement of fault would be for Parliament to re-enact an offence, such as the constructive murder offence, notwithstanding section 7 of the *Charter*. This section 33 override would be politically unpopular and would have to be re-enacted by Parliament after a five-year period.

A constitutional requirement of *mens rea* under section 7 of the *Charter* is much more difficult for Parliament to overcome than a common law presumption. All Parliament need do in response to a common law presumption of subjective *mens rea* is to indicate clearly that the common law presumptions are not desired. A constitutional requirement of *mens rea* can only be overcome by satisfying the rigorous and almost impossible standards for substituting elements under section 11(d) of the *Charter* or the equally difficult burden of justifying a violation of section 7 of the *Charter* under section 1. This may help explain

---

48   *R. v. Sit* (1991), 61 C.C.C. (3d) 449 (S.C.C.).

49   *B.C. Motor Vehicle Reference*, above note 20 at 518; *R. v. Heywood*, [1994] 3 S.C.R. 761 at 802; *New Brunswick v. G.(J.)*, [1999] 3 S.C.R. 46 at para. 99; *R. v. Ruzic*, 2001 SCC 24 at para. 92.

why the Supreme Court has been relatively cautious in constitutionalizing subjective *mens rea* under section 7 of the *Charter* while it did not hesitate before the *Charter* to apply robust common law presumptions of subjective *mens rea*. It should be remembered that constitutional requirements are a bare minimum. As the content of constitutional requirements become more minimal, the common law presumptions will become more important.

5) Fault Elements in Relation to the Defences of Mistake of Fact and Intoxication

Understanding fault elements is sometimes confused by reference to the "defences" of mistake of fact and intoxication. The availability of both defences depends on the fault element of the specific offence being absent. In other words, both defences operate to raise a reasonable doubt as to whether the accused had the requisite fault element rather than the existence of some other factor, such as self-defence, which may excuse or justify the commission of a crime that is committed with the required fault.

Both mistake of fact and intoxication defences are primarily derived from the fault element of the particular offence. As will be discussed in depth in chapter 7, evidence that the accused was intoxicated may raise a reasonable doubt whether the accused had the required mental element for a specific intent offence such as murder or robbery. The Supreme Court has made clear that the issue is the accused's actual intent, not his or her capacity for the intent.[50] The relation of the intoxication defence to the fault element is less clear for offences that are classified as general intent offences. General intent offences such as assault are thought to involve less complex mental processes. Only extreme intoxication may negate such mental elements.[51] It might also be thought that intoxication may never be relevant to offences that only require an objective fault element because the reasonable person would not be intoxicated. Nevertheless, extreme intoxication may raise a reasonable doubt as to whether the accused had voluntarily committed the *actus reus*.[52]

The derivative nature of the mistake of fact defence is revealed by comparing the availability of the defence for crimes with various and no fault elements. Mistake of fact will not be an issue for an ab-

---

50   *R. v. Robinson* (1996), 105 C.C.C. (3d) 97 (S.C.C.).

51   *R. v. Daviault* (1994), 93 C.C.C. (3d) 21 (S.C.C.).

52   See ch. 3(B)(4), "Voluntariness of the Act," and ch. 7(E), "Extreme Intoxication and General Intent Offences," for more discussion of this proposition.

solute liability offence because the only issue is whether the accused has committed the *actus reus*. What the particular accused thought or even what a reasonable person in the accused's position would have perceived is not relevant. If objective negligence is the fault element, a mistake of fact will only prevent a conviction if it is one that a reasonable person would have made. In other words, a mistake of fact would have to be honest and reasonable. If the offence requires a subjective fault element, this opens up the possibility that an honest but not necessarily reasonable mistake of fact will suffice. The issue is what the actual accused perceived, not what a reasonable person perceived. The more unreasonable the accused's mistake, the less likely the jury will be to accept it as genuine and honest, but the ultimate issue is the perceptions of the particular accused. As will be seen later in this chapter, it is possible to combine subjective and objective fault elements and require that a mistake of fact be based on reasonable behaviour given the accused's actual subjective knowledge of the circumstances.

B. THE DEGREES OF SUBJECTIVE *MENS REA*

There are important practical differences among the various forms of subjective *mens rea*. A person who might not be guilty of acting with the purpose or intent to commit a crime might, nevertheless, have acted with subjective knowledge that the prohibited result would occur. Similarly, a person who cannot be said to have acted with subjective knowledge that the prohibited result would occur may, nevertheless, have acted with subjective recklessness in adverting to or being conscious of a risk that the prohibited result could occur or the prohibited circumstances might be present. Such a person could also be wilfully blind by not inquiring into the prohibited risk, when he or she knows there is need for further inquiry. References to "subjective *mens rea*" are unhelpful, and the exact degree of subjective fault must be specified.

1) Intent, Purpose, or Wilfulness

The highest level of subjective *mens rea* is that which requires the accused to act with the intent or purpose to achieve the prohibited result, or to wilfully pursue such a result. An example would be section 229(a) (i), which prohibits murder where the accused "means to cause . . . death." This high level of *mens rea* is used relatively infrequently. Common law presumptions and even constitutional requirements of subjective *mens rea* do not require proof of intent and are satisfied by lower forms of *mens rea* such as knowledge and even recklessness. Where Parliament has specifically used the words "with intent," this will generally exclude lower forms of subjective *mens rea* such as recklessness.[53]

Proof of purpose is required under the various parties' provisions in the *Criminal Code*. As examined in the last chapter, these provisions can make a person guilty of an offence even though he or she did not actually commit the offence and thus it makes sense to require a fairly high level of *mens rea*. Section 21(1)(b) requires a party to do or omit "to do anything for the purpose of aiding any person" to commit an offence, and section 21(2) requires the formation of an "unlawful purpose." Similarly, attempts require "an intent to commit the offence," and an accessory after the fact must act for the purpose of enabling a known criminal to escape. The more peripheral the accused's involvement to the completed crime, the more sense it makes to require a higher form of subjective *mens rea*.

The potential difference between guilty intent and guilty knowledge can be illustrated in cases where the accused knowingly engages in prohibited conduct, but does so for another purpose such as avoiding harm. In *R. v. Steane*, the accused was charged with assisting the enemy with the "intent to assist the enemy" after he made wartime propaganda broadcasts. The Court of Appeal held that, given the intent required for the offence, it was wrong for the trial judge to have left the jury with the impression that "a man must be taken to intend the natural consequences of his acts." It was possible that Steane acted not with the intent to assist the enemy, but rather with "the innocent intent of a desire to save his wife and children from a concentration camp."[54] In *R. v. Paquette*,[55] the Supreme Court similarly indicated:

> A person whose actions have been dictated by fear of death or of grievous bodily injury cannot be said to have formed a genuine common intent to carry out an unlawful purpose with the person who has threatened him with those consequences if he fails to co-operate.

In that case, the accused was held not to have formed a common intent under section 21(2) to rob a store when he drove the robbers to the store after being threatened at gunpoint. In both cases, the accused certainly acted with the knowledge that his actions would contribute to the prohibited result. The difficult issue is whether the accused acted with the intent or purpose to achieve the prohibited result.

---

53 *R. v. Chartrand* (1994), 91 C.C.C. (3d) 396 (S.C.C.) [*Chartrand*].
54 [1947] K.B. 997 at 1006 (C.A.) [*Steane*].
55 (1976), 30 C.C.C. (2d) 417 at 423 (S.C.C.) [*Paquette*].

The Supreme Court in *R. v. Hibbert*,[56] has overruled *Paquette* on the basis that it confused intent and purpose with motive and desire. Lamer C.J. stated that a person, like Paquette, who participates in a robbery because of threats to his life nevertheless forms an "unlawful purpose" under section 21(2) to commit the robbery. His desire or motive of saving his own life does not prevent the formation of the unlawful purpose of intentionally committing the robbery. Similarly, Paquette would act with the purpose of assisting the robbery required under section 21(1)(b) if he intended to drive the getaway car and by doing so assist the robbery. It would not matter to the question of *mens rea* that Paquette's desire or motive was to save his own life. The Supreme Court has rejected the idea that intent or purpose under section 21 should be equated with the accused's desires and motivations. Some caution is in order before applying this ruling to all forms of subjective *mens rea*. The Court made clear it only reached these conclusions for section 21 in large part because an accused who responded to threats could still claim a common law defence of duress.[57] Depending on how the offence was structured, the fact that a person acted as a result of threats could in some instances be relevant to the question of whether he or she possessed the *mens rea* necessary to commit the offence. Thus, a person in Steane's position could perhaps still argue that he did not wilfully act with an intent or purpose to assist the enemy even though he surely knew that his actions would have that effect.

Knowledge that something is very certain to occur, however, may be equated with an intent or a purpose to achieve the prohibited result. In *Buzzanga*,[58] Martin J.A. stated that "as a general rule, a person who foresees that a consequence is certain or substantially certain to result from an act which he does to achieve some other purpose, intends that consequence." Consistent with the presumption of innocence, however, an accused should be allowed to raise a reasonable doubt as to whether he or she intended the consequence, if that is the required mental element.

A requirement that the accused wilfully achieve a prohibited result imposes a high degree of subjective *mens rea*. In *Buzzanga*,[59] the Ontario Court of Appeal interpreted a prohibition against wilfully promoting hatred against an identifiable group as requiring proof that the accused's "conscious purpose in distributing the document was to promote hatred against that group," or knowledge that the promotion

---

56   *R. v. Hibbert* (1995), 99 C.C.C. (3d) 193 (S.C.C.) [*Hibbert*].

57   See ch. 9(D), "Duress."

58   *Buzzanga*, above note 7 at 384–85, approved in *Chartrand*, above note 53 at 415.

59   *Buzzanga*, *ibid.* at 385. This analysis has been approved with reference to a "with intent" requirement. *Chartrand*, *ibid.*

of hatred "was certain or morally certain" to result from their actions. This requires knowledge of a much higher degree of probability of the prohibited act than either knowledge that requires that the accused know that the prohibited act is probable or recklessness that requires knowledge that the prohibited act is possible.

In *R. v. Docherty*,[60] the Supreme Court stated that the word "wilfully" "stresses intention in relation to the achievement of a purpose. It can be contrasted with lesser forms of guilty knowledge, such as 'negligently' or even 'recklessly.' In short, the use of the word 'wilfully' denotes a legislative concern for a relatively high level of *mens rea*." In that case, the accused was held not to have wilfully breached his probation order because he believed that what he was doing, sitting in the driver's seat of a motionless car while drunk, was not a crime that would place him in breach of probation. Parliament subsequently deleted the requirement that the prosecutor prove that the accused "wilfully" breached parole. Instead there is a simple prohibition against breaching parole without a reasonable excuse.[61]

In *R. v. Carker (No. 2)*,[62] a prisoner was convicted of wilfully damaging public property when he smashed plumbing fixtures in his cell during a prison riot, even though he only performed the act after fellow prisoners had threatened to injure him if he did not. On the basis of *Steane* and *Paquette*, it could be argued that Carker did not truly intend to damage public property because he was acting for the purpose of self-preservation. Carker was, however, found to have the necessary *mens rea*, because wilful was defined for the purpose of the offence as including knowledge or recklessness that the prohibited result would occur.[63] Carker knew he was damaging public property, even though his ultimate purpose or intent may have been to save his life. Given the Supreme Court's overruling of *Paquette*, however, it is possible that a court might dismiss Carker's desire to protect his own life as a matter of motive or desire not relevant to the determination of his intent.[64] In another prison case, a majority of the Court in *R. v. Kerr*[65] interpreted

---

60 (1989), 51 C.C.C. (3d) 1 at 7 (S.C.C.).
61 *Code*, above note 2, s. 733.1. Applying the common law presumption of subjective *mens rea* discussed above, this new offence would only require proof that accused recklessly breached probation by being aware of the risk that their actions would breach probation.
62 (1966), [1967] 2 C.C.C. 190 (S.C.C.).
63 *Code*, above note 2, s. 429(1).
64 Even if Carker had the required fault element, he could argue that he had a defence of duress. As discussed in ch. 9, however, s. 17 of the *Code, ibid.*, as interpreted in this case placed severe restrictions on the availability of this defence.
65 [2004] 2 S.C.R. 371.

the offence of possession of weapon for a purpose dangerous to the public peace in a manner that seemed to equate purpose with knowledge[66] and even with recklessness.[67] It can no longer be maintained with great confidence that a *mens rea* requirement of intent, purpose, or wilfulness will be sharply differentiated from a requirement of knowledge.

2) Intent, Purpose, or Wilfulness Distinguished from Motive

The criminal law does not require proof of a motive for a crime, and an argument that the accused had no motive or some innocent motivation will not exonerate one who has otherwise committed the crime with the necessary guilty intent. As Dickson J. has stated,

> In ordinary parlance, the words "intent" and "motive" are frequently used interchangeably, but in the criminal law they are distinct. In most criminal trials, the mental element, the *mens rea* with which the Court is concerned, relates to "intent," i.e., the exercise of a free will to use particular means to produce a particular result, rather than with "motive," i.e., that which precedes and induces the exercise of the will. The mental element of a crime ordinarily involves no reference to motive.[68]

The Crown does not have to prove motive, but evidence relating to motive can be relevant in a criminal trial and can assist the Crown and sometimes the accused. In *Buzzanga*, the fact that the accused may have intended to counter apathy among francophones when they circulated an anti-French document was relevant in determining whether they were wilfully promoting hatred against that group. On the other hand, Martin J.A. indicated that if the accused were indeed intentionally promoting hatred against francophones, they would be guilty even

---

66   *Ibid.* at para. 55, Bastarache J. (Major J. concurring). Justice Bastarache held that the accused did not have the purpose requirement because he possessed the shank in order to defend himself.

67   *Ibid.* at para. 77, LeBel J. (Arbour J. concurring). Justice LeBel elaborated: "Criminal liability under s. 88(1) thus applies not only to an accused who intends to do harm to persons or property, but also an accused who is aware of a risk of harm to persons or property and persists with his or her intention despite that risk. It does not establish an objective standard of dangerousness however." *Ibid.* at para. 88. He held that the accused did possess the weapon for a purpose dangerous to the public peace, but ruled that the offence was excused because of the defence of necessity.

68   *R. v. Lewis* (1979), 47 C.C.C. (2d) 24 at 33 (S.C.C.).

if their motive was to produce a reaction that would help establish a French language school.

Motive can be difficult to distinguish from intent, and cases on this issue have not always been consistent. In a 1936 case, the Supreme Court held that a person who assisted in a robbery had formed a common intent to commit the crime. The fact that his motivation may have been to avoid threats of death from his accomplices was irrelevant to the issue of *mens rea.*[69] In 1976, however, the Court indicated that a person who assisted in a robbery in response to threats of death could not have formed a genuine intent to carry out the unlawful purpose.[70] In 1995, however, the Supreme Court reverted to its former approach when it overruled the 1976 case on the basis that a person could act with the purpose of assisting a crime under section 21(1)(b) or form a common intent to carry out an unlawful purpose to engage in a crime under section 21(2), even though his or her motives and desires were to avoid threats from accomplices.[71] The Court indicated that in most cases, the motive of avoiding harm to self or others would not negate the issue of intent.

The Supreme Court has continued to draw a broad distinction between motive and intent. Cory and Iacobucci JJ. have stated that "[i]t does not matter to society, in its efforts to secure social peace and order, what an accused's motive was, but only what the accused intended to do. It is no consolation to one whose car has been stolen that the thief stole the car intending to sell it to purchase food for a food bank.[72] Good motive is no defence to intentional crimes. It may, however, be relevant to the exercise of prosecutorial or sentencing discretion.

The criminal law's general lack of concern about motive may also help explain the ignorance of the law is not an excuse principle found in section 19 of the *Criminal Code* and discussed previously in chapter 3. This principle means that accused who have formed honest and even reasonable but mistaken beliefs that their actions are legal may still be found to have the necessary *mens rea* to commit the offence. In most cases, *mens rea* relates only to the accused's intent or knowledge in relation to the commission of the immediate act and not to more elaborate processes relating either to why the accused acted or whether the accused thought that the act was legal. This may help explain why mistakes about the legality and legal consequences of actions are generally

---

69 *Dunbar v. R.* (1936), 67 C.C.C. 20 (S.C.C.).
70 *Paquette*, above note 55.
71 *Hibbert*, above note 56.
72 *United States of America v. Dynar* (1997), 115 C.C.C. (3d) 481 at 509 (S.C.C.) [*Dynar*].

not an excuse, but a mistake about the existence of the more immediate factual elements of the offences may, as will be discussed later in this chapter, be a factor that will prevent the prosecutor from establishing *mens rea.*

As in many areas, there are some exceptions. The *mens reas* of some offences, notably theft, are defined in a robust way that allows the accused's mistaken beliefs about legal claims to the property to be relevant to proof of *mens rea.* Section 322 (1) of the *Code* provides a particularly high level of *mens reas* which requires proof that an accused who commits theft "fraudulently and without colour of right" takes or converts property.[73] The courts have held that an accused's mistaken belief about his legal entitlement to the property can prevent proof of *mens rea* for this particular crime.[74] Consistent with the focus on the accused's mental state, the issue is the accused's belief in legal entitlement and not the actual legal entitlement[75] and mistaken beliefs about legal entitlement can prevent the proof of this particular fault element. This is another reminder about the need to be specific about the precise nature of *mens rea* for specific offences. Although neither motive nor beliefs about legality are relevant for most criminal offences, they may be relevant to some offences such as theft and other property offences that allow a colour of right defence.

One exception to the principle that motive is not an essential element of offences are the terrorism offences created by Parliament at the end of 2001. The prosecutor must not only prove various forms of intent beyond a reasonable doubt but also that the act was "committed in whole or in part for a political, religious, or ideological purpose, objective or cause.[76] In other words, a political or religious motive is an essential element of crimes involving the commission of a terrorist activity. The motive requirement was defended as necessary to distinguish terrorism from ordinary crime. This seems unlikely given that the activities also have to be committed with the intent to intimidate the public or compel governments or persons to act. Concerns were raised that the motive requirement would require the police to investigate the politics and religion of terrorist suspects and that these matters would be front and centre in any terrorist trial. In response, Parliament enacted section 83.01(1.1), which provides that "the expression of a

---

73   The colour of right concept will not be read into other crimes that do not contain such language. See *R. v. Jones,* [1991] 3 S.C.R. 110 (not reading in colour of right concept into offence of operating unlicensed bingo).

74   *R. v. Howson,* [1966] 3 C.C.C. 348 (Ont. C.A.); *R. v. Dorosh* 2003 SKCA 134.

75   *R. v. Lilly,* [1983] 1 SCR 794 at 798–99.

76   *Code,* above note 2, s. 83.01(1)(b)(I)(A).

political, religious, or ideological thought, belief or opinion" would not fall under the definition of terrorist activity unless the other intent requirements were satisfied. The Ontario Court of Appeal has upheld the use of the political and religious motive requirement on the basis that no rule prevents Parliament from including motive in the definition of a crime and also on the basis that the particular use of political and religious motive in relation to the definition of terrorist activities did not limit freedom of expression or religion or did so in a manner that constituted a reasonable limit on the rights.[77]

3) Knowledge

Knowledge is a slightly lower form of subjective *mens rea* than intent or purpose. Section 229(c) of the *Criminal Code* states that a person is guilty of murder if he "knows" that he "is likely to cause death to a human being, notwithstanding that he desires to effect his object without causing death or bodily harm to any human being."[78] Similarly, section 229(a)(ii) also emphasizes the requirement of guilty knowledge by providing that a person who intentionally causes bodily harm is guilty of murder if he or she knows that the harm is likely to result in death. This requirement of guilty knowledge of the likelihood of death has been held to be sufficient under section 7 of the *Charter* to sustain a murder conviction.[79] A person may have guilty knowledge that his or her victim will die without necessarily desiring or having the motive of causing death or even intending or meaning to cause death under section 229(a)(i).

Knowledge is a common form of *mens rea* for possession-based offences. In *Beaver*,[80] the Supreme Court held that a person in physical possession of a substance could not be said to possess that substance unless he or she knew the nature of the substance. Cartwright J. explained that a person with an honest belief that a substance was baking soda would not have the *mens rea* for possession even if the substance turned out to be heroin. "The essence of the crime is the possession of

77   *R. v. Khawaja*, 2010 ONCA 862.

78   The reference in that section to objective foreseeability that occurs when the accused ought to know that his or her actions would cause death is unconstitutional because s. 7 of the *Canadian Charter of Rights and Freedoms*, Part I of the *Constitution Act, 1982*, being Schedule B to the *Canada Act 1982* (U.K.), 1982, c. 11 [*Charter*] has been interpreted as requiring a minimal *mens rea* for murder of knowledge that death is likely to occur. *Martineau*, above note 6.

79   *Martineau, ibid.*, discussed in ch. 2(B)(4)(e), "Fault Requirements."

80   *Beaver*, above note 15.

the forbidden substance and in a criminal case there is in law no possession without knowledge of the character of the forbidden substance."[81]
As discussed in chapter 3, however, a person who makes a mistake
about whether a particular drug is illegal would not have a defence
because ignorance of the law is no excuse.

In *Lucas*,[82] the Supreme Court interpreted the requirement that the
prosecutor prove that an accused who has been charged with defamatory libel know that the statements were false as requiring proof of the
accused's subjective knowledge. The Court then qualified this correct
statement by indicating that the accused's

> subjective understanding of the statements . . . should not be deter-
> minative if this position was adopted, it would always be open to an
> accused to argue that the "real" meaning which they believed to be
> true was quite different from the meaning which would be object-
> ively attributed to it by any reasonable reader. Rather the question
> should be whether the appellants knew that the message, as it would
> be understood by a reasonable person, was false.

This formulation runs the risk of confusing subjective and objective
standards of liability and diluting the relatively high level of subjective *mens rea* required by proof of guilty knowledge. Knowledge is a
subjective form of *mens rea* and a person who claims to ignore what a
reasonable person would know runs the real risk of being found guilty.
Nevertheless, the ultimate issue is the particular accused's knowledge,
not what a reasonable person would know.

In *Dynar*,[83] the Supreme Court observed that knowledge has "two
components—truth and belief" and that only belief is relevant to the
determination of a subjective *mens rea*. The truth of the matter is an
objective fact that is required to establish the *actus reus* not the *mens
rea*. Thus, an accused who stabbed a manikin believing it to be human
would have the subjective *mens rea* of murder. Because the manikin
was not in truth a human being, however, there would be no *actus reus*
for murder. Even though the accused had the *mens rea* required for
murder, he or she could only be charged with attempted murder.

---

81   *Ibid.* at 140.
82   *R. v. Lucas* (1998), 123 C.C.C. (3d) 97 at 131 (S.C.C.).
83   *Dynar*, above note 72 at 506.

4) Wilful Blindness

A more recent and controversial form of subjective *mens rea* is wilful blindness, which is now seen as a substitute for knowledge in cases where an accused subjectively sees the need for further inquiries about the existence of prohibited consequences or circumstances but deliberately fails to make such inquiries because he or she does not want to know the truth.[84] The Supreme Court stated in *Sansregret*:

> Wilful blindness is distinct from recklessness because, while recklessness involves knowledge of a danger or a risk and persistence in a course of conduct which creates a risk that the prohibited result will occur, wilful blindness arises when a person who has become aware of the need for some inquiry declines to make the inquiry because he does not wish to know the truth. He would prefer to remain ignorant. The culpability in recklessness is justified by consciousness of the risk and by proceeding in the face of it, while in wilful blindness it is justified by the accused's fault in deliberately failing to inquire when he knows there is reason for inquiry.[85]

On the facts of the case, the trial judge had acquitted the accused of rape on the basis that while the risk that the complainant had not consented would have been obvious to anyone "in his right mind," it was not to the accused, who "saw what he wanted to see, heard what he wanted to hear, believed what he wanted to believe." The Supreme Court reversed and entered a conviction on the basis that the accused was wilfully blind to the lack of consent because he "was aware of the likelihood of the complainant's reaction to his threats." To proceed in the circumstances was "self-deception to the point of wilful blindness. . . . Where the accused is deliberately ignorant as a result of blinding himself to reality the law presumes knowledge, in this case knowledge of the nature of the consent."[86]

Some commentators have argued that if the accused in *Sansregret* genuinely believed that the complainant consented, there was no reason for him to make the inquiry, and the Court was actually imposing liability on the basis of negligence. This interpretation seems strained, given the facts of the case, which included a break-in and violence, as well as a similar encounter less than a month earlier in which the same complainant had reported that she had been raped by the accused. The Supreme Court seems to suggest that given these facts, the accused

---

84   *R. v. Briscoe*, [2010] 1 S.C.R. 411 at paras. 21 and 24 [*Briscoe*].
85   *Sansregret*, above note 18 at 235.
86   *Ibid.*

knew there was a likelihood that the complainant was not consenting, but he deliberately blinded himself to that possibility. This reading is supported by the Court's reliance on Glanville Williams's text in *Sansregret* where he states that "a court can only properly find wilful blindness only where it can almost be said that the defendant actually knew. He suspected the fact, he realized its probability, but he refrained from obtaining the final confirmation because he wanted in any event to be able to deny knowledge."[87]

In subsequent cases, the Supreme Court has defined wilful blindness as "deliberately choosing not to know" when the accused strongly suspects that such an inquiry would fix them with guilty knowledge.[88] The Court has made clear that a mere failure to inquire, though it may be evidence of negligence, will not be enough for a finding of wilful blindness. In *R. v. Briscoe*, the Court adopted Professor Don Stuart's description of wilful blindness as deliberate ignorance and ruled in *Briscoe* that the trial judge erred in not instructing the jury that wilful blindness was available as a substitute fault element for knowledge in a case where the accused had a "strong, well-founded suspicion" that the victim would be sexually assaulted and killed but had declared: "[W]hatever you guys wanna do just do it. Don't do it around me. I don't want to see nothing."[89]

The Court has made clear that wilful blindess is a subjective form of fault, distinct and greater than both recklessness and negligence. At the same time, wilful blindness is still a difficult concept to administer especially with respect to the ambiguous statement that an accused will only be wilfully blind if they "suspect" the prohibited consequence or circumstance.[90] It is clear that the accused must subjectively suspect,

---

87   Glanville Williams, *Criminal Law: The General Part*, 2d ed. (London: Stevens, 1961) at 159, cited in *Sansregret*, above note 18 at 586 and *Briscoe*, above note 84 at para. 22.

88   *R. v. Jorgensen* (1995), 102 C.C.C. (3d) 97 at 135 (S.C.C.).

89   *Briscoe*, above note 84 at para. 25.

90   The Quebec Court of Appeal has stressed the subjective nature of wilful blindness by stating that the issue was not whether the accused "'*should*' have known or should '*normally*' have known from the suspicious circumstances that her husband was probably involved in a conspiracy to import cocaine. The question was whether the circumstances were such that she, herself, was, in fact, suspicious that this was the case, but deliberately refrained from making inquiries so that she could remain in ignorance as to the truth." *R. v. Comtois Barbeau* (1996), 110 C.C.C. (3d) 69 at 95 (Que. C.A.) [emphasis in original]. The Ontario Court of Appeal has similarly stressed that "culpability on the basis of wilful blindness rests on a finding of deliberate ignorance. An accused who suspects that property is stolen but declines to make the inquiries that will confirm that suspicion, preferring instead to remain ignorant is culpable." *R. v. Lagace* (2003),

but it is still not clear whether the subjective suspicion must relate to the mere possibility or probability that the prohibited consequences or circumstances exist. In order to be equated with knowledge and distinguished from recklessness, wilful blindness should require more than a subjective suspicion about a mere possibility but rather a well founded suspicion that is closer to knowledge of a probability that the prohibited circumstances or consequences will occur. The fact that the accused should have been suspicious or only recognized the possibility as opposed to the probability of the unlawful act occurring should not be sufficient if wilful blindness is truly to be the equivalent of guilty knowledge.

5) Recklessness

Recklessness is a lower form of *mens rea* than intent, purpose, wilfulness, knowledge, or wilful blindness, but in Canada it is still a form of subjective *mens rea*. In Canadian criminal law, a person acts recklessly if he or she has adverted to or become aware of the risk of the prohibited conduct. In *Sansregret*,[91] the Supreme Court stressed the importance of distinguishing recklessness from negligence:

> In accordance with well-established principles for the determination of criminal liability, recklessness, to form a part of the criminal *mens rea*, must have an element of the subjective. It is found in the attitude of one who, aware that there is danger that his conduct could bring about the result prohibited by the criminal law, nevertheless persists, despite the risk. It is, in other words, the conduct of one who sees the risk and who takes the chance.

Recklessness requires subjective advertence to the prohibited risk and can be distinguished from negligence, which requires only that a reasonable person in the accused's circumstances would have recognized the risk.[92] A person recklessly commits sexual assault if he recognizes the risk that the woman is not consenting, while a person would negligently commit sexual assault if a reasonable person in his circumstances would have known there was a risk that the woman does not

---

181 C.C.C. (3d) 12 at para. 28 (Ont. C.A.). The Court of Appeal also referred to "actual suspicion, combined with a conscious decision not to make inquiries which could confirm that suspicion, is equated in the eyes of criminal law with knowledge." *R. v. Duong* (1998), 124 C.C.C.(3d) 392 at para. 23.

91   *Sansregret*, above note 18 at 233.
92   *O'Grady v. Sparling* (1960), 128 C.C.C. 1 at 13 (S.C.C.).

consent. As will be seen, the actual fault element for sexual assault falls somewhere in between recklessness and negligence.

Recklessness requires that the accused is subjectively aware of the possibility of the prohibited act, whereas knowledge requires that the accused be aware of the probability of the prohibited act. Recklessness is a common form of subjective *mens rea*. Martin J.A. has stated that "the general *mens rea* which is required and which suffices for most crimes where no mental element is mentioned in the definition of the crime, is either the intentional or reckless bringing about of the result which the law, in creating the offence, seeks to prevent."[93] Similarly, the common law presumption in Sault Ste. Marie[94] that a criminal offence have subjective *mens rea* includes recklessness. Recklessness requires only subjective awareness of the risk of the prohibited act, as opposed to knowledge of the likelihood of the prohibited act.

6) Transferred Subjective *Mens Rea*

Section 229(b) codifies the common law doctrine of transferred intent. The *mens rea* of intentionally or knowingly causing death to one person is transferred to the killing of the victim, even though the accused "does not mean to cause death or bodily harm" to the victim and does so "by accident or mistake." This provision was applied in R. v. Droste (No. 2)[95] to convict an accused who, in a deliberate attempt to kill his wife, set fire to a car, causing two children buckled in the back seat to die of asphyxiation. The Court concluded that because the attempted murder of the accused's wife was planned and deliberate, the intent of planning and deliberation, as well as the guilty knowledge that death would result, could be transferred to the childrens' deaths. The Manitoba Court of Appeal has decided that section 229(b) should not be applied when the accused intends to kill himself but ends up killing another person. The Court of Appeal held that a person who intends to kill himself does not have the same moral blameworthiness as a person who intends to kill another person, but then kills yet another person by accident or mistake.[96]

The courts may transfer intent in other contexts. An accused has been convicted of assault causing bodily harm when, in an attempt to

---

93   *Buzzanga*, above note 7 at 381.

94   *Sault Ste. Marie*, above note 14 at 362.

95   (1984), 10 C.C.C. (3d) 404 (S.C.C.).

96   R. v. *Fontaine* (2002), 162 C.C.C. (3d) 360 at paras. 40–45 (Man. C.A.), rejecting R. v. *Brown* (1983), 4 C.C.C. (3d) 571 (Ont. H.C.) holding that an intent to commit suicide could be transferred under s. 229(b) of the *Code*.

strike another person, he caused bodily harm to a bystander.[97] Statutory and common law doctrines of transferred intent allow *mens rea* directed towards one person to be transferred to an *actus reus* that occurs in relation to another person.

C. THE DEGREES OF OBJECTIVE *MENS REA*

The Supreme Court has indicated that objective, as opposed to subjective, fault is constitutionally sufficient for unlawful act manslaughter and other criminal offences less serious than murder, attempted murder, and war crimes. Despite increasing acceptance of objective fault as a form of *mens rea*, there has been some uncertainty about how such a standard should be applied in a criminal prosecution. This topic raises some of the same dilemmas encountered when the courts apply objective standards to defences such as self-defence.[98] The central issue is how to adjust the objective standard so that it does not apply to those who cannot reasonably be held responsible for satisfying that standard, while not collapsing objective standards into subjective ones.

1) Who Is the Reasonable Person?

Some judges have been attracted to the idea of making the reasonable person resemble the accused, but this has yet to win majority support in the Supreme Court. In *Tutton*,[99] Lamer J. would have applied an objective standard to determine criminal negligence, but he would have modified it by making "'a generous allowance' for factors which are particular to the accused, such as youth, mental development, education." He noted that if this was done, "the adoption of a subjective or an objective test will, in practice, nearly if not always produce the same result."[100] In *Creighton*,[101] Lamer C.J. elaborated his views and held that the reasonable person used to determine objective liability should be invested with "any human frailties which might have rendered the accused incapable of having foreseen what the reasonable person would have foreseen," as well as any "enhanced foresight" derived from the accused's special knowledge or skill. Human frailties were defined as

---

97 *R. v. Deakin* (1974), 16 C.C.C. (2d) 1 (Man. C.A.).
98 See ch. 9, "Self-Defence, Necessity, and Duress."
99 *Tutton*, above note 11 at 140.
100 *Ibid.* at 143.
101 *Creighton*, above note 3 at 359–60.

"personal characteristics habitually affecting an accused's awareness of the circumstances which create risk."[102] They had to be characteristics that the accused could not control or manage in the circumstances. On the one hand, Lamer C.J. would have factored in the inexperience, youth, and lack of education of a mother who did not provide the necessities of life to her child,[103] while on the other hand, he would have considered the enhanced foresight of risk that an experienced drug or gun user would have when dealing with those dangerous objects.[104] Making the reasonable person more like the accused could make it more difficult to convict an accused who habitually was unaware of prohibited risks, while it could also make it easier to convict an accused who was more sensitive to the prohibited risk than the reasonable person.

The Lamer approach to individualizing the reasonable person has not been accepted by a majority of the Supreme Court.[105] In *Creighton*,[106] McLachlin J. for a 5:4 majority rejected the Lamer approach on the basis that it "personalizes the objective test to the point where it devolves into a subjective test, thus eroding the minimum standard of care which Parliament has laid down by the enactment of offenses of manslaughter and penal negligence." The only personal characteristics of the accused that are relevant in the majority's approach would be those that establish incapacity to appreciate the nature and quality of the prohibited conduct and consequences. Justice McLachlin elaborated:

> Mental disabilities short of incapacity generally do not suffice to negative criminal liability for criminal negligence. The explanations for why a person fails to advert to the risk inherent in the activity he or she is undertaking are legion. They range from simple absent-mindedness to attributes related to age, education and culture. To permit such a subjective assessment would be "co-extensive with the judgment of each individual, which would be as variable as the length of the foot of each individual" leaving "so vague a line as to afford no

---

102 *Ibid.* at 362–63.
103 *Naglik*, above note 30.
104 *Creighton*, above note 3; *Gosset*, above note 29.
105 In *Hundal*, above note 11 at 104, there was some recognition that "[t]he potential harshness of the objective standard may be lessened by the consideration of certain personal factors." These were, however, held inapplicable to the offence of dangerous driving because licensing requirements ensure "that all who drive have a reasonable standard of physical health and capability, mental health and a knowledge of the reasonable standard required of all licensed drivers." *Ibid.* at 108.
106 *Creighton*, above note 3 at 381–82.

rule at all, the degree of judgment belonging to each individual being infinitely various." . . . Provided the capacity to appreciate the risk is present, lack of education and psychological predispositions serve as no excuse for criminal conduct, although they may be important factors to consider in sentencing.[107]

In short, the reasonable person will not be invested with the personal characteristics of the accused unless the characteristics are so extreme as to create an incapacity to appreciate the prohibited risk or the quality of the prohibited conduct. An example given by McLachlin J. of a relevant personal characteristic when applying objective standards would be the accused's illiteracy if he or she was charged with a crime stemming from the mishandling of a marked container containing a dangerous substance. The accused's age and level of education, however, would not normally be considered when applying the reasonable person standard.

Chief Justice Lamer subsequently accepted this unmodified objective approach and justified it on the basis that it applied to those who make a voluntary decision to perform conduct that is subject to punishment for negligence.[108] The Court has continued in *Beatty* to apply a strict reasonable person standard with respect to crimes of negligence:

> Short of incapacity to appreciate the risk or incapacity to avoid creating it, personal attributes such as age, experience, and education are not relevant. The standard against which the conduct must be measured is always the same—it is the conduct expected of the reasonably prudent person in the circumstances.[109]

As will be seen in chapter 9, however, Chief Justice Lamer's modified objective approach of endowing the reasonable person with similar characteristics, frailties, and experiences as the accused has won the day with respect to defences in which the accused is held up to standards of reasonable conduct. The justification for the different approaches would appear to be that an accused who commits a crime with a valid defence such as provocation, self-defence, duress, or necessity does not voluntarily commit the crime and that the accused's characteristics and experiences must be considered in determining whether he or she had no realistic choice but to commit the crime.

---

107 *Ibid.* at 390–91.
108 *Hibbert*, above note 56.
109 *Beatty*, above note 12 at para. 40.

2) Degree of Negligence

Another manner of adapting a negligence standard to the criminal context is to require not only unreasonable conduct or simple negligence, but also conduct that amounts to a marked departure from that of the reasonable person. In *Tutton*,[110] McIntyre J. stated that criminal negligence required "proof of conduct which reveals a *marked and significant departure* from the standard which could be expected of a reasonably prudent person in the circumstances," as opposed to simple negligence. In *Hundal*,[111] the Court indicated that although dangerous driving was to be determined on an objective basis, "the trier of fact should be satisfied that the conduct amounted to a *marked departure* from the standard of care that a reasonable person would observe in the accused's situation." In *Beatty*, the Supreme Court suggested that a requirement of a *marked departure* from reasonable standards was necessary to distinguish criminal from civil negligence and to ensure restraint in the use of the criminal law.[112]

The Supreme Court has required a marked departure from the conduct of a reasonable person even when a criminal offence seems to require simple negligence. In *Finlay*[113] and *Gosset*,[114] the Supreme Court considered manslaughter charges based on the unlawful act of careless use of a firearm. The Court required that a person demonstrate a marked departure from the standard of care of a reasonably prudent person in the circumstances, even though the offence seemed only to require careless use of a firearm. A legislated careless or simple negligence standard was essentially read up to require a more severe form of negligence.[115] This is an important development that is now constitutionally required given the Court's recognition in *Beatty* that a marked departure standard is required under section 7 of the *Charter*. A constitutional requirement would justify the court in disregarding Parliament's intent to criminalize simple carelessness in the use of a firearm and essentially to read the careless standard up to require a marked departure from reasonable conduct.

---

110 *Tutton*, above note 11 at 140 [emphasis added]. See also *R. v. Waite* (1989), 48 C.C.C. (3d) 1 at 5 (S.C.C.) [*Waite*] making reference to a "marked and substantial departure."
111 *Hundal*, above note 11 at 108 [emphasis added].
112 *Beatty*, above note 12. See also the discussion in ch. 2.
113 *Finlay*, above note 29 at para. 24.
114 *Gosset*, above note 29.
115 *Gosset*, *ibid.*, at 505, Lamer C.J.; at 512, McLachlin J. See also *R. v. Gunning*, [2005] 1 S.C.R. 627 at para. 21 stating: "[T]he gravamen of the offence is conduct that constitutes a marked departure from the standard of care of a reasonably prudent person."

In *R. v. J.F.*,[116] the Supreme Court distinguished the *marked departure* standard that, following *Beatty* as well as *Finlay* and *Gosset*, applies as a minimal fault requirement to all forms of negligence used for purposes of criminal liability, from a slightly higher standard of *marked and substantial* departure that applies to criminal negligence. The Court cited a number of cases in which appellate courts had distinguished criminal negligence causing death or bodily harm from dangerous driving, on the basis that criminal negligence requires a marked and substantial departure from reasonable conduct whereas dangerous driving only required a marked departure.[117] In the result, the Court held that the offence of failing to provide necessities of life required "a marked departure" from the standard of a reasonable caregiver whereas offences of criminal negligence causing death or bodily harm would require "*a marked and substantial departure* (as opposed to a *marked departure*) from the conduct of a reasonably prudent parent in the circumstances . . . ."[118] The Court justified its approach by noting that criminal negligence was subject to more serious maximum sentences than failing to provide the necessities of life. In addition, the definition of criminal negligence in section 219 of the *Code*[119] underlines the severity of the fault of criminal negligence by defining it as conduct that "shows wanton or reckless disregard for the lives or safety of other persons" and McIntyre J. had previously defined criminal negligence as required a marked and substantial departure from reasonable conduct.[120]

The decision in *J.F.* recognizes subtle and fine distinctions in the degrees of objective fault between the general rule of proof of a marked departure from reasonable conduct, and the higher standard of marked and substantial departures from reasonable conduct that is required for criminal negligence. This complicates the law, but in a not altogether

---

116 2008 SCC 60.

117 See *R. v. L.(J.)* (2006), 204 C.C.C. (3d) 324 (Ont. C.A.); *R. v. Fortier* (1998), 127 C.C.C. (3d) 217 at 223 (Que. C.A.); *R. v. Palin* (1999), 135 C.C.C. (3d) 119 (Que. C.A.).

118 *R. v. J.F.*, above note 116 at para. 9 [emphasis in original]. The Court did note, however, that the actual case which concluded that a conviction of criminal negligence causing death was inconsistent with an acquittal of failing to provide the necessities of life, did "not turn on the nature or extent of the difference between the two standards." *Ibid.* at para. 10.

119 Above note 2.

120 *Waite*, above note 110 at 5. In *Tutton*, above note 11 at 140, he formulated the criminal negligence standard slightly differently as a "marked and significant departure" from that expected of a reasonable person. His interchangeable use of "significant" and "substantial" in these two cases suggests that there is no real difference between the two terms.

different way than distinctions between the various degrees of subjective fault. It also means that the fault required for manslaughter may differ depending on whether manslaughter by criminal negligence is charged (requiring marked and substantial departures) or manslaughter by the commission of an unlawful act (requiring a marked departure) is charged.[121]

3) The Relevance of Subjective Perceptions and Exculpatory Factors to Objective Fault

Another manner of mitigating the potential harshness of objective standards is to factor in the accused's subjective perception of the surrounding circumstances and other subjective but exculpatory factors when determining whether the reasonable person would have been aware of the risk of the prohibited conduct. In the pre-*Charter* case of *R. v. Vasil*,[122] the Supreme Court held that although section 229(c) allowed an accused to be convicted of murder on the basis that he or she ought to have known death was likely to result, this objective standard was to be applied with respect to the circumstances known to the accused at that time. Thus, the jury would be allowed to consider subjective factors, including the accused's intoxication, in determining whether he actually knew that children were sleeping in a house that he set afire.

In *Tutton*,[123] McIntyre J. seemed to indicate that an accused's subjective perception of circumstances could be relevant in determining whether he or she acted with criminal negligence. He warned "the application of an objective test . . . may not be made in a vacuum" because:

> Events occur within the framework of other events and actions and when deciding on the nature of the questioned conduct, surrounding circumstances must be considered. The decision must be made on a consideration of the facts existing at the time and in relation to the accused's perception of those facts. Since the test is objective, the accused's perception of the facts is not to be considered for the purpose of assessing malice or intention on the accused's part but only to form a basis for a conclusion as to whether or not the accused's conduct, *in view of his perception of the facts*, was reasonable.[124]

---

121 See ch. 10(A)(6), "Manslaughter."
122 (1981), 58 C.C.C. (2d) 97 (S.C.C.).
123 *Tutton*, above note 11.
124 *Ibid.* at 141 [emphasis added].

Although the accused must live up to the standard of a reasonable person, that standard of conduct could be determined on the basis of the accused's own perception of the circumstances. An example cited by McIntyre J., which has recently been cited with approval by the Court in *Beatty*, is the need to factor in information provided to the accused that there was no combustible or explosive material stored near the site of welding.[125] The Court indicated that "a reasonably held mistake of fact may provide a complete defence if, based on the accused's reasonable perception of the facts, the conduct measured up to the requisite standard of care."[126]

In a case dealing with the offence of dangerous driving causing death, Cory J. maintained that objective fault must be determined in the context of the events surrounding the incident. However, Cory J. did not stress, as McIntyre J. had, that the accused's own perception of the facts should be considered. Rather, Cory J. stated:

> Although an objective test must be applied to the offence of dangerous driving, it will remain open to the accused to raise a reasonable doubt that a reasonable person would have been aware of the risks in the accused's conduct . . . .
>
> . . . [I]n order to convict, the trier of fact must be satisfied that a reasonable person in similar circumstances ought to have been aware of the risk and danger involved in the conduct manifested by the accused.[127]

These comments suggest that the issue is whether the reasonable person in the same circumstances as the accused would have been aware of the risk of the prohibited act. The Court in *Beatty* cited with approval the reference by Cory J. about the need to take a contextualized approach that considers, for example, whether the accused has suffered an unexpected heart attack, seizure, or detached retina.[128] At the same time and as discussed in chapter 3, the majority of the Court rejected the approach of the dissenters who would have applied the marked departure standard to the *actus reus* and would have held that a momentary lapse produced by falling asleep at the wheel without more did not satisfy either the *actus reus* or the *mens rea* of dangerous driving.[129]

The Court's decision in *Beatty* suggests that courts should not ignore factors subjective to the accused when determining whether the accused has a criminal *mens rea* based on negligence. The Court re-

---

125 *Beatty*, above note 12 at para. 38.
126 *Ibid.*
127 *Hundal*, above note 11 at 106–8.
128 *Beatty*, above note 12 at para. 37.
129 *Ibid.* at para. 72 per McLachlin C.J. in dissent.

ferred to situations where the presumption that a reasonable person in the accused's situation would have been aware of the risk "cannot be sustained because a reasonable person in the position of the accused would not have been aware of the risk or, alternatively, would not have been able to avoid creating the danger."[130] Consistent with basic criminal law principles including the presumption of innocence, the *mens rea* cannot be automatically deduced from the commission of the criminal act even if the act such as driving on the wrong side of the road is itself dangerous or a marked departure from reasonable conduct.[131] Relevant factors to be considered in determining *mens rea* may include the accused's perception of the circumstances, including mistaken belief that the prohibited circumstances or consequences did not exist. The trier of fact should also consider other explanations offered by the accused and contextual factors such as the accused's sudden incapacity. Although this requirement runs some risk of confusing a jury (and students) about the distinction between subjective and objective fault, it makes sense given the need to consider all relevant evidence when assessing *mens rea*. For example, it would be overly harsh not to allow the accused to lead evidence that he subjectively but mistakenly believed the situation to be safe even though this mistake of fact may not absolve the accused of responsibility under objective fault standards based on marked departure from reasonable standards.

The purpose of examining factors subjective to the accused is not to determine whether the accused was subjectively at fault but only to determine whether there is a reasonable doubt about whether the accused's conduct in the circumstances constituted a marked departure from standards of reasonable care. The Court in *Beatty* warned that the same standard of reasonable conduct will be applied to all accused and that the accused will not be exonerated simply because he or she did not subjectively advert to the risk. *Beatty* makes clear that the mere fact that the accused has engaged in a dangerous act, such as driving on the wrong side of the road, is not determinative of the fault of a marked departure. Courts should consider all the evidence including the accused's actual state of mind and any explanation offered by the accused in determining whether the Crown has proven a marked departure from reasonable conduct beyond a reasonable doubt.

---

130 *Ibid.*

131 I disagree with Manning and Sankoff's assertion that "once it is determined that the accused's conduct was sufficiently dangerous to rise to the standard of criminal negligence, any other aspect of the analysis is simply going to be a formality." M. Manning & P. Sankoff, *Criminal Law*, 4th ed. (Markham, ON: LexisNexis, 2009) at 201.

The Supreme Court subsequently affirmed its approach in *Beatty* of requiring a marked departure from a reasonable standard of care and not deducing such fault simply from the commission of an objectively dangerous act. In *R. v Roy*,[132] the Court unanimously acquitted a person of dangerous driving causing death after he drove into the path of an oncoming tractor-trailer when entering a highway at a difficult intersection in foggy and snowy weather. The Court stressed the seriousness of the criminal offence and the need to establish fault and not simply deduce it from the commission of an objectively dangerous act. Even at the *actus reus* stage, it emphasized that triers of fact should not reason backwards from the tragic consequences of traffic accidents, but rather should conduct a meaningful inquiry to determine whether the manner of driving was dangerous to the public given all the circumstances.[133] In addition, the trier of fact must find fault going beyond mere carelessness and amounting to a marked departure from the standard of care expected from a reasonable person. All the circumstances, including any evidence of the accused's state of mind or any explanation given for the commission of the *actus reus*,[134] should be considered in making this fault determination. At the same time, the ultimate issue is whether there was a marked departure from the standard of care that a reasonable person would take in the circumstances. Consistent with *Creighton*,[135] the accused's age, experience, or education is not relevant unless it rendered the accused incapable of appreciating the risk.[136] The Court has thus stressed the importance of finding fault in addition to an *actus reus* and the need for a marked departure from reasonable conduct as a means of ensuring that any objective standard of fault is appropriate for determining criminal liability. This case solidifies the majority decision in *Beatty* by indicating that only a marked departure from reasonable conduct and not mere carelessness will be sufficient to establish criminal liability, and that all the evidence must be examined and fault should not be automatically deduced even from a dangerous act.

---

132 2012 SCC 26. The Court acquitted the accused on the basis that "[t]he record here discloses a single and momentary error in judgment with tragic consequences. It does not support a reasonable inference that the appellant displayed a marked departure from the standard of care expected of a reasonable person in the same circumstances so as to justify conviction for the serious criminal offence of dangerous driving causing death." *Ibid.* at para. 55.

133 *Ibid.* at para. 34.

134 *Ibid.* at para. 39.

135 Above note 3.

136 Above note 132 at para. 38.

D. MISTAKE OF FACT

Mistake of fact is a controversial defence that conceptually depends on the *mens rea* of the particular offence. If subjective awareness of prohibited circumstances is required, the Crown will not be able to establish the fault element if the accused honestly, but not necessarily reasonably, believes those circumstances do not exist. On the other hand, if the fault element of the offence requires only that a reasonable person would have recognized the prohibited circumstance or risk, then any defence based on mistake must be honest *and* reasonable. Finally, even a reasonable mistake of fact would not be a defence to an absolute liability offence. All that would matter would be whether the accused in fact committed the prohibited act.

Deducing the existence and nature of a mistake of fact defence from the fault element of the offence may, however, be too mechanical. It is possible that a mistake of fact may be based on a combination of subjective and objective factors. For example, section 273.2(b) of the *Criminal Code* now provides that the accused's belief that the complainant consented to the sexual activity is not a defence if the accused did not take reasonable steps, in the circumstances known to him at the time, to ascertain that the complainant was consenting. As will be discussed below, this creatively combines objective and subjective fault elements.

1) Early Cases

Mistake of fact defences have frequently been influenced by policy concerns not derived from the fault element of the particular offence. Courts were initially reluctant to accept mistake of fact as a defence. In R. v. Prince,[137] an accused was convicted of unlawfully abducting an unmarried girl under sixteen years of age without her parents' permission, even though he had an honest *and* reasonable belief that the girl was eighteen. Bramwell B. concluded: "The legislature has enacted that if anyone does this wrong act, he does it at the risk of her turning out to be under sixteen."[138] He did, however, concede that an accused would have no *mens rea* if he made a subjective mistake about other elements of the offence, such as whether he had received permission from the parents. Only one judge would have acquitted the accused on the basis that

---

137 (1875), L.R. 2 C.C.R. 154.
138 *Ibid.* at 175.

a mistake of facts, on reasonable grounds, to the extent that if the facts were as believed the acts of the prisoner would make him guilty of no criminal offence at all, is an excuse, and that such excuse is implied in every criminal charge and every criminal enactment in England.[139]

The above passage was adopted in the subsequent case of *Tolson*,[140] so that a mistake of fact was originally recognized as a defence on the basis that it must be both honest *and* reasonable.

2) Mistake Related to the Degree of Fault

With the rise of subjective *mens rea*, courts began to recognize the possibility that an accused could have an honest but not necessarily reasonable belief in a state of circumstances that would make his activity innocent. In *R. v. Rees*,[141] the accused was charged with knowingly contributing to the delinquency of a person under eighteen who he believed to be older. Cartwright J. concluded:

> [T]he essential question is whether the belief entertained by the accused is an honest one and that the existence or non-existence of reasonable grounds for such a belief is merely relevant evidence to be weighed by the tribunal of fact in determining such essential question.

He conceded that the issue might be different if Parliament had not used the word "knowingly," or had specifically excluded a mistake about the girl's age as a possible defence. A year later, Cartwright J. acquitted an accused found in possession of an illegal drug because the accused thought that the substance was harmless. He stressed that the offence required subjective *mens rea*, and that "in a criminal case there is in law no possession without knowledge of the character of the forbidden substance."[142] Two judges dissented, on the basis that Parliament had intended to enact an absolute prohibition of being in possession of the illegal drugs. An absolute liability offence would, of course, allow no defence of mistake of fact.[143] An offence based on negligence would af-

---

139 *Ibid.* at 170.
140 *Tolson*, above note 1 at 181 and 189. In *D.P.P. v. Morgan* (1975), [1976] A.C. 182 (H.L.) the House of Lords reversed this decision and held in a 3:2 decision that the accused's mistaken belief in a woman's consent must be honest, but not necessarily reasonable, to be a defence to rape.
141 *Rees*, above note 15 at 11.
142 *Beaver*, above note 15.
143 *R. v. Pierce Fisheries Ltd.*, [1970] 5 C.C.C. 193 (S.C.C.).

ford a defence of mistake of fact "if the accused *reasonably* believed in a mistaken set of facts which, if true, would render the act or omission innocent."[144] As will be seen in chapter 6, a reasonable mistake of fact is necessary when the accused is charged with a regulatory offence that requires strict liability.

3) Mistake of Fact and Drug Offences

As discussed above, an accused would have a defence of mistake of fact if he or she believed that a substance was a harmless substance and not illegal drugs.[145] Courts have, however, been unwilling to apply this strict logic when an accused makes a mistake as to the nature of an illegal drug. In *R. v. Burgess*,[146] an accused was convicted of possession of opium, even though he thought the drug was hashish. This reasoning was extended in *R. v. Kundeus*,[147] when an accused was convicted of trafficking in LSD that he thought was mescaline. Mescaline was a prohibited drug, but not one carrying as serious a penalty as LSD. Laskin C.J.C. dissented on the basis that it was unfair to convict an accused of a more serious offence when he had the *mens rea* only for the commission of the less serious offence. In his view, the accused did not have the *mens rea* required to be convicted of selling LSD because he never thought he was selling LSD.

4) Mistake of Fact and Sexual Assault

Although the contours of a mistake of fact defence can be deduced at a conceptual level from the fault requirement of the specific offence, there may be a case for combining elements of subjective and objective fault for mistake of fact in some contexts. A purely subjective mistake of fact defence may not adequately protect victims of crime and social interests in giving people incentives to avoid unnecessary and harmful mistakes of fact, while a purely objective mistake of fact defence may punish those who, given their failure to correctly perceive circumstances, proceeded in a manner that did not indicate a flagrant disregard for the law.

In *R. v. Pappajohn*,[148] the Supreme Court held that an accused in a rape trial could have a defence of honest but not necessarily reason-

---

144 *Sault Ste. Marie*, above note 14 at 374 [emphasis added].
145 *Beaver*, above note 15.
146 [1970] 3 C.C.C. 268 (Ont. C.A.).
147 (1975), 24 C.C.C. (2d) 276 (S.C.C.).
148 (1980), 52 C.C.C. (2d) 481 (S.C.C.) [*Pappajohn*].

able mistake that the complainant consented. Dickson J. derived the defence of mistake of fact from the *mens rea* of the particular offence. He concluded that because the *mens rea* of rape was subjective intent or recklessness relating to all the elements of the offence, it was not necessary that an accused's mistaken belief about consent be reasonable. He stated:

> It is not clear how one can properly relate reasonableness (an element in offences of negligence) to rape (a "true crime" and not an offence of negligence). To do so, one must, I think, take the view that the *mens rea* only goes to the physical act of intercourse and not to non-consent, and acquittal comes only if the mistake is reasonable. This, upon the authorities, is not a correct view, the intent in rape being not merely to have intercourse, but to have it with a non-consenting woman. If the jury finds that mistake, whether reasonable or unreasonable, there should be no conviction. If, upon the entire record, there is evidence of mistake to cast a reasonable doubt upon the existence of a criminal mind, then the prosecution has failed to make its case.[149]

Dickson J. added that although the accused's belief did not have to be reasonable, its reasonableness would be evidence considered by the jury to determine whether the accused actually had an honest belief in consent. The *Criminal Code* was subsequently amended to provide that the judge "shall instruct the jury, when reviewing all the evidence relating to the determination of the honesty of the accused's belief, to consider the presence or absence of reasonable ground for that belief."[150]

Although, the Supreme Court agreed on the conceptual nature of the defence of mistake of fact and its relation to the *mens rea* of the particular offence, it disagreed on its application in particular cases. In *Pappajohn*, Dickson J. was in dissent in concluding that the jury should have been instructed to consider the defence of mistake of fact. McIntyre J. for the majority held that the only realistic issue that could arise on the facts of the case was whether there was consent or no consent, not a third option of a mistaken belief in consent. In his view, there should be something more than the accused's assertion that he believed the complainant consented to justify instructing the jury on the mistaken belief defence.

---

149 *Ibid.* at 497.
150 *Code*, above note 2, s. 265(4). This was held to be consistent with ss. 7, 11(d) and (f) of the *Charter* in *R. v. Osolin* (1994), 86 C.C.C. (3d) 481 (S.C.C.).

The *Pappajohn* defence of an honest but not necessarily reasonable mistaken belief in consent remained controversial. This controversy was increased when the Supreme Court struck down so-called rape shield restrictions on the admission of the complainant's prior sexual conduct as a violation of the accused's *Charter* right to make full answer and defence, in part because the restrictions could deprive the accused of evidence to support the *Pappajohn* defence. McLachlin J. stated that the *Pappajohn* defence

> rests on the concept that the accused may honestly but mistakenly (and not necessarily reasonably) have believed that the complainant was consenting to the sexual act. If the accused can raise a reasonable doubt as to his intention on the basis that he honestly held such a belief, he is not guilty under our law and is entitled to an acquittal. The basis of the accused's honest belief in the complainant's consent may be sexual acts performed by the complainant at some other time or place.[151]

In dissent, L'Heureux-Dubé J. argued that the complainant's prior sexual activity with a person other than the accused would never provide an air of reality for the jury to consider a defence of mistake of fact, if they were "operating in an intellectual environment that is free of rape myth and stereotype about women."[152]

In response to *Seaboyer*, the law of sexual assault was amended in 1992 to restrict the availability of the mistake of fact defence. Section 273.2 now states that the accused's belief that the complainant consented is not a defence if it arose from the accused's "self-induced intoxication," his "recklessness or wilful blindness," or if "the accused did not take reasonable steps, in the circumstances known to the accused at the time, to ascertain that the complainant was consenting." This provision will be discussed in greater detail in chapter 10, which examines sexual assault among other offences, but it is also relevant to the various levels of fault.

The reference to recklessness contemplates that an accused who adverted to the risk that the complainant did not consent has always had the *mens rea* required for sexual assault. The reference to wilful blindness would seem to codify *Sansregret* and preclude the defence when an accused is subjectively aware of the need to inquire into consent, but deliberately declines to inquire because he does not wish to

---

151 *R. v. Seaboyer* (1992), 66 C.C.C. (3d) 321 at 393 (S.C.C.).
152 *Ibid.* at 363.

know the truth. It will be recalled that in *Sansregret*,[153] the trial judge acquitted the accused on the basis of *Pappajohn*, even though she found that anyone in his right mind, but not the accused, would have been aware of the risk that the complainant was not consenting to the sexual activity. The Supreme Court reversed and entered a conviction on the basis that even if the accused was not subjectively aware that there was no consent, he was wilfully blind to that prohibited risk. The culpability in wilful blindness was the accused's refusal to inquire whether the complainant was consenting, when he was "aware of the need for some inquiry . . . [but declined] to make the inquiry because he . . . [does] not wish to know the truth."[154] *Sansregret* narrowed the *Pappajohn* defence by holding that the accused was presumed to have guilty knowledge of the absence of consent when, knowing the need for inquiry as to consent, he remained deliberately ignorant.

The denial in section 273.2(b) of the mistake of fact unless the accused takes reasonable steps in the circumstances known to him at the time to ascertain whether the complainant was consenting to the activity in question combines subjective and objective fault elements in a novel and creative manner. As such, it breaks away from the idea in *Pappajohn* that the contours of the mistake of fact defence can be deduced from the fault element of the offence and it represents a fault level that blends subjective and objective fault. On the one hand, section 273.2(b) bases the accused's obligation to take reasonable steps to ascertain consent on the basis of what the accused subjectively knows of the circumstances. The accused's obligation to take reasonable steps is only based on what he subjectively knows at the time. On the other hand, section 273.2(b) requires the accused to act as a reasonable person would in the circumstances by taking reasonable steps to ascertain whether the complainant was consenting. Further issues relating to the interpretation and constitutionality of section 273.2 will be discussed in chapter 10 when the offence of sexual assault is examined in more detail.

---

153 *Sansregret*, above note 18.

154 *Ibid.* at 235. The accused had broken into his ex-girlfriend's apartment and threatened her with a knife. Less than a month earlier, the complainant had reported a rape after a similar incident with the accused.

E. MIXED SUBJECTIVE AND OBJECTIVE FAULT ELEMENTS

The classification of fault elements as subjective or objective adds analytical clarity and precision, but it would be a mistake to conclude that a particular offence must necessarily be completely subjective or objective. Some offences contain multiple elements and there is little reason why some of these elements may not require proof of subjective fault while others only require proof of objective fault. Justice L'Heureux-Dubé has stated "that the *mens rea* of a particular offence is composed of the totality of its component fault elements. The mere fact that most criminal offences require some subjective component does not mean that every element of the offence requires such a state of mind."[155] A mixed approach allows the fault requirement to be tailored to the particular element of the offence, but it also requires judges and juries to understand clearly that for some elements of an offence they must consider all the evidence that is relevant to determining the accused's subjective state of mind, whereas for other elements of the same offence, all they need to consider is how the accused's conduct measures up to the reasonable person standard.[156] Justice Dickson in *Pappajohn*[157] argued that it was "unfair to the jury, and to the accused, to speak in terms of two beliefs, one entertained by the accused, the other by the reasonable man." Mixed fault elements require such an approach. Despite the added complexity,[158] both the Supreme Court and Parliament have been attracted in recent years to mixed forms of liability so that some elements of the offence require proof of subjective fault while others require proof of objective fault.

In *R. v. Lohnes*,[159] the Supreme Court interpreted the offence of disturbing the peace as requiring proof of subjective fault as to the underlying act such as fighting or yelling, but objective fault in relation to the actual disturbance of the peace. Similarly, the offence of conspiracy to unduly lessen competition requires a subjective intention among the parties to agree on a course of action and the objective fault that it is reasonably foreseeable that the course of action would unduly lessen

---

155   *R. v. Hinchey* (1996), 111 C.C.C. (3d) 353 at 385 (S.C.C.).

156   Assuming that the accused is not incapable of perceiving the prohibited risk or circumstances. See *Creighton* discussed above, note 3.

157   *Pappajohn*, above note 148.

158   The complexity can be overstated given the practical reality that even in determining a subjective *mens rea*, the jury must rely in part on inferences about what is reasonable.

159   (1992), 69 C.C.C. (3d) 289 (S.C.C.).

competition.[160] In both of these cases, the objective fault elements dominate and the subjective fault only seems to preclude a conviction if the accused unintentionally and almost accidentally engages in an act that disturbs that peace or lessens competition.

A more integrated blending of subjective and objective fault elements is found in section 273.2(b), which provides that the accused's subjective belief that the complainant consented is not a defence to a sexual assault charge if "the accused did not take reasonable steps, in the circumstances known to the accused at the time, to ascertain that the complainant was consenting." The accused's defence of mistake of fact is in part based on the accused's own subjective perception of the circumstances, provided they are not based on self-induced intoxication, recklessness, or wilful blindness.[161] At the same time, the accused's obligation to take reasonable steps is an objective fault element that requires the accused to act as a reasonable person would in situations where consent is not clear. This is a mixed standard of subjective and objective fault and one that may strike the appropriate balance in the circumstances. Those engaged in sexual activity are being required to take reasonable steps to ascertain consent, but they are only required to do what is reasonable given their own subjective perception or knowledge of the circumstances. Another integrated blending of subjective and objective fault elements is found in the new section 22.2(c) of the *Code*, which provides for organizational fault on the basis that a senior officer of a corporation subjectively knows that a representative of the organization is or is about to be a party to a subjective intent offence, but fails to take all reasonable measures to stop the representative from being a party to the offence.[162]

CONCLUSION

Many of the uncertainties surrounding the fault element for crimes could be addressed by legislative reform that provides generic definitions of the various levels of fault, that explains their relation to the *actus reus*, and that specifies what level of fault is required should Parliament not specifically address the issue in the drafting of a particular offence. The general rule should be that *mens rea* will relate to all aspects of the *actus reus* and that the lowest form of subjective *mens rea*, namely recklessness, should be the minimum form of fault for offences

---

160 R. v. *Nova Scotia Pharamaceutical Society* (1992), 74 C.C.C. (3d) 289 (S.C.C.).
161 *Code*, above note 2, s. 273.2(a).
162 This provision will be examined in ch. 6, "Section 22.2 of the *Criminal Code*."

in the *Criminal Code*.[163] These standards are based on well-established common law presumptions. They are not constitutional standards under section 7 of the *Charter*, and Parliament can clearly depart from them when drafting particular offences.

Although not all levels of fault are the same, the number of fault elements could be reduced. Given the Court's determination to distinguish intent from motive or purpose[164] and its requirement that knowledge of the prohibited act is the constitutionally required fault element for murder,[165] it could be argued that knowledge, as opposed to intent, purpose, or wilfulness should be the highest level of subjective *mens rea*. At the same time, an intent *mens rea* may still be valuable with respect to crimes of peripheral involvement and other crimes, such as wilful promotion of hatred, in which caution should be exercised before employing the criminal sanction. Knowledge should be defined as the accused's certain belief that the prohibited consequences or circumstances exist. Recklessness, the lowest form of subjective *mens rea*, should be defined as an awareness of the risk that the prohibited circumstances or consequences exist but if included it should be a form of subjective fault based on deliberate ignorance and knowledge of the probability, not the mere possibility, that the prohibited act exists. A reformed *Criminal Code* could probably dispense with wilful blindness.

Negligence is a constitutionally sufficient fault element for most criminal offences. The Court has indicated that it should be interpreted to require a marked departure from the standard of care that a reasonable person would have taken in the circumstances. The Court in *Beatty* stressed that it was constitutionally necessary to clearly distinguish criminal negligence from civil negligence or the negligence that is presumed when a person or corporation charged with a regulatory offence fails to establish a defence of due diligence. It also stressed that courts should consider all the evidence including the accused's subjective state of mind and explanations offered by the accused to see if they raise a reasonable doubt about whether the accused engaged in a marked departure from standards of reasonable care. In other words, courts should not automatically deduce the mens rea of negligence from the commission of a negligent or dangerous actus reus. The courts have spent much time adapting negligence for the purpose of criminal liability. They have drawn some fine distinctions between degrees of negligence that are sufficient for purposes of criminal liability, distin-

---

163 *Sault Ste Marie*, above note 14 at 362.
164 *Hibbert*, above note 56.
165 *Martineau*, above note 6.

guishing the requirement of a marked departure that is necessary for all criminal uses of objective fault from an additional requirement of a marked and substantial departure that is required for criminal negligence.

In some cases, subjective and objective standards can be blended. An example would be section 273.2(b), which requires the accused to take reasonable steps to ascertain the complainant's consent to sexual activity (that is, act as a reasonable person would have), but only based on the circumstances subjectively known to the accused at the time. Section 22.2(c) similarly requires that a senior officer know that a representative of an organization is committing an offence, but then requires the senior officer to take all reasonable steps to stop the offence from being committed. Blended fault levels may make sense in a particular context, but they may present a challenge to juries and judges who must administer them.

A final issue is whether the reasonable person standard used to determine criminal negligence can be made to account for the frailties and capacities of the particular accused without collapsing the distinction between individual and subjective fault elements. As will be seen in chapter 9, the courts now consider the experience and characteristics of the accused when determining whether he or she acted reasonably for the purposes of most defences. In contrast, the Court in *Creighton* and in *Beatty* held that the characteristics of the accused are not relevant in determining whether there is a marked departure from the standard of care that a reasonable person would have taken in the circumstances except in the rare event that those characteristics render the accused incapable of appreciating or controlling the prohibited risk. The divide between the modified reasonable person used for defences and the unmodified reasonable person used to determine fault has, however, been contracted by cases which remind courts to consider all the evidence, including evidence relating to the accused's subjective state of mind, in determining whether an accused had the fault of negligence.[166] The divide has also been narrowed by cases that stress that the modified objective standard used in defences is designed to place triggering events in context, but not to alter the reasonable standard of conduct demanded of all persons.[167]

---

166 *Beatty*, above note 12.
167 See *R. v. Tran*, [2010] 3 S.C.R. 350, discussed in ch. 10(A)(4).

FURTHER READINGS

BRUDNER, A., "Guilt under the *Charter*: The Lure of Parliamentary Supremacy" (1998) 40 Crim. L.Q. 287

CAIRNS-WAY, R., "The *Charter*, the Supreme Court and the Invisible Politics of Fault" (1992) 12 Windsor Y.B. Access Just. 128

COLVIN, E., & S. ANAND, *Principles of Criminal Law*, 3d ed. (Toronto: Thomson Carswell, 2007) ch. 5

EDWARDS, J. LL.J., "The Criminal Degrees of Knowledge" (1954) 17 Mod. L. Rev. 295

MANNING, M., & P. SANKOFF, *Criminal Law*, 4th ed. (Markham: LexisNexis, 2009) ch.4

PACIOCCO, D., "Subjective and Objective Standards of Fault for Offences and Defences" (1995) 59 Sask. L. Rev. 271

PICKARD, T., "Culpable Mistakes and Rape" (1980) 30 U.T.L.J. 75

ROACH, K., "Mind the Gap: Canada's Different Criminal and Constitutional Standards of Fault" (2011) 61 U.T.L.J. 545.

SRIBOPOLOUS, J., "The Constitutionalization of 'Fault' in Canada: A Normative Critique" (1999) 41 Crim. L.Q. 227

STEWART, H., *Fundamental Justice: Section 7 of the Charter* (Toronto: Irwin Law, 2011) ch. 4

STUART, D., *Canadian Criminal Law: A Treatise*, 5th ed. (Toronto: Thomson Carswell, 2007) chs. 3 & 4

———, R.J. DELISLE, & A. MANSON, eds., *Towards a Just and Clear Criminal Law: A Criminal Reports Forum* (Toronto: Carswell, 1999)

CHAPTER 6

REGULATORY OFFENCES AND CORPORATE CRIME

Regulatory offences are enacted by the federal, provincial, and municipal governments and they far outnumber offences under the *Criminal Code*. Regulatory or public welfare offences emphasize the protection of the public from the risk of harm and the regulatory interests of the modern state, as opposed to the punishment of inherently wrongful and harmful conduct. A person or a corporation is convicted for performing a regulated activity without a licence or for failing to take specified safety prosecutions not because such non-compliance must be denounced and punished, but because it frustrates the regulatory ambitions of the modern state and creates a danger of harm. Courts have fashioned distinct rules to make it easier for the state to investigate and prosecute regulatory offences.

Traditionally, Canadian courts were faced with the stark choice of interpreting a regulatory offence to require either absolute liability, in which a conviction followed from the commission of the prohibited act, or proof beyond a reasonable doubt of a subjective fault element. The former standard could impose liability without fault, while the latter might frustrate the objectives of the regulatory scheme by requiring the Crown to prove that someone in a large organization had guilty knowledge. A third option, strict liability, has now emerged to dominate the field. Absolute liability offences are now vulnerable under section 7 of the *Charter*, at least when they deprive individuals of life, liberty, or security of the person by imposing terms of imprisonment.

Strict liability offences require fault based on negligence, and for this reason they satisfy the requirement under section 7 of the *Charter* that the morally innocent who act without fault not be punished. They do, however, violate the presumption of innocence under section 11(d) of the *Charter*. After the Crown proves the prohibited act of a strict liability offence beyond a reasonable doubt, negligence is presumed, and the accused must establish that it was not negligent. The accused makes its case by establishing on a balance of probabilities a defence of due diligence or reasonable mistake of fact. This approach violates the presumption of innocence by allowing a conviction even if there is a reasonable doubt about whether the accused was negligent. Nevertheless, it has been held to be justified because of the danger of acquitting an accused who has entered a regulated field and committed an *actus reus* when there is only a reasonable doubt about negligence. An accused who enters a regulated field can be expected to bear the burden of establishing that it was not negligent in allowing a harmful or dangerous act to occur.

Regulatory offences frequently apply to corporations that have engaged in harmful conduct such as pollution, misleading advertising, or violations of health, safety, or licensing requirements. The difficulty of establishing fault in a large organization is one of the reasons why it is the accused who must establish a lack of negligence when charged with a strict liability offence. Negligence for regulatory offences also does not have to be the marked departure from reasonable standards required when negligence is required for a criminal offence. When a corporation is charged with a criminal offence, however, it is necessary to find someone within the corporation who has the required fault. That individual must have enough responsibility within the corporation so that his or her fault can be attributed to the corporation and the Crown must prove fault beyond a reasonable doubt. This makes it considerably more difficult to convict a corporation of a criminal offence than a regulatory offence.

Until recently, only the fault of a "directing mind" of the corporation could be attributed to the corporation for the purpose of establishing its criminal liability. At the end of 2003, Parliament introduced extensive reforms designed to make it easier to convict and punish corporations and other organizations for criminal offences. The common law concept of a "directing mind," which had previously been restricted to those who had enough power to establish corporate policy, was replaced by a new statutory concept of a corporate "senior officer." This position includes not only those who play an important role in establishing a corporation's policies, including its board of directors, chief executive officer, and chief financial officer, but also those who are "responsible for managing an important aspect of the organization's activities."[1] Parliament also specified the fault required by the senior officer in order to convict the corporation of a negligence-based criminal offence[2] and a subjective intent criminal offence.[3] The criminal liability of corporations and other organizations is still based on the attribution of the fault of individuals to the organizations, but Parliament has replaced the common law definition of a corporation's directing mind with a broader concept that allows the fault of its senior officers to be attributed to the organization.

A. ABSOLUTE LIABILITY OFFENCES

An absolute liability offence requires the Crown to prove the commission of the prohibited act beyond a reasonable doubt, but does not require proof of any additional fault element such as guilty knowledge or negligence. For offences of absolute liability, "it is not open to the accused to exculpate himself by showing that he was free of fault."[4] This form of liability has been controversial. Supporters of absolute liability argue that its imposition can persuade a person or an organization to take additional measures to prevent the prohibited act. Opponents stress that the imposition of absolute liability can punish the morally innocent, and that one who has not acted with subjective fault or negligence cannot be expected to do anything more to prevent the prohibited act.[5]

Courts have recognized offences as requiring absolute liability when they have been convinced that the legislature did not intend the Crown to prove fault or that such a requirement would frustrate the

---

1   *Criminal Code*, R.S.C. 1985, c. C-46, [*Code*], s. 2 (as amended by S.C. 2003, c. 21).
2   *Ibid.*, s. 22.1.
3   *Ibid.*, s. 22.2.
4   *R. v. Sault Ste. Marie (City)* (1978), 40 C.C.C. (2d) 353 at 374, [1978] 2 S.C.R. 1299 (S.C.C.) [*Sault Ste. Marie*].
5   In *R. v. Hess* (1990), 59 C.C.C. (3d) 161 (S.C.C.) [*Hess*], Wilson J. argued for the majority that an absolute liability offence for statutory rape served no useful purpose and was unfair to the accused who believed that the girl was over fourteen years of age. In dissent, McLachlin J. would have upheld the offence under s. 1 of the *Canadian Charter of Rights and Freedoms*, Part I of the *Constitution Act, 1982*, being Schedule B to the *Canada Act 1982* (U.K.), 1982, c. 11 on the basis that it would discourage men from having sex with girls who might be under fourteen years of age.

purpose of the statute. In *R. v. Pierce Fisheries Ltd.*,[6] the Supreme Court held that the possession of undersized lobsters contrary to regulations under the *Fisheries Act* was an absolute liability offence. Ritchie J. refused to apply the Court's previous decision in *R. v. Beaver*[7] that a person could not be held to possess drugs without subjective knowledge. He reasoned:

> I do not think that a new crime was added to our criminal law by making regulations which prohibit persons from having undersized lobsters in their possession, nor do I think that the stigma of having been convicted of a criminal offence would attach to a person found to have been in breach of these regulations.[8]

This approach recognized that regulatory offences did not carry with them the same stigma as criminal offences and that it would be difficult to achieve the objectives of regulatory offences if proof of subjective fault was required. Cartwright J. dissented and, following *Beaver*, would have required proof that the accused knew about the undersized lobsters.

There are problems with both the decisions in *Pierce Fisheries*. Under the minority's approach of requiring subjective *mens rea*, it would be difficult, if not impossible, to establish that individuals who were directing minds of the corporation[9] knew that they were catching undersized lobsters. Under the majority's absolute liability approach, however, the corporation could have been convicted even if it had taken reasonable precautions to ensure that undersized lobsters were not caught by, for example, training its employees properly and using proper equipment. The majority imposed absolute liability that could punish without fault while the minority insisted on proof of subjective fault that would often be very difficult for the state to establish beyond a reasonable doubt in the regulatory context.

---

6   [1970] 5 C.C.C. 193 (S.C.C.) [*Pierce Fisheries*].

7   (1957), 118 C.C.C. 129 (S.C.C.).

8   *Pierce Fisheries*, above note 6 at 201.

9   Only the subjective *mens rea* of a person classified as one of the corporation's directing mind could be attributed to the corporation. See ch. 6(D)(1), "The Common Law Directing Mind Approach." Now the fault of senior officers, including important managers, could be attributed to the corporation.

1) The Common Law Presumption against Absolute Liability

In *Sault Ste. Marie*,[10] the Supreme Court indicated that it would not interpret public welfare or regulatory offences as absolute liability offences unless "the Legislature has made it clear that guilt would follow proof merely of the proscribed act." The Court, in effect, created a common law or judge-made presumption that regulatory offences would be interpreted as requiring strict liability unless the legislature clearly indicated that the offence was an absolute liability offence that would punish the accused who had acted reasonably and with due diligence.

In the actual case, the Court held that the offence of causing or permitting the discharge of pollution was a strict liability as opposed to an absolute liability or subjective *mens rea* offence. This meant that the accused had an opportunity to establish that it had acted reasonably or with due diligence to avoid the commission of the *actus reus*. The accused could also establish that it had made a reasonable mistake of fact. The Crown, however, did not have to prove subjective fault or even the fault of negligence beyond a reasonable doubt. The Supreme Court applied its new common law presumption against absolute liability in another case to hold that a prohibition on hunting within a quarter mile of a baited area was a strict liability offence.[11] The accused would again have an opportunity to demonstrate that it had exercised due diligence to avoid the prohibited act or made a reasonable mistake of fact. Negligence would be inferred as the fault element in these regulatory offences, even though it was not specifically mentioned in these offences. Under the *Charter*, the courts have generally been reluctant to interpret a statute as imposing absolute liability, unless the legislature has clearly indicated that this is its intent.[12] As will be seen, an absolute liability offence when combined with imprisonment may violate the *Charter*.

Offences will, however, be recognized as absolute liability offences if the legislature clearly indicates an intent that they not be interpreted as offences of strict liability. In making this determination courts examine multiple factors, including the subject matter and regulatory pattern of the legislation, the language used to define the offence, and

---

10   *Sault Ste. Marie*, above note 4 at 374 (C.C.C.).

11   *R. v. Chapin* (1979), 45 C.C.C. (2d) 333 (S.C.C.).

12   *R. v. I.L.W.U., Local 500*, [1994] 1 S.C.R. 150; *R. v. Rube* (1992), 75 C.C.C. (3d) 575 (S.C.C.); *R. v. Nickel City Transport (Sudbury) Ltd.* (1993), 82 C.C.C. (3d) 541 (Ont. C.A.) [*Nickel City Transport*]. But see *R. v. Polewsky* (2005), 202 C.C.C. (3d) 257 (Ont. C.A.), holding speeding offences to be absolute liability in part because the risk of imprisonment was remote.

the penalties. In the B.C. *Motor Vehicle Reference*, the legislature clearly indicated such an intent by stating that the offence of driving with a suspended driver's licence was "an absolute liability offence in which guilt is established by proof of driving, whether or not the defendant knew of the prohibition or suspension."[13] As will be discussed later, the Court ruled that absolute liability offences, when combined with imprisonment, violated section 7 of the *Charter* and could not be justified under section 1 especially as compared with the alternative of a strict liability offence.

Even after the British Columbia legislature deleted the specific reference to the offence of driving with a suspended driver's licence being an offence of absolute liability, the Supreme Court held in a 5:4 decision that the offence remained one of absolute liability.[14] The majority stressed that the offence applied when the accused had his or her licence "automatically and without notice" suspended after conviction of a number of offences. Given that any mistake that the accused made about whether his or her licence was suspended would be classified as a mistake of law and hence prohibited as a defence,[15] the majority concluded that the offence was one of absolute liability. The minority in this case, however, would have interpreted the offence as one of strict liability. Thus, the minority would allow a defence of due diligence in ascertaining whether the accused had been convicted of a driving offence and a defence of reasonable mistake of fact about the existence of such a conviction. It also warned that the majority was making an incursion into the principle that ignorance of the law was not an excuse by holding that the legislation effectively deprived the accused of a due diligence defence. *Pontes*[16] suggests that it is possible for an offence that does not clearly state it is one of absolute liability still to be classified as one.

In *Lévis (City) v. Tétreault*,[17] the Supreme Court indicated that it would "be better to return to the clear analytical framework and classification approach adopted in *Sault Ste Marie*," which requires "clear proof of legislative intent" for an absolute liability offence and does not ask the additional question of whether the legislature intended a due diligence defence to be available. Therefore, there is a presumption that

---

13 *Motor Vehicle Act*, R.S.B.C. 1979, c. 288, s. 94(2).

14 *R. v. Pontes* (1995), 100 C.C.C. (3d) 353 (S.C.C.) [*Pontes*]. As will be examined below, the absolute liability offence was not struck down, but the Court indicated that no one could be imprisoned for its violation.

15 See ch. 3(A)(4), "Ignorance of the Law," on the principle that ignorance or mistake of law do not constitute an excuse.

16 *Pontes*, above note 14.

17 [2006] 1 S.C.R. 420 at paras. 19 and 17 respectively [*Lévis*].

all regulatory offences are strict liability offences that allow a defence of due diligence. This presumption has subsequently been applied to hold that relatively minor motor vehicle offences that have been phrased as simple prohibitions are not absolute liability and allow a defence of due diligence.[18] As will be seen, interpreting a regulatory offence as an absolute liability offence raises constitutional problems that will not occur if the offence is interpreted as a strict liability offence.

2) The *Charter* and Absolute Liability

As discussed in chapter 2, the Supreme Court of Canada held in the *B.C. Motor Vehicle Reference*[19] that absolute liability offences offend the principles of fundamental justice by allowing the conviction of the morally innocent. Justice Lamer observed that "it is because absolute liability offends the principles of fundamental justice that this Court [in *Sault Ste. Marie*] created presumptions against Legislatures having intended to enact offences of a regulatory nature falling within that category." Yet the Court also held that an absolute liability offence would violate section 7 of the *Charter* "only if and to the extent that it has the potential of depriving of life, liberty, and security of the person." Lamer J. suggested that a person's liberty would be broadly construed to include not only the mandatory imprisonment that was at issue in the case, but also probation orders.[20] Other courts have concluded that a fine threatens a person's liberty if there is a possibility of imprisonment if the fine is not paid.[21]

The Supreme Court has refused to strike down an absolute liability offence in *Pontes* on the basis of a general provision in British Columbia's legislation that provided that no one could be imprisoned for violation of an absolute liability offence. Cory J. indicated that "generally speaking, an offence of absolute liability is not likely to offend the *Charter* unless a prison sanction is provided" and refused to strike down an

---

18   *R. v. Kanda*, 2008 ONCA 22 (highway traffic offence of not having children wear seat belts interpreted as strict liability offence); *R. v. Raham*, 2010 ONCA 206 (highway traffic offence of street racing 50 km over speed limit interpreted as strict liability offence).

19   *Reference re Motor Vehicle Act (British Columbia) S. 94(2)* (1985), 23 C.C.C. (3d) 289 at 311 (S.C.C.) [*B.C. Motor Vehicle Reference*].

20   Lamer J. stated: "Obviously, imprisonment (including probation orders) deprives persons of their liberty. An offence has that potential as of the moment it is open to the judge to impose imprisonment. There is no need that imprisonment, as in s. 94(2), be made mandatory." *Ibid.*

21   *R. v. Burt* (1987), 38 C.C.C. (3d) 299 (Sask. C.A.) [*Burt*]; *Nickel City Transport*, above note 12 at 572.

absolute liability offence on the basis that an individual convicted of driving without a licence "faces no risk of imprisonment and there is, accordingly, no violation of the right to life, liberty and security of the person under s. 7 of the Charter."[22] The Ontario Court of Appeal subsequently refused to strike down an absolute liability offence that provided for the operator of a commercial motor vehicle to be fined at least $2,000 and not more than $50,000 when a wheel becomes detached from a vehicle on a highway. Although an absolute liability offence violates the principles of fundamental justice, there was no section 7 violation because the rights of life, liberty, and security of the person were not affected since the offence provided that no one could be imprisoned or placed on probation for violation of the offence. The Court of Appeal concluded that the offence did not involve state-imposed serious psychological stress on the accused that would trigger section 7 of the Charter. "The right to security of the person does not protect the individual operating in the highly regulated context of commercial trucking for profit from the ordinary stresses and anxieties that a reasonable person would suffer as a result of government regulation of that industry."[23] In the commercial context at least, significant and mandatory fines, as well as the stigma that may accompany conviction for regulatory offences associated with deaths, appear not to engage the rights to life, liberty, and security of the person under section 7 of the Charter.

In the *B.C. Motor Vehicle Reference*, Lamer J. suggested that an absolute liability offence would rarely, if ever, be justified under section 1 of the *Charter*, because only in exceptional cases "such as natural disasters, the outbreak of war, epidemics and the like" should the liberty or security of a person "be sacrificed to administrative expediency."[24] In *Hess*,[25] the Supreme Court held that a statutory rape offence of having sexual intercourse with a girl under fourteen years of age constituted an absolute liability offence because Parliament had specifically provided for the accused's guilt upon proof of the *actus reus* "whether or not he believes that she is fourteen years of age or more." The offence was one of absolute liability because the Crown was not required to establish subjective fault such as knowledge or objective fault such as negligence concerning an essential element of the statutory rape offence. The majority of the Court held that the offence was an unjustified violation of section 7 of the *Charter* when compared to a less restrictive alternative that would allow the accused a limited defence that he took all reason-

---

22   *Pontes*, above note 14.
23   *R. v. 1260448 Ontario Inc.* (2003), 68 O.R. (3d) 51 (C.A.).
24   *B.C. Motor Vehicle Reference*, above note 19 at 311.
25   *Hess*, above note 5.

able steps to ascertain the age of the complainant[26] and would thus require objective fault or negligence. In *R. v. Wholesale Travel Group Inc.*,[27] the Court concluded that provisions that required the prompt correction of misleading advertising, even in cases where it was not reasonable for the accused to know that the advertising was misleading, amounted to absolute liability that could not be justified under section 1.

3) Corporations and the *Charter*

In the *B.C. Motor Vehicle Reference*, Lamer J. recognized that there might be a case for the use of absolute liability offences against corporations "in certain sensitive areas such as the preservation of our vital environment and our natural resources." He hinted, however, that such concerns "might well be dispelled were it to be decided, given the proper case, that s. 7 affords protection to human persons only and does not extend to corporations."[28] Subsequently, the Court held that corporations were not protected under section 7 of the *Charter*, on the basis that only human beings can enjoy life, liberty, and security of the person and that it would be "nonsensical to speak of a corporation being put in jail.[29] Despite this conclusion, a corporate accused can, when charged with an offence, bring a *Charter* challenge on the basis that the offence violates the section 7 rights of individuals who might be charged.[30] Legislatures can insulate absolute liability offences from invalidation under section 7 of the *Charter* by enacting offences that apply only to corporations. So far, legislatures have not made extensive use of this option to insulate absolute liability offences from *Charter* review. As will be seen, however, new provisions for organizational liability under the *Criminal Code* may be immune from section 7 review because they do not apply to natural persons who enjoy rights to life, liberty, and security of the person under section 7 of the *Charter*.

4) Corporate Liability for Absolute Liability Offences

Corporations have "automatic primary responsibility[31] for absolute liability offences. A corporation may be guilty whenever one of its em-

---

26   *Code*, above note 1, s. 150.1(4).
27   [1991] 3 S.C.R. 154, 67 C.C.C. (3d) 193 at 214–15 [*Wholesale Travel Group*].
28   *B.C. Motor Vehicle Reference*, above note 19 at 314.
29   *Irwin Toy Ltd. v. Quebec (A.G.)*, [1989] 1 S.C.R. 927 at 1003 [*Irwin*].
30   *Wholesale Travel Group*, above note 27.
31   *Canadian Dredge & Dock Co. v. R.* (1985), 19 C.C.C. (3d) 1 at 8 (S.C.C.) [*Canadian Dredge & Dock*].

ployees or someone under its control commits the prohibited act.[32] In a sense, this is a form of vicarious liability because it attributes the acts of the employee to the corporation. Courts have not seen this as a problem, however, because it is only the acts of the employees that are attributed to the corporation, and not some fault element. Corporations can also be guilty if they had an ability to control the commission of the *actus reus* by an independent contractor. In *Sault Ste. Marie*,[33] Justice Dickson indicated that although a homeowner who hires a company to collect garbage is probably not responsible for polluting if the company dumps the garbage in a river, a corporation or a municipality may well be.

5) Defences to Absolute Liability Offences

A defence of honest or even reasonable mistake of fact will not be a defence to an absolute liability offence. Thus, an accused's subjective reliance on a faulty speedometer would not be a valid defence even if the reliance was reasonable.[34] The defences of automatism, mental disorder, or extreme intoxication might possibly apply to an absolute liability offence, because they would indicate that the accused acted in an involuntary manner that is inconsistent with proof of the *actus reus*.[35] There is also some authority that the defence of necessity might apply to a person who committed an absolute liability offence such as speeding because of an urgent need to save a life.[36]

B. STRICT LIABILITY OFFENCES

A strict liability[37] offence requires the Crown to prove the prohibited act beyond a reasonable doubt, but then gives the accused an oppor-

---

32 A corporation will not be guilty if an independent operator on its premises commits a crime. *R. v. F.W. Woolworth Co.* (1974), 18 C.C.C. (2d) 23 (Ont. C.A.).

33 *Sault Ste. Marie*, above note 4.

34 *R. v. Hickey* (1976), 30 C.C.C. (2d) 416 (Ont. C.A.).

35 In *R. v. Daviault* (1994), 93 C.C.C. (3d) 21 at 25 (S.C.C.), Lamer C.J.C. stated that he preferred to characterize the mental element involved in voluntary and conscious activity "as relating more to the *actus reus* than the *mens rea*, so that the defence clearly be available in strict liability offences." The same logic should apply to absolute liability offences.

36 *R. v. Kennedy* (1972), 7 C.C.C. (2d) 42 (N.S. Co. Ct.); *R. v. Walker* (1979), 48 C.C.C. (2d) 126 (Ont. Co. Ct.).

37 Note that this terminology is distinctly Canadian, so that what other jurisdictions call strict liability would in Canada be classified as absolute liability. Simi-

tunity to prove due diligence or absence of negligence on a balance of probabilities. Strict liability offences are a halfway house between absolute liability offences and full *mens rea* offences. They "seek a middle position, fulfilling the goals of public welfare offences while still not punishing the entirely blameless."[38] In 1978 the Supreme Court indicated that all regulatory offences would be presumed to be strict liability offences, unless there was a clear indication from the legislature that either absolute liability or subjective *mens rea* was intended.

1) Simple Negligence

The blameworthiness of a strict liability offence is negligence. The Crown does not have to prove this fault element; rather, the accused is given an opportunity to establish on a balance of probabilities that it was not negligent.[39] In *Sault Ste. Marie*, Dickson J. contemplated that an accused who took all reasonable care, but still committed the prohibited act, would not be convicted of a strict liability offence. Given that regulatory offences are designed to encourage people and corporations to take appropriate safeguards to avoid harmful results, such as pollution or workplace accidents, courts should not require negligence to amount to a marked departure from the conduct of a reasonable person, as they do when applying negligence in criminal offences.[40] The reasonableness of the accused's conduct also should be determined on the basis of the circumstances that a reasonable person would have seen, not the circumstances that the accused actually perceived. Thus, any mistake of fact would have to be both honest and reasonable. To avoid a conviction for a regulatory offence, the corporation would have to demonstrate that it took reasonable steps to avoid the prohibited act or that it made an honest and reasonable mistake of fact.[41] It is important that the accused be given the opportunity to demonstrate that it was not negligent in order to avoid a strict liability offence becoming an absolute liability offence in which guilt is established simply by the prosecution proving the prohibited act beyond a reasonable doubt.

---

larly, strict liability in tort law is analogous to absolute liability in Canadian criminal law.

38   *Sault Ste. Marie*, above note 4 at 374 (C.C.C.).
39   *R. v. Timminco Ltd.* (2001), 42 C.R. (5th) 279 (Ont. C.A.).
40   See ch. 5(C)(2), "Degree of Negligence."
41   *R. v. MacMillan Bloedel Ltd.*, 2002 BCCA 510.

2) Negligence and the *Charter*

In *Wholesale Travel Group*,[42] the Supreme Court unanimously upheld negligence as a sufficient fault element for an offence of false or misleading advertising. The accused had argued that subjective *mens rea* was required because of the stigma that would accompany a conviction, and it relied upon *dicta* in *Vaillancourt*, which had suggested that proof of subjective *mens rea* might be required because of the stigma attached to theft. Lamer C.J. stated that a conviction for misleading advertising will not "brand the accused as being dishonest," but, in many cases, would indicate that the accused had been careless. Negligence was sufficient, even if the accused faced imprisonment. Adoption of a higher fault element was a matter of public policy for the legislature. Cory J. similarly concluded that "the demands of s. 7 will be met in the regulatory context where liability is imposed for conduct which breaches the standard of reasonable care required of those operating in the regulated field."[43] Simple negligence will be a constitutionally sufficient fault element for all regulatory offences.

3) The Defence of Due Diligence

Although the fault element for a strict liability offence is negligence, the Crown need not prove negligence beyond a reasonable doubt. Rather, the accused must prove a defence of due diligence or lack of negligence on a balance of probabilities. Once the Crown has proved the wrongful act beyond a reasonable doubt, the fault element of negligence is presumed, unless the accused can demonstrate that it took reasonable care or acted under a reasonable mistake of fact. In *Sault Ste. Marie*,[44] Dickson J. stressed that the burden of establishing due diligence should fall upon the accused, because it "will generally have the means of proof." This is especially true when, as in the case, it was alleged that "a large and complex corporation" caused pollution. He concluded that the burden was not unfair, "as the alternative is absolute liability which denies an accused any defence whatsoever," and the accused need only prove the defence on a balance of probabilities. The burden on the accused is an important component of the halfway house approach of strict liability offences, because it means that the Crown is not required to prove negligence beyond a reasonable doubt and that the accused is not acquitted because there is a reasonable doubt as to negligence.

---

42 *Wholesale Travel Group*, above note 27.
43 *Ibid.* at 252. See also *R. v. Eurosport Auto Co.* (2002), 11 C.R. (6th) 327 (B.C.C.A.).
44 *Sault Ste. Marie*, above note 4 at 373 (C.C.C.).

The due diligence defence requires more than passivity from the accused. In *Lévis (City) v. Tétreault*,[45] the Supreme Court rejected the idea that an accused who thought that the date on his licence was a renewal notice as opposed to an expiry date had a defence of due diligence. The Court stated that the courts below, which had acquitted the accused on the basis of due diligence, had

> confused passivity with diligence .... He proved no action or attempt to obtain information. The concept of diligence is based on the acceptance of a citizen's civic duty to take action to find out what his or her obligations are. Passive ignorance is not a valid defence ....[46]

Due diligence requires an active and reasonable attempt to prevent the commission of the prohibited act.

The courts look to a large range of factors in determining whether the accused has established a defence of due diligence to a regulatory offence. Some factors look to the likelihood and gravity of the risk, including whether it was foreseeable and the effect that it could have on vulnerable people and neighbourhoods. Other factors look to the ability of the accused to control or manage the risk of the prohibited act from occurring. Factors such as alternative solutions, regulatory compliance, industry standards and preventive systems, efforts made to address the problem, and the promptness of the accused's response are significant. Other matters such as factors beyond the control of the accused, technological limitations, skill level expected of the accused, complexities involved, and economic considerations can be relevant in determining whether the accused has taken all reasonable steps to prevent the risk.[47] The accused must be given an opportunity to establish due diligence in order to ensure that a strict liability offence does not become an absolute liability offence in which a conviction follows automatically from the fact that the risk sought to be managed has been realized and the prohibited act occurred.

---

45   Above note 17 at paras. 17 and 19.

46   *Ibid.* at para. 30.

47   These factors are taken from *R. v. Commander Business Furniture* (1992), 9 C.E.L.R. (N.S.) 185 (Ont. Prov. Div.). They are discussed at greater length in T. Archibald, K. Jull, & K. Roach, *Regulatory and Corporate Liability: From Due Diligence to Risk Management*, looseleaf (Aurora, ON: Canada Law Book, 2004–) ch. 4, where it is suggested that the due diligence defence may require reasonable risk management.

4) The Defence of Due Diligence and the *Charter*

In *Wholesale Travel Group*, the Supreme Court in a 5:4 decision upheld a statutory defence that required those who committed the wrongful act of false or misleading advertising to prove on a balance of probabilities that they exercised due diligence to prevent the occurrence of such error. Seven judges agreed that placing such a burden on the accused violated the presumption of innocence as protected under section 11(d) of the *Charter* because it allowed an accused to be convicted, even though there was a reasonable doubt as to whether it acted in a negligent fashion. Lamer C.J., with three other judges in dissent, found that this restriction on section 11(d) could not be justified under section 1, because the legislature could achieve its objective by means of an evidential as opposed to a persuasive burden. He contemplated a mandatory presumption of negligence following proof of the *actus reus*, but one that could be rebutted by evidence that could raise a reasonable doubt as to whether the accused was negligent. Such a mandatory presumption would violate section 11(d) of the *Charter* but would constitute a less drastic means of advancing the legislature's objectives.[48]

However, a majority of the Court concluded that imposing the burden on the accused to establish due diligence on a balance of probabilities could be justified. Iacobucci J. stated that an evidential burden "would shift to the accused the burden of simply raising a reasonable doubt as to due diligence and would not thereby allow the effective pursuit of the regulatory objective."[49] He argued that the accused, as participants in regulated activities, "are in the best position to prove due diligence, since they possess in most cases the required information" to prove that they were not negligent. Cory J. also stressed that the accused would be in the best position to prove whether it exercised reasonable care, and concluded, "in the regulatory context, there is nothing unfair about imposing that onus; indeed, it is essential for the protection of our vulnerable society."[50] He feared that with only an evidential burden, the accused would always be able to point to some evidence of measures it had taken to prevent the prohibited act, and the Crown would then have the difficult task of proving beyond a reasonable doubt that the accused was negligent.

The majority's judgment in *Wholesale Travel Group* endorses the functional justification given in *Sault Ste. Marie* for requiring the ac-

---

48 *R. v. Downey* (1992), 72 C.C.C. (3d) 1 (S.C.C.); *R. v. Laba* (1994), 94 C.C.C. (3d) 385 (S.C.C.), discussed in ch. 2(B)(3)(f), "Right to Be Presumed Innocent."

49 *Wholesale Travel Group*, above note 27 at 267 (C.C.C.).

50 *Ibid.* at 256–57.

cused to prove the defence of due diligence or lack of negligence. Although it is technically necessary to justify each reverse burden under section 1, the Court has applied the section 1 analysis used in *Wholesale Travel Group* to other regulatory offences in different contexts.[51]

5) Corporate Liability for Strict Liability Offences

The same considerations apply when holding corporations accountable for strict liability offences as apply for absolute liability offences. In *Canadian Dredge & Dock*,[52] Estey J. stated:

> As in the case of an absolute liability offence, it matters not whether the accused is corporate or unincorporated, because the liability is primary . . . . It is not dependent upon the attribution to the accused of the misconduct of others . . . . [T]he corporation and the natural defendant are in the same position. In both cases liability is not vicarious but primary.

As with absolute liability offences, this approach suggests that the corporation will have committed the *actus reus* when one of its employees or another person subject to its control has committed the prohibited act. In *Sault Ste. Marie*, the accused could be liable, even though it had contracted out the pollution-causing activity to another company.

The primary liability of a corporation for a strict liability offence suggests the corollary that the corporation must establish a defence of due diligence for the organization. In *Sault Ste. Marie*,[53] however, Dickson J. suggested that "the availability of a defence to a corporation will depend on whether such due diligence was taken by those who are the directing mind and will of the corporation, whose acts are therefore in law the acts of the corporation itself." As will be seen, this standard is no longer used for attributing subjective fault to a corporation and has been replaced by a broader concept of a senior officer who exercises policy-making or important managerial functions within the organization. There may be cases in large organizations where the directing mind or even the senior officers act with due diligence, but the corporation as a complex organization does not. An example of this would occur when no one informed a directing mind or senior officer about certain problems or warning signs that the *actus reus* was likely to occur. In that case, it is possible that the directing mind or senior

---

51   *R. v. Ellis-Don Ltd.* (1992), 71 C.C.C. (3d) 63 (S.C.C.); *R. v. Martin* (1992), 71 C.C.C. (3d) 572 (S.C.C.).

52   *Canadian Dredge & Dock*, above note 31 at 9.

53   *Sault Ste. Marie*, above note 4 at 377–78 (C.C.C.).

officer will be found not to be negligent (unless he or she should have made inquiries) even though the corporation as an organization might be negligent. It would be more consistent with the logic of strict liability offences to require the corporation as an organization to prove a due diligence defence.

6) Requirements of Fault beyond Negligence in Regulatory Offences

The Court in *Sault Ste Marie*[54] contemplated that while regulatory offences would be presumed to be offences of strict liability, they could also require proof of fault if the legislature specifically provided for fault elements such as knowledge, wilfulness, or recklessness. It held that the use of the words "cause" and "permit" in environmental legislation were not sufficient to move the regulatory offence into the full *mens rea* category.[55] In *Strasser v. Roberge*,[56] the Supreme Court disagreed about whether there was an intent requirement with respect to the offence under Quebec labour legislation of participating in an illegal strike. The Court in *Strasser* divided 4:3 on the classification of the offence, with Beetz J. holding for the majority that the offence was one of strict liability that required the accused to bear the burden of establishing the lack of intent and Dickson J. in dissent holding that the offence was a *mens rea* offence that required the Crown to prove intent. The majority decision in *Strasser* has been criticized primarily for reversing the burden of proof. In a decision by Fish J.A. (as he then was), the Quebec Court of Appeal finessed the *Strasser* precedent by reading down the persuasive burden that Beetz J. had placed on the accused to establish lack of intent to an evidential burden that only requires the accused to point to evidence capable of raising a reasonable doubt about intent.[57]

The primary issue in these cases seems to be the proper characterization of the offence. If it is accepted that the offence remains one of strict liability even though the legislature has required fault above negligence, then *Wholesale Travel Group* should justify the reversal of proof that requires the accused to establish lack of intent. On the other hand, the dissenting position of Dickson J. that regulatory offences can still be classified as *mens rea* offences if they require proof of fault beyond

---

54   *Ibid.*
55   *Ibid.* at 1327–28 (S.C.R.).
56   [1979] 2 S.C.R. 953.
57   *R. v. Bergeron* (1995), 101 C.C.C. (3d) 69 (Que. C.A.).

negligence is attractive. With respect to such offences, the ordinary burden of proof should apply and the Crown should have to establish fault beyond a reasonable doubt. The halfway house created by the Quebec Court of Appeal by reading down *Strasser* to only require an evidential burden is difficult to justify except perhaps on the basis that it constitutes a less drastic violation of the presumption of innocence than the full burden of establishing no intent required by the majority in *Strasser*. The better approach may be to follow Dickson J. and simply recognize the small subset of regulatory offences that specifically require subjective fault as *mens rea* offences where the Crown has to establish both the prohibited act and the fault requirement beyond a reasonable doubt.

C. VICARIOUS LIABILITY

Vicarious liability occurs when the acts and fault of another person are attributed to the accused for the purpose of determining liability. It is used in tort law as a means of ensuring that employers are not allowed to profit from civil wrongs committed by their employees. Even before the *Charter*, courts resisted this doctrine on the basis that "criminal law regards a person as responsible for his own crimes only."[58] A judge-made or common law presumption against holding a person responsible for the acts and faults of another could, however, be displaced by clear legislative intent.[59] As will be seen in relation to corporate liability for *mens rea* offences, Canadian courts struggled to avoid holding corporations vicariously liable for crimes committed by their employees.

1) Vicarious Liability and the *Charter*

In *Bhatnager v. Canada (Minister of Employment & Immigration)*,[60] the Supreme Court suggested that it might violate section 7 to hold ministers of the government vicariously liable for acts of criminal contempt committed by their officials without their knowledge. Several *Charter* cases have considered statutes that make the owners of automobiles

---

58   *Tesco Supermarkets Ltd. v. Nattrass* (1971), [1972] A.C. 153 at 199 (H.L.); *R. v. Stevanovich* (1983), 7 C.C.C. (3d) 307 at 311 (Ont. C.A.).

59   *R. v. Budget Car Rentals (Toronto) Ltd.* (1981), 57 C.C.C. (2d) 201 (Ont. C.A.).

60   [1990] 2 S.C.R. 217.

vicariously liable for violations committed by any person driving their cars. In *Burt*,[61] the Saskatchewan Court of Appeal concluded:

> The principles of fundamental justice simply do not recognize the as-cribing to one person of another's state of mind. Accordingly, where a statute purports to make one person vicariously liable for another's *mens rea* offence the statute may be said to offend . . . the principles of fundamental justice.

An offence that bases the accused's liability on the acts and faults of another may be found to be an absolute liability offence that punishes the accused without fault. At a minimum, a person could not be impris-oned for such an offence.[62] Many motor vehicle offences that impose vicarious liability on the owner of a vehicle for offences committed with the vehicle contain a limited defence allowing the owner to es-tablish that the vehicle was taken without his or her consent. Courts of Appeal are divided on whether this limited defence make a vicari-ous liability offence one of absolute or strict liability.[63] The statutory defence does allow the owner a limited opportunity to show that he or she was not at fault. At the same time, however, it does not exhaust the range of due diligence defences that an accused would ordinarily have to a strict liability offence. Thus, the better view is that even with this limited defence, the offence remains one of absolute liability because it can convict an accused who was not at fault. The accused may still be convicted but not imprisoned for the violation of a vicarious liability offence that imposes absolute liability.

D. CORPORATIONS AND *MENS REA* OFFENCES

1) The Common Law Directing Mind Approach

Canadian courts resisted holding corporations vicariously liable for the *mens rea* offences of their employees. Instead, they identified the cor-

---

61   *Burt*, above note 21 at 311. See also *R. v. Pellerin* (1989), 47 C.C.C. (3d) 35 (Ont. C.A.).

62   *R. v. Gray* (1988), 44 C.C.C. (3d) 222 (Man. C.A.); *R. v. Smith* (1989), 14 M.V.R. (2d) 166 (Y.C.A.); *R. v. Free* (1990), 110 A.R. 241 (Q.B.).

63   The British Columbia Court of Appeal has held that such a vicarious liability offence remains one of absolute liability while the Nova Scotia Court of Appeal has held that it makes the offence one of strict liability. *R. v. Geraghty* (1990), 55 C.C.C. (3d) 460 (B.C.C.A.); *R. v. Sutherland* (1990), 55 C.C.C. (3d) 265 (N.S.C.A.).

poration with a senior official who acts as the corporation's directing mind and attributed the fault or mental element of that person to the corporation for the purpose of determining the corporation's liability for a criminal offence. In doing so, they followed English authorities that suggest that a corporation is liable only for what is done by "the directing mind and will of the corporation, the very ego and centre of the personality of the corporation."[64] Under this identification or alter ego theory, the wrongful action of the directing mind is attributed to the corporation so that the corporation has primary, not vicarious, liability for the acts and mind of an official who is a directing mind of the corporation.

A corporation could not insulate itself from the crimes committed by a directing mind by claiming ignorance or issuing instructions that the crime not be committed. Thus, the Supreme Court has stated: "Acts of the ego of a corporation taken within the assigned managerial area may give rise to the corporate criminal responsibility, whether or not there be formal delegation; whether or not there be awareness of the activity in the board of directors or the officers of the company, and . . . whether or not there be express prohibition."[65] One relatively narrow exception was that a corporation would not be held liable if the directing mind acted wholly in fraud and against the interest of the corporation. In that case, the corporation would be the victim of the crime, not responsible for it. The Court has restricted this principle so that the corporation remains liable if the directing mind's activities were "by design or result partly for the benefit of the company."[66] Thus, a corporation may be guilty of fraud if it receives kickbacks, even though the directing mind fraudulently keeps some of the kickbacks from the corporation.

Canadian courts defined the directing mind of the corporation somewhat more broadly than English courts, in part because of the decentralized nature of much corporate activity in Canada. In the leading case of *Canadian Dredge & Dock*, the Supreme Court made clear that there could be more than one directing mind of a corporation. Directing minds could include "the board of directors, the managing director, the superintendent, the manager or anyone else delegated . . . the governing executive authority of the corporation." In *R. v. Waterloo*

---

64   *Lennard's Carrying Co. Ltd. v. Asiatic Petroleum Co. Ltd.*, [1915] A.C. 705 at 713 (H.L.). Note that s. 2 of the *Code*, above note 1, defines "everyone" to include corporations and fines are generally available to punish corporations.

65   *Canadian Dredge & Dock*, above note 31 at 17.

66   *Ibid.* at 38.

Mercury Sales Ltd.,[67] the manager of a used car lot was held to be the corporation's directing mind for the purpose of determining whether it had committed fraud by rolling back odometers, even though the president of the corporation had no knowledge of the acts and had circulated written instructions not to roll back odometers. The manager was acting as the corporation's directing mind within the field of operation assigned to him. An employee with lesser responsibility, such as a salesperson or a mechanic, would not be a directing mind.

In the 1990s, Canadian courts placed limits on who might be classified as a corporation's directing mind. A directing mind must be an officer or manager of a corporation, acting in the scope of his or her responsibility. A directing mind must also have an express or implied delegation of executive authority to design and supervise the implementation of corporate policy rather than simply to carry out such policy.[68] Under this test, both a tug captain who exercised considerable discretion[69] and a truck driver who was a corporation's sole representative in an area[70] were held not to be directing minds of their corporations. The courts reasoned that these employees did not have the power to design or supervise the implementation of corporate policy and that their fault could not be attributed to the corporation. This trend made it difficult to hold corporations criminally accountable for crimes committed in Canada. Not infrequently, those with the degree of responsibility required of a directing mind would be sheltered within the corporate hierarchy and not have the required fault, while those with the required fault would not have enough policy-making power within the corporation to be classified as the corporation's directing mind. The designers and even the supervisors of corporate policies in a large and economically dependent country such as Canada often were so far away from any criminal acts that took place that they did not have the *mens rea* required for the particular crime. Those closer to the ground who would have the required fault were not classified as directing minds because they did not design or supervise the implementation of corporate policy, even though they exercised an important managerial role in the corporation.

---

67 (1974), 18 C.C.C. (2d) 248 (Alta. Dist. Ct.).
68 *"Rhone" (The) v. "Peter A.B. Widener" (The)*, [1993] 1 S.C.R. 497 at 521 [*Rhone*].
69 *Ibid.*
70 *R. v. Safety Kleen Canada Inc.* (1997), 114 C.C.C. (3d) 214 (Ont. C.A.) [*Safety Kleen*].

2) New Statutory Provisions for Corporate Criminal Liability

There were many calls to abandon the identification, alter ego, or directing mind approach in favour of less restrictive approaches. One option would be to hold corporations vicariously responsible for the actions of all their employees and agents as is done in some American jurisdictions. This would run against the criminal law's reluctance to impose vicarious liability based on the fault of another. Such vicarious liability likely offends the principles of fundamental justice, but it may not violate section 7 of the *Charter* because corporations have no rights to life, liberty, and security of the person. In any event, vicarious liability would still only attribute the fault of individuals to corporations. Another option would have been to to impose liability on corporations based on their organizational fault or "corporate culture," as is done in some Australian jurisdictions.[71] The focus under such proposals would not be on the fault of individuals within the corporation, but the fault of the corporation as a whole.

In late 2003, Parliament enacted Bill C-45 that amended the *Criminal Code* to provide a new regime to determine when corporations and other organizations were guilty of criminal offences and its provisions took effect at the end of March 2004. The Bill also provided a new punishment regime to allow courts not simply to fine corporations, but also to place them on probation in an attempt to ensure that the offences were not repeated. This new regime is a fundamental change to corporate criminal liability in response to corporate misconduct that led to the death of twenty-six miners in the Westray Mine disaster, as well as events such as the Enron scandal.

The new regime replaces the common law concept of a directing mind with a new and broader statutory concept of a senior officer, which now includes those who are responsible for managing an important aspect of the corporation's activities. At the same time, the new regime retains the idea that a senior officer of the corporation must be at fault before that person's fault can be attributed to the corporation for either a negligence or subjective fault offence under the *Criminal Code*. The new provisions do, however, allow an organization to be found criminally liable for crimes of negligence because of the aggregate actions of more than one of its representatives and the aggregate or collective fault of more than one of its senior officers. It does not go as far

---

71   D. Stuart, "A Case for a General Part" in D. Stuart, R.J. Delisle, & A. Manson, eds., *Towards a Clear and Just Criminal Law: A Criminal Reports Forum* (Toronto: Carswell, 1999) 135–38.

as vicarious liability for the fault of all employees or fault that inheres in the corporation as an organization including "corporate culture" as opposed to the senior officers of the corporation.

The new regime also lends some structure to the *Criminal Code* by providing a separate provision for determining organizational liability for criminal offences of negligence and for criminal offences of subjective fault. It also builds on the parties provisions of the *Criminal Code* by tying organizational liability to individuals in the organization being a party to the specific offence. This underlines the reality that in many cases both individuals within the organization and the organization itself may face criminal charges. Nevertheless, it does make the new sections complex and can in some circumstances result in the corporation being found guilty for a subjective intent offence because its senior officers ought to have known that the offence would be committed or did not take reasonable steps to prevent an offence that they knew was being committed by representatives of the corporation.

a) Organizational Liability

The new provisions apply not only to corporations, but also any "public body, body corporate, society, company, firm, partnership, trade union or municipality."[72] This makes sense because municipalities have long been held liable for regulatory offences and there is no reason in principle why other public bodies and alternatives to formal corporations should not be held responsible under the *Criminal Code*. All of these entities are united in not being natural persons who enjoy a right to life, liberty, and security of the person under section 7 of the *Charter*.[73]

The new provisions also apply to a less formal association that is "created for a common purpose, has an operational structure and holds itself out to the public as an association of persons."[74] This suggests that the formal legal status of the organization will not be determinative with respect to the applicability of the new principles. It also raises the novel possibility that prosecutors could charge associations like criminal gangs with a criminal offence as a means of fining the organization or placing the organization itself on probation as opposed to relying solely on prosecutions of individuals within the informal association.

---

72 *Code*, above note 1, s. 2.
73 *Irwin*, above note 29.
74 *Code*, above note 1, s. 2.

b)   Representatives of an Organization

The prohibited act or *actus reus* must be committed by one or more of the organization's "representatives." Representatives are defined broadly in section 2 of the *Criminal Code* as including not only the directors, partners, employees, and members of the organization, but also its agents and contractors. A public body or a corporation that contracts out work to non-employees can still be held liable for prohibited acts performed by the contractor or agent.

c)   Senior Officers of an Organization

In general, the required fault element or *mens rea* for the offence must be found in a senior officer of the organization. The definition of a senior officer in section 2 of the *Criminal Code* is perhaps the most crucial feature of the new regime because the new statutory concept of a senior officer replaces the old common law concept of the corporation's directing mind. Senior officer is defined as a

> [r]epresentative who plays an important role in the establishment of the organization's policies or is responsible for managing an important aspect of the organization's activities and, in the case of a body corporate, includes a director, its chief executive officer and its chief financial officer.[75]

This definition follows the common law concept of directing mind to the extent that it provides that 1) directors, chief executive and chief financial officers, and 2) those who play an important role in the establishment of policies are senior enough in the organization that their fault can fairly be attributed to the corporation. The most important difference between the old directing mind concept and the new senior officer concept is that the latter also covers those responsible for managing an important part of the organization's activities. This last aspect of the definition of a senior officer overrules previous cases that suggested that those who exercised important managerial functions in an organization were not high enough in the corporate hierarchy to represent the corporation for the purpose of determining fault. Thus, it is likely the tugboat captain in *Rhone*[76] and the truck driver who represented a waste disposal corporation in *Safety Kleen*[77] would now be found to be senior officers whose fault could be attributed to the corporation. Even though such persons were held not to be directing minds because they

---

75   *Ibid.*
76   *Rhone*, above note 68.
77   *Safety Kleen*, above note 70.

did not play an important role in establishing corporate policy, they did manage an important aspect of the corporation's activities and on that basis would satisfy the expanded definition of senior officer in section 2 of the *Criminal Code*. At the same time, the new concept of a senior officer is limited to managers and not mere employees and the manager must be responsible for managing an important aspect of the organization's activities.

d) Section 22.1 of the *Criminal Code* and Organizational Fault for Negligence Offences

As mentioned above, the new regime differentiates between organizational fault for criminal offences based on negligence and subjective intent. This helpfully differentiates between the two main varieties of criminal fault. As will be seen, the new legislation also incorporates the idea that negligence in the criminal context requires more than unreasonable conduct or simple negligence. Following cases such as *Creighton*, *Beatty*, and *Roy*, discussed in chapter 5, the new regime requires a marked departure from a standard of reasonable care. Section 22.1 provides:

> In respect of an offence that requires the prosecution to prove negligence, an organization is a party to the offence if:
> a)   acting within the scope of their authority
>   i)   one of its representatives is a party to the offence, or
>   ii) two or more of its representatives engage in conduct, whether by act or omission, such that, if it had been the conduct of only one representative, that representative would have been a party to the offence; and
> b)   the senior officer who is responsible for the aspect of the organization's activities that is relevant to the offence departs—or the senior officers, collectively, depart—markedly from the standard of care that, in the circumstances, could reasonably be expected to prevent a representative of the organization from being a party to the offence.

Section 22.1(a) defines how the representative(s) of the organization can commit the prohibited act or *actus reus* of the offence whereas section 22.1(b) defines how the senior officer(s) of the organization will have the required fault element for a negligence-based criminal offence.

Such offences could include causing death or causing bodily harm by criminal negligence.[78]

i)   The Commission of the Prohibited Act by the Organization's Representative(s)

Section 22.1(a) requires that the representative(s) of the organization commit the prohibited act. The first requirement is that the representative(s) be acting in the scope of their authority. A corporation thus will not be liable for something done by employees, agents, or contractors outside the scope of their authority. For example, a corporation would not be guilty of criminal negligence causing death should an employee be involved in a fatal accident after he or she had stolen the company's truck.

In many cases, one representative of an organization acting within the scope of his or her authority will commit the prohibited act. Section 22.1(a)(ii), however, provides that multiple representatives of the organization may culmulatively be held responsible for commission of the prohibited act. This provision recognizes the corporate misconduct can often be the aggregate of the behaviour of separate individuals, each of whom taken by themselves may not have committed the prohibited act. A mining disaster, for example, may be caused by the combination of two or more individuals failing to take safety precautions. The failure of each may not have caused death, but the combined actions of the individuals may be sufficient to cause death.

ii)   Marked Departure from Reasonable Standards by the Organization's Senior Officer(s)

Section 22.1(b) requires that senior officer(s) of the organization have the fault of departing markedly from the standard of care that could reasonably be expected to prevent a representative from being a party to the offence. The fault element does not require that a senior officer necessarily know that a representative of the organization was committing the offence. Nevertheless, it does require more than simple negligence or a lack of due diligence by the senior officer. The fault element that is required is criminal negligence in the sense that the departure from reasonable conduct must be a marked departure. This follows

---

78   *Code*, above note 1, ss. 220 & 221. Criminal negligence under s. 219(b) can also be found on the basis of omissions. Section 217.1 of the *Code* now provides that "every one who undertakes, or has the authority, to direct how another person does work or performs a task is under a legal duty to take reasonable steps to prevent bodily harm to that person, or any other person, arising from that work or task."

from the Supreme Court's repeated statements that negligence in the criminal context must be "marked."[79]

The relevant standard is the standard of care that in the circumstances could reasonably be expected to prevent a representative of the organization from being a party to the offence. This suggests that all organizations should establish systems designed to prevent their representatives from committing offences based on negligence, such as causing death or bodily injury by criminal negligence. The exact contours of this standard of care will depend on the particular circumstances and may be informed by some of the factors discussed above in relation to the due diligence defence.

In general, the requisite degree of negligence will be found in the conduct of the senior officer "who is responsible for the aspect of the organization's activities that is relevant to the offence." For example, the senior officer responsible for mine safety would generally be the relevant person in determining whether the mining company had acted with criminal negligence in the causing of death or bodily harm. It will be recalled that this senior officer need not establish corporate policy; it is sufficient under the definition of senior officer in section 2 of the *Criminal Code* that he or she be responsible for managing an important part of the organization's activities. This could include a mine manager in Canada even though corporate policy is established in head office in some other country.

Section 22.1(b) also provides for an innovative form of aggregate fault by multiple senior officers. In a sense this mirrors the concept of the aggregate commission of the prohibited act by multiple representatives of the organization in section 22.1(a). Section 22.1(b) contemplates a conviction of an organization if "the senior officers, collectively, depart markedly from the standard of care that, in the circumstances, could reasonably be expected to prevent a representative of the organization from being a party to the offence." Even if the required criminal negligence cannot be located in one senior officer, it may be found in the collective fault of the senior officers, including the board of directors, the chief executive, and those who play an important role in establishing corporate policies or managing an important aspect of the organization's activities. Thus, in a case where no one at a mine is responsible for safety, the required level of criminal negligence might

---

79   See *R. v. Creighton* (1993), 83 C.C.C. (3d) 346 at 382–83 (S.C.C.); *R. v. Hundal*, [1993] 1 S.C.R. 867; *R. v. Finlay*, [1993] 3 S.C.R. 103; *R. v. Beatty*, 2008 SCC 5; *R. v. Roy*, 2012 SCC 26, discussed in ch. 5(C)(2), "Degree of Negligence."

be found in the collective conduct of the senior officers of the mining company.

Corporate liability for criminal offences of negligence may in practice blur with corporate liability for strict liability regulatory offences as discussed above. Both are offences based on negligence in allowing a prohibited act to occur. The differences, however, are that criminal offences under section 22.1 of the *Criminal Code* must be based on 1) a marked departure from the standard of care and 2) the Crown must prove beyond a reasonable doubt that senior officer(s) had this fault whereas it is the accused corporation who must demonstrate that it took all reasonable steps to prevent the prohibited act from occurring when the offence is a regulatory offence of strict liability or simple negligence.

e) Section 22.2 of the *Criminal Code* and Organizational Fault for Subjective Intent Offences

Section 22.2 applies to organizational liability for all criminal offences other than those based on negligence. In other words, it applies when the organization is charged with a subjective intent offence such as fraud, obscenity, or facilitating terrorism. Section 22.2 provides:

> In respect of an offence that requires the prosecution to prove fault—other than negligence—an organization is a party to the offence if, with the intent at least in part to benefit the organization, one of its senior officers
>
> a) acting within the scope of their authority, is a party to the offence;
>
> b) having the mental state required to be a party to the offence and acting within the scope of their authority, directs the work of other representatives of the organization so that they do the act or make the omission specified in the offence; or
>
> c) knowing that a representative of the organization is or is about to be a party to the offence, does not take all reasonable measures to stop them from being a party to the offence.

Section 22.2 contemplates subjective intent offences being committed by 1) senior officers acting on their own within the scope of their authority; 2) senior officers directing representatives so that they commit the offence; or 3) senior officers knowing that representatives are or will commit offences but failing to take all reasonable measures to stop them from doing so. Unlike section 22.1, it does not contemplate fault based on the collective or aggregate fault of multiple senior officers. In other words, one responsible senior officer must have the fault under section 22.2, which is then attributed to the organization.

i)   Senior Officers Being a Party to the Offence

The simplest form of organizational liability for a subjective intent offence is when the senior officer commits the offence. The only restrictions under section 22.2(a) are that the senior officer must 1) be acting within the scope of his or her authority and 2) have the intent at least in part to benefit the organization. The latter requirement codifies the holding in *Canadian Dredge & Dock*[80] that a corporation will not be held responsible if the senior officer acts totally in fraud of the corporation. Nevertheless, corporations can be held criminally responsible when they receive some benefits from the senior officer's activities, even though the senior officer is also defrauding the corporation.

Under section 22.2(a) the senior officer does not necessarily have to be the person who actually commits the offence. All that is required is that the senior officer be a party to the offence, which as discussed in chapter 4 includes aiding and abetting under section 21(1)(b) and (c), common unlawful intent under section 21(2), and counselling the commission of an offence under section 22. Thus the corporation could be liable for a subjective intent offence under section 22.2(a) on the basis that its senior officer intentionally assisted or counselled a representative of the corporation to commit the offence. Indeed, sections 21(2) and 22(2) suggest that in some circumstances a senior officer may be a party to a subjective intent offence on the basis that he or she ought to have known that the offence would be committed as a result of the carrying out of an unlawful purpose or as a result of intentionally counselling the commission of another offence.

ii)   Senior Officers Directing Representatives to Commit the Offence

Section 22.2(b) is a complex provision that makes the corporation liable when a senior officer directs other representatives of the corporation so that they commit an offence. As under section 22.2(a), the senior officer must be acting within the scope of his or her authority. The senior officer must also be "directing the work of other representatives of the organization so that they do the act or make the omission specified in the offence." This requires not only that the senior officer directs the work of representatives, but also directs them in such a manner that they commit the prohibited act or omission. The wording of this provision, as well as the requirement that the senior officer must also have "the mental state required to be party to an offence," suggests that the reference to directing the work of representatives so that they commit the *actus reus* of the offence is a broader concept than counselling the

---

80   *Canadian Dredge & Dock*, above note 31.

commission of the offence. Indeed, a senior officer who intentionally and successfully counselled the commission of the offence under section 22 would be a party to the offence counselled and would already be covered by section 22.2(a) discussed above.

In addition to the direction requirement, the senior officer must "have the mental state required to be a party to the offence." As with section 22.2(a) discussed above, this incorporates the party provisions of sections 21 and 22 of the *Criminal Code* into the new corporate criminal liability provisions. Section 21(1)(b) and (c) make a senior officer liable if he or she intentionally and knowingly assists in the commission of a crime. The fact that the senior officer may have been motivated by a desire to save his or her job will not negate this fault element. Section 21(2) extends liability to offences that the senior officer either knew or ought to have known would be a probable consequence of carrying out a common unlawful purpose that was intentionally formed with at least one other person. Thus, if a senior officer intentionally forms an unlawful purpose to commit a fraud with another person, the corporation will also be liable for other offences that the senior officer either knew or ought to have known would be committed in carrying out that unlawful purpose. A senior officer would have the mental state required under section 22(1) if he or she counselled another person to commit an offence that is then in fact committed. Section 22(2) extends liability to include every offence that the senior officer would have known or ought to have known would have been carried out as a likely consequence of the counselling.

Both sections 21(2) and 22(2) could be applied to make an organization liable for an subjective intent criminal offence even though its senior officer only had objective fault in relation to that particular offence. In other words, the corporation could be liable if its senior officer, having formed a common unlawful purpose or having counselled the commission of an offence, ought to have known that some further offence would be committed. Any illogic or unfairness in this state of affairs is the fault of the party provisions incorporated as an important part of the new organizational liability provision of section 22.2 and have only been partially mitigated by cases such as *Logan*[81] that hold that the objective arm of section 21(2) should not be applied for offences such as murder and attempted murder that constitutionally require subjective fault.

---

81   *R. v. Logan* (1990), 58 C.C.C. (3d) 391 (S.C.C.). See ch. 4(F), "Common Intention to Commit an Unlawful Purpose and Section 21(2)."

iii) Senior Officers Failing to Prevent Representatives from Committing the Offence

The organization's liability for subjective intent offence is further extended by section 22.2(c), which applies when a senior officer knows that a representative of the organization is or is about to be a party to the offence but fails "to take all reasonable measures" to stop the representative[82] from being a party to the offence. This section requires subjective fault in the form of guilty knowledge by the senior officer about the commission of an offence. As discussed in chapter 5, knowledge is a fairly high form of subjective knowledge and does not encompass recklessness or wilful blindness.

Section 22.2(c) also requires objective fault by the senior officer in the form of a failure to take all reasonable steps to stop the commission of the offence. The requirement of liability for a failure to take all reasonable steps is one usually associated with regulatory offences as opposed to criminal offences of subjective fault.[83] Indeed, this requirement is quite close to the due diligence requirement for strict liability offences and courts may well look to the multiple factors that are relevant in determining due diligence in order to determine whether a senior officer took all reasonable steps to prevent a representative from committing or continuing to commit the offence.

There are still some differences between section 22.2(c) as it applies to organizations charged with a criminal offence of subjective intent and the due diligence available to corporations charged with a regulatory offence. One difference is that an organization will not be liable under section 22.2(c) unless its senior officer also had guilty knowledge that a representative of the organization was committing or was about to commit the offence. A second difference is that the failure of the senior officer to take all reasonable steps must be proven beyond a reasonable doubt. Organizations are made liable under this section through a combination of subjective and objective fault elements,[84] both of which must be proven beyond a reasonable doubt.

---

82 The section at first refers to "a representative" but later uses the plural "them" in reference to the representative. This is confusing but fails to clearly introduce the novel concept of aggregate liability found in s. 22.1, which applies to criminal offences of negligence.

83 But see s. 150.1(4), requiring an accused to have taken "all reasonable steps" to ascertain the age of a complainant under the age of fourteen for the purpose of various sexual offences.

84 See the discussion of s. 273.2(b) in ch. 5(D)(4), "Mistake of Fact and Sexual Assault," for a somewhat similar combination of subjective and objective fault that requires a person arguing mistaken belief in consent to take "reasonable steps,

CONCLUSION

Although the Supreme Court has disapproved of absolute liability offences since its decision in *Sault Ste. Marie*[85] and declared them contrary to the principles of fundamental justice in the *B.C. Motor Vehicle Reference*,[86] it appears that such offences are constitutionally permissible so long as no imprisonment is imposed.[87] Absolute liability offences would also be permissible if only applied to corporations, which do not enjoy the rights to life, liberty, and security of the person protected under section 7 of the *Charter*. The Supreme Court has recently affirmed the common law presumption that regulatory offences should be assumed not to be absolute liability but rather to be strict liability offences that allow a defence of due diligence. The defence of due diligence requires an active attempt to prevent the commission of the prohibited act and not mere passivity.[88]

Strict liability offences have survived *Charter* challenge. The courts have not disapproved of the fault element of simple negligence, but they have noted that the mandatory presumption that the accused is negligent unless it establishes a defence of due diligence on a balance of probabilities does violate the presumption of innocence under section 11(d) of the *Charter*. The Court in *Wholesale Travel Group* did not accept that the less drastic alternative of an evidential as opposed to a persuasive burden would adequately advance the objectives of regulatory offences. It expressed concerns that regulatory objectives could be frustrated if accused were acquitted simply because there was a reasonable doubt whether they were negligent in allowing an *actus reus* to occur.

When a corporation is charged with a criminal offence, the required fault must now under new statutory provisions designed to facilitate the prosecution of corporations be attributed to senior officer(s) who either play an important role in establishing policy or who are responsible for managing an important aspect of its activities. If the criminal offence is based on negligence, the prohibited act under section 22.1 of the *Criminal Code* must be committed by representative(s) of the corporation (not only employees but also agents and contractors) acting within their scope of authority. No one individual need be responsible for the prohibited act, which can be committed in aggregate by multiple

---

in the circumstances known to the accused at the time, to ascertain that the complainant was consenting."

85 *Sault Ste. Marie*, above note 4.
86 *B.C. Motor Vehicle Reference*, above note 19.
87 *Pontes*, above note 14.
88 *Lévis*, above note 17.

representatives. Either the responsible senior officer or the senior officers collectively must be at fault in the sense of a marked departure from the standard of care that could reasonably be expected to prevent the commission of the offence.

If the criminal offence requires subjective fault, a senior officer acting within the scope of his or her authority must be 1) a party to the offence; or 2) direct the work of the organization's representatives so that they commit the offence; or 3) fail to take all reasonable steps to stop the commission of the offence when he or she knows that representatives of the organization are committing an offence. Sections 22.1 and 22.2 of the *Criminal Code* are complex and still untested provisions designed to facilitate the process of holding organizations responsible for criminal offences in a manner consistent with the requirements of objective and subjective fault found in the criminal law.

FURTHER READINGS

ARCHIBALD, T., K. JULL, & K. ROACH, "The Changed Face of Corporate Criminal Liability" (2004) 48 Crim. L.Q. 367

————, *Corporate and Regulatory Liability: From Due Diligence to Risk Management*, looseleaf (Aurora, ON: Canada Law Book, 2004–)

BRAITHWAITE, J., *Responsive Regulation and Restorative Justice* (Oxford: Oxford University Press, 2002)

COLVIN, E., & S. ANAND, *Principles of Criminal Law*, 3d ed. (Toronto: Thomson Carswell, 2007) chs. 3 and 6

EDWARDS, J. LL.J., *Mens Rea in Statutory Offences* (London: Stevens, 1955)

FISSE, B., "Corporate Criminal Responsibility" (1991) 15 Crim. L.J. 166

HANNA, D., "Corporate Criminal Liability" (1989) 31 Crim. L.Q. 452

HARVARD LAW REVIEW ASSOCIATION, "Corporate Crime: Regulating Corporate Behavior through Criminal Sanctions" (1979) 92 Harv. L. Rev. 1227

MACPHERSON, D.L., "Extending Corporate Criminal Liability" (2004) 30 Man. L.J. 253

MANNING, M., & P. SANKOFF, *Criminal Law*, 4th ed. (Markham: LexisNexis, 2009) chs. 5 and 6.

ONTARIO LAW REFORM COMMISSION, *Report on Provincial Offences* (Toronto: Queen's Printer, 1992)

RUBY, C., & K. JULL, "The *Charter* and Regulatory Offences: A Wholesale Revision" (1992) 14 C.R. (4th) 226

STUART, D., *Canadian Criminal Law: A Treatise*, 5th ed. (Scarborough, ON: Thomson Carswell, 2007) chs. 4 and 11

STUESSER, L., "Convicting the Innocent Owner: Vicarious Liability under Highway Traffic Legislation" (1989) 67 C.R. (3d) 316

WELLS, C., *Corporations and Criminal Responsibility*, 2d ed. (Oxford: Oxford University Press, 2001)

CHAPTER 7

INTOXICATION

Intoxication from alcohol or drugs may be a condition that prevents the Crown from proving that the accused had the fault element required for a particular offence (see chapter 5). Some extreme forms of intoxication may even result in involuntary conduct which, as discussed in chapter 3, is increasingly seen as inconsistent with proof of the prohibited act. Nevertheless, the intoxication defence has been influenced by policy considerations beyond those that relate to the fault element or the prohibited act of the particular offence. For these reasons, it will be examined here in a separate chapter.

Intoxication was historically considered an aggravating factor to a crime because it "was occasioned by [the accused's] own act and folly, and he might have avoided it."[1] In the nineteenth century, as greater emphasis was placed on subjective *mens rea*, courts became more concerned about the relevance of intoxication as a possible defence. The object was not to determine whether the accused was intoxicated, but whether intoxication, combined with any other factors, prevented the formation of the fault element required for the particular offence. At the same time, however, courts never completely abandoned the older idea that an intoxicated offender was not morally innocent, and they placed restrictions on the availability of the intoxication defence. Intoxication was admissible and could raise a reasonable doubt to the mental element for specific intent offences, which required an ulterior objective beyond

---

1   *Reniger v. Fogossa* (1548), 75 E.R. 1 (Ex.).

the immediate act. It was not, however, admissible when the accused was charged with general intent offences, which required proof only of an intent to perform the immediate act. In practice, this meant that intoxication could be a defence to more serious crimes such as murder and robbery, but not to less serious offences such as manslaughter and assault.

The distinction between general and specific intent offences has frequently been criticized. As examined in chapter 5, there are different levels of *mens rea*, but fault elements are not usually classified as either general or specific intent. At best, the general/specific intent dichotomy serves as a rough and ready distinction between the various degrees of subjective *mens rea* and how they may be affected by the accused's intoxication. The classification of a particular fault element as general or specific intent may be uncertain and will likely be driven by policy concerns about the ultimate disposition of the accused. In any event, the classification of intent as either general or specific remains a relevant factor in the administration of the intoxication defence. Its continued relevance reveals concerns about whether voluntary intoxication by the accused should lead to a complete acquittal. As will be seen in this and the next two chapters, defences are often influenced by concerns about the ultimate disposition of the accused.

A. BEARD'S CASE

The genesis of the modern defence of intoxication is found in the House of Lords' 1920 decision in *D.P.P. v. Beard*.[2] In that case, the Court articulated the following propositions:

1) "[T]hat intoxication could be a ground for an insanity defence if it produced a disease of the mind."

2) "That evidence of drunkenness which renders the accused incapable of forming the specific intent essential to constitute the crime should be taken into consideration with the other facts proved in order to determine whether or not he had this intent."

3) "That evidence of drunkenness falling short of a proved incapacity in the accused to form the intent necessary to constitute the crime, and merely establishing that his mind was affected by drink so that he more readily gave way to some violent passion,

---

2   [1920] A.C. 479 (H.L.) [*Beard*].

does not rebut the presumption that a man intends the natural consequences of his acts."[3]

In the actual case, Beard had been drinking when he killed a woman in the course of a rape. Shortly after the killing, he was accepted into a trade union after answering "not unintelligently certain questions which were put to him." The House of Lords confirmed his conviction for constructive murder in the course of a rape by stating: "[D]runkenness in this case could be no defence unless it could be established that Beard at the time of committing the rape was so drunk that he was incapable of forming the intent to commit it, which was not in fact, and manifestly, having regard to the evidence, could not be contended."[4]

B. THE DISTINCTION BETWEEN GENERAL AND SPECIFIC INTENT OFFENCES

Courts in England and Canada have taken the reference in *Beard* to "forming the specific intent essential to commit the crime" as drawing a distinction between crimes of specific intent and those of general intent. It is arguable, however, that the word "specific" was used in *Beard* only to refer to the particular crime, and not to a distinct category of offences. No reference is made in *Beard* to "general intent" offences as a category of offences distinct from "specific intent" offences. Moreover, the relevance of intoxication to rape was considered even though that offence has subsequently been classified as a general intent offence. Nevertheless, *Beard* has been interpreted in England and Canada as establishing a distinction between crimes of specific and general intent, with intoxication traditionally being a defence only with respect to the former.

In *R. v. George*, the Supreme Court held that robbery was a specific intent offence to which drunkenness was relevant, but assault was

---

3   *Ibid.* at 500–2.

4   *Ibid.* at 504–5. Constructive or felony murder bases liability for murder on the commission of a serious underlying offence such as rape, whether or not the accused intended to kill the victim or knew that death was likely. If *Beard*'s case arose today in Canada, he could not be charged with constructive murder. See *R. v. Vaillancourt* (1987), 39 C.C.C. (3d) 118 (S.C.C.) and *R. v. Martineau* (1990), 58 C.C.C. (3d) 353 (S.C.C.), discussed in chs. 2 and 5. Evidence of intoxication would be relevant in determining not whether Beard would have the intent for sexual assault, but for murder. The focus today would be on intent, not capacity for intent. In other words, the question would be whether given the evidence of intoxication and any other factors, the prosecutor had established that Beard knew that his victim was likely to die.

a general intent offence to which evidence of intoxication was rarely, if ever, relevant. Fauteux J. explained: "In considering the question of *mens rea*, a distinction is to be made between (i) intention as applied to acts considered in relation to their purposes and (ii) intention as applied to acts apart from their purposes."[5] Robbery fell into the first category because it required the application of force in order to facilitate the taking of property, while assault fell into the second category because it required only the minimal intent required for the application of force without consent. Ritchie J. similarly distinguished

> between "intention" as applied to acts done to achieve an immediate end on the one hand and acts done with the specific and ulterior motive and intention of furthering or achieving an illegal object on the other hand. Illegal acts of the former kind are done "intentionally" in the sense that they are not done by accident or through honest mistake, but acts of the latter kind are the product of preconception and deliberate steps taken towards an illegal goal.[6]

In the result, the intoxicated accused was acquitted of robbery, but convicted of the included offence of assault.

In *R. v. Bernard*,[7] McIntyre J. stressed that specific intent offences require the mind to focus on an objective further to the immediate one at hand, while general intent offences require only a conscious doing of the prohibited act. In that case, the majority held that the offence of sexual assault causing bodily harm was a general intent offence. In a companion case, breaking and entering and committing the indictable offence of assault was held to be a general intent offence. It was suggested, however, that the different offence of breaking and entering with the intent to commit an indictable offence was a specific intent offence, because it required proof of an ulterior intent beyond the immediate prohibited acts.[8] In dissent, Dickson C.J. argued that the distinction between general and specific intent offences was an artificial, uncertain, and confusing device to exclude relevant information from the jury's consideration. He also argued that the distinction was not necessary to ensure social protection.[9] Juries could be relied on not to accept specious claims that the accused's intoxication deprived him or her of the intent required for the particular crime.

---

5   *R. v. George* (1960), 128 C.C.C. 289 at 301 (S.C.C) [*George*].
6   *Ibid.* at 306.
7   (1988), 45 C.C.C. (3d) 1 at 24–25 (S.C.C.) [*Bernard*].
8   *R. v. Quin* (1988), 44 C.C.C. (3d) 570 (S.C.C.) [*Quin*].
9   *Bernard*, above note 7 at 9–13; *Quin*, *ibid.* at 574.

The distinction between general and specific intent has been criticized as illogical and difficult to apply. The Supreme Court has recognized that the distinction is largely driven by policy concerns. In *R. v. Daviault*,[10] Sopinka J. noted that specific intent offences were generally more serious offences requiring some ulterior intent, and that "failure to prove the added element will often result in conviction of a lesser offence for which the added element is not required. One example is the offence of assault to resist or prevent arrest which is a specific intent offence. Absent the intent to resist arrest, the accused would be convicted of assault *simpliciter*, a general intent offence."[11] The distinction between specific and general intent offences has often served the practical purpose of ensuring that even if the accused's voluntary intoxication prevents conviction for the specific intent offence, the accused will normally still be convicted of a less serious general intent offence. A classic example is when evidence of intoxication raises a reasonable doubt about the intent for murder, but the accused is then convicted of the general intent offence of manslaughter.

Murder, theft, robbery, aiding and abetting a crime, and attempted crimes have all been held to be specific intent offences, on the basis that they require proof of an ulterior objective beyond the immediate act. Thus, intoxication is admissible and can raise a reasonable doubt about the mental element for these offences. Manslaughter, assault, sexual assault, assault causing bodily harm, and mischief, however, have all been classified as general intent offences on the basis that they require proof only of intent in relation to the prohibited act. In addition, crimes based on an objective fault element would also seem to preclude considering the accused's intoxication as a defence. Recent developments, however, suggest that extreme intoxication may be a defence to general intent offences. To the extent that extreme intoxication negates the voluntariness of the accused's actions it may also be a defence to crimes that require objective fault and even absolute liability offences.

C. THE INTOXICATION DEFENCE FOR SPECIFIC INTENT OFFENCES

Since *Beard*,[12] it has been possible for an accused to be acquitted of a specific intent offence where evidence of intoxication alone or in com-

---

10   (1994), 93 C.C.C. (3d) 21 (S.C.C.) [*Daviault*].

11   *Ibid.* at 41 (in dissent, but not on this issue).

12   *Beard*, above note 2.

bination with other factors produced a reasonable doubt as to whether he or she had the intent required for the offence. The role of the intoxication defence in relation to specific intent offences has not been as controversial as the possibility that extreme intoxication might be a defence to a general intent offence. The practical reason is that an accused acquitted of a specific intent offence because of intoxication will almost always be convicted of a lesser general intent offence. For example, evidence of intoxication could raise a reasonable doubt to the specific intent of murder, but would normally not be considered in determining whether the accused was guilty of the general intent offence of manslaughter. In *George*, the accused was acquitted of the specific intent offence of robbery because of intoxication, but was convicted of assault because his intoxication was not so extreme as to prevent the Crown from proving the minimal intent required for that general intent offence.

1) Intent Not Capacity to Commit the Offence

In *Beard*, the House of Lords referred to evidence of intoxication that would render the accused incapable of forming a specific intent. This seems to require the trier of fact to have a reasonable doubt about whether the accused was capable of forming an intent, whereas general *mens rea* principles would suggest that the actual intent, not the capacity for intent, should be the issue. Nevertheless, in a long line of cases, Canadian courts followed *Beard* and held that the issue was whether evidence of drunkenness raised a reasonable doubt as to the accused's capacity to form a specific intent.[13]

In *R. v. Robinson*,[14] the Supreme Court held that the *Beard* rules violated sections 7 and 11(d) of the *Charter* because they required the jury to convict even if it had a reasonable doubt about the accused's actual intent. In other words, the Court was concerned that an accused who was not so intoxicated as to lack the capacity to form the intent may nevertheless have not exercised that capacity and formed the specific intent. A conclusion that evidence of intoxication did not raise a reasonable doubt as to the accused's capacity to form the specific intent did not lead inexorably to the conclusion that the Crown had proven beyond a reasonable doubt that the accused had actually exercised that capacity and had the required intent. The *Beard* rule concerning cap-

---

13   *R. v. MacAskill* (1931), 55 C.C.C. 81 at 84 (S.C.C.); *R. v. Leary* (1977), 33 C.C.C. (2d) 473 at 482–84 (S.C.C.) [*Leary*]; *Bernard*, above note 7 at 26.

14   (1996), 105 C.C.C. (3d) 97 (S.C.C.) [*Robinson*].

acity could not be justified under section 1 because social protection could be achieved without casting the net of liability so far as to convict all those who had the capacity to form the requisite intent, but who may nevertheless not have had the intent required for a murder conviction. The Court was less deferential to judge-made common law rules that infringed *Charter* rights than to legislation enacted by Parliament. The Court also noted that the capacity rule was not necessary because the intent rule only reduced the accused's culpability from murder to manslaughter.

After *Robinson*, judges could still instruct the jury to consider the accused's capacity to form the intent if evidence, such as expert evidence, was directed to the issue of capacity. Nevertheless, a judge who instructs on capacity has an onerous obligation to make sure that at the end of the day the jury understands that the ultimate issue is whether evidence of intoxication raised a reasonable doubt as to the accused's actual intent and not his or her capacity to form the intent. A new trial will be ordered if the jury is misled into thinking that the accused's capacity to form that intent was the ultimate issue because this could result in convicting an accused even though there might still be a reasonable doubt as to his or her actual intent.[15] In 2007, however, a majority of the Court in *R. v. Daley* indicated that henceforth judges should only instruct the jury to consider whether intoxication raises a reasonable doubt with respect to actual intent and that they should not make reference to capacity so as not to confuse the jury.[16] This approach has simplified charges to the jury and is consistent with basic *mens rea* principles in focusing on the issue of intent.

2) Threshold Air of Reality Tests

In cases involving either general or specific intent offences, the accused must establish that there is an air of reality that justifies instructing the trier of fact about the intoxication defence. Threshold air of reality tests are designed to ensure that the jury is not instructed about irrelevant defences. They have not generally been seen as presenting presumption of innocence problems. Nevertheless, they can keep the jury from considering defences such as mistake of fact, intoxication, and necessity and they may play an important role in the criminal trial.

---

15   See, e.g., *R. v. McMaster* (1996), 105 C.C.C. (3d) 193 (S.C.C.).

16   *R. v. Daley*, [2007] 3 S.C.R. 523 at para. 102 [*Daley*]. Four judges dissented on the facts of the case and held that the trial judge should have done more to instruct the jury about the evidence of intoxication and the *mens rea* requirements.

With respect to murder, the threshold test is whether "the evidence of drunkenness was sufficient to permit a reasonable inference that the accused may not in fact have foreseen that his act of firing the gun at the deceased would cause her death."[17] This threshold was not satisfied in the murder case of *Lemky* where an accused with a blood alcohol level slightly above the legal limit for driving was capable before and after the shooting of being aware of the consequences of his actions and who argued at trial that his shooting of the deceased was not done without *mens rea*, but was the result of an accident. With respect to specific intent offences the evidential threshold is focused on actual intent and not capacity. With respect to the *Daviault* test of extreme intoxication to a general intent offence however, the threshold issue should be the capacity to have the minimal intent associated with general intent offences as opposed to the actual intent. A judge at the stage of applying the air of reality test should focus on whether a properly instructed jury could reasonably acquit on the evidence. The judge should not determine the credibility of the evidence or keep the defence from the jury on the basis that the accused may not be able to establish the defence on a balance of probabilities.[18]

D. LIABILITY FOR THE INTOXICATED COMMISSION OF GENERAL INTENT OFFENCES

In *R. v. Leary*,[19] the Supreme Court followed *R. v. Majewski*[20] and decided that intoxication could not be a defence to a general intent offence. In *Majewski*, Lord Elywn-Jones relied on the controversial proposition that the accused, by becoming voluntarily intoxicated, had committed the *mens rea* for a general intent offence such as assault causing bodily harm. He stated:

---

17   *R. v. Lemky* (1996), 105 C.C.C. (3d) 137 at 144 (S.C.C.). In *Robinson*, above note 14 at 116, the Court articulated the threshold standard in a seemingly less restrictive manner by stating that the trial judge must instruct the jury concerning intoxication if "the effect of the intoxication was such that its effect *might* have impaired the accused's foresight of consequences sufficient to raise a reasonable doubt" [emphasis in original].

18   See *R. v. Fontaine*, 2004 SCC 27 discussed in chs. 2 and 8.

19   *Leary*, above note 13.

20   (1976), 62 Cr. App. Rep. 262 (H.L.).

If a man of his own volition takes a substance which causes him to cast off the restraints of reason and conscience, no wrong is done to him by holding him answerable criminally for any injury he may do while in that condition. His course of conduct in reducing himself by drugs and drink to that condition in my view supplies the evidence of *mens rea*, of guilty mind certainly sufficient for crimes of basic intent. It is a reckless course of conduct and recklessness is enough to constitute the necessary *mens rea* in assault cases.[21]

Under this approach, the recklessness of becoming drunk is deemed to be sufficient to supply the fault element for the commission of the particular general intent offence. This creates an exception to the general proposition, examined in chapter 3, that the fault element should occur at the same time as the *actus reus*. The fault element would be formed not when the assault took place, but before that time while the accused was becoming intoxicated. At the time the assault was committed, the accused would have no fault element. It also creates an exception to the general proposition, examined in chapter 5, that the fault element should be directed towards the *actus reus*. An extremely intoxicated person may not necessarily have formed the intent to commit the general intent offence while he or she was becoming intoxicated.

In a strong dissent in *Leary*,[22] Dickson J. argued that the recklessness in becoming intoxicated was not legally sufficient because "recklessness in a legal sense imports foresight. Recklessness cannot exist in the air; it must have reference to the consequences of a particular act," namely, the crime charged. He argued that the dichotomy between general and specific intent was irrational and that evidence of drunkenness should be left to the jury regardless of the offence charged. "In the case of an intoxicated or drugged accused, the jury may have little difficulty in drawing an inference of intent or recklessness in the relevant sense, but that remains an issue of fact for the jury to determine in each particular case."[23] New Zealand and Australia follow this approach and allow evidence of intoxication to be considered by the trier of fact in all cases and without regard to the classification of offences as general or specific intent.[24]

---

21 *Ibid.* at 270.
22 *Leary*, above note 13 at 494.
23 *Ibid.* at 495.
24 R. v. *Kamipeli*, [1975] 2 N.Z.L.R. 610 (C.A.); R. v. *O'Connor* (1980), 54 A.L.J.R. 349 (H.C.).

E. EXTREME INTOXICATION AND GENERAL INTENT OFFENCES

1) The Development of the *Daviault* Defence

The rule in *Leary* that holds that becoming intoxicated could supply the *mens rea* for general intent offences was vulnerable under the *Charter* because 1) it departed from the requirement that the *mens rea* occur at the same time as the *actus reus*; 2) it transferred the general or at-large fault of becoming intoxicated for the fault of the particular general intent offence; and 3) it would allow the conviction of a person who was so severely intoxicated that he or she acted involuntarily or without the intent required for the particular general intent offence.

The Supreme Court first considered the constitutionality of the *Leary* rule in *Bernard*.[25] The Court was deeply divided. Two judges would have upheld the *Leary* rule in its full vigour so that even if the accused "was so intoxicated as to raise doubts as to the voluntary nature of his conduct," the Crown could demonstrate the necessary *mens rea* from the fact of voluntary self-intoxication. McIntyre J. argued for the traditional position that proof of the accused's "voluntary drunkenness can be proof of his guilty mind"[26] even though this fault would not necessarily be present when the prohibited act was committed, or have been directed at the prohibited act.

At the other end of the spectrum, Chief Justice Dickson, with the concurrence of Justices Lamer and La Forest, not only adhered to his strong dissent in *Leary*, but argued that the *Leary* rule violated sections 7 and 11(d) of the *Charter* by substituting the intent of becoming intoxicated for the intent of the particular general intent offence. He concluded:

> The effect of the majority holding in *Leary* is to impose a form of absolute liability on intoxicated offenders, which is entirely inconsistent with the basic requirement for a blameworthy state of mind as a prerequisite to the imposition of the penalty of imprisonment [under section 7 of the *Charter*] . . . .
>
> The majority holding in *Leary* also runs counter to the s. 11(d) right to be presumed innocent until proven guilty. With respect to crimes of general intent, guilty intent is in effect presumed upon

---

25 *Bernard*, above note 7.
26 *Ibid.* at 36.

proof of the fact of intoxication. Moreover, the presumption of guilt created by the *Leary* rule is irrebutable.[27]

The exclusion of evidence of intoxication converted general intent offences to absolute liability offences by not considering a potentially crucial factor in determining whether the accused had the required *mens rea.* In addition, the presumption of innocence was violated when the fault of becoming intoxicated was substituted for the fault of the particular general intent offence. Dickson C.J. also concluded that the *Leary* rule could not be justified under section 1 of the *Charter* because it would require people to be convicted for unintended or unforeseen crimes. He argued: "[I]t has not been demonstrated that risk of imprisonment of a few innocent persons is required to attain the goal of protecting the public from drunken offenders."[28] If public protection required special measures to deal with intoxicated offenders, that should be done by Parliament, not the courts. This could be done through the creation of an offence that punished the accused for being drunk and dangerous.

Justice Wilson fashioned a novel compromise position that was later to command support from a majority of the Court in *Daviault.* Unlike Dickson C.J., she retained the distinction between general and specific intent offences. In most cases, the minimal intent required for the commission of a general intent offence could be inferred from the commission of the act. In *Bernard*, for example, the accused was guilty of the general intent offence of sexual assault causing bodily harm because it was clear that he engaged in "intentional and voluntary, as opposed to accidental or involuntary, application of force."[29] Wilson J. also disagreed with Dickson C.J. that the *Leary* rule violated section 7 of the *Charter.* An accused who voluntarily became so intoxicated as not to have the minimal awareness required for a general intent offence was not a morally innocent person who should be protected from conviction under section 7 of the *Charter.*[30] However, the "real concern" for Wilson J. arose under section 11(d) because the fault of becoming

---

27   *Ibid.* at 16–17.

28   *Ibid.* at 18.

29   She concluded: "There is no evidence that we are dealing here with extreme intoxication, verging on insanity or automatism, and as such capable of negating the inference that the minimal intent to apply force was present. . . . The evidence of intoxication in this case was simply not capable of raising a reasonable doubt as to the existence of the minimal intent required." *Ibid.* at 39–40.

30   Such persons would nevertheless have rights under ss. 7 and 12 of the *Canadian Charter of Rights and Freedoms*, Part I of the *Constitution Act, 1982*, being Schedule B to the *Canada Act 1982* (U.K.), 1982, c. 11 [*Charter*] "to be protected

drunk would under the *Leary* rule be substituted for the fault of the particular offence charged. Wilson J. elaborated:

> While this court has recognized that in some cases proof of an essential element of a criminal offence can be replaced by proof of a different element, it has placed stringent limitations on when this can happen . . . . In my tentative view, it is unlikely that in those cases in which it is necessary to resort to self-induced intoxication as the substituted element for the minimal intent, proof of the substituted element will "inexorably" lead to the conclusion that the essential element of the minimal intent existed at the time the criminal act was committed.[31]

Wilson J. would apply the basic *Leary* rule in a more flexible fashion that would allow "evidence of extreme intoxication involving an absence of awareness akin to a state of insanity or automatism" to go to the trier of fact in "those rare cases in which the intoxication is extreme enough to raise doubts as to the existence of the minimal intent which characterizes conscious and volitional conduct."[32]

Six years later, Justice Wilson's approach, with some variations, commanded support from a majority of the Supreme Court. In *Daviault*,[33] the Supreme Court decided that extreme intoxication could in rare cases be a defence to general intent offences such as assault or sexual assault. In such cases, the minimal intent required for a general intent offence could not be inferred from the commission of the prohibited act because "the very voluntariness or consciousness of that act may be put in question by the extreme intoxication of the accused."[34] The focus in *Daviault* was on extreme intoxication that negated the accused's capacity for voluntary conduct and the minimal *mens rea* necessary for a general intent offence as opposed to evidence of intoxication that could raise a reasonable doubt about the more complex mental processes required in specific intent offences. Moreover, the application of the *Leary* and *Majewski* rule would violate both sections 7 and 11(d) of the *Charter* by substituting the intent of becoming intoxicated for the intent of the offence. Cory J. concluded:

So does extreme intoxication negate general intent or voluntariness of actus reus?

> against punishment that is disproportionate to their crime and degree of culpability." *Ibid.* at 43–44.

31   *Ibid.* at 44.
32   *Ibid.* at 42–43.
33   *Daviault*, above note 10.
34   *Ibid.* at 58.

The consumption of alcohol simply cannot lead inexorably to the *S11(A)* conclusion that the accused possessed the requisite mental element to commit a sexual assault, or any other crime. Rather, the substituted *mens rea* rule has the effect of eliminating the minimal mental element required for sexual assault. Furthermore, *mens rea* for a *S7* crime is so well recognized that to eliminate that mental element, an integral part of the crime, would be to deprive an accused of fundamental justice.[35]

Not considering evidence of intoxication in cases of extreme intoxication could lead to conviction without proof that the accused had the *mens rea* required for the general intent offence. Whatever fault element could be inferred from becoming intoxicated did not prove beyond a reasonable doubt that the accused had the fault element for a general intent offence, in this case, sexual assault.

In *Daviault*, the Supreme Court purported to adopt Wilson J.'s position in *Bernard*, but the Court's reasoning differed in two respects. First, the Court held that the *Leary* rule violated not only section 11(d), but also section 7 of the *Charter*. In contrast, Wilson J. suggested in *Bernard* that a person who voluntarily became so intoxicated that he or she did not have the minimal intent necessary to commit a general intent offence was not a morally innocent person protected from punishment under section 7 of the *Charter*.[36] This is not a doctrinal quibble given that the courts have been much more willing to uphold violations of section 11(d) under section 1 than violations of section 7 of the *Charter*.[37]

Second, the Court in *Daviault* required an accused to prove extreme intoxication as a defence to a general intent crime on a balance of probabilities, whereas Wilson J. would have allowed such evidence to rebut the Crown's usual duty to prove the fault element beyond a reasonable doubt. Cory J. explained that the burden on the accused to prove extreme intoxication violated the presumption of innocence in section 11(d), but was justified because "it is only the accused who can give evidence as to the amount of alcohol consumed and its effect upon him. Expert evidence would be required to confirm that the accused was probably in a state akin to automatism or insanity as a

---

35   *Ibid.* at 60.

36   Wilson J., however, contemplated that such a person would be protected from disproportionate punishment under both s. 7 and s. 12 of the *Charter*, above note 30.

37   See ch. 2(B)(3)(f), "Right to Be Presumed Innocent."

result of his drinking."[38] Because of concerns about social protection, the Supreme Court violated the presumption of innocence in its own development of the common law. As will be seen in chapter 8, an accused wishing to take advantage of the mental disorder or automatism defences must also prove the defence on a balance of probabilities. At the same time, the reversal of the burden can be criticized as unprincipled. In countries such as Australia and New Zealand, which have abandoned the specific and general intent distinction, the accused has no burden to establish the defence of intoxication and will be acquitted whenever the evidence of intoxication raises a reasonable doubt about the intent of the offence charged. There is no compelling evidence that social protection has been sacrificed by maintaining the presumption of innocence.

The defence contemplated in *Daviault* applies only if the accused is extremely intoxicated. Cory J. argued:

> those who are a "little" drunk can readily form the requisite mental element to commit the offence. The alcohol-induced relaxation of both inhibitions and socially acceptable behaviour has never been accepted as a factor or excuse in determining whether the accused possessed the requisite *mens rea*. Given the minimal nature of the mental element required for crimes of general intent, even those who are significantly drunk will usually be able to form the requisite *mens rea* and will be found to have acted voluntarily. . . .
>
> It is obvious that it will only be on rare occasions that evidence of such an extreme state of intoxication can be advanced and perhaps only on still rarer occasions is it likely to be successful.[39]

Despite evidence suggesting that Daviault, a chronic alcoholic, had a blood alcohol level that would kill most people, and the trial judge's acquittal, the Court sent the case back for a new trial to require the accused to establish the defence of extreme intoxication on a balance of probabilities.

Daviault dealt with the crime of sexual assault, which, at the time, required subjective *mens rea*.[40] Other general intent offences, notably

---

38 *Daviault*, above note 10.

39 *Ibid.* at 67–68.

40 Subsequent amendments to sexual assault have introduced objective components in relation to the defence of mistake of fact and have affirmed that self-induced intoxication should not be considered in relation to that defence. *Criminal Code*, R.S.C. 1985, c. C-46 [*Code*], s. 273.2(b). In his dissent, Sopinka J. concluded "sexual assault does not fall into the category of offences for which either the stigma or the available penalties demand as a constitutional require-

unlawful act manslaughter, require only proof of an objective fault element. An extremely intoxicated accused could still have objective fault if his or her conduct demonstrated a marked and substantial departure from what a reasonable person would have done in the circumstances. If, however, the extreme intoxication negates the voluntariness required for the *actus reus*, the accused may have a defence because he or she did not consciously and voluntarily commit the criminal act. In *Daviault*, Cory J. indicated that when extreme intoxication produced a state akin to automatism it would "render an accused incapable of either performing a willed act or of forming the minimal intent required for a general intent offence." In their concurrences, both Lamer C.J. and La Forest J. indicated that such extreme intoxication would also raise a reasonable doubt as to the commission of the *actus reus*.[41]

Daviault raises the possibility that extreme intoxication would be a defence not only to general intent offences but to absolute or strict liability offences. The extreme intoxication contemplated under *Daviault* may negate the voluntariness that is increasingly seen as part of the *actus reus*.[42] Cory J. recognized that "the mental aspect involved in willed or voluntary conduct may overlap to some extent in both the concept of *mens rea* and *actus reus*."[43] In their concurrences, both Lamer C.J. and La Forest J. stated that they preferred to characterize the minimal mental element of general intent offences "as relating more to the *actus reus* than the *mens rea*, so that the defence [of extreme intoxication akin to automatism] clearly be available in strict liability offences."[44] In such cases, it would not matter that the accused could not prove a defence of due diligence because of his or her negligence in becoming drunk,

---

ment subjective intent to commit the *actus reus*. . . . I cannot see how the stigma and punishment associated with the offence of sexual assault are disproportionate to the moral blameworthiness of a person like the appellant who commits the offence after voluntarily becoming so intoxicated as to be incapable of knowing what he is doing. The fact that the *Leary* rules permit an individual to be convicted despite the absence of symmetry between the *actus reus* and the mental element of blameworthiness does not violate a principle of fundamental justice." *Daviault, ibid.* at 37–38.

41   In Australia, extreme intoxication can be a defence to manslaughter if it indicates that the accused's acts were not voluntary. *R. v. Martin* (1984), 51 A.L.R. 540 (H.C.). Presumably, a similar defence would apply in Canada after *Daviault*, above note 10, albeit one that requires the accused to prove on a balance of probabilities that the unlawful act for the manslaughter was not voluntary because of extreme intoxication.

42   See ch. 3(B)(4), "Voluntariness of the Act."

43   *Daviault*, above note 10 at 49.

44   *Ibid.* at 25. The Chief Justice's reasoning would also seem to apply to absolute liability offences to the extent that they survive *Charter* scrutiny.

since the *actus reus* necessary for conviction would not be present. The accused would still bear the burden of proving the defence of extreme intoxication on a balance of probabilities even though extreme intoxication might prevent the Crown from proving the commission of the *actus reus* beyond a reasonable doubt.

Daviault did not abolish the much criticized distinction between general and specific intent offences, and it introduced two distinct intoxication defences with different burdens of proof. When an accused is charged with a specific intent offence such as murder, the ordinary intoxication defence will apply if it raises a reasonable doubt about whether the accused had the required intent. In many cases, however, the accused would still have to face a charge on a general intent offence such as manslaughter or assault. With respect to general intent offences, evidence of intoxication will be relevant only in rare cases supported by expert evidence. The accused must prove on a balance of probabilities that he or she was so extremely intoxicated as to be incapable of having the minimal intent required for a general intent offence. An accused with the extreme intoxication defence may, however, not be convicted of any offences, because there are generally no lesser included offences to convict a person acquitted of a general intent offence.[45] For example, while a person acquitted because of intoxication of the specific intent offence of murder will often be convicted of manslaughter, a person acquitted of manslaughter, assault, or sexual assault because of extreme intoxication will often not be guilty of any lesser crime.

2) The Legislative Response to *Daviault*: Section 33.1

Although the Supreme Court believed the *Daviault* defence would apply only in rare cases, it recognized that Parliament might wish to respond to the social danger of an acquittal of a severely intoxicated accused who committed a general intent offence. The Court indicated that "it is always open to Parliament to fashion a remedy which would make

---

45   One exception may be offences such as impaired driving, which have intoxication as an essential element. See *R. v. Penno* (1990), 59 C.C.C. (3d) 344 (S.C.C.) [*Penno*], discussed below at note 47. On the other hand, it could be argued that an accused should still have a *Daviault* defence, because the extreme intoxication prevents the voluntary commission of even the *actus reus* required for intoxication-based offences. This is also suggested by the Court's recognition that involuntary intoxication may be a defence to impaired driving. See *R. v. King* (1962), 133 C.C.C. 1 (S.C.C.) [*King*].

it a crime to commit a prohibited act while drunk."[46] There are many ways that such legislation could be formulated. Parliament could have provided a new offence of being "drunk and dangerous," committing harm while extremely intoxicated, or committing a specific wrongful act while extremely intoxicated. All these options would mean that an extremely intoxicated person who did not have the minimal intent to commit a general intent offence would be acquitted of that offence, but convicted of a new offence that contained intoxication as an essential element. Such offences have long been proposed as a means to ensure public safety should the courts abolish the common law distinction between specific and general intent offences, and allow evidence of intoxication to go to the jury in all cases. An offence that included intoxication as an element would undoubtedly be held consistent with the *Charter*. In *Penno*,[47] the Supreme Court rejected the notion that intoxication could be a defence to a crime of intoxicated driving and it has in several subsequent cases indicated that the denial of a defence that would be at odds with the very mischief that the offence seeks to prohibit would not violate the *Charter*.[48]

Another alternative would be to treat those with a *Daviault* defence in the same manner as a mentally disordered offender. They would then be found not criminally responsible but be subject to further detention and treatment if they are a significant danger to the public. The House of Lords in *Beard* seemed to contemplate that drunkenness could produce a state of insanity, but Canadian courts have been reluctant to hold that self-induced intoxication and other transitory states should qualify for the insanity or mental disorder defence.[49] In his dissent in *Daviault*, Sopinka J. explicitly rejected this mental disorder option and argued that those who voluntarily become extremely intoxicated "deserve to be punished for their crimes" because their condition was self-induced and avoidable.[50]

---

46   *Daviault*, above note 10 at 68.
47   Above note 45. Only Lamer C.J. found that the denial of the intoxication defence might violate ss. 7 and 11(d) of the *Charter* because it could convict a person on the basis of an involuntary act, but he held that such violations were justified under s. 1 of the *Charter*. The rest of the judges found no *Charter* violation.
48   *R. v. Finta*, [1994] 1 S.C.R. 701 at 865 [*Finta*]; *R. v. Ruzic*, 2001 SCC 24 at para. 23 [*Ruzic*]; *Canadian Foundation for Children, Youth and the Law v. Canada (A.G.)*, 2004 SCC 4 [*Canadian Foundation for Children*].
49   *R. v. Cooper* (1979), 51 C.C.C. (2d) 129 (S.C.C.); *R. v. Bouchard-Lebrun*, [2011] 3 S.C.R. 575 [*Bouchard-Lebrun*]. See ch. 8(C), "Mental Disorder or Disease of the Mind."
50   *Daviault*, above note 10 at 45.

In any event, Parliament did not respond to *Daviault* through the creation of a new intoxication-based offence or by creating a treatment disposition. Rather, it amended the *Criminal Code* so that those with a *Daviault* defence will be convicted of the same violent general intent offences that they would have been convicted of before the Court's decision.[51] Section 33.1(1) and (2) of the *Criminal Code* now contemplates that it will not be a defence that the accused "by reason of self-induced intoxication, lacked the general intent or the voluntariness required to commit the offence," because

> a person departs markedly from the standard of reasonable care generally recognized in Canadian society and is thereby criminally at fault where the person, while in a state of self-induced intoxication that renders the person unaware of, or incapable of consciously controlling, their behaviour, voluntarily or involuntarily interferes or threatens to interfere with the bodily integrity of another person.[52]

This confusing provision seems to deem that a person who has become so drunk as to engage in involuntary violence has departed markedly from an at-large standard of reasonable care "generally recognized in Canadian society." This marked departure from the standard of reasonable care is then substituted for the intent required to commit the particular general intent offence charged whether it be assault or sexual assault. This seems to be a legislative reaffirmation of the controversial proposition in *Majewski* and *Leary* that if an accused charged with a general intent offence does not have the necessary *mens rea* at the time that the offence was committed, his actions and mind in voluntarily becoming so intoxicated can be substituted for the *mens rea* or the voluntary *actus reus* required for the particular offence. The only extra step is that the *Criminal Code* now deems that becoming so intoxicated is a marked departure from "the standard of reasonable care generally recognized in Canadian society." In a sense, what Dickson J. originally criticized in *Leary* as "recklessness at large" has been codified for general intent offences, which involve assaults or other interference or threat of interference with bodily integrity. The following chart demonstrates the similarities between the *Leary* rule and section 33.1.

---

51 Section 33.1(3) of the *Code*, above note 40, applies only to offences that include "as an element an assault or any other interference or threat of interference by a person with the bodily integrity of another person." An accused could still raise a *Daviault* defence and be acquitted of a general intent property crime such as mischief.

52 *Code, ibid.*, s. 33.1(2).

Leary **Rule**

Becoming intoxicated   ⎯⎯⎯⎯⎯→   fault for any general intent offence
"recklessness in the air"

Section 33.1

Becoming intoxicated   ⎯⎯⎯⎯⎯→   fault for any general intent offence
that includes an assault or threat of
interference with bodily integrity
(section 33.1(3))

Deemed to constitute marked
departure from standard of
reasonable care generally recognized in Canadian society
(section 33.1(2))

It is important to stress, however, that section 33.1 does not apply to general intent offences that do not involve an assault or threat of interference with bodily integrity. In a recent case in which it applied section 33.1 but was not asked to rule on its constitutional validity, the Supreme Court observed that "the principles set out in *Daviault* still represent the state of the law in Canada, subject, of course, to the significant restriction set out in section 33.1 *Cr. C. Daviault* would still apply today, for example, to enable an accused charged with a property offence to plead extreme intoxication."[53]

3) The Constitutionality of Section 33.1

The Supreme Court has not ruled on the constitutionality of Parliament's "in your face" reply that takes away the *Daviault* defence for violent general intent offences. The Court has, however, applied section 33.1 to convict a person of the general intent offence of aggravated assault even though the person was acting in an involuntary manner and without intent as a result of a toxic psychosis produced by his voluntary consumption of a drug. The Court stressed that section 33.1 applies even to extreme intoxication and "toxic psychosis" produced by drugs that would render the accused incapable of knowing that his or her acts were wrong. The Court explained that section 33.1 "applies where three conditions are met: 1) the accused was intoxicated at the material time; 2) the intoxication was selfinduced; and 3) the accused departed from the standard of reasonable care generally recognized in Canadian society by interfering or threatening to interfere with the bodily integ-

---

53   *Bouchard-Lebrun*, above note 49 at para. 35.

rity of another person. Where these three things are proved, it is not a defence that the accused lacked the general intent or the voluntariness required to commit the offence."[54]

There is still no definitive ruling of the constitutionality of section 33.1 almost twenty years after its enactment. This may be a product of the rarity of the defence. The trend in lower courts has been to uphold section 33.1 usually under section 1 of the *Charter* while concluding that its substitution of the fault of becoming extremely intoxicated for the fault and voluntariness of the general intent crime of violence violates sections 7 and 11(d) of the *Charter*. The fault of becoming extremely intoxicated does not lead inexorably to the intent required for a particular general intent offence. Thus, the provision violates section 11(d) of the *Charter* by substituting the fault of becoming intoxicated for the fault of the particular general intent offence. The fact that Parliament has deemed such intoxication as departing from the standard of care generally recognized in Canadian society does not alter the fact that such fault is not the fault that Parliament has required for assault and sexual assault or any other general intent offences of violence covered by section 33.1.

Unless the Court reverts to Justice Wilson's position in *Daviault* that a person who commits a general intent offence while in an involuntary state produced by self-induced intoxication is not morally innocent, it would also seem that section 33.1 violates section 7 of the *Charter*. Even if a person who becomes extremely intoxicated is not morally innocent, a person who commits a crime in either a physically or morally involuntary manner would also be protected under section 7 of the *Charter*.[55] Section 33.1 clearly allows a person to be convicted of a crime even though he or she "lacked the general intent or the voluntariness required to commit the offence" and was "incapable of consciously controlling" the behaviour. The Court in both *Daviault* and a number of other non-intoxication cases has confirmed that it would violate the fundamental principles of justice to convict a person for involuntary actions.[56]

If section 33.1 violates sections 7 and 11(d) of the *Charter*, its fate will be decided under section 1 of the *Charter*. When enacting section 33.1, Parliament included a lengthy preamble emphasizing the legislative objective of responding to intoxicated violence. It expressed a particular concern that such "violence has a particularly disadvantaging

---

54   *Ibid.* at para. 89.
55   *Ruzic*, above note 48.
56   *R. v. Stone*, [1999] 2 S.C.R. 290 at paras. 155–58; *Ruzic, ibid.* at paras. 42–43.

impact on the equal participation of women and children in society and on the rights of women and children to security of the person and to equal protection and benefit of the law as guaranteed by sections 7, 15, and 28 of the *Canadian Charter of Rights and Freedoms*."[57] Such considerations may be used to urge the Court to view a *Charter* challenge to section 33.1 through a framework of reconciling competing rights, as was done when the Court upheld a law restricting access to the therapeutic records of complainants in sexual assault cases,[58] even though the legislation, like section 33.1, seemed at odds with a previous *Charter* decision of the Court.[59] Such a reconciliation of rights approaches runs the risk of undermining the obligation placed on the state under section 1 of the *Charter* to justify restrictions on rights and of ignoring the extent to which legislation may infringe one of the competing rights including, in this case, the basic principle that a person should not be convicted for involuntary conduct.

One judge who has held that section 33.1 was an unjustified violation of sections 7 and 11(d) of the *Charter* has been quite critical of the preamble, concluding that "victim's rights are, undoubtedly, a component of society's interests but society's interests must also include a system of law, governed by the principles of fundamental justice . . . . The section cannot accurately be said to address victim's section 7 rights; nor does it address any special needs of women or of children; rather, it sets out to protect victims against intoxicated automatons who act violently."[60] Section 33.1 does indeed apply to forms of violence committed by the accused and is not as specifically tailored to the interests of women and children as the legislation restricting access to confidential records in sexual offence cases.

A better approach than attempting to reconcile the rights of the accused and the victim may be to determine whether the infringements of sections 7 and 11(d) of the *Charter* in section 33.1 can be justified under section 1 of the *Charter*. A threshold issue will be whether a violation of section 7 of the *Charter* can ever be saved under section 1 of

---

57 The preamble generally speaks more to the importance of the objective rather than to the crucial issue of the proportionality of the means used to advance the objective. It does, however, refer to Parliament sharing with Canadians "the moral view that people who, while in a state of self-induced intoxication, violate the physical integrity of others are blameworthy in relation to their harmful conduct and should be held criminally accountable for it." See *An Act to Amend the Criminal Code (Self-Induced Intoxication)*, S.C. 1995, c. 32 [*Code Amendment*].

58 *R. v. Mills*, [1999] 3 S.C.R. 668.

59 *R. v. O'Connor*, [1995] 4 S.C.R. 1411.

60 *R. v. Dunn* (1999), 28 C.R. (5th) 295 at 303 (Ont. S.C.J.) [*Dunn*].

the *Charter*. The Court has suggested that a violation of section 7 could only be justified in "exceptional circumstances, such as the outbreak of war or a national emergency."[61] Such an approach runs the danger of undermining the structure of the *Charter* in contemplating that legislatures can place and then justify limits on all *Charter* rights.

The first step in a section 1 analysis would be to determine the objective of section 33.1 and whether it is important enough to justify limitations on the relevant *Charter* rights. Responding to alcohol-induced violence that could result in the complete acquittal of the accused is obviously a compelling objective that could justify the infringement of *Charter* rights. The fundamental question under section 1 of the *Charter* will be whether section 33.1 is a proportionate response to these important objectives.

The Crown will argue that Parliament has adopted a more tailored rule than the previous common law rule. Thus, section 33.1 does not transfer the fault of becoming extremely intoxicated for the *mens rea* or voluntariness of all general intent offences as contemplated under the *Leary* rule, but only for crimes involving violence. Moreover, it will be argued that Parliament's policy decision not to respond to *Daviault* by introducing a new intoxication-based crime or treatment disposition deserves more judicial deference than the Court's previous common law rule in *Leary*.[62] It may be assumed that Parliament examined other options such as introducing new intoxication-based crimes but found them wanting for a variety of reasons, including their possible effects on police discretion and plea bargaining and the perceived need to label and punish a drunken sexual assaulter or assaulter as a person who nevertheless committed a sexual assault or an assault.[63] Parliament also heard evidence suggesting that alcohol cannot produce involuntary behaviour. This evidence, however, does not relate to other drugs. One judge has dismissed such scientific concerns: "[T]he issue is not whether an accused can scientifically prove [automatism]; the issue is whether it is constitutionally permissible to deny an accused

---

61 *Ruzic*, above note 48 at para. 92.

62 In *R. v. Swain* (1991), 63 C.C.C. (3d) 481 (S.C.C.), the Supreme Court indicated that "where a common law, judge-made rule is challenged under the *Charter*, there is no room for judicial deference" that can apply when Parliament as an elected body places limits on *Charter* rights.

63 The preamble for example states that Parliament "shares with Canadians the moral view that people who, while in a state of self-induced intoxication, violate the physical integrity of others are blameworthy in relation to their harmful conduct and should be held criminally accountable for it." See *Code Amendment*, above note 57.

even the opportunity to try to prove it just because his or her intoxication was self-induced. In my opinion, it is not."[64]

The accused will argue that Parliament rejected a number of more proportionate responses when it introduced new legislation that effectively reversed *Daviault* for general intent offences of violence. Section 33.1 follows the minority in *Daviault* and the *Leary* rule by substituting the fault of voluntarily becoming drunk for the fault of the general intent offence. It labels the drunken automaton as guilty of the same crime as the person who consciously committed an assault or sexual assault with the required *mens rea* at the time the offence was committed. It may thus run afoul of the principles that those who cause harm intentionally be punished more severely than those who cause harm unintentionally and that punishment be morally proportionate to the gravity of the offence.[65] There were other ways that Parliament could have advanced its interest in social protection that were more respectful of the accused's rights under sections 7 and 11(d) of the *Charter*. For example, a new intoxication-based crime would recognize that an accused with a *Daviault* defence did not have the voluntariness or *mens rea* required for an assault or a sexual assault even though he committed an act that caused harm and required punishment. It will also be argued that the harm caused by convicting an accused who acted involuntarily and without *mens rea* outweighs the benefits of section 33.1, especially with regard to the dubious proposition of deterring severely intoxicated people from violence and the rarity that an accused will be so extremely intoxicated as to be able to establish a *Daviault* defence on a balance of probabilities.

The constitutionality of section 33.1 has been considered in a few cases. In *Vickberg*,[66] a trial judge found that section 33.1 violated sections 7 and 11(d) of the *Charter* because it substituted "proof of voluntary intoxication for proof of the intent to commit an offence of general intent, most commonly assault." Nevertheless, these violations were held to be justified under section 1 of the *Charter* as a proportionate means to ensure accountability for violence related with intoxication.[67] In the actual case, however, the trial judge did not apply section 33.1 to convict the accused who committed an assault while in a state of drug-

---

64   *R. v. Brenton* (1999), 28 C.R. (5th) 308 at 331 (N.W.T.S.C.), rev'd on other grounds, 2001 NWTCA 1 [*Brenton*].

65   *R. v. Creighton* (1993), 83 C.C.C. (3d) 346 (S.C.C.). See ch. 5(A)(4), "Constitutional Requirements of *Mens Rea*."

66   *R. v. Vickberg* (1998), 16 C.R. (5th) 164 at 193 (B.C.S.C.) [*Vickberg*].

67   See also *R. v. Decaire*, [1998] O.J. No. 6339 (Gen. Div.), holding that s. 33.1 of the *Code*, above note 40, is justified under s. 1 of the *Charter* to deal with the harms of voluntary intoxication.

induced automatism. Section 33.1 only substitutes the fault of being intoxicated for the fault of the offence if the intoxication is self-induced. The trial judge found that the accused's intoxication in *Vickberg* (an overdose of drugs prescribed to treat his heroin addiction) constituted involuntary intoxication producing non-mental disorder automatism leading to a verdict of acquittal. This is an interesting finding given that on its face section 33.1 applies to "self-induced intoxication," which arguably could be seen as a broader concept than voluntary intoxication.[68] Although section 33.1 was not struck down as an unconstitutional reversal of *Daviault*, it was also not applied to an accused who committed a general intent offence in a state of drug-induced automatism. Should section 33.1 be held to be constitutional, it will be important that courts, as in *Vickberg*, expand the defence of involuntary intoxication to apply to unanticipated effects of self-induced drugs.[69]

In two recent cases, trial judges have held that section 33.1 violated section 7 of the *Charter* but was a justified response because the alternatives of an intoxication-based offence were problematic both with respect to penalties and the accountability of the offender. In one case, the judge stressed that Parliament acted on evidence that the notion of extreme intoxication producing involuntary conduct (as opposed to simply an alcoholic black out and failure to remember) was a "dodgy scientific proposition."[70] The judge also concluded that "reasonable people do not agree with the prevailing view in *Daviault* that the criminal mind and the criminal act must be precisely contemporaneous" but rather with the dissent that holds that the act of becoming extremely intoxicated is sufficiently blameworthy and renders the

---

68   The judge in *Vickberg*, above note 66 at para. 68 stated: "I am in agreement with the defence that 'self-induced' must mean something more than simply the accused himself ingesting the pills, as opposed to someone else administering them. I am satisfied that for intoxication to be self-induced, the accused must intend to become intoxicated, either by volvoluntarily ingesting a substance knowing or having reasonable grounds to know it might be dangerous, or by recklessly ingesting such a substance." The Court applied *King*, above note 45. The Nova Scotia Court of Appeal also applied the *King* test for involuntary intoxication to "self-induced intoxication" under s. 33.1 in *R. v. Chaulk* (2007), 223 C.C.C. (3d) 174 at para. 47 [*Chaulk*] (N.S.C.A.) at para. 46. As discussed in ch. 8(C), "Mental Disorder or Disease of the Mind," courts have been reluctant to classify transitory states of intoxication as a mental disorder for the purposes of s. 16 of the *Code*, *ibid.*

69   In *Brenton*, above note 64, the court held that unanticipated effects of marijuana consumption did not result in involuntary intoxication. The court, however, found that s. 33.1 was an unjustified violation of the *Charter* and acquitted the accused on the basis of the *Daviault* defence.

70   *R. v. S.N.*, 2012 NUCJ 2 at para. 114.

accused less than "morally innocent."[71] In another case, the trial judge stressed that section 33.1 was a proportionate limit on section 7 rights because it "only relates to a limited number of offences, namely crimes of general intent including, as an element, an assault or any other interference or threat of interference by a person with the bodily integrity of another person. This leaves the defence of voluntary extreme intoxication akin to automatism or insanity available for all other general intent offences."[72] Section 33.1 has been held to be constitutional in another case on the basis that "the act of becoming voluntarily intoxicated to the extent of being incapable of controlling one's behaviour, constitutes criminal culpability sufficient to found criminal liability for offences committed against the bodily integrity of others . . . . The public outcry and the Parliamentary response to the *Daviault* case . . . strongly indicate that such a provision is not only consistent with the objectives of the *Charter* but is justifiable and essential in a free and democratic society."[73] The judge in that case also stated that a judge could use sentencing discretion to distinguish between "offences that were deliberately committed and those that were committed involuntarily because of self-induced intoxication."[74]

In some other cases, trial judges have found section 33.1 to be unconstitutional. In *Dunn*,[75] the judge stressed the importance of focusing on the objective of limiting the sections 7 and 11(d) rights as articulated in *Daviault*. The judge doubted that the objective of removing the *Daviault* defence for violent general intent offences was important enough to limit the accused's rights, but in any event concluded that the good of convicting such accused did not outweigh the harms of convicting a person who acted in an involuntary manner. "When an accused can be convicted without proof that he intended his actions or without proof that his actions were voluntary, then absolute liability has become a component of Canadian criminal justice, the presumption of innocence is eroded and the principles of fundamental justice

---

71   *Ibid.* at para. 111.

72   *R. v. Dow*, 2010 QCSC 4276 at para. 144.

73   *R. v. B.J.T.*, [2001] 4 W.W.R. 741 at para. 35 (Sask. Q.B.).

74   *Ibid.* at para. 36.

75   *Dunn*, above note 60. See also *R. v. Cedono* (2005), 195 C.C.C. (3d) 468 at paras. 35–36 (Ont. Ct. J.), finding that s. 33.1 was unconstitutional but that the *Daviault* defence did not apply because the accused had not established it on a balance of probabilities with expert evidence. In the result, the accused was convicted of sexual assault even though the judge would otherwise have had a reasonable doubt that the intoxicated accused had the necessary intent.

are seriously compromised."[76] In *Brenton*,[77] section 33.1 was also struck down with the judge stressing that it "in effect re-enacts as legislation the very same common law rule that was held unconstitutional" in *Daviault*. By eliminating the need to prove either intent or voluntariness at the time the offence was committed, Parliament had created an absolute liability provision and ignored the more proportionate response of enacting a new offence based on the accused's intoxication. This decision was subsequently reversed on appeal on the basis that the constitutionality of section 33.1 did not arise on the facts of the case because the accused who had consumed marijuana had not established the *Daviault* defence of extreme intoxication on a balance of probabilities.[78] In *R. v. Jensen*,[79] the trial judge concluded that section 33.1 was an unjustified violation of sections 7 and 11(d). The accused's murder conviction was subsequently upheld with the Ontario Court of Appeal stating that it "may have been preferable for the trial judge to have explicitly instructed the jury that the level of intoxication required to negate the specific intent to kill could be less than intoxication akin to automatism"[80] that would be required to establish the *Daviault* defence with respect to manslaughter.

The Supreme Court will ultimately decide the fate of section 33.1. Although it is rare that violations of section 7 of the *Charter* will be held to be justified under section 1 of the *Charter*, it is possible that courts will defer to this strong articulation of legislative will. Section 33.1 is more narrowly tailored than the common law *Leary* rule because it is restricted to general intent crimes of violence. In addition, unexpected forms of intoxication may be exempted from section 33.1 should they continue to be classified as involuntary intoxication that is not truly self-induced and as such not affected by section 33.1. The new legislation deserves a greater margin of deference than the previous judge-made common law rule.

The Court may also hold that section 33.1 engages conflicting rights, even though such an approach would overestimate what the section actually accomplishes in convicting the rare accused who will be able to establish intoxicated automatism. The reconciliation of rights approach will also diminish the heavy burden that the Crown should bear in justifying the violation of the accused's sections 7 and 11(d) rights where the result is to convict someone who has acted in an involuntary manner and to base the conviction on the prior and unfocused fault of becoming

---

76   *Dunn, ibid.* at 307.
77   *Brenton*, above note 64.
78   *Ibid.* (N.W.T.C.A.).
79   [2000] O.J. No. 4870 (S.C.J.).
80   *R. v. Jensen* (2005), 195 C.C.C. (3d) 14 at para. 22 (Ont. C.A.).

extremely intoxicated. To uphold section 33.1 would require the Court to back down from its previous and controversial decision in *Daviault*.

G. INVOLUNTARY INTOXICATION

Under section 33.1 as well as the traditional approach taken in *Leary*, an accused may be convicted of a general intent offence on the basis of the fault or recklessness of voluntarily becoming intoxicated. This raises the question of what should the courts do if the accused becomes involuntarily intoxicated through no fault of his or her own? If the accused is to be held at fault for a general intent offence for voluntarily becoming intoxicated, it is only fair that he or she not be convicted if the intoxication was not the accused's fault.[81]

1) Involuntary Intoxication as an Independent Defence

The Supreme Court has long recognized that involuntary intoxication raises special issues. In *R. v. King*,[82] the Court indicated that an accused who had been impaired by a drug given to him by his dentist should not be convicted of impaired driving if he "became impaired through no act of his own will and could not reasonably be expected to have known that his ability was impaired or might thereafter become impaired when he undertook to drive and drove his motor vehicle." It is also significant that the 1962 case of *King* seems to acknowledge that there could be a degree of intoxication that is inconsistent with the formation of the *mens rea* of a general intent offence such as impaired driving. *King* is consistent with *Daviault* in suggesting that involuntary intoxication can be a defence that may negate either the *mens rea* or the *actus reus* of a general intent offence. Evidence of either voluntary or involuntary intoxication could also be considered in determining whether the accused had the *mens rea* of a specific intent offence. At the same time, *King* places a restriction on the involuntary intoxication defence by requiring not simply that the accused not know that the substance might impair, but also that the accused could not reasonably know that the substance would impair.

King has been applied in a case in which the accused went into an automatic state and assaulted another person after overdosing on

---

81   Courts in England have, however, convicted an accused despite his involuntary consumption of drugs. *R. v. Kingston*, [1994] 3 W.L.R. 519 (H.L.).

82   Above note 45.

prescription pills that contained no specific warnings[83] or was surreptitiously given vodka in his drink.[84] It has been distinguished in cases in which the accused were convicted of impaired driving caused by overdoses of cold medication;[85] and by a deliberate overdose of prescription pills in an attempt to commit suicide.[86]

2) Involuntary Intoxication and Section 33.1

As discussed above, section 33.1 limits the *Daviault* defence of extreme intoxication to a general intent offence of violence by deeming that the fault of "self-induced intoxication" constitutes a marked departure from standards of reasonable care that can supply the fault for such offences even if the accused does not have *mens rea* and acts involuntarily at the time that the crime is committed. This raises the issue of whether involuntary and unexpected intoxication constitutes "self-induced intoxication" under section 33.1 or whether section 33.1 can be read down not to apply to such forms of intoxication.

In *Vickberg*, a trial judge held that the reference to "self-induced intoxication" in section 33.1 required voluntary intoxication. The judge decided that section 33.1 did not apply in the case because the accused became involuntarily intoxicated since he did not know and could not reasonably be expected to know that a drug he was given to assist with heroin withdrawal would intoxicate him.[87] In *Brenton* a similar argument was made by the accused on the basis that smoking marijuana had an unexpected effect on the accused, but it was rejected by the courts on the basis that the accused knew that marijuana was intoxicating and that smoking it constituted self-induced intoxication under section 33.1.[88]

The Nova Scotia Court of Appeal has concluded that consumption of drugs or alcohol will be excluded as self-induced intoxication under section 33.1 only if the accused did not know and could not reasonably be expected to know the risk of becoming intoxicated. The Court of Appeal stressed that since *King* "courts have consistently held that 'voluntary intoxication' means the consuming of a substance where the person knew or ought to have had reasonable grounds for believing

---

83   *Vickberg*, above note 66 at 184. Section 33.1 of the *Code* places restrictions on when "self-induced intoxication" will be a defence.

84   *R. v. Tramble* (1983), 33 C.R. (3d) 264 (Ont. Co. Ct.).

85   *R. v. Rushton* (1963), [1964] 1 C.C.C. 382 (N.S.C.A.).

86   *R. v. Honish* (1991), 68 C.C.C. (3d) 329 (Alta. C.A.).

87   *Vickberg*, above note 66 at paras. 68–70.

88   *Brenton*, above note 64 at 320.

such might cause him to be impaired."[89] There is support in *King* for the proposition that intoxication may be held to be voluntary when the accused ought to have known that the substance was intoxicating even though he or she did not subjectively have that knowledge. Such an approach errs on the side of social protection, but fails to ensure subjective fault for voluntary intoxication.

Summary Chart of Intoxication Defences

Defence	Issues
Ordinary intoxication defence to specific intent offences (i.e., murder, robbery)	Is there a reasonable doubt about intent?
Extreme intoxication defence to non-violent general intent offences (i.e., mischief)	Has the accused established on a balance of probabilities lack of capacity for minimal *mens rea* or involuntary conduct?
Extreme intoxication defence to violent general intent offences (i.e., assault, sexual assault)	Has the accused established on a balance of probabilities lack of capacity for minimal *mens rea* or involuntary conduct? Does the deeming of the fault of becoming extremely intoxicated as sufficient for the fault and voluntariness of the offence in s.33.1 of the *Criminal Code* violate sections 7 and 11(d) of the *Charter*? Can it be justified under section 1?
Involuntary intoxication defence to specific or general intent offences	Did the accused know or ought to have known the intoxicating effect of the substance(s)? If the intoxication is involuntary, is it "self-induced intoxication" under section 33.1 or does section 33.1 not apply to involuntary intoxication?

---

89   *Chaulk*, above note 68 at para. 45 (N.S.C.A.).

CONCLUSION

The Canadian law concerning intoxication is not only intensely controversial, but complex. There are four different ways in which intoxication can operate as a "defence" or more accurately prevent proof of the required fault for various criminal offences. The first and simplest is that evidence of intoxication can raise a reasonable doubt as to whether the accused had the intent required for a specific intent offence such as murder or robbery. The issue is the accused's actual intent, not whether intoxication impaired the accused's capacity to form the required intent.[90] The only difficult issues may be whether a particular offence will be classified as a specific intent offence that requires an intent directed at some purpose beyond the immediate action and whether there is an air of reality to justify instructing the jury about this defence.

The second intoxication defence is the *Daviault* defence of extreme intoxication to general intent offences that do not include an element of an assault or any other interference or threat of interference with of the bodily integrity of another person.[91] The accused must establish the *Daviault* defence of extreme intoxication to a general intent crime on a balance of probabilities and with expert evidence. The issue seems to be whether the accused was capable of forming the minimal intent required for general intent offences and not whether the accused actually had that intent, as in the case with the first intoxication defence to specific intent offences. The *Daviault* defence only exists unimpeded by legislation when the accused is charged with a general intent offence such as mischief to property that does not involve an assault or threat of violence.[92] If the accused establishes the *Daviault* defence to such a general intent crime on a balance of probabilities, he or she will be acquitted. The *Daviault* defence does not apply to crimes that require intoxication as an element of the offence because such a defence would be inconsistent with the mischief of the offence.[93]

The third and most controversial intoxication defence is when the accused raises a *Daviault* defence to a violent general intent offence such as manslaughter, assault, or sexual assault. The Supreme Court's decision in *Daviault* suggests that it would violate the accused's rights under sections 7 and 11(d) of the *Charter* to convict a person who was

---

90   *Robinson*, above note 14; *Daley*, above note 16.

91   *Code*, above note 40, s. 33.1(3).

92   *Ibid.*

93   *Penno*, above note 45; *Finta*, above note 48; *Ruzic*, above note 48; *Canadian Foundation for Children*, above note 48. But see *King*, above note 45, recognizing involuntary intoxication as a defence to impaired driving.

so extremely intoxicated at the time of the criminal act that he or she acted involuntarily and without the minimal intent required for a general intent offence. Parliament's reply to *Daviault* in section 33.1 of the *Criminal Code*, however, adds legislative support to the traditional rule in *Leary*. Section 33.1 substitutes the fault of becoming extremely intoxicated for the fault of committing the general intent crime of violence, even though the accused may have acted involuntarily at the time the assault occurs. It remains to be seen whether the Supreme Court will find that section 33.1 can be upheld under the *Charter*.

On the one hand, the substitution of the fault of becoming intoxicated for the fault of committing the general intent offence offends principles that require fault to be related to the *actus reus* and to overlap in time with the *actus reus*. As suggested by Justice Wilson in *Bernard*, this is mainly a substitution problem under section 11(d). In *Daviault*, the Supreme Court also held that basing the fault of sexual assault on the fault of becoming extremely intoxicated also violated section 7 of the *Charter* by punishing an accused who had no *mens rea* at the time of the act and who acted involuntarily. By deeming voluntary intoxication a marked departure from reasonable standards of conduct, s.33.1 may substitute objective fault for a subjective intent crime in possible violation of s.7 of the Charter. Although courts frequently accept violations of the presumption of innocence under section 11(d) as reasonable limits, they have been reluctant to accept violations of section 7 under section 1 of the *Charter*. The section 1 defence will likely focus on the fact that substitution of the fault of becoming extremely intoxicated for the fault of the particular offence is restricted under section 33.1 to general intent crimes of violence and that an intoxication-based offence may be less effective than s.33.1 in responding to intoxicated violence.

The time may have passed for general reforms that would abolish the much criticized distinction between general and specific intent offences and allow intoxication as a defence to all offences that require subjective *mens rea*. Such reform proposals were usually accompanied by proposals for the introduction of separate intoxication-based offences. After *Daviault*, there was reluctance to introduce new intoxication-based offences, in part because of a concern that a person who commits assault or sexual assault while intoxicated should still be labelled as an assaulter or sexual assaulter, and in part because of concerns about the impact of broad intoxication-based offences on the discretion of police and prosecutors in laying and reducing charges. There is no easy solution to the many dilemmas produced by the various intoxication defences and the most important immediate issue is whether section 33.1, restricted as it is to general intent offences of violence, will survive a *Charter* challenge.

The fourth intoxication defence is the rare defence of involuntary intoxication. It could apply to prevent the conviction of a person charged with a general intent offence who involuntarily becomes intoxicated and commits a criminal act,[94] as well as to a specific intent offence. Those who are involuntarily intoxicated, for example by a drug slipped into a drink, might also be exempted from s.33.1 which applies only to self-induced intoxication. The defence of involuntary intoxication is based on the logic that if the fault of becoming voluntarily intoxicated can supply or be substituted for the fault for the particular offence, then a person who becomes intoxicated through no fault of his or her own should not be held culpable. In other words, the substitution of the fault of becoming intoxicated for the fault of the particular offence should not occur if the accused was without fault in becoming intoxicated. The involuntary intoxication defence may only benefit those who ought not to have known about the intoxicating effects of the substance they ingested.

FURTHER READINGS

COLVIN, E., & S. ANAND, *Principles of Criminal Law*, 3d ed. (Toronto: Thomson Carswell, 2007) ch. 8

"Criminal Reports Forum on *Daviault*" (1995) 33 C.R. (4th) 269

GRANT, I., "Second Chances: Bill C-72 and the *Charter*" (1996) 33 Osgoode Hall L.J. 379

HEALY, P., "Intoxication and the Codification of Canadian Criminal Law" (1994) 73 Can. Bar Rev. 515

————, "*Beard* Still Not Cut Off" (1996) 46 C.R. (4th) 65

MANNING, M., & P. SANKOFF, *Criminal Law*, 4th ed. (Markham: LexisNexis, 2009) ch. 10

QUIGLEY, T., "Reform of the Intoxication Defence" (1987) 33 McGill L.J. 1

SHAFFER, M., "*R. v. Daviault*: A Principled Approach to Drunkenness or a Lapse of Common Sense?" (1996) 3 Rev. Const. Stud. 311

---

94 *King*, above note 45; *Vickberg*, above note 66.

SMITH, K., "Section 33.1: Denial of the *Daviault* Defence Should Be Held Constitutional" (2000) 28 C.R. (5th) 350

STUART, D., *Canadian Criminal Law: A Treatise*, 5th ed. (Toronto: Thomson Carswell, 2007) ch. 6

WILKINSON, J., "The Possibility of Alcoholic Automatism: Some Empirical Evidence" (1997) 2 Can. Crim. L. Rev. 217

CHAPTER 8

MENTAL DISORDER AND AUTOMATISM

Like intoxication, the defences of mental disorder and automatism apply to accused who commit criminal acts, but who cannot be found criminally responsible because their mental processes were impaired. It has long been accepted that an offender who, because of a mental disorder, is incapable of appreciating the nature and quality of a criminal act, or of knowing that it is wrong, should not be convicted. The verdict is not a pure acquittal, but rather a verdict of not criminally responsible on account of mental disorder or what used to be called not guilty by reason of insanity. The accused does not automatically go free and can be subject to detention or release with conditions until he or she is determined no longer to be a significant danger to society. In Canada, the mental disorder defence is set out in section 16 of the *Criminal Code*, and has been revised by both the Supreme Court and Parliament to take into account various *Charter* concerns.

The defence of automatism is more novel, and applies to an accused who has committed a criminal act while in a state of impaired consciousness that results in involuntary behaviour. If that state is caused by a mental disorder, the accused will be held not criminally responsible by reason of mental disorder. If the cause of the automatism is some other factor such as a blow to the head, the present disposition is to acquit the accused. The defence of non-mental disorder automatism is a common law defence that is not codified. If the cause of automatism producing involuntary behaviour is self-induced intoxication by alcohol or drugs, then the provisions of the intoxication defence discussed in chapter 7 will apply.

Section 16(3) of the *Criminal Code* requires that the mental disorder defence be established on a balance of probabilities and the Supreme Court has also required the accused to establish the defences of both intoxicated and non-mental disorder automatism on a balance of probabilities. This violates the presumption of innocence in section 11(d) of the *Charter* by allowing a person to be convicted even though there is a reasonable doubt about guilt. Nevertheless, it has been held to be justified as a reasonable limit on the presumption of innocence on the basis that accused persons will be in the best position to adduce evidence about the impairment of their mental processes.[1]

A. PROCEDURAL CONSIDERATIONS IN THE MENTAL DISORDER DEFENCE

1) Unfitness to Stand Trial

The mental disorder defence applies to an accused who, at the time that the criminal act was committed, suffered from a mental disorder that made him or her incapable of appreciating the nature or quality of the act or omission or of knowing that it was wrong. It is possible that a person who suffered from a mental disorder at the time of the crime will continue to suffer from that condition and be found unfit to stand trial. Conversely, a person who was sane when the crime was committed might subsequently suffer a severe mental disorder that would make it unfair to have a trial. Section 672.23(1) allows the court on its own motion, or on an application from the accused or the prosecutor, to determine whether an accused is fit to be tried. A person is unfit to stand trial if he or she is

> unable on account of mental disorder to conduct a defence at any stage of the proceedings before a verdict is rendered or to instruct counsel to do so, and, in particular, unable on account of mental disorder to
>
> (a) understand the nature or object of the proceedings,
> (b) understand the possible consequences of the proceedings, or
> (c) communicate with counsel.[2]

---

1   *R. v. Chaulk*, [1990] 3 S.C.R. 1303 [*Chaulk*] (mental disorder defence); *R. v. Daviault*, [1994] 3 S.C.R. 63 [*Daviault*] (extreme intoxication defence); *R. v. Stone*, [1999] 2 S.C.R. 290 [*Stone*].

2   *Criminal Code*, R.S.C. 1985, c. C-46, s. 2 [*Code*].

The accused is presumed to be fit to stand trial, and unfitness must be proven on a balance of probabilities.[3] It is not necessary that a person be able to act in his or her own best interests or to employ analytical reasoning, but it is necessary that he or she have "limited cognitive capacity to understand the process and to communicate with counsel."[4] This standard is a legal one that focuses on the fairness of the trial process and the accused's ability to participate in the trial process and not whether the accused clinically requires psychiatric treatment. A person who satisfies the minimal standards of the cognitive capacity test may still be found at trial to have a mental disorder defence. Courts of Appeal have found that accused who lack testimonial competence and could not remember the crime were nevertheless fit to stand trial. They have found that accused with the permanent brain injury caused by fetal alcohol spectrum disorder were also fit to stand trial as were accused who were delusional.[5] Some lower courts, however, have argued for higher standards that would require accused persons be able to make rational decisions especially in relation to their defence.[6]

A person found unfit to stand trial is subject to the same disposition hearing as a person found not criminally responsible because of a mental disorder. The difference, however, is that where an accused is found unfit to stand trial, the Crown may not have proven beyond a reasonable doubt that the accused committed the criminal act. For this reason, judges have the power to postpone the determination of fitness until the Crown has made its case and the accused has been found not to be entitled to an acquittal or a discharge. If the accused is found unfit to stand trial, the Crown is required to establish a *prima facie* case against the accused every two years until the accused is either found fit to be tried or is acquitted because the Crown cannot establish a *prima facie* case.[7] These safeguards are designed to ensure that a factually in-

---

3   *Code, ibid.*, ss. 672.22 & 672.23. The burden placed on the accused when the accused argues unfitness to stand trial has been held to be justified under the *Charter. R. v. Morrissey* (2002), 8 C.R. (6th) 41 (Ont. S.C.J.), aff'd on other grounds 2007 ONCA 770. As will be seen, similar burdens on the accused to establish the mental disorder and automatism defences have also been held to be justified under the *Charter.*

4   *R. v. Whittle* (1994), 92 C.C.C. (3d) 11 at 25 (S.C.C.) approving of *R. v. Taylor* (1992), 77 C.C.C. (3d) 551 (Ont. C.A.).

5   *R. v. Morrissey,* 2007 ONCA 770; *R. v. Jobb,* 2008 SKCA 156; *R. v. Krivicic,* 2011 ONCA 703.

6   *R. v. Steele* (1991), 63 C.C.C. (3d) 149 (Que. C.A.); see also *Dusky v. United States,* 362 U.S. 402 (1960).

7   *Code,* above note 2, s. 672.33. The unavailability of an absolute discharge for a permanently unfit accused who does not pose a significant threat to society

nocent accused is not subject to detention in the same manner as an accused who committed the criminal act, but was found not guilty by reason of a mental disorder.

Rv Demers 2004 (SCC) A person with Down's Syndrome accused of sexual assault who was found unfit to stand trial and released after two months challenged the constitutionality of the provisions. The Supreme Court found Parliament had jurisdiction under the division of powers to legislate with respect to those unfit to stand trial because of concerns about trying the accused and also about preventing crime by the mentally disordered accused. The Court also rejected the accused's argument that subjecting him to review board proceedings violated the presumption of innocence under section 11(d) of the *Charter* given that the aim of review proceedings was not to punish the accused. The Court did, however, find the unfitness to stand trial scheme violated section 7 of the *Charter* because it did not provide for an absolute discharge for an accused who is permanently unfit to stand trial and who did not present a continuing danger to the public. The Court ruled that the scheme was overbroad to the objectives of social protection by effectively providing that such a person could only be released subject to indeterminate conditions.[8] Parliament responded to this ruling with a new provision that allows a trial court to enter a stay of proceedings in such circumstances where an accused is not likely to ever become fit to stand trial, but also does not pose a significant threat to the safety of the public.[9]

2) Who Can Raise the Mental Disorder Defence?

Canadian courts have been more willing than British or American courts to allow the prosecutor to raise the mental disorder defence. The rationale is that society has an interest in not convicting an accused who may not be responsible because of a mental disorder, but who has chosen not to advance the insanity defence. This latitude presents dangers that 1) the Crown could bolster a weak case by presenting evidence of the accused's mental disorder, and 2) an accused could be

---

violates s. 7 of the *Charter. R. v. Demers*, 2004 SCC 46 [*Demers*].

8   *Demers, ibid.*

9   *Code*, above note 2, s. 672.851. The court may make this determination on its own initiative or with representations from the review board. To enter a stay the court must conclude not only that the accused is not likely ever to be fit to stand trial and that he or she does not pose a significant threat to the safety of the public, but also that a stay is in the best interests of the proper administration of justice considering factors such as the seriousness of the offence and any harm of a stay to public confidence in the administration of justice.

exposed to indeterminate detention as a person found not guilty on grounds of mental disorder when he or she wishes either to plead guilty or to contest his or her innocence.

In *R. v. Swain*,[10] the Supreme Court found that the common law practice of allowing the Crown to raise the insanity defence violated the accused's right under section 7 of the *Charter* to control his or her own defence. Lamer C.J. stated:

> The mere fact that the Crown is able to raise a defence which the accused does not wish to raise, and thereby to trigger a special verdict which the accused does not wish to trigger, means that the accused has lost a degree of control over the conduct of his or her defence.[11]

The Court concluded that the principles of fundamental justice generally would allow the Crown to raise the insanity defence only after the accused had otherwise been found guilty. A permissible exception is that the Crown can raise the insanity defence in rebuttal if the accused has placed his or her capacity for criminal intent in issue. For example, if the accused raised a defence of non-mental disorder automatism, the Crown could then raise the defence of mental disorder and introduce evidence to indicate that section 16 of the *Code* should apply and the verdict should be not criminally responsible on account of mental disorder. An accused who argued that he or she went into a state of automatism because of a severe emotional blow may find the Crown arguing that the cause of the automatism was a mental disorder and that the appropriate disposition is further detention and treatment, not a complete acquittal.[12] It is even possible that the court will determine that there is no air of reality to the non-mental disorder automatism defence and only the mental disorder defence will be left for the jury to consider.[13]

3) Burden of Proof

Sections 16(2) and 16(3) of the *Criminal Code* provide that every person is presumed not to suffer from a mental disorder so as to be exempt from criminal responsibility and that the party who raises this issue

---

10   (1991), 63 C.C.C. (3d) 481 (S.C.C.) [*Swain*].

11   *Ibid.* at 506.

12   See, e.g., *R. v. K.* (1970), 3 C.C.C. (3d) 84 (Ont. H.C.J.) [*K.*]; *R. v. Rabey* (1977), 37 C.C.C. (2d) 461 (Ont. C.A.), aff'd (1980), 54 C.C.C. (2d) 1 (S.C.C.) [*Rabey*], discussed later in this chapter.

13   See, e.g., *Stone*, above note 1, discussed later in this chapter.

must prove it on the balance of probabilities. In *R. v. Chaulk*,[14] the Supreme Court found that the requirement that an accused prove the defence of insanity on a balance of probabilities violated the presumption of innocence under section 11(d) of the *Charter*, because it allowed the conviction of an accused in spite of a reasonable doubt as to a factor essential to guilt, namely sanity. Lamer C.J. reasoned:

> Whether the claim of insanity is characterized as a denial of *mens rea*, an excusing defence or, more generally, as an exemption based on criminal incapacity, the fact remains that sanity is essential for guilt. [The section] allows a factor which is essential for guilt to be presumed, rather than proven by the Crown beyond a reasonable doubt. Moreover, it requires an accused to disprove sanity (or prove insanity) on a balance of probabilities; it therefore violates the presumption of innocence because it permits a conviction in spite of a reasonable doubt in the mind of the trier of fact as to the guilt of the accused.[15]

The Chief Justice went on, however, to find that the statutory requirement that an accused prove the insanity defence on a balance of probabilities was justified under section 1 of the *Charter* because of the difficulties that the Crown would have proving beyond a reasonable doubt that an accused was sane. Wilson J. dissented and held that, as in some American jurisdictions, once the accused produced some evidence of insanity, the prosecutor should bear the burden of proving beyond a reasonable doubt that the insanity defence did not apply.

The Court did not consider the burden of proof if the prosecutor raises the mental disorder defence. Section 16(3) suggests that the prosecutor, like the accused, would have to prove the defence on a balance of probabilities. Normally, however, the prosecutor must prove its case against the accused beyond a reasonable doubt. Given this general principle and the fact that the prosecutor would only be required to establish a mental disorder defence against an accused who did not wish to rely on such a defence, it would be best if the prosecutor was required to establish a mental disorder defence by proof beyond a reasonable doubt.

There must also be an air of reality before the mental disorder defence is even put to the jury. This requires some evidence that if believed by the jury would support the essential requirements of the mental disorder defence, namely the existence of a mental disorder that

---

14   *Chaulk*, above note 1.
15   *Ibid.* at 213.

renders an accused incapable of appreciating the nature and quality of the act or incapable of knowing that the act is wrong.

4) Disposition of an Accused Acquitted by Reason of Mental Disorder

An accused acquitted on grounds of insanity used to be subject to automatic indeterminate detention at the pleasure of the Lieutenant Governor in Council. In practice, this meant detention until a review board determined that release was in the accused's interests and not contrary to the public interest. In *Swain*,[16] the Supreme Court held that such automatic detention without a hearing and with no criteria to authorize detention violated the accused's rights under sections 7 and 9 of the *Charter*. That case raised the issue because the accused, who did not wish to plead insanity as a defence, was found to have been insane at the time of the crime but had successfully been treated with anti-psychotic drugs at the time of sentencing. Lamer C.J. noted, however, that some automatic detention and delay following an acquittal by reason of insanity is a "practical reality," because the evidence of insanity at trial relates to the mental condition of the accused at the time of the offence and not the accused's "present mental condition and dangerousness."[17]

Amendments to the *Criminal Code* in the wake of *Swain* now instruct the court to hold, if possible, a disposition hearing for the accused when the accused is found unfit to stand trial or not criminally responsible on account of mental disorder.[18] In any event, a review board of a judge and two mental health professionals is required to hold such a hearing "as soon as is practicable but not later than forty-five days after the verdict was rendered."[19] At the disposition hearing, the court or review board is instructed to discharge the accused absolutely if "the accused is not a significant threat to the safety of the public."[20] The Supreme Court has interpreted this provision to require an absolute discharge unless the court or review board finds that release would present a significant risk to the safety of the public by the commission of a crime that presents a real risk of physical or psychological harm that is not merely trivial or annoying.[21]

---

16   *Swain*, above note 10.
17   *Ibid.* at 539.
18   *Code*, above note 2, s. 672.45.
19   *Ibid.*, s. 672.47(1).
20   *Ibid.*, s. 672.54(a).
21   *Winko v. British Columbia (Forensic Psychiatric Institute)* (1999), 135 C.C.C. (3d) 129 (S.C.C.) [*Winko*].

If an absolute discharge is not warranted, the court or review board is instructed under section 672.54 to make the disposition "that is the least onerous and least restrictive to the accused," considering "the need to protect the public from dangerous persons, the mental condition of the accused, the reintegration of the accused into society and the other needs of the accused."[22] The Supreme Court has stressed that there is no presumption that a person found not criminally responsible by reason of mental disorder is dangerous. Courts or review boards no longer are faced with the draconian disposition of automatic indeterminate detention and should impose the least restrictive conditions compatible with public safety.[23] There is no burden or onus of proof on either the accused or the Crown. The court or review board may consider and seek evidence from a broad range of sources. The Supreme Court also found that this scheme does not violate sections 7 and 15 of the *Charter* in large part because it avoids stereotypical assumptions about those who suffer a mental disorder and requires individual assessment of each and every person found not criminally responsible by reason of mental disorder and unconditional release if they do not present a significant threat to the safety of the public.[24]

Continued detention or conditions placed on those found not criminally responsible by reason of mental disorder are subject to yearly reviews by the review board.[25] The review board can order provincial authorities to provide an independent evaluation of a person's diagnosis, safety risk, treatment plan, and to make assertive efforts to enroll an Aboriginal person in a culturally appropriate treatment plan as an incident to its powers to supervise and make available treatment. At the same time, the review board does not have the power to order treatment for the person, such powers being within provincial authority with respect to the hospital where the person is detained.[26]

There were provisions in the *Criminal Code* never proclaimed in force that would have capped the ultimate period of time a person could be detained, or could be subject to conditions, based on the seriousness of the offence charged[27] while also allowing the Crown to apply to have a person declared a dangerous mentally disordered accused, subject

---

22   *Code*, above note 2, s. 672.54.
23   *Penetanguishene Mental Health Centre v. Ontario (A.G.)*, 2004 SCC 20.
24   *Winko*, above note 21.
25   *Code*, above note 2, s. 672.81(1).
26   *Mazzei v. British Columbia (Director of Adult Forensic Psychiatric Services)*, [2006] 1 S.C.R. 326.
27   *Code*, above note 2, s. 672.64, repealed S.C. 2005, c. 22, s. 24.

to a disposition cap of life.[28] The Supreme Court has disapproved of a Court of Appeal decision that held that the failure to proclaim the capping provisions produced overbreadth and disproportionality in the criminal law that violated section 7 of the *Charter*.[29] As a result, an accused found not criminally responsible still remains subject to potentially indeterminate detention or indeterminate conditional restraints on liberty. At the same time, the accused should be subject to the least restrictive disposition and they should be released without conditions if they are not a significant threat to the safety of the public.[30] The potential for indeterminate detention or indeterminate conditions, as well as the generally restrictive nature of the defence, help explain why the mental disorder defence is rarely invoked despite evidence that many in our prisons suffer from a mental disorder of some form.

B. THE *M'NAGHTEN* RULES AND THEIR CODIFICATION

The substantive rules governing the insanity or mental disorder defence are derived from the 1843 decision of the House of Lords in *M'Naghten's Case*.[31] In that case, the accused was found by a jury to be not guilty by reason of insanity of murdering the prime minister's secretary. He suffered from delusions of persecution from the government. Subsequent controversy led to a reference to the House of Lords, which affirmed the availability of the insanity defence if it was "clearly proved that, at the time of the committing of the act, the party accused was labouring under such a defect of reason, from disease of the mind, as not to know the nature and quality of the act he was doing, or, if did know it, that he did not know he was doing what was wrong."[32] The House of Lords added that an accused suffering from delusions should have his responsibility determined on the basis that the delusions were real. Thus, an accused who killed another, supposing himself under deadly attack, may not be responsible, but one imagining only an injury to his character would be guilty of murder.[33]

---

28 *Ibid.*, s. 672.65, repealed S.C. 2005, c. 22, s. 24.
29 *Winko*, above note 21 at para. 70, disapproving of *R. v. Hoeppner* (1999), 25 C.R. (5th) 91 (Man. C.A.).
30 *Code*, above note 2, s. 672.54.
31 (1843), 8 E.R. 718 (H.L.).
32 *Ibid.* at 722.
33 This provision was codified in Canada until its repeal. S.C. 1991, c. 43, s. 2. Delusions would now be considered with reference to whether the accused was

In 1892 the *M'Naghten* rules were embodied in the *Criminal Code* of Canada with some variations. A person was defined as legally insane if he or she laboured "in a state of natural imbecility or disease of the mind, to such an extent as to render him incapable of appreciating the nature and quality of an act or omission, and of knowing that such an act or omission was wrong." This introduced the idea that an accused would have an insanity defence if he or she did not "appreciate," as opposed to "know," the nature and quality of the act. The 1892 *Code* also required the accused to be incapable of both appreciating the nature and quality of the act and of knowing that it was wrong. This was corrected as a misreading of the disjunctive *M'Naghten* rules.[34] Thus, either a failure to appreciate the nature and quality of the criminal act or to know that it was wrong will suffice to ground the mental disorder defence.

In 1992 the insanity defence was renamed the mental disorder defence, and the verdict of not guilty by reason of insanity was renamed the verdict of not criminally responsible by reason of mental disorder. The mental disorder defence now provides:

> No person is criminally responsible for an act committed or an omission made while suffering from a mental disorder that rendered the person incapable of appreciating the nature and quality of the act or omission or of knowing that it was wrong.[35]

This provision indicates more clearly that the accused must have committed the act or omission charged, but other changes are more cosmetic. Section 2 of the *Criminal Code* defines mental disorder as a disease of the mind, preserving the old jurisprudence on that issue. Section 16(1) preserves the traditional two-prong test that allows the defence on the basis that 1) a mental disorder "rendered the person incapable of appreciating the nature and quality of the act or omission," or 2) a mental disorder "rendered the person incapable . . . of knowing that it was wrong." The most significant changes in the 1992 amendments related not to the substantive defence, but rather to the abolition of automatic indeterminate detention as discussed above. For example, the 1992 amendments did not embrace American reforms that attempt to broaden the insanity defence so that it applied to crimes that were a

---

able to appreciate the nature and quality of the act or was able to know that it was wrong. See *R. v. Landry* (1991), 62 C.C.C. (3d) 117 (S.C.C.) [*Landry*]; *R. v. Oommen* (1994), 91 C.C.C. (3d) 8 (S.C.C.) [*Oommen*], discussed below for two cases considering mental disorder defences based on the accused's delusions.

34   *R. v. Cracknell* (1931), 56 C.C.C. 190 (Ont. C.A.).

35   *Code*, above note 2, s. 16(1).

product of mental disorder or to offenders whose mental disorder made them unable to obey the law.

Although Parliament could reformulate the mental disorder defence as it did in 1992, it could not repeal it in response to some controversial finding that a person cannot be convicted because of the mental disorder defence. The Supreme Court had indicated that a person who is incapable because of a mental disorder of appreciating the nature and quality of their actions or of knowing that they are wrong acts in a morally involuntary manner. In other words, the acts are "not actually the product of his or her free will" and the court's refusal to convict such persons is "therefore consistent with the principles of fundamental justice" under section 7 of the *Charter*.[36] That said, the scope of the mental disorder defence should not be overestimated. It is not enough to establish that the accused has a mental disorder or even that the mental disorder caused the crime. The mental disorder must be so severe that it prevented the accused from either appreciating the consequences of his or her actions or of knowing that they were wrong.

C. MENTAL DISORDER OR DISEASE OF THE MIND

In order for the defence to apply, an accused must suffer from a disease of the mind or a mental disorder. A person who is unable to appreciate the nature and quality of an act or is incapable of knowing that the act is wrong, but does not suffer from a mental disorder, will not qualify for the defence.[37] However, holding that a person suffers from a mental disorder is not sufficient. As mentioned, the condition must be severe enough to render the person incapable of appreciating the nature and quality of the act, or incapable of knowing that it was wrong.

1) Policy Considerations

The categories of disease of the mind have expanded since 1843 when the *M'Naghten* rules were first defined. Judicial interpretation of what constitutes a disease of the mind will be influenced by medical developments, but it remains a question of law for the courts to define and may involve policy considerations not known to the discipline of psychiatry.

---

36   R. v. *Bouchard-Lebrun*, 2011 SCC 58 at para. 51 [*Bouchard-Lebrun*].

37   As will be discussed later, they may have the common law defence of non-mental disorder automatism.

These policy factors relate to concerns about how wide the mental disorder defence should be and the need to protect the public "by the control and treatment of persons who have caused serious harms while in a mentally disordered or disturbed state."[38] The Supreme Court in *Stone* has stated that it is open to trial judges to find new policy considerations to influence their interpretation of what constitutes a disease of the mind. "Policy concerns assist trial judges in answering the fundamental question of mixed law and fact which is at the centre of the disease of the mind inquiry: whether society requires protection from the accused and, consequently, whether the accused should be subject to evaluation under the regime contained in Part XX.1 of the Code."[39] The Court in that case endorsed a "holistic" approach to determining disease of the mind that includes an open-ended list of policy factors, including whether the accused presents a continuing danger and whether his or her conduct can be explained by an internal as opposed to an external cause.

2) Continuing Danger and Internal Causes

A disease of the mind has often been defined in relation to whether there is a continuing danger to the public,[40] or whether the disturbance is related to an internal cause stemming from the psychological makeup of the accused as opposed to an external factor.[41] La Forest J. has warned against exclusive reliance on either the continuing danger or the internal cause theories, but has noted that they are united in their common concern for recurrence. In his view, however, even "recurrence is but one of a number of factors to be considered in the policy phase of the disease of the mind inquiry," and "the absence of a danger of recurrence will not automatically exclude the possibility of a finding of insanity."[42] Nevertheless, the danger of recurrence does seem to be the most important policy factor in determining whether a particular condition constitutes a disease of the mind. It is related to concerns about both the need to protect public safety and to treat and rehabilitate the accused.

---

38   *Rabey*, above note 12.
39   *Stone*, above note 1 at 441.
40   *Bratty v. A.G. for Northern Ireland* (1961), [1963] A.C. 386 (H.L.).
41   *R. v. Quick*, [1973] 3 All E.R. 347 (C.A.) [*Quick*]; *Rabey*, above note 12.
42   *R. v. Parks* (1992), 75 C.C.C. (3d) 287 at 310 (S.C.C.) [*Parks*]; *Stone*, above note 1 at 438. See also *R. v. Sullivan* (1983), [1984] A.G. 156 (H.L.) [*Sullivan*].

In *Stone*,[43] the Supreme Court confirmed that the existence of a continuing danger or an internal cause are legitimate and non-mutually exclusive factors indicating that the accused may suffer from a mental disorder. The psychiatric history of the accused and the likelihood of the recurrence of violence or the stimulus that triggered violence in the past are important considerations in determining whether the accused is a continuing danger. "The greater the anticipated frequency of the trigger in the accused's life, the greater the risk posed to the public and, consequently, the more likely it is that the condition alleged by the accused is a disease of the mind."[44] Thus, an accused who goes into an automatic state[45] and assaults or kills another because of ordinary teasing or nagging is more likely to be classified as having a disease of the mind than a person who goes into an automatic state after a rare stimulus such as seeing a loved one assaulted or killed. At the same time, the Court warned that the absence of a continuing danger does not preclude a finding of a mental disorder or a disease of the mind.

The existence of an internal cause will be most relevant in cases of psychological blow automatism discussed later in this chapter. An internal cause may reveal itself when the accused goes into an automatic state when faced with something less than "an extremely shocking trigger"[46] that would send "a normal person" in similar circumstances into an automatic state. Comparing how the accused reacted with how a normal person would have acted in similar circumstances is motivated by concerns about public safety when an accused responds atypically and violently to what may be the ordinary stresses and disappointments of life. There may be cases where a focus on internal causes is not helpful and the accused will be found not to suffer from a mental disorder even though there might be an internal cause to his or her actions. As will be discussed later in this chapter, sleepwalking may be an internal cause of automatic behaviour, but it may not be classified as a disease of the mind. Conversely, a person might be classified as having a disease of the mind even though there is no apparent internal cause.

The existence of either a continuing danger or an internal cause are simply factors that suggest the accused may have a mental disorder.

---

43   *Stone*, ibid.
44   *Ibid.* at 440.
45   It is assumed that such a state will by definition produce a situation in which the accused is incapable of appreciating the nature and quality of his or her actions or knowing that they are wrong. The crucial issue in determining whether the mental disorder defence applies or not will be determining whether the accused suffers from a mental disorder or disease of the mind.
46   *Stone*, above note 1 at 436.

The absence of these factors does not mean that for other policy reasons, concerning the need to protect the public by potentially indeterminate detention or conditions placed on a person found not criminally responsible by reason of mental disorder, an accused will not be classified as having a disease of the mind. In a fundamental sense, the definition of whether a person has a mental disorder or disease of the mind is driven by policy and public safety concerns about the ultimate disposition of the accused.

3) The *Cooper* Definition

In *R. v. Cooper*,[47] Dickson J. defined disease of the mind as

> any illness, disorder or abnormal condition which impairs the human mind and its functioning, excluding however, self-induced states caused by alcohol or drugs, as well as transitory mental states such as hysteria or concussion.

This is a broad definition of disease of the mind that includes all medically recognized disorders except those in which transitory disturbances are caused by external factors such as drugs. Psychopathic personalities[48] or personality disorders[49] have been recognized as diseases of the mind. Brain damage including fetal alcohol spectrum disorder and severe mental disability may also be considered diseases of the mind.[50] *Delirium tremens*, or deterioration of the brain cells produced by chronic alcoholism have also been recognized as diseases of the mind.[51] Thus, alcohol or drug use will generally only fall under the mental disorder defence when it produces a permanent condition as opposed to temporary intoxication.

The Supreme Court has held that sleepwalking is not a disease of the mind, so that a person rendered unconscious by this condition was entitled to a complete acquittal, rather than possible detention as a per-

---

47 (1979), 51 C.C.C. (2d) 129 at 144 (S.C.C.) [*Cooper*].

48 *R. v. Simpson* (1977), 35 C.C.C. (2d) 337 (Ont. C.A.) [*Simpson*].

49 *Rabey*, above note 12.

50 *R. v. Revelle* (1979), 48 C.C.C. (2d) 267 (Ont. C.A.), aff'd (1981), 21 C.R. (3d) 225 (S.C.C.) [*Revelle*]; *R. v. R.(M.S.)* (1996), 112 C.C.C. (3d) 406 (Ont. Gen. Div.); *R. v. C.P.F.*, 2006 NLCA 70. In the last case, the permanent brain damage caused by fetal alcohol spectrum disorder was found to be a mental disorder but not one that satisfied the other requirements of the mental disorder defence, namely that the mental disorder render the accused incapable of appreciating the physical consequences of his or her actions or knowing that they were wrong.

51 *R. v. Malcolm* (1989), 50 C.C.C. (3d) 172 (Man. C.A.); *R. v. Mailloux* (1985), 25 C.C.C. (3d) 171 (Ont. C.A.), aff'd (1988), 45 C.C.C. (3d) 193 (S.C.C.).

son found not guilty by reason of insanity.[52] This suggests that even though a condition might fall within the broad contours of an illness or abnormal condition that impairs the human mind, it will not necessarily be classified as a disease of the mind.

4) Mental Disorder and Transitory States

The House of Lords in *Beard* suggested that "if actual insanity in fact supervenes, as the result of alcoholic excess, it furnishes as complete an answer to a criminal charge as insanity induced by any other cause."[53] Canadian courts have not been willing to apply the section 16 defence in cases involving self-induced intoxication. The *Cooper* definition excludes self-induced states caused by alcohol and other drugs as a disease of the mind. In R. v. *Bouchard-Lebrun*,[54] the Supreme Court held that an accused who brutally assaulted a person after taking the ecstasy drug was not suffering from a mental disorder even though he was in a state of "toxic psychosis" that both Crown and defence experts agreed rendered him unable to know that the assaults were wrong. The accused had made religious comments during the assault about the coming of the Apocalypse and the devil. The Court stopped short of holding that "toxic psychosis" produced by intoxication could never be a mental disorder. Nevertheless, applying the holistic test in *Stone*, the Court concluded that the drugs acted as an external cause of the behaviour and there was no evidence of a danger of recurrence if the accused did not take similar drugs.[55] It indicated that the mental disorder defence and various intoxication defences are "mutually exclusive"[56] as a matter of law even though they may overlap in a clinical or medical sense. The Court's refusal to find a mental disorder meant that the accused was convicted of aggravated assault even though at the time he committed the assault he was acting in an involuntary, delusional, and psychotic state and did not know that his acts were wrong. This seems to base his fault not on what he did at the time, but on the act of becoming voluntarily intoxicated. It should also be noted that the accused

---

52 *Parks*, above note 42. The Court based this decision on the evidence presented in the particular case and suggested that it could reconsider its decision on different evidence.

53 *D.P.P. v. Beard*, [1920] A.C. 479 at 500 (H.L.).

54 2011 SCC 58.

55 In the specific case, the accused was guilty of aggravated assault by virtue of the restrictions on the extreme intoxication defence in s. 33.1 of the *Code* as examined in ch. 7.

56 *Ibid.* at para. 37.

appeared to rely on the mental disorder defence and did not challenge section 33.1 of the *Code* under the *Charter*, which as discussed in the last chapter, substitutes the fault of becoming extremely intoxicated for the fault and voluntariness of violent general intent offences such as aggravated assault.

The *Cooper* definition of disease of the mind also excludes "transitory mental states such as hysteria or concussion." Those subject to a one-time mental disturbance because of external factors such as a blow to a head or an extraordinary trauma should probably not be subject to potential indeterminate detention or conditions as a person found not criminally responsible on account of a mental disorder. However, this more intrusive disposition may be appropriate when the accused's inability to appreciate the nature and quality of the acts or to know that they are wrong is caused by a "malfunctioning of the mind arising from some cause that is primarily internal to the accused, having its source in his psychological or emotional make-up, or in some organic pathology, as opposed to a malfunctioning of the mind which is the transient effect produced by some external factor such as, for example, concussion."[57] In *Rabey*, a disassociative state produced by the accused's disappointment at being romantically rejected was found to have been derived from internal factors within the accused that could constitute a disease of the mind. However, if the accused had been subjected to "extraordinary external events" such as being involved in a serious accident, escaping a murderous attack, or seeing a loved one killed, then a disassociative state could perhaps be explained "without reference to the subjective make-up of the person exposed to such experience."[58] In such a case, the disassociation would not be likely to recur, because of the extraordinary nature of the external factor. As such, it would be unduly intrusive to subject the accused to possible detention and treatment as a person found not criminally responsible on account of mental disorder.

5) Mental Disorder and Organic Conditions

A focus on factors internal to the accused has led English courts to conclude that various conditions that are not commonly considered mental disorders are nevertheless diseases of the mind for the purpose of the insanity defence. For example, epilepsy has been found to constitute a

---

57   *Rabey*, above note 12 at 477–78.
58   *Ibid.* at 482–83.

disease of the mind,[59] as has arteriosclerosis.[60] The focus on internal factors has produced strange results where diabetics are concerned. If the accused takes insulin and does not eat, the resulting disassociative state has been held not to be a disease of the mind, because it was caused "by an external factor and not by a bodily disorder in the nature of a disease which disturbed the working of the mind."[61] If, however, a diabetic goes into a disassociative state because he or she has not taken insulin, then the resulting condition is a disease of the mind because it is caused by the internal factor of the accused's diabetes.[62] In such cases, it would be better not to focus on whether the cause of the state was internal or external, but whether it was likely to recur and to present a continuing danger.

The Supreme Court's holistic approach to categorizing a disease of the mind suggests that a focus on whether the cause was internal can and should be dispensed with in those cases in which it will produce an absurd result not necessary for public safety. In *Parks*,[63] sleepwalking was not classified as a disease of the mind even though it could be seen as an organic or hereditary condition internal to the accused. Canadian courts should not classify organic conditions such as epilepsy or diabetes as diseases of the mind simply because they are internal causes that explain the accused's behaviour. The ultimate issue should be whether the public requires protection through potentially indeterminate conditions or detention imposed on those found not criminally responsible on account of mental disorder. In a case subsequent to *Parks*, however, the Ontario Court of Appeal held that sleepwalking should be considered a mental disorder under the holistic *Stone* test because it was a matter internal to the accused, it was not triggered by specific external stimuli, and there was a continuing danger to the public from a risk of recurrence.[64] This case certainly underlines the tension between the Court's decision in *Parks* that sleepwalking was not a mental disorder and its more open-ended and holistic approach to defining a mental disorder in *Stone*.

---

59   R. v. O'Brien, [1966] 3 C.C.C. 288 (N.B.C.A.) [O'Brien]; Sullivan, above note 42.
60   R. v. Kemp (1956), [1957] 1 Q.B. 399.
61   Quick, above note 41.
62   R. v. Hennessy, [1989] 2 All E.R. 9 (C.A.) [Hennessy].
63   Parks, above note 42.
64   R. v. Luedecke, 2008 ONCA 716 [Luedecke].

D. CAPACITY TO APPRECIATE THE NATURE AND QUALITY OF THE ACT

Even if the accused is held to suffer from a mental disorder or disease of the mind, he or she must qualify under one of the two arms of the mental disorder defence. Canadian courts have stressed that section 16 of the *Criminal Code* refers to an inability to *appreciate* the nature and quality of acts, as opposed to the *M'Naghten* rules, which refer to an inability to *know* the nature and quality of the act. The ability to appreciate the nature and quality of an act involves more than knowledge or cognition that the act is being committed. It includes the capacity to measure and foresee the consequences of the conduct. In *Cooper*, Dickson J. stated:

> The requirement, unique to Canada, is that of perception, an ability to perceive the consequences, impact, and results of a physical act. An accused may be aware of the physical character of his action (i.e., in choking) without necessarily having the capacity to appreciate that, in nature and quality, the act will result in the death of a human being.[65]

An accused who is unable to appreciate the physical consequences of his or her actions because of a mental disorder will have a valid section 16 defence. In a murder case, this also mirrors the *mens rea* requirement that the accused subjectively know that his or her actions would cause death. Of course, a successful section 16 defence could result in a disposition far more intrusive than an acquittal in a murder case.

The courts have not expanded the defence to apply to those who, because of mental disorder, were unable emotionally to appreciate the effect of their actions on the victim. In *Simpson*,[66] Martin J.A. stated that the defence did not apply to an accused

> who has the necessary understanding of the nature, character and consequences of the act, but merely lacks appropriate feelings for the victim or lacks feelings of remorse or guilt for what he has done, even though such lack of feeling stems from "disease of the mind." Appreciation of the nature and quality of the act does not import a requirement that the act be accompanied by appropriate feeling about the effect of the act on other people . . . . No doubt the absence of such

---

65 *Cooper*, above note 47 at 147.
66 *Simpson*, above note 48 at 355.

feelings is a common characteristic of many persons who engage in repeated and serious criminal conduct.

An inability to appreciate that a victim may die can result in a mental disorder defence. An inability to have appropriate emotions about the death of another person, however, does not result in a section 16 defence, even if it is an indication of a mental disorder such as a psychopathic personality.

The courts have also held that an inability to appreciate the penal consequences of an act does not render an accused incapable of appreciating the physical consequences of the act. In *R. v. Abbey*,[67] the accused believed that he was protected by an external force from punishment for importing narcotics. The Supreme Court held that the trial judge had erred in law "in holding that a person who by reason of disease of the mind does not 'appreciate' the penal consequences of his actions is insane."

In *Landry*,[68] the Supreme Court rejected the Quebec Court of Appeal's conclusion that an accused who killed while under the delusion that he was God, and the victim, Satan, did not appreciate the nature and circumstances of the act. Lamer C.J. reasoned that the prior precedents had clearly established that an accused would have an insanity defence only if a mental disorder prevented him from appreciating the physical, as opposed to the moral, consequences of the act. He also added that the Court of Appeal had erred in holding that section 7 of the *Charter* required it "to modify the established interpretation of this statutory provision."[69] As will be seen later in this chapter, however, the majority of the Supreme Court affirmed the verdict of not guilty by reason of insanity on the alternative basis that the accused's severe psychosis and resulting delusion rendered him incapable of knowing that the killing was wrong. It is important to be sensitive to how the two alternative arms of the mental disorder defence interact.

E. CAPACITY TO KNOW THAT THE ACT IS WRONG

Section 16(1) of the *Criminal Code* provides two alternative arms or formulations of the mental disorder defence. The first, discussed above,

---

67   (1982), 68 C.C.C. (2d) 394 at 405–6 (S.C.C.) [*Abbey*].
68   *Landry*, above note 33.
69   *Ibid.* at 124.

applies when a mental disorder renders the accused incapable of appreciating the physical consequences of the act. The second is when the disease of the mind renders the accused incapable of knowing that the act was wrong.

In *R. v. Schwartz*,[70] the Supreme Court divided 5:4, with the majority holding that an accused must be unable to know that an act was legally wrong. Martland J. for the majority concluded that the test "is not as to whether the accused, by reason of mental disease, could or could not calmly consider whether or not the crime which he committed was morally wrong. He is not to be considered as insane . . . if he knew what he was doing and also knew that he was committing a criminal act."[71] Dickson J. in his dissent seemed more concerned with giving the insanity defence a generous reading. He noted that Parliament had chosen in section 16 to use the word "wrong," which could refer to either legal or moral wrong. In most cases, there would be no practical difference, but he was concerned about a case in which an accused was capable of knowing that his or her acts were illegal but was not capable of knowing they were morally wrong. He cited the example of an accused who knew that it was legally wrong to kill but did so believing that his killing followed a divine order and therefore was not morally wrong. Dickson J. held that the reference to wrong in section 16 should be interpreted to mean morally wrong. In his view, this broader definition would not give the amoral offender a defence, because the incapacity to know that an act was morally wrong must stem from a disease of the mind and indicate a complete loss of the "ability to make moral distinctions."[72]

In *Chaulk*,[73] the Supreme Court reversed *Schwartz* and concluded that accused should have an insanity defence if, because of a disease of the mind, they were incapable of knowing that an act was morally wrong, even if they were capable of knowing that the act was legally wrong. Lamer C.J. argued for the majority that this broader reading of the insanity defence

> will not open the floodgates to amoral offenders or to offenders who relieve themselves of all moral considerations. First, the incapacity to make moral judgments must be causally linked to a disease of the mind . . . . Secondly, as was pointed out by Dickson J. in *Schwartz*, *supra*, "'moral wrong' is not to be judged by the personal standards

---

70   (1977), 29 C.C.C. (2d) 1 (S.C.C.) [*Schwartz*].
71   *Ibid.* at 12.
72   *Ibid.* at 22.
73   *Chaulk*, above note 14.

of the offender but by his awareness that society regards the act as wrong.'" . . . The accused will not benefit from substituting his own moral code for that of society. Instead, he will be protected by s. 16(2) if he is incapable of understanding that the act is wrong according to the ordinary moral standards of reasonable members of society.[74]

This distinction between the accused's own moral code and his or her ability to know society's moral standards may be difficult to draw in some cases. In *Chaulk*, the accused were young boys suffering from a paranoid psychosis that made them believe that they had the power to rule the world and that killing was necessary. It was clear that they did not have a defence under *Schwartz*, because they knew that killing was illegal. Unfortunately, the Supreme Court did not rule on the crucial issue of whether their belief that the law was irrelevant to them constituted an inability to know that what they did was morally wrong in the eyes of society.[75]

A subsequent case suggested that the insanity defence would not apply to a "psychopath or a person following a deviant moral code" if such a person "is capable of knowing that his or her acts are wrong in the eyes of society, and despite such knowledge, chooses to commit them."[76] The insanity defence will also not apply if the act was motivated by a delusion but the accused was still capable of knowing "that the act in the particular circumstances would have been morally condemned by reasonable members of society."[77] In another case, the Supreme Court upheld the denial of the section 16 defence because there was some evidence that the accused knew killing was morally wrong even though he shot a woman while suffering from a delusion that by killing her unborn child he would save the world.[78] The section 16 defence will also not apply if the accused understands society's views about right and wrong but, because of a delusion, chooses to do the wrong thing.[79] All of these cases indicated that the section 16 defence does not apply to many mentally disturbed offenders despite the Court's ruling in *Chaulk* that the defence should apply if the accused was because of a mental disorder incapable of knowing that an act was morally wrong.

---

74   *Ibid.* at 232–33.
75   The insanity defence did succeed at their subsequent trial.
76   *Oommen*, above note 33 at 19.
77   *R. v. Ratti* (1991), 62 C.C.C. (3d) 105 at 113 (S.C.C.) [emphasis in original].
78   *R. v. Baker*, [2010] 1 S.C.R. 329.
79   *R. v. W.(J.M.)* (1998), 123 C.C.C. (3d) 245 (B.C.C.A.).

The Supreme Court applied the new moral wrong standard in *Landry*,[80] when it concluded that the accused had an insanity defence because his disease of the mind produced a delusion that he was God killing Satan. This condition rendered him "incapable of knowing that the act was morally wrong in the circumstances." The Court was presumably satisfied that the mental disorder was so severe that the accused was not capable of knowing that society would consider the killing immoral. In *Oommen*,[81] the Supreme Court indicated that an accused, even though he was generally capable of knowing that killing was wrong, could have an insanity defence if his paranoid delusion "at the time of the act deprived him of the capacity for rational perception and hence rational choice about the rightness or wrongness of the act." The focus is on the accused's capacity for rational choice about the particular criminal act at the time the act was committed, not his or her general intellectual ability to know right from wrong.

F. IRRESISTIBLE IMPULSE

Canadian courts have long refused to recognize irresistible impulse as a separate category of the insanity defence. At the same time, however, evidence of an irresistible impulse, like evidence of delusions, may be relevant in determining whether an accused otherwise qualifies for the mental disorder defence.[82] Categorical rejections of the relevance of irresistible impulsion to the mental disorder defence would be especially inadvisable given the Court's statements that convicting a person who did not act through a voluntary expression of free will would violate the principle of fundamental justice that a person should not be convicted for a morally involuntary action. The section 16 defence should protect those who act in an morally involuntary manner because of a mental disorder and a person who faces a genuine irresistible impulse because of a mental disorder may well qualify for the defence.[83]

Evidence of "irresistible impulse" may also be relevant to proof of non-mental disorder automatism or of the required *mens rea*. In a case of multiple killings where the accused testified that he "lost control," the trial judge was correct in telling the jury to consider such testimony in relation to the Crown's burden to prove intent in relation to

---

80 *Landry*, above note 33 at 124.
81 *Oommen*, above note 33 at 18.
82 *Abbey*, above note 67; *Chaulk*, above note 14.
83 *Bouchard-Lebrun*, above note 36 at para. 51.

each killing and in relation to the accused's claims to have acted in a disassociative state.[84]

G. EFFECT OF A MENTAL DISTURBANCE SHORT OF INSANITY ON *MENS REA*

Evidence of a mental disorder may fall short of establishing a mental disorder defence but may raise a reasonable doubt as to whether the accused had a subjective mental element required for a particular offence. The insanity defence focuses on capacity and has to be proven on a balance of probabilities, whereas the mental element focuses on actual intent and is rebutted by any evidence that raises a reasonable doubt. Thus, it should not be surprising that evidence of mental disturbance, short of establishing a full section 16 defence, could still raise a reasonable doubt about some forms of *mens rea*.

In *R. v. Baltzer*,[85] Macdonald J.A. reasoned that in order to determine what was in the accused's mind, the jury must have evidence of the accused's "whole personality and background including evidence of any mental illness or disorder that he may have suffered from at the material time." It is an error of law for a judge to instruct the jury to disregard evidence of mental disorder if the defence of insanity fails.[86] All the evidence, including that of mental disorder, should be considered in determining whether the accused had the requisite intent. The higher the degree of *mens rea*, the more likely it is that mental disorder may raise a reasonable doubt about the particular intent. For example, evidence of mental disorder short of establishing the insanity defence may raise a reasonable doubt as to whether murder was planned and deliberate.[87]

Some judges have confused the relevance of evidence of mental disturbance to the determination of *mens rea* with the separate issue of Parliament's choice not to create a defence of diminished responsibility to reduce a killing from murder to manslaughter.[88] Although there is no defence of diminished responsibility in Canadian criminal law, the growing consensus is that evidence of mental disturbance or illness

---

84   *R. v. Ng* (2006), 212 C.C.C. (3d) 277 at paras. 28–31 (Alta. C.A.).

85   (1974), 27 C.C.C. (2d) 118 at 141 (N.S.C.A.).

86   *R. v. Allard* (1990), 57 C.C.C. (3d) 397 (Que. C.A.); *R. v. Jacquard* (1997), 113 C.C.C. (3d) 1 (S.C.C.) [*Jacquard*].

87   *Jacquard*, *ibid.* at 14; *R. v. McMartin* (1964), [1965] 1 C.C.C. 142 (S.C.C.); *More v. R.*, [1963] 3 C.C.C. 289 (S.C.C.).

88   This is a defence in England. *Homicide Act 1957* (U.K.), c. 11, s. 2.

should be considered when determining whether the accused had the required *mens rea*. Such evidence may prevent the Crown from proving that the accused had the subjective foresight of death required for a murder conviction. In such a case, an accused could be acquitted of murder but could still be found to have the *mens rea* necessary for manslaughter. This would occur through ordinary *mens rea* principles and not through the recognition of a separate defence of diminished responsibility.

H. AUTOMATISM

Automatism is a legal term that refers to unconscious or involuntary behaviour. The Supreme Court has defined automatism as "unconscious, involuntary behaviour, the state of a person who, though capable of action, is not conscious of what he is doing. It means an unconscious, involuntary act, where the mind does not go with what is being done."[89] More recently, the Court has noted that an accused acting as an automaton may not necessarily be actually unconscious, but that his or her consciousness must be so impaired that he or she "has no voluntary control over that action."[90] Those who act while sleepwalking or in a dazed condition from a concussion are examples of those who may be acting in an automatic state.

1) Relation to Mental Disorder and Consequences of an Automatism Defence

Automatism is related to the mental disorder defence because both involve conditions in which the accused cannot be held criminally responsible for his or her actions owing to a lack of mental capacity. If an accused leads evidence of automatism, the Crown can counter with evidence that the cause of the automatism was a mental disorder. Because an accused who acts in an automatic state will generally satisfy either arm of the mental disorder defence, the crucial issue in automatism cases is whether the cause of the automatism is a mental disorder or some other factor. If it is established that the cause of the automatism is a disease of the mind, the accused is held not criminally responsible by reason of a mental disorder and is subject to a disposition hearing

---

89   *Rabey*, above note 12 at 6.
90   *Stone*, above note 1 at 417.

and potential indeterminate detention or conditions as outlined above in relation to the mental disorder defence.

If the accused's automatism is not caused by a mental disorder, however, then the verdict is a simple acquittal. In *R. v. Bleta*,[91] the Supreme Court affirmed the acquittal of an accused who, while in a dazed condition following a severe blow to his head, killed another person. The Court concluded that "the question of whether or not an accused person was in a state of automatism so as not to be legally responsible at the time when he committed the acts with which he is charged, is a question of fact"[92] for the jury. In *Parks*,[93] an accused successfully raised a defence of automatism after he stabbed two people, killing one of them. The cause of his automatism was sleepwalking, and the Supreme Court found this condition, on the evidence presented to it, not to be a disease of the mind. The accused was acquitted and was not subject to a disposition hearing or any form of treatment. Lamer C.J. expressed concerns about setting the accused "free without any consideration of measures to protect the public, or indeed the accused himself, from the possibility of a repetition of such unfortunate occurrences."[94] The majority of the Court held, however, that in the absence of a verdict of not criminally responsible on account of mental disorder, the courts did not have jurisdiction to make preventive orders.

The Supreme Court has also speculated that "anger conceivably could, in extreme circumstances, cause someone to enter a state of automatism in which that person does not know what he or she is doing, thus negating the voluntary component of the *actus reus*."[95] In such a circumstance, the Court noted that the appropriate disposition would be an acquittal. The possibility that the accused's state of automatism may negate either the voluntary commission of the prohibited act or the required fault element makes it even more anomalous that, as will be discussed below, the accused has the burden of establishing the defence of automatism on a balance of probabilities.[96]

Federal proposals to amend the *Criminal Code*, made in 1993 but not implemented, would have made an accused acquitted on the basis of non-insane automatism subject to the same disposition hearing and possible conditions or detention as a person held not criminally responsible by reason of mental disorder. If enacted, it would have for all

---

91   (1964), [1965] 1 C.C.C. 1 (S.C.C.) [*Bleta*].
92   *Ibid.* at 58.
93   *Parks*, above note 42.
94   *Ibid.* at 299.
95   *R. v. Parent* (2001), 154 C.C.C. (3d) 1 at para. 10 (S.C.C.).
96   *Stone*, above note 1.

practical purposes eliminated the present distinction between a defence of mental disorder or non-mental disorder automatism by eliminating the different dispositions for the two defences. As will be seen, the Supreme Court subsequently in *Stone*[97] narrowed the distance between the two defences by requiring the accused to establish the defence of non-mental disorder automatism on a balance of probabilities and by indicating that automatism will be presumed to be caused by mental disorder unless the accused establishes otherwise. Nevertheless, non-mental disorder automatism still results in an acquittal.

2) Air of Reality and Persuasive Burdens of Proof

As late as 1992, the Supreme Court held that an accused who raised a defence of non-insane automatism was entitled to an acquittal if the evidence presented at trial raised a reasonable doubt as to whether the accused acted in a voluntary or conscious manner.[98] This was because such evidence would raise a reasonable doubt as to whether the accused acted with the required fault element (including the capacity to live up to an objective fault element) or, alternatively, whether the accused consciously and voluntarily committed the *actus reus*.

In the 1999 case of *Stone*,[99] however, the Supreme Court held that an accused claiming a non-mental disorder defence of automatism must establish on a balance of probabilities that he or she acted in an involuntary manner. The majority of the Court was concerned that an automatism defence might easily be faked under the traditional law that allowed the defence to go to the jury so long as the accused pointed to some evidence, that if believed, would raise a reasonable doubt about the voluntariness of his or her actions. The Court was also concerned about consistency in allocating burdens of proof given that the accused had the onus to establish on a balance of probabilities the *Daviault* defence of extreme intoxication producing a state akin to automatism and the mental disorder defence under section 16(3) of the *Criminal Code*.

The Court in *Stone* also concluded that the new persuasive burden on the accused to establish the automatism defence on a balance of probabilities also influenced the threshold decision by trial judges about whether there was a sufficient air of reality to justify instructing the jury about the defence. On the facts in *Stone*, the Court held that

---

97 *Ibid.*
98 *Parks*, above note 42. The accused would have had an air of reality burden to point to some evidence in the case that makes automatism a viable issue, but not a persuasive burden.
99 Above note 1.

a trial judge was justified in not instructing the jury on the defence of non-mental disorder automatism because there was no "evidence upon which a properly instructed jury could find that the accused acted involuntarily on a balance of probabilities."[100] The Court indicated that even to satisfy this threshold air of reality burden, the accused will not only have to assert involuntariness, but also produce collaborating psychiatric evidence. Even these two factors will not necessarily suffice. Other relevant factors that should be considered include the severity of the triggering stimulus, the corroborating evidence of bystanders, the corroborating evidence of the accused being in states of automatism at other times, whether there was a motive for the crime, and whether the alleged trigger of automatism was also the victim of the crime. Finally, if the crime could be explained without reference to automatism, this suggested that the automatism defence should not be put to the jury. The Court not only imposed a novel persuasive burden on the accused to establish non-mental disorder automatism, but also raised the threshold air of reality burden considerably.

In a strong dissent joined by three other members of the Court, Binnie J. noted the virtues of the traditional law in giving the accused the benefit of a reasonable doubt about the voluntariness of his or her actions. He persuasively argued that the majority's decision on the threshold air of reality test would deprive the accused of having claims of non-insane automatism considered by the jury. *Stone* indeed suggested a stringent test that may significantly reduce the number of claims of non-mental disorder automatism that are considered by the jury especially in cases in which the accused argues that he or she went into an automatic state because of an emotional blow.

In *R. v. Fontaine*,[101] the Supreme Court qualified *Stone* as it relates to the threshold air of reality burden but not the persuasive burden on the accused to establish automatism. Fish J. stated for an unanimous Court that "there is language in *Stone* that may be understood to invite an assessment by the trial judge as to the likely success of the defence. This in turn, may be seen to require the judge to weigh the evidence in order to determine whether it establishes, on a balance of probabilities, that the accused perpetrated the criminal act charged in a state of automatism." The Court, however, held that a trial judge who followed such an approach erred and that the factors set out in *Stone* were better used to guide the trier of fact in deciding whether the automatism defence had been established on a balance of probabilities. A trial judge should not weigh evi-

---

100 *Ibid.* at 426.
101 2004 SCC 27 at para. 63 [*Fontaine*].

dence or judge its credibility in deciding whether there is an air of reality that justifies leaving the defence to the jury. The question should rather be whether there is "in the record any evidence upon which a reasonable trier of fact, properly instructed in law and acting judicially, could conclude that the defence succeeds."[102] The Court stressed that judges should not lightly deny the accused an opportunity to have a jury consider the defence. In this case, the Court determined that the jury should have been instructed about the defence of mental disorder automatism. The accused gave detailed evidence that he acted in an involuntary manner and did not simply assert that the defence existed in law. A psychiatrist also testified that the accused was suffering from a psychotic episode induced by substance abuse and was "seeing things" when he shot the victim. *Fontaine* lowers the air of reality burden in *Stone* but leaves intact the assignment of a persuasive burden on the accused to establish the defence of non-mental disorder automatism on a balance of probabilities.

If the accused or the Crown raises a defence of mental disorder automatism, then, under section 16(3) of the *Criminal Code*, that party must prove on a balance of probabilities that the accused suffers from a mental disorder and that this condition rendered the accused incapable of appreciating the physical consequences of his or her actions or of knowing that they were morally wrong. The jury can be left with a choice between mental disorder and non-mental disorder automatism if, for example, the accused places his or her capacity for the mental element in issue by claiming non-insane automatism, and the Crown argues that the cause of any automatism is a mental disorder.[103] After the Court's decision in *Stone*, however, it will be more difficult for the accused to satisfy the threshold air of reality burden to have the jury instructed about non-mental disorder automatism. As in *Stone* and in *Fontaine*, the

---

102 *Ibid.* at para. 57. Note, however, that other parts of this judgment suggest that the fact that the accused has to establish automatism on a balance of probabilities may still influence the threshold air of reality decision. Fish J. stated: "In the case of 'reverse onus' defences, such as mental disorder automatism, it is the accused who bears both the persuasive and the evidential burdens. Here the persuasive burden is discharged by evidence on the balance of probabilities, a lesser standard than proof beyond a reasonable doubt. Reverse onus defences will therefore go to the jury where there is any evidence upon which a properly instructed jury, acting judicially, could reasonably conclude *that the defence has been established in accordance with this lesser standard.*" *Ibid.* at para. 54 [emphasis added]. The rest of the judgment, however, stresses the need to apply a consistent air of reality test to all defences regardless of whether the accused has a persuasive burden to establish the defence on a balance of probabilities or whether the Crown has to prove beyond a reasonable doubt that the defence does not exist.

103 See, e.g., *K.*, above note 12.

judge may frequently be justified in only leaving the defence of mental disorder automatism to the jury. In such cases, a jury that accepts the accused committed the crime will only be left with the options of a guilty verdict, or if it finds the crime was committed while the accused was in an automatic state, a verdict of not criminally responsible on account of mental disorder.

3) Automatism and Sleepwalking

An early American case recognized that sleepwalking could produce a defence of non-insane automatism because the "law only punishes for overt acts done by responsible moral agents. If the prisoner was unconscious when he killed the deceased, he cannot be punished for that act." An unconscious accused could not be held guilty for killing a person who tried to rouse him from a deep sleep even if the accused had committed "a grave breach of social duty in going to sleep in the public room of a hotel with a deadly weapon on his person."[104]

In *Parks*,[105] the Supreme Court upheld the acquittal of a man who drove 23 kilometres to his in-laws' house and attacked them with a knife, fatally wounding one of them. The jury had obviously concluded that the accused was acting in an involuntary or unconscious manner at the time of the attacks. Lamer C.J. concluded that the trial judge had acted properly in not instructing the jury on the defence of insanity because there was uncontradicted evidence that "sleepwalking is not a neurological, psychiatric, or other illness," but rather a sleep disorder from which "there is no medical treatment as such, apart from good health practices, especially as regards sleep."[106] The Supreme Court's definition of a disease of the mind in *Parks* does not follow English law, which somewhat mechanically assesses sleepwalking, like epilepsy, as a disease of the mind because it is a cause that is internal to the accused.[107] The Supreme Court stressed medical issues in *Parks*, not policy issues concerning whether the accused's condition was prone to recur or presented a danger to the public. However, the Court left open the possibility that, on different evidence, sleepwalking could be held to be a disease of the mind.

The Court's decision in *Stone* does not overrule *Parks*, but it does encourage judges to use policy concerns about the need to protect the public as a factor in concluding that the accused suffers from a disease

---

104 *Fain v. Commonwealth of Kentucky*, 78 Ky. Rptr. 183 at 189 and 193 (C.A. 1879).
105 *Parks*, above note 42.
106 *Ibid.* at 297.
107 *R. v. Burgess*, [1991] 2 Q.B. 92 (C.A.).

of the mind. Indeed, in one case subsequent to *Stone*, the trial judge held that sleepwalking was a mental disorder because it was a factor internal to the accused that was not triggered by specific external factors and because of the risk of recurrence and public danger. The trial judge also expressed a greater confidence about holding that sleepwalking is a mental disorder because of reforms to the disposition of those found not criminally responsible that require the least restrictive conditions be placed on a person found not criminally responsible because of a mental disorder.[108]

In *R. v. Luedecke*,[109] the Ontario Court of Appeal held that a trial judge had erred when following *Parks*; he had classified sleepwalking as a basis for non-mental disorder automatism in a case where an accused sexually assaulted a woman at a party while asleep. As in *Parks*, there was uncontradicted medical evidence led by the accused that a person could perform complex actions while sleepwalking and that sleepwalking was not a mental disorder.[110] The trial judge determined that there was no continuing danger under *Stone*, in part because the accused had accepted a plan of sleep hygiene, modest alcohol consumption, and medication that "would reduce the risk of recurrence."[111] The trial judgment in this case is more consistent with the medicalized approach taken by the Court in *Parks* to determine the existence of a mental disorder than the focus on public safety in *Stone*.[112]

The Ontario Court of Appeal reversed and held that sleepwalking should for policy reasons be characterized as a mental disorder. In doing so, the Court of Appeal rejected the medicalized approach in *Parks* and followed the public safety approach taken in *Stone*. It candidly recognized that the accused was not mentally ill and "the criminal law uses the concept of mental disorder very differently than the medical profession."[113] The Court of Appeal stressed that *Stone* required it to assume that automatism was caused by a mental disorder and to focus on the risk of recurrence of not simply violence, but the factors that caused the sleepwalking. It concluded that "social defence concerns, inevitably present in such cases, must to a large degree drive the analysis in automatism cases after *Stone*."[114] The Court of Appeal stressed dangers of recurrence given

---

108   *Canada v. Campbell* (2000), 35 C.R. (5th) 314 (Ont. S.C.J.) [*Campbell*].
109   2008 ONCA 716.
110   *R. v. Luedecke* (2005), 35 C.R. (6th) 205 (Ont. Ct. J.).
111   *Ibid.* at para. 48.
112   E. Colvin & S. Anand, *Principles of Criminal Law*, 3d ed. (Toronto: Thomson Carswell, 2007) at 451–54.
113   *Luedecke*, above note 64 at para. 7.
114   *Ibid.* at para. 93.

that the accused had a history of sexual activities in his sleep, albeit in situations with former girlfriends that did not lead to criminal charges. Finally, the Court of Appeal expressed confidence that reforms to the disposition process examined above would ensure that a sleepwalking accused found not criminally responsible because of mental disorder would not be detained or subject to conditions or stereotyped as dangerous unless he was a significant threat to the public.[115] The accused consented to a verdict of not criminally responsible on account of mental disorder at a new trial and subsequently received an absolute discharge from the Review Board. The result in this case is inconsistent with *Parks* and could only be justified on the basis that *Stone* overrules *Parks*, a decision that the Supreme Court has yet to make.

4) Automatism and Emotional Blows

In *Rabey*,[116] the Supreme Court considered whether an accused who committed a criminal act while in an automatic state caused by an emotional or psychological blow should have a defence of insane or non-insane automatism. The majority, following Martin J.A. in the Ontario Court of Appeal, decided that an accused would only have a defence of non-insane automatism if he or she went into an automatic state because of an "extraordinary event" such as being in a serious accident or seeing a loved one killed. Such an event "might reasonably be presumed to affect the average normal person without reference to the subjective make-up of the person exposed to such experience." The accused, who assaulted a fellow student a day after learning that she was not romantically interested in him, was held not to have a defence of non-insane automatism. The Court determined that the accused was only being exposed to "the ordinary stresses and disappointments of life which are the common lot of mankind."[117] If he had gone into an automatic state, the defence would have to be insane automatism because his "disassociative state must be considered as having its source primarily in the respondent's psychological or emotional make-up."[118]

Dickson J. dissented in *Rabey* on the basis that the medical evidence in the case suggested that the accused did not suffer from psychosis, neurosis, personality disorder, or an organic disease of the brain and that his violence "was an isolated event" and "the prospect of re-

---

115 *Ibid.* at para. 101. See Section A(4), earlier in this chapter.
116 *Rabey*, above note 12 at 7.
117 *Ibid.*
118 *Ibid.*

currence of disassociation is extremely remote."[119] In its reliance on medical evidence, this dissent bears some resemblance to the Supreme Court's decision in *Parks*. Dickson J. also objected to placing an objective threshold on when an emotional blow should be allowed as a basis for a defence of non-insane automatism. He stressed that "the fact that other people would not have reacted as [Rabey] did should not obscure the reality that the external psychological blow did cause a loss of consciousness."[120] He noted that in the case of a physical as opposed to a psychological blow, the only issue would be whether the particular accused, not a reasonable person, went into a disassociative state.[121]

In *Stone*,[122] the Supreme Court followed *Rabey* in holding that a trial judge did not err by refusing to instruct the jury about the defence of non-mental disorder automatism in a case in which an accused, after being provoked by his wife's verbal insults, felt a "whoosh sensation" and stabbed her forty-seven times before disposing of her body and fleeing to a foreign country. The Court indicated that trial judges should start from the proposition that involuntary and automatic behaviour was caused by a disease of the mind. They should only instruct the jury about non-insane automatism if there was confirming psychiatric evidence that established an air of reality for the defence of non-mental disorder automatism.[123] The Court held that the requirement in *Rabey* that the trigger of the involuntary conduct be an extraordinary event that could send a "normal person" in similar circumstances into an automatic state did not violate sections 7 and 11(d) of the *Charter*. The majority reasoned that the objective standard only affected the classification of the defence as mental disorder or non-mental disorder automatism and not whether the Crown had proven that the accused had voluntarily committed the offence as a matter relating to proof of the *actus reus* or the *mens rea*. This distinction is a fine and somewhat artificial one given that 1) the presumption of innocence applies to defences as well as to elements of the offence; 2) the different dispositions for the two automatism defences; and 3) the Court's novel imposition of a persuasive burden on the accused to establish automatism on a balance of probabilities. In any event, *Stone* reaffirms that the definition of disease of the mind, and the characterization of automatism as insane

---

119 *Ibid.* at 27.

120 *Ibid.* at 29.

121 See, e.g., *Bleta*, above note 91.

122 *Stone*, above note 1.

123 As discussed earlier, the air of reality burden on the accused was onerous and reflected a new persuasive burden that the accused must establish a defence of non-mental disorder automatism on a balance of probabilities.

or non-insane, is driven by policy concerns about the ultimate disposition of the accused. Even if, as in *Rabey* and *Stone*, a psychiatrist would not agree that the accused suffered from a mental disorder, courts are reluctant to hold that an accused who responds violently but perhaps involuntarily to non-extraordinary emotional blows should receive the complete acquittal that follows a verdict of non-mental disorder automatism.

Justice Binnie's dissent in *Stone* followed Justice Dickson's dissent in *Rabey* in stressing that there was no medical evidence before the court that the accused was suffering from a mental disorder and arguing that the accused had a right to have his defence of non-mental disorder automatism considered by the jury. Both judges were confident that juries would reject frivolous and untruthful claims of non-insane automatism. Binnie J. also strongly argued against the majority's decision to require the accused to prove the defence of non-mental disorder automatism on a balance of probabilities. He was concerned that the Court's decision would deprive the accused of the traditional right to be acquitted if there was a reasonable doubt as to whether he or she acted in a voluntary manner.

5) Automatism and Organic Conditions

As discussed above, accused suffering from conditions such as epilepsy, diabetes, or sleepwalking have been held by English courts to have a disease of the mind. Even if their condition caused them to act in an automatic state and there was little or no need for possible indeterminate detention, their defence has been limited to insanity.[124] These results have most often been justified with reference to a conclusion that the automatic state was the product of a cause internal to the accused. These English cases should not be followed under the holistic Canadian approach to defining a disease of the mind. In *Stone*,[125] the Supreme Court indicated that whether automatic conduct was caused by an internal cause is only one factor in a holistic test to determine whether there is a disease of the mind. A focus on internal causes can and should be discarded when it would not accord with the underlying policy concerns, most importantly the need to protect the public through potentially indeterminate detention or conditions that can be applied following a verdict of not criminally responsible by reason of mental disorder.

---

124 *O'Brien*, above note 59; *Sullivan*, above note 42; *Hennessy*, above note 62.
125 *Stone*, above note 1 at 438.

6) Automatism and Intoxication

Before *Daviault*,[126] courts were reluctant to allow the defence of non-insane automatism to go to the jury when the accused's mental condition was a product of voluntary intoxication. In *Revelle*,[127] the Supreme Court upheld a decision of Martin J.A. that concluded:

> It is well established that if automatism is produced solely by drunkenness only the defence of drunkenness, which is limited to crimes of specific intent, need be left to the jury.

An accused who became voluntarily intoxicated to the state of automatism could use this condition to raise a reasonable doubt to a specific intent offence such as murder, but such self-induced automatism could not be used as a defence to a general intent offence such as manslaughter.

As discussed in chapter 7, the Supreme Court's decision in *Daviault* opened the possibility that a voluntarily intoxicated accused could be acquitted of a general intent offence if he or she established, on a balance of probabilities, that the intoxication was severe enough to produce an unconscious condition similar to automatism or insanity. Parliament responded to *Daviault* with section 33.1, which takes away the *Daviault* defence in cases of general intent offences that involve violence. The Supreme Court in *Bouchard-Lebrun*[128] held that there was no mental disorder in a case where an accused who took drugs acted in a toxic psychosis and brutally assaulted persons in part because of religious delusions. The Court's restrictive reading of mental disorder in this case is at odds with its broad reading of mental disorder in *Stone* which as discussed earlier has been applied to cover even cases of sleepwalking. Self-induced intoxication thus seems to be a special case to which Canadian courts are reluctant to apply the mental disorder defence.

Long before *Daviault*, the Supreme Court seemed prepared to consider that involuntary intoxication might produce a state of automatism that could be a defence to any criminal offence. In *R. v. King*,[129] an accused drove while still under the influence of a drug given to him by his dentist. In his concurring judgment, Taschereau J. came close to recognizing a defence of non-insane automatism when he stated "there can be no *actus reus* unless it is the result of a willing mind at liberty to

---

126 *Daviault*, above note 1.
127 *Revelle*, above note 50.
128 Above note 36.
129 (1962), 133 C.C.C. 1 (S.C.C.) [*King*].

make a definite choice or decision, or in other words, there must be a willpower to do an act."[130] An accused who acted in an automatic state because of *involuntary* intoxication would still have a defence that could lead to an acquittal of a general intent offence such as impaired driving. Unlike in *King*, however, the accused would now have to establish the automatism defence on a balance of probabilities. The scenario is more complex and less certain for an accused who acted in an automatic state because of *voluntary* intoxication. *Daviault* itself would suggest the defence could be established by the accused on a balance of probabilities, but section 33.1 of the *Criminal Code* may deny the defence when the general intent offence involves an assault or threat of interference with bodily integrity. A further complication is that involuntary intoxication of the type seen in *King* or in other situations where the accused could not reasonably be expected to contemplate the intoxication may not qualify as self-induced intoxication under section 33.1. In such cases, the accused may be able to establish a defence of automatism that is not affected by that provision[131] and that under *Bouchard-Lebrun* would presumably be classified as non-mental disorder automatism leading to an acquittal.

7) Automatism and Other Defences

In *R. v. Stone*, the majority of the Court cautioned against leaving both mental disorder and non-mental disorder automatism to the jury. As suggested earlier in the chapter, *Stone* may require that the court classify the cause of automatism as a mental disorder in many cases for reasons relating more to public safety than medical diagnosis or the need for continued treatment. Indeed, courts have used *Stone* as a reason for classifying sleepwalking as a mental disorder that can only produce a finding of not criminally responsible by reason of mental disorder should the trier of fact accept that the accused acted in an involuntary automatic state at the time that the *actus reus* was committed.[132] In such cases, an accused with an automatism defence will be exposed to the potentially indeterminate detention for those held not responsible on account of mental disorder.

In *R. v. Graveline*,[133] the Supreme Court upheld the jury's acquittal of a severely battered woman after the judge had left the defence of non-mental disorder automatism and self-defence to the jury with re-

---

130 *Ibid.* at 3.
131 See ch. 7 for an examination of section 33.1.
132 *Campbell*, above note 108; *Luedecke*, above note 64.
133 [2006] 1 S.C.R. 609, rev'g (2005), 200 C.C.C. (3d) 247 (Que. C.A.).

spect to her actions in shooting her sleeping husband. It was accepted that the accused had no memory of her actions, but the Crown's expert testified that this amnesia occurred after the shooting. The Court held that the Crown was not entitled to a new trial simply because the judge had left both defences to the jury. Fish J. in dissent concluded that a new trial was necessary in part because the defences were "fundamentally inconsistent"[134] and there was no air of reality with respect to self-defence. The majority of the Quebec Court of Appeal had upheld the acquittal, despite the fact that the trial judge had not reviewed policy factors relating to the feigning of the defence of automatism, the accused's motive, or the alleged trigger for the behaviour said to be involuntary and unconscious. The decision may have limited precedential value because the Crown had conceded that there was an air of reality to justify putting the non-mental disorder automatism defence to the jury.

CONCLUSION

The classification of diseases of the mind has been the most dynamic and uncertain feature of the law defining the defences of mental disorder and automatism. In *Parks*,[135] the Supreme Court held that sleepwalking was not a disease of the mind and indicated that the proper verdict, if the jury found that the accused had acted in an involuntary state, was an acquittal. This remains the law today with the important exception that the accused would now have the burden of establishing his defence of non-mental disorder automatism on a balance of probabilities. In *Stone*,[136] the Supreme Court not only imposed a burden on the accused of establishing an automatism defence on a balance of probabilities, but also followed *Rabey*[137] by indicating that only extraordinary emotional blows that would cause an average person to go into a disassociative state would produce a defence of non-mental disorder automatism and its consequent verdict of acquittal. In all but the most extraordinary cases, an emotional blow producing an automatic state will result in a verdict of not criminally responsible by reason of mental disorder, even if the accused was not diagnosed by a psychiatrist with a mental disorder. In contrast to its earlier decision in *Parks*,

---

134 *Ibid.* at para. 24 (S.C.R.).
135 *Parks*, above note 42.
136 *Stone*, above note 1.
137 *Rabey*, above note 12.

the Court in *Stone* has significantly restricted the defence of non-insane automatism. In doing so, the Court has made it much less likely that the jury will ever get to consider such a defence even in cases such as *Parks* where the accused commits a crime while sleepwalking. This is unfortunate because there was no evidence that the defence was being abused in the period between *Parks* and *Stone*.

The only virtue of *Stone* is its recognition of a holistic and policy-driven approach to defining a disease of the mind. In this, the Court has been consistent with *Parks* and wisely avoided the absurd results that English courts, given their exclusive reliance on internal cause theories, have produced in cases holding that sleepwalkers, epileptics, and diabetics who act while in an automatic state should be forced into the insanity defence. Canadian courts will only use the presence of internal causes as a factor in determining disease of the mind. They may, as in *Parks*, depart from reliance on that factor if it does not accord with the overall policy objectives of using the mental disorder defence to protect the public.

The exact contours of the two alternative arms of the section 16 defence are relatively settled. The Court has limited the reference to a mental disorder producing an inability to appreciate the consequences of actions to physical consequences as opposed to emotional or penal consequences. The Court is understandably concerned that the mental disorder defence not be expanded so far as to apply to psychopaths who lack empathy for victims and foresight of penal consequences.

Less clear are the exact contours of the accused being incapable of knowing that his or her acts were morally wrong. In *Chaulk*,[138] the Court indicated that the accused could not benefit by substituting his or her own moral code for that of society. Except in extreme cases such as *Landry*,[139] it is not always easy to distinguish the accused's own moral code from his or her ability to know what society generally regards as wrong. The reference in *Oommen*[140] to the defence applying if the accused did not have a capacity for rational perception and choice about the rightness or wrongness of the act does not clarify matters or respond to the danger of expanding the defence so far as to apply to psychopaths who assert their own moral code over society's. If the psychopath is capable of discerning society's moral code but decides to follow his or her own deviant moral code, the mental disorder defence should not apply because punishment, not treatment, would be the appropriate disposition.

---

138 *Chaulk*, above note 14.
139 *Landry*, above note 33.
140 *Oommen*, above note 33.

FURTHER READINGS

BARRETT, J., & R. SHANDLER, *Mental Disorder in Canadian Criminal Law* (Toronto: Thomson Carswell, 2006)

BLOOM, H., & R. SCHNEIDER, *Mental Disorder and the Law* (Toronto: Irwin Law, 2006)

BRUDNER, A., "Insane Automatism: A Proposal for Reform" (2000) 45 McGill L.J. 67

COLVIN, E., & S. ANAND, *Principles of Criminal Law*, 3d ed. (Toronto: Thomson Carswell, 2007) ch. 8

GRANT, I., D. CHUNN, & C. BOYLE, *The Law of Homicide* (Toronto: Carswell, 1994) ch. 6

HEALY, P., "Automatism Confined" (2000) 45 McGill L.J. 87

HOLLAND, W., "Automatism and Criminal Responsibility" (1982) 25 Crim. L.Q. 95

MARTIN, G.A., "The Insanity Defence" (1989) 10 Criminal Lawyers Association Newsletter 19

MANNING, M., & P. SANKOFF, *Criminal Law*, 4th ed. (Markham: LexisNexis, 2009)) chs. 12 & 13

McSHERRY, B., "Criminal Responsibility, 'Fleeting' States of Mental Impairment and the Powers of Self-Control" (2004) 27 Int'l J. L. & Psychiatry 445

O'MARRA, A.J.C., "*Hadfield* to *Swain*: The *Criminal Code* Amendments Dealing with the Mentally Disordered Accused" (1994) 36 Crim. L.Q. 49

SCHNEIDER, R., & D. NUSSBAUM, "Can the Bad Be Mad?" (2007) 53 Crim. L.Q. 206

STUART, D., *Canadian Criminal Law: A Treatise*, 5th ed. (Toronto: Thomson Carswell, 2007) at 115–31 and 385–430

TOLLEFSON, E.A., & B. STARKMAN, *Mental Disorder in Criminal Proceedings* (Toronto: Carswell, 1993)

CHAPTER 9

SELF-DEFENCE, NECESSITY, AND DURESS

This chapter will outline a variety of defences that may apply when the accused faces external threats or pressures. Unlike mistake of fact or intoxication, these defences are not derived from the fault element of the particular offence, and they can apply even though the accused committed the *actus reus* in a physically voluntary manner and had the *mens rea* required for the offence. For example, a person who intentionally kills another may nevertheless have a defence of self-defence. A person who intentionally breaks into a house to save him- or herself from freezing to death may have a defence of necessity and a person who intentionally assists in a robbery because of death threats may still have a defence of duress.

All the defences examined in this chapter operate as complete defences that result in the accused's acquittal. In each case, there must be a reasonable doubt about each requirement of the defence. Unlike in the cases of mental disorder, automatism, or extreme intoxication, the accused does not have to establish self-defence, necessity, or duress on a balance of probabilities.

All three defences require a person to have acted reasonably in response to external pressures. In self-defence, these external pressures are violence, or threats of violence from the victim; in duress, threats of serious harm from third parties; and in necessity, dire circumstances of peril. The Supreme Court has observed that self-defence, necessity, and duress "all arise under circumstances where a person is subjected to an external danger, and commits an act that would otherwise be criminal as a way of avoiding the harm the danger presents."[1]

The common requirement that the accused respond to these pressures in a reasonable fashion raises the familiar issue of how objective standards should be applied to ensure fairness towards individual accused. This issue first arose in the context of self-defence claims by women who killed abusive partners. The Court's landmark decision in R. v. Lavallee[2] to consider particular experiences and circumstances that the accused faced in determining whether the accused acted reasonably has had implications for all the defences examined in this chapter. The Supreme Court has accepted a contextual objective standard that invests the reasonable person with the relevant characteristics and experiences of the accused for all three defences examined in this chapter, as well as the defence of provocation, which will be examined in chapter 10, because it provides a partial defence that reduces murder to manslaughter. This approach to endowing the reasonable person with similar characteristics and experiences as the accused stands in contrast to the Court's decision that a modified objective standard based on an individuated or contextual reasonable person is generally not appropriate in applying the objective fault standards discussed in chapter 5.[3] The modified objective standard used to administer these defences responds to the danger of holding accused to unreasonable standards of restraint, but it also risks blurring the distinction between subjective and objective standards and undermining social interests in requiring people to satisfy general standards of reasonable conduct.

Some of the defences examined in this chapter—self-defence, defence of property, and duress (as applied to principal offenders)—are codified, whereas others such as necessity and duress (as applied to secondary parties) are common law defences that the courts have recognized and developed.[4] Overly restrictive statutory or common law defences may violate section 7 of the Charter by allowing those who have acted in a morally involuntary manner to be punished and defences should not be subject to any special deference under the Charter.[5]

---

1   R. v. Hibbert (1995), 99 C.C.C. (3d) 193 (S.C.C.) [Hibbert].

2   (1990), 55 C.C.C. (3d) 97 (S.C.C.) [Lavallee], discussed below.

3   R. v. Creighton (1993), 83 C.C.C. (3d) 346 (S.C.C.) [Creighton], discussed in ch. 5(C)(1), "Who Is the Reasonable Person?"

4   Section 8(3) of the Criminal Code, R.S.C. 1985, c. C-46 [Code] has been interpreted as allowing courts to develop and recognize new defences. Entrapment, which was examined in ch. 2, "The Charter and the Investigation of Crime," has been developed as a common law defence.

5   R. v. Ruzic (2001), 153 C.C.C. (3d) 1 (S.C.C.) [Ruzic].

The Supreme Court has struck out the requirement in the statutory defence of duress that the threats must be of immediate death or bodily harm and that the threat must be from a person who is present at the time that the accused commits the crime under duress on the basis that they could result in the conviction of a person who has no other reasonable choice but to commit a crime.[6] As examined in chapter 7, common law restrictions on the defence of intoxication have also been found to be unconstitutional.[7]

A. CONCEPTUAL CONSIDERATIONS

1) Excuses and Justifications

Criminal law defences are sometimes classified as excuses or justifications. A defence that excuses a crime is one that acknowledges the wrongfulness of the action but holds that in the circumstances the accused should not be punished for the crime. The Supreme Court has stated that excuses rest

> on a realistic assessment of human weakness, recognizing that a liberal and humane criminal law cannot hold people to the strict obedience of laws in emergency situations where normal human instincts, whether of self-preservation or altruism, overwhelmingly impel disobedience . . . . Praise is indeed not bestowed, but pardon is, when one does a wrongful act under pressure which . . . "overstrains human nature and no one could withstand . . . . At the heart of [necessity conceptualized as an excuse] is the perceived injustice of punishing violations of the law in circumstances in which the person has no other viable or reasonable choice available; the act was wrong but it is excused because it was unavoidable."[8]

In other words, "excuses absolve the accused of personal accountability by focussing, not on the wrongful act, but on the circumstances of the act and the accused's personal capacity to avoid it." Because the accused has no realistic choice but to commit the crime, "criminal attribution points not to the accused but to the exigent circumstances facing him."[9] Section 17 of the *Criminal Code* provides that a person

---

6   *Ibid.*
7   *R. v. Daviault* (1994), 93 C.C.C. (3d) 21 (S.C.C.).
8   *Perka v. R.* (1984), 14 C.C.C. (3d) 385 at 398, [1984] 2 S.C.R. 232 [*Perka*].
9   *Ruzic*, above note 5 at paras. 40 and 46.

who commits a crime under duress from threats is "excused" from the commission of crimes.

In contrast, a defence that acts as a justification "challenges the wrongfulness of an action which technically constitutes a crime." The accused is not punished because, in the circumstances, "the values of society, indeed of the criminal law itself, are better promoted by disobeying a given statute than by observing it."[10] A justification is not conceived as a concession to normal human weakness. Most would classify self-defence as a justification on the basis that people have rights to defend their persons and their property. Indeed, until very recently the *Criminal Code* specifically stated that an accused who acts in self-defence or defence of property was "justified" in committing offences and in some cases the concept of justification was used as a reason to restrict the defence.[11]

As will be seen in the case of necessity and duress, whether a defence is conceptualized as an excuse or a justification can have a practical effect on its availability. Excuses are inherently limited by what is thought necessary for a realistic concession to reasonable human weaknesses whereas justifications are more wide-ranging in holding that certain values are so important that they justify disobeying the law. In addition, the Supreme Court has accepted the idea that a conviction of a person who committed a crime in a morally involuntary manner because the circumstances were so exigent that there was no realistic choice but to commit the crime would offend section 7 of the *Charter.* This acceptance is largely based on the self-defining and self-limiting nature of the juristic category of an excuse.[12] Nevertheless, the classification of a defence as an excuse or a justification does not affect the disposition of the accused. Duress and necessity are commonly seen as excuses, yet they lead to a complete acquittal just as the justification of self-defence does.

The distinction between excuses and justifications can be become blurred in some circumstances. A proportional relation between the harm inflicted by the accused and the harm avoided is commonly thought to be one of the defining features of a justification that makes an act taken, for example, in proportionate self-defence to be rightful. As will be seen, however, Canadian courts and legislatures have imposed proportionality requirements as part of necessity and duress

---

10   *Perka*, above note 8 at 396–97.

11   *R. v. Ryan*, 2011 NSCA 30 at para. 71 refusing to allow self-defence to go to a jury because a battered woman could not be justified in hiring a hit man to kill her abuser but allowing the excuse of duress to go to the jury.

12   *Ruzic*, above note 5.

defences, even though they are commonly seen as excuses. Recent reforms to self-defence and defence of property have dropped the language of justification that previously appeared in the *Criminal Code* perhaps in recognition that proportionality is only one element to determine whether self-defence was reasonable. This may recognize that some forms of self-defence may have elements of excuses as realistic concessions to human weaknesses and not simply act as a justification that challenges the wrongfulness of the act. It does, however, produce the paradoxical result that proportionality between the harm threatened and the harm inflicted is now required in Canadian criminal law for the so-called excuses of duress and necessity, but it is not absolutely required for the so-called justification of self-defence or defence of property.

2) Relation to Fault Element

The defences examined in this chapter are not conceived as an absence of *mens rea* in the same way as the mistake of fact or intoxication defences examined in previous chapters. At the same time, however, evidence relating to these defences could conceivably be relevant to proof of the mental element of some crimes. Evidence of self-defence, necessity, or duress, perhaps when combined with other factors, could possibly lead the jury to have a reasonable doubt as to whether the accused had the fault element for a particular crime. This would usually be possible only for offences with a high subjective level of *mens rea*. As discussed in chapter 5, the Supreme Court has indicated that duress will not negate the formation of a common intent under section 21(2) or the intent required under section 21(1)(b) when a party performs an act or omission for the purpose of aiding another person to commit an offence.[13]

3) Subjective and Objective Components

In order to qualify for the defences of self-defence, necessity, or common law duress, the accused must not only subjectively and honestly perceive the need to respond to the relevant external pressures or threats, but the accused must also act reasonably.[14] The Supreme Court has

---

13 *Hibbert*, above note 1.

14 A reasonable basis for the accused's perceptions is not required under s. 17 of the *Code*, above note 4, which codifies the statutory defence of duress. As will be seen, however, this defence is made restrictive in other more categorical ways, such as excluding a long list of offences and requiring the accused to

explained that it is "society's concern that reasonable and non-violent behaviour be encouraged that prompts the law to endorse the objective standard."[15] This restriction makes sense when it is recognized that an accused who qualifies for these defences will nevertheless have committed a crime, frequently one involving violence, with the required fault element.

At the same time, the use of objective standards raises the challenge of ensuring that accused with particular characteristics and experiences can fairly be expected to live up to the objective standard required by the law. The dilemma is to make the objective standard fair, without collapsing it into a subjective standard. This task can be attempted in several ways. One approach is to endow the reasonable person with some of the characteristics of the particular accused, such as the accused's age or sex. As examined in chapter 5, the Supreme Court has rejected such a modified objective approach for administering objective fault elements in offences. The Court was concerned that such an approach could undermine the purpose of objective fault requirements in requiring that all persons abide by the same standard of conduct. As will be seen in this chapter, the Court has been more willing to factor in characteristics of the accused such as age and gender when applying objective standards to defences. At the same time, however, the Court has recently warned that such an approach should not be taken so far as "to subvert the logic of the objective test" so that objective standards imposed on defences fail to accomplish their purpose in encouraging that all persons act whenever possible in a reasonable and non-violent manner.[16]

Both with respect to objective fault elements and reasonableness requirements in defences, there is greater consensus that objective standards must be contextualized to reflect the particular circumstances that the accused faced. For example, the Court has recognized that evidence of past battering and expert evidence concerning how battered women respond to cycles of violence is relevant in assessing the reasonableness of claims of self-defence.[17] Such evidence may also be

---

face threats of immediate death or bodily harm from a person present when the crime is committed. The Supreme Court has severed the requirements of immediate death or bodily harm and that the person who threatens be present when the crime was committed in *Ruzic* and the viability of the rest of s. 17 of the *Code* is very much in doubt.

15   *R. v. Hill* (1986), 25 C.C.C. (3d) 322 at 330 (S.C.C.) [*Hill*].

16   *R. v. Tran*, [2010] 3 S.C.R. 350 at paras. 33–34 [*Tran*] in relation to the ordinary person standard used in the provocation defence examined in ch. 10.

17   *Lavallee*, above note 2; *R. v. Malott* (1997), 121 C.C.C. (3d) 457 (S.C.C.) [*Malott*].

relevant to determining "the reasonableness of a battered woman's actions or perceptions" when provocation, duress, or necessity defences are claimed. It has been suggested that such evidence is a means of ensuring that "the perspectives of women, which have historically been ignored, . . . equally inform the 'objective' standard of the reasonable person in relation to self-defence."[18] This contextual approach also suggests that the accused's particular experiences may be relevant to placing the external pressure faced by the accused in its proper context. The emphasis is on how the accused's experiences affect context, not the level of self-control that the law expects. The fact that the accused had previously been beaten would not speak to the level of self-control expected, but could be considered so that the jury could fully understand the implications of the threats that the accused faced. For example, the fact that a woman had been previously battered by a man she assaults or kills may be relevant in determining whether she had a reasonable basis for believing that she was being assaulted by the man and that the violence she used was reasonable. Of course, considering the full context of the pressures that the accused faced may have the practical result of making it easier to excuse the accused's conduct. The distinction[19] between modifying the objective standard in order to place the events in context and individualizing it in a manner that lowers the standard of reasonable conduct expected is a critical but sometimes difficult distinction to maintain.

4) Burden of Proof

Although the extreme intoxication, mental disorder, and automatism defences examined in the last two chapters must be proven by the accused on a balance of probabilities, the defences examined in this chapter must be disproved by the Crown as part of its burden to prove guilt beyond a reasonable doubt. Thus, if the jury has a reasonable doubt that an accused acted in self-defence, or under duress or necessity, it must acquit. In *R. v. Pétel*,[20] Lamer C.J. stated that in a case of self-defence, "it is the accused's state of mind that must be examined, and it is the accused (and not the victim) who must be given the benefit of a reasonable doubt." The same is true with respect to the partial defence

18   *Malott, ibid.* at 470–71, L' Heureux-Dubé J. (McLachlin J. concurring).

19   In *Tran*, above note 16 at para. 35, the Court warned "there is an important distinction between contextualizing the objective standard, which is necessary and proper, and individualizing it, which only serves to defeat its purpose" in encouraging reasonable behaviour.

20   (1994), 87 C.C.C. (3d) 97 at 104 (S.C.C.) [*Pétel*].

of provocation examined in the next chapter. A new trial was necessary in *R. v. Thibert*[21] because the trial judge failed to explain to the jury that the accused need not prove the defence of provocation, but rather that "it rested upon the Crown to establish beyond a reasonable doubt that there had not been provocation." In order to acquit, there must be a reasonable doubt about each of the requited elements of self-defence, necessity, and duress.

5) Air of Reality

The judge does not, however, have to instruct the jury about every defence in every case. The accused has to overcome a threshold air of reality burden in every case. In *R. v. Cinous*,[22] the Supreme Court indicated that a standard air of reality test should apply to all defences. The appropriate air of reality test was whether a properly instructed jury acting reasonably could acquit on the basis of the evidence. This requires evidence on each necessary element of the defence and that a properly instructed jury acting reasonably could acquit on the basis of the evidence. In administering the air of reality test, the judge should assume that evidence is true and leave the determination of its credibilty to the jury.

The air of reality test does not impose a persuasive burden on the accused. Once a judge determined there is an air of reality to any of the defences examined in this chapter, the jury should be instructed to acquit if it has a reasonable doubt about the existence of the defence. The majority of the Court in *Cinous*, however, held that there was no air of reality to the accused's claim that he acted in self-defence when he shot the victim in the back of the head. Thus, the jury should not have even been instructed about self-defence.

B. SELF-DEFENCE

The statutory provisions in the *Criminal Code* governing self-defence were notoriously complex. In 1995, the Supreme Court criticized them as "highly technical," "excessively detailed," and "internally inconsistent" and stated that "legislative action is required to clarify the *Criminal Code*'s self-defence regime."[23] The old provisions attempted

---

21   *R. v. Thibert* (1996), 104 C.C.C. (3d) 1 at 5 (S.C.C.) [*Thibert*].

22   (2002), 162 C.C.C. (3d) 129 (S.C.C.) [*Cinous*].

23   *R. v. McIntosh*, [1995] 1 S.C.R. 686 at para. 18.

to define the various circumstances in which an accused might act in self-defence. They drew distinctions on the basis of whether the accused intended to cause death or grievous bodily harm, or had no such intent. They also drew distinctions on the basis of whether the accused had assaulted or provoked the person against whom he or she claimed self-defence. In some cases, they imposed specific duties of retreat on accused. They also contained distinctions between self-defence and defence of third parties under the protection of the accused and between the protection of personal property and dwelling houses. Although not without any defenders, these attempts to classify the various situations in which a claim of self-defence might arise were often criticized as artificial and unnecessary.

Amendments to the *Criminal Code* in 2012, however, adopt a simpler approach based on one encompassing provision in a new section 34, governing defence of self and others, and a new section 35, governing defence of all forms of property. These new provisions simplify self-defence and defence of property considerably though at some expense to the predictability of the defences. As will be seen, the new self-defence provisions are less demanding of the accused than the defences of necessity and duress, which explicitly require proportionality between the harm inflicted and the harm caused and that there be no legal way out. The new provisions instead simply require that the acts of self-defence and defence of property be reasonable in the circumstances.

The new provisions retain the basic structure of the previous self-defence provisions because they require both that the accused act with the subjective purpose of defending self or others and that they must act reasonably both with respect to the perceptions of the threat and the response to the threat. A fully subjective approach to self-defence, though used in some jurisdictions,[24] could encourage hot-headed and unnecessary resort to violent self-help. The defences of necessity, duress, and provocation also similarly blend subjective and objective requirements. At the same time, the need for reasonable grounds and

---

24   For a subjective approach to self-defence, see *Beckford v. R.* (1987), [1988] A.C. 130 (P.C.). In *People v. Goetz*, 497 N.E.2d 41 at 50 (1986), the New York Court of Appeals stated that to base self-defence solely on the accused's subjective beliefs "would allow citizens to set their own standards for the permissible use of force" and risk acquitting individuals who use violence "no matter how aberrational or bizarre his thought patterns." At the same time, however, there is some evidence that contrary to the instructions it received from the judge in that case, that the jury applied a subjective test in acquitting Goetz, the so-called subway vigilante, for shooting four African-American youths who approached him in the New York subway and asked him for $5; George Fletcher, *A Crime of Self-Defence* (New York: Free Press, 1988) at 186–88.

conduct in self-defence raises the difficult issue of whether and how objective standards should be contextualized to reflect the accused's circumstances and characteristics. The new section 34(2) continues the trend in recent self-defence jurisprudence to allow objective standards to be contextualized to reflect the accused's characteristics and history. It requires judges and juries to consider a variety of factors including the imminence and nature of the threat, whether there were other means to respond, and the proportionality of the force used by the accused to the force threatened against the accused while at the end of the day simply requiring that any act of self-defence be reasonable in all the circumstances. The new section 34 provides:

34. (1) A person is not guilty of an offence if

(a) they believe on reasonable grounds that force is being used against them or another person or that a threat of force is being made against them or another person;

(b) the act that constitutes the offence is committed for the purpose of defending or protecting themselves or the other person from that use or threat of force; and

(c) the act committed is reasonable in the circumstances.

(2) In determining whether the act committed is reasonable in the circumstances, the court shall consider the relevant circumstances of the person, the other parties and the act, including, but not limited to, the following factors:

(a) the nature of the force or threat;

(b) the extent to which the use of force was imminent and whether there were other means available to respond to the potential use of force;

(c) the person's role in the incident;

(d) whether any party to the incident used or threatened to use a weapon;

(e) the size, age, gender and physical capabilities of the parties to the incident;

(f) the nature, duration and history of any relationship between the parties to the incident, including any prior use or threat of force and the nature of that force or threat;

(f.1) any history of interaction or communication between the parties to the incident;

(g) the nature and proportionality of the person's response to the use or threat of force; and

(h)   whether the act committed was in response to a use or threat of force that the person knew was lawful.[25]

1)   Self-Defence and Defence of Others in the New Section 34

Section 34(1) now contains one defence for self-defence and defence of others. It provides that accused are not guilty of an offence if a) they believe on reasonable grounds that force is being used against them or another person or that a threat of force is being made against them or another person; b) the act is committed for the purpose of defending or protecting themselves or the other person from the use or threat of force; and c) the act committed is reasonable in the circumstances.[26]

a)   Self-Defence Applies to a Broad and Expanded Range of Offences

The new provision makes clear that self-defence can be claimed not only as a defence to charges of violent crimes such as assault or murder undertaken in self-defence, but also to any offence. Thus self-defence could apply if an accused stole a vehicle in order to protect him- or herself or others. In such circumstances, the theft could be justified under the new section 34 provided that the accused reasonably believed he or she was threatened and the theft was reasonable in the circumstances. This expansion of self-defence makes sense given that the alternative offence would often be a more proportionate response to real or threatened violence than the use of actual violence. The existence of less drastic means to respond to the potential use of force and the proportionality of the response are specifically enumerated factors under section 34(2)(b) and (g) in determining the reasonableness of self-defence. In some cases, the commission of a property or other offences to facilitate escape could be a preferred means of responding to a threat of violence than violent self-defence. The approach taken in Florida and a number of other states of extending the so-called Castle doctrine of no retreat beyond the home is ill-advised and can encourage unnecessary violent self-help.

---

25   Section 34(3) addresses self-defence in the context of legally authorized actions and provides:

> 3) Subsection (1) does not apply if the force is used or threatened by another person for the purpose of doing something that they are required or authorized by law to do in the administration or enforcement of the law, unless the person who commits the act that constitutes the offence believes on reasonable grounds that the other person is acting unlawfully.

26   *Code*, above note 4, s. 34 as amended by S.C. 2012, c. 9.

There are no restrictions on the offences to which section 34 can apply and, as under the old law, self-defence can apply to the most serious crimes including murder. As will be seen, it is an open question whether necessity or duress would be available to murder because of the explicit requirement of proportionality between the force threatened and the force used. In this way, self-defence is less demanding on the accused than common law duress and necessity perhaps because the victim in self-defence will usually be an aggressor.

The new section 34 departs from the old law in not making the accused's intent to cause death or grievous bodily harm specifically relevant to the self-defence claim. Such determinations are best left to the determination of whether the accused has the fault required for the offence. The accused's intent may be relevant in determining the reasonableness of the self-defence, but it is not enumerated in the non-exclusive list of factors in section 34(2). At most, the accused's intent will be one among a range of factors that is relevant in determining the reasonableness of the act of self-defence.

b) No Specific Reference to Self-Defence as a Justification

The previous law on both self-defence and defence of property specifically incorporated the language of justification. As previously discussed, the Canadian courts have recognized a distinction between excuses conceived of as realistic concessions to human weaknesses and justifications which are challenges to the wrongfulness of the act.[27] Self-defence has traditionally been seen as a justification and not an excuse on the basis that accused have rights to defend themselves and their property. Those who act in proportionate self-defence are seen as right in defending themselves and not as persons who must be excused for committing a crime under dire circumstances. At the same time, Canadian criminal law is not entirely consistent in this regard and requires that crimes committed under duress and necessity be proportionate to the harm threatened even though those defences are characterized as excuses and not justifications.

The new defences in both sections 34 and 35 replace the reference that an accused who acts in self-defence or defence of property is justified with a more generic reference to such a person not being guilty of an offence. What effect, if any, will this change have? In most cases, acts of proportionate self-defence can still be seen as a justification, but the new approach recognizes that the theoretical distinction between justification and excuse can become blurred in some contexts. For

---

27   *R. v. Ruzic*, [2001] 1 S.C.R. 687; *Perka*, above note 8.

example, the Supreme Court disapproved in 1990 of a case in which appellate courts had held that a battered woman could not claim self-defence or defence of others when she shot her sleeping husband.[28] If self-defence was recognized in such a case, it would bear some resemblance to an excuse that accommodated human frailties as opposed to a justification that would apply to rightful conduct. Although the Court has appealed to the concept of an excuse to limit necessity and to some extent duress, they have generally not appealed to the concept of a justification to limit self-defence.[29] In this respect, the omission of the concept of justification in the new section 34 is consistent with recent developments in self-defence especially in the context of battered women.

The omission of the language of justification with respect to the new defence of property may, however, break new ground. Justifications require some proportionality between the threatened harm and that caused by the accused. For example, it is difficult to say that killing someone simply to defend property is justified or rightful given that life is far more important than property. As will be seen later in this chapter, the new section 35 opens up this possibility both in its refusal to incorporate the concept of justification and by its omission of proportionality as one of the enumerated factors in determining whether any particular defence of property is reasonable in the circumstances.

c) First Requirement: Belief on Reasonable Grounds that Force or Threat of Force Is Being Used under Section 34(1)(a)

An accused under section 34(1)(a) must believe on reasonable grounds that force or the threat of force is being used against them or another person. In *R. v. Reilly*,[30] Ritchie J. explained that in applying a similarly dual objective and subjective standard in the old law of self-defence that the jury can be guided by the accused's subjective beliefs "so long as there exists an objectively verifiable basis for his perception." A mistake by the accused as to the existence of force or threat of force is not fatal to a self-defence claim, but the mistake must be reasonable.

---

28 *R. v. Whynot*, (1983), 9 C.C.C. (3d 449 (N.S.C.A.) disapproved of in *Lavallee*, above note 2 at 116.

29 But see *R. v. Ryan*, 2011 NSCA 30 at para. 71 refusing to allow self-defence to go to a jury because a battered woman could not be justified in hiring a hit man to kill her abuser but allowing the excuse of duress to go to the jury. To the extent that this decision relies on the statutory concept of justification in the old self-defence provisions, it should no longer be viewed as valid given that the new s. 34 does not employ the language of justification.

30 *R. v. Reilly* (1984), 15 C.C.C. (3d) 1 at 7 (S.C.C.) [emphasis in original] [*Reilly*].

The old law of self-defence generally referred to unlawful assault or assaults as the triggering factor whereas section 34(1)(a) now refers to force or the threat of force. This approach should simplify matters by avoiding having to resort to the definitions of assault and the classification of unlawful assaults. The concept of responding to the threat of force may expand self-defence somewhat, but the old law rejected the idea that the accused must wait until an assault was underway in order to respond with self-defence.[31]

The new concept of a threat of force could be applied in a case such as R. v. Petel in which the Supreme Court held that an accused can qualify for a self-defence claim even though he or she was in fact not being unlawfully assaulted. The case arose when a woman who had been threatened by one of two men shot both of them after one of them had given her his gun. She claimed that she reasonably, but perhaps mistakenly, believed she was being unlawfully assaulted by both men. Lamer C.J. stated:

> An honest but reasonable mistake as to the existence of an assault is . . . permitted . . . . The existence of an assault must not be made a kind of prerequisite for the exercise of self-defence to be assessed without regard to the perception of the accused. This would amount in a sense to trying the victim before the accused.[32]

The question for the jury is not "'was the accused unlawfully assaulted?' but rather 'did the accused reasonably believe, in the circumstances, that she was being unlawfully assaulted?'"[33] In determining the reasonableness of the belief, the jury could consider prior threats and violence received by the accused from the victim[34] and expert evidence concerning battered woman syndrome.[35] Under the new section 34(1), the relevant question for the jury would now be whether the accused reasonably believed that she faced force or a threat of force. As before, reasonable mistakes will not defeat a self-defence claim and past acts might be relevant in determining whether the accused reasonably perceived that force or the threat of force was being used.

The new concept of a threat of force is also consistent with the Supreme Court's landmark decision in R. v. Lavallee.[36] In that case, the

---

31 Lavallee, above note 2 at 116.
32 Pétel, above note 20 at 104.
33 Malott, above note 17 at 464. See also R. v. Currie (2002), 166 C.C.C. (3d) 190 (Ont. C.A.).
34 Pétel, above note 20.
35 Malott, above note 17.
36 Lavallee, above note 2.

Court held that there was no legal requirement that the accused wait until she faced an imminent attack from the deceased. In doing so, the Court upheld the acquittal of a woman who had shot her abusive partner in the back of the head after he had threatened that she would be harmed after guests had left their house. Wilson J. stated that expert testimony about the effects of battering on women can cast doubt on the view expressed in a previous case that it was "inherently unreasonable to apprehend death or grievous bodily harm unless and until the physical assault is actually in progress."[37] Expert evidence may suggest "it may in fact be possible for a battered spouse to accurately predict the onset of violence before the first blow is struck, even if an outsider to the relationship cannot." She stressed

> [t]he issue is not, however, what an outsider would have reasonably perceived but what the accused reasonably perceived, given her situation and her experience . . . .
>   . . . I do not think it is an unwarranted generalization to say that due to their size, strength, socialization and lack of training, women are typically no match for men in hand-to-hand combat. The requirement . . . that a battered woman wait until the physical assault is "underway" before her apprehensions can be validated in law would . . . be tantamount to sentencing her to "murder by installment."[38]

In the context of spousal battering, "the definition of what is reasonable must be adapted to circumstances which are, by and large, foreign to the world inhabited by the hypothetical 'reasonable man.'"[39]

In subsequent cases, the Supreme Court affirmed that evidence of prior threats and beatings would be relevant to the determination of whether the accused could perceive danger from an abuser.[40] The accused's knowledge of the complainant's propensity for violence is also relevant.[41] Although the history of the relationship between the parties to the incident is only mentioned explicitly in section 34(2)(f.1) as a factor to be considered in determining whether the act of self-defence was reasonable in the circumstances, it should also be relevant in determining whether the accused believed on reasonable grounds that he or she faced force or a threat of force.

Although the imminence of the force is likewise only mentioned in section 34(2)(b) as a factor in determining the reasonableness of the act

---

37   *Ibid.* at 116, citing *R. v. Whynot* (1983), 9 C.C.C. (3d) 449 (N.S.C.A.) [*Whynot*].
38   *Lavallee*, above note 2 at 120.
39   *Ibid.* at 114.
40   *Pétel*, above note 20; *Malott*, above note 17.
41   *R. v. Pintar* (1996), 110 C.C.C. (3d) 402 (Ont. C.A.) at 435.

and there is no legal requirement of an imminent attack, the presence or absence of an imminent threat is a factor that can be considered in determining whether the accused had a reasonable belief of force or threat of force.[42] The concept of a threat of force extends the law of self-defence but only so far.

The jury should not be instructed about self-defence if there is no air of reality to the accused's claim that he had a reasonable belief that he or she was subject to force or a threat of force. For example, cases under the old law decided that an adult son could not claim to have reasonably apprehended that his frail, asthmatic seventy-five-year-old father presented a realistic danger of inflicting death or grievous bodily harm.[43] The question under the new section 34(1) would be whether a jury could reasonably conclude that there was a reasonable basis for the accused's belief that he or she faced force or threat of force from the victim.

d) The Protection of Others

Self-defence has been expanded in section 34(1)(a) not only by refer-ence to threats of force, but also by the inclusion of force or threats of force against "another person." The old provision for the defence of others was limited to the defence of persons under the accused's protec-tion. This term was not defined in the *Code* or the Canadian caselaw, but was commonly thought to include family members and others to whom the accused owed a duty of care. Now, defence of others could be claimed with respect to unrelated third parties, for example, in cir-cumstances where an accused came across a stranger being beaten or threatened by others and acted in defence of that person. In this way, section 34(1)(a) has broadened self-defence to include the defence of all other persons. As such it now also supplements the more narrow pro-visions in section 27 that provide a separate defence for using reason-able force to prevent a commission of offences subject to arrest without warrant and that are likely to cause immediate and serious injury to persons or property.

Good Samaritans will be able to act in defence of all others, but they must under section 34(1)(a) believe on reasonable grounds that the other person is faced with force or the threat of force. They must also under section 34(1)(b) act with the subjective purpose of defending the other person. Moreover, the force they use under section 34(1)(c) must be reasonable in the circumstances. These requirements should

---

42   *Cinous*, above note 22.
43   *R. v. Hebert* (1996), 107 C.C.C. (3d) 42 at 50 (S.C.C.) [*Hebert*].

exclude violent persons who are "itching for a fight" and who may use real or imagined threats to third parties as an excuse for violence. That said, a mistaken belief that a third party is threatened by force or threat of force may still qualify under section 34(1) if it is a reasonable mistake in the circumstances.

e) Second Requirement: Subjective Purpose of Defending Oneself or Others under Section 34(1)(b)

Section 34(1)(b) requires that those claiming self-defence have the subjective purpose of defending themselves or others. In most cases, this subjective inquiry will be the least challenging requirement for the accused of the three requirements of self-defence. It will, however, exclude those accused who do not subjectively intend to defend themselves or others but rather desire to seek vengeance, punishment, or vindicate honour against someone who has used force against them or threatened to do so. The more difficult cases will be those where such improper subjective purposes are combined with the required subjective purposes of defending self or others. In such cases, the accused may satisfy the second requirement and the fate of the self-defence claim may rest on whether the accused's response was reasonable in the circumstances. (34(1)(c))

The separation out of the inquiry into the accused's subjective purpose under section 34(1)(b) will make it important that the jury is clearly instructed that the subjective purpose of self-defence is not sufficient and that the accused must in addition have both a reasonable belief that they are threatened and that they respond reasonably. A completely subjective approach to self-defence could allow people who act on unreasonable, inaccurate, and even racist perceptions of threats from others to be acquitted.

f) Third Requirement: Acts Done in Self-Defence Must Be Reasonable in the Circumstances under Section 34(1)(c)

In most self-defence cases, the critical issue will be whether the act done by the accused was reasonable in the circumstances. Section 34(1)(c) provides a more general and open-ended standard than the old law of self-defence which in some contexts specifically required that the accused use no more force than was necessary or use self-defence that was necessary to preserve the accused from death or grievous bodily harm. The new section 34(1) essentially delegates to the judge and the jury the issue of determining whether self-defence is reasonable in the circumstances.

Section 34(2) provides that the "court shall consider the relevant circumstances of the person, the other parties and the act, including, but not limited to" nine specified factors. As originally introduced in Parliament, section 34(2) simply provided that the court may consider such factors. The mandatory nature of the requirements now means that the jury should consider all relevant circumstances as they relate to the accused, other persons, and the act that is claimed to be self-defence and that they must consider the nine specified factors.

Although all relevant factors including the nine listed factors must be considered, it would be quite onerous to require either an air of reality or a reasonable doubt about all nine listed factors. As suggested previously, the three elements of self-defence remain those three factors listed in section 34(1), namely, the requirements of 1) a belief on reasonable grounds of force or threat of force; 2) subjective purpose of defending self or others; and 3) that the act be reasonable in the circumstances. Section 34(2) merely provides guidance to courts in determining whether the third requirement exists. Judges should read the long list in section 34(2) to the jury and the jury should consider all the listed factors, but they can also consider other relevant factors relating to the accused, the parties, and the act. This open-ended approach allows courts and juries to consider new factors that may be relevant. At the same time, however, it also makes self-defence less predictable and less structured and demanding than the necessity and common law duress defences that require proportionality between the harm threatened and inflicted and that there be no legal alternative.

g) Contextual Objective Standard and the History of the Relationship between the Parties to the Incident

As under the old law of self-defence, a contextual objective standard should be used in determining whether acts of self-defence are reasonable in the circumstances. This standard should account for the history of the relationship of the parties to the incident. *Lavallee* is the landmark case in this regard because it was the Supreme Court's first decision embracing a contextual objective approach that considered the accused's situation and experience. *Lavallee* has, however, sometimes been misunderstood as making the accused's status as a battered woman (or not) determinative of the self-defence claim. This is unfortunate because Wilson J. specifically warned:

> [T]he fact that the accused was a battered woman does not entitle her to an acquittal. Battered women may well kill their partners other than in self-defence. The focus is not on who the woman is, but on

what she did. . . . Ultimately, it is up to the jury to decide whether, in fact, the accused's perceptions and actions were reasonable.[44]

The converse of the above proposition should also be true. A woman may act in self-defence against a threatening partner even if she does not satisfy clinical definitions of being a battered woman.

The contextual objective standard articulated in *Lavallee* was not limited to issues of gender and past battering. In *Nelson*[45] the Ontario Court of Appeal held that an accused's diminished intelligence should be considered in determining whether he had a self-defence claim. The Court of Appeal stated that an accused with an intellectual impairment relating to his or her ability to perceive and react to an assault "may be in a position similar to that of the accused in *Lavallee* in that his or her apprehension and belief could not be fairly measured against the perceptions of an 'ordinary man.'" In another case, the Nova Scotia Court of Appeal indicated that the jury should have been instructed about both past altercations between the accused and the victim and that the accused had Asperger's Syndrome, which may have impaired his social functioning and made him anxious, paranoid, and distrustful.[46] The Supreme Court has approved of a decision that factored in expert evidence about prison environment in determining whether an inmate faced a threat from other inmates.[47] In general, the jury should be instructed to consider a reasonable person with any of the characteristics and experiences that are relevant to the accused's ability to perceive harm and to respond to it. The accused's age, gender, physical capabilities, and past interaction and communication with the person who presents a threat may be relevant to both his or her perception of the harm under section 34(1)(a) and must be considered in determining the reasonableness of the response to threatened harm under section 34(1)(c).[48] This approach allows for contextualization, but there must still be a reasonable basis for the accused's perceptions and actions.

The reference to the reasonableness of the accused's response in section 34(1)(c) should be read in light of the Court's use of the contextual objective standard since *Lavallee*. In addition, there are some specifically enumerated factors in section 34(2) which must be con-

44   *Lavallee*, above note 2 at 126.
45   *R. v. Nelson* (1992), 71 C.C.C. (3d) 449 at 467 (Ont. C.A.) [*Nelson*].
46   *R. v. Kagan* (2004), 185 C.C.C. (3d) 417 (N.S.C.A.).
47   *R. v. McConnell*, [1996] 1 S.C.R. 1075.
48   There is no need for a modified objective standard under s. 34(1)(b) which focuses on whether the accused acts with the subjective purpose of defending oneself or others.

sidered and which support the use of the contextual objective standard. These include the reference in section 34(2)(e) to the "size, age, gender and physical capabilities of the parties to the incident"; in section 34(2)(f) to "the nature, duration and history of any relationship between the parties to the incident, including any prior use or threat of force and the nature of that force or threat"; and in section 34(2)(f.1) to "any history of interaction or communication between the parties to the incident." It could be argued that the specific reference to size, age, physical capabilities, and gender is exhaustive of the contextual objective standard, but this would be a mistake given both the specifically non-exhaustive nature of the section 34(2) factors and the development of the modified objective standard to incorporate other factors that the accused cannot control such as mental disabilities. Indeed, limiting the modified objective standard to size, age, gender, and physical capabilities might even result in a successful equality rights challenge on that basis.

The reference in section 34(2)(f) and (f.1) to the relationship between the parties including the use of force and threats between the parties and the history of their interaction and communication reflects a series of cases involving claims of self-defence by battered women. In *Lavallee*, the Supreme Court held that evidence of battering and expert evidence on the effects of battering was relevant in determining the reasonableness of the response. Such evidence would be particularly relevant in explaining why a woman did not leave an abusive relationship sooner. Wilson J. stressed that "the jury must ask itself is whether, given the history, circumstances and perceptions of the [accused], her belief that she could not preserve herself from being killed by [the deceased] that night except by killing him first was reasonable.[49] In *Pétel*, the Supreme Court affirmed that the prior assaults suffered by the accused and her daughter would be relevant to determining the reasonableness of her "belief that she could not extricate herself otherwise than by killing the attacker."[50] In *Malott*,[51] the Court again affirmed that evidence with respect to past battering may be relevant to determine the reasonableness of the accused's response. The modified objective standard thus includes not only the size, age, gender and other non-controllable characteristics of the accused, but also the history of the accused's relationship with the victim including any prior force or threat of force.

---

49   *Ibid.* at 125.
50   *Pétel*, above note 20 at 104.
51   *Malott*, above note 17.

One characteristic of the particular accused that should not be considered is his or her intoxication. In *Reilly*,[52] the Supreme Court held that the accused's intoxication could not be considered in determining whether he reasonably apprehended harm. The Court concluded:

> The perspective of the reasonable man which the language of s. 34(2) places in issue here is the objective standard the law commonly adopts to measure a man's conduct. A reasonable man is a man in full possession of his faculties. In contrast, a drunken man is one whose ability to reason and to perceive are diminished by the alcohol he has consumed.

The Court left open the possibility that an intoxicated accused could have a valid self-defence claim provided that he or she still had reasonable grounds for his or her beliefs. Although the new section 34(2) allows a non-exhaustive use of factors to be considered, intoxication is simply not relevant to determining whether an act of self-defence is reasonable in the circumstances.

The reference to particular characteristics and past circumstances in sections 34(2)(e) and (f) are not limited to those of the accused but extend to those of all parties to the incident. This recognizes the fact that it is relevant in cases such as *Lavallee* that the victim is a larger male with a past history of beating and threatening the female accused. At the same time, sections 34(2)(d) and (e) suggest that the old age or small size of a victim and the use or absence of a weapon could also be relevant to whether the accused responded reasonably to force or a threat of force. At the end of the day, however, the focus should be on the accused and the accused should be given the benefit of the doubt about whether he or she acted in self-defence.

h) Retreat from Homes and Other Situations

The concept of whether the accused should retreat before using self-defence has been controversial. The Supreme Court in *Lavallee* affirmed that there is no requirement that the accused retreat from his or her home.[53] The origins of this concept are in the old common law notion that "a man's home is his castle."[54] Wilson J. argued that a "man's home"

---

52   *Reilly*, above note 30 at 8.

53   A statutory duty to retreat was formerly imposed under the old s. 35(c) on those accused who committed the initial assault or provoked it.

54   *Semayne's Case* (1604), 77 E.R. 194 (K.B.). See also *R. v. Antley*, [1964] 2 C.C.C. 142 at 147 (Ont. C.A.) [*Antley*]; *R. v. Deegan* (1979), 49 C.C.C. (2d) 417 (Alta. C.A.) [*Deegan*], affirming the concept in the context of intruders on the accused's property.

may be his castle but it is also the woman's home even if it seems to her more like a prison in the circumstances."[55] Courts of Appeal have held that the jury should be instructed that retreat is not a reasonable option for those attacked in their homes.[56] This doctrine is not specifically mentioned in the new section 34, as it was under the old section 35 of the *Code* which in some situations required the accused to retreat.

Any no retreat doctrine should, however, be administered cautiously because it could encourage unnecessary and perhaps disproportionate violent self-help. The new section 34(2)(b) suggests that courts may consider "whether there were other means available to respond to the potential use of force." These other means in some situations could include retreat. The fact that the new defence applies to all offences also means that it could provide a defence in situations where an accused stole a car or trespassed on other property in order to avoid a violent situation.

i) The Proportionality of the Act Done in Self-Defence

In determining the reasonableness of the act done in self-defence, the trier of fact shall consider a number of specifically enumerated factors including in section 34(2)(a) "the nature of the force or threat" to be avoided; whether the force "was imminent and whether there were other means available to respond" to it (section 34(2)(b)); whether weapons were used or threatened (section 34(2)(d)) and "the nature and proportionality of the person's response to the use or threat of force" (section 34(3)(g)). These factors can all be grouped under the general heading of the proportionality and relative harm of the force resisted or threatened and the force used by the accused. At the same time, the only absolute requirement in section 34(1) (c) is that the act done must be reasonable in the circumstances. There is no requirement that the force or threat faced by the accused must be imminent or even that the accused's response must be proportionate, though these factors must be considered in determining the reasonableness of the act done. Similarly, there is no requirement that the accused must retreat in all cases. This is consistent with the historical tendency of Canadian courts not to demand that all self-defence be strictly proportional or that the accused take all possible routes of retreat.[57]

Section 34(1)(c) is more generous than the old section 34(2) of the *Code* because it does not require accused to believe on reasonable

---

55 *Lavallee*, above note 2 at 124.

56 *R. v. Forde*, 2011 ONCA 592 at para. 56; *R. v. Proulx* (1998), 127 C.C.C. (3d) 511 at paras. 45–46 (B.C.C.A.); *R. v. Antley*, [1964] 1 O.R. 545 at para. 11; *Deegan*, above note 54.

57 *R. v. Kong*, 2006 SCC 40.

grounds that the act done in self-defence was the only way to protect themselves from death or grievous bodily harm. In *R. v. Cinous*,[58] the Supreme Court held that there was no air of reality to put self-defence to the jury in a case in which a man shot another man in the back of the head while they were stopped at a service station en route to steal computers together. The accused feared that the deceased and a companion were planning to kill him because they had put on latex gloves. The accused also testified that he believed he had no alternatives. He had tried to avoid the deceased and he did not think of calling the police to help because he had spent his whole life running from the police. McLachlin C.J. and Bastarache J. for the majority of the Court held that while the jury may reasonably have reached a conclusion that the accused reasonably apprehended an assault and death or grievous bodily harm, it could not have reasonably concluded that the accused reasonably believed he had no alternatives but killing the person. Unlike in *Lavallee*, there was no evidence supporting why the accused may have reasonably believed that there were no other alternatives. The fact that the accused may have reasonably believed that the police could not protect him was not enough. He could still have fled the scene: "Section 34(2) does not require that an accused rule out *a few* courses of action other than killing. The requirement is that the accused have believed on reasonable grounds that there was *no alternative course of action* open to him . . . . This defence is intended to cover situations of last resort."[59] Under the new section 34(1)(c), however, the relevant question would not be whether the accused believed *on reasonable grounds* that there was no other course of action, but only whether the accused's actions were reasonable in the circumstances. It may well be more difficult for a judge to hold that there is no air of reality to a self-defence claim under this new and less structured self-defence provision and the issue would ultimately fall to the jury to decide whether the accused's actions were reasonable in all the circumstances.

j) The Accused's Role in the Incident

The old defences drew complex distinctions between assaults that were unprovoked and assaults provoked by the accused. This required complex instructions to the jury on multiple defences. Section 34(2)(c)

---

58 *Cinous*, above note 22.

59 *Ibid.* at paras. 123–24 [emphasis in original]. See also *R. v. Pilon*, 2009 ONCA 248 at paras. 73 and 75 rejecting the idea that a criminal subculture of kill or be killed should be considered and that self-defence is a defence of last resort as measured by the standards of the ordinary community as represented by the jury.

much more simply allows the jury to consider "the person's role in the incident" in determining whether the act done in self-defence is reasonable in the circumstances. The jury will then apply their own judgment about the relevance and importance of what the accused may have done to provoke force or threats of force. This approach is certainly easier to administer, but underlines how self-defence claims under the general reasonableness standard of section 34(1)(c) may be more difficult to predict than under the old law.

k) Excessive Self-Defence

If excessive self-defence leads to a conclusion that the act was not reasonable in the circumstances, the accused will, as under the old law of self-defence, be convicted, at least absent another defence including one that may be based on a constitutionally claim of moral involuntariness.[60] Canadian courts have not recognized a partial defence for accused who engage in excessive and unreasonable self-defence, which in some other jurisdictions reduces murder to manslaughter. Dickson J. has concluded in the context of an unsuccessful self-defence claim under the old section 34(2):

> Where a killing has resulted from the excessive use of force in self-defence the accused loses the justification provided under s. 34. There is no partial justification open under the section. Once the jury reaches the conclusion that excessive force has been used, the defence of self-defence has failed.[61]

This decision is also supported by section 26 of the *Criminal Code*, which provides that everyone authorized by law to use force is criminally responsible for any excess of force. The result can make self-defence, especially when the accused has the intent required for murder, an all or nothing proposition. The options are either to acquit on the basis of self-defence or to convict the accused of the most serious offence with its mandatory penalty of life imprisonment. Concern about the ultimate disposition of an accused in cases such as *Lavallee* and *Pétel* may have influenced the development of the law of self-defence. It also places significant pressure on the accused to accept a plea bargain to manslaughter should one be offered.

---

60   Stephen Coughlan, "Duress, Necessity, Self-Defence and Provocation: Implications of Radical Change?" (2002) 7 Can. Crim. L. Rev. 146 at 199–200; E. Colvin & S. Anand, *Principles of Criminal Law*, 3d ed. (Toronto: Carswell, 2007) at 320–23.

61   *R. v. Faid* (1983), 2 C.C.C. (3d) 513 at 518 (S.C.C.).

l)   Section 34(3): Self-Defence against Law Enforcement Actions

Can a person use self-defence in resisting arrest or other law enforcement actions? Section 34(3) prevents such self-defence claims unless the accused "believes on reasonable grounds" that those enforcing the law are "acting unlawfully." This means that in order to claim self-defence against law enforcement actions the accused must both subjectively and reasonably believe that the law enforcement actions are unlawful. The requirements for both subjective and objective components are consistent with the general tenor of the self-defence provisions.

In many cases, the critical issue under section 34(3) will be whether the accused's belief that the law enforcement actions were unlawful is reasonable. The requirement of reasonableness is not a standard of perfection. The accused may have a reasonable belief that the police are acting unlawfully even though the police may actually be acting lawfully. The reasonableness standard should be a modified one at least to the extent of considering the history of the parties. The accused should also be given the benefit of the doubt as is the case with all other elements of self-defence. Even if the accused's belief that the law enforcement actions are unlawful is accepted as reasonable, accused must still under section 34(1)(a) have reasonable grounds to believe that they face force or threats of force; they must under section 34(1)(b) act for the purpose of defending themselves or others and the acts that they do must be reasonable in the circumstances under section 34(1)(c).

m)   Summary

The new section 34 is less structured and predictable than the old self-defence provisions or, as will be seen, the necessity and duress defences. Nevertheless, the new section 34 retains the basic elements of self-defence in that the accused must subjectively perceive a threat and respond for the purpose of defending themselves or others and there must be a reasonable basis both for the accused's perceptions of force and the accused's response in the circumstances. The trend towards a contextual application of objective standards also continues with specific reference to the characteristics and history of the parties to the incident.

In order for self-defence to be left to the jury there must be evidence upon which a jury acting reasonably could find 1) a belief on reasonable grounds that force or threat of force is being made against the accused or another; 2) that the act was done for the subjective purpose of defending the accused or the other person; and 3) that the act was reasonable in the circumstances. In order to justify an acquittal, there must be a reasonable doubt about each of those three requirements.

2) Defence of Property in the New Section 35

Section 35 now contains one defence for defence of property and makes no distinction between various forms of property and dwelling houses. The new section 35 provides:

> **35.** (1) A person is not guilty of an offence if
>
> (a)   they either believe on reasonable grounds that they are in peaceable possession of property or are acting under the authority of, or lawfully assisting, a person whom they believe on reasonable grounds is in peaceable possession of property;
>
> (b)   they believe on reasonable grounds that another person
>
>   (i)   is about to enter, is entering or has entered the property without being entitled by law to do so,
>
>   (ii)   is about to take the property, is doing so or has just done so, or
>
>   (iii)   is about to damage or destroy the property, or make it inoperative, or is doing so;
>
> (c)   the act that constitutes the offence is committed for the purpose of
>
>   (i)   preventing the other person from entering the property, or removing that person from the property, or
>
>   (ii)   preventing the other person from taking, damaging or destroying the property or from making it inoperative, or retaking the property from that person; and
>
> (d)   the act committed is reasonable in the circumstances
>
> 2) Subsection (1) does not apply if the person who believes on reasonable grounds that they are, or who is believed on reasonable grounds to be, in peaceable possession of the property does not have a claim of right to it and the other person is entitled to its possession by law.[62]

There are four requirements to defence of property and there must be an air of reality on all four elements to put the defence to the jury and there must be a reasonable doubt on all four elements to justify an acquittal. The first requirement is that the accused under section 35(1)(a) must believe on reasonable grounds that they are in peaceable possession of property (or reasonably believe that they are acting under the authority of or lawfully assisting such a person). The second

---

62   Section 35(3) addresses the defence of property against law enforcement and provides that there is no defence, "unless the person who commits the act that constitutes the offence believes on reasonable grounds that the other person is acting unlawfully."

is that under section 35(1)(b) the accused must also believe on reasonable grounds that another person is entering, taking, damaging, or destroying the accused's property. The third requirement is that the offence under 35(1)(c) must be committed for the subjective purpose of protecting the property and the fourth and often most critical requirement under section 35(1)(d) is that that the offence committed by the accused must be reasonable in the circumstances.

a) Defence of Property Applies to a Broad and Expanded Range of Offences

As with the new self-defence provision, the new defence of property applies not only to assaults and other acts of force done to protect property, but any other offence. Unlike in self-defence, however, proportionality is not a specifically enumerated factor in defence of property. This omission creates the potential that the section 35 defence might be claimed, not as under section 34 as a defence to less serious crimes such as stealing a vehicle to flee an attacker, but to more serious offences of violence. In any event, an act of defence of property must under section 35(1)(c) be done for the subjective purpose of protecting property and must under section 35(1)(d) be reasonable in the circumstances. This latter requirement should disqualify attacks on people for reasons not related and reasonable to the defence of property.

b) No Specific Reference to Defence of Property as a Justification

As under the new section 34, there is no specific reference in section 35 to the concept that defence of property constitutes a justification of rightful conduct as opposed to an excuse that makes a realistic concession to human frailties. The omission of the concept of justification is more than a theoretical quibble with respect to defence of property because the new section 35 omits the concept of using no more force than necessary that was found in several of the old defence of property provisions relating to defence of dwellings. Section 35 does not specifically require the proportionality of the response be considered as one of the relevant factors in determining whether an act done to defend property is reasonable in the circumstances. One of the features of a justification is that the harm inflicted is less serious than the harm avoided and this makes the conduct rightful in the circumstances. As will be seen, it is possible that seriously injuring or even killing a person solely to defend property could be considered to be a valid defence of property under section 35. If such an extreme defence was recognized under section 35, it would operate more as an excuse for conduct that would still be wrongful given the value of human life and health and not as a justification of rightful conduct.

c) No Deeming of Assault but Continued Overlap between Defence of Property and Self-Defence

The old defence of property provisions provided that a trespasser who resisted an attempt to protect personal or real property would be deemed to have committed an assault. These complex provisions are not present in the new section 35. Nevertheless, this does not preclude frequent overlap between defence of property and self-defence provisions. For example, a person who is protecting property may also be able to claim self-defence if they have a reasonable belief that force or a threat of force is being made against them.

d) The Contextual and Modified Objective Standard

Several components of defence of property require that the accused must not only have the subjective purpose of protecting property but that there must also be a reasonable basis for the belief that the accused has possession of the property (section 35(1)(a)); that the property is being threatened (section 35(1)(b)); and that the accused's actions are reasonable in the circumstances (section 35(1)(d)). In principle, the contextual objective standard used with respect to self-defence should also be applied to defence of property. The accused's history and circumstances may be relevant to their belief in the peaceable possession of property and their belief that their property is being threatened. The age, size, gender, physical capabilities, and perhaps other personal characteristics of the parties may also be relevant to determining whether a particular act done in defence of property was reasonable in the circumstances. As always, care must be taken to ensure that the objective standard of reasonable conduct is contextualized but does not become a subjective standard or one that demands lower standards of restraint from some accused.

e) First Requirement: Reasonable Belief in Peaceable Possession and Claim of Right under Section 35(1)(a)

The first requirement for defence of property is a reasonable belief by the accused that they are in peaceable possession of property. The old defence of property provisions also used the concept of peaceable possession and it has been interpreted to include control of property that was peaceable because it was not seriously challenged by others. Aboriginal protesters who have occupied land have previously been held not to be in peaceable possession of the land.[63] The new section 35(1)(a) does not, as did the prior section, actually require peaceable possession of the property. It only requires that those claiming the defence and those assisting have a reasonable belief in such peaceable possession. This seems to open the door for a court to hold that a person claiming the defence had a reasonable belief in peaceable possession even if they were mistaken. This may be of particular relevance in cases such as Aboriginal occupations where the actual question of possession may be contested and difficult to determine. The concept of a reasonable belief in peaceable possession may also make relevant the history of the accused's claims to possession and even perhaps legal and other advice received about the possession.

Section 35(2), however, places an additional requirement by requiring that an accused who has a reasonable belief in peaceable possession will not have a defence if they do "not have a claim of right to it and the other person is entitled to its possession by law." A claim of right can include an honest mistake about entitlement even though the mistake is based on both fact and law.[64] In this way, the concepts of both reasonable belief in peaceable possession and claim of right represent some relaxation of the strict principle that ignorance or mistakes of law is not an excuse. At the same time, it is possible to read section 35(2) as denying the defence of property in cases in which the accused is not entitled to possession of the property. In my view, however, it would be unduly harsh to preclude a defence of property if the accused made a reasonable mistake about their entitlement to the property.

f) Second Requirement: Reasonable Belief That Property Is Being Threatened under Section 35(1)(b)

The second requirement for defence of property is that accused have a reasonable belief that the property in question is being threatened. This section specifies a number of ways in which property can be threatened including when a person is about to enter or enters property without being entitled in law to do so. This provision on its face seems to exclude defence of property as a defence if the accused wrongly, but even reasonably, believes that the person entering the property is not entitled by law to enter the property when in fact the person is so entitled. It would, however, seem to be within the general tenor of the defence provisions to allow an accused to have the benefit of a reason-

---

63 *R. v. George* (2000), 145 C.C.C. (3d) 405 (Ont. C.A.) [*George*]; *R. v. Born With A Tooth* (1992), 76 C.C.C. (3d) 169 (Alta. C.A.).

64 *R. v. Lei* (1997),120 C.C.C. (3d) 441, leave to appeal to S.C.C. refused (1998), 123 C.C.C. (3d) vi.

able mistake that a person was a trespasser on property or in a dwelling house even though section 35(1)(b)(i) seems to require that the person actually have no entitlement to enter the property. This section also does not apply in cases where another person may have just entered property, but is no longer on property.

Section 35(1)(b)(ii) applies in cases where an accused believes on reasonable grounds "that another person is about to take property, is doing so or has just done so." This provision expands defence of property to include acts done when the accused reasonably believes that a person has just taken property. It could apply to a security guard or shopkeeper who restrains a person outside the store on the basis of a reasonable belief that the person has just shoplifted.

Section 35(1)(b)(iii) applies in cases where an accused believes on reasonable grounds that "another person is about to damage or destroy property, or make it inoperative, or is doing so." This section clarifies that defence of property applies not only against trespass and theft of property but also vandalism. Like section 35(1)(b)(i), however, this section seems not to apply in cases where the accused has a reasonable belief that a person has just finished damaging property. On the one hand, it could be argued that in such cases the damage has been done and the proper response is to call the police. On the other hand, it is anomalous that the defence applies to those who have just taken property but not to those who have just entered or damaged property but are no longer doing so.

g) Third Requirement: Subjective Purpose of Protecting Property under Section 35(1)(c)

The third requirement for the defence of property is that the accused have the subjective purpose of protecting property. Depending on the circumstances, this will be a purpose in preventing a trespasser from entering property or removing a trespasser or retaking property or preventing its damage. In many cases, such subjective purposes will be obvious from the circumstances, but this provision would preclude a person who assaults a trespasser, thief, or vandal for the purpose of vengeance or punishment. The specific reference to accused removing trespassers or retaking property may raise issues about whether such potentially forceful actions by the accused are reasonable in the circumstances. As will be seen, the new section does not incorporate old statutory provisions that frequently required the accused to use no more force than necessary and had been interpreted by the Supreme Court in a number of cases to require a degree of proportionality between the harm inflicted by the accused in defence of property and the harm of the threat to property.[65]

h) Fourth Requirement: Act Must be Reasonable in the Circumstances under Section 35(1)(d)

As with the new self-defence provision, the most critical issue with respect to defence of property will often be whether the accused's actions were reasonable in the circumstances. Unlike in self-defence, section 35 of the *Code* provides no enumerated factors that must be considered by judges and juries in determining whether any particular act of defence of property is reasonable in the circumstances. In addition, section 35 does not follow the frequent references in the old defence of property provisions to the need to use no more force than necessary despite the fact that these phrases have been subject to extensive interpretation by the courts who had read them as requiring some proportionality between the force used to protect property and the harm to property interests that were avoided by the use of self-help.

The old jurisprudence on proportionality should inform determinations of the reasonableness of defence of property under section 35(1)(d). In *R. v. Gee*,[66] Dickson J. quoted with approval an authority that stated it "cannot be reasonable to kill another merely to prevent a crime which is directed only against property." The Supreme Court in *R. v. Gunning* held that the force used by a person in peaceable possession of a dwelling house to eject a trespasser "must have been reasonable in all the circumstances. . . . Where the defence arises on the facts, the onus is on the Crown to prove beyond a reasonable doubt that Mr. Gunning did *not* act in defence of property." The Court indicated that "the intentional killing of a trespasser could only be justified where the person in possession of the property is able to make out a case of self-defence." Thus the Court has concluded that it will always be unreasonable to intentionally kill a person in order to remove them as a trespasser.[67] In the subsequent case of *R. v. McKay*, however, the Court refused to extend such categorical rules when it explicitly stated that it did not endorse the view of the Manitoba Court of Appeal that "'defence of property alone will never justify the use of anything more than minor force being used against a trespasser or that, in all cases, 'the defence of

---

65   *R. v. Gunning*, [2005] 1 S.C.R. 627 at para. 25 [*Gunning*]; *R. v. Szczerbaniwicz*, [2010] 1 S.C.R. 455 at para. 20 [*Szczerbaniwicz*]. See also *George*, above note 63 at para. 49; *R. v. McKay*, 2009 MBCA 53 at para. 23.

66   (1982), 68 C.C.C. (2d) 516 at 528 (S.C.C.). See also *R. v. Clark* (1983), 5 C.C.C. (3d) 264 at 271 (Alta. C.A.).

67   *Ibid.* at paras. 25–26.

property alone will not justify the intentional use of a weapon against a trespasser.'"[68] The Court in that case did hold that aggravated assault was not justified by defence of property.

In *R. v. Szczerbaniwicz*[69] the majority of the Supreme Court held that a man had used more force than was necessary when he pushed his estranged wife as she was damaging his diploma. Justice Abella quoted with approval statements by Justice G.A. Martin to the effect that self-defence and defence provisions reflected the

> great principle of the common law that the use of force in such circumstances is subject to the restriction that the force used is necessary; that is, that the harm sought to be prevented could not be prevented by less violent means and that the injury or harm done by, or which might reasonably be anticipated from the force used is not disproportioned to the injury or harm it is intended to prevent.[70]

Justice Abella stressed that the "proportionality approach" requires both subjective and objective standards related to the harm caused to property and the harm inflicted in defence of property. Dissenting judges in *Szczerbaniwicz* also accepted that the accused "must have a subjective belief of the necessity, and the belief must be based on reasonable grounds," but stressed that in "'quick response' situations an accused is not expected to "weigh to a nicety" the exact measure of a defensive action or to stop and reflect upon the precise risk of consequences from such action."[71] The Court was united on the need for proportionate defence of property though they disagreed in how strictly proportionality should be required.

It remains to be seen whether courts will read a proportionality requirement into the bare reference in section 35(1)(d) of the need for the act to be reasonable in the circumstances and it is unfortunate that Parliament was silent on this issue. In my view, courts should read in such a proportionality requirement in the absence of clear legislation displacing the extensive proportionality jurisprudence. Although proportionality is only one of the enumerated factors in section 34(2) relating to self-defence, it has an important role in restraining disproportionately violent defences of property. Although some mechanical approaches to statutory interpretation might find that Parliament's failure to include proportionality in section 35 when it is mentioned in sec-

---

68   *R. v. McKay*, [2007] 1 S.C.R. 793 at para. 2.

69   Above note 65.

70   *R. v. Baxter* (1975), 27 C.C.C. (2d) 96 at 113 (Ont. C.A.) quoted with approval in *Szczerbaniwicz*, *ibid.* at para. 19.

71   *Ibid.* at paras. 33 and 35.

tion 34(2) would suggest that Parliament did not intend proportionality to be a factor in section 35, it would be anomalous to restrain defence of life and health with proportionality principles, but not to restrain defence of property. That said, it should also be noted that the courts have been relatively cautious about drawing categorical limits on proportionate defences of property, only having suggested in *Gunning* that defence of property alone would not justify an intentional killing.

i)   Section 35(3): Defence of Property against Law Enforcement Actions

Section 35(3) prevents a defence of property claim against law enforcement actions unless the "accused believes on reasonable grounds that the other person is acting unlawfully." This follows the same pattern as section 34(3) examined earlier in this chapter. Consistent with the general tenor of the defence of property provisions, it has both subjective and objective components that require that a person have both an honest and a reasonable belief that they are resisting unlawful law enforcement efforts. The requirement of reasonableness is not a standard of perfection and the accused may have a reasonable belief that the police are acting unlawfully even though the police may actually be acting lawfully. The reasonableness standard should be a modified one at least to the extent of considering the history of the parties. The accused should also be given the benefit of the doubt, as is the case with all elements of defence of property.

Even if the accused's belief that the law enforcement actions are unlawful is accepted as reasonable, accused must still under section 35(1)(a) have reasonable grounds to believe that they are in peaceable possession and have a legal right to the property; they must under section 35(1)(b) have a reasonable belief about a threat to property; they must under section 35(1)(c) have the subjective purpose of protecting property; and under section 35(1)(d) their acts done in defence of property must be reasonable in the circumstances. These should be adequate restraints against unreasonable attacks on law enforcement officials.

j)   Summary

The new section 35 is less structured and predictable than the old defence of property provisions, but it should be easier to apply. Section 35(1)(a) requires a reasonable belief in peaceable possession of the property defended, but section 35(2) may restrict the defence to at least require a claim of right and may even preclude the defence when the accused is not in fact entitled to the property. The accused must under section 35(1)(b) also believe on reasonable grounds that the property is threatened or that the accused has just taken the property. In addition, the accused must under section 35(1)(c) act for the subjective purpose of protecting the property and not for other purposes such as vengeance and punishment. Finally and most importantly, the act under section 35(1)(d) must be reasonable in the circumstances and courts may well read established principles of proportionality developed in defence of property cases under the old provisions. There must first be an air of reality on all four elements to justify putting the defence to the jury and there must be a reasonable doubt on all four elements to justify an acquittal.

The new sections 34 and 35 of the *Code* are overdue and are in many respects an improvement over the previous self-defence and defence of property provisions that were needlessly complex. They will make the life of judges, jurors, lawyers, and students easier. That said, however, the increased simplicity of these defences will come at a price of less certainty. Self-defence and defence of property are now less structured defences than the defences of necessity and common law duress, which clearly require proportionality between the harm inflicted and the harm avoided and that there be no legal alternative to breaking the law.

Previous law reform proposals explicitly required that a person use no more force than necessary and/or that the force used be proportionate to the harm avoided; in some cases it was explicitly stated that defence of property could not justify intentional causing of death or serious harm.[72] The government has chosen not to follow these proposals, but to use the more flexible requirement that self-defence and defence of property must simply be reasonable in the circumstances. To be sure, this does not go as far as a wholly subjective approach or the explicit no-retreat rule used in Florida and other American states. Nevertheless, it may open up new avenues for self-defence and defence of property. For example, cases like *Cinous* where self-defence was held not to have an air of reality because there was no evidence to support a reasonable belief in lack of alternatives could potentially be decided differently under the new section 34. The question at the air of reality stage will be whether there is evidence that would allow a jury acting reasonably to conclude that the act was reasonable in the circumstances. At the same time, courts are capable and may well be inclined to read requirements of proportionality and necessity back into self-defence and defence of property. Courts should do so especially with respect to de-

---

72   These previous proposals were made by the Law Reform Commission of Canada, the Canadian Bar Association, and by the government in a 1993 white paper. See Don Stuart, *Canadian Criminal Law*, 5th ed. (Toronto: Carswell, 2007) at 510–11 and 517.

fence of property because of the dangers of killing and maiming people simply to protect property interests and because of the lack of guidance provided by Parliament in respect of what constitutes reasonable force. With respect to self-defence, courts will continue to maintain the flexibility of the contextual objective standard embraced in *Lavallee* and clearly endorsed in the new section 34(2). This approach, as well as the omission of hard and fast proportionality and necessity requirements in the new section 34, also blurs the distinction between justifications and excuses and opens up the possibility that self-defence may in some circumstances operate more as an excuse and concession to human weakness than a justification that always requires that the force used be proportionate and necessary.

3) Related Defences

There are a number of other provisions that allow justifications for the use of force in specific situations. Section 43 justifies the use of force by way of correction by schoolteachers and parents towards children under their care, provided the force does not exceed what is reasonable under the circumstances. The Supreme Court has narrowly interpreted this controversial defence because it restricts the protection of the law afforded to young people from unconsented invasions of their physical security and dignity. It has held that section 43 does not apply to the discipline of mentally disabled adults and only applies when used with the intent and for the benefit of correction and education.[73]

In *Canadian Foundation for Children v. Canada*,[74] the Supreme Court upheld section 43 as not violating sections 7, 12, or 15 of the *Charter*. Although section 43 adversely affects children's security of the person, it was consistent with the principles of fundamental justice. The requirement that the force be reasonable in the circumstances was not unduly vague under section 7 of the *Charter*. The Court indicated that the force must be used for corrective purposes and not include corporal punishment for those under two or over twelve years of age, corporal punishment using objects, such as rulers or belts, or slaps or blows to the head.[75] The result of the decision is to place new restrictions on the section 43 defence. These restrictions are expressed in clear and categorical terms in the Court's judgment but not in the text of the section 43 defence. The majority of the Court justified this approach as

---

73   *R. v. Ogg-Moss* (1984), 14 C.C.C. (3d) 116 (S.C.C.).
74   *Canadian Foundation for Children, Youth and the Law v. Canada (A.G.)*, 2004 SCC 4.
75   *Ibid.* at paras. 37 and 40.

a proper interpretation of the defence in light of expert evidence and Canada's international obligations, while a minority argued that it was an impermissible reading down of a vague and overbroad defence that should have been struck down.

Section 45 justifies the performance of a surgical operation for a person's benefit if the operation was reasonable in the circumstances and performed with reasonable care. A doctor's actions in stopping respiratory support of a patient, at the patient's request that nature be allowed to take its course, has been held to be justified under this provision on the basis that the doctor's actions were reasonable.[76]

Sections 25 to 33 provide various justifications for the use of force to prevent criminal offences and to assist in enforcing the law. The Supreme Court has explained:

> Section 25(1) essentially provides that a police officer is justified in using force to effect a lawful arrest, provided that he or she acted on reasonable and probable grounds and used only as much force as was necessary in the circumstances. That is not the end of the matter. Section 25(3) also prohibits a police officer from using a greater degree of force, that is, that which is intended or likely to cause death or grievous bodily harm, unless he or she believes that it is necessary to protect him- or herself, or another person under his or her protection, from death or grievous bodily harm. The officer's belief must be objectively reasonable. This means that the use of force under section 25(3) is to be judged on a subjective-objective basis. If force of that degree is used to prevent a suspect from fleeing to avoid a lawful arrest, then it is justified under section 25(4), subject to the limitations described above and to the requirement that the flight could not reasonably have been prevented in a less violent manner.[77]

Although these provisions impose objective standards of using no more force than necessary, the Court has also indicated that police have demanding and difficult work and the amount of force should not be measured with exactitude.[78] A previous provision that authorized the shooting of fleeing felons without regard to whether or not they were dangerous was held to be an unjustified violation of section 7 of the *Charter* by threatening people's lives and security of the person in a disproportionate manner.[79]

---

76   B.(N.) v. Hôtel-Dieu de Québec (1992), 69 C.C.C. (3d) 450 (Que. S.C.).

77   R. v. Nasogaluak, 2010 SCC 6, [2010] 1 S.C.R. 206 at para. 34.

78   Ibid. at para. 35.

79   R. v. Lines, [1993] O.J. No. 3248 (Gen. Div.).

C. NECESSITY

Courts were historically reluctant to recognize necessity caused by dire circumstances of peril as either an excuse or a justification. In *R. v. Dudley*,[80] men who killed a boy and resorted to cannibalism when lost at sea were convicted of murder. Noting that it was "the weakest, the youngest, the most unresisting" who was chosen to die, the court declared that any defence of necessity "appeared to us to be at once dangerous, immoral, and opposed to all legal principle and analogy." The Court conceded that the accused were subject to great suffering, but concluded:

> We are often compelled to set up standards we cannot reach ourselves. ... [A] man has no right to declare temptation to be an excuse, though he might himself have yielded to it, nor allow compassion for the criminal to change or weaken in any matter the legal definition of the crime.[81]

The accused did not have a defence of necessity and they were convicted of murder. They were sentenced to death, but their sentences were commuted to six months' imprisonment in an exercise of royal mercy by the Queen.

In the 1970s, necessity was pleaded as a defence to the crime of performing an abortion without the approval of an abortion committee. Dickson J. stated for the Supreme Court that the defence of necessity was "ill-defined and elusive," and concluded that if it did exist in Canadian law, "it can go no further than to justify non-compliance in urgent situations of clear and imminent peril when compliance with the law is demonstrably impossible." He added that "no system of positive law can recognize any principle which would entitle a person to violate the law because on his view the law conflicted with some higher social value.[82] Laskin C.J. dissented and would have left the defence with the jury, allowing it to decide whether there was an immediate danger to the woman's life or health and whether it was certain that a legal and committee-approved abortion could be obtained to prevent that danger.

The Supreme Court finally recognized necessity as a common law defence in *Perka*,[83] which involved drug smugglers who were forced to

---

80 (1884), 14 Q.B.D. 273 at 287 (C.C.R.).
81 *Ibid.* at 288.
82 *R. v. Morgentaler (No. 5)* (1975), 20 C.C.C. (2d) 449 at 497 (S.C.C.) [*Morgentaler (No. 5)*].
83 *Perka*, above note 8.

① imminent
② no legal alternative
③ proportionate

come ashore in Canada because of dangerous seas. Dickson C.J. was careful to restrict necessity to "circumstances of imminent risk where the action was taken to avoid a direct and immediate peril"; where the act was "morally involuntary" as "measured on the basis of society's expectation of appropriate and normal resistance to pressure"; and where it was clear that there was no reasonable legal alternative to avoid the peril. The Court recognized necessity as an excuse for morally involuntary conduct but not as a justification that made conduct rightful. The idea that necessity excuses morally involuntary conduct now gives the common law defence a constitutional foundation, despite the fact that necessity was not recognized as a common law defence until 1984. In *Ruzic*,[84] the Supreme Court held that it was a principle of fundamental justice under section 7 of the *Charter* that a person who acts in a morally involuntary manner not be punished. In other words, those who commit an offence when there is no other realistic choice but to do so should not be punished because their actions are morally involuntary. This means that attempts by Parliament to abolish the common law defence, or perhaps even to restrict it by precluding its use for serious offences, would likely be found to violate the principle of fundamental justice that prevents the punishment of those who act in a morally involuntary manner.

1) Necessity an Excuse and Not a Justification

Dickson C.J. stressed in *Perka* that necessity could only operate as an excuse in the face of immediate and urgent circumstances, and that it should not be based on "the comparative social utility of breaking the law against importing as compared to obeying the law."[85] In her concurring opinion, Wilson J. would have left open the possibility that necessity could operate as a justification. In such a scenario, an accused could have the defence, even though he or she did not act in a morally involuntary manner in the face of an emergency. Rather, the accused could deliberate and decide that the "fulfillment of the legal duty to save persons entrusted to one's care is preferred over the lesser offences of trespass or petty theft."[86] The English Court of Appeal has recognized necessity as a justification to a deliberate and intentional killing in a case of the conjoined twins where it was certain that they would both

---

84 Above note 5.
85 *Ibid.* at 402. Thus, a moral belief that abortion was or was not moral could not be the basis for a necessity defence. *R. v. Bridges* (1990), 62 C.C.C. (3d) 455 (B.C.C.A.).
86 *Perka*, above note 8 at 420.

eventually die if they were not separated.[87] Whether necessity could be a justification as well as an excuse could have had a practical effect in the abortion context, where those who did not comply with the law had often made a deliberate decision to violate the law.

In *R. v. Morgentaler*,[88] the Ontario Court of Appeal held that the defence of necessity should not have been left to the jury when doctors were charged with violating a *Criminal Code* provision that required the approval of a hospital committee before an abortion was performed. The court stated that the doctors' deliberate and planned decision to violate the law was inconsistent with the morally involuntary response to an immediate peril to life or health that was required for a necessity defence. The Supreme Court[89] did not deal with this issue because it decided that the law requiring approval of an abortion by a hospital committee was an unjustified violation of the rights of women under section 7 of the *Charter*.

The conceptualization of necessity as an excuse may preclude pre-mediated and deliberate decisions to violate the law. At the same time, it also precludes a "clean hands" argument that would deny the necessity defence to those who were engaged in illegal activity when they were faced with circumstances of urgent and compelling necessity. In *Perka*, the Court rejected the argument that an accused who is engaged in illegal conduct should be disentitled to the necessity defence. This decision meant that the jury could consider the defence, even though the accused had been engaged in drug smuggling when a storm forced them to land on Canadian territory. This followed from the Court's conceptualization of the defence as an excuse that in no way justifies the conduct and the Court's focus on whether the accused had any realistic choice but to commit the crime. Nevertheless, Dickson C.J. indicated that the defence of necessity would not apply "if the necessitous situation was clearly foreseeable to the reasonable observer, if the actor contemplated or ought to have contemplated that his actions would likely give rise to an emergency requiring the breaking of the law."[90] In such circumstances, the defence would be denied, not because the accused was acting illegally, but because his or her conduct was not morally involuntary.

Necessity and duress are recognized in Canada only as excuses. Excuses have a self-defining feature because they are based on what

---

87   *A (Children) (Conjoined Twins: Surgical Separation)*, [2000] 4 All E.R. 961 (C.A.).

88   (1985), 22 C.C.C. (3d) 353 (Ont. C.A.).

89   *R. v. Morgentaler (No. 2)* (1988), 37 C.C.C. (3d) 449 (S.C.C.), discussed in ch. 2(B)(4)(b), "Principles of Fundamental Justice."

90   *Perka*, above note 8 at 403.

is required by a realistic concession to human weaknesses and do not normally involve a calculation of the respective harms that are avoided and harms that are inflicted.[91] Dickson C.J. elaborated that necessity conceptualized as an excuse "rests on a realistic assessment of human weakness, recognizing that a liberal and humane criminal law cannot hold people to the strict obedience of laws in emergency situations where normal human instincts, whether of self-preservation or of altruism, overwhelmingly impel disobedience."[92] The Court's rejection of necessity as a justification could cause injustice especially if the courts take a narrow and restrictive approach to the question of the imminence of peril.

The Supreme Court in R. v. Latimer[93] articulated three elements of necessity: 1) the requirement of imminent peril or danger; 2) the requirement of no reasonable legal alternative; and 3) the requirement of proportionality between the harm inflicted and the harm avoided. As will be discussed below, the first two requirements are evaluated according to the "modified objective standard . . . that takes into account the situation of the particular accused person"[94] while the third proportionality standard is assessed on a purely objective standard.

Before the jury is instructed to consider the necessity defence, the judge must determine that there is an air of reality to the defence. This means that there must be evidence relating to each of the three requirements of the test and that the evidence must be such that a properly instructed jury acting reasonably could acquit the accused. In Perka, the Court indicated that there was an air of reality to the necessity defence in a case where the accused put into shore with thirty-three tons of marijuana because they faced imminent peril on the ocean. In Latimer,[95] however, the Court unanimously held that there was no air of reality with respect to any of the elements of necessity when a father killed his daughter in order to prevent her from suffering severe pain that would be caused by a medically required operation.

---

91   As will be seen, however, a proportionality requirement was imposed in Perka, ibid., out of an abundance of caution.

92   Ibid. at 398.

93   R. v. Latimer (2001), 150 C.C.C. (3d) 129 (S.C.C.) [Latimer].

94   Ibid. at para. 32.

95   Ibid.

2) First Requirement: Reasonable Belief in Imminent Peril and Danger

Dickson C.J. indicated in *Perka* that necessity as an excuse only applied when the accused had no realistic choice but to violate the law. He suggested that "at minimum, the situation must be so emergent and the peril must be so pressing that normal human instincts cry out for action and make a counsel of patience unreasonable."[96] The requirement in *Perka* of an imminent peril might be in tension to the recognition six years later in *Lavallee* that some accused, because of their experience and situation, should not be required to wait until harm was just about to occur. Similarly, what may be a reasonable legal alternative for some accused may not be for others.[97]

In addition, the requirement in *Perka* that the peril be imminent might violate section 7 of the *Charter* if the accused responded in a morally involuntary fashion to a serious and unavoidable threat of future harm. In *Ruzic*,[98] a statutory requirement that the duress defence be limited to threats of immediate death or bodily harm was held to violate section 7 of the *Charter* because it could punish those who acted in a morally involuntary fashion.

Following *Ruzic*, the requirement of imminence in the related defence of necessity should not be restricted to immediate threats. It is difficult to distinguish between an accused who breaks into a cabin for food before he or she has reached a level of starvation or exposure that is life-threatening and one who waits until the peril is immediate. Similarly, it would be difficult to distinguish between a person who leaves a secluded location by driving while impaired to escape a serious attack that has not yet commenced and one who waits until the attack is actually underway. Both accused in these scenarios would have no safe avenue of escape and no realistic choice but to violate the law. A restrictive approach to the imminence requirement is particularly undesirable given the Court's categorical rejection of necessity as a justification that could apply to deliberate and well-thought-out decisions to break the law.

In *R. v. Latimer*,[99] the Supreme Court affirmed the requirement that "disaster must be imminent, or harm unavoidable and near. It is not enough that the peril is foreseeable or likely; it must be on the verge of

---

96   *Perka*, above note 8 at 399.
97   In *R. v. Lalonde* (1995), 37 C.R. (4th) 97 at 109 (Ont. Gen. Div.), *Lavallee*, above note 2, was applied to expand the common law defence of necessity.
98   *Ruzic*, above note 5.
99   *Latimer*, above note 93 at para. 29.

transpiring and virtually certain to occur." This restrictive formulation of the imminence requirement creates a risk that the peril may not be held to be imminent until the accused faces an immediate threat. As discussed above, a requirement of an immediate threat would be at odds with developments in self-defence and duress. At the same time, the Court was on firmer ground when it indicated that "where the situation of peril clearly should have been foreseen and avoided, an accused person cannot reasonably claim any immediate peril."[100] On the facts of the case, the Court held there was no imminent peril because Tracy Latimer's "ongoing pain did not constitute an emergency in this case" but was rather "'an obstinate and long-standing state of affairs'" and that the proposed surgery "did not pose an imminent threat to her life, nor did her medical condition."[101]

The accused's subjective belief that there is an imminent peril is not determinative. There must be a reasonable basis for that belief. Reasonableness will be determined on a modified objective standard. In *Latimer*, the Court held that there was no reasonable basis for Latimer's belief in imminence in part because "there was no evidence of a legitimate psychological condition that rendered him unable to perceive that there was no imminent peril."[102] Here an analogy to evidence of the ability of battered women to predict when another round of battering was imminent might be made. In the absence of such psychological evidence, however, the Court rejected Latimer's subjective belief in the imminence of the peril as unreasonable.

3) Second Requirement: Reasonable Belief in No Legal Way Out or Safe Avenue of Escape

In *Perka*,[103] the Court suggested that "if there is a reasonable legal alternative to disobeying the law, then the decision to disobey becomes a voluntary one, imperilled by some consideration beyond the dictates of 'necessity' and human instincts." In that case, there was no legal way out because the accused faced disaster and drowning at sea if they did not put ashore with their large cargo of drugs. Courts should not deny the necessity defence simply because the accused was acting illegally at the time that necessity arose, though they have denied the defence on the basis that it was foreseeable when the accused acted that the

---

100 *Ibid.*
101 *Ibid.* at para. 38.
102 *Ibid.*
103 Above note 8.

need to break the law would arise.[104] The principled focus should be on whether the accused acted in a morally involuntary manner at the time that the offence was committed.

In two *Morgentaler* cases,[105] there were legal ways out because a legal abortion could have been approved by a therapeutic abortion committee as then required under the *Criminal Code*. In *Latimer*,[106] the Court affirmed that "if there was a reasonable legal alternative to breaking the law, there is no necessity." It indicated that legal alternatives must be pursued even though they may be "demanding," "sad," and "unappealing."[107] In this case, the Court indicated that allowing Tracy Latimer to go through the required operation and inserting a feeding tube to assist with pain management were reasonable legal alternatives that the accused should have pursued. The determination of no reasonable legal alternative should be determined on a modified objective standard so that any past experiences that the accused had with the victim's pain, pain management, and surgeries should have been relevant in determining the reasonableness of legal alternatives.

There is some overlap in the determination of the imminence of the peril and the existence of reasonable legal alternatives. In both cases, courts should be careful before demanding that the accused wait until the peril is immediate. The defence of necessity has been denied in a case in which an accused engaged in impaired driving to flee a possible attack because there were other safe avenues of escape.[108] This makes sense because the accused had a reasonable legal way out. It would not, however, make sense to deny the defence to a person with no safe avenue of escape on the basis that she did not wait until the attack was underway to drive away while in an impaired state. It would also be inconsistent with *Lavallee* to deny the necessity defence until the attack was underway. In other cases, courts have found that impaired driving was the only way that the accused could escape attack.[109]

In *R. v. Kerr*, LeBel J. (Arbour J. concurring) would have found a valid defence of necessity to a weapons charge laid against a prisoner who carried a shank in a lawless prison and used the shank in self-

---

104 *Ibid.* at 256 (S.C.R.); *R. v. John Doe* (2007), 228 C.C.C. (3d) 302 (B.C.C.A.).

105 *Morgentaler (No. 5)*, above note 82; *R. v. Morgentaler* (1985), 22 C.C.C. (3d) 353 (Ont. C.A.).

106 *Latimer*, above note 93 at para. 30.

107 *Ibid.* at para. 38.

108 *R. v. Berriman* (1987), 45 M.V.R. 165 (Nfld. C.A.).

109 See cases described in D. Paciocco, "No-one Wants to Be Eaten: The Logic and Experience of the Law of Necessity and Duress" (2010) 56 Crim. L.Q. 249 at 258–59.

defence. They concluded that the accused "had a reasonable belief that the circumstances afforded him no legal way out. And the harm he sought to avoid—in the words of the trial judge, 'a lethal attack'—outweighed" the harm of the weapons offence.[110] Binnie J. stated in dissent that the "argument that violent self-help in breach of the peace can be justified as a 'necessity' has been rejected since medieval times as inimical to public order and should not be given new credence in 21st century Alberta."[111] This dissent discounts both the fact that necessity was considered a defence to the weapons charge and not the homicide charge and the fact that the authorities had lost control of a prison beset by warring gangs. As in self-defence, the contextual objective approach to both the imminent peril and no legal way out requirements of necessity should make allowances for the exigencies of the prison environment.[112]

4) Third Requirement: Proportionality between Harm Inflicted and Harm Avoided

Even though he conceptualized necessity as an excuse and not a justification, Dickson C.J. required that, as is the case with self-defence, there be proportionality between the harm sought to be avoided and the harm committed by the accused. He stated:

> Even if the requirements for urgency and "no legal way out" are met, there is clearly a further consideration. There must be some way of assuring proportionality. No rational criminal justice system, no matter how humane or liberal, could excuse the infliction of a greater harm to allow the actor to avert a lesser evil.[113]

In *Latimer*,[114] the Court affirmed the importance of the proportionality requirement and held that killing a person was "completely disproportionate" to "non-life-threatening suffering" should Tracy Latimer have had the proposed operation. This suggests that the Court saw the case as one "where proportionality can quickly be dismissed" so that it might not even be necessary to examine whether the above two requirements of the necessity defence can be applied. On the other hand, the Court recognized that "most situations fall into a grey area that re-

---

110   *R. v. Kerr*, [2004] 2 S.C.R. 371 at para. 96. The other members of the majority of the Court acquitted on the basis of lack of *mens rea*.

111   *Ibid.* at para. 68.

112   See *R. v. McConnell*, [1996] 1 S.C.R. 1075.

113   *Perka*, above note 8 at 400–1.

114   *Latimer*, above note 93 at para. 41.

quires a difficult balancing of harms." The Court warned that it was not necessary that the harm avoided "clearly outweigh" the harm inflicted, but only that the two harms be "of a comparable gravity."[115] In this vein, the Court declined to create an absolute rule that murder would be categorically excluded from the necessity defence as a disproportionate response to all possible perils. At the same time, the case stands for the proposition that killing is disproportionate to relieving non–life-threatening suffering.

5) Modified and Contextual Objective Standard for Imminence and No Legal Way Out but Not Proportionality

As in the other defences in this chapter, the reasonable person will generally be tailored to reflect the past experiences and frailties of the particular accused. In *Hibbert*,[116] Chief Justice Lamer observed that

> The defences of self-defence, duress and necessity are essentially similar, so much so that consistency demands that each defence's "reasonableness" requirement be assessed on the same basis . . . [namely an objective standard] that takes into account the particular circumstances and frailties of the accused. . . . [I]t is appropriate to employ an objective standard that takes into account the particular circumstances of the accused, including his or her ability to perceive the existence of alternative courses of actions.

In *R. v. Latimer*, the Court confirmed that a modified objective standard that takes into account the situation and characteristics of the accused should be used for determining 1) whether there was an imminent peril and 2) whether there was a reasonable legal alternative. It cautioned that the modified objective standard must be distinguished from the subjective standard. Thus, the fact that an accused like Robert Latimer subjectively believed that there was imminent peril and no reasonable legal alternative was not enough because his beliefs must also be "reasonable given his circumstances and attributes."[117] In the absence of psychological evidence about caregivers for children who lived in much pain, the use of the modified objective standard made little difference in *Latimer*.

---

115 *Ibid.* at para. 31.
116 *Hibbert*, above note 1 at 227.
117 *Latimer*, above note 93 at para. 33.

The Court in *Latimer* concluded that a modified objective standard should not be used when determining whether there was proportionality between the harm inflicted and the harm avoided. Proportionality was to be determined on a purely objective standard that is not modified by the characteristics and experiences of the accused or the victim. The Court was concerned that a modified objective standard would give too little weight to harms suffered by the victim who was severely disabled. Proportionality is a matter of the moral standards of the community and these standards are "infused with constitutional considerations (such as, in this case, the section 15(1) equality rights of the disabled)."[118]

D. DURESS

Like necessity, duress occurs when an accused commits a crime in response to external pressure. In the case of duress, the pressure is threats of harm by some other person. The classic case is the person who commits a crime or assists in the commission of a crime with a gun to his or her head.

The defence of duress in Canada is very complex, in large part because section 17 of the *Criminal Code* contains a very restrictive defence that requires threats of immediate death or bodily harm from a person present when the offence was committed and excludes a long list of offences ranging from murder to arson. Even before the *Charter*, the courts minimized the harsh impact of this restrictive defence by applying it only to principal offenders, and not parties to crime. Instead, the courts applied the more flexible common law defence to parties to a crime on the grounds that they were not covered by section 17, which applies only to "a person who commits an offence." This approach mitigated the harsh effects of section 17 because in many cases a person acting under duress would only be a party to a crime—by, for example, being forced to assist—and not the principal offender.

The Supreme Court has performed some major surgery on section 17 by holding that its requirement that threats must be of immediate death or bodily harm and made by a person who is present when the crime was committed violate section 7 of the *Charter* by denying the defence to those who have no realistic choice but to commit the offence and thus act in a morally involuntary manner.[119] Section 17 as reformu-

---

118 *Ibid.* at para. 34.
119 *Ruzic*, above note 5.

lated by the Court remains valid, albeit perhaps on life support. The Supreme Court has yet to rule whether the surviving parts of section 17 violate section 7 of the *Charter* because they categorically exclude from the defence those who commit offences such as murder, attempted murder, robbery, unlawfully causing bodily harm, and arson. It may well be that the categorical exclusion of such a long list of crimes will eventually be held to violate section 7 of the *Charter*. In such an eventuality, the common law defence of duress would apply not only to parties to a crime but also to principal offenders. The result would be to make the law considerably less complex and fairer to the accused.

The common law defence is less restrictive and more flexible than section 17 of the *Code*. The common law defence of duress applies when an accused commits a crime in a morally involuntary response to threats where there is no safe avenue of escape. The common law defence of duress, like the other defences examined in this chapter, is applied on the basis of a modified objective standard that makes allowance for the particular characteristics and attributes of the accused. It does not require the threats to be of immediate death or bodily harm or from a person who is present when the offence is committed. The courts have stressed that duress as a common law defence is similar to necessity and this suggests that, as with necessity, there is some requirement for proportionality between the harm threatened and the harm committed by the accused. Finally, circumstances of duress may prevent the Crown from proving some particularly high levels of subjective *mens rea* for a few crimes.

In short, duress can refer to 1) the statutory defence available under section 17 of the *Criminal Code* to the principal offender who commits the offence and as modified by section 7 of the *Charter*; 2) the common law defence available to parties to an offence (this common law defence would be available in all cases should section 17 be found in its entirety to violate section 7 of the *Charter*); and 3) a factor that may in rare cases prevent the Crown from proving the mental element for some crimes.

1) Section 17 as Applied to Principal Offenders

Section 17 of the *Criminal Code* provides that the defence of duress is available only when an accused "commits an offence under compulsion by threats of immediate death or bodily harm from a person who is present when the offence is committed." The courts interpreted the requirement of a threat of immediate death or bodily harm quite literally. In *R. v. Carker (No. 2)*,[120] an accused charged with wilfully damaging public property argued that he acted under duress because he was threatened with death and serious bodily harm by fellow prisoners during a prison riot. The Supreme Court held that the defence of duress was not available because the accused and the prisoners issuing the threats were locked in their respective cells. Although the accused acted under compulsion of threats of death and grievous bodily harm that were operative at the time the offence was committed, "they were not threats of 'immediate death' or 'immediate bodily harm' and none of the persons who delivered them was present in the cell with the [accused] when the offence was committed."[121] Likewise, in *R. v. Hébert*,[122] a witness did not face threats of immediate death or bodily harm when he gave false testimony in court, because he could have sought official protection from anonymous phone threats. The Supreme Court has observed that "the plain meaning of section 17 is quite restrictive in scope. Indeed, the section seems tailor-made for the situation in which a person is compelled to commit an offence at gun point."[123]

a) First Requirement: Threats of Death or Bodily Harm against the Accused or a Third Party

Section 17 required that the threats be of immediate death or bodily harm from a person who was present when the crime was committed. The Supreme Court held in *R. v. Ruzic* that the requirements of immediacy and presence violated section 7 of the *Charter* because they could result in the punishment of a person who committed a crime in a morally involuntary manner. In that case, the accused was charged with importing heroin after a person had threatened to kill her mother who lived in a foreign country, if she did not import the drugs. The Supreme Court in *R. v. Ruzic* clarified that threats of death or bodily harm against third parties such as the accused's family may be considered under section 17 of the *Criminal Code*.[124] This seems appropriate as threats to one's family or loved ones may be just as compelling as threats to oneself, and Parliament has not clearly excluded threats to third parties from section 17. In addition, other caselaw suggests that the threats need not be express from words or gestures but can be reasonably implied from the circumstances.[125] For example, there could be

---

120 [1967] 2 C.C.C. 190 (S.C.C.) [*Carker*].
121 *Ibid.*
122 (1989), 49 C.C.C. (3d) 59 (S.C.C.).
123 *Ruzic*, above note 5 at para. 50.
124 *Ibid.* at para. 54.
125 *R. v. Mena* (1987), 34 C.C.C. (3d) 304 at 320 (Ont. C.A.) [*Mena*].

an implied threat when a person instructs his cousin to assist him after the accused killed two other people.[126]

The more flexible common law defence of duress was not an option in *Ruzic* because the accused was the principal offender who brought drugs into Canada. Absent a successful *Charter* challenge, however, section 17 would also not excuse the offence because the threats faced by the accused were not threats of immediate death or bodily harm from a person who was present when the accused actually imported heroin into Canada. Justice LeBel for a unanimous Supreme Court held that a defence that punished morally involuntary behaviour would violate section 7 of the *Charter*. He reasoned:

> It is a principle of fundamental justice that only voluntary conduct—behaviour that is the product of a free will and controlled body, unhindered by external constraints—should attract the penalty and stigma of criminal liability. Depriving a person of liberty and branding her with the stigma of criminal liability would infringe the principles of fundamental justice if the accused did not have any realistic choice. The ensuing deprivation of liberty and stigma would have been imposed in violation of the tenets of fundamental justice and would thus infringe section 7 of the *Charter*.[127]

An accused could act in a morally involuntary manner even though he or she was not blameless or morally innocent and committed the *actus reus* of the crime in a physically voluntary manner and did so with the required *mens rea* or fault element.

Applying the principle that people should not be convicted for morally involuntary crimes, the Court in *Ruzic* found that the requirement in section 17 that the threats must be of immediate death or bodily harm from a person who is present violated section 7 of the *Charter*. In order to support its conclusions, the Court observed that the common law defence of duress in Canada and elsewhere did not have the restrictive requirements of a threat of immediate death or harm from a person present when the crime was committed. Rather, the focus under the common law was on whether there was "any safe avenue of escape in the eyes of a reasonable person, similarly situated."[128] The Court concluded that the requirements of immediacy and presence would prevent a person such as a battered woman or a hostage who acted in a morally involuntary manner from claiming the defence. The violations

---

126 *R. v. McRae* (2005), 77 O.R. (3d) 1 (C.A.).
127 *Ibid.* at para. 47.
128 *Ibid.* at para. 62.

of section 7 of the *Charter* were not justified under section 1 in part because of the unwillingness of the Court to hold that any violation of section 7 was justified under section 1 and in part because of the less restrictive alternative of the common law defence.

The Supreme Court did not, however, strike section 17 down in its entirety. Instead, it struck down only the immediacy and presence requirements. Although the situation is far from clear,[129] it would appear that section 17 remains in force and will be applied to those who commit offences as opposed to those who are parties who aid and abet offences. The reformulated section 17 defence thus applies to those who commit an offence "under compulsion by threats of death or bodily harm . . . if the person believes that the threats will be carried out and if the person is not party to a conspiracy or association whereby the person is subject to compulsion." Although this section on its face does not require the accused respond reasonably to threats, courts have read in a modified and contextual objective standard and have held that the purpose of the defence is to excuse morally involuntary conduct.[130] Without resort to such common law concepts, some judges fear that the section 17 duress defence will be too expansive because it only requires the accused subjectively to believe that he or she is threatened.[131] Reading section 17 as informed by common law concepts effectively erodes the distinction between the statutory defence that applies to principal offenders and the common law defence that applies to parties to an offence, with the exceptions of the constitutionally dubious list of excluded offences and categorical exclusion of accused who are a party to a conspiracy or association in which they are subject to compulsion. This may be good policy, but it would have been preferable for the Supreme Court to have clearly struck all of section 17 down.

In my view, the statutory section 17 defence prevails over the common law test except to the extent that it has been clearly struck down as unconstitutional. This follows the traditional hierarchy of law where statutes displace the common law unless and to the extent that they have been ruled unconstitutional. Some concerns have been raised that section 17 will be too liberal a defence after the removal of its requirement of threats of immediate death or bodily harm from a person who is present. This discounts the other robust statutory restrictions that

---

129   Some judges now apply the common law defence in all cases but apply the excluded offences under s. 17 in cases involving principal offenders. (*R. v. Wilson*, 2011 ONSC 3385 at paras. 57–60), or apply the s. 17 defence in a manner that is heavily informed by the common law defence (*R. v. Ryan*, 2011 NSCA 30).

130   *R. v. Ryan*, 2011 *ibid.*

131   *R. v. Wilson*, above note 131 at paras. 57–60.

are present on the section 17 defence. Indeed, these restrictions are so severe in categorically excluding offences and persons who have associated or conspired with those that later threaten them that these statutory restrictions may well eventually be held to violate section 7 of the *Charter* by punishing morally involuntary conduct in cases where an accused would have no realistic choice but to commit the crime. If this is indeed true, it would have been preferable to have simply struck down section 17 in total and apply the common law defence of duress to all accused.

In my view, the reformulated section 17 defence still exists minus the unconstitutional requirements of threats of immediate death from a person who is present. The section 17 defence is still restrained by the long list of excluded offences and it still will not apply if the accused was a party to a conspiracy or association whereby the accused was subject to compulsion. Under this approach, the section 17 defence as reformulated in *Ruzic* still applies to principal offenders while the common law defence still applies to parties. The result is the retention of the complex mixture of statutory and common law defences of duress.

b) Second Requirement: Subjective Belief That Threats Will Be Carried Out

Unlike self-defence, necessity, or, as will be seen, common law duress, section 17 of the *Code* requires only that the accused subjectively believe that the threats will be carried out and does not require a reasonable basis for such a belief.[132] Under the other defences, the reasonableness of the belief is determined on a modified and contextual objective standard that takes into account the accused's characteristics and experiences. The subjective approach of section 17 means that even an unreasonable belief by the accused about threats of death and bodily harm may be a sufficient basis for the statutory defence of duress. This raises the risk of people committing crimes on the basis of idiosyncratic and flawed perceptions of threats. The danger to social protection was lessened by the requirements that the threats be of immediate death or bodily harm from a person who is present, but these requirements have now been found unconstitutional and severed from section 17.

The section 17 defence, unlike the common law defence, does not explicitly require either that the accused have no safe avenue of escape or that there be proportionality between the harm threatened and the

---

132 *Mena*, above note 125; *R. v. Williams* (2002), 168 C.C.C. (3d) 67 at paras. 25–26 (B.C.C.A.).

harm caused by the accused. The main remaining restrictions in the section 17 defence are the list of offences that are categorically excluded from the statutory defence of duress and the exclusion of those who are threatened as a result of their criminal associations.

c)   No Section 17 Defence if Offences are Excluded

Section 17 is not available if the accused is charged with a long list of offences including murder, attempted murder, sexual assault, forcible abduction, assault with a weapon or causing bodily harm, aggravated assault, unlawfully causing bodily harm, robbery, arson, and abduction of a young person. The question that arises in light of the *Ruzic* decision is whether such categorical restrictions on the duress defence can be justified if the accused is truly placed in a position in which he or she has no realistic choice but to commit one of the excluded offences. The excluded offences in section 17 will have to be measured against the constitutional principle that it violates the principles of fundamental justice to convict a person who commits a crime in a morally involuntary manner. Although it can be argued that an accused should not be able to commit a crime such as murder that is clearly disproportionate to a threat of bodily harm, it is also doubtful that the exclusion of offences such as arson can be justified under section 7 of the *Charter* when the accused or a third party has been threatened with death. Subsequent to *Ruzic*, one court has held that the exclusion of robbery in section 17 of the *Code* violated the principle that no one should be convicted for a morally involuntary crime.[133]

It is not clear that even the exclusion of the most serious crimes such as murder and attempted murder from the section 17 defence can be justified in cases where the accused is threatened with death and commits the crime in a morally involuntary manner. The categorical exclusion of offences from the defence is a blunt and potentially overbroad means of ensuring social protection compared to the more proportionate approach of requiring true moral involuntariness as measured by the common law requirements of proportionality and no legal way out before a defence of duress is recognized for the commission of any crime.

d)   No Section 17 Defence If Accused Is Party to a Conspiracy or Criminal Association

An accused claiming a section 17 defence of duress must not be "a party to a conspiracy or association whereby the person is subject to

---

133   *R. v. Fraser* (2002), 6 C.R. (5th) 308 (N.S. Prov. Ct.).

compulsion." The use of the word "association" suggests that the accused may be deprived of the defence because of prior contact with those who issue the threats, even though he or she had not entered into an agreement to commit a crime. This is a more restrictive exclusion than that contemplated under the common law defence of necessity, where involvement in criminal activity does not disentitle the actor to the excuse of necessity.[134] The Ontario Court of Appeal has held that those who voluntarily associate with a criminal organization should be denied the common law defence of duress.[135] This reasoning would presumably also apply to section 17, but the Court of Appeal did not deal with the Supreme Court's statement in *Perka* that the accused's involvement in illegal activities did not preclude the related defence of necessity in circumstances of true moral involuntariness.

The broad exclusion from the section 17 defence of those who conspire or associate with those who subsequently threaten them may, like the excluded categories of offences, be found to violate section 7 of the *Charter* when applied to those who commit a crime under circumstances of true moral involuntariness. The focus should be on whether the accused had any realistic choice but to commit the offence at the time it was committed and not on the prior acts or associations of the accused. This is consistent with the general principles that the accused's fault and lack of fault as manifested by the defence should be determined at the time that the prohibited act occurs.

e) Summary

Although some judges have effectively killed off section 17 in light of *Ruzic*, the better view is that it remains on life support. Section 17 still applies to principal offenders as opposed to parties of a crime. It applies without the requirements of threats of immediate death or bodily harm from a person who is present that were found in *Ruzic* to punish morally involuntary behaviour. This raises concerns that section 17 is too broad especially because it does not require that the accused have a reasonable basis for beliefs that he or she faces threats of death or bodily harm. As will be seen, there is such a reasonableness requirement with respect for the common law defence. Nevertheless, section 17 still places robust restraints on the defence in the form of categorical exclusions of a long list of offences and of accused who conspired or associated with those who threaten them before the threats are made. These restrictions are so severe that they may themselves be found to violate

---

134 *Perka*, above note 8 at 403.
135 *R. v. Li* (2002), 162 C.C.C. (3d) 360 (Ont. C.A.).

section 7 of the *Charter* by punishing people who responded in a morally involuntary manner to threats where there was no other realistic option. The law would be simpler and more principled and consistent if section 17 were struck down in its entirety and the common law defence of duress applied to all offenders without regard to whether they are principal offenders or parties to the crime. Canadian law will eventually get there, but it is not there yet.

2) The Common Law Defence of Duress as It Applies to Parties to the Offence

Even before the *Charter*, the Supreme Court revived the common law defence of duress by concluding that "s. 17 is limited to cases in which the person seeking to rely upon it has himself committed an offence."[136] Section 17 was thus read down only to apply to principal offenders, and the common law defence of duress was held to apply to those who aided, abetted, or formed a common unlawful purpose to commit an offence.[137] It is not, however, always clear who was the principal offender and who only acted as a party or accomplice. Thus, juries sometimes have to be instructed about both the section 17 defence and the common law defence. The common law defence of duress continues to apply to all accused who act as accomplices to crimes under section 21(1)(b) and (c) and 21(2). In addition, it would apply to all accused should section 17 be held to be unconstitutional in its entirety.

The common law defence of duress has the same juridical basis and mirrors the common law defence of necessity.[138] Both defences are characterized by the general requirement that the accused respond reasonably and in a morally involuntary manner to threats of imminent death or harm when there is no safe avenue of escape or legal way out. Canadian courts have been cautious in applying both defences. They require in both defences a proportionality between the harm avoided and the harm inflicted, even though the concept of proportionality is normally associated with justifications such as self-defence that are based on a judgment that breaking the law can be correct in some cases as opposed to excuses which are a concession to human frailty that excuses wrongful conduct in extenuating circumstances. The distinction

---

136 The section uses the specific words "a person who commits an offence." It does not use the words "a person who is a party to an offence." *R. v. Paquette* (1976), 30 C.C.C. (2d) 417 at 421 (S.C.C.) [*Paquette*].

137 *Code*, above note 4, ss. 21(1)(b), (c) and 21(2). See ch. 4, "Unfulfilled Crimes and Participation in Crimes" for an explanation of these terms.

138 *Hibbert*, above note 1.

between excuses and justification is even more confused in Canada because the so-called justification of self-defence does not specifically require proportionality and necessity but only that the conduct be a reasonable response to reasonably perceived force or threat of force. One reason why the Canadian defences of necessity and common law duress are more restrictive than the law of self-defence is that the person harmed under duress and necessity may be an innocent third party whereas those harmed by acts of self-defence and defence of property may often be aggressors and trespassers. This distinction, however, needs to be approached with caution.

a) First Requirement: Reasonable Belief in Threats of Death or Bodily Harm

In *Ruzic*,[139] the Supreme Court indicated that threats need not be of immediate death or bodily harm or from a person who is present under the common law defence of duress in Canada. Indeed, such restrictive requirements in section 17 of the *Code* violated the principle under section 7 of the *Charter* that no one should be convicted for morally involuntary behaviour. The Court noted that the common law defence of duress in Canada and other countries, unlike section 17, had not traditionally required the threats to be immediate.

The Court in *Ruzic* did place some restrictions on the common law defence of duress by indicating that there was a "need for a close temporal connection between the threat and the harm threatened." This requirement serves a similar purpose as the requirement under the necessity defence that the peril be imminent. At the same time, the facts of *Ruzic* suggest that the Court will interpret the imminence requirement in a flexible manner and there is no magic in any particular time between receiving the threat and committing the crime. Ruzic was threatened over two months before she committed the crime of importing narcotics. It took her four days from receiving the heroin and a false passport to travel from Belgrade to Toronto via Budapest and Athens. The people who threatened her did not accompany Ruzic but they remained in Belgrade where threats to Ruzic's mother could have been carried out. As under section 17 of the *Code*, threats to third parties can be the basis for the common law defence of duress.

The requirement for a temporal connection between the threat and the harm threatened will interact with the second and primary requirement of the common law defence of duress: the requirement that the accused have no safe or realistic avenue of escape. As the Court in *Ru-*

139 *Ruzic*, above note 5 at para. 96.

zic indicated, a threat that was "far removed in time, would cast doubt on the seriousness of the threat and, more particularly, on claims of an absence of a safe avenue of escape."[140]

As in the common law defence of necessity and unlike in section 17 of the *Code*, the accused's subjective belief in the existence of threats is not enough and there must also be a reasonable basis for such a belief. As the Supreme Court observed in *Ruzic*[141] in its discussion of the common law defence of duress, the law "rejects a purely subjective assessment" of the threats and instead imposes a modified and objective assessment of both the threat faced and whether there is a safe avenue of escape.

b) Second Requirement: Reasonable Belief in No Legal Way Out or Safe Avenue of Escape

In *Hibbert*,[142] the Supreme Court concluded that the common law defence of duress will not apply to parties who had a safe avenue of escape and could have safely extricated themselves from the situation of duress. Lamer C.J. reasoned that the common law defence of duress, like necessity, applied only if the accused had no realistic choice when deciding whether or not to commit the crime. The lack of alternatives is not determined solely on the basis of the accused's subjective perception of the available choices, but on the basis of what a reasonable person in the accused's circumstances would have perceived as a safe avenue of escape and a legal way out. The accused will be obliged to seek a realistic and safe avenue of escape.

In another case, the common law defence of duress was kept from the jury even though the accused honestly believed he had no safe avenue of escape when he picked drugs up from an airport some four months after he was threatened. The Alberta Court of Appeal stated: "[t]he question is whether a reasonable person, with similar history, personal circumstances, abilities, capacities, and human frailties as the accused, would, in the particular circumstances, reasonably believe there was no safe avenue of escape and that he had no choice but to yield to the coercion," after having taken reasonable steps such as contacting the police, to discover his full range of options.[143]

---

140 *Ruzic, ibid.* at para. 65.
141 *Ibid.* at para. 61.
142 *Hibbert,* above note 1.
143 *R. v. Keller* (1999), 131 C.C.C. (3d) 59 at 68 (Alta. C.A.).

c) Third Requirement: Proportionality Between Harm Inflicted and Harm Avoided

In *Ruzic*,[144] the Supreme Court hinted that there may be a requirement of proportionality in the common law defence of duress. LeBel J. stated: "the law includes a requirement of proportionality between the threat and the criminal act to be executed, measured on the objective-subjective standard of the reasonable person similarly situated." The requirement of proportionality was not a live issue in *Ruzic* because the crime committed—importing drugs—was clearly not disproportionate to the threatened harm of physical violence.

As discussed above, the Supreme Court has stressed the similarities between necessity and duress and the third requirement of the necessity defence is that there be proportionality between the harm avoided and the harm caused by the accused. In *Latimer*, the Court also indicated that proportionality should be determined on a purely objective standard. *Ruzic* and *Latimer* are unfortunately inconsistent as the former suggests that a modified objective standard should be applied to the proportionality requirement while the latter suggests that a purely objective standard should be applied. The *Latimer* holding that a purely objective standard should apply is the more considered opinion of the two and arguably makes conceptual sense. Proportionality is based on the shared values of the community and should not be influenced by the subjective experiences and characteristics of either the accused or the victim.

At the same time, the courts should be cautious about applying a proportionality requirement to the defence of duress. A strict application of a purely objective test of proportionality could cast doubt on cases such as *Paquette*[145] and *Hibbert*[146] that hold that the common law defence of duress could be a defence to very serious crimes such as murder and attempted murder. In *Latimer*, the Court refused to rule out killing as always a disproportionate response. A murder could be a proportionate response to a threat that the accused or a third party would die if the accused did not kill. Those who assist in a killing, or perhaps even those who kill, under agonizing conditions produced by threats that even the reasonable person could not withstand and from which there was no safe avenue of escape should not be branded with the special stigma and penalty reserved for murderers or for those who attempt

---

144 *Ruzic*, above note 5 at para. 62.
145 *Paquette*, above note 136.
146 *Hibbert*, above note 1.

murders.[147] On the other hand, a murder would be a disproportionate response to a threat of the infliction of non–life-threatening pain.

d) Modified and Contextual Objective Standard

As with the other defences examined in this chapter, courts will be confronted with the issue of how the objective standard for duress should be tailored to the circumstances of particular individuals or groups. Following *Lavallee*,[148] the reasonable person standard in the common law defence of duress will be tailored to the past experiences and physical capabilities of the accused in order to ensure that the objective standard is administered fairly given the particular accused's capacities and abilities. In *Hibbert*,[149] the Supreme Court stated:

> The defences of self-defence, duress and necessity are essentially similar, so much so that consistency demands that each defence's "reasonableness" requirement be assessed on the same basis ... while the question of whether a "safe avenue of escape" was open to an accused who pleads duress should be assessed on an objective basis, the appropriate objective standard to be employed is one that takes into account the particular circumstances and human frailties of the accused . . . . When considering the perceptions of a "reasonable person" . . . the personal circumstances of the accused are relevant and important, and should be taken into account.

The Court distinguished the way that it contextualizes objective standards in defences to the way it applied objective standards in negligence-based offences on the basis the experiences and characteristics of the particular accused could be relevant in determining whether that person's only realistic choice was to commit a crime whereas all accused make a voluntary decision to undertake risky actions and that this justifies determining whether their conduct was negligent on the basis of a simple reasonable person or non-modified objective standard.

As in *R. v. Latimer*, the modified and contextual objective standard should be applied to both the issues of whether there was a sufficient connection between the crime and the harm threatened and whether there is a safe avenue of escape or legal way out. This approach blends

---

147 *R. v. Martineau* (1990), 58 C.C.C. (3d) 353 (S.C.C.); *R. v. Logan* (1990), 58 C.C.C. (3d) 391 (S.C.C.). But for a lower court case applying English and Australian law and holding that committing murder even as a party would always be disproportionate under the common law defence of duress, see *R. v. Sandham*, 2009 CanLII 58605 (Ont. S.C.J.).

148 *Lavallee*, above note 2.

149 *Hibbert*, above note 1 at 227–28.

subjective and objective standards and makes the accused's "perceptions of the surrounding facts . . . highly relevant to the determination of whether his or her conduct was reasonable under the circumstances, and thus whether his or her conduct is properly excusable."[150]

At the same time, as suggested above, proportionality between the threat and the harm inflicted should, consistent with *Latimer*, be judged on a purely objective standard, even though there is *dicta* in *Ruzic*[151] that suggests that proportionality should be "measured on the objective-subjective standard of the reasonable person similarly situated." The inconsistency in the law on this issue is surprising given that the cases were decided in the same year and the Court has stressed that the defences of necessity and duress should develop in tandem. Although there are arguments that proportionality should not be required for excuses, the Court does require proportionality. The purpose of a proportionality requirement is to ensure that excuses are administered in a manner that is consistent with social values and social protection. It is thus appropriate to apply an objective standard to proportionality because a modified objective standard could have the effect of diluting societal standards of reasonable behaviour.

3) Duress and *Mens Rea*

Although the common law defence of duress is on the ascendancy, the relevance of duress to *mens rea* is on a decline. As previously discussed in chapters 4 and 5, duress will not negate the *mens rea* required to be a party to an offence. The fate of those who reluctantly assist in crimes will depend on the common law defence of duress. Duress will only be relevant to high levels of *mens rea* and even then it remains to be seen whether courts will allow duress to negate *mens rea*. It is quite plausible that they will conclude that duress only speaks to the motive as opposed to the intent with which the accused commits the crime.

The Supreme Court held in *Carker*[152] that the accused did not qualify for the defence of duress under section 17 because he was threatened only with future not immediate death. The Court also rejected the accused's separate argument that the threats deprived him of the *mens rea* of wilfully damaging public property. Ritchie J. stated that while the evidence suggested "that the criminal act was committed to preserve . . . [the accused] from future harm . . . there is no sugges-

150 *Ibid.* at 228.
151 *Ruzic*, above note 5 at para. 62.
152 *Carker*, above note 120 at 195.

tion . . . that the accused did not know that what he was doing would 'probably cause' damage." If the *mens rea* of wilfulness had not been defined in the *Criminal Code* to include the lower subjective mental elements of knowledge or recklessness, there may have been a reasonable doubt about whether Carker wilfully destroyed the public property.[153] It might be possible, however, that a court would have concluded that Carker's motive was to avoid the threats of his fellow inmates and he still wilfully damaged the property.[154]

In *Hebert*,[155] the Supreme Court held that an accused charged with perjury did not have a section 17 defence of duress because he was not threatened with immediate death or bodily harm. The Court nevertheless gave the accused a new trial so that the effects of the threats could be considered in determining whether he had the *mens rea* required for perjury. The Court stressed that the mental element of perjury requires "more than a deliberate false statement. The statement must also have been made with intent to mislead. While it is true that someone who lies generally does so with the intent of being believed, it is not impossible, though it may be exceptional, for a person to deliberately lie without intending to mislead."[156] In this case, for example, the accused testified that he attempted to tell a deliberate lie so that the judge might be alerted to the fact that he had been threatened. Duress may well be relevant to the particular *mens rea* of perjury and other offences relating to interference with the administration of justice.

In *Hibbert*,[157] the Supreme Court narrowed the instances in which duress could raise a reasonable doubt about *mens rea*. It held that duress could not negate the accused's intent required to form an unlawful purpose under section 21(2) or the intent required for doing something for the purpose of aiding an offence under section 21(1)(b).[158] Given that duress will frequently arise in situations where the accused reluctantly assists in the commission of the crime, this decision suggests that duress will rarely be relevant to determining *mens rea*. The Court overruled its earlier decision in *Paquette*[159] to the extent that it suggested that

---

153 *Code*, above note 4, s. 429(1). See ch. 5(B), "The Degrees of Subjective *Mens Rea*" for further discussion of this aspect of the case.

154 On the distinction between motive and intent see ch. 5(B)(2), "Intent, Purpose, or Wilfulness Distinguished from Motive."

155 *Hebert*, above note 43.

156 *Ibid.* at 64.

157 *Hibbert*, above note 1.

158 See also *Dunbar v. R.* (1936), 67 C.C.C. 20 (S.C.C.) to a similar effect. See ch. 5(B), "The Degrees of Subjective *Mens Rea*" for further discussion of these cases.

159 *Paquette*, above note 136 at 423.

an accused who participated in a robbery under duress did not have the intent to carry out the unlawful purpose as required under section 21(2) of the *Criminal Code*. The Court suggested that the duress faced by Paquette explained his motives and desires in assisting in the robbery but could not negate or raise a reasonable doubt about his intent.

4) Summary

As discussed above, duress will rarely be relevant to the proof of fault. In most cases, duress will either be considered as part of the section 17 defence of duress or as part of the common law defence of duress. The former statutory defence applies to those who actually commit an offence while the latter common law defence applies to those who are parties to an offence. Although the Supreme Court has reformulated the section 17 defence by striking down the requirements of threats of immediate death or bodily harm from a person who is present, the common law defence in many ways remains superior. The categorical exclusion of many offences from the section 17 defence, as well as the categorical exclusion of those who had previously conspired or associated with those who threatened them, runs a serious risk of convicting people for morally involuntary conduct. An eventual finding that section 17 should be struck down in its entirety would simplify and improve the law. The common law defence would apply to all offenders regardless of whether they actually committed the offence or were parties to the offence.

The related common law defences of duress and necessity should develop in tandem. Both are available if the accused acts in a morally involuntary fashion in that he or she had no realistic choice but to violate the law and no safe avenue of escape. Unlike under section 17, the accused is required to act reasonably, but the court has made clear that the reasonable person will be invested with the same characteristics and experiences as the accused.Much would be gained in simplicity and justice were section 17 struck down in its entirety.

CONCLUSION

Unlike the defences of due diligence (chapter 6), extreme intoxication (chapter 7), mental disorder and automatism (chapter 8), accused do not have to establish the defences of self-defence, necessity, and duress on a balance of probabilities. They apply whenever there is a reasonable doubt about all of the requirements of the defence. The three defences examined in this chapter do not relate to the fault element of particular offences and they have both subjective and objective requirements. In general, they apply if the accused subjectively and reasonably responds to external pressures such as threats from other people (self-defence and duress), and circumstances of peril (necessity).

In administering the objective requirements of these defences, the Supreme Court has taken a modified and contextual objective approach that not only places the reasonable person in the same circumstances that the accused faced, but also invests the reasonable person with the same characteristics and experiences as the particular accused. This, of course, stands in contrast to the Court's unwillingess to consider such factors when applying objective standards of liability.[160] The landmark decision in contextualizing the reasonable person was *Lavallee*,[161] which recognized that a woman's past abuse could be relevant in determining whether she had a valid claim of self-defence against her abuser. This trend has been continued in the new section 34(2)(f) and (f.1) which requires consideration of the relationship and history of interaction including prior use or threat of force between the parties to the incident as well as section 34(2)(e) which requires consideration of the size, age, gender, and physical capabilities of the parties to the incident when determining whether an act of self-defence or defence of others was reasonable in the circumstances. The issue is not whether the accused can be classified as a battered woman, but whether in light of her experiences and characteristics, her actions and perceptions were reasonable.

New self-defence and defence of property provisions have replaced old provisions that the Supreme Court has candidly recognized were "unbelievably confusing."[162] The new provisions no longer attempt artificially to categorize and restrict self-defence. They are, however, based on the basic principles that an accused must 1) believe on reasonable grounds that either force or threat of force is being used against them or another person (section 34(1)(a)); 2) they must respond for the subjective purpose of defending themselves (section 34(1)(b)); and 3) they must respond in a manner that is reasonable in the circumstances (section 34(1)(c)). The new defence will be less predictable than the old defence or the common law defences of necessity and duress because factors relating to the necessity of the force used and the proportionality between the force used and the force threatened are only two of nine enumerated but non-exhaustive factors listed in section 34(2) that must

---

160 *Creighton*, above note 3.
161 *Lavallee*, above note 2.
162 *R. v. McIntosh* (1995), 95 C.C.C. (3d) 481 (S.C.C.) at 489.

be considered in determining whether self-defence is reasonable in the particular circumstances. Nevertheless, the use of general standards based on reasonableness in the circumstances seems inevitable in this context. A totally subjective approach to self-defence would excuse irrational, unnecessary resort to violent self-help. Most of the concerns about objective standards have been addressed by the Court's willingness to invest the reasonable person with the same characteristics and experiences as the accused. At the same time, the new self-defence provisions are more generous to the accused than the common law defences of duress and necessity because they do not explicitly require that there be no legal way or that the force used be proportional to the force avoided. This difference can only be explained by the fact that the victim of self-defence will usually, but not always, be an aggressor or a trespasser whereas the victims of necessity and duress will generally be innocent third parties. This justification cannot, however, be pushed too far given that self-defence and defence of property may still apply if the accused acts under a reasonable mistake with respect to the use of force or invasion of property.

The new defence of property provisions discard unnecessary distinctions between personal and real property in the old provisions. They require 1) a reasonable belief in peaceable possession of property combined with a claim of right to the property (section 35(1)(a), section 35(2)); 2) a reasonable belief that a person is threatening property (section 35(1)(b)); 3) that the accused must act for the subjective purpose of protecting property (section 35(1)(c)); and 4) that the act done in defence of property must be reasonable in the circumstances (section 35(1)(d)). There must be an air of reality for all four requirements to justify putting the defence to the jury and there must be a reasonable doubt about all four requirements for the accused to be acquitted. The new section 35 does not specifically include the proportionality requirement that the Supreme Court has elaborated in a number of defence of property cases, but courts should read in such a requirement to the critical requirement that acts done in defence of property be reasonable in the circumstances.

Common law duress and necessity are similar defences that are both more demanding of the accused than self-defence. In each case, there must be 1) a reasonable perception of a threat to life or safety; 2) no reasonable alternative; and 3) proportionality between the harm done and the harm avoided. The threat need not be immediate but it does have to be close in time to the commission of the crime. The first two requirements are judged on a contextual and modified objective standard that takes into account the accused's characteristics and past experiences, as does self-defence. Proportionality is measured on an objective standard but the courts have not ruled out that duress and necessity could be a defence to serious crimes including perhaps murder, if the accused's life was threatened. As with self-defence, there must be an air of reality and subsequently a reasonable doubt about all three requirements for the defence to succeed and result in an acquittal.

The Supreme Court in *Ruzic* struck down the restrictive requirements that there must be threats of immediate death or bodily harm from a person who is present when the crime is committed under the section 17 defence of duress, but unfortunately did not clearly strike out the entire restrictive statutory defence. In my view, it is doubtful that the remaining elements of section 17, namely its long list of excluded offences and its exclusion of those who are parties to a conspiracy or association, can survive section 7 review because they could result in the conviction of a person who acted in a morally involuntary manner. Striking down the entire section 17 defence on the basis that it violates section 7 of the *Charter* by allowing the conviction of a person who had no realistic choice but to commit the offence would be welcome. Such a development would simplify the law by allowing the common law defence of duress to be applied to all offenders, and not just parties to an offence. It would also eliminate the need in cases where it is not clear whether the accused actually committed the offence or was a party to the offence to instruct the jury about both the statutory and common law defences of duress and the uncertainty created by *Ruzic* about whether the section 17 defence should even be applied.

FURTHER READINGS

BERGER, B., "Emotions and the Veil of Voluntarism: The Loss of Judgment in Canadian Criminal Defences" (2006) 51 McGill L.J. 99

BRUDNER, A., "Constitutionalizing Self-Defence" (2011) 61 University of Toronto L.J. 867

COLVIN, E., & S. ANAND, *Principles of Criminal Law*, 3d ed. (Toronto: Thomson Carswell, 2007) ch. 7

COUGHLAN, S., "Duress, Necessity, Self-Defence and Provocation: Implications of Radical Change?" (2002) 7 Can. Crim. L. Rev. 147

"Forum on the *Latimer* Case" (2001) 39 C.R. (5th) 29*ff*

"Forum on the *Latimer* Case" (2001) 64 Sask. L. Rev. 469*ff*

GORMAN, W., "Provocation: The Jealous Husband Defence" (1999) 42 Crim. L.Q. 478

GRANT, I., D. CHUNN, & C. BOYLE, *The Law of Homicide* (Toronto: Carswell, 1994) ch. 6

HEALY, P., "Innocence and Defences" (1994) 19 C.R. (4th) 121

HORDER, J., "Self-Defence, Necessity and Duress: Understanding the Relationship" (1998) 11 Can. J.L. & Jur. 143

MANNING, M., & P. SANKOFF, *Criminal Law*, 4th ed. (Markham: LexisNexis, 2009) chs. 13 & 14

PACIOCCO, D., "Applying the Law of Self-Defence" (2007) 12 Can. Crim. L. Rev. 25

———, "No-one Wants to Be Eaten: The Logic and Experience of the Law of Necessity and Duress" (2010) 56 Crim. L.Q. 240

ROSENTHAL, P., "Duress in the Criminal Law" (1990) 32 Crim. L.Q. 199

SHAFFER, M., "The Battered Woman's Syndrome Revisited" (1997) 47 U.T.L.J. 1

———, "Scrutinizing Duress: The Constitutional Validity of S. 17 of the *Criminal Code*" (1998) 40 Crim. L.Q. 444

STUART, D., *Canadian Criminal Law: A Treatise*, 5th ed. (Toronto: Thomson Carswell, 2007) ch. 7

TROTTER, G., "Necessity and Death: Lessons from *Latimer* and the Case of the Conjoined Twins" (2003) 40 Alta. L. Rev. 817

YEO, S., "Challenging Moral Involuntariness as a Principle of Fundamental Justice" (2002) 28 Queen's L.J. 335

———, "Defining Duress" (2002) 46 Crim. L.Q. 293

———, "Revisiting Necessity" (2010) 56 Crim. L.Q. 13

THE SPECIAL PART: HOMICIDE, SEXUAL, PROPERTY, AND TERRORISM OFFENCES

This book has so far provided an overview of the general principles of criminal liability and defences. These principles are sometimes called the general part of the criminal law because they provide general principles, excuses, and justifications that apply to all offences. It is important to have a sense of the principles that apply to all criminal offences. Such general principles also inform how the courts interpret the principles of fundamental justice found in section 7 of the *Charter*.

That said, the criminal law, as well as *Charter* jurisprudence, has in recent years taken a more contextual approach. The increased emphasis on context makes it helpful to have a sense of how the courts interpret some specific offences. Those parts of the *Criminal Code* that set out specific offences are often referred to as the special part of the *Code*.

As discussed in previous chapters, it is important when examining specific offences to distinguish between matters relating to the prohibited act or *actus reus* and matters relating to the required fault element or *mens rea*. In addition, there is one defence—provocation—that belongs to the special part because it only applies when a person is charged with murder. Unlike the other defences examined in the previous chapters, a successful provocation defence does not produce an acquittal: it only reduces murder to manslaughter.

Any attempt to discuss the special part, especially in a book such as this that is designed to provide a concise introduction to criminal law, must be selective. To this end, this chapter will only examine homicide, some sexual, some property, and some terrorism offences. Each of these offences could merit a book in its own right and there are indeed books on each of these subjects. The offences examined in this chapter have been selected because they are some of the most important offences and they have been informed by contextual considerations that may not naturally be discussed in the general part with its focus on the general principles of criminal liability, excuses, and justifications. Because of their severity, homicide, sexual, and terrorism offences are subject to frequent litigation in the appellate courts and amendment by Parliament.

A. HOMICIDE OFFENCES

There are three homicide offences: murder, manslaughter, and infanticide. Section 234 of the *Criminal Code* provides that manslaughter is the residual offence so that culpable homicide that is not murder or infanticide is manslaughter. All murder convictions carry with them a mandatory penalty of life imprisonment, whereas manslaughter without the use of a firearm and infanticide have no mandatory minimum penalty. Murder is classified as either first or second degree with first-degree murder under section 231 of the *Code* requiring that the accused serve twenty-five years in prison before being eligible for parole. Section 232 provides a defence of provocation that reduces murder to manslaughter. Murder with its special stigma and mandatory penalty of life imprisonment is distinguished from manslaughter or infanticide mainly on the basis of its higher requirements of subjective fault involving as a minimum the accused's subjective knowledge that the victim would die.

1) The *Actus Reus* of Causing Death

The common *actus reus* for all homicide offences is the causing of the death of a human being. A human being is defined as a child who has completely proceeded from its mother in a living state whether or not the child has breathed, has an independent circulation, or has had its navel string severed.[1] A person can commit homicide if he or she causes injury to a child before or during its birth and the child dies as a result after becoming a human being as defined above.[2]

---

1 *Criminal Code*, R.S.C. 1985, c. C–46, s. 223(1) [*Code*].
2 *Ibid.*, s. 223(2). Section 238 also provides a separate offence punishable by up to life imprisonment for causing death in the act of birth before the fetus becomes

a) Statutory Provisions in Homicide Cases

Section 222(1) of the *Code* provides that a person commits homicide when, directly or indirectly, by any means, he or she causes the death of a human being. This is a broad definition that has been satisfied in a case where an accused abducted a child who subsequently was left in a car and died of hypothermia.[3]

There are a variety of specific statutory rules relating to causation in homicide cases. Section 224 provides that a person is responsible for a death even though it might have been prevented by resorting to proper means. This section would apply where victims die as a result of a wound but could have been saved if they had accepted or received proper medical treatment.[4] A person who stabs another in a remote location will be held responsible for causing that person's death even though the very same wound may not have been life-threatening if inflicted in a place with medical facilities.

Section 225 provides that a person who causes a dangerous injury is responsible for death, notwithstanding that the immediate cause of death is proper or improper treatment rendered in good faith. A person who stabs another will be responsible for causing death even though the immediate cause of death might be negligent treatment of the wound by a doctor. Indeed, section 225 might be less favourable to the accused than judge-made common law, which has held that very bad treatment that overtakes the initial wound can break the chain of causation, so that it is unfair to conclude that the accused caused the death.[5]

Under section 226, a person is deemed to have caused death even though the bodily injury that results in death accelerates a pre-existing disease. This provision suggests that an accused must assume responsibility if the victim's "thin skull" takes the form of a pre-existing disease. Section 222(5)(c) provides that a person commits homicide when he or she causes another person by threats, fear of violence, or by deception to do anything that causes the person's death. The Supreme Court has

---

a human being, as defined in s. 223 with an exemption for acts done in good faith to preserve the life of the mother. This offence is distinct from infanticide.

3   R. v. *Younger* (2004), 186 C.C.C. (3d) 454 (Man. C.A.). In that case, the accused was also convicted of first-degree murder under the stricter requirement that his actions were the "substantial cause" of the child's death. This requirement will be examined later in this chapter.

4   In R. v. *Blaue*, [1975] 1 W.L.R. 1411 (C.A.), a manslaughter conviction was upheld when the victim refused a blood transfusion because of her religious beliefs. In R. v. *Smith* (1959), 43 Cr. App. Rep. 121 (C.A.), the accused was held to have caused death even though proper medical treatment would have probably saved the victim's life.

5   R. v. *Jordan* (1956), 40 Cr. App. Rep. 152 (C.C.A.).

observed that "these statutory provisions and others like them preempt any speculation as to whether the triggering of a chain of events was then interrupted by an intervening cause which serves to distance and exonerate the accused from any responsibility for the consequences."[6]

b) General Principles of Causation in Homicide Cases

The *Criminal Code* does not comprehensively codify all causation issues that may arise in a homicide case. As the Supreme Court has stated, "[w]here the factual situation does not fall within one of the statutory rules of causation in the *Code*, the common law general principles of criminal law apply to resolve any causation issues that may arise."[7]

In *R. v. Smithers*,[8] the Supreme Court upheld a manslaughter conviction on the basis that the accused's action of kicking the deceased in the stomach "was at least a contributing cause of death, outside the *de minimis* range," even though the death was in part caused by the victim's malfunctioning epiglottis, which caused him to choke to death on his own vomit. Dickson J. upheld the applicability of the thin skull principle in the criminal law of homicide by stating:

> Death may have been unexpected, and the physical reactions of the victim unforeseen, but that does not relieve the [accused]. . . .
>
> It is a well-recognized principle that one who assaults another must take his victim as he finds him.[9]

This test has been applied in a case to hold that the accused caused a victim's death by a minor assault that was followed by a fatal heart attack even though the victim had a history of severe heart disease.[10] The accused had to accept that the victim had a "thin skull," in this case heart disease and anxiety that may have led to the heart attack.

Despite its breadth, the *Smithers* approach to causation in homicide cases has survived under the *Charter*. In *R. v. Cribbin*,[11] the Ontario Court of Appeal concluded that the *de minimis* causation test and thin skull principles approved in *Smithers* are consistent with the principles of fundamental justice that forbid the punishment of the morally innocent. Arbour J.A. stated:

---

6   *R. v. Nette*, [2001] 3 S.C.R. 488 at para. 48 [*Nette*]. See also *R. v. Maybin*, 2012 SCC 24 at para 52.
7   *Ibid.*
8   (1977), 34 C.C.C. (2d) 427 (S.C.C.) [*Smithers*].
9   *Ibid.* at 437.
10 *R. v. Shanks* (1996), 4 C.R. (5th) 79 (Ont. C.A.).
11 (1994), 89 C.C.C. (3d) 67 (Ont. C.A.) [*Cribbin*].

As the law of manslaughter stands, if a person commits an unlawful dangerous act, in circumstances where a reasonable person would have foreseen the risk of bodily harm which is neither trivial nor transitory, and the unlawful act is at least a contributing cause of the victim's death, outside the *de minimis* range, then the person is guilty of manslaughter. Both causation and the fault element must be proved beyond a reasonable doubt before the prosecution can succeed. Combined in that fashion, both requirements satisfy the principles of fundamental justice in that any risk that the *de minimis* test could engage the criminal responsibility of the morally innocent is removed by the additional requirement of objective foresight.[12]

The result is that a person could be convicted of manslaughter on the basis that his or her unlawful acts played more than a minimal role in the death, even though death was not reasonably foreseeable. A manslaughter conviction was upheld in *Cribbin* because the accused's assault had contributed to the victim's death, even though the victim had been subject to more serious assaults by another person and had died because he drowned in his own blood.

In *R. v. Nette*,[13] the Supreme Court held that "the causation standard expressed in *Smithers* is still valid and applicable to all forms of homicide" (that is, murder, manslaughter, and infanticide) but that to make it easier to explain to the jury it should be described as a requirement that the accused's act be a "significant contributing cause" to death.[14]

L'Heureux-Dubé J. with three other judges dissented and would have maintained the negative formulation of a not insignificant cause contemplated under *Smithers*. She argued that "[t]here is a meaningful difference between expressing the standard as 'a contributing cause that is not trivial or insignificant' and expressing it as a 'significant contributing cause.'"[15]

All the judges in *Nette* were agreed, however, that the accused had caused the death of a ninety-five-year-old widow he had left hog-tied and alone after robbing her home. The victim died of asphyxiation some twenty-four to forty-eight hours later. Medical evidence showed that a number of factors contributed to the death, including the hog-tied position, a moderately tight ligature that the accused had left around the victim's neck, as well as the victim's age, asthma, and congestive heart failure. Arbour J. concluded that "the fact that the appellant's actions

---

12   *Ibid.* at 88.
13   *Nette*, above note 6.
14   *Ibid.* at para. 71.
15   *Ibid.* at para. 6.

might not have caused death in a different person, or that death might have taken longer to occur in the case of a younger victim, does not transform this case into one involving multiple causes."[16]

Courts now articulate causation in the positive terms of whether the accused's actions were a significant contributing cause of death as opposed to the older formulation of a cause that is not trivial, *de minimis*, or insignificant.[17] There are some signs that the verbal reformulation of the test has produced a more demanding standard of causation. For example, the Ontario Court of Appeal has held that "evidence that an act was possibly a cause of death cannot provide the evidentiary basis for a finding beyond a reasonable doubt that the act significantly contributed to the death." Thus a kick to the head was found not to be a significant cause of death when the deceased was punched in self-defence and fell to the ground hitting his head.[18] As will be seen below, courts after *Nette* have been more willing to contemplate that the accused's responsibility for causing death has been broken or interrupted by an intervening event. That said, it is not necessary to establish that the accused's actions were the sole or even a substantial cause of death.[19] An accused involved in a gun fight can be a significant cause of the death of a victim caught in the crossfire even if the accused's bullet did not strike the victim.[20] In addition, the specific statutory rules in sections 224 to 226 of the *Criminal Code* that specifically address some issues involving thin skulls and intervening events should not be forgotten. They remain valid unless successfully challenged under section 7 of the *Charter* as infringing a principle of fundamental justice as they might relate to the requirement that an accused's action be a cause of the victim's death. Section 225 might be vulnerable to *Charter* challenge to the extent that it holds an accused who caused a dangerous but relatively minor bodily injury such as a stabbing accountable for a death that is really caused by grossly improper treatment such as giving the victim drugs that caused a severe allergic reaction.

---

16 *Ibid.* at para. 81. See also *R. v. Knight*, [2003] 1 S.C.R. 156.
17 *R. v. Pangowish* (2003), 171 C.C.C. (3d) 506 (B.C.C.A.), leave to appeal to S.C.C. refused (2003), 176 C.C.C. (3d) vi.
18 *R. v. Talbot* (2007), 217 C.C.C. (3d) 415 at para. 82 (Ont. C.A.).
19 See, e.g., *R. v. Reid and Stratton* (2003), 180 C.C.C. (3d) 151 (N.S.C.A.) [*Reid and Stratton*], discussed below in this chapter.
20 *R. v. J.S.R.*, 2008 ONCA 544 at paras. 30–34 [*J.S.R.*].

c) **Substantial Cause Requirements for Some Forms of First-Degree Murder**

Although the Supreme Court stressed in *Nette* that there is one causation test for all homicide cases, it also recognized that section 231(5) contemplates an additional and more stringent causation test for that particular form of first-degree murder. Section 231(5) requires that the death "be caused by the accused while the accused is committing or attempting to commit a list of enumerated offences, including sexual assault, kidnapping, and hostage-taking. As a result of recent amendments, the same phrase "caused by that person" is now also found in sections 231(6), 231(6.01), (6.1), and (6.2) that apply when the accused causes the death of a person by committing other serious crimes, such as criminal harassment, a terrorist activity, a crime for a criminal organization, or the intimidation of a justice system participant. In *Harbottle*, the Supreme Court concluded that an accused may only be convicted of first-degree murder under section 231(5) if his or her actions "form an essential, substantial and integral part of the killing of the victim." Cory J. elaborated:

> The substantial causation test requires that the accused play a very active role—usually a physical role—in the killing. . . . Obviously, this requirement is much higher than that described in *R. v. Smithers* . . . which dealt with the offence of manslaughter. There it was held . . . that sufficient causation existed where the actions of the accused were "a contributing cause of death, outside the *de minimis* range." That case demonstrates the distinctions in the degree of causation required for the different homicide offences.[21]

The Court found that there was substantial causation in *Harbottle* because the accused had held the victim's legs to stop her from struggling while his co-accused strangled her to death. The Court rejected an even stricter causation test that would have required the Crown to prove that the accused's acts were a physical cause of death, because it would lead to impractical and non-purposive distinctions. On the facts of the case, it was impossible "to distinguish between the blameworthiness of an accused who holds the victim's legs, thus allowing his co-accused to strangle her, and the accused who performs the act of strangulation."[22] At the same time, section 231(5) will in most cases require the accused to play a physical role in the killing.

---

21   *R. v. Harbottle* (1993), 84 C.C.C. (3d) 1 at 13–14 (S.C.C.) [*Harbottle*].
22   *Ibid.* at 12.

In *Nette*,[23] the Supreme Court rejected the idea that the substantial causation standard articulated in *Harbottle* should apply in all homicide cases. Rather, it was restricted to those sections that use the statutory phrase when death "is caused by that person." In such cases, the jury must be given two different causation tests. The first that applies to the causing of death is "that the acts of the accused have to have made a 'significant' contribution to the victim's death to trigger culpability for the homicide." The second causation test under sections 231(5), (6.01), (6.1), and (6.2) is that "the accused's actions must have been an essential, substantial and integral part of the killing of the victim."[24] Multiple causation tests, especially those that hinge on the fine distinction between "significant" and "substantial" causation, may be difficult for the jury to understand.

To further complicate matters, the *Harbottle* substantial cause test does not apply to all forms of first-degree murder. There is no substantial cause requirement in section 231(2) that provides for planned and deliberate murders, section 231(3) that applies to contract murders, and section 231(4) that applies to murders of police officers and prison guards. The substantial cause requirement for some forms of first-degree murder can be defended as a restriction on the most serious offence in the *Criminal Code* that requires the accused to be a substantial cause and usually play a physical role in the death. The substantial causation requirement recognizes that the ordinary causation test of the accused being a significant cause of death is quite broad. At the same time, the substantial cause requirement complicates the law and requires the trial judge to instruct the jury on two different causation tests in many first degree-murder cases.

d) Concurrent Causes of Death and New Acts That Break the Chain of Causation

Courts have concluded that an accused caused death when he or she set off a chain of events that ended in a person's death, even though the immediate cause of death had not been at the accused's hands. In *R. v. Kitching*,[25] an accused who had assaulted the victim, causing his "brain death," was held responsible, even though the immediate cause of death was the medical withdrawal of life support. The accused's conduct "need not be shown to be the sole or 'effective' cause of a crime . . . there may be two or more independent operative causes of death." An

---

23   *Nette*, above note 6.
24   *Ibid.* at paras. 73 and 82.
25   (1976), 32 C.C.C. (2d) 159 at 175 (Man. C.A.).

accused who shot a person who then cut his own throat was still held to have caused the person's death.[26] In this respect it is no longer necessary that death must occur within a year of the accused's act.

In *R. v. Maybin*,[27] the Supreme Court recognized that some intervening causes may break the legal chain of causation even if it was possible to still conclude as a factual matter that the victim would not have died but for the accused's actions. In that case, the Court held a trial judge erred when he acquitted two brothers and a bouncer who had assaulted a victim within a minute of one another during a bar room brawl on the basis that it could not be proven beyond a reasonable doubt which one caused the victim's death through a bleed in the brain. Karakatsanis J. for the Court held that the tests in the law of whether the harm caused by the accused's actions was reasonably foreseeable from the accused's actions and whether the intervening act was independent of the accused's acts were only non-determinative analytical aids in determining the ultimate question of whether the accused's actions were a significant cause of the death. In this case, it was reasonably foreseeable that either a bouncer or some other patron might strike the victim once the brothers initially assaulted the victim. It could not be said that the bouncer's actions were so independent of the brothers' initial assault that they rendered the accused's actions "so remote to suggest that they were morally innocent of the death."[28]

Maybin suggests that the significant cause of death standard is a broad test of causation that is not easily broken by intervening acts especially if those acts are connected and not independent of the accused's acts or they produce a harm that was reasonably foreseeable at the time of the accused's actions even though the exact manner in which the subsequent harm was caused might not be foreseeable. In another case, the Supreme Court, in a 4:3 decision, reversed a murder conviction and ordered a new trial where the victim, who was shot in the stomach and barely survived, died as a result of a blood clot a few days after being released from hospital. A new trial would include the possible verdict of attempted murder because even though the pathologist would not rule out the possibility that the blood clot was probably related to the shooting, it could have been caused by cocaine ingested by the victim shortly before his death.[29]

---

26   *People v. Lewis*, 57 P. 470 (S.C. Cal. 1899).

27   2012 SCC 24

28   *Ibid.* at para. 59.

29   *R. v. Sarrazin*, 2011 SCC 54 at paras. 6, 20, and 42.

A new trial was ordered in another case in which the accused caused the victim to become unconscious because of a headlock, but the victim died when his friends' attempts at resuscitation had the unfortunate effect of causing the victim to choke to death on his own vomit. The Nova Scotia Court of Appeal concluded that the jury should be asked whether it was "satisfied beyond a reasonable doubt that the actions [of the accused] are so connected to the death . . . that they can be said to have had a significant causal effect which continued up to the time of his death, without having been interrupted" by the intervening act of the botched resuscitation. The Court of Appeal added that the jury must not be convinced that the accused's actions were "the sole cause" of the death but rather, consistent with *Nette*, that they were "a significant contributing cause."[30] At the same time, however, the Court of Appeal indicated that it was not sufficient to instruct the jury on the *Nette* test of causation; the jury must also be instructed about the intervening event and asked to determine if the accused's actions remained a significant contributing cause of death. As in the subsequent *Maybin* case, the Court focused on the statutory test of whether the accused's actions were a significant cause of death. The accused's actions do not have to be the sole cause of death, but there may be situations where the chain of causation will be broken so that the accused's actions are no longer the significant cause of death.

2) Murder

The main offence for murder is section 229. Any person charged with murder, even first-degree murder, must now be charged under section 229. It provides:

Culpable homicide is murder
a) where the person who causes the death of a human being
   i) means to cause his death or
   ii) means to cause him bodily harm that he knows is likely to cause his death and is reckless whether death ensues or not;
b) where a person, meaning to cause death to a human being or meaning to cause him bodily harm that he knows is likely to cause his death, and being reckless whether death ensues or not, by accident or mistake causes death to another human being, notwithstanding that he desires to effect his object without causing death or bodily harm to any human being; or

---

30   *Reid and Stratton*, above note 19 at para. 89.

c)   where a person, for an unlawful object, does anything that he knows or ought to know is likely to cause death, and thereby causes death to a human being, notwithstanding that he desires to effect his object without causing death or bodily harm to any human being.

a)   The Constitutionally Required Fault for Murder

As discussed in chapter 2, the Supreme Court has interpreted section 7 of the *Charter* to require that a few offences because of the special stigma and penalty require a minimum form of *mens rea* or fault element. The constitutionally required minimum *mens rea* for murder is subjective knowledge of the likelihood or probability of death. In *R. v. Martineau*, the majority of the Court explained:

> A conviction for murder carries with it the most severe stigma and punishment of any crime in our society. The principles of fundamental justice require, because of the special nature of the stigma attached to a conviction for murder, and the available penalties, a *mens rea* reflecting the particular nature of that crime. . . . The rationale underlying the principle that subjective foresight of death is required before a person is labelled and punished as a murderer is linked to the more general principle that criminal liability for a particular result is not justified except where the actor possesses a culpable mental state in respect of that result . . . . In my view, in a free and democratic society that values the autonomy and free will of the individual, the stigma and punishment attaching to the most serious of crimes, murder, should be reserved for those who choose to intentionally cause death or who choose to inflict bodily harm that they know is likely to cause death. The essential role of requiring subjective foresight of death in the context of murder is to maintain a proportionality between the stigma and punishment attached to a murder conviction and the moral blameworthiness of the offender. Murder has long been recognized as the "worst" and most heinous of peace time crimes. It is, therefore, essential that to satisfy the principles of fundamental justice, the stigma and punishment attaching to a murder conviction must be reserved for those who either intend to cause death or who intend to cause bodily harm that they know will likely cause death.[31]

In that case, the Court struck down section 230(a) of the *Criminal Code*. That section provided for a murder conviction where the accused caused

---

31   *R. v. Martineau*, [1990] 2 S.C.R. 633 at 645 [*Martineau*].

death while committing or attempting to commit one of a long list of serious crimes if he or she meant to cause bodily harm for the purpose of facilitating the underlying offence or escape from it. The Court held that section 230(a) violated sections 7 and 11(d) of the *Charter* because it substituted the intent to commit the underlying offence and to cause bodily harm for the constitutionally required *mens rea* of subjective knowledge of the likelihood of death. Proof of the intent to cause bodily harm would not lead inexorably to proof of the constitutionally required fault element of knowledge of the likelihood of death.

The Supreme Court in *Martineau* held that the violation of sections 7 and 11(d) could not be justified under section 1 of the *Charter*. Even though the deterrence of violence during the commission of serious crimes was an important objective, it could be pursued in a more proportionate way. Chief Justice Lamer commented:

> Very stiff sentences for the infliction of bodily harm leading to death in appropriate cases would sufficiently meet any deterrence objective that Parliament might have in mind. The more flexible sentencing scheme under a conviction for manslaughter is in accord with the principle that punishment be meted out with regard to the level of moral blameworthiness of the offender. To label and punish a person as a murderer who did not intend or foresee death unnecessarily stigmatizes and punishes those whose moral blameworthiness is not that of a murderer and thereby unnecessarily impairs the rights guaranteed by ss. 7 and 11(d) of the *Charter*. In my view then, s. 213(a) [now s. 230(a)], indeed all of s. 213 [now s. 230], cannot be saved by s. 1 of the *Charter*.[32]

One judge, Justice L'Heureux-Dubé, dissented in *Martineau* and would have maintained that the constitutionally required fault for murder was only objective foresight of death. She stressed the need to consider not only fault, but also the harm caused by the *actus reus* of death and the fact that other democracies including the United Kingdom and the United States used "felony murder" or constructive murder provisions that applied even though an accused who killed while committing a serious crime would not have known that the victim would die. Justice L'Heureux-Dubé held that the fault requirement of objective foresight of death would be satisfied by proof of a subjective intent to cause bodily harm while committing another serious offence, but Justice Sopinka disputed this conclusion even though he otherwise agreed that the constitutionally required fault for murder should only be object-

---

32   *Ibid.* at 647.

ive foresight of death. This disagreement underlines the malleability of judgments about objective foresight. In any event, the majority of the Court clearly established that the constitutionally required fault for murder is subjective knowledge of the likelihood of death and the objective foresight of death standard would not have maintained an appropriate distinction between murder as the intentional infliction of death and manslaughter as a negligent killing.

In a previous case, *R. v. Vaillancourt*, the Supreme Court had struck down section 230(d), which had provided for a murder offence when death results from the use or possession of a firearm while committing one of a long list of serious offences, on the limited basis that it did not even guarantee that there would be objective foreseeability of death in a case, for example, where a firearm accidentally discharged during a robbery.[33] In a subsequent case, the Court also held that section 230(c) violated sections 7 and 11(d) of the *Charter* by substituting proof of wilfully stopping the breath of a human for the constitutionally required fault of subjective knowledge of the likelihood of death.[34] In most cases, a person who wilfully stopped another's breath would know that the victim was likely to die, but this might not be true in every case. Consistent with concerns about the presumption of innocence and any presumptions that could prevent the jury from having a reasonable doubt, the Court struck down this provision. In the result, section 230 has been rendered a dead letter that is no longer used even though Parliament has only formally repealed section 230(d). Hence, all people charged with murder have to be charged under section 229. Those charged with first-degree murder will be charged under section 229, but the Crown will also have to prove additional fault under section 231.

b) Section 229(a)(i)

Section 229(a)(i) requires that the person who causes the death of a human being means to cause death. "This clearly requires that the accused have actual subjective foresight of the likelihood of causing death coupled with the intention to cause that death." This fault requirement has been described as "the most morally blameworthy state of mind in our system."[35] It could be argued that a person who plants a bomb to achieve some political objective does not mean to cause the death of those killed by the bomb but rather means to cause the advancement of the political objective. Courts would likely reject this argument based

---

33   *R. v. Vaillancourt*, [1987] 2 S.C.R. 636 [*Vaillancourt*].
34   *R. v. Sit*, [1991] 3 S.C.R. 124.
35   *Vaillancourt*, above note 33 at para. 10.

on the distinction between motive and intention discussed in chapter 5 on fault.

c) Section 229(a)(ii)

Section 229(a)(ii) requires that the person who causes the death means to cause the victim "bodily harm that he knows is likely to cause his death and is reckless whether death ensures or not." This offence requires proof of a) subjective intent to cause bodily harm; and b) subjective knowledge that the bodily harm is of such a nature that it is likely to result in death. The Supreme Court has explained that the reference to recklessness in section 229(a)(ii) is an "afterthought"[36] because a person who knows of the probability of death will of necessity have the lesser form of fault of being reckless in the sense of subjectively adverting to the possibility of death. The reference to recklessness in this section is not only superfluous but dangerous. New trials have been ordered in cases in which trial judges erroneously left the jury with the impression that recklessness was a sufficient form of fault for a murder conviction or that the accused need only be aware of a danger or risk as opposed to the likelihood of death.[37]

Section 229(a)(ii) requires proof of subjective knowledge that the victim is likely to die. As Martin J.A. explained,

> An intention to cause bodily harm that the offender ought to have known was likely to cause death is merely evidence from which, along with all the other circumstances, the jury may infer that the accused actually had the requisite intention and knowledge .... It does not, however, constitute the requisite state of mind.[38]

As with all crimes, there must be some degree of correspondence between the commission of the *actus reus* of causing death and the *mens rea* required under section 229. That said, the Supreme Court in *R. v. Cooper*[39] indicated that so long as the accused knew at some point during two minutes of strangulation that the victim was likely to die, then there was a sufficient overlap between the *actus reus* and the *mens rea*. In other words, "if death results from a series of wrongful acts that are part of a single transaction then it must be established that the requisite intent coincided at some point with the wrongful acts." As

---

36   R. v. Nygaard, [1989] 2 S.C.R. 1074 at 1088 [Nygaard].

37   R. v. Czibulka (2004), 189 C.C.C. (3d) 199 (Ont. C.A.); R. v. Patterson (2006), 205 C.C.C. (3d) 171 (Ont. C.A.).

38   R. v. Simpson (1981), 58 C.C.C. (2d) 122 (Ont. C.A.).

39   (1993), 78 C.C.C. (3d) 289 (S.C.C.) [Cooper].

long as the *mens rea* existed at some point in the transaction leading to death, it would not matter that the victim died some time later.[40]

d)   Section 229(b) and Transferred Intent

Section 229(b) codifies the common law doctrine of transferred intent. The *mens rea* of intentionally or knowingly causing death to one person is transferred to the killing of the victim, even though the accused "does not mean to cause death or bodily harm" to the victim and does so "by accident or mistake." This provision was applied in R. v. *Droste* (No. 2)[41] to convict an accused who, in a deliberate attempt to kill his wife, set fire to a car, causing two children buckled in the back seat to die of asphyxiation. The Supreme Court concluded that because the attempted murder of the accused's wife was planned and deliberate, the intent of planning and deliberation, as well as the guilty knowledge that death would result, could be transferred to the children's deaths.

The Manitoba Court of Appeal has decided that section 229(b) should not be applied when the accused intends to kill himself but ends up killing another person. The Court of Appeal held that a person who intends to kill himself does not have the same moral blameworthiness as a person who intends to kill another person, but then kills yet another person by accident or mistake.[42] The Court of Appeal also stated that "section 229(b) is ambiguous in its interpretation as to whether it is intended to be limited to the killing of another or to include the killing of oneself. Where ambiguity is present in a piece of penal legislation, the statutory interpretation rule of strict construction should be applied because of the potential for serious interference with individual rights."[43] This conclusion invoked the principle of strict construction of the criminal law discussed in chapter 3. The Ontario Court of Appeal has even further restricted section 229(b) by holding that it did not apply in a case where an innocent bystander was killed during a gun fight on Toronto's Yonge Street on the basis that the accused did nothing by accident or mistake that caused the bystander's death.[44] It could, however, be argued that the killing was by accident and mistake,

---

40   *Meli v. The Queen,* [1954] 1 W.L.R. 228 (P.C.), cited with approval in *Cooper, ibid.* at 297.

41   (1984), 10 C.C.C. (3d) 404 (S.C.C.).

42   R. v. *Fontaine* (2002), 168 C.C.C. (3d) 263 at paras. 40–45 (Man. C.A.) [*Fontaine*], rejecting R. v. *Brown* (1983), 4 C.C.C. (3d) 571 (Ont. H.C.), holding that an intent to commit suicide could be transferred under s. 229(b) of the *Code,* above note 1.

43   *Fontaine, ibid.* at para. 34.

44   *J.S.R.,* above note 20 at para. 38.

and that any intent to kill a rival gang member could be transferred to killing of the bystander.

e) Section 229(c)

Section 229(c) provides that a person is guilty of murder where he or she does 1) for an unlawful object 2) anything that he or she knows 3) or ought to know is likely to cause death and 4) causes death 5) notwithstanding that he or she desires to effect his or her object without causing death or bodily harm. In R. v. Vasil,[45] the Supreme Court held that the unlawful object must be the pursuit of a serious crime "clearly distinct from the immediate object of the dangerous (unlawful) act." This requirement is necessary to ensure that section 229(c) does not eclipse other murder provisions. For example, if an assault that resulted in death was a sufficient unlawful object then there might not be much of a need for section 229(a). Courts have continued to confirm that the unlawful object be distinct and not merge with the dangerous act that caused the victim's death.[46]

In R. v. Martineau,[47] the Supreme Court ruled that the objective arm of section 229(c) violated sections 7 and 11(d) of the Charter because it substituted proof of objective foresight of death for subjective knowledge of the likelihood of death, which was constitutionally required because of the stigma and penalty of murder.[48] The Court also indicated that it would be difficult to justify the objective arm of section 229(c) under section 1 given that there were other more proportionate means to deter the use of violence in pursuing an unlawful objective.

The courts have been using section 229(c) more often minus its objective arm that has unfortunately[49] still not been repealed by Parliament. In R. v. Meiler,[50] section 229(c) was applied to an accused who killed a person while pursuing the unlawful objective of attempting to kill another person. He was approaching his intended victim, but was

---

45   [1981] 1 S.C.R. 469 at 500.

46   R. v. Roks, 2011 ONCA 526 at paras. 126–27 [Roks].

47   Martineau, above note 31.

48   Justice Lamer explained: "In my view, subjective foresight of death must be proven beyond a reasonable doubt before a conviction for murder can be sustained, and as a result, it is obvious the part of s. 212(c) of the Code allowing for a conviction upon proof that the accused ought to have known that death was likely to result violates ss. 7 and 11(d) of the Charter." Martineau, ibid. at 648.

49   New trials have had to be ordered in a number of cases in which trial judges left juries with copies of the Criminal Code section including the unconstitutional "ought" to know section. See Kent Roach, "The Problematic Revival of Murder under Section 229(c) of the Criminal Code" (2010) 47 Alta. L. Rev. 675 at 685–86.

50   (1999) 136 C.C.C. (3d) 11 (Ont. C.A.).

tackled by another person and the accused's gun went off, killing the victim. The application of section 229(c) in these circumstances comes perilously close to the old section 230 under which killings during the course of certain crimes could result in murder convictions. The critical distinction, however, is that s.229 (c) requires not only the pursuit of an unlawful object, but also subjective knowledge that death is likely to occur in the pursuit of the unlawful object. Knowledge that death is likely to occur requires that the accused know that death is probable, not simply that it is possible, a risk, a danger, foreseeable or a chance.[51] The courts also applied section 229 (c) in a case in which a bystander was killed in the course of a gun battle on a busy Toronto street noting that the accused was doing a dangerous act in shooting in pursuit of the unlawful objective of killing a rival gang member when he knew that firing shots in the crowded street was likely to cause the death of someone other than his intended target. The transferred intent provisions of section 229(b) which apply to the killing of an unintended victim "by accident or mistake" were strangely held not to apply in that case.[52] The courts have, however, held that section 229(c) did not apply in a case where an arson planned for insurance fraud purposes unexpectedly led to the death of one of the arsonists. The Ontario Court of Appeal stressed the importance of proving that the accused must know at the time of the act that death was probable and the dangers of reasoning backwards from the fact that a death resulted.[53] In the result the accused who had planned the fire was convicted of manslaughter, not murder.

In *R v. Shand*[54] the Ontario Court of Appeal held that section 229(c) minus the objective arm was consistent with section 7 of the *Charter* but stressed the importance of the subjective foresight of death requirement. In other words "vague realization that death is possible is not sufficient."[55] The accused must know that death was likely to occur and not simply a risk or a possibility. Section 229(c) applied in that case in which the accused pointed a gun that accidentally discharged during a robbery. The murder conviction was sustained because the trial judge made it clear to the jury that the accused must actually know that the unlawful act was likely to cause someone's death.[56]

The recent revival of section 229(c) carries many dangers. One danger that the Ontario Court of Appeal recognized was that the jury

---

51   *Roks*, above note 46 at paras. 134 and 146 .
52   *J.S.R.*, above note 20.
53   *Roks*, above note 46 at paras. 134–35.
54   2011 ONCA 5.
55   *Ibid.* at para. 152.
56   *Ibid.* at para. 203.

might engage in "the logical fallacy of assuming that, because the victim died, the appellant must have known that death was likely. This type of analysis essentially amounts to the constitutionally prohibited reasoning that the accused 'ought to have known' that his or her act was likely to cause death."[57] The critical distinction between subjective and objective fault can be blurred especially in cases where knowledge of death is extended to a broad range of victims. Another danger in section 229(c) is that accidental deaths will be punished as murder in large part because the accused was pursuing an unlawful object at the time of the accidental death. Long before the *Charter*, the Supreme Court took care not to allow section 229(c) to be applied to accidental deaths[58] and such a possibility violates the principle of fundamental justice that unintentional harm should not be punished as severely as intentional harm.[59] Accidental or non-intentional deaths should not be punished with the high stigma and penalty of murder. When using section 229(c), judges and juries should be careful to require knowledge of the probability of death and not reason backwards from the fact that a death occurred during the commission of an unlawful object.

f) Parties to Murder Offences

As discussed in chapter 4, section 21(1) makes a person guilty of an offence both if they actually commit it and if they aid and abet the commission of an offence. The *Thatcher* case underlines that it is not necessary for the Crown to specify whether a person is guilty as the principal offender or as an aider or abettor of the offence.[60] The *Pickton* serial murder case goes even farther as it upheld a murder conviction in a case where the trial judge had initially and according to the Crown's theory of the case instructed the jury that Pickton personally shot his multiple victims, but later in response to a question from the jury on its sixth day of deliberation said that Pickton would be guilty if he was "otherwise an active participant" in the killings and indicated that it was not necessary that he be the actual shooter to be guilty of murder. Relying on the *Thatcher* case, the Court stressed that section 21(1) was designed to put the aider or abettor on the same footing as the person who actually committed the crime.[61] A number of accused could be convicted of murder

---

57   *Ibid.* at para. 210.
58   *R. v. Hughes*, [1942] S.C.R. 517 at 523.
59   *R. v. Creighton*, [1993] 3 S.C.R. 3 at 49 [*Creighton*].
60   *R. v. Thatcher* (1987), 32 C.C.C. (3d) 481 (S.C.C.).
61   *R. v. Pickton*, [2010] 2 S.C.R. 198 at para. 33. Charron J. for the majority indicated that it would have been preferable had the jury been instructed specifically about aiding and abetting but that the omission of such an instruction

if they all knowingly assisted in the victim's death even though it was unclear which one of the accused actually killed the victim.[62]

If charged as an aider or abettor of murder, the Crown must prove that the accused performed an *actus reus* that rendered aid, assistance, or encouragement to the killing and something more than mere presence and passive acquiescence. In *Kirkness*,[63] the Supreme Court stated that an accused aiding or abetting a murder "must intend that death ensue or intend that he or the perpetrator cause bodily harm of a kind likely to result in death and be reckless whether death ensues or not." The above holding ensures that no one will be convicted of murder without proof of at least subjective foresight of death. In the actual case, the Supreme Court affirmed the acquittal of an accused who during a break-in had not participated in suffocating the victim and had told the accused to stop choking the victim.

In *R. v. Briscoe*,[64] the Supreme Court held that wilful blindness as a form of "deliberate ignorance" could be substituted for this knowledge requirement even with respect to murder. Thus, an accused will be guilty of aiding and abetting murder if the accused 1) purposively aids and abets, and 2) knows or is wilfully blind that the victim will die. An accomplice that satisfies the above requirements could be held guilty of murder through aiding and abetting even if the principal offender was not guilty of murder, for example, because he or she had a defence such as provocation or intoxication that reduced murder to manslaughter. The basic principle is that accused must intend to aid and abet and also have the requisite fault of knowledge or wilful blindness of death for murder. In cases where the aider or abettor intends to assist, but does not know and is not wilfully blind that death was likely to occur, a manslaughter conviction may be possible and that form of liability will be discussed later in this chapter.

---

could only have benefited the accused, *ibid.* at para. 12. The dissenters in the case agreed that the alternatives of aiding and abetting could be put to the jury, but stated that "the phrases 'active participation,' 'acting in concert,' or 'joint venture' do not in and of themselves adequately convey the law of party liability to a trier of fact." *Ibid.* at para. 38.

62 *Chow Bew v. The Queen*, [1956] S.C.R. 124; *R. v. Issac*, [1984] 1 S.C.R. 74 at 80–81; *R. v. McMaster*, [1996] 1 S.C.R. 740 at para. 33; *R. v. McQuaid*, [1998] 1 S.C.R. 244; *R. v. Biniaris*, [2000] 1 S.C.R. 381; *R. v. Suzack* (2000), 141 C.C.C. (3d) 449 (Ont. C.A.); *R. v. H.(L.I.)* (2003), 17 C.R. (6th) 338 at para. 60 (Man. C.A.); *R. v. Portillo* (2003), 17 C.R. (6th) 362 at para. 71 (Ont. C.A.); *R. v. J.F.D.* (2005), 196 C.C.C. (3d) 316 at para. 14 (B.C.C.A.); *R. v. Rojos* (2006), 208 C.C.C. (3d) 13 (B.C.C.A.).

63 *R. v. Kirkness* (1990), 60 C.C.C. (3d) 97 at 127 (S.C.C.).

64 *R. v. Briscoe*, [2010] 1 S.C.R. 411 at paras. 22–25 [*Briscoe*].

Special caution must be employed with liability for murder under the common purpose doctrine of section 21(2). In *Logan*,[65] the Supreme Court declared the phrase "ought to have known" to be an unjustified violation of the *Charter* when the accused is charged with murder or attempted murder on the basis that stigma and punishment of those offences require no less than proof of subjective knowledge of the probability that death would result.

In cases of murder and attempted murder, the objective arm of section 21(2) should not be left to the jury and the jury should only convict if a party has actual foresight or knowledge that the principal offender would kill a person while carrying out their common unlawful purpose.[66]

3) First-Degree Murder

First-degree murder is technically a sentencing classification that has its origins in the now-abolished offence of capital murder. A person charged with first-degree murder will be charged with murder under section 229, but also with murder under section 231. Section 231 requires the proof of more fault and prohibited acts than contemplated in section 229[67] and thus section 231 has been interpreted as if it were an offence. All murder convictions result in a mandatory sentence of life imprisonment, but a first-degree murder conviction results in ineligibility for parole for twenty-five years though an accused previously could apply for eligibility for parole after fifteen years' imprisonment.[68]

a) Planned and Deliberate Murder under Sections 231(2) and (3)

The purest form of first-degree murder is a planned and deliberate killing. The accused is subject to increased punishment because of the increased culpability of killing in a calculated and planned manner as opposed to a more impulsive murder. A planned and deliberate murder is more than an intentional murder. It must be "considered, not impulsive"[69] and it requires planning and consideration beforehand.[70] A lesser degree of intoxication or mental disturbance may be sufficient to raise a reasonable doubt about planning and deliberation under sec-

---

65 (1990), 58 C.C.C. (3d) 391 (S.C.C.).
66 R. v. *Rodney* (1990), 58 C.C.C. (3d) 408 (S.C.C.); R. v. *Laliberty* (1997), 117 C.C.C. (3d) 97 at 108 (Ont. C.A.); R. v. *Portillo* (2003), 17 C.R. (6th) 362 at paras. 72–73 (Ont. C.A.).
67 R. v. *Luxton*, [1990] 2 S.C.R. 711.
68 *Code*, above note 1, ss. 745–746.1.
69 R. v. *More*, [1963] 3 C.C.C. 289 at 291 (S.C.C.).
70 R. v. *Ruptash* (1982), 68 C.C.C. (2d) 182 (Alta. C.A.).

tion 231 than knowledge of the likelihood of death under section 229. There is no requirement that juries always be instructed to that effect, but the differences between the relevance of intoxication in raising a reasonable doubt about planning and deliberation and the less complex mental element of knowledge should be made clear to the jury.[71] Although a person with a mental disorder can still engage in a planned and deliberate murder,[72] evidence of mental disorder well short of establishing the mental disorder defence may still raise a reasonable doubt about planning and deliberation.

Murders under section 229(a)(ii)[73] and under section 229(b)[74] may be planned and deliberate. In the former case, the accused could have planned and deliberated to have given the victim a sustained beating in order to collect debts that he knew was likely to result in the accused's death. It should be clear that what is planned is not simply a beating, but a beating that the accused knew was likely to cause death.[75] In the latter case, the accused could have planned and deliberated to kill one person but then by accident or mistake have killed another person. It is also possible that a murder under section 229(c) might be planned and deliberate if the accused planned and deliberated the commission of an unlawful object that he knew would result in death.

Section 231(3) provides as a specific example of planned and deliberate killings a contract killing where money or anything of value is promised, passed, or is intended to be passed in exchange for causing, assisting in causing, or counselling another person to do any act causing or assisting in causing death.

b) Killing Police Officers and Other Officials in the Execution of Their Duties

Section 231(4) provides that murder is first-degree murder where the victim is a police officer acting in the course of his or her duties or other law enforcement officials acting in the course of their duties, including those working in prisons. This provision was enacted in order to provide additional protection to such officials. It has been interpreted in a purposive manner to apply to a whole tour of duty, including breaks and other periods when police officers are not necessarily actively

---

71 R. v. Wallen, [1990] 1 S.C.R. 827.

72 R. v. Kirkby (1985), 21 C.C.C. (3d) 31 (Ont. C.A.).

73 Nygaard, above note 36.

74 R. v. Droste (No. 2), [1984] 1 S.C.R. 208.

75 R. v. Banwait, 2011 SCC 55, rev'd 2010 ONCA 869 at paras. 178–89 and approving of MacPherson J.A.'s judgment in dissent.

engaged in exercising their powers or duties[76] and courts have understandably been reluctant to conclude that on-duty police officers were not exercising their powers or duties because of allegations that the police had engaged in excessive force.[77]

As with many offences, section 231(4) is completely silent on the fault issue of whether the accused must know or be reckless with respect to the elements of the prohibited act, in this case the fact that the person killed was a police officer or other justice official acting in the course of his or her duties. The Ontario Court of Appeal has held that the normal common law presumption of fault should apply to section 231(4) even though the section is technically a sentencing classification and the accused must also be found guilty under section 229. Thus under section 231(4), the Crown must prove that the accused either knew or was reckless by subjectively adverting to the possibility that the victim was a police officer.[78] The Court of Appeal reasoned that some degree of subjective fault with respect to the identity of the police officer was necessary to justify the enhanced culpability and punishment of first-degree murder as well as to satisfy the purpose of the section in deterring violence against the police officer. It is not necessary, however, that the accused know for certain that the victim is a police officer acting in the course of his or her duties. Some subjective advertence to the risk, for example, that a person is an undercover officer should be sufficient to satisfy the fault requirement of recklessness.

c) Killing While Committing Other Serious Crimes

Section 231(5) provides that killing is first-degree murder "when the death is caused by that person while committing or attempting to commit" a short list of serious offences including hijacking an aircraft, hostage-taking, kidnapping and forcible confinement, and sexual assault including aggravated forms of sexual assault. Although the Supreme Court struck down a similar formulation under section 230, the constructive or "felony" first-degree murder provisions in the *Code* have been upheld under section 7 of the *Charter* on the basis that any person convicted of first-degree murder under section 231(5) would also have been convicted of murder under section 229. The requirement for a conviction under section 229 would guarantee that the accused would have the constitutionally required fault of subjective knowledge

---

76   *R. v. Prevost* (1988), 42 C.C.C. (3d) 314 (Ont. C.A.).

77   *R. v. Boucher*, 2006 QCCA 1079; *R. v. Jaw*, 2008 NUCA 2, aff'd on other grounds [2009] 3 S.C.R. 326.

78   *R. v. Munro* (1983), 8 C.C.C. (3d) 260 (Ont. C.A.); *R. v. Collins* (1989), 48 C.C.C. (3d) 343 (Ont. C.A.).

that the victim would die. The Court also ruled that basing the harsher punishment provided for murders under section 231(5) on the commission of a serious crime was not arbitrary or cruel and unusual.[79] Parliament has in recent years effectively added to the list of serious crimes through the enactment of sections 231(6) to 231(6.2), which now apply to serious and well-publicized crimes such as criminal harassment, terrorism offences, intimidation of a justice system participant, and offences for a criminal organization.

The most controversial of the underlying offences in section 231(5) has been forcible confinement. The Alberta and Quebec Courts of Appeal have stressed that there must be some evidence of unlawful domination that goes beyond the violence inherent in a robbery, which in itself is not an offence listed under section 231(5).[80] The Supreme Court, however, rejected this restrictive approach and held that section 231(5) applies as long as there is some element of unlawful confinement distinct from the killing and that this unlawful confinement can arise in the course of a robbery.[81]

The Supreme Court has also taken a broad approach to section 231(5) in other cases. In R. v. Paré,[82] it indicated that the section would apply so long as the sexual assault was committed during a continuous transaction of illegal domination and that it need not occur at exactly the same time as the killing. Appeal courts have taken an even broader approach and held that the section applies even in cases where the accused commits sexual assault shortly after and in the same transaction as killing the victim.[83] In R. v. Russell,[84] the Court went farther and held that the underlying offence could be committed against a person other than the murder victim so long as there was a temporal and causal connection between the commission of the underlying offence and the killing. The Court stressed that Parliament had not precluded the application of section 231(5) in cases where there are multiple victims as it has in section 231(6) which specifically states that the person murdered must also be the victim of the underlying offence of criminal harassment. It stressed that Parliament wanted to punish more

---

79   R. v. Arkell, [1990] 2 S.C.R. 695.
80   R. v. Strong (1990), 60 C.C.C. (3d) 516 (Alta. C.A.); R. v. Kingsley (1995), 105 C.C.C. (3d) 85 (Que. C.A.).
81   R. v. Pritchard, [2008] 3 S.C.R. 195 at paras. 27–28.
82   [1987] 2 S.C.R. 618.
83   R. v. Muchikekwanape (2002), 166 C.C.C. (3d) 144 (Man. C.A.); R. v. Richer (1993), 82 C.C.C. (3d) 385, aff'd on other grounds [1994] 2 S.C.R. 486.
84   [2001] 2 S.C.R. 804.

severely killings while the accused also committed one of the listed serious crimes.

As discussed earlier in this chapter, in *R. v. Harbottle*,[85] the Supreme Court held that the phrase "caused by that person" in section 231(5) requires that the accused be a substantial cause of the victim's death. The Court in that case did not preclude the application of section 231(5) to co-accused and held that an accused who held the victim's legs while another accused strangled her to death still was a substantial and integral cause of the victim's death. As suggested above, the substantial cause requirement in section 231(5) applies to sections 231 (6)(6.01), (6.1), and (6.2) pursuant to recent amendments.

4) Provocation

Provocation is a partial defence that reduces murder to manslaughter. As defined in section 232 of the *Criminal Code*, provocation requires 1) a wrongful act or insult that is not provoked by the accused or the result of a victim exercising a legal right;[86] 2) sudden provocation; 3) subjective provocation;[87] and 4) the wrongful act or insult must be "of such a nature as to be sufficient to deprive an ordinary person of the power of self-control."[88]

Anger alone will not suffice[89] and the provocation defence will not apply when the accused has acted in a calculated manner to retaliate to some perceived insult or wrong. The ordinary person standard is designed to encourage reasonable and non-violent behaviour that is in accord with contemporary norms and values including equality under the *Charter*.[90] The ordinary person standard has been contextualized so that the ordinary person has the same age and gender of the accused and the

---

85   [1993] 3 S.C.R. 306.

86   Section 232(3) provides in part that "no one shall be deemed to have given provocation to another by doing anything that he had a legal right to do, or by doing anything that the accused incited him to do in order to provide the accused with an excuse for causing death or bodily harm to any human being."

87   Section 232(1) uses the archaic phrase that the accused must act "in the heat of passion caused by sudden provocation."

88   *Code*, above note 1, s. 232(2). The proper formulation is whether the ordinary person would, rather than could, have lost self-control. *Hill*, below note 90 at 330; *Hibbert*, below note 282 at para. 24; *R. v. Lees* (2001), 156 C.C.C. (3d) 421 at paras. 15–16 (B.C.C.A.).

89   *R. v. Parent*, [2001] 1 S.C.R. 761 [*Parent*].

90   *R. v. Hill*, [1986] 1 S.C.R. 313 at 324 [*Hill*]; *R. v. Tran*, [2010] 3 S.C.R. 350 at para. 34 [*Tran*].

same relevant experiences.[91] This led to concerns that the individuated reasonable person may diminish the level of self-control and afford defences in particular to jealous or homophobic males. The Supreme Court responded to many of these concerns in *R. v. Tran*[92] by holding that the ordinary person should only be modified to place the act or insult in context but not "to shift the ordinary person standard to suit the individual accused" or to individualize the ordinary person so as to defeat its purpose in encouraging self-control and non-violent behaviour.

Like the defences discussed in chapter 9, the provocation defence will apply if there is a reasonable doubt about all of its elements. It should only be left to the jury when there is an "air of reality" to the defence and some evidence that if believed by the jury would allow them acting judicially to have a reasonable doubt about each element of the defence. In order for the provocation defence to apply, the jury must have a reasonable doubt about each of its constituent elements.[93] Unlike self-defence, necessity, and duress, however, a successful provocation defence does not result in the acquittal of the accused. Provocation only reduces murder to manslaughter. Nevertheless, this is an important distinction that avoids the mandatory life imprisonment that accompanies a murder conviction.

As a partial defence that reduces murder to manslaughter, provocation does not fit easily into the excuse/justification framework discussed in chapter 9. The Supreme Court has stated that the "provocation . . . neither justifies nor excuses the act of homicide. But the law accounts the act and the violent feelings which prompted it, less blamable because of the passion aroused by the provocation."[94] Provocation could be said to operate as a partial excuse out of compassion to human frailty when an accused kills another person while in a rage provoked by a sudden act or insult. Although the origins of the provocation defence lie in the distinction between capital and non-capital murder, today it flows from the distinction between mandatory life imprisonment for murder and more discretionary penalties for manslaughter.[95]

Provocation is a controversial defence. Its origins lay in traditions of mitigating violent responses to marital infidelities and other affronts to "honour" and it contains archaic phrases about excusing a person who acts in the heat of passion. Some argue that it should be abolished as a defence because it allows deadly rage and violence, often directed

---

91   *R. v. Thibert* (1996), 104 C.C.C. (3d) 1 (S.C.C.) [*Thibert*].
92   *Tran*, above note 90 at para. 35.
93   *Ibid.* at para. 41.
94   *R. v. Manchuk* (1937), 69 C.C.C. 172 at 173 (S.C.C.) [*Manchuk*].
95   *Tran*, above note 90 at paras. 21–22.

against women and gay people, to be treated less seriously than other intentional killings. The Supreme Court has, however, indicated that the provocation defence should accord with contemporary norms and reject sexist and homophobic beliefs and "inappropriate conceptualizations of 'honor.'"[96] Others argue that the provocation defence reflects the special significance of murder and the fact that murder, unlike manslaughter, carries a fixed penalty. Still others argue that the defence of provocation should apply to all crimes, not only murder. Still others question why provocation privileges emotions such as rage and loss of self-control but not other emotions such as compassion and despair that may also prompt killings.

a) A Wrongful Act or Insult that Is Not Incited by the Accused or the Result of the Victim Exercising a Legal Right

The courts had traditionally interpreted the requirement of a wrongful act or insult broadly to include scornful and contemptuous remarks and a broad range of wrongful acts including assaults. For example, a wife's denial of an affair and slapping her husband was considered a wrongful act or insult[97] as were a victim's actions in holding the accused's wife in front of him and saying "come on big fellow shoot me."[98] In one controversial case, the victim's statement that she would not marry the accused because he was black was not considered a wrongful act or insult but only on the basis that the accused testified at trial that he had not heard the remark.[99]

In *Tran*, the Court took a more restrictive approach to the threshold requirement of whether there was an act or insult. It found that there was no wrongful act or insult when the accused entered the apartment of his estranged wife to find her naked with another man. The behaviour of the two lovers "was not only lawful, it was discreet and private and entirely passive vis-à-vis" the accused. There was no wrongful act or insult defined as scornful abuse or offences to modesty or self-respect.[100] What in previous generations may have been considered to be the paradigmatic act of provocation—the discovery of evidence of

---

96   *Ibid.* at para. 34.

97   *Taylor v. The King*, [1947] S.C.R. 462.

98   *Thibert*, above note 91. Two judges dissented on this issue and argued that the words and actions were not contemptuous or scornful but legitimate reactions to being confronted by the accused who was pointing a loaded rifle. *Ibid.* at para. 63.

99   *Parnekar v. The Queen*, [1974] S.C.R. 449. Chief Justice Laskin in dissent would have left the provocation defence to the jury.

100   *Tran*, above note 90 at para. 44.

adultery and a sudden violent response to that evidence—has now been held by the Court not even to constitute a wrongful act or insult capable of being an act of provocation. This part of *Tran* imposes a categorical restriction on the provocation defence.

At the same time, the Court also suggested that the provocation defence might fail in *Tran* on the other subjective and objective elements of the provocation defence. The accused in the case was not provoked suddenly given that he had known about the state of affairs. He also took the initiative in entering his estranged wife's apartment and in retrieving butcher knives and stabbing the deceased seventeen times.[101] With respect to the objective standard, the Court also stressed in *Tran* the need for it to be informed by contemporary social norms and values and for it to reject sexist attitudes that saw adultery as "the highest invasion of propriety."[102]

There are other restrictions on what may constitute a wrongful act or insult. Section 232(3) states that there is no provocation when the accused has incited the victim to commit the act or insult claimed to be provocation. In *R. v. Squire*,[103] an accused who was an aggressor in a fight was held not to have been provoked even if he had been kicked during the fight. The accused should not be allowed to argue provocation when he or she incited the act or insult claimed to be provocation. Provocation was, however, established in *Thibert*[104] even though the accused, by pursuing an opportunity to speak to his estranged wife while armed, created the opportunity for the deceased to insult him by challenging the accused to shoot.

Section 232(3) also restricts the definition of provocation by providing that "no one shall be deemed to have given provocation to another by doing anything he has a legal right to do."[105] The legal right exception to provocation has been interpreted narrowly by the courts. In *R. v. Galgay*,[106] the Ontario Court of Appeal held that a trial judge had erred when he informed the jury that the victim's telling the accused that he was no good and she was going to leave him could not be provocation because the victim was only exercising her legal rights. In reversing the trial judge, Kelly J.A. stated that section 232(3) "does

---

101 *Ibid.* at para. 46.

102 *Ibid.* at para. 34 disapproving of *R. v. Mawgridge* (1707), 84 E.R. 1107 at 1115.

103 (1977), 29 C.C.C. (2d) 497 (S.C.C.).

104 *Thibert*, above note 91.

105 Section 232(4) provides that an arrest that exceeds an individual's or a police officer's legal powers is not necessarily provocation, "but the fact that the illegality of the arrest was known to the accused may be evidence of provocation."

106 (1972), 6 C.C.C. (2d) 539 at 553 (Ont. C.A.) [*Galgay*].

not apply to remove from a verbal insult offered by the provoker the provocative quality of the insult." Brooke J.A. added that although the victim had a legal right to leave the accused, she had no legal right to insult him. The absence of a legal remedy for an insult in private does not mean that the victim was exercising a legal right under this section. The approach in *Galgay* limits this exception to cases where the victim was exercising legal rights such as self-defence. It could be rethought if courts consider the domestic violence context in which many provocation defences arise. It could be argued that people have a legal right to leave relationships and even to make disparaging comments about ex-partners. The Court's continued refusal to recognize this broader interpretation of a legal right could deny women the equal protection and benefit of the law.

The restrictive approach in *Galgay* has been adopted by a three-judge plurality of the Supreme Court in *Thibert*.[107] In that case, the deceased was held not to have a legal right to tell the accused to shoot him while holding onto the accused's wife. Cory J. explained: "In the context of the provocation defence, the phrase 'legal right' has been defined as something which is sanctioned by law as distinct from something which a person may do without incurring legal liability." This restricts the meaning of legal right to matters such as self-defence. Even then, the Court took a restrictive approach and held that the deceased's actions in walking towards the accused while the accused was pointing a gun at him "could well be found not to be acts of self-defence."[108] It seems that a deceased will only be held to be exercising a legal right that cannot constitute provocation in the clearest cases of self-defence. This is unfortunate because a broader reading of the deceased's legal rights could respond to many of the concerns that have been expressed about the provocation defence excusing violence in response to rather trivial acts or insults or when women tell men that they are leaving a relationship. This criticism of the legal right exception to provocation has been considered but rejected by the Supreme Court in *R. v. Tran*[109] which has upheld the idea that legal right only applies to conduct such as self-defence specifically authorized by law and not to freedoms that are not specifically prohibited by law. The Court noted that while a spouse has a legal right to leave his or her partner, it was still possible that he or she might suddenly insult the other during the course of leaving. The Court did note, however, that the fact that the victim had

---

107   *Thibert*, above note 91 at 14.
108   *Ibid.*
109   [2010] 3 S.C.R. 350 at para. 29.

"the 'legal right,' in the broad sense of the term to leave the relationship is an important consideration" in determining whether the insult would have deprived an ordinary person of self-control.

b) Sudden Provocation

The Supreme Court has stated that "'suddenness' must characterize both the insult and the act of retaliation."[110] On this basis, the Court has denied the defence to an accused who had prior knowledge of his wife's unfaithfulness and abortion but had killed her when she informed him of these previously known facts;[111] to an accused who commenced an argument with his wife and followed her into a room and called her a name;[112] and to an accused who kidnapped the victim, who later provoked the accused by hitting him with a hammer.[113] Most recently in *Tran*, the Court held there was no sudden provocation when an accused who previously knew that his estranged wife was seeing another man entered the wife's locked apartment to find her in bed with the other man and when the accused responded to seeing his wife with another man by retrieving butcher knives from the kitchen and stabbing the man seventeen times. Both the wrongful act or insult and the accused's response to it must be sudden and unexpected; it cannot be a manifestation of a grudge, the affirmation of suspected conduct or a foreseeable response to something that the accused has initiated. In a series of cases, provincial appellate courts have held that the defence of provocation should not be left to the jury if there was no sudden provocation that would make an unexpected impact on the accused's mind.[114]

The Supreme Court in a divided decision in *Thibert*[115] allowed a provocation defence in response to taunts by the deceased to shoot him,

---

110   R. v. *Tripodi* (1955), 112 C.C.C. 66 at 68 (S.C.C.); *Tran*, above note 90 at para. 38.
111   *Ibid.*
112   *Salamon v. R.* (1959), 123 C.C.C. 1 at 12 (S.C.C.) [*Salamon*].
113   R. v. *Louison* (1975), 26 C.C.C. (2d) 266 (Sask. C.A.), aff'd (1978), 51 C.C.C. (2d) 479 (S.C.C.).
114   There was no sudden provocation when a man knew for four hours that his wife was leaving him. R. v. *Young* (1993), 78 C.C.C. (3d) 538 (N.S.C.A.), leave to appeal to S.C.C. refused (1993), 81 C.C.C. (3d) vi (S.C.C.). There was no provocation when a battered woman shot her husband sometime after he had choked her and they had argued. R. v. *Malott* (1996), 110 C.C.C. (3d) 499 (Ont. C.A.), aff'd on other grounds (1998), 121 C.C.C. (3d) 457 (S.C.C.) [*Malott*]. See also R. v. *Gibson* (2001), 41 C.R. (5th) 213 (B.C.C.A.); R. v. *Merasty* (2000), 30 C.R. (5th) 274 (B.C.C.A.); R. v. *Pawliuk* (2001), 40 C.R. (5th) 28 (B.C.C.A.).
115   Above note 91 at 17. In his dissent, Major J. argued that the provocation was not sudden because the accused knew of his wife's involvement with the deceased and had seen them together that day. "It cannot be said that . . . [Thibert's]

even though the accused apparently had known for some time that the deceased was involved in an extramarital affair with the accused's wife, and the accused was pursuing (while armed) an opportunity to speak to his wife alone. This case suggests that sudden provocation in the form of a taunt can still be found even though the accused has taken the initiative, has produced a confrontation with the victim, and had prior knowledge of the victim's relationship with his wife. *Thibert* can only be distinguished from the more recent and unanimous judgment in *Tran* on the basis that the accused in *Thibert* was reacting on the sudden to unexpected taunts from the accused whereas the victim and the wife said nothing and did not insult the accused when he took the initiative and confronted them in his estranged wife's apartment.

The act or insult that constitutes provocation must generally come from the victim. Provocation cannot be used when the accused knows that the victim was not involved in the act or insult.[116] Provocation may, however, be available when the victim participated with a third person in the act or insult, or where the accused makes a reasonable mistake that the victim was involved in the provocation.[117] Cases of transferred intent under section 229(b) of the *Criminal Code* in which the accused intends to kill one person but kills another by accident or mistake may be mitigated by the provocation defence even though the accused was provoked by the person he or she intended to kill and not the person actually killed.[118]

c)   Subjective Provocation

In addition to sudden provocation, the accused must act "before there was time for his passion to cool." This test "is called subjective because it involves an assessment of what actually occurred in the mind of the accused. . . . [The] task at this point is to ascertain whether the accused was in fact acting as a result of provocation."[119] The accused must not only be angry and excited but must have subjectively lost self-control.[120] In determining this subjective component of the provocation defence, all factors particular to the accused can be considered,

---

mind was unprepared for the sight of his wife and the deceased such that he was taken by surprise and his passions were set aflame."

116 *Manchuk*, above note 94

117 *R. v. Hansford* (1987), 33 C.C.C. (3d) 74 (Alta. C.A.).

118 *R. v. Droste* (1981), 63 C.C.C. (3d) 418 (Ont. C.A.), aff'd on other grounds (*sub nom. R. v. Droste (No. 2)*), above note 74.

119 *Hill*, above note 90 at 336.

120 *Tran*, above note 90 at para. 46.

including intoxication,[121] his or her "mental state and psychological temperament,"[122] and the history of the accused's relationship with the deceased.[123]

In many cases, the objective test for provocation to be discussed below will be the most difficult for the accused to raise a reasonable doubt about. The accused may, however, fail to raise a reasonable doubt about the subjective test if the killing involved an element of deliberation inconsistent with acting on the sudden and in the heat of passion. In *Malott*,[124] the Ontario Court of Appeal held that a battered woman did not qualify for the provocation defence in part because she had deliberately obtained a gun to shoot her husband and her "behaviour following the shooting was characterized by a lack of passion." At the same time, the accused in *Thibert* was held to have been subjectively provoked by an insult while he was pursuing an opportunity to talk with his wife without the deceased being present. The history of the relationship between the accused and the deceased may be considered so long as there was a sudden act or insult added to the mix such as the deceased goading the accused to shoot him or the throwing of a bottle.[125] In many ways, the requirement that the accused be subjectively provoked complements the requirement that the provocation be sudden.

d) Objective Standard That the Wrongful Act or Insult Is Capable of Depriving an Ordinary Person of Self-Control

The most important limitation on what acts and insults can amount to provocation is the requirement in section 232(2) that they be "of such a nature as to deprive an ordinary person of self-control." Dickson C.J. has stated that it is

> society's concern that reasonable and non-violent behaviour be encouraged that prompts the law to endorse the objective standard. The criminal law is concerned among other things with fixing standards for human behaviour. We seek to encourage conduct that complies with certain societal standards of reasonableness and responsibility. In doing so, the law quite logically employs the objective standard of the reasonable person.[126]

---

121 *Salamon*, above note 112.
122 *Hill*, above note 90.
123 R. v. *Sheridan* (1991), 65 C.C.C. (3d) 319 (S.C.C.), rev'g (1990), 55 C.C.C. (3d) 313 at 321 (Alta. C.A.); *Thibert*, above note 91 at 10–11.
124 *Malott*, above note 114.
125 *Thibert*, above note 91.
126 *Hill*, above note 90 at 330.

The same could be said about self-defence, necessity, and the common law defence of duress, which also employ objective standards. A peaceful society does not want to excuse violence solely on the basis of the accused's subjective and perhaps idiosyncratic perceptions and reactions to the ordinary stresses and strains of modern life. The challenge, as is the case with objective standards for *mens rea*, is to ensure that the particular accused can reasonably be required to live up to the objective standard of self-control and reasonable and non-violent behaviour. There is no meaningful distinction between the ordinary person standard used for provocation and the reasonable person standard used for self-defence, necessity, and duress, except to the extent the ordinary person standard used in provocation may be slightly less demanding of the accused in reflection of the fact that provocation is only a partial defence that reduces murder to manslaughter and not a full defence that results in the accused going free.[127]

Courts in Canada and England[128] traditionally interpreted the ordinary person without any reference to the accused's circumstances or characteristics. In *R. v. Wright*,[129] the Supreme Court held that the fact that the accused was insulted by his father should not be considered when determining whether an ordinary person would have lost self-control. In *R. v. Parnerkar*,[130] the Saskatchewan Court of Appeal held that the accused's race was not relevant in determining whether an ordinary person would have lost self-control, even though the accused had been told by the victim that she was "not going to marry you because you are a black man." This approach was harsh because it did not allow the Court to consider the relevant context and circumstances behind the act or insult,[131] and could, in the case of a young accused, require "old heads be placed upon young shoulders."[132]

In *Hill*,[133] the majority of the Supreme Court upheld a murder conviction of a sixteen-year-old boy who killed the victim after he claimed

---

127   *Tran*, above note 90 at para. 30.
128   *Bedder v. D.P.P.*, [1954] 2 All E.R. 801 (H.L.), overruled in *D.P.P. v. Camplin*, [1978] 2 W.L.R. 679 (H.L.) [*Camplin*].
129   [1969] 3 C.C.C. 258 (S.C.C.) [*Wright*].
130   (1972), 5 C.C.C. (2d) 11 (Sask. C.A.), aff'd (1973), 10 C.C.C. (2d) 253 (S.C.C.).
131   Lord Diplock stated that the jury should be able to "take into consideration all those factors which in their opinion would affect the gravity of taunts or insults" when applied to the accused, in part because "[t]o taunt a person because of his race, his physical infirmities or some shameful incident in his past may well be considered by the jury to be more offensive to the person addressed . . . if the facts on which the taunt is founded are true." *Camplin*, above note 128 at 717.
132   *Ibid.*
133   *Hill*, above note 90.

the male victim made sexual advances. The trial judge, following *Wright* and *Parnerkar*, had instructed the jury that, in determining whether the acts and words constituted provocation, "you are not to consider the particular mental make-up of the accused; rather the standard is that of the ordinary person."[134]

For the majority of the Court, Dickson C.J. stated that it would be fair to consider the accused's youth as an "important contextual consideration." He warned, however, that the accused's personal characteristics will not always be relevant. For example, an accused's race would not be relevant if he or she was faced with an insult about a physical disability. The accused's sex would not be relevant if the insult was directed at his or her race. Even with regard to the accused's youth, Dickson C.J. held that the charge to the jury was acceptable and it was not necessary for the judge to instruct the jury to consider whether an ordinary sixteen year old would have lost self-control. He explained:

> [T]he "collective good sense" of the jury will naturally lead it to ascribe to the ordinary person any general characteristics relevant to the provocation in question. For example, if the provocation is a racial slur, the jury will think of an ordinary person with the racial background that forms the substance of the insult. To this extent, particular characteristics will be ascribed to the ordinary person.[135]

Although he did not require the jury to be instructed to consider the accused's youth, Dickson C.J. did not seem to believe that considering youth was inconsistent with the purposes of the objective standard in encouraging reasonable and non-violent behaviour. Subsequent cases have considered the accused's youth when determining whether an ordinary person would have lost self-control.[136] Indeed, it would now be an error of law not to instruct the jury to consider the reactions of an ordinary person of the accused's own age when considering whether an ordinary person would have been deprived of the power of self-control.[137]

Three judges dissented in *Hill* and would have ordered a new trial. Le Dain and Lamer JJ. dissented on the grounds that the trial judge's charge would have left the jury with the impression that it could not consider the accused's age when determining whether an ordinary person would have lost self-control. Wilson J. also dissented and stated

---

134 *Ibid.* at 327–28. They could consider the accused's emotional and physical conditions and his age when determining if he had acted suddenly, before his passion had cooled.

135 *Ibid.* at 335.

136 *R. v. Jackson* (1991), 68 C.C.C. (3d) 385 at 410 (Ont. C.A.) [*Jackson*].

137 *Thibert*, above note 91.

that a specific instruction about the accused's youth and sex was necessary in this case. She reasoned that it was appropriate to consider the accused's youth because "the law does not attribute to individuals in the developmental stage of their youth the same degree of responsibility as is attributed to fully adult actors."[138] She cautioned against allowing other factors, including the accused's sex, to determine the amount of self-control expected. In her view, "the underlying principles of equality and individual responsibility cannot be undermined by importing the accused's subjective level of self-control into the 'ordinary person' test."[139] She believed, however, that the accused's sex was relevant as a factor "to put the wrongful act or insult into context for the purposes of assessing its gravity," so that the jury would determine the effect of the act or insult on "the ordinary person similarly situated and similarly insulted" as the accused.[140]

Subsequent cases have affirmed that the jury should be instructed to consider an ordinary person of the same age and sex of the accused. This includes the concerns expressed by the dissenting judges in *Hill* about the relevance of age, but not always Justice Wilson's careful distinction between the relevance of gender as a factor that may, depending on the circumstances, place an act or insult in context but a factor that should not influence the level of self-control expected by society. This is unfortunate because the Wilson approach addresses real concerns about the provocation defence being used partially to excuse rage and violence that does occur with males but rarely with females. The key to applying objective standards in a fair manner seems to be to apply the same standard of conduct to all while also making appropriate adjustment to ensure that the context of the act or insult to the person is properly appreciated. In *R. v. Tran*,[141] the Court may have implicitly adopted the Wilson approach by drawing a distinction between the need to modify the ordinary person to place the wrongful act or insult in context while at the same time not allowing this contextual process "to shift the ordinary person standard to suit the individual accused" or to individualize the ordinary person so as to defeat its purpose in encouraging self-control and non-violent behaviour. The Court indicated that the ordinary person standard should not be modified by the fact that the accused was "homophobic" or held "antiquated beliefs" about "honour" or adultery being "the highest invasion of property."

---

138 *Hill*, above note 90 at 352.
139 *Ibid.*
140 *Ibid.*
141 [2010] 3 S.C.R. 350 at paras. 34–35.

i)   The Modified Objective and Contextual Standard

In *Thibert*,[142] a three-judge plurality of the Court went beyond the relatively cautious approach taken by the majority in *Hill* or even by Justice Wilson in that case to relating the accused's characteristics to those of the ordinary person and concluded:

> The "ordinary person" must be of the same age, and sex, and share with the accused such other factors as would give the act or insult in question a special significance and have experienced the same series of acts or insults as those experienced by the accused.

This definition of the ordinary person meant that the accused in the case was held up to the same standard of self-control as would be possessed by a "married man, faced with the breakup of his marriage"[143] who had previously convinced his wife to return to the marriage. The majority concluded that this ordinary man would have lost his powers of self-control when the deceased taunted him to shoot him while holding the accused's wife in front of him. A two-judge minority dissented on the basis that the breakup of a marriage due to an extramarital affair and the deceased's participation in the affair should not be considered as wrongful acts or insults capable of depriving an ordinary person of the power of self-control.

The proper focus in administering a defence that requires a sudden response to acts or insults should be on the deceased's taunts just before the shooting,[144] but the majority's approach makes the breakup of the marriage and indeed much of the history of the marriage relevant. Such information could well be relevant in appreciating the context of the particular taunt. The problem, however, is that it could be used by the trier of fact to adjust the standard of self-control or reasonable conduct required of the accused. In other words, it could demand not the standard of self-control expected of ordinary persons including women and men, single and married people, but only the self-control expected from the ordinary married man whose marriage is breaking up.

It is not clear from the majority's decision whether the accused's gender is relevant to place the act or insult in context or to determine the level of self-control or to both. It should be recalled that both Chief Justice Dickson and Justice Wilson in *Hill* expressed caution about

---

142   *Thibert*, above note 91 at 10.

143   *Ibid.* at 12.

144   To this end, Cory J. indicated that if the accused had simply brooded over his rejection and gone and shot the deceased, "the history of the deceased's relationship with the wife of the accused could not be used as a basis for a defence of provocation because the necessary final act of provocation was missing." *Ibid.* at 13.

including gender as a factor that may be relevant to the level of self-control expected from the ordinary person. Although Justice Wilson was more explicit, both judges would have considered the accused's gender to be relevant only when it was necessary to place the wrongful act or insult in context. The Court's decision in *Thibert* to judge conduct by the standard of the married man may too easily excuse male violence towards women simply because of a breakup of a relationship. This concern has been partially addressed by the unanimous decision in *Tran* that a man who entered his estranged wife's apartment to find her naked in bed with another man was not provoked because he did not experience a sudden wrongful act or insult. *Tran*[145] also specifically warns "that it would not be appropriate to ascribe to the ordinary person the characteristic of being homophobic if the accused were a recipient of a homosexual advance." This is undoubtedly correct and helpful. Nevertheless, it stops short of addressing whether the ordinary person in such a context should be of the same gender as the accused. Both the decisions in *Hill* and especially *Thibert* suggest that the ordinary person should be the same gender as the accused. When this is done, however, judges following *Tran* should make clear that the jury must apply contemporary norms including equality rights in the *Charter* and not allow sexism or homophobia to influence their application of the modified objective test.

Although *Thibert* was problematic on the gender issue, the other aspects of the plurality's judgment are less controversial. The Supreme Court clearly indicates that the age of the accused should be factored into the ordinary person test and this is an improvement on *Hill* where there was a danger that the jury may not have considered the fact that the accused was only sixteen years old when applying the ordinary person standard. It also seems appropriate that the ordinary person should "share with the accused such other factors as would give the act or insult in question a special significance and have experienced the same series of acts or insults as those experienced by the accused." The accused should be expected to demonstrate reasonable self-control, but it would not be fair to judge the accused's reactions against those of an ordinary person that did have the same factors as give the act or insult special significance. A slur about a person's race or sexuality only takes on full meaning when that person's particular characteristics and history are considered. In addition, past acts and insults exchanged between the accused and the deceased may be relevant to determine the

---

145 [2010] 3 S.C.R. 350 at para. 34.

gravity of the final act or insult.[146] The requirement for sudden provocation should prevent the accused from acting on old grudges.

In summary, the ordinary person should be defined in a contextual manner that ensures the ordinary person is endowed with those characteristics and past experiences that are necessary to place the act or insult in context. It also suggests that the ordinary person should be the same age and gender as the accused. This makes clear the idea implicit in *Hill* that youth is relevant to the degree of self-control that can reasonably be expected. At the same time, however, it may make the accused's gender relevant both to place the act or insult in context and more problematically to the degree of self-control expected from the accused. *Tran* now makes clear that *Charter* equality values should inform the ordinary person standard and that homophobia and sexism should not influence the standard of self-control expected of the ordinary person.

ii) Factors Not Relevant to an Ordinary Person

It is clear that factors such as intoxication and temper that may affect an accused's self-control are not relevant in determining whether an ordinary person would have lost self-control. Courts have not been clear about whether and why the accused's sex should be considered when applying the objective test. In *R. v. Fraser*,[147] McDermid J.A. argued in dissent that a reasonable person would not respond with violence to homosexual advances, given contemporary attitudes towards sexuality. This argument is appealing in principle[148] and is now supported by the Supreme Court's decision in *Tran* that homophobia has no place under section 232. At the same time, it must be reconciled with Dickson C.J.'s implicit and Wilson J.'s explicit indications that the accused's sex in *Hill* was a consideration that was relevant to place the male deceased's sexual advances towards the sixteen-year-old male accused in context. The Supreme Court's decision in *Thibert*[149] suggests that the ordinary person should always share the same gender as the accused and does not clearly differentiate when gender is relevant to placing an act or insult in context and when gender is relevant to the degree of self-control expected. *Tran* now provides new and unanimous support from the

---

146 *Ibid.*
147 (1980), 55 C.C.C. (2d) 503 (Alta. C.A.).
148 Especially given that sexual orientation has been included by courts as a prohibited ground for denying gays and lesbians the equal protection and benefit of the law under s. 15 of the *Canadian Charter of Rights and Freedoms*, Part I of the *Constitution Act, 1982*, being Schedule B to the *Canada Act 1982* (U.K.), 1982, c. 11 [*Charter*].
149 *Thibert*, above note 91.

Supreme Court for the need to make such distinctions, as difficult as that may be.

The Court in *Tran*[150] also helpfully addressed this issue outside the difficult context of gender when it stated that the context that an accused was insulted by being wrongfully fired from a position was relevant, but that the ordinary person standard "does not vary depending on the accused's particular relationship or particular feelings about his employer or his employment." This may qualify the individualization process contemplated by the Court in *Thibert* which by asking the jury to consider how the ordinary married man would have reacted may have made the troubled history of the marriage relevant. The Court has been restrictive with the provocation defence in other non-gendered contexts. For example, it has held that there was no objective ground for provocation when the accused was sworn at and threatened in a commercial dispute that could have led to the destruction of his house and barn.[151]

iii) Cultural Background of the Accused

In *R. v. Ly*,[152] an accused born and raised in Vietnam argued that his cultural background should be considered when determining whether an ordinary person would have lost self-control when his wife returned home early in the morning and told him that where she had been was none of his business. The British Columbia Court of Appeal held that the accused's cultural background was not relevant to place the act or insult in context because a racial slur had not been used.[153] Under this approach, an accused's cultural background can only be considered if necessary to determine the gravity of the insult. It should not be used to determine the degree of self-control expected from the ordinary person. This approach is appealing in principle and seems to follow the path set by Justice Wilson in *Hill* and recently confirmed by the Supreme Court in *Tran* where the Court did not consider a similar cultural background of the accused.

Under the generous contextual approach taken by the plurality in *Thibert*,[154] it could be argued that the accused's cultural background in *Ly* should have been considered and was necessary to place the deceased's words in context. Indeed, the British Columbia Court of Ap-

---

150 [2010] 3 S.C.R. 350 at para. 35.

151 *R. v. Roberts*, [2005] 1 S.C.R. 22. Fish J. dissented, however, on the basis that the jury could have had a reasonable doubt that the accused was provoked.

152 (1987), 33 C.C.C. (3d) 31 (B.C.C.A.) [*Ly*].

153 *Ibid.* at 38.

154 *Thibert*, above note 91. Recall that in that case, an "ordinary married man" person was applied by the majority.

peal in R. v. *Nahar* has subsequently noted that *Ly* was decided before *Thibert* and has indicated that

> in assessing the objective element, on what was said in R. v. *Thibert*, those factors that would give the wrongful act or insult a special significance to the accused are to be taken into account as being shared by the ordinary person. While that case involved no consideration of cultural background, factors that give an act or insult a special significance could be said to include the implications of an accused person having been raised in a particular culture.[155]

On the facts of the case, however, the Court of Appeal upheld the murder conviction of a Sikh accused on the basis that his estranged wife's statements that she would continue to do as she pleased did not satisfy the objective arm of the provocation test. As in *Tran*, the victim's behaviour had been known to the accused for some time and the Court of Appeal stressed the need for both a sudden provocation and a sudden response.

The Ontario Court of Appeal took a more restrictive approach to the relevance of cultural factors in R. v. *Humaid*, in upholding a murder conviction after the trial judge had specifically instructed the jury that while it could consider the accused's age, gender, and other factors that would give an insult a special significance, it should not consider "any peculiar or idiosyncratic traits" arising from the accused's Muslim faith or culture. The accused had stabbed his wife nineteen times after apparently learning that she had sexual intercourse with a business associate, but there was also some evidence that he had planned to kill her and the jury convicted the man of first-degree murder. The Ontario Court of Appeal held that there was no evidence that the accused had cultural and religious beliefs that would have added to the significance of his wife's admission of infidelity. Doherty J.A. also added:

> Provocation does not shield an accused who has not lost self-control, but has instead acted out of a sense of revenge or a culturally driven sense of the appropriate response to someone else's misconduct. An accused who acts out of a sense of retribution fuelled by a belief system that entitles a husband to punish his wife's perceived infidelity has not lost control, but has taken action that, according to his belief system, is a justified response to the situation.[156]

155 R. v. *Nahar* (2004), 181 C.C.C. (3d) 449 at para. 34 (B.C.C.A.) [*Nahar*].
156 R. v. *Humaid* (2006), 37 C.R. (6th) 347 at para. 85 (Ont. C.A.), leave to appeal to S.C.C. refused, 2006 SCCA No. 232 [*Humaid*].

As in *Nahar*, the above quote underlines how attention to traditional limitations on the provocation defence—namely, the requirement for sudden loss of self-control in response to a sudden insult or wrongful act—can exclude some claims made by jealous or possessive husbands. The interest in social protection and encouraging law-abiding behaviour can often be satisfied by attention to these traditional requirements of the provocation defence.

But should the accused's cultural background be included in the Court's modified objective and contextual approach to assessing whether an ordinary person would have lost self-control? The Ontario Court of Appeal appears to favour the more restrictive *Ly* approach when it stressed that the alleged insult in this case did not directly target the accused's religion or culture. This seems to be an overly narrow and simplistic approach to the question of when consideration of the accused's characteristics are necessary to place the insult in context. Although an accused's religion should be considered in determining whether a religious insult would cause a person to lose self-control, such an approach does not exhaust the significance of a person's religion to his or her behaviour. The British Columbia Court of Appeal's approach in *Nahar* of factoring religious and cultural factors that are relevant to the marriage relationship appears more realistic and consistent with *Thibert*. It could also be made consistent with *Tran* if care were taken to stress that the accused's religious and cultural background should not affect the level of self-control expected even though it may influence the context and gravity of an act or insult. The holding in *Nahar* that the accused was not provoked also underlines that the provocation defence should not apply when the accused acts violently to a woman's assertion of autonomy or when the accused seeks calculated revenge for infidelity. The same standard of reasonable conduct is expected for all as part of the rule of law that applies to all.

The Ontario Court of Appeal in *Humaid* also stated that the "beliefs which give the insult added gravity are premised on the notion that women are inferior to men and that violence against women is in some circumstances accepted, if not encouraged. These beliefs are antithetical to fundamental Canadian values, including gender equality."[157] Without reference to this statement, the Supreme Court in *Tran*[158] subsequently made similar statements that "the ordinary person standard must be informed by contemporary norms of behaviour, including fundamental values such as the commitment to equality provided for in

---

157 *Ibid.* at para. 93.
158 [2010] 3 S.C.R. 350 at para. 34.

the *Canadian Charter of Rights and Freedoms*." This approach suggests that the ordinary person standard should be applied in a manner that supports and incorporates *Charter* and other contemporary norms of behaviour. *Tran* explicitly states that homophobia should not influence the standard of control promoted by the ordinary person standard and implicitly suggests that sexist and cultural values that are out of sync with contemporary norms of behaviour including the equality of men and women should not dilute the standard of reasonable behaviour required by the ordinary person standard.

The Supreme Court recently dealt with a case that may have had a cultural dimension. It held that the fact that a woman had immigrated to Canada from Sri Lanka in the same year she killed her sister-in-law was relevant because such an accused might have a heightened sensitivity to insults relating to her education and ability to integrate into a new country. At the same time, the Court unanimously concluded that there was no air of reality to the accused's argument that an ordinary person in those circumstances would have lost self-control when ridiculed about her lack of education. In other words, the accused's characteristics, "while relevant, do not transform her conduct [in stabbing the deceased forty-five times] into an act an ordinary person would have committed."[159] This case appropriately does not reject the relevance of the accused's particular circumstances even when applying the ordinary person standard. At the same time, it maintains the distinction in *Tran* about not allowing a contextual objective standard to be so individualized that it becomes a subjective one that fails to serve the purpose of the objective standard in promoting reasonable and non-violent behaviour.

e) Proportionality Not Required

The courts in England stress proportionality when they state the issue is "not merely whether such person would in like circumstances be provoked to lose his self-control but would also react to the provocation as the accused did."[160] Proportionality also figures in the Canadian law applying to self-defence, necessity, and common law duress discussed in chapter 9. Nevertheless, under the section 232 provocation defence, Canadian courts have focused only on whether an ordinary person in the circumstances would have lost self-control, not whether he or she would have done what the accused did.[161] This approach seems to elim-

---

159 *R. v. Mayuran*, 2012 SCC 31 at paras. 30–31.
160 *Camplin*, above note 128 at 686.
161 *R. v. Carpenter* (1993), 83 C.C.C. (3d) 193 at 197 (Ont. C.A.).

inate any requirement that the accused's acts be even roughly proportionate to the act or insult. It also discounts the real possibility that a particularly cutting insult may cause an ordinary person to lose self-control, but perhaps not to engage in a vicious and deliberate killing. At the same time, this approach follows the wording of section 232, which refers only to whether an ordinary person would have lost self-control.

f)   Provocation and the *Charter*

There are a number of issues raised by the interaction of the provocation defence with the *Charter*. The first is whether the objective standard discussed above violates section 7 of the *Charter*. The second is whether abolition or tightening of the provocation defence violates section 7 of the *Charter*.

The requirement that an act or insult be sufficient to deprive an ordinary person of self-control has been challenged as inconsistent with section 7 of the *Charter* and, in particular, the constitutional requirement that there be subjective fault for a murder conviction. In *R. v. Cameron*,[162] Doherty J.A. concluded:

> The argument misconceives the effect of section 232. The section does not detract from or negative the fault requirement for murder, but serves as a partial excuse for those who commit what would be murder but for the existence of the partial defence created by section 232. . . .
>
> The statutory defence of provocation does not detract from the *mens rea* required to establish murder . . . .
>
> The objective component of the statutory defence of provocation serves a valid societal purpose . . . and cannot be said to be contrary to the principles of fundamental justice.

An objective standard for the defence of provocation does not relieve the Crown of the burden of proving that the accused subjectively knew that the victim was likely to die.

As recognized in *Hill*, the objective standard in section 232 is designed to encourage reasonable and non-violent behaviour. The courts have accepted objective standards as constitutionally sufficient for many offences[163] and it is likely that they will continue to uphold ob-

---

162   (1992), 71 C.C.C. (3d) 272 at 273–74 (Ont. C.A.). A majority of the Supreme Court has relied on this case and its reasoning that objective standards in a defence did not affect the Crown's obligations to prove the voluntary commission of the *actus reus* with the required *mens rea*. *R. v. Stone* (1999), 134 C.C.C. (3d) 353 at 437 (S.C.C.) [*Stone*]. See ch. 8(H), "Automatism."

163   See ch. 5, "The Fault Element, or *Mens Rea*."

jective standards in defences. This is especially true given the generously contextual and individuated approach taken in *Thibert* to apply objective standards of self-control.

② Serious thought has recently been given to abolishing the defence of provocation. This raises the issue of whether the absence of a provocation defence would violate section 7 of the *Charter*. A person who kills while provoked is not a morally innocent person. He or she will have the minimum *mens rea* of subjective foresight of death, which is constitutionally required for murder.[164] Moreover, he or she will likely not be acting in a morally involuntary manner in response to a compelling threat that cannot be reasonably resisted so that it could be said that he or she had no realistic choice but to kill the victim. It thus appears as if the abolition of the provocation defence would not violate section 7 of the *Charter* by allowing the conviction of the morally innocent or a person who acts in a morally involuntary manner.

The abolition of the provocation defence would mean under the present law that a person who killed while provoked would be subject to mandatory life imprisonment. It could be argued that because the person had the *mens rea* required for murder that such punishment was appropriate. On the other hand, it could be argued that the automatic life imprisonment that follows a murder conviction could be disproportionate in cases where the accused responded to a sudden and extraordinary insult. Life imprisonment may go beyond what is necessary to recognize the gravity of the offence and the person's responsibility for it and may not be necessary to protect the public and ensure that the person does not violate the law again. The *Charter* jurisprudence concerning what constitutes cruel and unusual punishment will be examined in chapter 11, but absent such a finding, it is likely that courts would find that the abolition of the provocation defence would not violate the *Charter*.

> A less drastic alternative to abolishing the provocation defence is to make it more restrictive. More attention should be paid to the existing statutory requirements that provocation be sudden and that an act or insult cannot constitute provocation if the deceased was exercising a legal right. Parliament might want to consider specifying particular behaviour that should not be considered provocation. It might also want to require that the accused's response to the act or insult be roughly proportionate to the act or insult. Another alternative would be to abolish mandatory life imprisonment that follows from a murder convic-

---

164 The Ontario Court of Appeal has observed that "the defence of provocation, unlike duress, does not raise an issue of moral blameworthiness because, even if successful, it does not lead to an acquittal." *R. v. Ruzic* (1998), 128 C.C.C (3d) 97 at 122.

tion. As will be seen in the next chapter on sentencing, violence in the domestic context and violence motivated by hatred are aggravating factors that can increase an accused's sentence even when a mandatory sentence does not apply.

g) Relation of Provocation to the Fault Element

As noted earlier, the defence of provocation applies even though the accused has killed with subjective foresight of the likelihood of death.[165] In such a case, the defence of provocation reduces murder to manslaughter. It is possible, however, that evidence of provocation could prevent the Crown from proving the mental element of murder or even other crimes. Martin J.A. recognized this possibility in R. v. Campbell,[166] when he stated there may "be cases where the conduct of the victim amounting to provocation produces in the accused a state of excitement, anger or disturbance as a result of which he might not contemplate the consequences of his acts and might not, in fact, intend to bring about those consequences. . . . Provocation in that aspect, however, does not operate as a 'defence' but rather as a relevant item of evidence on the issue of intent." Provocation is more likely to raise a reasonable doubt about the higher levels of *mens rea.* An accused who damages property in a rage at an act or insult, for example, may not act with the intent or purpose to damage property. The accused would, however, probably be aware of the risk that the property would be damaged and, as such, could be said to have recklessly caused the damage.

In R. v. Parent,[167] the Supreme Court held that a trial judge had erred when he left the jury with the impression that anger alone could reduce murder to manslaughter even when the defence of provocation did not apply. The Supreme Court unfortunately did not discuss Justice Martin's statement in *Campbell* or other statements by the Ontario Court of Appeal suggesting that evidence relating to provocation, perhaps combined with other evidence such as evidence relating to intoxication, could be relevant to reasonable doubt of *mens rea* for murder.[168]

Parent should be restricted to the idea that anger is not in itself "a stand-alone defence."[169] Unfortunately, the Alberta Court of Appeal has interpreted *Parent* for the categorical proposition that "after *Parent*, anger felt by an accused, short of provocation, cannot negative the intent to commit murder. It is an irrelevant factor under section 229(a)

165 R. v. *Oickle* (1984), 11 C.C.C. (3d) 180 (N.S.C.A.).

166 (1977), 38 C.C.C. (2d) 6 at 16 (Ont. C.A.) [*Campbell*].

167 *Parent*, above note 89.

168 R. v. *Nealy* (1986), 30 C.C.C. (3d) 460 (Ont. C.A.) [*Nealy*].

169 *Parent*, above note 89 at para. 10.

and it is an error of law to consider it, whether alone or in combination with other factors."[170] The idea that anger combined with other factors can never raise a reasonable doubt about whether the accused had the constitutionally required fault element of knowledge of the probability of death should be rejected as inconsistent with the concept of subjective fault and the presumption of innocence that gives the accused the benefit of a reasonable doubt. It may well be that an angry accused who has been provoked will have the required fault element in most cases, but that is ultimately an issue to be proven by the Crown beyond a reasonable doubt and determined by the jury.

Anger itself does not automatically reduce murder to manslaughter, but anger should still be considered relevant evidence with respect to subjective fault elements. It may well be that anger will not likely raise a reasonable doubt that a person accused of murder intended that the accused would die or knew that the victim was likely to die,[171] but it should be considered with all other relevant evidence in determining whether the Crown has proved the required level of subjective fault beyond a reasonable doubt. It would be contrary to the principle of subjective fault to exclude consideration of any factor particular to the accused when determining whether the accused subjectively had guilty knowledge.

h) Relation of Provocation to Other Defences

If provocation resulted in automatism that could only be explained with reference to the accused's internal emotional make-up or that required the public to be protected from a continuing danger, then the defence would be mental disorder automatism. If the provocation could be explained on the basis of extraordinary external factors such as seeing a loved one killed or harmed, the defence might be non-mental disorder automatism, leading to a complete acquittal.[172] Either variety of automatism must be established by the accused on a balance of probabilities as opposed to the provocation defence that applies if there is a reasonable doubt about all the elements of the provocation defence. Evidence of intoxication and provocation combined might prevent the Crown from proving the intent of murder beyond a reasonable

---

170   *R. v. Walle* (2007), 230 C.C.C. (3d) 181 at para. 31 (Alta. C.A.).

171   For an argument that anger is more likely to raise a reasonable doubt with respect to the knowledge of death-based fault element in s. 229(a)(ii), rather than the intent to cause death fault requirement in s. 229(a)(i), see Sanjeev Anand, "A Provocative Perspective on the Influence of Anger on the *Mens Rea* for Murder: The Alberta Court of Appeal's Interpretation of *Parent*" (2008) 54 Crim. L.Q. 27.

172   *R. v. Rabey* (1980), 54 C.C.C. (2d) 1 (S.C.C.); *Stone*, above note 161. See ch. 8(H), "Automatism."

doubt, even though the evidence considered separately would not be capable of producing either an intoxication or a provocation defence.[173] This follows the logic of subjective *mens rea*, which is open to the effects that all evidence might have on whether the particular accused had the required mental element.

5) Infanticide

Infanticide is a separate homicide offence punishable by no more than five years' imprisonment that applies when a woman by wilful act or omission causes the death of her newly born child when, by reason of not fully being recovered from childbirth, her mind is disturbed.[174] There must be a causal connection between giving birth or lactation and the disturbance of the mind, but surprisingly not necessarily between the disturbance of the mind and the killing of the newly born which under section 2 of the *Code* is a child under one year of age.

Infanticide functions both as a stand alone offence and a partial defence to murder. As an offence, the Ontario Court of Appeal interpreted infanticide as requiring the same *mens rea* as manslaughter, namely, objective foresight of bodily harm despite the reference to the commission of a "wilful act or omission" and the Supreme Court's prior *dicta* characterizing infanticide as an intentional killing.[175] The Court of Appeal's approach is consistent with the reduced penalty and stigma of infanticide and its status as an included offence to murder.[176] Section 663 of the *Code* is poorly drafted. It seems to suggest that an accused can be convicted of infanticide where the evidence demonstrates that the mother caused the death, but does not establish that she was not fully recovered from childbirth and that her mind was disturbed as a result. In such circumstances, the mother can be convicted of infanticide, though section 663 recognizes that she will be acquitted if the evidence establishes that her acts or omissions are not wilful, as also is required in section 233.

Infanticide also operates as a partial defence to murder. Once an air of reality has been established for the defence, the Crown must then disprove the defence beyond a reasonable doubt.[177] The jury should consider infanticide before murder and convict the accused of the

---

173 *Nealy*, above note 168; *R. v. Friesen* (1995), 101 C.C.C. (3d) 167 (Alta. C.A.).
174 *Code*, above note 1, s. 233.
175 *R. v. L.B.*, 2011 ONCA 153 at para. 121 [*L.B.*] dismissing reference in *Creighton*, above note 59 at 41–42 to infanticide as an "intentional killing."
176 *Code*, above note 1, s. 662(3).
177 *L.B.*, above note 175 at para. 137; *R. v. Effert*, 2011 ABCA 134 at para. 21.

lesser offence of infanticide and not murder unless the Crown proves beyond a reasonable doubt that the accused was fully recovered from the effects of giving birth or her mind was not disturbed as an effect of giving birth. If the jury has even a reasonable doubt about those factors, it should only convict the accused of the lesser offence of infanticide even though the accused might also have the guilt required for murder. In *R. v. Effert*,[178] the Alberta Court of Appeal substituted an infanticide conviction for a second-degree murder conviction in a case in which a nineteen-year-old mother, who had hidden her pregnancy, strangled her newborn and there was expert evidence that her mind was disturbed. It stressed that "the issue is not . . . whether a properly instructed jury must have found a 'disturbed mind' on a balance of probabilities, but whether such a jury would not even have been left with a doubt on the issue." Here as with infanticide as a stand alone offence, Parliament does not require that the mother's disturbed mind be related to the killing, but assumes that such a connection exists and that it significantly diminishes the blameworthiness of the killing. Infanticide is thus an alternative to murder with its mandatory penalties.[179] As with provocation, infanticide emerges as a partial excuse driven more by concerns about the ultimate disposition of the accused because of human frailties than clear principles.

6) Manslaughter

Manslaughter is the residual offence for culpable homicides that are not murders or infanticides. Manslaughter is a much broader offence than either murder or infanticide. It can include killings that are only a reasonable doubt short of murder to killings that are only slightly more than accidents but that involve marked departures from standards of reasonable conduct.

a) Unlawful Act Manslaughter under Section 222(5)(a)

Section 222(5)(a) provides that a person commits culpable homicide when he or she causes the death of a human being by means of an unlawful act. The *actus reus* for this offence is causing death and, as discussed earlier, this requires that the Crown establish that the accused's act was a significant cause of the death.

---

178 *Ibid.* at para. 24.

179 Section 238 also provides a separate offence of killing an unborn child during birth that while subject to punishment of life imprisonment avoids the mandatory penalty of life imprisonment that follows a murder conviction.

The unlawful act can include any federal or provincial offence provided that it is not an absolute liability offence and it is objectively dangerous.[180] At the same time, the Court indicated in *R. v. Gosset*[181] that there was a requirement of a marked departure from a reasonable standard of care even when the unlawful act was one such as careless use of a firearm that seemed on its face to contemplate a lesser form of negligence. If they form the basis for an unlawful act in a manslaughter charge, strict liability offences would be read up to require the Crown to prove a marked departure from a standard of reasonable conduct, even though the accused would have to establish the defence of due diligence if only charged with the regulatory offence. This approach is reaffirmed in *R. v. Beatty*,[182] which suggests that a marked departure from standards of reasonable care is required whenever negligence is used as a form of criminal liability that could result in a deprivation of liberty.

In addition to the act and fault of the underlying act, the majority of the Supreme Court in *R. v. Creighton*[183] established that the Crown must establish the independent fault that there is a reasonable foreseeability of the risk of bodily harm that is not trivial or transitory. The majority rejected the minority's position that the fault element should relate to all aspects of the prohibited act, holding that such a requirement was not a principle of fundamental justice.[184] McLachlin J. held that the lesser stigma of a manslaughter offence did not require a fault element in relation to the foresight of death. The idea that fault elements should relate to all aspects of the *actus reus* was characterized as criminal law "theory." There were sufficient exceptions to this theory that it did not constitute a principle of fundamental justice under section 7 of the *Charter*.[185] The

---

180 *R. v. DeSousa*, [1992] 2 S.C.R. 944.

181 [1993] 3 S.C.R. 76. See also *R. v. Finlay*, [1993] 3 S.C.R. 103 and *R. v. Naglik*, [1993] 3 S.C.R. 122.

182 2008 SCC 5 [*Beatty*].

183 *Creighton*, above note 59.

184 McLachlin J. concluded: "It is important to distinguish between criminal law theory, which seeks the ideal of absolute symmetry between *actus reus* and *mens rea*, and the constitutional requirements of the *Charter* . . . the Constitution does not always guarantee the 'ideal.'" *Ibid.* at para. 98.

185 McLachlin J. concluded: "It would shock the public's conscience to think that a person could be convicted of manslaughter absent any moral fault based on foreseeability of harm. Conversely, it might well shock the public's conscience to convict a person who has killed another only of aggravated assault—the result of requiring foreseeability of death—on the sole basis that the risk of death was not reasonably foreseeable. The terrible consequence of death demands more. In short, the *mens rea* requirement which the common law has adopted—foreseeability of harm—is entirely appropriate to the stigma associated with the offence of manslaughter." *Ibid.* at para. 85.

majority also sought to justify its approach in only requiring objective foresight of bodily harm as consistent with the thin skull principle that informs the Court's broad approach to causation in homicide cases.

In *Creighton*, the Court divided 5:4 on the proper approach to the reasonable person, with the majority holding that the reasonable person should not have the same characteristics as the accused. The majority stressed the need to encourage common standards of reasonable behaviour. It would only make an exception in cases where the accused's characteristics rendered the accused incapable of appreciating the relevant risk. McLachlin J. reasoned that "even those who lack the advantages of age, experience and education" may properly be held to standards of reasonable conduct when they engage in dangerous activities. She added:

> Mental disabilities short of incapacity generally do not suffice to negative criminal liability for criminal negligence. The explanations for why a person fails to advert to the risk inherent in the activity he or she is undertaking are legion. They range from simple absentmindedness to attributes related to age, education, and culture. To permit such a subjective assessment would be "co-extensive with the judgment of each individual, which would be as variable as the length of the foot of each individual" leaving "so vague a line as to afford no rule at all, the degree of judgment belonging to each individual being infinitely various": *Vaughan v. Menlove* (1837), 3 Bing. (N.C.) 468, 132 E.R. 490, at p. 475; see A.M. Linden, *Canadian Tort Law* (4th ed. 1988), at pp. 116–17. Provided the capacity to appreciate the risk is present, lack of education and psychological predispositions serve as no excuse for criminal conduct, although they may be important factors to consider in sentencing.
>
> This is not to say that the question of guilt is determined in a factual vacuum. While the legal duty of the accused is not particularized by his or her personal characteristics short of incapacity, it is particularized in application by the nature of the activity and the circumstances surrounding the accused's failure to take the requisite care.[186]

The Supreme Court has subsequently affirmed this approach while also stating that attention should be paid to the accused's actual state of mind in order to determine whether it suggests that the accused was incapable of appreciating the risk or whether there is a reasonable doubt that the accused was negligent.[187] The purpose of this approach is not

---

186 *Ibid.* at para. 137.
187 *Beatty*, above note 182. See also *R. v. Roy*, 2012 SCC 26.

to individualize the reasonable person in the manner that is done with respect to defences, but rather to accommodate sudden and unexpected events such as a heart attack or a detached retina and all other relevant circumstances that may have to be considered even when administering the objective standard.

b) Criminal Negligence Manslaughter under Sections 222(5)(b) and 220

Section 222(5)(b) provides that culpable homicide is manslaughter when a person causes death by criminal negligence, and section 220 provides a separate but identical offence of causing death by criminal negligence. Criminal negligence is defined in section 219 of the *Code* as doing anything or omitting to do anything that "shows wanton or reckless disregard for the lives or safety of other persons."

In 1989, the Supreme Court split 3:3 whether criminal negligence was an objective or subjective form of fault, with three judges stressing the idea that the conduct has to show negligence and three judges stressing the presumption of subjective fault and the concept of wanton and reckless disregard.[188] With the decision in *Creighton*, however, it is now settled that criminal negligence is an objective form of fault that requires a marked and substantial departure from the standard of reasonable care expected of a reasonable person in the circumstances.

Following the majority judgment of Justice McLachlin, the reasonable person would not have the characteristics of the accused, such as age and education, unless the characteristics would render the accused incapable of appreciating the relevant risk.[189] In addition, objective foresight of death is not required. As discussed earlier, the majority of the Court in *Creighton*[190] rejected the idea that it is a principle of fundamental justice that the fault element must relate to all aspects of the *actus reus* or that the stigma of manslaughter was sufficient to require objective foresight of death. The conclusion that objective foresight of death is not required for manslaughter by criminal negligence is also supported by the definition of criminal negligence in section 219 of the *Code*, which refers to conduct that "shows wanton or reckless disregard for the lives *or* safety of other persons" (emphasis added).

---

188 *R. v. Tutton*, [1989] 1 S.C.R. 1392.

189 *R. v. Ubhi* (1994), 27 C.R. (4th) 332 (B.C.C.A.). The majority's decision in *Creighton* casts doubt on prior cases that would apply the standard of a reasonable sixteen year old. *R. v. Barron* (1985), 23 C.C.C. (3d) 544 (Ont. C.A.).

190 *Creighton*, above note 59.

The Supreme Court's decision in *R. v. J.F.*[191] indicates that the fault element for manslaughter by criminal negligence is proof of a *marked and substantial departure* from the conduct of a reasonable person. This appears to be a slightly higher fault requirement than that required for unlawful act manslaughter where the unlawful act is a negligence-based offence such as failing to provide the necessities of life or careless use of a firearm. As discussed above, the fault requirement for those forms of unlawful act manslaughter is only a *marked departure* from reasonable conduct. In *J.F.*, the Court reversed a conviction of manslaughter by criminal negligence on the basis that it was inconsistent with the jury's decision to acquit the caregiver of manslaughter by the unlawful act of failing to provide the necessities of life. In other words, it was inconsistent for a jury to acquit a person of the unlawful act manslaughter offence that required a lower degree of fault (i.e., marked departure) but then convict that person of a criminal negligence manslaughter offence that required a slightly higher level of fault (i.e., marked and substantial departure). This approach is quite complex and will require that the different degrees of negligence be carefully explained to the jury.

The additional requirement of proof of a marked *and substantial* departure from reasonable conduct is the main distinction between criminal negligence manslaughter and unlawful act manslaughter, at least where the unlawful act is a crime of negligence which, as discussed above, only requires a *marked* departure from standards of reasonable conduct. In other respects the two manslaughter offences are similar. They both require reasonable foresight of harm but not necessarily death and they both apply a non-individuated reasonable person standard that does not consider the characteristics of the accused unless they render the accused incapable of appreciating the risk. The *actus reus* of both manslaughter offences are identical in requiring that the accused's actions be a significant cause of death.

c) Manslaughter under Sections 222(5)(c) and (d)

Sections 222(5)(c) and (d) are archaic sections that refer to manslaughter by causing a person's death by threats or fear of violence or by deception or by wilfully frightening a child or sick person. These offences are at most articulation of broad causation rules that would apply to the two primary manslaughter offences articulated above.

---

191   2008 SCC 60 at para. 9 [*J.F.*].

d) Parties to a Manslaughter Offence

As discussed earlier in this chapter, an accused will be acquitted of aiding or abetting a murder if he or she does not have subjective foresight of death or wilful blindness as a form of deliberate ignorance that is the equivalent of knowledge. At the same time, however, an accused could be convicted of aiding or abetting manslaughter if "a reasonable person in all the circumstances would have appreciated that bodily harm was the foreseeable consequence of the dangerous act which was being undertaken."[192] This follows from the fault element of manslaughter, which is satisfied by objective foreseeability of bodily harm.[193] In order to be guilty of aiding and abetting manslaughter, however, "it would still be necessary to establish that the accused did or omitted to do something for the purpose of aiding the principal to commit the offence."[194] Thus, an accused who acted with the subjective purpose of aiding an assault would be found guilty of manslaughter if there was objective foreseeability that the victim would be harmed. Such a person could be found guilty of aiding and abetting manslaughter even though the principal offender was guilty of murder.

7) Suicide and Assisted Suicide

Section 14 of the *Code* provides that no person can consent to death and that consent does not affect the criminal responsibility of those who assist a willing person to commit suicide. This means that a person who agrees to assist another person, including a loved one, to commit suicide could be liable to prosecution for murder, including in cases of planning and deliberation of first-degree murder. As with infanticide, issues of prosecutorial discretion and the proper disposition of the accused are often more important than the legal definition of the offence.

Section 241 provides a separate offence of counselling or aiding and abetting a person to commit suicide whether or not suicide itself ensues. The offences of suicide and attempted suicide have been abolished so that it is only those who assist or counsel others to commit suicide who remain liable to criminal prosecution and punishment. The section 241 offence is punishable for terms of imprisonment up to fourteen years but no mandatory minimum sentence. This offence was unsuccessfully challenged under the *Charter* by Sue Rodriguez who argued that it infringed her equality rights because as a result of her terminal disease

---

192 *Jackson*, above note 136 at 391.
193 *Creighton*, above note 59.
194 R. v. *Helsdon* (2007), 216 C.C.C. (3d) 1 at para. 37 (Ont. C.A.).

she would be physically unable to take her own life.[195] The majority of the Supreme Court stressed the role of the offence in protecting the vulnerable and protecting life. A trial judge has subsequently struck down section 241(b) on the basis that the government could not justify how it discriminated against those who were not physically able to take their own life and because the absolute prohibition on assisted suicide was overbroad and grossly disproportionate as it applied to such persons. The latter two section 7 grounds had not been considered by the Supreme Court in *Rodriguez*. The judge suspended the declaration of invalidity for a year to allow Parliament to address the issue, but recognized an exemption from the law for one of the applicants who, like Sue Rodriguez, had the degenerative ALS disease resulting in total paralysis, in order to ensure an effective remedy.[196]

B. SEXUAL OFFENCES

1) Sexual Assault Offences

Sexual offences have been the site of much controversy and change over the past three decades of Canadian criminal law. In 1982, Parliament abolished the offence of rape and replaced it with three new offences of sexual assault. The offences—sexual assault under section 271; sexual assault with a weapon, threats to a third party, or causing bodily harm under section 272; and aggravated sexual assault under section 273—were deliberately modelled after the corresponding assault offences in sections 266 to 268 of the *Code* in an attempt to emphasize that sexual assault is a crime of violence. The *actus reus* was broadened from rape to sexual assault and the new offences, unlike the old offence of rape, applied to both genders and to a man who sexually assaulted his wife.

In 1992, Parliament again reformed the offence of sexual assault in order to emphasize factors that were particular to the context of sexual encounters and violence. Parliament defined consent to mean the voluntary agreement to engage in the sexual activity in question. It provided a "no means no" law that states that there will be no consent if the complainant, having initially consented to engage in sexual activity, expresses by words or conduct, a lack of agreement. The law also provides that there will be no consent if the complainant is incapable

---

195 *Rodriguez v. British Columbia (A.G.)*, [1993] 3 S.C.R. 519.
196 *Carter v. Canada (Attorney General)*, 2012 BCSC 886.

of consenting, is induced to consent by an abuse of a position of trust, power, or authority, or if a third party purports to provide consent.[197] S273 l The law also addressed the *mens rea* for sexual assault by placing a series of restrictions on the defence that the accused had a mistaken belief that the complainant was consenting to the sexual activity.

There are other sexual offences that relate specifically to sexual activity with children. In 1990, the Supreme Court struck down the offence of statutory rape of a girl under fourteen years of age regardless of the accused's belief about the girl's age or the girl's consent. The Court concluded that the offence was an absolute liability offence because it required no fault in relation to the age of the girl.[198] It also concluded that the legitimate objective of protecting children could be satisfied by new and broader offences of sexual interference that would protect both boys and girls and provide the accused a limited defence if he or she took all reasonable steps to ascertain the age of the child,[199] as S150.4 (4) well as a defence in cases where the accused was close in age to the S 150.1(l) child.[200] These new offences, like the 1982 sexual assault reforms, expand the *actus reus*. They apply to sexual interference, invitation to sexual touching, and sexual exploitation.[201] The age of consent, including for those offences, has recently been raised from fourteen to sixteen years of age.[202]

2) The *Actus Reus* of Sexual Assault

The *actus reus* of sexual assault is extremely complex because it involves a generic definition of assault, a specific definition of what constitutes consent for the purpose of sexual assault offences, the Court's interpretation of consent as depending on the subjective views of the complainant, as well as common law restrictions that vitiate consent.

a) Assaults under Section 265

Section 265 provides a generic definition that defines all assaults to include the intentional application of force, directly or indirectly, to another person without that person's consent[203] or attempting or threatening by acts or gestures to apply force if it causes the other person to

---

197 *Code*, above note 1, s. 273.1.
198 *R. v. Hess*, [1990] 2 S.C.R. 906.
199 *Code*, above note 1, s. 150.1(4).
200 *Ibid.*, s. 150.1(1).
201 *Ibid.*, ss. 151, 152, & 153.
202 *Ibid.*, s. 150.1(2).
203 *Ibid.*, s. 265(1).

§265(2) believe upon reasonable grounds that the accused has the ability to effect his or her purpose.[204] These two provisions define different ways of committing an assault.[205] The result is a broad definition of assault that can include any touching without consent.

b) Sexual Assaults Distinguished from Other Assaults and Sexual Offences

The courts have distinguished sexual assaults from assaults on the basis of whether the circumstances viewed objectively are sexual. The intent or motive of the accused to obtain sexual gratification may be a factor, but it is not a requirement. Sexual assault differs from the sexual offences with respect to young persons in sections 151 through 153.1 of the *Code* because it does not require that the touching be for a sexual purpose.[206] The courts will examine all the circumstances including "the part of the body touched, the nature of the conduct, the words and gestures accompanying the act and all other circumstances surrounding the conduct[207] in determining whether the assault is sexual. The Supreme Court has determined that a man grabbing a fifteen year old around her breasts and shoulders while saying "Come on, dear, don't hit me, I know you want it" was an assault of a sexual nature.[208] More controversially, that Court has also held that a father's actions in grabbing his three-year-old son's genitals causing bruising and severe pain in an attempt to discipline the child who had been grabbing the private parts of others was a sexual assault because it invaded the child's sexual integrity. Sopinka J. dissented on the basis that the father's actions constituted assault, not sexual assault.[209] The Court has continued to confirm that with respect to sexual assault "the Crown need not prove that the accused had any *mens rea* with respect to the sexual nature of his or her behaviour."[210]

c) Consent under Section 273.1

In 1992, Parliament enacted section 273.1, which defines consent for the purposes of the sexual offences as "the voluntary agreement of the complainant to engage in the sexual activity in question." There is, for ex-

---

204   *Ibid.*, s. 265(2).
205   *R. v. MacKay*, [2005] 3 S.C.R. 725.
206   *R. v. Lutoslawski*, 2010 SCC 49, [2010] 3 S.C.R. 60.
207   *R. v. Chase*, [1987] 2 S.C.R. 293.
208   *Ibid.*
209   *R. v. V.(K.B.)*, [1993] 2 S.C.R. 857.
210   *R. v. Ewanchuk*, [1999] 1 S.C.R. 330 at para. 25 [*Ewanchuk*].

ample, no voluntary consent when the accused threatened to distribute nude photographs of his ex-girlfriend if she did not have sex with him.[211]

As will be discussed in greater detail later in this chapter, the 1992 reforms were called the "no means no" reforms because they also provide a concrete list of circumstances in which consent would not be obtained. The idea was to provide a legal definition of what did and did not constitute consent. A person who thought that no meant yes or that consent could be given by a third party or by a person who was not capable of giving consent would arguably have a mistaken belief about the law, which, as discussed in chapter 3, cannot be an excuse for criminal conduct.

d) Consent in *Ewanchuk*

In a very important decision rendered in 1999, *R. v. Ewanchuk*,[212] the Supreme Court interpreted the *actus reus* of sexual assault as requiring proof of three elements "i) touching, ii) the sexual nature of the conduct, and iii) the absence of consent." The Court held that the touching and sexual nature were determined on an objective basis, but that the third factor of absence of consent "is subjective and determined by reference to the complainant's internal state of mind towards the touching at the time that it occurred."[213] If the complainant says that she did not consent, the only issue is whether she is a credible complainant. The accused's perception of the complainant's state of mind is not relevant"[214] when determining whether there was consent for the purpose of determining whether the *actus reus* has been committed. The accused's belief that the complainant consented is only relevant to determine the *mens rea* of the offence.

The Supreme Court in *Ewanchuk* rejected the defence of implied consent to sexual assault.[215] In other words, it rejected the idea that although the complainant did not actually consent, her conduct satisfied an objective standard of implied consent. Thus, as a matter of determining the *actus reus* of consent "[t]he absence of consent . . . is subjective and determined by reference to the complainant's subjective internal state of mind toward the touching, at the time it occurred."[216] The trier of fact "may only come to one of two conclusions: the complainant either consented or not. There is no third option. If the trier of fact accepts the complain-

---

211 *R. v. D.S.* (2004), 72 O.R. (3d) 223 (C.A.), aff'd [2005] 1 S.C.R. 914.
212 Above note 208 at para. 25.
213 *Ibid.* at para. 26.
214 *Ibid.* at para. 30.
215 *Ibid.*
216 *Ibid.* at para. 26.

ant's testimony that she did not consent, no matter how strongly her conduct may contradict that claim, the absence of consent is established."[217]

On the facts of *Ewanchuk*, the Court reversed an acquittal in a case where a man repeatedly made sexual advances to a seventeen-year-old woman who was applying for a job. The Court held that the judge's determination that the woman subjectively did not consent to the repeated sexual touching and that she subjectively feared force from the accused should have been determinative that there was no consent for the purpose of determining whether the *actus reus* of sexual assault had occurred.

The existence of consent for the purpose of defining the *actus reus* of sexual assault as a result of *Ewanchuk* depends on the subjective perceptions of the victim as opposed to external and objective standards of law. Similarly, consent will be negated by the complainant's fear of the application of force regardless of the reasonableness of the fear or whether it was communicated to the accused. A statement by the victim that she did not consent or did so because of fear will be determinative unless it is found not to be a credible statement of her state of mind at the time the offence occurred. The Court is understandably concerned about maximizing the physical and sexual integrity of women and rejecting the rape myths that women implicitly consent to sexual activity unless they protest or resist or clearly expressly fear. The Court's vehicle for rejecting these myths is to make the issue of consent for the purpose of defining *actus reus* dependent on the subjective perceptions of the complainant even if they are uncommunicated and unreasonable.

e)   Specific Instances Where Consent Is Not Valid

Various provisions of the *Criminal Code*, as well as the common law, deem that consent even if apparently given by the complainant will not be valid in certain circumstances.

Section 265(3) of the *Code* provides that

> no consent is obtained where the complainant submits or does not resist by reason of
> a)   the application of force to the complainant or to a person other than the complainant;
> b)   threats or fear of the application of force to the complainant or to a person other than the complainant;
> c)   fraud; or
> d)   the exercise of authority.

---

217   *Ibid.* at para. 31.

In R. v. *Ewanchuk*, the Supreme Court held that under section 265(3) (b) "the complainant's fear need not be reasonable, nor must it be communicated to the accused in order for consent to be vitiated. While the plausibility of the alleged fear, and any overt expressions of it, are obviously relevant to assessing the credibility of the complainant's claim that she consented out of fear, the approach is subjective."[218]

Traditionally, consent has only been vitiated by fraud that relates to the nature of the act itself or the identity of the person conducting the act. This would mean that a person who has sex with another without disclosing the existence of a sexually transmitted disease would not be found guilty of assault or sexual assault. The Court has understandably revisited this idea in the era of AIDS. In R. v. *Cuerrier*[219] Cory J., with the concurrence of three other judges, held that fraud could negate consent in a case where a dishonest act in the form of falsehoods or a failure to disclose would have "the effect of exposing the person consenting to a significant risk of serious bodily harm." The Crown must also prove that the complainant would have refused to engage in unprotected sex with the accused had she been informed that he was HIV-positive. Justice McLachlin with the concurrence of Justice Gonthier would have expanded the traditional notion of fraud as to the nature and quality of the act to include the transmission of sexually transmitted diseases where there is a high risk of infection and the accused knew or ought to have known that fraud induced consent to unprotected sex. Justice L'Heureux Dubé would have interpreted fraud even more broadly to include all deceptions that induced consent to the touching. Some courts have applied *Cuerrier* broadly, for example, holding that deceptive conduct about the use of contraception could vitiate consent in a case where a woman did not want to become pregnant.[220]

In addition to defining consent for the purpose of sexual offences as the voluntary agreement to engage in the sexual activity in question, Parliament in 1992 provided in section 273.1(2) that no consent is obtained where

a)   the agreement is expressed by the words or conduct of a person other than the complainant;

---

218   *Ibid.* at para. 39.

219   [1998] 2 S.C.R. 371.

220   R. v. *Hutchinson*, 2010 NSCA 3. The Court of Appeal also indicated that no consent to the sexual activity might exist because the complainant only consented to sexual activity with contraception. *Ibid.* at para. 38. Bateman J.A. dissented on the basis that there was no authority for the proposition that "a lie about the use of contraceptives or having been vasectomized is a matter for the criminal law." *Ibid.* at para. 157.

b)   the complainant is incapable of consenting to the activity;

c)   the accused induces the complainant to engage in the activity by abusing a position of trust, power or authority;

d)   the complainant expresses, by words or conduct, a lack of agreement to engage in the activity; or

e)   the complainant, having consented to engage in sexual activity, expresses, by words or conduct, a lack of agreement to engage in the activity.[221]

This provision defines certain examples where the accused will be precluded from arguing that the prohibited act of sexual assault did not occur because the complainant consented. It establishes as an objective statement of law that there cannot be consent if a) agreement is given by a third party; b) the complainant is incapable of consenting; c) the complainant is induced to participate by abuse of a position of trust, power, or authority; or (d, e) the complainant, expresses a lack of agreement, by either words or comments, to engage or continue to engage in sexual activity. The above examples of deemed non-consent are not exhaustive. It should be noted that the accused can still argue that although there was no consent in these situations and the *actus reus* was committed, he or she still did not have the *mens rea* to commit sexual assault.

In *R. v. J.A*,[222] a majority of the Supreme Court held that consent required the conscious agreement of the complainant to the sexual activity in question and that there was no consent in a case where a complainant consented in advance to choking and sexual experimentation while she was unconscious. The majority stressed that Parliament "defined consent in a way that requires the complainant to be conscious throughout the sexual activity in question."[223] The rejection of advance consent was justified in part by reference to section 273.1(2)(d) and (e), which contemplate that the complainants can revoke consent at any time as well as vulnerability of an unconscious complainant. McLachlin C.J. explained: "When the complainant loses consciousness, she loses the ability to either oppose or consent to the sexual activity that occurs. Finding that such a person is consenting would effectively negate the right of the complainant to change her mind at any point in the sexual encounter."[224] The Court stressed the need for vigilance

---

221   *Code*, above note 1, s. 273.1, introduced in *An Act to Amend the Criminal Code (Sexual Assault)*, S.C. 1992, c. 38, s. 1.

222   [2011] 2 S.C.R. 440.

223   *Ibid.* at para. 33.

224   *Ibid.* at para. 53.

about consent in the context of sexual assault that might not be applicable to other contexts such as the consent that an unconscious person may give to surgery. It recognized, however, that this doctrine may seem "unrealistic" in trusting relationships where one partner would be unable legally to consent in advance to sexual activity including kissing while that person is asleep. Nevertheless, the Court held that Parliament's requirement for conscious consent to the sexual activity in question "produces just results in the vast majority of cases" and helps combat stereotypes that have "undermined the law's ability to address the crime of sexual assault." [225] The Court also declined to create a *de minimis* exception because "even mild non-consensual touching of a sexual nature can have profound implications for the complainant."[226] Justice Fish with two others dissented and argued that the Court's rejection of advance consent unreasonably limited sexual autonomy and overshot Parliament's policy concerns which were to protect women "who said no"[227] and not the complainant who agreed in advance to the sexual activity in question.

Finally, courts have applied the *Jobidon* principle that consent can be vitiated for policy reasons when the accused intends to and causes serious bodily harm to forms of sexual activity that are intended and do cause such harms. In a case where a complainant sustained bruising from a beating with a belt and bleeding from her rectum for a number of days (and also claimed that she did not consent), the Ontario Court of Appeal held that Parliament had not exhaustively defined consent for the purpose of sexual assault. It held that "the consent of the complainant, assuming it was given, cannot detract from the inherently degrading and dehumanizing nature of the conduct. Although the law must recognize individual freedom and autonomy, when the activity in question involves pursuing sexual gratification by deliberately inflicting pain upon another that gives rise to bodily harm, then the personal interest of the individuals involved must yield to the more compelling societal interests which are challenged by such behaviour."[228] The court noted that the exemptions for socially desirable activities in *Jobidon* did not include sexual activities. Today, such a case would for the purpose of determining the *actus reus* of consent likely be decided on the basis of the complainant's subjective perceptions that there was not consent.

---

225   *Ibid.* at para. 65.
226   *Ibid.* at para. 63.
227   *Ibid.* at para. 112.
228   *R. v. Welch* (1995), 101 C.C.C. (3d) 216 at 239 (Ont. C.A.). See also *R. v. Robinson* (2001), 153 C.C.C. (3d) 398 at para. 62 (Ont. C.A.), extending this to less serious harms that deliberately inflicted pain causing bodily harm.

3) The *Mens Rea* of Sexual Assault

The *mens rea* of sexual assault requires an intentional application of force without consent. There is no requirement to demonstrate that the accused had a motive of sexual gratification. Traditionally, the *mens rea* for sexual assault has in accordance with common law presumptions been interpreted as requiring proof of subjective fault in relation to all aspects of the prohibited act of applying force without consent. Recklessness,[229] as well as knowledge and wilful blindness,[230] has traditionally been held to be a sufficient form of fault.

a) Mistaken Belief in Consent

Before the 1992 reforms, the Court applied the traditional common law presumption of subjective *mens rea* to hold that the Crown had to establish that the accused had subjective fault in relation to all aspects of the *actus reus* of the crime of sexual assault. In *R. v. Pappajohn*,[231] the Supreme Court held that an accused in a rape trial could have a defence of honest but not necessarily reasonable mistake that the complainant consented. Dickson J. derived the defence of mistake of fact from the *mens rea* of the particular offence. He concluded that because the *mens rea* of rape was subjective intent or recklessness relating to all the elements of the offence, it was not necessary that an accused's mistaken belief about consent be reasonable. He stated:

> It is not clear how one can properly relate reasonableness (an element in offences of negligence) to rape (a "true crime" and not an offence of negligence). To do so, one must, I think, take the view that the *mens rea* only goes to the physical act of intercourse and not to non-consent, and acquittal comes only if the mistake is reasonable. This, upon the authorities, is not a correct view, the intent in rape being not merely to have intercourse, but to have it with a non-consenting woman. If the jury finds that mistake, whether reasonable or unreasonable, there should be no conviction. If, upon the entire record, there is evidence of mistake to cast a reasonable doubt upon the existence of a criminal mind, then the prosecution has failed to make its case.[232]

Although the accused's belief did not have to be reasonable, its reasonableness would be evidence considered by the jury to determine wheth-

---

229 *R. v. Pappajohn* (1980), 52 C.C.C. (2d) 481 (S.C.C.) [*Pappajohn*].
230 *R. v. Sansregret*, [1985] 1 S.C.R. 570 [*Sansregret*].
231 *Pappajohn*, above note 227.
232 *Ibid.* at 497.

er the accused actually had an honest belief in consent. The *Criminal Code* was subsequently amended to provide that the judge "shall instruct the jury, when reviewing all the evidence relating to the determination of the honesty of the accused's belief, to consider the presence or absence of reasonable ground for that belief."[233]

b) Establishing an Air of Reality for a Mistake of Fact Defence

Although, the Supreme Court agreed on the conceptual nature of the defence of mistake of fact and its relation to the *mens rea* of the particular offence, it disagreed on its application in particular cases. In *Pappajohn*, Dickson J. was in dissent in concluding that the jury should have been instructed to consider the defence of mistake of fact. McIntyre J. for the majority held that the only realistic issue that could arise on the facts of the case was whether there was consent or no consent, not a third option of a mistaken belief in consent. In his view, there should be something more than the accused's assertion that he believed the complainant consented to justify instructing the jury on the mistaken belief defence. In a subsequent case, however, a majority of the Court indicated that there need not be evidence independent of the accused to support a mistake of fact. It was possible that the defence could arise when the accused alleged consent, and the complainant alleged no consent.[234] At the same time, there must be some plausible evidence to support a claim of mistake of fact, and a bare assertion by the accused of a mistaken belief is not sufficient.[235] In one case, a majority of the Court found there to be an air of reality to the defence of mistaken belief in consent when the accused testified to consent and the complainant testified to absence of memory. Both Justices McLachlin and L'Heureux-Dubé dissented on the basis that there was no plausible evidence of ambiguous conduct that could create the basis for the defence of mistake about consent.[236]

The controversy about when the jury should be instructed about the defence of mistaken belief in the complainant's consent continues. As will be seen, however, this debate should be influenced by 1992 changes to the sexual assault offence. There will now not be an air of reality with respect to the mistake of fact defence unless the complainant in some way communicated an agreement to engage in sexual

---

233 *Code*, above note 1, s. 265(4). This was held to be consistent with ss. 7, 11(d), and 11(f) of the *Charter*, above note 148, in R. v. *Osolin* (1994), 86 C.C.C. (3d) 481 (S.C.C.) [*Osolin*].

234 *Osolin, ibid.*

235 R. v. *Park* (1995), 99 C.C.C. (3d) 1 (S.C.C.).

236 R. v. *Esau*, [1997] 2 S.C.R. 777.

activity with the accused.[237] For example, there would be no air of reality to a mistaken belief in consent defence in a case where an accused relies on consent given by an unconscious complainant in advance. The Court explained it would be impossible for the accused to take reasonable steps to ascertain consent at the moment that the *actus reus* occurs because the complainant would be unconscious. During that time, the accused could not believe that the complainant had said yes and communicated consent to engage in the sexual activity.[238] This demanding approach to mistaken belief in consent follows from the definition of consent in section 273.1(1) as the voluntary agreement of the complainant to engage in the sexual activity in question. Even if there is the belief based in some words or actions of the complainant, section 273.2(b) would still require the accused to take reasonable steps in the circumstances known to him or her at the time to ascertain whether the complainant was consenting. This requirement could influence the determination of whether there was an air of reality to the mistake of fact, for example, in a case where there is no evidence that the accused took any steps to ascertain whether the complainant consented.

c) Wilful Blindness in Relation to Consent

In *Sansregret*,[239] the Supreme Court entered a conviction for rape despite the fact that the trial judge had found that at the time that the accused had sex with his ex-girlfriend with whom he had lived that he honestly believed that she consented even though he had terrorized her with a knife and blows after having broken into her house in the middle of the night. In an effort to calm down the accused after an hour of this behaviour, the complainant pretended that there was some hope of reconciliation and they had intercourse. A similar incident had occurred a month before and the complainant had reported the inci-

---

237 *Ewanchuk*, above note 210.

238 Chief Justice McLachlin has explained: "In *Ewanchuk*, this Court held that it is not sufficient for the accused to have believed that the complainant was subjectively consenting in her mind: 'In order to cloak the accused's actions in moral innocence, the evidence must show that he believed that the complainant communicated consent to engage in the sexual activity in question.' It thus is not sufficient for the accused to have believed the complainant was consenting: he must also take reasonable steps to ascertain consent, and must believe that the complainant communicated her consent to engage in the sexual activity in question. This is impossible if the complainant is unconscious." *R. v. J.A.*, [2011] 2 S.C.R. 440 at para. 48. Fish J. in dissent argued that he "read s. 273.2 differently" so that it could apply to a belief in prior consent and ascertainment of prior consent. *Ibid.* at para. 107.

239 *Sansregret*, above note 230.

dent to the police. The trial judge had found that "no one in his right mind could have believed that the complainant's dramatic about-face stemmed from anything other than fear. But the accused did. He saw what he wanted to see, heard what he wanted to hear and believed what he wanted to believe."

The Supreme Court reversed the acquittal and entered a conviction, holding that the accused should have been convicted on the basis that the accused was wilfully blind to the lack of consent. The Court explained that in the circumstances, the accused had engaged in "self-deception to the point of willful blindness" and that "where the accused becomes deliberately blind to the existing facts, he is fixed by law with actual knowledge" on the basis that he is at fault "in deliberately failing to inquire when he knows there is a reason for inquiry."[240] In subsequent cases, the Court has affirmed that wilful blindness is a form of deliberate ignorance equivalent to knowledge and distinct from both recklessness and negligence and not satisfied by the accused's mere failure to inquire into whether prohibited circumstances or consequences exist.[241]

d) Restrictions on the *Pappajohn* Mistake of Fact Defence under Section 273.2

The Supreme Court struck down so-called rape shield restrictions on the admission of the complainant's prior sexual conduct as a violation of the accused's *Charter* right to make full answer and defence, in part because the restrictions could deprive the accused of evidence to support the *Pappajohn* defence. McLachlin J. stated that the *Pappajohn* defence

> rests on the concept that the accused may honestly but mistakenly (and not necessarily reasonably) have believed that the complainant was consenting to the sexual act. If the accused can raise a reasonable doubt as to his intention on the basis that he honestly held such a belief, he is not guilty under our law and is entitled to an acquittal. The basis of the accused's honest belief in the complainant's consent may be sexual acts performed by the complainant at some other time or place.[242]

In dissent, L'Heureux-Dubé J. argued that the complainant's prior sexual activity with a person other than the accused would never provide an air of reality for the jury to consider a defence of mistake of fact,

---

240 *Ibid.* at 584.
241 *Briscoe*, above note 64 at para. 24.
242 *R. v. Seaboyer* (1991), 66 C.C.C. (3d) 321 at 393 (S.C.C.) [*Seaboyer*].

if it were "operating in an intellectual environment that is free of rape myth and stereotype about women."[243]

In response to *Seaboyer*, the law of sexual assault was amended in 1992 to restrict the availability of the mistake of fact defence. Section 273.2 provides:

> It is not a defence to a charge under section 271, 272 or 273 that the accused believed that the complainant consented to the activity that forms the subject-matter of the charge, where
> a) the accused's belief arise from the accused's
>   i) self-induced intoxication or
>   ii) recklessness or willful blindness; or
> b) the accused did not take reasonable steps, in the circumstances known to him at the time, to ascertain whether the complainant was consenting.

The accused's belief that the complainant consented is not a defence if it arose from the accused's "self-induced intoxication," his "recklessness or willful blindness," or if "the accused did not take reasonable steps, in the circumstances known to the accused at the time, to ascertain that the complainant was consenting."

The reference to recklessness contemplates that an accused who adverted to the risk that the complainant did not consent has always had the *mens rea* required for sexual assault. The reference to self-induced intoxication not being relevant represents traditional but constitutionally suspect law that provides that intoxication may never be a defence to crimes classified as general intent.[244] This issue will be discussed in greater detail later in this chapter.

The reference to wilful blindness codifies *Sansregret* and precludes the defence when an accused is subjectively aware of the need to inquire into consent but deliberately declines to inquire because he does not wish to know the truth. The culpability in wilful blindness was the accused's refusal to inquire whether the complainant was consenting, when he was "aware of the need for some inquiry . . . [but declined] to

---

243 *Ibid.* at 363.

244 *R. v. Leary* (1977), 33 C.C.C. (2d) 473 (S.C.C.). But for a recognition of a possible defence of extreme intoxication see *Daviault*, below note 265. In addition, s. 33.1 of the *Code*, above note 1, would deem the fault of self-induced intoxication sufficient to form the fault of sexual assault and other general intent offences involving an assault or interference or threat of interference with the bodily integrity of another person. See ch. 7(E), "Extreme Intoxication and General Intent Offences" for further discussion.

make the inquiry because he . . . [does] not wish to know the truth."[245] *Sansregret* narrowed the *Pappajohn* defence by holding that the accused was presumed to have guilty knowledge of the absence of consent when, knowing the need for inquiry as to consent, he remained ignorant.

e) The Requirement of Reasonable Steps in Section 273.2(b)

The denial in section 273.2(b) of the mistake of fact unless the accused takes reasonable steps in the circumstances known to him or her at the time to ascertain whether the complainant was consenting to the activity in question combines subjective and objective fault elements in a novel and creative manner. As such, it breaks away from the idea in *Pappajohn* that the contours of the mistake of fact can be deduced from the fault element of the offence. On the one hand, section 273.2(b) bases the accused's obligation to take reasonable steps to ascertain consent on the basis of what the accused subjectively knows of the circumstances. The accused's obligation to take reasonable steps is only based on what he subjectively knows at the time. On the other hand, section 273.2(b) requires the accused to act as a reasonable person would in the circumstances by taking reasonable steps to ascertain whether the complainant was consenting. Much will depend on the courts' view of what reasonable steps are necessary to ascertain consent. Some judges may find that positive steps are required in most, if not all, situations regardless of the accused's subjective perception of the circumstances. Others may only require such steps if the complainant has indicated resistance or lack of consent in some way that is subjectively known to the accused.

In *R. v. Ewanchuk*,[246] the majority of the Court did not directly apply section 273.2 despite the fact pointed out by the dissenters that it applied to the sexual assault in question.[247] Major J. for the majority followed the traditional *Pappajohn* view that mistake of fact was a denial of *mens rea* and was necessary to protect the morally innocent. In part drawing on the new definition of consent, however, he indicated:

---

245 *Sansregret*, above note 230 at para. 22. The accused had broken into his ex-girl-friend's apartment and threatened her with a knife. Less than a month earlier, the complainant had reported a rape after a similar incident with the accused.

246 Above note 210.

247 L'Heureux-Dubé J. argued that the mistake of fact defence would not arise unless the accused took reasonable steps to ascertain consent. She indicated that moving from a massage to sexual touching without inquiring about consent was not reasonable and that once that complainant had expressed non-consent "the accused has a corresponding escalating obligation to take additional steps to ascertain consent." *Ibid.* at para. 99.

In order to cloak the accused's actions in moral innocence, the evidence must show that he believed that the complainant *communicated consent to engage in the sexual activity in question.* A belief by the accused that the complainant, in her own mind, wanted him to touch her, but did not express that desire, is not a defence. The accused's speculation as to what was going on in the complainant's mind provides no defence.[248]

The above statement would seem to restrict the mistaken belief in consent defence to cases in which the complainant communicated in an ambiguous manner that she consented to sexual activity. The mistake of fact defence was thus influenced more by statutory definitions of consent in section 273.1 as the voluntary agreement to engage in sexual activity than the reasonable steps requirement in section 273.2. *Ewanchuk* suggests that the accused may only have a mistaken belief defence when he mistakenly believes that the victim said yes through her words or actions. The accused may not have a mistaken belief defence if he only claims not to have heard the victim say no. This would mean that the accused would only have a defence in mistaken belief in consent if 1) he believed the victim communicated consent to the sexual activity in question and 2) he had taken reasonable steps, given the circumstances known to him at the time, to discover whether the victim consented to the sexual activity in question.

In any event, the mistake of fact defence was denied in *Ewanchuk* because the complainant said no and "there is nothing on the record to support the accused's claim that he continued to believe her to be consenting, or that he re-established consent before resuming physical contact."[249] In another case, the Ontario Court of Appeal stressed that the complainant's prior rejection of the accused's advances, as well as her objections when the accused entered her apartment and tried to kiss her, required the accused to take reasonable steps before he engaged in sexual intercourse: "The legislative scheme replaces the assumptions traditionally—and inappropriately—associated with passivity."[250]

The Supreme Court has yet to interpret the new requirement in section 273.2(b) that the accused take reasonable steps in the circumstances known to him or her to ascertain consent. The Manitoba Court of Appeal has described it as "a quasi-objective" provision that requires the court to ascertain what circumstances the accused knew about and then to ask "if a reasonable man was aware of the same cir-

248 *Ibid.* at para. 46 [emphasis in original].
249 *Ibid.* at para. 58.
250 *R. v. Cornejo* (2003), 68 O.R. (3d) 117 at para. 21 (C.A.) [*Cornejo*].

cumstances, would he take further steps before proceeding with the sexual activity?"[251] In her concurring judgment in *Ewanchuk*, Justice L'Heureux-Dubé interpreted section 273.2(b) to require that the accused take reasonable steps to ascertain consent in all cases when she stated that "until an accused first takes reasonable steps to assure that there is consent, the defence of honest but mistaken belief in consent does not arise."[252] She indicated that the fact that the complainant did not refuse a message from the accused was not a reasonable step because "the accused cannot rely on the complainant's silence or ambiguous conduct to initiate sexual contact."[253] This approach could require some sign of consent in all cases. In a case where a co-worker had made numerous sexual advances to a woman and been rejected, the Ontario Court of Appeal also indicated that there was a need for "steps *before* he engaged in sexual activity to ascertain whether she was consenting."[254] Although some might criticize a requirement to take positive steps in all cases as unrealistic, it is also supported by the idea expressed by the majority of the Court in *Ewanchuk* that an accused cannot take silence, passivity, or ambiguous conduct as consent and must believe that the complainant has affirmatively communicated consent through words or actions. In any event, it is clear that the requirement to take reasonable steps will be tailored to the overall circumstances known to the accused.

It is also clear that section 273.2(b) contemplates what has been described as "a proportionate relationship"[255] between the circumstances known to the accused and the reasonable steps that are required. Once a complainant has expressed an unwillingness to engage in sexual activity, the accused must make certain that the complainant has changed her mind. In such circumstances, the accused cannot rely on lapse of time, silence, or equivalent conduct.[256] As Justice L'Heureux Dubé indicated in *Ewanchuk*, "where a complainant expresses non-consent, the accused has a corresponding escalating obligation to take additional steps to ascertain consent."[257]

---

251 R. v. *Malcolm* (2000), 147 C.C.C. (3d) 34 at para. 24 (Man. C.A.), leave to appeal to S.C.C. refused (2000), 150 C.C.C. (3d) vi.
252 *Ewanchuk*, above note 210 at para. 99.
253 *Ibid*.
254 *Cornejo*, above note 250 at para. 32 [emphasis in original].
255 R. v. *G.(R.)* (1994), 38 C.R. (4th) 123 at para. 29 (B.C.C.A.).
256 *Ewanchuk*, above note 210.
257 *Ibid*. at para. 99.

f) Mistake of Fact Precluded if Based on a Mistake of Law

The 1992 amendments not only altered the mistake of fact defence by introducing a requirement in section 273.2(b) that the accused take reasonable steps in the circumstances known to him at the time to ascertain consent, but it also may have eliminated some claims of mistaken belief in consent as errors of law through the definition of consent and specific instances of non-consent in section 273.1. As discussed earlier in this chapter, section 273.1(1) defines consent as the voluntary agreement of the complainant to engage in the sexual activity in question and section 273.2(2) provides a list of circumstances where consent is not valid. The Supreme Court has subsequently indicated that the accused's "belief that silence, passivity or ambiguous conduct constitutes consent is a mistake of law and provides no defence."[258] This means that an accused who argued that he mistakenly believed the complainant consented because he thought that no meant yes or that he thought that yes to one sexual activity meant yes to another would be precluded from arguing this as a mistake of fact because it now constitutes a mistake of law. Given the Supreme Court's ruling in J.A. that advance consent by a complainant who was unconscious at the time of the sexual activity was not legally valid, the accused's claim of mistaken belief in consent in such a situation may also now be precluded as a mistake of law.[259]

g) The Constitutionality of Section 273.2(b)

The Ontario Court of Appeal upheld the constitutionality of section 273.2(b) in R. v. Darrach.[260] Although the provision introduced an "objective component into the mental element of the offence," it was "personalized according to the subjective awareness of the accused at the time" and did not require the accused to take all reasonable steps to ascertain whether the complainant consented. Morden A.C.J.O. concluded that the subjective mens rea requirement "remains largely intact" and that the new provision did not require a mistaken belief to be reasonable. He posited a situation in which an accused who made an unreasonable mistake about consent could be acquitted because he took reasonable steps to ascertain that the complainant was consenting. Although it is true that the provision combines subjective and objective fault elements, the likelihood that any mistake that remains after

---

258 Ewanchuk , above note 210 at para. 51.
259 The majority of the Court in R. v. J.A., above note 238, did not directly address this point, but Fish J. in his dissent stated that the majority's position meant that the accused's belief in the validity of advance consent "would constitute a mistake of law, which cannot avail as a defence." Ibid. at para. 118.
260 (1998), 122 C.C.C. (3d) 225 at 252 (Ont. C.A.) [Darrach].

reasonable steps have been taken would still be unreasonable must be very small. The Supreme Court unfortunately did not deal with section 273.2(b) when it dismissed the accused's appeal in this case.[261]

Some have warned that section 273.2(b) is vulnerable under the *Charter* because it does not on its face require a marked departure from reasonable standards.[262] To the extent that section 273.2(b) bases liability on a failure to take reasonable steps to ascertain that the complainant is consenting, it can be argued that there is a need for the accused to engage in a marked departure from what would be reasonable in the circumstances as now required in *Beatty*[263] whenever negligence is used as a form of criminal liability. On the other hand, section 273.2(b) can be interpreted as it was by the Ontario Court of Appeal in *Darrach* to stress subjective fault based on what circumstances are actually known to the accused. Such an interpretation might, however, add little to the already existing law that the accused's mistaken belief in consent is not a valid defence if it is based on wilful blindness.

It has also been argued that section 273.2(b) may violate the principle of fundamental justice that intentional conduct should be punished more seriously than negligent conduct as articulated by the Court in *Creighton*.[264] This is a clearly established principle of fundamental justice that is invoked by those who argue that the appropriate way to have restricted the mistake of fact defence would have been to create a separate offence of negligent sexual assault.[265] This principle of fundamental justice would, however, only clearly apply if section 273.2(b) would convict the accused simply on the basis that he or she ought to have known that the victim was not consenting. As discussed above, section 273.2(b) is an innovative blended form of subjective and objective fault that has been interpreted in a manner that stresses its subjective components. As such, the principle of fundamental justice that requires the different culpability of intentional and negligent conduct is not clearly engaged. In addition, one practical reason for not introducing a new offence of negligent sexual assault would be concerns that in a criminal justice system where most cases do not receive a full trial that many cases would be resolved by guilty pleas to this less serious offence.

---

261 *R. v. Darrach* (2000), 148 C.C.C. (3d) 97 (S.C.C.).
262 D. Stuart, *Canadian Criminal Law*, 5th ed. (Toronto: Thomson Carswell, 2007) at 325 [Stuart].
263 *Beatty*, above note 182.
264 *Creighton*, above note 59.
265 Stuart, above note 262 at 326.

h) Sexual Assault and Intoxication

Sexual assault has been held to be a crime of general intent where the intent does not go beyond the commission of the immediate act. This interpretation stresses the idea that sexual assault is a crime of violence that need not be committed for an ulterior purpose such as the achievement of sexual gratification.[266] As discussed in chapter 7, the normal rule is that evidence of intoxication is not considered capable of raising a reasonable doubt about a general intent offence such as sexual assault.

The Court's decision in *R. v. Daviault*[267] raised the possibility that an accused charged with sexual assault could raise a defence of extreme intoxication. *Daviault* was a sexual assault case and the accused at the new trial ordered by the Court would have had an opportunity to establish on a balance of probabilties a defence of extreme intoxication producing involuntary conduct. Such a defence would also have to be supported with expert evidence about the degree of intoxication. If successful, the defence would have produced a complete acquittal in contrast to the traditional intoxication defence that operates to raise a reasonable doubt about a specific intent offence, such as murder or robbery, but would not affect the ability to convict the accused of lesser included general intent offences such as manslaughter and assault.

As discussed in chapter 7, concerns about possible acquittals in cases following *Daviault* led to the quick enactment of sections 33.1 to 33.3 of the *Code*. These provisions deny the *Daviault* defence in cases where an accused was charged with sexual assault or indeed any offence involving an assault or interference with bodily integrity. Parliament resisted the Court's suggestion that it enact a new intoxication-based offence to cover such cases in part because it was thought important to convict voluntarily intoxicated accused of sexual assault and not some other intoxication-based offence that would be regarded as a less serious offence. As discussed earlier in this chapter, similar concerns influenced the decision not to enact a new offence of negligent sexual assault as a means to restrict the mistaken belief in consent defence.

An accused charged with sexual assault would not have an intoxication defence absent a successful *Charter* challenge to sections 33.1 to 33.3 of the *Criminal Code* and the proof on a balance of probabilities of the *Daviault* defence of extreme intoxication.

---

266 *R. v. Bernard*, [1988] 2 S.C.R. 833.
267 [1994] 3 S.C.R. 63 [*Daviault*].

C. PROPERTY OFFENCES

A broad array of property crimes are found in the *Criminal Code* and it is only possible to examine a few here. As with all criminal offences, it is important to distinguish the prohibited act and the prohibited fault elements. As will be seen, both theft and fraud follow trends to broadly defined act requirements. At the same time, theft has a particularly high *mens rea* requirement. Fraud has a slightly lower fault requirement that includes some forms of recklessness and does not require subjective appreciation that one is acting dishonestly.

1) Theft

The *actus reus* of theft under section 322 of the *Criminal Code* requires the taking or conversion of anything.[268] Anything must be a type of property that can be converted in a manner that deprives the victim. It does not include confidential information that has not been reduced to a list or other tangible thing.[269] Conversion can be affected by delivery of goods or the conversion of property to the accused's own use with the intent to deprive the other person of the property.[270] Section 322(2) broadens the *actus reus* by providing that a person commits theft when, with the intent to steal, he or she begins to cause anything to move or to become moveable. Section 322(4) provides that it is not material whether the person in possession of the property is in lawful possession of the property.[271] It could be argued that a person who knowingly receives double payment for his or her services or who buys something from a store does not commit the *actus reus* of the theft because there is no taking of property. Such approaches, however, ignore the breadth of the *actus reus* of theft, which includes not only taking but also conversion of property for one's own use.[272] Any concern about overreaching in defining the *actus reus* of theft should be addressed by the high *mens rea* requirement of the offence.

The *mens rea* of theft requires that a person take or convert something "fraudulently and without colour of right." The requirement of a fraudulent intent requires deceit, or an intention to deceive, and dis-

---

268 *Code*, above note 1, s. 322.
269 *R. v. Stewart*, [1988] 1 S.C.R. 963. Note, however, that there are many other separate theft-based offences, including the offence of unauthorized use of a computer and theft of telecommunications signals. *Code, ibid.*, ss. 342.1 and 326.
270 *R. v. Milne*, [1992] 1 S.C.R. 697 [*Milne*].
271 See also *Code*, above note 1, s. 328.
272 *Milne*, above note 270; *R. v. Dawond* (1975), 27 C.C.C. (2d) 300 (Alta. C.A.).

honesty.[273] A colour of right is, as discussed in chapter 3, a form of *mens rea* that provides something of an exception to the general principle that ignorance or mistake of law is not an excuse. A person who has an honestly asserted proprietary or possessory claim to a thing may have a colour of right even if the claim is not founded in the law.[274]

In addition, the prosecution must establish that the accused intended to deprive the owner of the property either temporarily or permanently. This includes actions such as pledging the property in security or altering or dealing with it in a manner so that it cannot be restored to its original condition.

2) Fraud

The *actus reus* of fraud under section 380 of the *Criminal Code* is 1) a prohibited act of deceit, falsehood, or some other fraudulent means that 2) has the prohibited consequence of causing a deprivation either in the form of an actual loss or placing the victim's pecuniary interests at risk. What constitutes other fraudulent means will be determined objectively on the basis of what a reasonable person would consider to be dishonest even if these acts do not involve deceit or falsehood.[275] They can include the use of corporate funds for personal purposes, the unauthorized diversion of funds, and non-disclosure of material facts. In one case, other fraudulent means were defined to include the gambling practices of the accused with respect to money that was necessary to pay the accused's creditors.[276]

The *actus reus* has been defined in a broad but purposive manner that is driven by the focus on dishonesty. In addition to dishonesty, however, there has to be a deprivation that produces either an actual loss or the placing of the victim's interest at risk. In the case of a risk to financial interests, "proof of actual loss is irrelevant. Proof of risk to the economic interest of the victim is sufficient.[277] The dishonest act must play a significant role in the deprivation, but consistent with causation principles examined in chapter 3, it need not be the exclusive or only cause. Thus, the fact that the victim may have been deprived in part because of his or her own actions or truthful representations by the accused does not necessarily mean that an accused will not have committed the *actus reus* of fraud if the accused's dishonest act was a

---

273 R. v. *Howson*, [1966] 2 O.R. 63 (C.A.).
274 R. v. *DeMarco* (1973), 13 C.C.C. (2d) 369 (Ont. C.A.); R. v. *Lilly*, [1983] 1 S.C.R. 794.
275 R. v. *Olan*, [1978] 2 S.C.R. 1175.
276 R. v. *Zlatic*, [1993] 2 S.C.R. 29 [*Zlatic*].
277 R. v. *Drabinsky*, 2011 ONCA 582 at para. 82.

significant cause of the deprivation. As with other offences, an accused could be charged with an attempt in a case where the *actus reus* of the completed offence, in this case dishonest conduct that causes a deprivation, is not present.

The *mens rea* of fraud was interpreted in *Théroux*[278] to only require subjective knowledge of the prohibited act combined with subjective knowledge that the act could result in a deprivation including the placing of the victim's pecuniary interest at risk. McLachlin J. stated:

> The prohibited act is deceit, falsehood, or some other dishonest act. The prohibited consequence is depriving another of what is or should be his, which may, as we have seen, consist in merely placing another's property at risk. The *mens rea* would then consist in the subjective awareness that one was undertaking a prohibited act (the deceit, falsehood or other dishonest act) which could cause deprivation in the sense of depriving another of property or putting that property at risk. If this is shown, the crime is complete. The fact that the accused may have hoped the deprivation would not take place, or may have felt there was nothing wrong with what he or she was doing, provides no defence. To put it another way, following the traditional criminal law principle that the mental state necessary to the offence must be determined by reference to the external acts which constitute the *actus* of the offence (see Williams, *supra*, c. 3), the proper focus in determining the *mens rea* of fraud is to ask whether the accused intentionally committed the prohibited acts (deceit, falsehood, or other dishonest act) knowing or desiring the consequences proscribed by the offence (deprivation, including the risk of deprivation). The personal feeling of the accused about the morality or honesty of the act or its consequences is no more relevant to the analysis than is the accused's awareness that the particular acts undertaken constitute a criminal offence.[279]

McLachlin J. added that "[r]ecklessness presupposes knowledge of the likelihood of the prohibited consequences. It is established when it is shown that the accused, with such knowledge, commits acts which may bring about these prohibited consequences, while being reckless as to whether or not they ensue."[280]

The Supreme Court justified the above articulation of the fault element for fraud, which does not require that the accused subjectively

---

278 R. v. *Théroux*, [1993] 2 S.C.R. 579 [*Théroux*].
279 *Ibid.* at para. 24.
280 *Ibid.* at para. 26.

know that his or her conduct was dishonest as relating to the breadth of the *actus reus*. The Court built on a number of earlier decisions that had made clear the fact that the accused's belief that he had done nothing wrong because he would return the property[281] or that the fraud had been encouraged by others[282] did not prevent the formation of the criminal fault. It concluded that the *mens rea* would not catch negligent misstatements or sharp business practices: "to establish the *mens rea* of fraud the Crown must prove that the accused knowingly undertook the acts which constitute the falsehood, deceit or other fraudulent means, and that the accused was aware that deprivation could result from such conduct."[283] The Court's approach accords with a trend towards thinner versions of intentional *mens rea* that is seen in the Court's decision that the intent to assist a party in a crime or to commit an unlawful purpose is not negated by the fact that the accused has been threatened and commits intentional acts in the hope of avoiding the threat.[284]

The Court upheld a conviction for fraud in *Théroux* on the basis that the accused had lied about insurance protection for deposits paid towards the construction of new homes. The deprivation of not receiving the insurance protection was a sufficient *actus reus*, as was the risk that the victims could lose the deposit money. The *mens rea* was also present because the accused knew that he did not have insurance protection for the deposits and that he would be depriving the depositors of that protection even though he honestly believed that the houses would be built and the risk to the deposit money would not materialize.[285] Sopinka J. agreed with this result but warned that there may not be *mens rea* in a case where a deprivation would only occur in the event of some future event and the accused honestly believed that such an event would not occur.

This difference of opinion with respect to the fault element was soon revealed in a companion case. In *Zlatic*,[286] the majority of the Supreme Court held that the accused had the necessary *mens rea* because he subjectively knew that when he gambled with money that was re-

---

281 *Lafrance v. The Queen*, [1975] 2 S.C.R. 201.

282 *R. v. Lemire*, [1965] S.C.R. 174.

283 *Théroux*, above note 278 at para. 39.

284 See *R. v. Hibbert*, [1995] 2 S.C.R. 973 [*Hibbert*], discussed in ch. 5.

285 The Ontario Court of Appeal has applied this reasoning to conclude that an accused's "assertion that he believed that no one would be hurt by his conduct is no defence, because a subjective intent to mislead is not an essential element of the offence of fraud. Instead, all that is required is subjective knowledge of the prohibited act, and that the act could have as a consequence the deprivation of another." *R. v. Eizenga*, 2011 ONCA 113 at para. 81.

286 Above note 276.

quired by creditors that he was placing their financial interests at risk even though he also believed that he would win at the casinos and be able to repay his creditors. Chief Justice Lamer and Justice Sopinka dissented on the basis that there was no finding that the accused was reckless or knew that his gambling would place the creditors' interest at risk. Indeed, the trial judge had made findings that the accused honestly believed that he would be able to pay off his creditors after the gambling. The majority, however, rejected the relevance of these findings on the basis of its thinner understanding of criminal fault as only relating to the commission of the *actus reus* and not including the accused's belief that the risk to the creditors' money would not be realized.

D. TERRORISM OFFENCES

The terrorism offences quickly enacted after 9/11 are of interest in their own right; but for the purpose of a book on the fundamental principles of criminal law, they are of special interest in the way that they create new offences for conduct that would otherwise be prosecuted as inchoate offences, such as conspiracy, attempts, and counselling a crime that is not committed, or as forms of participation, such as aiding or abetting or committing crimes as a result of common unlawful purposes. Whatever the arguments at the time that existing offences would be adequate should terrorist plots be discovered, it is now clear that such conduct, as well as additional conduct, can be prosecuted as completed crimes of terrorism under Part II.1 of the *Criminal Code*.

The new terrorism offences are also of interest to the extent that they built on previous and problematic extensions of criminal liability under sections 467.11 to 467.13 with respect to participation in a criminal organization or gang, instructing the commission of an offence, and committing an offence for a criminal organization. These offences have been criticized for criminalizing conduct that may only remotely be connected with organized crime but have so far been upheld by the courts as neither vague nor overbroad, according to the Supreme Court's rather deferential approach to reviewing criminal offences on these bases.[287] Taken together, these offences demonstrate a reluctance

---

287 *R. v. Terezakis* (2007), 223 C.C.C. (3d) 344 (B.C.C.A.); *R. v. Lindsay* (2004), 182 C.C.C. (3d) 301 (Ont. S.C.J.). For criticism, see Stuart, above note 262 at 731*ff.* See also D. Freedman, "The New Law of Criminal Organizations in Canada" (2006) 85 Can. Bar Rev. 171.

to rely on the traditional inchoate offences and principles of party liability and a willingness to create broadly defined new crimes.

1) The Offence of Participation in a Terrorist Group

With respect to both organized crime and terrorist groups, a decision was taken not to criminalize mere membership in those groups. In this way, Parliament decided not to create pure status-based crimes but instead to create offences that provided a broadly worded prohibited act but also required intent. Section 83.18(1) provides:

> Every one who knowingly participates in or contributes to, directly or indirectly, any activity of a terrorist group for the purpose of enhancing the ability of any terrorist group to facilitate or carry out a terrorist activity is guilty of an indictable offence and liable to imprisonment for a term not exceeding ten years.

The *mens rea* of this offence requires that a person both knowingly participate or contribute to the activities of a terrorist group and have the purpose of enhancing its ability to facilitate or carry out a terrorist activity. Taken by itself, the dual requirements of knowledge and purpose are high subjective fault standards that would be sufficient even if the courts determined that terrorism crimes because of their stigma and penalty should, like murder, attempted murder, and war crimes, require proof of subjective fault in relation to all elements of the prohibited act.[288]

The more problematic aspects of this offence are found in its definition of an *actus reus*. The *actus reus* involves participation or contribution to any activity of a terrorist group and includes a long but non-exclusive list of examples of participating in section 83.18(3). As with the *actus reus* of attempted crime, the *actus reus* here may involve otherwise legal activity that is not a crime or a social mischief. In addition, the offence incorporates the broad and problematic definitions of a terrorist group and terrorist activities in section 83.01 of the *Criminal Code*. In addition, the reference to facilitating the carrying out of a terrorist activity in section 83.18 has been interpreted to include the broad definition of facilitation in section 83.19(2), which does not require the accused to know any particulars about a planned terrorist activity.

The Ontario Court of Appeal has upheld this offence from challenge under section 7 of the *Charter*. It held that "[p]utting the *actus reus* and *mens rea* together, section 83.18 applies to persons who, by their acts,

---

288   See ch. 2 for a discussion of constitutionally required fault elements.

contribute to or participate in what they know to be activities of a terrorist group. In addition, those acts must be done for the specific purpose of enhancing the ability of that terrorist group to facilitate or carry out activity that falls within the definition of terrorist activity."[289] It stressed that there was no reason why Parliament could not criminalize acts in preparation for terrorism as serious substantive crimes in their own right. It concluded that the offence did not violate section 7 by being vague or grossly disproportionate because it "does not criminalize mere participation in or contribution to activities of a terrorist group, but criminalizes only that participation or contribution that is done for the specific purpose of improving the terrorist group's ability to facilitate or carry out terrorist activity as defined in section 83.01. Conduct that falls within the prohibition of section 83.18 is both inherently dangerous and potentially preparatory to other very dangerous acts."[290]

2) Definition of a Terrorist Group

What constitutes a terrorist group? A terrorist group is defined under section 83.01 as either a group that has been listed by the Cabinet as a terrorist group under section 83.05 or "an entity that has as one of its purposes or activities facilitating or carrying out any terrorist activity." The listed entity part of this definition effectively substitutes a judgment made by the Cabinet as part of the executive without trial or adversarial challenge and on the basis of secret intelligence for proof beyond a reasonable doubt in a criminal trial that the group is a terrorist group. The second part of this definition is very broad because it incorporates the definition of terrorist activities in section 83.01 as well as the definition of facilitation under section 83.19, which as examined below has a highly qualified fault element in relation to knowledge of the nature of the terrorist activity.

3) Definition of Terrorist Activities

Terrorist activities are defined in section 83.01(a) as a number of extraterritorial offences to the extent that they implement various listed international conventions against terrorism that Canada has signed. This means that the full ambit of the criminal sanction cannot be interpreted without consulting both domestic and international law.

---

289 *United States of America v. Nadarajah*, 2010 ONCA 859 at para. 28 [*Nadarajah*].
290 *Ibid.* at para. 33.

An alternative definition of terrorist activity is found in section 83.01(b), which provides:

an act or omission, in or outside Canada,

(i)   that is committed

(A)   in whole or in part for a political, religious or ideological purpose, objective or cause, and

(B)   in whole or in part with the intention of intimidating the public, or a segment of the public, with regard to its security, including its economic security, or compelling a person, a government or a domestic or an international organization to do or to refrain from doing any act, whether the public or the person, government or organization is inside or outside Canada, and

(ii)   that intentionally

(A)   causes death or serious bodily harm to a person by the use of violence,

(B)   endangers a person's life,

(C)   causes a serious risk to the health or safety of the public or any segment of the public,

(D)   causes substantial property damage, whether to public or private property, if causing such damage is likely to result in the conduct or harm referred to in any of clauses (A) to (C), or

(E)   causes serious interference with or serious disruption of an essential service, facility or system, whether public or private, other than as a result of advocacy, protest, dissent or stoppage of work that is not intended to result in the conduct or harm referred to in any of clauses (A) to (C),

and includes a conspiracy, attempt or threat to commit any such act or omission, or being an accessory after the fact or counselling in relation to any such act or omission, but, for greater certainty, does not include an act or omission that is committed during an armed conflict and that, at the time and in the place of its commission, is in accordance with customary international law or conventional international law applicable to the conflict, or the activities undertaken by military forces of a state in the exercise of their official duties, to the extent that those activities are governed by other rules of international law.

This definition has been upheld from vagueness and overbreadth challenge on the basis that Parliament had provided enough guidance to restrain law enforcement discretion and provide notice to the accused. The harms defined in section 83.01(1)(b)(ii)A–E are "all clearly undesirable, adequately comprehensible and not at all surprising objectives of criminal sanctions."[291] Justice Rutherford also rejected the idea that the definition was overbroad to the state's legitimate goal of preventing terrorism by concluding that hypothetical examples of overbreadth, especially in relation to intentional disruption of public or private services, could be avoided by case-by-case adjudication of the offence, including the exemption of advocacy, protest, dissent, or stoppage of work that is not intended to result in death, serious bodily harm by violence, danger to life, or a serious risk to health or safety. He also did not have a problem with the reference to security and economic security despite the vague and potentially broad meaning of these terms. The judge was not deterred by the fact that the Supreme Court in a decision upholding investigative hearings in terrorism investigations expressed its unease with relying on the phrase "national security" as a justification for the *Anti-terrorism Act* given that "courts must not fall prey to the rhetorical urgency of a perceived emergency or an altered security paradigm."[292]

The conclusion that the above definition of terrorist activity is not unconstitutionally vague or overbroad is not surprising in light of the jurisprudence that has demonstrated a distinct reluctance to strike down offences on the grounds of vagueness. The Supreme Court's jurisprudence has increasingly focused on whether legislation provides a basis for further interpretation of the law and not on whether the legislation itself provides fair notice or limits law enforcement discretion.[293] Although the Court has expressed concerns about fair notice and the limitation of law enforcement discretion, it has not demanded that laws necessarily advance these values without the benefit of further judicial interpretation, even though such a deferential approach undermines the actual notice or limits on law enforcement discretion provided by the offence.

Overbreadth has been a more potent ground for challenging laws under section 7 of the *Charter* than vagueness. Justice Rutherford did not fully consider the accused's overbreadth claims and reduced them to claims of hypotheticals that could be resolved by sensible case-by-case adjudication. This approach, however, avoided the central question of overbreadth analysis, which is whether the legislature's choice of means overshoots its objective and whether the legislature has restricted liberty in ways that are unnecessary to fulfill the objective of the law. If the objective of the law is to prevent acts of terrorism, then

---

291 R. v. Khawaja (2006), 214 C.C.C. (3d) 399 at para. 18 (Ont. S.C.J.) [Khawaja (2006)], aff'd on other grounds 2010 ONCA 862 at para. 64 [Khawaja (2010)]. See also R. v. Ahmad (2009), 257 C.C.C. (3d) 199 (Ont. S.C.J.).

292 R. v. Bagri, [2004] 2 S.C.R. 248 at para. 39.

293 See discussion in ch. 3(A)(3), "Unconstitutionally Vague and Overbroad Laws."

it is questionable that targeting serious disruptions of essential public or private services is necessary. Although the Ontario Court of Appeal has affirmed that the participation offence in section 83.18 that incorporates the definition of terrorist activities in section 83.01 is not overbroad, its decision relied on high *mens rea* requirement specific to the section 83.18 offence.[294]

Another area that may be vulnerable is Parliament's inclusion of conspiracies, counselling, and threats to commit a terrorist activity in its definition of terrorist activities. This could result in a process in which inchoate forms of liability are combined with crimes that punish acts of preparation for terrorism. In other words, inchoate forms of liability would be added to crimes that are in substance inchoate crimes in a way that the Supreme Court has resisted with respect to other crimes such as attempted conspiracies.[295] At the same time, most of the other terrorism offences can probably withstand overbreadth scrutiny because of their relation to preventing terrorist activities.

4) The Requirement of Political or Religious Motive

The Ontario Court of Appeal reversed a trial judge who held that the political or religious motive requirement in section 83.01(b)(i)(A) was an unjustified violation of fundamental freedoms and should be severed from the other parts of the definition of terrorist activities. The Court of Appeal stated that there was no impediment under section 7 to requiring proof of motive as an essential element of a crime.[296] It held that even assuming that some of the activity captured by the broad definition of terrorist activity was not violent activity excluded from protection under section 2 of the *Charter*, that none of the activity was protected because it did not advance any of the purposes of freedom of expression. For example, "counselling someone to engage in conduct that would cause death or serious bodily harm hardly encourages the pursuit of truth, participation in the community or individual self-fulfillment."[297] The Court of Appeal also indicated that there was no evidence that the political and religious motive would chill the fundamental freedoms of those who might have similar political or religious views as those caught by the section, and that if it did, any chill was caused by social attitudes and the actions of terrorists and not the law. It also added that any chill from the law should be displaced by section 83.01(1.1) which "clearly

---

294 *Nadarajah*, above note 289 at para. 28.
295 *R. v. Déry*, 2006 SCC 53, discussed in ch. 4(B) "Conspiracy."
296 *Khawaja* (2010), above note 291 at para. 91.
297 *Ibid.* at para. 116.

declares that one need not fear expressing any political, religious or ideological belief as long as one does not engage in conduct that falls within the meaning of "terrorist activity." The accused appealed this decision to the Supreme Court and a decision is pending.[298]

5) Fault Elements in Other Terrorism Offences

Justice Rutherford rejected arguments that the various terrorism offences under sections 83.18, 83.19, and 83.21 of the *Code* violated section 7 of the *Charter* by not providing for sufficient levels of subjective fault. The accused argued that the interpretative subsections found in sections 83.18(2), 83.19(2), and 83.21(2) undermined the fault requirements of knowledge of a terrorist activity or the purpose of enhancing the ability to carry out a terrorist activity by not requiring that the knowledge or purpose relate to any particular or specific terrorist activity. The government argued that these provisions were necessary given the realities of modern cell-based terrorism in which members of the cell may not know the particular nature of the terrorist acts that they will perform until the last minute. Justice Rutherford accepted the government's justification and concluded that "it is unnecessary that an accused be shown to have knowledge of the specific nature of terrorist activity he intends to aid, support, enhance or facilitate, so long as he knows it is terrorist activity in a general way."[299] The new terrorism offences apply to conduct that would not amount to a conspiracy because there is no agreement to commit an offence and to conduct that would probably not attract party liability under section 21 of the *Criminal Code*.

Justice Rutherford's trial judgment in *Khawaja* suggests but does not clearly hold that terrorism offences because of their special stigma and punishment require a knowledge fault requirement under section 7 of the *Charter*. Although many have criticized the Supreme Court's stigma jurisprudence as circular and question-begging, it makes some intuitive sense to single out crimes of murder, attempted murder, war crimes, and now terrorism as particularly serious and requiring offenders to have subjective fault in relation to the defining features of those crimes. Justice Rutherford's decision that knowledge is sufficient as the constitutional form of fault is also defensible given that knowledge is what is constitutionally required for murder and attempted murder. At the same time, however, inchoate offences such as attempted murder and conspiracy to commit murder generally require the higher fault requirement of

---

298   *Ibid.* at para. 128.
299   *Khawaja* (2006), above note 291 at para. 39.

intent to commit the completed offence and this is arguably appropriate where the ultimate objective of a terrorist act has not been achieved. Although the terrorism offences are defined as completed offences in their own right, they are, in essence, instances of various forms of preparation to commit complete crimes. Thus, proof of something more than the *Charter* minimum of knowledge may be desirable. Indeed, the offences in sections 83.18 and 83.21 require in addition to guilty knowledge, a higher subjective purpose of enhancing the ability of any terrorist group to facilitate or carry out a terrorist activity.

Section 83.19, however, does not require purpose or intent, but only that there be knowing facilitation of a terrorist activity. In itself, this satisfies the constitutional minimum of knowledge. Section 83.19(2)(b), however, qualifies the constitutionally required knowledge requirement by providing that a terrorist activity can be facilitated "whether or not . . . any particular terrorist activity was foreseen or planned at the time it was facilitated." This raises the question of how can the accused know under section 83.19(1)(a) that he or she is facilitating a terrorist activity but not know under section 83.19(2)(b) that *any* particular terrorist activity was foreseen or planned? Any remaining knowledge of a terrorist activity would have to be extremely tenuous, abstract, and hypothetical. It could amount to just reckless and angry talk. Indeed, there is a danger that knowledge of a terrorist activity could be nothing more than bad talk and extreme political or religious views about past or future acts of terrorism or about known terrorists. Section 83.19 could be applied to those who are on the periphery of terrorist conspiracies, who do not necessarily have the intent to assist the group in preparing for any particular terrorist act. The *actus reus* of section 83.19 is broad and can include facilitation of activities by otherwise legal acts. Given the breadth of the offence, it is extremely important that the minimal fault requirement of knowledge in relation to the facilitation of terrorist activities not be diluted. Unlike section 83.18, it is not necessary to prove under section 83.19 that the accused know that the group is a terrorist group or have the purpose of enhancing its ability to facilitate or carry out a terrorist activity. Section 83.19 has been characterized as a "basket charge" that can cover a broad range of actions such as supplying money, material and training in a way that was "knowingly intended to promote, help forward or assist the terrorist purposes of the group,"[300] even if those purposes are not related to any particular terrorist activity.

---

300 *R. v. Khawaja*, [2008] O.J. No. 4244 at para. 139 (Ont. S.C.J.).

Although some accommodations have to be made with respect to the fact that those in a terrorist cell may not know the specifics of their operation until the last minute, this is done in a better tailored manner in both sections 83.18(1)(c) and 83.21(2)(g), which provide that it is not necessary to establish that "the accused knows the specific nature of any terrorist activity that may be facilitated or carried out by a terrorist group." There is a difference between not knowing the *specific nature* of a planned terrorist activity and not knowing that *any* particular terrorist activity is planned or foreseen at the time it was facilitated. In the former case, the accused knows that an act of terrorism is coming but does not know the details; in the latter case, the accused may only discuss terrorism in general and not know that any particular terrorist act will occur.

Justice Rutherford's conclusion that section 83.19 satisfies constitutional fault standards on the basis that: "I see nothing wrong in asking, indeed expecting law-abiding citizens to avoid any knowing activity that aids, supports or advances terrorist activity or a group engaged in such activity"[301] runs the risk of blurring the distinction between punishing accused as terrorists for their subjective fault or for their negligence in not taking reasonable steps to avoid assisting terrorists. A conclusion that negligent involvement with terrorists would be sufficient would be inconsistent with any conclusion that there is a constitutionally required *mens rea* of knowledge for terrorism offences. It would also raise concerns about exposing negligent intentional assisters of terrorism to the same liability and punishment as facilitators of terrorism.

CONCLUSION

This chapter has provided an overview of a few selected offences in order to illustrate how the general principles of criminal liability play out in some different contexts. With respect to homicide, the general principle of fault in relation to all elements of the *actus reus* is satisfied with respect to murder but not manslaughter. The Supreme Court has held as a principle of fundamental justice under section 7 of the *Charter* that murder requires proof of at least knowledge of the probability that the victim will die. This fault element is designed to reflect the stigma and mandatory life imprisonment that follows from a murder conviction. At the same time, the Court has held that objective foresight of bodily harm is a sufficient fault element for manslaughter and has rejected the idea that it is a principle of fundamental justice

---

301 *Khawaja* (2006), above note 291 at para. 36.

protected under section 7 of the *Charter* that the fault element must correspond with the prohibited act of causing death. In addition, the Court has held that the idea that the accused must take the risk that a victim may unexpectedly die as a matter of determining whether the accused caused death should also be reflected in the fault element of manslaughter. In recent years, however, the Court has articulated the causation requirement as requiring the accused's acts to be a significant cause of death. It is also now necessary for the Crown to demonstrate that the accused has engaged in a marked departure from standards of reasonable care with regard to negligence-based unlawful acts. It is necessary to demonstrate a marked and substantial departure for manslaughter by criminal negligence.

Although it is technically a sentencing classification, first-degree murder under section 231 of the *Criminal Code* has been influenced by principles of criminal liability. The courts have recognized that planning and deliberation under section 231(2) may be negated by lesser forms of intoxication or other mental disturbance than the *mens rea* of requirements of section 229. The courts have followed the traditional presumption of subjective fault by reading in a requirement that the accused must either know or be reckless that the victim was a police officer or other justice official under section 231(4) of the *Code*. The Supreme Court has interpreted section 231(5) to require stricter causation than in other homicide cases so that the Crown must establish that the accused was a substantial, and not only the significant, cause of the victim's death. Even here, though, it is not necessary to prove that the accused was the only cause of the victim's death.

The defence of provocation in section 232 is unique because it only applies when an accused is charged with murder. If there is a reasonable doubt that the accused was provoked, murder is reduced to manslaughter. As with self-defence, there are both subjective and objective arms of the provocation defence. The objective arm has, as in self-defence, been held to a modified objective standard based on a reasonable person of the same age, gender, and relevant experience as the accused.

Sexual offences have been the subject of much legislative and judicial reform. The trend towards broad definition of the prohibited act can be seen in the replacement of rape with broader crimes of sexual assault and by the replacement of statutory rape with broader offences of sexual interference with children. In 1992, Parliament also provided objective definitions of consent and specific examples of situations that would not constitute valid consent to sexual activity. The Supreme Court has subsequently interpreted consent as a matter of *actus reus* to be based on the subjective views of the complainant regardless of whether they were communicated or reasonable.

By applying basic principles of subjective fault, the courts reached the conclusion that the accused's honest belief that the complainant consented would raise a reasonable doubt about fault even if the belief was unreasonable in the circumstances. The courts were, however, hesitant about some of the logical implications of this conclusion and held in a number of cases that there was no air of reality that required the jury to be instructed about the mistake of fact defence. They also held that a mistaken belief in consent could not be based on either wilful blindness or self-induced intoxication. In 1992, Parliament modified the defence of honest but not necessarily reasonable mistaken belief in consent by providing that the accused must take reasonable steps in the circumstances known to him or her at the time to ascertain whether the complainant consented to the sexual activity in question. This approach blends subjective and objective fault requirements and has been held to be consistent with the *Charter*, if not always enthusiastically applied by the courts.

Property offences remain an important part of the criminal law. For an offence that is less serious than homicide and sexual offences, theft has surprisingly high fault requirements that the accused act both fraudulently and without colour of right. The latter concept constitutes a partial exception to the principle that ignorance or mistake of law does not constitute an excuse because it allows the accused's honest but mistaken belief in his or her legal entitlement to the property to be a defence to a theft charge. Although some aspects of the *actus reus* or prohibited act of theft follow general trends towards broad definitions of the prohibited act, the idea that information has to be reduced to a tangible item to be capable of being stolen is a curiously narrow and, some would suggest, archaic view of the *actus reus*.

Fraud has a broad *actus reus* that includes an open-ended range of dishonest conduct that results in deprivation or risks to the financial interests of others. The Supreme Court has required subjective fault in relation to the commission of the broadly defined *actus reus* but not to the point of requiring that the accused subjectively recognize the dishonesty of his or her actions. This is consistent with the Court's reluctance to incorporate matters that can be described as motive in fault or *mens rea* requirements.

The new terrorism offences created after 9/11 demonstrate how Parliament can enact new crimes for what may otherwise be inchoate crimes or forms of participation in crimes and how it can expand criminal liability beyond those established forms of inchoate and party liability. The prohibited acts of these new crimes are quite broad, including their incorporation of the broadly defined concepts of terrorist groups and terrorist activities. The fault element for these crimes generally requires subjective intent and knowledge. Indeed, knowledge may be a constitutionally required fault element given the stigma and punishment of terrorism offences. That said, Parliament has qualified these fault elements, especially with respect to the degree of knowledge that the accused must have about the specific terrorist activity that is planned or contemplated. The result has been that people who would not have been found guilty of being a party or of conspiracy to a terrorist plot have been found guilty of new terrorism offences.

FURTHER READINGS

BOYLE, C., *Sexual Assault* (Toronto: Carswell, 1984)

———, D. CHUNN, & I. GRANT, *The Law of Homicide*, looseleaf (Toronto: Carswell, 1994–1999)

HOLLAND, W., *The Law of Theft and Related Offences* (Toronto: Carswell, 1998)

MANNING, M., & P. SANKOFF, *Criminal Law*, 4th ed. (Markham, ON: LexisNexus, 2009), pt. 4

NIGHTINGALE, B., *The Law of Fraud and Related Offences*, looseleaf (Toronto: Carswell, 1996)

QUIGLEY, T., "Battered Women and the Defence of Provocation" (1991) 55 Sask. L. Rev. 223

———, "Deciphering the Defence of Provocation" (1989) 38 U.N.B.L.J. 11

ROACH, K., "The New Terrorism Offences," in D. Daubney *et al.*, eds., *Terrorism, Law & Democracy: How Is Canada Changing Following September 11?* (Montreal: Éditions Thémis, 2002)

STEWART, H., *Sexual Offences in Canadian Law*, looseleaf (Aurora, ON: Canada Law Book, 2004)

TROTTER, G., "Provocation, Anger and Intent for Murder" (2002) 47 McGill L.J. 669

WILSON, L., "Too Many Manslaughters" (2007) 52 Crim. L.Q. 433

SENTENCING

The Supreme Court has recognized that "sentencing is, in respect of most offenders, the only significant decision the criminal justice system is called upon to make."[1] Sentencing in Canada has traditionally been a matter of judicial discretion because Parliament frequently defines offences broadly to cover behaviour of varying degrees of culpability and has generally only set high and infrequently used maximum penalties to limit the judge's sentencing discretion. In contrast, many American jurisdictions rely more on statutory gradations of crimes and minimum sentences attached to each degree of any particular crime. Such attempts to limit sentencing discretion may transfer discretion from the sentencing judge to the prosecutor, when he or she accepts a guilty plea to a particular charge. There is a recent trend in Canada towards the use of more mandatory sentences.

Sentencing is a discretionary process because a judge can emphasize multiple purposes or justifications for punishment. The basic purposes and principles of sentencing were first outlined in the *Criminal Code* in 1996. The fundamental principle of sentencing, as defined in section 718.1 of the *Code*, is that the sentence "must be proportionate to the gravity of the offence and the degree of responsibility of the offender." This is an important first principle, owing to the wide variety of conduct that may be caught by some crimes. For example, a person who planned and executed a robbery should receive a more severe

---

1   *R. v. Gardiner* (1982), 68 C.C.C. (2d) 477 at 514 (S.C.C.) [*Gardiner*].

sentence than a person who reluctantly assisted the robbery in some manner. The fundamental principle of proportionality also counters the danger that a judge might punish an offender more than the crime deserves because of concerns about deterrence and future danger. It directs the judge to look backwards at the seriousness of the crime and the offender's role in it.

Nevertheless, the *Criminal Code* recognizes other concerns as legitimate purposes in sentencing. Section 718 provides:

> The fundamental purpose of sentencing is to contribute, along with crime prevention initiatives, to respect for the law and the maintenance of a just, peaceful and safe society by imposing just sanctions that have one or more of the following objectives:
> (a) to denounce unlawful conduct;
> (b) to deter the offender and other persons from committing offences;
> (c) to separate offenders from society, where necessary;
> (d) to assist in rehabilitating offenders;
> (e) to provide reparations for harm done to victims or to the community; and
> (f) to promote a sense of responsibility in offenders, and acknowledgement of the harm done to victims and the community.

This provision allows courts to sentence in order to deter the offender or others from committing crimes in the future; to remove an offender from society where necessary to prevent future crimes; and to tailor the punishment to further the rehabilitation of the offender in the future or the ability of the offender to provide reparations for the harm done to victims and the community. Concerns about rehabilitation and reparation may also suggest the use of alternatives to imprisonment, such as probation, restitution, or fines. Different purposes suggest different sentences. For example, a sentence of imprisonment might be thought necessary to deter the accused and others from committing a crime, but it may well not assist in rehabilitating the offender or providing reparation to the victims of crime. Much will depend on what sentencing purposes a judge believes are most important in any particular case and the Supreme Court has observed that "[n]o one sentencing objective trumps the others and it falls to the sentencing judge to determine which objective or objectives merit the greatest weight, given the particulars of the case."[2]

In addition to these multiple purposes, Parliament has also codified some other sentencing principles. The principle of parity in sec-

---

2   *R v. Nasogaluak*, 2010 SCC 6, [2010] 1 S.C.R. 206 at para. 43 [*Nasogaluak*].

tion 718.2(b) of the *Criminal Code* requires that a sentence "should be similar to sentences imposed on similar offenders for similar offences committed in similar circumstances." This is a broad principle of parity because it focuses not only on the crime committed, but also on the offender and his or her circumstances. Offenders are often found guilty of two or more offences at one time and section 718.2(c) codifies the totality principle by instructing judges that where consecutive sentences are imposed, "the combined sentence should not be unduly long or harsh." Absent specific statutory direction to the contrary,[3] Canadian judges have the discretion to allow offenders to serve separate sentences on a concurrent basis, a matter that has led to controversy in some circles. Section 718.21 sets out specific factors that are to be taken into consideration in the sentencing of corporations and other organizations.

Sections 718.2(d) and (e) codify the principle of restraint in punishment by instructing judges not to deprive the offender of liberty "if less restrictive sanctions may be appropriate in the circumstances" and to consider "all available sanctions other than imprisonment that are reasonable in the circumstances . . . with particular attention to the circumstances of aboriginal offenders." Canada has one of the highest rates of imprisonment of industrialized countries as well as gross overrepresentation of Aboriginal people in prison.[4] These principles, as well as a broad array of community sanctions that may not result in actual imprisonment, encourage judges to use alternatives to imprisonment whenever appropriate. The conditional sentence of imprisonment, a sanction that allows an offender to serve a shorter imprisonment term in the community often under conditions of partial house arrest, was added to the *Criminal Code* in the 1996 sentencing reforms. It has been used frequently, but Parliament has increasingly placed restrictions on its use.

---

3   *Criminal Code*, R.S.C. 1985, c. C-46, s. 718.3 [*Code*].

4   The Supreme Court has observed that "although the United States has by far the highest rate of incarceration among industrialized democracies, at over 600 inmates per 100,000 population, Canada's rate of approximately 130 per 100,000 population places it second or third highest." *R. v. Gladue* (1999), 133 C.C.C. (3d) 385 at 406 (S.C.C.) [*Gladue*]. It also noted that in 1997, Aboriginal people constituted 12 percent of federal inmates but only 3 percent of the total population and that they constituted the majority of prisoners in provincial institutions in Manitoba and Saskatchewan. In 2008–09, Aboriginal offenders accounted for 27 percent of provincial admissions and 18 percent of federal admissions to custody: (2010) 30:3 Juristat at 11.

A. PROCEDURAL CONSIDERATIONS

1) The Guilty Plea

In most cases, the accused pleads guilty to an offence. A guilty plea by the accused means that there will be no formal determination of whether the Crown can prove the accused's guilt beyond a reasonable doubt, and the trial process will move directly to the sentencing stage. An early guilty plea is an important mitigating factor in sentencing, on the grounds that it indicates remorse and saves the victim and the state the costs of a trial.[5] Courts have held that an accused who is sentenced after a full trial is not deprived of his or her *Charter* rights by not having the advantage of a guilty plea considered in mitigation of sentence.[6] Sometimes a guilty plea is accompanied by a joint submission by the Crown and the accused concerning sentencing. This submission does not, however, bind the trial judge from exercising his or her sentencing discretion.[7]

Canadian courts have not required trial judges to determine whether there is a factual basis for a guilty plea and whether the guilty plea is truly voluntary and unequivocal. In the disturbing case of *Brosseau v. R.*,[8] the Supreme Court did not allow a young Aboriginal accused to withdraw his plea to non-capital murder, even though the accused claimed that he did not understand the consequences of entering the guilty plea. Cartwright C.J. indicated that a trial judge should usually make inquiries if there is a doubt as to whether the accused understands what he is doing, but concluded: "[I]t cannot be said that where, as in the case at bar, an accused is represented by counsel and tenders a plea of guilty to non-capital murder, the trial Judge before accepting it is bound, as a matter of law, to interrogate the accused."[9] In that case, the accused's lawyer had indicated to the judge after sentencing that he did not pretend to have any understanding of his client's intent, a matter quite relevant to whether the accused was guilty of murder.

In a subsequent case, the Supreme Court affirmed the *laissez-faire* approach of *Brosseau* over a strong dissent by Laskin C.J., who argued that judges should be required by law to ensure that the guilty plea "be made voluntarily and upon a full understanding of the nature of

---

5   *R. v. Johnston*, [1970] 4 C.C.C. 64 (Ont. C.A.).

6   *R. v. M.(C.B.)* (1992), 99 Nfld. & P.E.I.R. 280 (P.E.I.C.A.).

7   *R. v. Rubenstein* (1987), 41 C.C.C. (3d) 91 (Ont. C.A.).

8   [1969] 3 C.C.C. 129 (S.C.C.) [*Brosseau*].

9   *Ibid.* at 138–39.

the charge and its consequences and that it be unequivocal."[10] Laskin C.J. would also have required that in cases of doubt, the trial judge should ensure that there was a factual basis for the guilty plea. The Laskin approach, at least with respect to determining whether the guilty plea is voluntary and made in full awareness of the consequences, may be more appropriate under the *Charter*, because a person who pleads guilty is waiving his or her rights under the *Charter* to a fair trial. Section 36 of the *Youth Criminal Justice Act* provides a model for reform: it requires the court to be satisfied that the facts support the charge but 606 (1.1) of the *Code* only requires that the plea be made voluntarily by an accused who admits to the essential elements of the offence and who understands the nature and consequences of the plea including that the court is not bound by any agreement made between the accused and the prosecutor. A failure of the court to inquire into even these conditions does not affect the validity of the plea. There have been cases where innocent accused have pled guilty in order to receive a more favourable sentencing and courts have subsequently allowed them to introduce fresh evidence relating to their innocence.[11]

2) The Sentencing Hearing

The sentencing hearing is less formal than the trial because of the greater range of information that is relevant when sentencing an offender. The accused does, however, retain procedural rights, such as the right to call evidence, cross-examine witnesses, and address the court. Judges may accept as proved any information disclosed at trial or at the sentencing hearing or any facts agreed by the prosecutor and the offender. If there is a dispute, the party wishing to rely on the disputed fact must establish it on a balance of probabilities. The prosecutor, however, must establish an aggravating factor or a previous conviction beyond a reasonable doubt.[12]

---

10   *Adgey v. R.* (1975), 13 C.C.C. (2d) 177 at 183 (S.C.C.).

11   *R. v. Marshall*, 2005 QCCA 852; *R. v. Hannemaayer*, 2008 ONCA 580 at para. 18 where Rosenberg J.A. recognized that "the court cannot ignore the terrible dilemma facing the appellant. He has spent eight months in jail awaiting trial and was facing the prospect of a further six years in the penitentiary if he was convicted. . . . The justice system held out to the appellant a powerful inducement that by pleading guilty he would not receive a penitentiary sentence." See also *R. v. Sheratt Robinson*, 2009 ONCA 886; *R. v. C.F.*, 2010 ONCA 691; *R. v. C.M.*, 2010 ONCA 690; *R. v. Kumar*, 2011 ONCA 120; *R. v. Brant*, 2011 ONCA 362 (parents pled guilty to reduced homicide in the child's death in the face of forensic pathology evidence later shown to be unreliable).

12   *Code*, above note 3, s. 724; *Gardiner*, above note 1.

Sentencing judges have a discretion to require the production of evidence and compel the attendance of witnesses at sentencing hearings[13] and they are required to provide reasons for their sentence.[14] Sentencing judges are "bound by the express and implied factual implications" of the verdict. For example, they cannot consider a person's death to be an aggravating factor when the accused was charged with dangerous driving causing death but convicted only of dangerous driving. They can in some cases consider that the accused has since conviction been charged with new offences, but only for purposes related to sentencing for the offence of which the accused has been convicted.[15]

Victim impact statements and reports by probation officers may be introduced as evidence in the sentencing hearing. Recent amendments require judges to inquire whether victims have been informed of the availability of victim impact statements and allow victims to give their impact statements orally.[16] Judges in some cases have used sentencing circles, in which offenders, victims, and community and family members are allowed to speak informally as a means to enhance community participation and improve the quality of information when sentencing Aboriginal offenders.[17]

The Supreme Court decided in a 5:4 decision that a presumption that young offenders should receive an adult sentence when convicted of murder, attempted murder, manslaughter, or aggravated sexual assault violates section 7 of the *Charter*. Abella J. for the majority indicated that the principles that young offenders are presumed less morally culpable than adult offenders and that the state has to establish aggravating factors at sentencing beyond a reasonable doubt qualified as principles of fundamental justice.[18]

3) Sentencing Appeals

Unless the sentence has been fixed by law, both the accused and the Crown can appeal a sentence. The Court of Appeal has a broad jurisdiction to consider the fitness of the sentence and vary the sentence within the limits prescribed by law.[19] The Supreme Court has, however,

---

13   *Code, ibid.*, s. 723.

14   *Ibid.*, s. 726.2.

15   *R. v. Brown* (1991), 66 C.C.C. (3d) 1 at 5 (S.C.C.); *R. v. Angelillo*, [2006] 2 S.C.R. 728.

16   *Code*, above note 3, s. 722.

17   *R. v. Moses* (1992), 71 C.C.C. (3d) 347 (Y. Terr. Ct.).

18   *R. v. D.B.*, 2008 SCC 25.

19   *Code,* above note 3, s. 687.

counselled deference to the decisions of sentencing judges and held that absent 1) an error in principle, 2) failure to consider a relevant factor, or 3) an overemphasis of the appropriate factor, a Court of Appeal should not normally intervene.[20] It is not necessary to find "the worst offender committing the worst offence" if the statutory maximum can be justified on the basis of the purposes and principles of sentencing.[21] Courts of Appeal may intervene if the sentence is demonstrably unfit and a marked and substantial departure from the sentences imposed for similar offenders committing similar crimes. A departure from a starting point established by the Court of Appeal for a particular offence or type of offence, by itself, is not a sufficient reason to overturn the sentence.[22] Sentencing appeals allow Courts of Appeal to develop legal principles to govern sentencing, but absent an error in principle, deference is accorded the decision of the sentencing judge. In recent years, the Supreme Court has also been much more active in sentencing when hearing appeals that raise questions of law of national importance. This, along with the new sentencing provisions in the *Criminal Code*, may bring a greater degree of national uniformity to sentencing. Nevertheless, much will still depend on the discretion of trial judges.

B. THE PRINCIPLES AND PURPOSES OF SENTENCING

In 1953 the Ontario Court of Appeal referred to "three principles of criminal justice requiring earnest consideration in the determination of punishment, viz., deterrence, reformation and retribution."[23] The first two factors, deterrence and reformation, look to the future, while retribution looks to the past and the severity of the crime committed. Although the terms have changed, these remain the primary purposes of sentencing, with some new concerns being introduced about reparation. The Supreme Court has recently explained:

> Far from being an exact science or an inflexible predetermined procedure, sentencing is primarily a matter for the trial judge's compe-

---

20 *R. v. M.(C.A.)* (1996), 105 C.C.C. (3d) 327 (S.C.C.) [*M.(C.A.)*]; *R. v. L.M.*, 2008 SCC 31 at para. 14 [*L.M.*].

21 *R. v. Solowan*, [2008] 3 S.C.R. 309; *R. v. Cheddesingh*, [2004] 1 S.C.R. 433 [*Cheddesingh*]; *L.M.*, ibid.

22 *Ibid.*; *R. v. Shropshire* (1995), 102 C.C.C. (3d) 193 (S.C.C.); *R. v. M.(T.E.)* (1997), 114 C.C.C. (3d) 436 (S.C.C.).

23 *R. v. Willaert* (1953), 105 C.C.C. 172 at 175 (Ont. C.A.).

tence and expertise. The trial judge enjoys considerable discretion because of the individualized nature of the process.[24] To arrive at an appropriate sentence in light of the complexity of the factors related to the nature of the offence and the personal characteristics of the offender, the judge must weigh the normative principles set out by Parliament in the *Criminal Code*:

- the objectives of denunciation, deterrence, separation of offenders from society, rehabilitation of offenders, and acknowledgement of and reparations for the harm they have done (*Criminal Code*, section 718);
- the fundamental principle that a sentence must be proportionate to the gravity of the offence and the degree of responsibility of the offender (*Criminal Code*, section 718.1); and
- the principles that a sentence should be increased or reduced to account for aggravating or mitigating circumstances, that a sentence should be similar to other sentences imposed in similar circumstances, that the least restrictive sanctions should be identified, and that available sanctions other than imprisonment should be considered (*Criminal Code*, section 718.2).[25]

One difficulty with the multiple purposes of sentencing is that much depends on what purpose is stressed. For example, in some cases imprisonment might be thought necessary to achieve retribution for a past wrong and perhaps to deter others from committing a crime in the future. At the same time, such a sentence may not be necessary and may even be counterproductive in achieving the purposes of rehabilitation or deterring the particular offender or allowing the offender to provide reparation to the victim.

1) The Fundamental Principle of Proportionality

Parliament has raised one principle above the others by designating the principle of proportionality as the fundamental principle of sentencing. Section 718.1 provides that "a sentence must be proportionate to the gravity of the offence and the degree of responsibility of the offender." This principle contemplates not only that punishment be proportionate to the crime committed, but also to the responsibility or blameworthiness of the offender. This directs judges to pay attention to the offend-

---

24   *Code*, above note 3, s. 718.3; *R. v. Johnson*, [2003] 2 S.C.R. 357 at para. 22; *R. v. Proulx*, [2000] 1 S.C.R. 61 at para. 82 [*Proulx*].

25   *L.M.*, above note 20 at para. 17.

er's actual conduct. The person who reluctantly acted as a lookout for a robbery does not require the same punishment as the person who planned and executed the robbery even though both may be convicted of the offence of robbery.

Before the enactment of section 718.1, the Supreme Court stated:

> It is a well-established tenet of our criminal law that the quantum of sentence imposed should be broadly commensurate with the gravity of the offence committed and the moral blameworthiness of the offender . . . the principle of proportionality in punishment is fundamentally connected to the general principle of criminal liability which holds that the criminal sanction may only be imposed on those actors who possess a morally culpable state of mind.[26]

This approach should guide the way courts approach the new fundamental principle of proportionality. Punishment should never exceed that which is required to recognize the blameworthiness of the offender's crime and his or her conduct. Proportionality restrains and limits punishment based on the offender's moral culpability and the need to punish "the offender no more than is necessary." At the same time, it also authorizes punishment through a "just deserts" philosophy of sentencing, which seeks to ensure that offenders are held responsible for their actions and that the sentence properly reflects and condemns their role in the offence and the harm they caused and imposes "a form of judicial and social censure."[27] The Court has recognized the dual nature of proportionality as the fundamental purpose of sentence. On the one hand, it "reflects the gravity of the offence" and as such is related to denunciation, "justice for victims and public confidence in the justice system." On the other hand, it "ensures that a sentence does not exceed what is appropriate, given the moral blameworthiness of the offender" and, in this sense, "serves a limiting or restraining function and ensures justice for the offender."[28]

---

26   M.(C.A.), above note 20 at 348. The Court also quoted with approval Justice Wilson's statement in the *Reference re Motor Vehicle Act (British Columbia) S. 94(2)* (1985), 23 C.C.C. (3d) 289 at 325 (S.C.C.): "It is basic to any theory of punishment that the sentence imposed bear some relationship to the offence; it must be a 'fit' sentence proportionate to the seriousness of the offence. Only if this is so can the public be satisfied that the offender 'deserved' the punishment he received and feel a confidence in the fairness and rationality of the system." In that case, she held that a mandatory term of seven days of imprisonment was disproportionate to the absolute liability offence of driving with a suspended licence.

27   *Nasogaluak*, above note 2 at para. 42.

28   *R. v. Ipeelee*, 2012 SCC 13 at para. 37.

Proportionality is a retributive concept that focuses on the offender's past conduct as opposed to utilitarian concerns about the future effects of the punishment on the offender or others through deterrence or rehabilitation. Retribution is a legitimate concern in sentencing, but it should not be confused with revenge or vengeance, which produces an unrestrained and "uncalibrated act of harm upon another, frequently motivated by emotion and anger." In contrast, retribution is "an objective, reasoned and measured determination of an appropriate punishment which properly reflects the *moral culpability* of the offender." It restrains punishment to ensure "the imposition of a just and appropriate punishment, and *nothing more*."[29] As will be seen, a grossly disproportionate sentence may also be unconstitutional and struck down as cruel and unusual punishment prohibited by section 12 of the *Charter*. Proportionality should restrain punishment by ensuring that offenders do not receive undeserved punishment for their own good or other social objectives. The existence of other sentencing purposes, some of which are utilitarian and forward-looking, however, suggests that retribution or "just deserts" restrains but does not determine punishment. The Supreme Court has indicated that the award of a maximum sentence under the law should be rare, but that it is not necessarily reserved for "the worst offender." Rather, it should be justified after consideration of all the multiple purposes of sentencing.[30]

2) The Fundamental Purpose of Sentencing

Section 718 states that the "fundamental purpose of sentencing is to contribute, along with crime prevention initiatives, to respect for the law and the maintenance of a just, peaceful and safe society by imposing just sanctions." Courts often pass over this vague and inspirational purpose to focus on the enumerated objectives. Nevertheless, it should be given some meaning. It combines concerns about proportionality by its reference to just sanctions with concerns about the future through its concern for promoting a peaceful and safe society. It also recognizes sentencing discretion through its recognition that appropriate and just sanctions may have one or more of the enumerated objectives. The Supreme Court has indicated that retribution alone does not determine punishment, and other legitimate purposes such as deterrence, rehabilitation, and the protection of society should be considered. The

---

29   *M.(C.A.)*, above note 20 at 368–69 [emphasis in original].
30   *Cheddesingh*, above note 21 at 433; *L.M.*, above note 20.

relative importance of these multiple factors will vary with the crime, the circumstances of the offender, and the needs of the community.[31]

3) Denouncing Unlawful Conduct

Like proportionality, denunciation is a retributive concept that focuses on the past. Unlike proportionality, however, the emphasis is on expressing society's disapproval of the crime committed as opposed to judging the culpability of the particular offender. The Supreme Court has stated:

> The objective of denunciation mandates that a sentence should also communicate society's condemnation of that particular offender's conduct. In short, a sentence with a denunciatory element represents a symbolic, collective statement that the offender's conduct should be punished for encroaching on our society's basic code of values as enshrined within our substantive criminal law.[32]

A concern about denunciation, as well as deterrence, has motivated some courts to indicate that a custodial sentence should normally be imposed for domestic violence.[33]

Another way of achieving the aim of denunciation is to enact a mandatory minimum sentence for a crime. For example, the mandatory sentence for murder is life imprisonment. Problems may arise, however, because such mandatory sentences apply to the most sympathetic and least blameworthy person that nevertheless has committed the crime with the required act and fault and without a valid defence. As discussed in chapter 3, crimes are often defined quite broadly and capture both the actual perpetrator and those who may have assisted the perpetrator. As discussed in chapter 5, a good motive is also no defence to a crime but may be relevant in determining punishment.

4) Deterring and Incapacitating Offenders

Section 718 draws a distinction between general deterrence, which is concerned with the effect of punishment in deterring others from committing similar offences, and specific deterrence, which is concerned with the effect of punishment in deterring the particular offender from committing subsequent crimes. The latter concern may also embrace

---

31   M.(C.A.), above note 20 at 368–69.
32   Ibid. at 369.
33   R. v. Brown (1992), 73 C.C.C. (3d) 242 (Alta. C.A.); R. v. Inwood (1989), 48 C.C.C. (3d) 173 (Ont. C.A.).

concerns about the incapacitation or rehabilitation of the offender, if that is the only way to prevent him or her from committing future crimes/The effectiveness of any strategy designed to deter future conduct is commonly thought to depend on a combination of the certainty, speed, and severity of punishment. Courts at the sentencing stage focus on the severity of punishment, because they have little control over the certainty and speed of punishment.

a) General Deterrence

Courts have accepted that the deterrence of others is a legitimate objective of sentencing. In *R. v. Sweeney*,[34] Wood J.A. stated:

> The theory behind the general deterrence goal of sentencing is that the legal sanction imposed on actual offenders will discourage potential offenders. While there is little empirical evidence to support such a theory, common sense tells us that, to some extent, that must be so. Indeed, there can be little doubt that the very existence of a criminal justice system acts as a deterrent which prevents many people from engaging in criminal conduct.

Courts often consider general deterrence as a factor in crimes such as drunk driving, sexual assault, and domestic violence, where there is widespread concern about the prevalence of such crimes and a desire to change human behaviour. Section 718(b) recognizes the desire to deter both the offender and other persons from committing offences as a legitimate objective of the sentencing process. In addition, section 718.2 also indicates a concern with general deterrence, by stating that hate crimes, spousal and child abuse, and crimes based on the abuse of a position of trust or authority should be punished more severely.

b) Specific Deterrence

Specific deterrence refers to the goal of preventing the offender from committing another criminal offence. This requires courts to consider the offender's history and other information that may help predict future dangerousness. One court has stated that if the concern is general deterrence, then judges should focus on "the gravity of the offence, the incidence of the crime in the community, the harm caused by it either to the individual or the community and the public attitude toward it," whereas if specific deterrence is the goal, "greater consideration must be given to the individual, his record and attitude, his motivation and

---

34   (1992), 71 C.C.C. (3d) 82 at 98 (B.C.C.A.).

his reformation and rehabilitation."[35] Concerns about specific deterrence can blur into concerns about rehabilitation when the best way to ensure that an offender does not reoffend is to help get that person's life back on track. A more punitive approach to specific deterrence would advocate harsher punishments as a means to prevent future crimes. If it was relatively certain that an offender was bound to reoffend, incapacitation of the offender by imprisonment might be considered the only way to prevent the commission of an offence during that time. Section 718(c) recognizes this concern by naming the separation of offenders from society "where necessary" as a legitimate objective of sentencing. Separation or incapacitation may be necessary in the case of the most dangerous offenders, but it is an expensive strategy and one that does not necessarily protect fellow prisoners or guards from violence in prison.

Provisions in the *Criminal Code* providing for indeterminate detention of repeat dangerous offenders are largely concerned with the incapacitation of repeat violent offenders.[36] They have been upheld under the *Charter*, with the Supreme Court stressing that concerns about preventing future crimes "play a role in a very significant number of sentences. . . . Indeed, when society incarcerates a robber for, say, 10 years, it is clear that its goal is both to punish the person and prevent the recurrence of such conduct during that period."[37] La Forest J. also stated that it did not offend the principles of fundamental justice to punish people for preventive purposes, "which are not entirely reactive or based on a 'just deserts' rationale."[38] In 1997, the dangerous offender provisions were toughened to remove a judicial discretion to impose a determinate sentence on a person found to be a dangerous offender[39] and to delay the first parole hearing to determine if the offender is no longer a danger from three to seven years with subsequent hearings every two years after.[40] This new regime is significantly harsher than that upheld in *Lyons* or the regime for the detention of those found not criminally responsible by reason of mental disorder.[41] The new amendments also allowed long-term sexual offenders who present a substantial risk to reoffend to be sentenced to a minimum of two years

35   *R. v. Morrissette* (1970), 1 C.C.C. (2d) 307 at 310 (Sask. C.A.).
36   Part XXIV of the *Code*, above note 3.
37   *R. v. Lyons* (1987), 37 C.C.C. (3d) 1 at 22 (S.C.C.) [*Lyons*].
38   *Ibid.*
39   *Code*, above note 3, s. 753.
40   *Ibid.*, s. 761.
41   See ch. 8, "Mental Disorder and Automatism."

and then supervised in the community for up to ten years after their release.[42]

5) Rehabilitating Offenders

Section 718(d) of the *Criminal Code* provides that one of the objectives of sentencing is "to assist in rehabilitating offenders." Sections 718.2(d) and (e) encourage courts not to deprive offenders of their liberty or to imprison them, when less restrictive sanctions are appropriate and reasonable in the circumstances.

Although less popular than in the past, rehabilitation remains a valid consideration in sentencing, especially in cases where there is a prospect of not imprisoning the offender. In *R. v. Preston*,[43] the British Columbia Court of Appeal upheld a suspended sentence, with probation orders, for the possession of heroin on the basis that "the principle of deterrence should yield to any reasonable chance of rehabilitation which may show itself to the court imposing sentence." Wood J.A. stated:

> The notion that rehabilitation is a legitimate goal of the sentencing process is neither new nor experimental. Every Royal Commission, official report and extensive study done on sentencing in this country . . . has stressed the obvious, namely, that the ultimate protection of the public lies in the successful rehabilitation of those who transgress society's laws. Those same authorities have also unanimously concluded that rehabilitation is unlikely to occur while the offender is incarcerated.[44]

Given the fundamental principle of proportionality, a concern for rehabilitation should not be used to deprive the accused of greater liberty than is necessary to punish the offender. The traditional justification for restraint in punishment has been a concern about preserving as much of the offender's liberty as possible. In recent years, concerns about the costs of imprisonment and the disproportionate imprisonment of Aboriginal people have also been raised.

---

42   *Code*, above note 3, s. 753.1.
43   *R. v. Preston* (1990), 79 C.R. (3d) 61 (B.C.C.A.) [*Preston*].
44   *Ibid.* at 78.

6) Providing Reparations and Promoting a Sense of Responsibility

Section 718(e) provides that one of the purposes of sentencing is to provide reparations for harm done to victims or to the community. The idea that an offender should provide reparation for crime is quite ancient and was prevalent in both Aboriginal societies and England before the monarchy asserted its power. Nevertheless, it is a relatively new concept in modern criminal law and, as will be discussed later in this chapter, there are limited means by which judges can require offenders to make reparation to victims. Judges may stress the idea of reparation to the community more than reparation to the victim, and this may be used to support retributive and denunciatory sanctions.

Section 718(f) provides that another purpose of sentencing is "to promote a sense of responsibility in offenders, and acknowledgement of the harm done to victims and to the community." This provision could also be used to support punitive measures, but it can be better advanced by sentences designed to achieve restorative justice among offenders, victims, and the community. The Supreme Court in R. v. Gladue noted that sections 718(e) and (f) introduce new concerns to sentencing, which along with rehabilitation and the need to examine alternatives to incarceration, promote restorative justice. "Restorative sentencing goals do not usually correlate with the use of prison as a sanction," but generally involve "some form of restitution and re-integration into the community."[45] Justices Cory and Iacobucci have explained:

> In general terms, restorative justice may be described as an approach to remedying crime in which it is understood that all things are interrelated and that crime disrupts the harmony which existed prior to its occurrence, or at least which it is felt should exist. The appropriateness of a particular sanction is largely determined by the needs of the victims, and the community, as well as the offender.[46]

In the subsequent case of R. v. Proulx, the Supreme Court affirmed that the 1996 sentencing reforms including sections 718(e) and (f) were designed to reduce reliance on incarceration and advance the restorative principles of sentencing. Lamer C.J. explained:

> Restorative justice is concerned with the restoration of the parties that are affected by the commission of an offence. Crime generally

---

45   *Gladue*, above note 4 at 403.
46   *Ibid.* at 414.

affects at least three parties: the victim, the community, and the offender. A restorative approach seeks to remedy the adverse effects of crime in a manner that addresses the needs of all parties involved. This is accomplished, in part, through the rehabilitation of the offender, reparations to the victim and to the community, and promotion of a sense of responsibility in the offender and acknowledgment of the harm done to victims and the community.[47]

The Supreme Court has indicated that restorative sentencing purposes should be considered for all offenders, but especially for Aboriginal offenders because of their overincarceration and the primary emphasis upon the ideals of restorative justice in Aboriginal traditions.

7) Sentencing Aboriginal Offenders

Section 718.2(e) instructs judges to consider "all available sanctions other than imprisonment that are reasonable in the circumstances" for all offenders but "with particular attention to the circumstances of Aboriginal offenders." The Supreme Court has held that this provision is designed to remedy the overincarceration of Aboriginal people and requires judges to pay attention to the unique circumstances of Aboriginal offenders, including systemic discrimination that may explain why the offender has been brought to court. It also requires courts to consider the availability of restorative and other approaches that may be appropriate because of the offender's Aboriginal heritage or connection. The Court also stated that "the more violent and serious the offence,"[48] the more likely it will be that Aboriginal offenders will receive the same sentence as non-Aboriginal offenders. In the actual case, the Court did not allow the accused's appeal from a three-year sentence of imprisonment for manslaughter in part because the accused had been granted day parole after six months on conditions that she reside with her father, comply with electronic monitoring, and take alcohol and substance abuse counselling. In a subsequent case, the Court upheld a sentence of imprisonment of an Aboriginal offender convicted of sexual assault.[49]

In R. v. Ipeelee,[50] the Supreme Court expressed concerns about the growing percentage of Aboriginal offenders in jail in the course of holding that trial judges had erred by sentencing two long-term vio-

---

47   *Proulx*, above note 24 at para. 18.
48   *Gladue*, above note 4 at 417.
49   R. v. Wells (2000), 141 C.C.C. (3d) 368 (S.C.C.).
50   2012 SCC 13.

lent offenders to three-year imprisonment for breaching non-intoxicant provisions in their long-term offender designation. The Supreme Court reaffirmed that courts must take judicial notice of systemic and background factors affecting Aboriginal people to explain why the Aboriginal offender is before the court and what sentencing objectives and procedures should be used. The Court stressed that section 718.2(e) imposes mandatory duties on all trial judges and that it continues to apply in cases that are serious and violent. In the result, the Court held that one-year sentences of imprisonment would be appropriate and not the three years ordered by the trial judges.

C. AGGRAVATING AND MITIGATING FACTORS IN SENTENCING

Courts consider a wide range of aggravating and mitigating factors in connection with the particular crime and the offender. They often consider the offender's degree of participation in a crime. This consideration is important because criminal offences are often defined to catch a broad range of conduct and people can be convicted of a crime as parties even though they did not actually commit the crime. Courts also consider planning and deliberation, breach of trust, use of violence and weapons, and harm to victims as aggravating factors. Section 718.2 directs the court to consider aggravating factors such as whether the crime "was motivated by bias, prejudice or hate" on group characterstics, involved spousal or child abuse, or involved an abuse of a position of trust or authority.

Prior convictions are usually considered an aggravating factor, while the accused's good character, youth, old age, ill health, remorse, and early guilty plea will generally be considered mitigating factors. Even though it also operates as a partial defence that reduces murder to manslaughter, provocation can be considered a mitigating factor in sentencing for manslaughter[51] and presumably other crimes. The use of alcohol and drugs can either be a mitigating factor or an aggravating factor, depending on the circumstances and the purposes of punishment that are stressed. The same can be said of the accused's social status, which may be related to either prospects for rehabilitation and future danger or to the goals of general deterrence and denunciation. Courts also consider time served in custody, and the combined effect of consecutive sentences.

---

51   *R. v. Stone* (1999), 134 C.C.C. (3d) 353 (S.C.C.).

Charter breaches and other abuses of state power may be mitigating factors at sentencing subject to other sentencing rules and statutory minimums and "provided that the impugned conduct relates to the individual offender and the circumstances of his or her offence." The Supreme Court has justified this approach in part through reference to section 718 which provides that "the fundamental purpose of sentencing is to contribute . . . to respect for the law and the maintenance of a just, peaceful and safe society." It upheld the entry of a conditional discharge to guilty pleas to impaired driving and flight from the police, in part because of excessive force by the police in the arrest which broke the accused's ribs and punctured his lung.[52]

D. CONSTITUTIONAL CONSIDERATIONS

Punishment is restricted by section 12 of the *Charter*, which prohibits cruel and unusual treatment or punishment.[53] In *R. v. Smith*,[54] the Supreme Court held that a mandatory minimum sentence of seven years for importing narcotics violated section 12 and could not be justified under section 1 of the *Charter* because it could in some cases result in punishment that was grossly disproportionate to both the offence and the offender. Lamer J. noted that the offence covered a wide variety of behaviour, so that it could hypothetically catch a person importing one joint of marijuana. He also noted that it could be applied to a range of offenders, including a young person with no prior convictions. He stated that, in determining whether a sentence was "grossly disproportionate,"

> the court must first consider the gravity of the offence, the personal characteristics of the offender and the particular circumstances of the case in order to determine what range of sentences would have been appropriate to punish, rehabilitate or deter this particular offender or to protect the public from this particular offender.[55]

Punishment that is disproportionate for the particular offender, but which may be necessary to deter others, must be justified under section 1 of the *Charter*.

---

52 *Nasogaluak*, above note 2 at para. 49.
53 See ch. 2, "The Criminal Law and the Constitution."
54 (1987), 34 C.C.C. (3d) 97 (S.C.C.) [*Smith*].
55 *Ibid.* at 139.

The Supreme Court has subsequently upheld minimum sentences of seven days' imprisonment for driving with a suspended licence on the basis that the Court should only consider how a sentence would affect reasonable hypothetical offenders and not remote or extreme examples.[56] If such a remote example actually arose, the courts would then have to consider whether imposing the mandatory penalty would result in cruel and unusual punishment. The Supreme Court eventually held that because the driving without a licence offence remained one of absolute liability, judges could not constitutionally imprison a person for its violation.[57] The Court also has upheld a mandatory minimum sentence of four years' imprisonment for the crime of criminal negligence causing death when a firearm is used. The Court deferred to Parliament's attempts to deter the use of firearms during the commission of crimes.[58] The Court subsequently held that the four-year mandatory minimum sentence for manslaughter with a firearm was not cruel and unusual when applied to a police officer who shot a person in his custody. The Court also ruled that constitutional exemptions were not an appropriate remedy with respect to mandatory sentences because they would be inconsistent with Parliament's attempt to limit a judge's sentencing discretion and send a clear deterrent message to offenders. The Court was also concerned that case-by-case constitutional exemptions would undermine the certainty, clarity, and predictability of the law by creating a gap between the mandatory sentence on the books and the actual sentences below that minimum that were ordered as a constitutional exemption.[59]

The Supreme Court of Canada has held that mandatory firearm prohibitions upon the conviction of offences do not constitute grossly disproportionate cruel and unusual treatment in light of a statutory provision that allows exemptions for employment and sustenance reasons.[60] In light of the Court's decision that judges cannot order constitutional exemptions from mandatory sentences, the presence or absence of such statutory exemptions will often be determinative. If a

---

56 R. v. Goltz (1991), 67 C.C.C. (3d) 481 (S.C.C.). See also R. v. Brown (1994), 93 C.C.C. (3d) 97 (S.C.C.) upholding a then minimum one-year sentence for using a gun in a robbery. Most Courts of Appeal have upheld an increased minimum four-year sentence for using a gun in a robbery. R. v. Wust (1998), 125 C.C.C. (3d) 43 (B.C.C.A.); R. v. Lapierre (1998), 123 C.C.C. (3d) 332 (Que. C.A.); R. v. McDonald (1998), 127 C.C.C. (3d) 57 (Ont. C.A.).

57 R. v. Pontes (1995), 100 C.C.C. (3d) 353 (S.C.C.).

58 R. v. Morrisey (2000), 148 C.C.C. (3d) 1 (S.C.C.).

59 R. v. Ferguson, 2008 SCC 6.

60 R. v. Wiles, [2005] 3 S.C.R. 895 at para. 10. See s. 113 of the Code, above note 3.

judge determines that a mandatory sentence will be grossly disproportionate and cruel and unusual either in a particular case or on the basis
of a reasonable hypothetical case, the judge now has no alternative but
to strike down the mandatory sentence as it applies to all offenders.

The Supreme Court has held that life imprisonment for first-degree murder, without eligibility of parole for twenty-five years, does
not violate section 12 of the *Charter*, because of the seriousness of the
crime committed and the possibility that after fifteen years a jury will
allow the accused to be considered for early parole, royal mercy, and
absences from custody for humanitarian and rehabilitative purposes.[61]
Since that time, the availability of controversial faint hope hearings has
been eliminated. The Supreme Court in *R. v. Latimer* also upheld the
mandatory sentence of life imprisonment with ten years' ineligibility
for parole for the offence of second-degree murder. It stressed the seriousness of the crime and the constitutional requirements of subjective
mens rea. The Court rejected arguments that the accused's altruistic
motives in killing his daughter to prevent her suffering from a needed
operation was relevant to the proportionality of the punishment.[62] The
problem with mandatory sentences is that by definition they will apply
to the most sympathetic and least blameworthy person who nevertheless committed the criminal act with the required fault. In any event,
since the 1987 case of *Smith*, the Supreme Court has deferred to Parliament's decision to employ mandatory sentences.

Legislation providing for the indeterminate detention of repeat
violent offenders has been held not to violate the *Charter* because of
its relation to society's legitimate interest in punishing, rehabilitating,
deterring, and incapacitating repeat violent offenders.[63] At the same
time, the Supreme Court stressed that regular reviews are necessary to
ensure that continued detention was not disproportionate to the legitimate aims of punishment. The Court subsequently authorized, by the
writ of *habeas corpus*, the release of an offender who served thirty-sev-
en years for sexual offences and who, in its view, no longer presented a
danger to society.[64]

---

61   *R. v. Luxton* (1990), 58 C.C.C. (3d) 449 (S.C.C.).

62   *R. v. Latimer* (2001), 150 C.C.C. (3d) 129 (S.C.C.).

63   *Lyons*, above note 37.

64   *Steele v. Mountain Institution* (1990), 60 C.C.C. (3d) 1 (S.C.C.).

E. SENTENCES OTHER THAN IMPRISONMENT

1) Alternative Measures

Alternative measures allow an accused who accepts responsibility for a crime to engage in supervised activities in the community, without a formal determination of guilt or innocence at trial. They are contemplated under section 10 of the *Youth Criminal Justice Act* and under section 717 of the *Criminal Code*. There must be sufficient evidence to proceed with the charge; the accused must accept responsibility for the offence charged and voluntarily agree to the alternative measures. There are a great variety of alternative measures. Some may focus on various forms of community service and/or education for the offender while others may be based on restorative justice.

2) Absolute and Conditional Discharges

When the accused is charged with an offence not subject to imprisonment for fourteen years or life and without a minimum sentence, the court can, instead of convicting the accused, order an absolute or conditional discharge if "it considers it to be in the best interest of the accused and not contrary to the public interest."[65] The best interests of the accused include the accused's good character and the harm that can follow from a conviction. The public interest includes society's interest in the general deterrence of the offence. Absolute or conditional discharges do not apply only to trivial or technical violations of the *Code*, but they should not routinely be applied to any particular offence.[66] If the conditions of a conditional discharge are breached, the offender may be sentenced for the original offence as well as for the crime of breaching the probation order.

3) Suspended Sentences and Probation

After convicting an accused, the court can suspend sentence and make a probation order, or make a probation order in addition to a fine or sentence of imprisonment of not more than two years. Probation orders can be made even though the accused's sentence would normally have been more than two years in the absence of consideration of time that

---

65   *Code*, above note 3, s. 730.
66   *R. v. Fallofield* (1973), 13 C.C.C. (2d) 450 (B.C.C.A.).

the accused spent in pre-trial custody.[67] Probation orders may also be entered after absolute or conditional discharges.

Courts make probation orders "having regard to the age and character of the offender, the nature of the offence and the circumstances surrounding its commission."[68] Compulsory conditions of a probation order are that the offender keep the peace and be of good behaviour, appear before the court when required and notify the court or probation officer of changes of address or employment. Optional conditions are regular reports to the probation officer, abstaining from the consumption of alcohol or other drugs, abstaining from possessing a gun, supporting dependants, performing up to 240 hours of community service, and complying with other reasonable conditions designed to protect society and facilitate the offender's successful reintegration into the community.[69] The court does not have the power to require an offender to provide bodily substances for testing as part of an abstention order.[70] It is an offence not to comply with a probation order without a reasonable excuse.[71] Corporations and other organizations can now be placed on probation under section 732.1 of the *Code*.

In *Preston*,[72] the British Columbia Court of Appeal upheld a suspended sentence for an accused convicted of three counts of possession of heroin. The accused's probation orders required her to attend a drug rehabilitation facility and perform fifty hours of community service. Wood J.A. reasoned that only overcoming the accused's addiction would break her cycle of crime. He presumed that there would be adequate resources to supervise the accused while on probation and that she would be brought back before the court if she breached her probation order.

4) Conditional Sentences of Imprisonment

If the court imposes a sentence of imprisonment of less than two years, it may, under section 742.1, order that the sentence be served in the community if the court is satisfied that this would not endanger the safety of the community and would not be inconsistent with the fundamental purpose and principles of sentencing set out in sections 718 to

---

67   *R. v. Mathieu*, 2008 SCC 21 [*Mathieu*].
68   *Code*, above note 3, s. 731.
69   *Ibid.*, s. 732.1.
70   *R. v. Shoker*, [2006] 2 S.C.R. 399.
71   *Code*, above note 3, s. 733.1.
72   *Preston*, above note 43.

718.2. In *R. v. Proulx*,[73] the Supreme Court indicated that only offences with a mandatory minimum sentence of imprisonment are categorically excluded from conditional sentences, but section 742.1 of the *Code* now categorically excludes a long list of serious personal injury offences defined in section 752 and terrorism and criminal organization offences prosecuted by indictment.

The Supreme Court restricted the availability of conditional sentences in *R. v. Fice*[74] when it held that in determining whether a conditional sentence is excluded because the offender faces a penitentiary sentence of two years' imprisonment or more, the trial judge should include time spent in pre-trial custody. In other words, pre-trial detention should be considered part of the offender's punishment for determining whether the threshold for a conditional sentence is satisfied even though pre-trial detention may ordinarily be used to reduce the final sentence. This approach restricts the availability of conditional sentences in a manner that is not done with respect to probation orders. As discussed above, probation orders can be made even if the accused's sentence was only reduced below two years' imprisonment because of time the accused spent in pre-trial custody.[75]

Conditional sentences should be a more punitive sentence than a probation order and will generally include punitive conditions such as house arrest. In addition, a conditional sentence can be longer than an actual term of imprisonment. The judge must determine that the particular offender will not present a danger to the community, but the conditions imposed on the offender will be considered in determining the risk of reoffending and the gravity of the damage caused by reoffending.[76] A conditional sentence can fulfill both the restorative and punitive purposes of sentencing, but imprisonment may be required for offences where the objectives of denunciation and deterrence are particularly important.

The conditions imposed as part of the conditional sentence of imprisonment are very similar to those imposed by probation orders. Unlike probation orders, however, the offender can be required to take a treatment program and some courts have imposed restrictive conditions such as "house arrest" except for limited purposes such as employment. Breaches of the conditions only have to be proven on a balance

---

73 *Proulx*, above note 24.
74 [2005] 1 S.C.R. 742.
75 *Mathieu*, above note 67.
76 *R. v. Knoblauch* (2000), 149 C.C.C. (3d) 1 (S.C.C.).

of probabilities and can result in the offender serving the duration of the conditional sentence in prison or having the conditions changed.[77]

5) Fines

Fines are commonly used in addition to, or as an alternative to, imprisonment. There are no limits to the amount fined except in respect of summary conviction offences, which are generally limited to $5,000 for individuals[78] or $100,000 for organizations.[79] If fines are not paid, an offender may be imprisoned. In the past, significant numbers of those serving short imprisonment terms were serving time because of a failure to pay their fines. Provinces may provide fine option programs to allow an offender who cannot pay a fine to work off the fine. Section 734(2) of the *Criminal Code* now provides that a court should order fines only when satisfied that an offender will be able to pay the fine or to work off the fine in a fine option program. In *R. v. Topp*,[80] the Supreme Court stressed that as a practical matter a party seeking a fine must satisfy the court on a balance of probabilities that the offender has the ability to pay and there must be an affirmative finding to this effect.

Imprisonment for failure to pay parking tickets has been held to be cruel and unusual punishment contrary to section 12 of the *Charter*.[81] As discussed in chapter 6, a person convicted of an absolute liability offence cannot constitutionally be imprisoned.[82] A more drastic sentence, such as a conditional sentence, should not be used because the offender is unable to pay a fine.[83] Although a judge has no discretion to take the ability to pay principle into account when ordering a fine as an alternative to the forfeiture of the proceeds of crime, such a principle will be considered when determining the time that is required to pay the fine and whether imprisonment for failure to pay the fine is warranted.[84]

There are victim fine surcharges on fines, but these do not have to be assessed if they would cause hardship to offenders.[85] The provinces can use the proceeds to provide assistance to victims of offences. Part

---

77   *Code*, above note 3, s. 742.6.
78   *Ibid.*, s. 787.
79   *Ibid.*, s. 735(1)(b).
80   2011 SCC 43 at paras. 20–22.
81   *R. v. Joe* (1993), 87 C.C.C. (3d) 234 (Man. C.A.).
82   See ch. 6(A), "Absolute Liability Offences."
83   *R. v. Wu* (2003), 180 C.C.C. (3d) 97 (S.C.C.).
84   *R. v. Lavigne*, [2006] 1 S.C.R. 392.
85   *Code*, above note 3, s. 737.

XII.2 of the *Criminal Code* provides an elaborate scheme for the forfeiture to the state of the proceeds of many crimes.

6) Restitution

Section 738 of the *Criminal Code* allows judges to order restitution for property damage, pecuniary damage arising from offences involving bodily harm, and reasonable and readily ascertainable expenses when a spouse and children move from an offender's household in cases involving bodily harm or the threat of bodily harm to the spouse or child. The Supreme Court has cautioned that the restitution provisions should not be used as a substitute for the civil process.[86] Nevertheless, "in appropriate cases, compensation orders provide an extremely useful and effective tool in the sentencing procedure" that can help rehabilitate the accused, provide benefits for victims in a "speedy and inexpensive manner," and benefits for society by reducing the use of imprisonment. They can also provide "for the reintegration of the convicted person as a useful and responsible member of the community at the earliest possible date. The practical efficacy and immediacy of the order will help to preserve the confidence of the community in the legal system."[87]

Restitution orders are generally enforced as civil judgments. This can make them difficult to enforce. Restitution can be better ensured by requiring it as a condition of probation or a conditional sentence. Provinces, however, have the option under section 738(2) of enacting regulations to preclude judges from imposing restitution as a condition of probation or a conditional sentence. Although reparation to victims is now recognized as a purpose of sentencing, judges have limited instruments with which to pursue this purpose.

7) Forfeiture

There are various provisions that allow for the forfeiture of property that is the proceeds of crime or was offence-related property. In certain drug and criminal organization cases, forfeiture can be ordered of any property of the offender. The state is generally only required to establish on a balance of probabilities that the property is related to crime[88] and in some cases, the accused has to establish on a balance of probabilities that it was not so obtained.[89]

---

86 *R. v. Zelensky*, [1978] 2 S.C.R. 940.
87 *R. v. Fitzgibbon*, [1990] 1 S.C.R. 1005 at 1013.
88 *Code*, above note 3, ss. 462.37(1) and 490.1.
89 *Ibid.*, s. 463.37 (2.03).

CONCLUSION

Sentencing is the most important and visible aspect of the criminal law. The 1996 amendments to the *Criminal Code* have created a statutory framework for the exercise of sentencing discretion, but much discretion remains. The fundamental principle is that the sentence must be proportionate to the gravity of the offence and the offender's degree of responsibility. The offender's crime and responsibility, however, do not determine punishment, and judges are instructed to be concerned about a wide range of other factors including specific and general deterrence, rehabilitation, reparation, and promoting a sense of responsibility. The last three purposes, combined with other instructions to consider alternatives to imprisonment, suggest that restorative justice is a legitimate and important approach to sentencing, especially, but not exclusively, with respect to Aboriginal offenders. There are a wide variety of alternatives to actual imprisonment including pre-trial diversion, probation, restitution, and conditional sentences that allow offenders to be punished and held accountable while remaining in the community.

Courts will strike down grossly disproportionate sentences as cruel and unusual punishment, but in recent years they have been more willing to uphold mandatory minimum sentences that by definition apply to the most sympathetic offenders and least blameworthy crimes that are caught under often broad definitions of crime. Parliament has also moved in a more punitive direction by enacting more mandatory minimum sentences, restricting credit for "dead time" served in pre-trial custody and placing more restrictions on the use of conditional sentences of imprisonment.

FURTHER READINGS

ARCHIBALD, B., & J. LLEWELLYN, "The Challenges of Institutionalizing Restorative Justice" (2006) 29 Dal. L.J. 297

BROCKMAN, J., "An Offer You Can't Refuse: Pleading Guilty When Innocent" (2010) 56 Crim. L.Q. 116

CANADIAN SENTENCING COMMISSION, *Sentencing Reform: A Canadian Approach* (Ottawa: Queen's Printer, 1987)

CAYLEY, D., *The Expanding Prison* (Toronto: Anansi, 1998)

Cole, D., & J. Roberts, *Making Sense of Sentencing* (Toronto: University of Toronto Press, 1999)

Fitzgerald, O., *The Guilty Plea and Summary Justice* (Toronto: Carswell, 1990)

Healy, P., & H. Dumont, *Dawn or Dusk in Sentencing* (Montreal: Thémis, 1998)

Manson, A., *The Law of Sentencing* (Toronto: Irwin Law, 2001)

Roach, K., "Changing Punishment at the Turn of the Century: Restorative Justice on the Rise" (2000) 42 Can. J. Crim. 249

———, "Searching for *Smith*: The Constitutionality of Mandatory Minimum Sentences" (2001) 39 Osgoode Hall L.J. 367

Roberts, J., & A. von Hirsch, "Sentencing Reform in Canada: Recent Developments" (1992) 23 R.G.D. 319

———, "Statutory Sentencing Reform: The Purpose and Principles of Sentencing" (1995) 37 Crim. L.Q. 220

Roberts, J., & R. Melchers, "The Incarceration of Aboriginal Offenders: Trends from 1978 to 2001" (2003) 45 Can. J. Crim. 211

Roberts, J., & K. Roach, "Restorative Justice in Canada: From Sentencing Circles to Sentencing Principles" in A. Von Hirsch *et al.*, eds., *Restorative Justice and Criminal Justice* (Oxford: Hart, 2003)

Ruby, C., *et al.*, *Sentencing*, 6th ed. (Toronto: Butterworths, 2004)

Rudin, J., & K. Roach, "Broken Promises: A Response to Stenning and Roberts' 'Empty Promises'" (2002) 65 Sask. L. Rev. 3

Stenning, P., & J. Roberts, "Empty Promises: Parliament, the Supreme Court and the Sentencing of Aboriginal Offenders" (2001) 64 Sask. L. Rev. 137

CONCLUSION

The criminal law in Canada has undergone significant changes in the past three decades. The most visible change has been the enactment of the *Canadian Charter of Rights and Freedoms*. As examined in chapter 2, the *Charter* causes criminal courts to be concerned not only with the accused's factual guilt, but also with whether the police and prosecutors complied with the accused's legal rights in the investigative and trial process. Non-compliance with *Charter* rights can lead to the exclusion of relevant evidence. Entrapment that would bring the administration of justice into disrepute can result in a stay of proceedings even though the accused may have committed the crime with the required *mens rea*.

The *Charter* guarantees the presumption of innocence. It has been interpreted to be breached whenever the accused bears the burden of establishing an element of an offence, a defence, or a collateral factor. It can even be breached when the accused must satisfy an evidential burden to overcome a mandatory presumption. It is not breached, however, when a judge makes a preliminary decision about whether there is an air of reality to justify putting a defence to a jury. In addition, the *Charter* has provided new substantive standards of fairness by which to measure criminal and regulatory offences and the availability of defences. Constructive murder has been struck down as inconsistent with the minimum *mens rea* for murder and absolute liability offences have been found to be unconstitutional when they result in imprisonment. The intoxication and duress defences have also been expanded in response to *Charter* concerns.

Although some of the effects of the *Charter* on the criminal law have been unexpected, the overall effect can be overstated, particularly in relation to substantive criminal law, which has been the focus of this work. Most cases in which the broad presumption of innocence has been violated have nevertheless been sustained under section 1 of the *Charter* as reasonable and proportionate limits on *Charter* rights. The Supreme Court has approved the pre-*Charter* compromise of strict liability for regulatory offences, including the requirement that the accused rebut a presumption of negligence by establishing a defence of due diligence. The courts have also found that no-fault absolute liability offences will not violate section 7 of the *Charter* if they do not result in imprisonment. The Court has even violated the presumption of innocence itself by requiring the accused to establish the defences of extreme intoxication, non-mental disorder automatism, and officially induced error on a balance of probabilities.

The *Charter* has in some respects protected fault principles less robustly than the common law. Before the *Charter*, the courts under the common law applied common law presumptions of subjective fault in relation to all the elements of the *actus reus*. Under section 7 of the *Charter*, the courts have only required subjective fault in relation to the prohibited result for murder, attempted murder, and war crimes. It has decided that the principle that fault be proven in relation to all aspects of the prohibited act or that there be symmetry between the *actus reus* and *mens rea* is a matter of criminal law "theory" but not a principle of fundamental justice under section 7 of the *Charter*. The Court has approved the use of objective fault standards for many criminal offences. Moreover, there is no constitutional requirement that the reasonable person used to administer objective fault standards have the same characteristics as the particular offender or that fault be proven for all aspects of the *actus reus*. That said, the Court has recently interpreted section 7 of the *Charter* to require that there be a marked departure whenever negligence is used as a form of criminal liability and that courts at least consider whether the subjective position of the accused raises a reasonable doubt about the accused's negligence.[1]

Even when the Supreme Court has ruled in favour of the *Charter* rights of the accused, Parliament has frequently responded with new legislation that reaffirms the public interest and the interests of victims and potential victims of crime. The most dramatic example is section 33.1 of the *Criminal Code*, which attempts to overrule the Court's decision in *Daviault*, so that an extremely intoxicated accused who acted

---

1   *R. v. Beatty*, 2008 SCC 5 [*Beatty*], *R. v. Roy*, 2012 SCC 26.

in an involuntary or unconscious manner would still be convicted of crimes such as assault and sexual assault. In an attempt to ensure that "no means no," Parliament has in sections 273.1 and 273.2 of the *Code* defined consent for the purpose of sexual assault not to include specific conduct and has restricted the *Pappajohn* mistake of fact defence to require the accused to take reasonable steps, given the circumstances known to him, to ascertain whether a complainant consents to sexual activity. In its preambles to these new provisions, Parliament has asserted that the *Charter* rights of women and children as potential victims of sexual and domestic assault should be balanced with the *Charter* rights of the accused. *Charter* decisions striking down warrantless searches have led Parliament to create new warrant provisions and to authorize some warrantless searches. Parliament revived tertiary grounds relating to public confidence in the administration of justice for the denial of bail after they were struck down by the Supreme Court and it has restricted credit for remand custody when an accused has been denied bail. The Court's decision that the unavailability of an absolute discharge for those found permanently unfit to stand trial because of a mental disorder but of no significant danger to the public has been cured by legislation, but the new legislation requires judges to consider any adverse effects on the administration of justice including any adverse effect on public confidence in the administration of justice. The *Charter* has not prevented Parliament from responding to court decisions. Legislative replies may be challenged under the *Charter*, but Parliament frequently has had the last word in its dialogue with the courts over the values of the criminal law.

A. THE CHARTER AND THE CRIMINAL LAW

1) The *Charter* and the Due Process Model

In his landmark study of the criminal process, Herbert Packer outlined two contrasting models of the criminal process.[2] In the crime control model, the justice system resembled an assembly line, with the police and prosecutors being able to identify the factually guilty and to secure a guilty plea. In contrast, he saw an emerging due process model that resembled an obstacle course, because it required the state to comply with various legal rights in the investigative and trial process before

---

2   H.L. Packer, *The Limits of the Criminal Sanction* (Stanford, CA: Stanford University Press, 1968) Part II.

it could secure a conviction. If the police or prosecutor violated the accused's legal rights, courts were prepared to exclude evidence or terminate the case regardless of whether the accused was factually guilty of the crime charged.

The *Charter*, as interpreted by the Supreme Court of Canada, has injected due process elements into the Canadian criminal process. As discussed in chapter 2, suspects now have constitutional rights against unreasonable searches, arbitrary detentions, and the right to counsel. If the police do not comply with these rights, the evidence they obtain can be excluded under section 24(2) of the *Charter*. An accused also has rights in the criminal trial process not to be denied reasonable bail without just cause, to be tried within a reasonable time, to receive disclosure of relevant evidence in the Crown's possession, and to be presumed innocent. The Court has interpreted the last right broadly, but governments have been able to justify many limitations on that right under section 1 of the *Charter* as reasonable and necessary means to facilitate the prosecution of various crimes.

The due process model describes some elements of the criminal justice system under the *Charter*. At the same time, the *Charter* era has not demonstrated the skepticism towards the use of the criminal sanction with respect to so-called victimless crime that Packer associated with the due process model. The Supreme Court has refused to constitutionalize the liberal principle that the criminal sanction only be used to respond to proven harms and it has upheld broad laws targeting prostitution, assisted-suicide, and pornography from *Charter* challenge. Although they have crafted some exemptions for medical use of marijuana, the courts have not invalidated drug laws. It is telling that recent challenges to the prostitution laws have not been based on liberty-based arguments or open skepticism about the criminal sanction, but on arguments that prostitution laws harm the safety and equality rights of sex workers and section 9 equality rights of the physically disabled. In other words, due process and liberty claims are supplemented with claims about equality and victimization.

As Packer observed, the due process model was nurtured by the appellate courts, most notably the Supreme Court, and was dependent on changes within that institution. In recent years, there has been a trend, albeit not invariable, to more deference to police actions. The Court has created police powers of investigative detention while at the same time holding them to *Charter* limits. It has also allowed the police to engage in prolonged interrogation of suspects who have invoked the right to silence. Counsel does not have to be present so long as they have been given a reasonable opportunity to contact counsel and the statement obtained is involuntary. These cases provide some support for the critical comments that "due process is for crime control" in that they demonstrate how due process both enables and restrains law enforcement. The courts have also stopped short of requiring that police interrogations be recorded. Recent changes to the exclusion of unconstitutionally obtained evidence under section 24(2) underline that such evidence should never be automatically excluded.

Prison populations have increased significantly in the *Charter* era and will probably expand more in the future given increased Parliament use of minimum sentences and restrictions on conditional sentences and enhanced credit for "dead time" spent in remand when a person is denied bail pending trial. Moreover, the accused is not the only actor in the criminal process that has claimed *Charter* rights, and a number of cases have been influenced by concerns about the rights of crime victims and groups such as women, children, and minorities who may be disproportionately subject to some crimes. Indeed, the criminal sanction has been enthusiastically used as a means to respond to risks of crime and as a means to respond to even slight risks of harm.

2) The *Charter* and the Crime Control Model

The enactment of the *Charter* has not eclipsed the utility of Packer's description of the crime control model. Most criminal cases continue to end with guilty pleas that are not well supervised by judges. An early entry of a guilty plea remains an important mitigating factor in sentencing. Although Packer predicted that the due process model would contribute to skepticism about the use of the criminal sanction, this outcome has not proven to be the case in Canada. With the exceptions of abortion where courts have avoided imposing criminal sanctions, and recent rulings that the refusal to grant an exemption from drug laws for a safe injection site contravenes the principles of fundamental justice guaranteed by s. 7 of the *Charter* [3] and that bawdy house laws violate the *Charter* because they harm the safety of sex workers,[4] there seems to be more enthusiasm about the use of the criminal sanction in the *Charter* era. Since the enactment of the *Charter*, offences against sexual assault, proceeds obtained by crime; war crimes; impaired driving causing death or bodily harm; sexual interference with children; the possession of drug instruments, drug literature, and child pornog-

---

3   *Canada (Attorney General) v. PHS Community Services*, 2011 SCC 44 [*PHS Community Services*].

4   *A.G. Canada v. Bedford*, 2012 ONCA 186 (bawdy house and living off the avails offences ruled to violate the *Charter*).

raphy; and committing a crime for a criminal organization have all been passed. In the wake of September 11, Parliament enacted many new crimes of terrorism. It also expanded the provisions for holding corporations and other organizations criminally liable as a response to the Westray Mine disaster. The Supreme Court has rejected a *Charter* challenge to the criminal offence of possession of marijuana and the proposed decriminalization of such activity has fallen off the policy agenda. New sentencing provisions require crimes motivated by hate against identifiable groups and involving child or spousal abuse, or abuse of positions of trust or authority, to be punished more severely and some new hate-crime provisions were created as part of the *Anti-terrorism Act*. Sections 15 and 28 of the *Charter* have also been invoked by Parliament in support of claims that the criminal sanction is necessary to protect the rights of women, children, and other vulnerable groups.

Judicial interpretation of the *Charter* has not been oblivious to crime control values. The Court has accepted that random stops and roadside denials of counsel are reasonable limits necessary to deter drunk driving. Violations of the presumption of innocence protected under section 11(d) of the *Charter* have frequently been upheld to facilitate the prosecution of crimes such as drunk driving, living off the avails of prostitution, hate propaganda, and regulatory offences. The Supreme Court has required proof of subjective foresight of the likelihood of death for murder but has approved of manslaughter convictions when death was unforeseen by the accused and may have been unforeseeable by the reasonable person. The Court has based this latter ruling on the fact that the accused was acting unlawfully and should accept responsibility for the victim's "thin skull."[5] Except in a few excessive cases, the *Charter* has had relatively little impact on sentencing and punishment, with the Court ruling that constitutional exemptions could not be used to mitigate the increasing use of mandatory minimum sentences.[6]

The *Charter* has changed the way conflicting interests are described and balanced in the criminal justice system, but it has not done away with the need to balance these interests. Parliament still plays a leading role in defining the prohibited act, the fault element, and the punishment available for most criminal offences. Enthusiasm for the use of the criminal sanction has not diminished under the *Charter*, and the criminal law is used as a practical and symbolic response to a wide

---

5   *R. v. Creighton* (1993), 83 C.C.C. (3d) 346 (S.C.C.) [*Creighton*].
6   *R. v. Ferguson*, 2008 SCC 6.

range of social issues, including drunk driving, domestic violence, hate literature, hate crimes, degrading pornography, terrorism, sexual violence towards women and children, and corporate misconduct.

3) The *Charter* and the Punitive Model of Victims' Rights

In a few cases, the *Charter* has encouraged courts to consider the effects of laws in protecting victims of crime, and in particular women and minorities who may disproportionately be the victims of certain crimes. In *R. v. Keegstra*,[7] the Supreme Court upheld hate propaganda offences that violated freedom of expression and the presumption of innocence in large part because the law attempted to protect vulnerable minorities from being the targets of wilful promotion of hatred. In *R. v. Butler*,[8] the Court reinterpreted obscenity provisions so that they prohibited material that was found to be violent, or degrading, or dehumanizing, particularly in relation to its portrayal of women and children. In the *Prostitution Reference*,[9] the Court upheld a new crime of soliciting in a public place for the purpose of prostitution in part because of concerns for communities and women victimized by prostitution. A concern that disabled people might be coerced into suicide in part motivated the Court's decision in *Rodriguez v. British Columbia (A.G.)*[10] not to strike down the offence of assisting suicide.

Parliament and the provincial legislatures have been more active than the courts in protecting the interests of victims of crimes. They have enacted various laws designed to provide compensation for the victims of crime. The new sexual assault provisions enacted in response to *R. v. Seaboyer*,[11] and the legislative response to *R. v. Daviault*,[12] both include preambles that state that the laws were designed in part to promote the full protection of rights guaranteed under sections 7 and 15 of the *Charter* and to deal with the prevalence of sexual assault and other violence against women and children.

---

7   (1990), 61 C.C.C. (3d) 1 (S.C.C.).

8   *R. v. Butler* (1992), 70 C.C.C. (3d) 129 (S.C.C.).

9   *Reference re ss. 193 & 195.1(1)(c) of the Criminal Code (Canada)* (1990), 56 C.C.C. (3d) 65 (S.C.C.) [*Prostitution Reference*].

10   *Rodriguez v. British Columbia (A.G.)* (1993), 85 C.C.C. (3d) 15 (S.C.C.) [*Rodriguez*].

11   (1992), 66 C.C.C. (3d) 321 (S.C.C.). See *Criminal Code*, R.S.C. 1985, c. C-46, ss. 273.1–273.2 and 276.1–276.5 [*Code*].

12   *R. v. Daviault* (1994), 93 C.C.C. (3d) 21 (S.C.C.) [*Daviault*]. See *Code, ibid.*, ss. 33.1–33.3.

There are real limits, however, as to how far victim interests will be integrated into the present criminal justice system. The *Charter* provides no explicit rights for crime victims and the interests of victims have to be squeezed into the interests protected under sections 7 and 15. In *Canadian Foundation for Children*,[13] the Supreme Court preemptorily rejected arguments that section 43 of the *Code* violated procedural and equality rights of children by authorizing the use of reasonable force by way of correction against them. McLachlin C.J. stated: "[T]hus far, the jurisprudence has not recognized procedural rights for the alleged victim of an offence" and that assuming that such rights existed, "the child's interests are represented at trial by the Crown. . . . There is no reason to suppose that, as in other offences involving children as victims or witnesses, the Crown will not discharge that duty properly. Nor is there any reason to conclude . . . that providing separate representation for the child is either necessary or useful."[14] This case sets real limits on the extent to which the rights of crime victims will be recognized within the existing criminal justice system.

4) The Non-Punitive Model of Victims' Rights

The *R. v. Gladue*[15] decision has recognized the role of restorative justice in sentencing and its ability to respond to the needs of victims as well as offenders. *Gladue* represents a non-punitive model of victims' rights that places less emphasis on competing claims of rights and the imposition of punishment. Other examples of a non-punitive model would include the use of family conferences and victim offender mediation and a greater emphasis on crime prevention. In *R. v. Proulx*,[16] Lamer C.J. explained that restorative justice was a new objective of sentencing that applies to all offenders and was associated with the rehabilitation of the offender and reparation and acknowledgment of the harm done to the victims and the community. The Chief Justice explained:

> Restorative justice is concerned with the restoration of the parties that are affected by the commission of an offence. Crime generally affects at least three parties: the victim, the community, and the offender. A restorative approach seeks to remedy the adverse effects of crime in a manner that addresses the needs of all parties involved.

---

13 *Canadian Foundation for Children, Youth and the Law v. Canada (A.G.)*, 2004 SCC 4 [*Canadian Foundation for Children*].
14 *Ibid.* at para. 6.
15 *R. v. Gladue* (1999), 133 C.C.C. (3d) 385 (S.C.C.).
16 (2000), 140 C.C.C. (3d) 449 (S.C.C.).

This is accomplished, in part, through the rehabilitation of the offender, reparations to the victim and to the community, and promotion of a sense of responsibility in the offender and acknowledgment
of the harm done to victims and the community.[17]

Restorative approaches that attempt to rehabilitate the offender depend
on the willingness of prosecutors to divert cases out of the system and
of Parliament not to restrict alternatives to imprisonment through mandatory minimum sentences and restrictions on conditional sentences.

The non-punitive model of victims is also open to the possibility
that an offender's conduct may be related to his or her prior victimization even if such victimization does not excuse the conduct. The
Supreme Court in the *PHS Community Services* case rejected the government's argument that the use of illegal drugs was simply a matter of
choice. It held that the refusal of the Minister of Health to continue to
grant a statutory exemption from drug laws to continue to allow a safe
injection site to operate on Vancouver's Downtown Eastside violated
section 7 of the *Charter* because it was arbitrary and grossly disproportionate given evidence that it helped save the lives of addicts who
might be infected with HIV by dirty needles while not increasing crime
in the community.[18] In *R. v. Ipeelee*,[19] the Court stressed that judges
must take judicial notice of distinct background factors including the
residential school experience that may help explain why Aboriginal
offenders commit offences and may provide background to determine
what sentence is appropriate.

Crime prevention strategies are another example of a concern about
preventing crime victimization that do not rely on the threat or imposition of punishment. Another example is the development of an all-risk
strategy to respond not only to the crime of terrorism, but also to other
harms that can be caused by natural and man-made disasters. Should
the possession of marijuana be decriminalized by Parliament sometime in the future, it will be important that the government attempts to
educate the populace about the health and safety hazards of the drug,
as well as other drugs. A non-punitive approach to victimization would
often take a public health approach to minimizing the harms of not
only crime, but also other threats to human security. It would also
emphasize the importance of healthy infant and school experiences in
decreasing crime and the many costs of crime.

---

17   *Ibid.* at para. 18.
18   *PHS Community Services*, above note 3.
19   2012 SCC 13.

B. TRENDS IN THE CRIMINAL LAW

1) Definition of Crimes

The *Charter* has had a limited effect on the ability of legislatures to define what conduct is illegal. A crime that prohibits some activity protected under the *Charter*, such as freedom of expression, must be justified under section 1 of the *Charter*. No crime should be so vague or overbroad that it fails to provide notice to the accused or limit law enforcement discretion.

The criminal law as enacted by Parliament sets a fairly wide net of criminal liability by defining criminal acts quite broadly. Courts will interpret prohibited acts in a purposive fashion, before resorting to the doctrine of strict construction of the criminal law that gives the accused the benefit of reasonable ambiguities. As examined in chapter 4, people can be held guilty as parties to an offence for a wide range of conduct, including aiding, abetting, or counselling a crime, or forming a common unlawful purpose with either subjective or objective foresight that the crime charged will occur.[20] Separate offences of conspiracy, counselling a crime that is not committed, and being an accessory after the fact also exist. Courts have defined the prohibited act of attempted crimes broadly, so that anything beyond preparation will suffice, even if it is not otherwise illegal or harmful. The accused may be guilty of an attempted crime even though it was impossible to commit the complete crime and his or her actions were quite remote from the complete crime.[21] At the same time, courts have stressed that the Crown must prove that the accused acted with the intent to commit the crime. Another alternative to inchoate crimes is to criminalize activities that are preparatory to the commission of crimes. Parliament has taken this approach with organized crime and terrorism offences that apply to financial transactions and participation in groups that may occur well in advance to the commission of any crime and to activity that might not attract inchoate or party liability.

Various sexual offences have been defined by Parliament broadly in an attempt to protect the sexual integrity of women and children. Parliament has defined consent for the purpose of sexual assault not to

---

20   If the crime is murder or attempted murder, there must be subjective foresight that death will result from the carrying out of the unlawful purpose with an accomplice. *R. v. Logan* (1990), 58 C.C.C. (3d) 391 (S.C.C.) [*Logan*].

21   *R. v. Deutsch* (1986), 27 C.C.C. (3d) 385 (S.C.C.); *United States of America v. Dynar* (1997), 115 C.C.C. (3d) 481 (S.C.C.).

include specific conduct[22] and the Supreme Court has held that consent as a matter of *actus reus* depends solely on the subjective intent of the complainant[23] and also cannot be given by an unconscious complainant.[24] In *R. v. Jobidon*,[25] the Supreme Court held that, for the purposes of assault, a person could not consent to the intentional infliction of serious hurt or non-trivial bodily harm. This has effectively expanded the law of assault to include consensual fights that result in injury. In *Rodriguez v. British Columbia (A.G.)*,[26] the Court upheld a *Criminal Code* provision that a person could not consent to his or her death. There has also been some relaxation of the traditional requirement that the prohibited act and the fault element occur at the same time. There seems to be less reluctance to criminalize the omission to perform specific legal duties. In the future it appears likely that Parliament will continue to define many crimes broadly, and the manner in which crimes are defined will be an important policy component of the criminal law.

2) Subjective and Objective Fault Elements

It appears that proof of subjective *mens rea* in relation to the prohibited result of a crime will be a constitutional requirement for only a few offences, such as murder, attempted murder, and war crimes. The Supreme Court has stressed that the penalties and stigma that accompany these offences require proof beyond a reasonable doubt of subjective *mens rea* in relation to the prohibited result. It has struck down the constructive (or felony) murder provisions in section 230 of the *Criminal Code*, because they allowed accused who caused death while committing serious crimes to be convicted of murder even if they did not have subjective foresight that death would occur. Liability for murder based on objective, as opposed to subjective, foresight of death contemplated in sections 229(c) and 21(2) has also been struck down.[27] In a controversial decision, the Supreme Court held in *R. v. Finta* that section 7 of the *Charter* required proof of knowledge or at least wilful blindness in relation to the conditions that would make a war crime constitute a war crime. The Court has recently affirmed this approach but also indicated that recklessness may be a sufficient form of fault.[28]

---

22 *Code*, above note 11, s. 273.1.
23 *R. v. Ewanchuk* (1999), 131 C.C.C. (3d) 481 (S.C.C.).
24 *R. v. J.A.*, [2011] 2 S.C.R. 440.
25 *R. v. Jobidon* (1991), 66 C.C.C. (3d) 454 (S.C.C.).
26 *Rodriguez*, above note 10.
27 *R. v. Martineau* (1990), 58 C.C.C. (3d) 353 (S.C.C.); *Logan*, above note 20.
28 *Mugesera v. Canada (Minister of Citizenship and Immigration)*, [2005] 2 S.C.R. 100.

Terrorism may, like war crimes, be found to be a stigma crime that requires subjective fault in relation to the prohibited act, but so far the courts have upheld the main terrorism offences including broad offences with qualified forms of subjective fault such as the facilitation of terrorism offence under section 83.19 of the *Criminal Code*. The Ontario Court of Appeal reversed a trial judge's decision that the political or religious motive violated the *Charter* and stressed that the law was not responsible for any chill on religious or political freedoms.[29] For non-stigma offences, however, the *Charter* prohibits only imprisonment for absolute liability that follows from the commission of the prohibited act and without regard to either subjective or objective fault.

The Supreme Court has rejected, as a constitutional requirement, the principle that the fault element should relate to all aspects of the *actus reus*. Thus, the fault element of manslaughter relates not to the causing of death but the causing of non-trivial bodily harm. Many other crimes are based on the consequences of the accused's actions even though the accused may not have had subjective or objective fault in relation to those consequences. The Court has upheld the constitutionality of objective standards of liability for serious crimes, including unlawful act manslaughter, unlawfully causing bodily harm, and dangerous driving. The courts have accepted the legitimacy of the use of objective fault standards in the criminal law while also holding that section 7 of the *Charter* requires more than simple negligence, but rather a marked departure from the standard of care expected from a reasonable person in the circumstances so that negligence as a form of criminal fault is adequately distinguished from mere civil negligence.[30] The new section 22.1 of the *Criminal Code*, for example, requires that senior officer(s) of a corporation demonstrate a marked departure from the standard of care necessary to prevent representatives of the corporation from committing a criminal offence based on negligence. The marked departure standard, as well as the onus on the Crown to prove fault beyond a reasonable doubt, is an important distinction between criminal and regulatory offences.

In *Creighton*,[31] a 5:4 majority of the Supreme Court rejected attempts to tailor objective standards to a particular accused by endowing the reasonable person with personal characteristics such as the accused's age and intelligence. The majority did keep open the possibility of considering the characteristics of individual accused but only if they meant

---

29   R. v. *Khawaja*, 2010 ONCA 862. See also R. v. *Roy*, 2012 SCC 26.
30   *Beatty*, above note 1.
31   *Creighton*, above note 5.

that the accused lacked the capacity to appreciate the prohibited risk. In most cases, however, the reasonable person used to administer objective standards will not have the same characteristics as the accused and the Court has expressed concerns about not blurring the distinction between subjective and objective standards of liability. This distinction has been reaffirmed in more recent cases that require a marked departure and consideration of whether the accused's own mental state raises a reasonable doubt about negligence.[32] In cases dealing with defences, however, the Court has indicated that courts should consider the particular accused's past experiences, characteristics, and frailties when determining whether perceptions and actions are reasonable.[33] This leads to more generous defences, but some blurring of the distinctions between subjective and objective standards.

The different approaches to applying objective standards and defining the reasonable person introduce inconsistency in the law. A possible rationale for the divergent approach is that many accused will make a voluntary choice to undertake activities that are judged on a negligence-based standard, whereas the objective standard in defences must be modified to account for the characteristics and experiences of the particular accused in order to ensure that he or she is not found guilty for morally involuntary conduct. In other words, accused's characteristics and experiences may be relevant to determine whether the only realistic choice open to them in particular circumstances was to violate the law.

3) Regulatory Offences and Corporate Crime

Following *R. v. Sault Ste. Marie (City)*,[34] most regulatory offences are interpreted as strict liability offences that require the Crown to prove the prohibited act, but then presume the existence of negligence unless the accused can establish a defence of due diligence on a balance of probabilities. This important presumption was affirmed by the Court in 2006.[35] In *R. v. Wholesale Travel Group Inc.*,[36] the Supreme Court held that the fault element of negligence was constitutionally sufficient for

---

32 *Beatty*, above note 1.

33 R. v. *Lavallee* (1990), 55 C.C.C. (3d) 97 (S.C.C.) [*Lavallee*]; R. v. *Pétel* (1994), 87 C.C.C. (3d) 97 (S.C.C.) [*Pétel*]; R. v . *Hibbert* (1995), 99 C.C.C. (3d) 193 (S.C.C.) [*Hibbert*]; R. v. *Thibert* (1996), 104 C.C.C. (3d) 1 (S.C.C.) [*Thibert*], discussed in ch. 9, "Self-Defence, Necessity, and Duress."

34 (1978), 40 C.C.C. (2d) 353 (S.C.C.).

35 *Lévis (City) v. Tétreault*, [2006] 1 S.C.R. 420 [*Lévis*].

36 (1991), 67 C.C.C. (3d) 193 (S.C.C.).

a regulatory offence of misleading advertising, and it approved the requirement that the accused demonstrate that it was not negligent by proving a defence of due diligence on a balance of probabilities. Absolute liability in which the Crown must prove only the prohibited act is unconstitutional when there is imprisonment.

The Supreme Court's decision in R. v. *Pontes*[37] suggests that offences may be interpreted as absolute liability offences if the ignorance of the law is no excuse principle would deprive the accused of his or her only possible defence. The Court has made a minimal intrusion into section 19 of the *Criminal Code* by recognizing a defence of officially induced error,[38] but while maintaining the distinction that mistakes about the law will not excuse while mistakes about facts often will. The courts have also interpreted the *actus reus* of fraud quite broadly to apply to cases that produce even a risk of deprivation of property while interpreting the *mens rea* relatively restrictively to require subjective awareness of the risk of deprivation of property, but not subjective awareness of dishonesty or knowledge of actual deprivation.[39] Parliament has also provided for enhanced penalties for so-called white-collar crime so any deficiency in the prosecution of such crimes seems more related to investigations and trials, rather than to the substantive criminal law.

Sections 22.1 and 22.2 of the *Criminal Code* now have replaced the old common law that only attributed the fault of a corporation's directing mind to the corporation for the purpose of determining criminal liability. Now the fault of senior officers can be attributed to the corporation. Unlike the old directing mind concept, a senior officer may include someone who manages an important aspect of the company's operations even when that person does not set corporate policy. Section 22.1 applies to criminal offences of negligence and requires that senior officer(s) depart markedly from the standard of care that would prevent representatives of the corporation from being a party to the offence. Section 22.2 applies to criminal offences of subjective fault and requires the senior officer to be a party to the offence or direct a representative so that he or she commits an offence or to fail to take all reasonable steps to prevent a representative from committing an offence when the senior officer knows that an offence is being committed. It remains to be seen whether these new provisions, as well as new sentencing provisions that allow a corporation to be placed on probation, will increase criminal charges and convictions against corpora-

---

37   (1995), 100 C.C.C. (3d) 353 (S.C.C.).
38   *Lévis*, above note 35.
39   *R. v. Théroux*, [1993] 2 S.C.R. 5.

tions and other organizations and whether this will effectively deter corporate misconduct.

4) Intoxication, Mental Disorder, and Other Defences

Some recent cases have expanded the range of defences open to accused. In *Daviault*,[40] the Supreme Court recognized a defence of extreme intoxication akin to automatism. Such a rare state would deprive an accused of the voluntary and conscious behaviour necessary for general intent offences such as assault and sexual assault. Unlike evidence of intoxication, which can always raise a reasonable doubt about the mental element of specific intent offences such as murder or robbery, the defence of extreme intoxication to a general intent offence must be proved by the accused on a balance of probabilities. Parliament responded with section 33.1 of the *Criminal Code*. It attempts to eliminate the *Daviault* defence with respect to violent offences by deeming that the marked departure from reasonable conduct involved in becoming extremely intoxicated can be substituted for the voluntary and conscious behaviour and fault required to convict a person of assault, sexual assault, or other violent general intent offences. The constitutionality of this provision has not yet been finally settled, but most courts have found that it violates the presumption of innocence by substituting the fault of becoming extremely intoxicated for the fault of committing the crime and that it violates the principles of fundamental justice by allowing the conviction of a person who commits a crime in an involuntary manner. The Supreme Court, however, had no trouble finding that the section 33.1 applied and denied a defence in a case where an accused committed an aggravated assault while subject to a "toxic psychosis" produced by drugs even though that condition produced delusions normally associated with mental illness.[41] The Supreme Court has also held that the traditional intoxication defence for specific intent crimes violates the *Charter* by requiring a reasonable doubt about the accused's capacity to form the intent rather than the actual formation of the intent.[42]

The mental disorder defence applies to a wide range of mental disorders, but only when the mental disorder renders the accused incapable of appreciating the physical consequences of his or her actions or knowing that they are wrong. The courts have not, however, extended

---

40   *Daviault*, above note 12.

41   *R. v. Bouchard-Lebrun*, 2011 SCC 58 at paras 89-91 [*Bouchard-Lebrun*].

42   *R. v. Robinson* (1996), 105 C.C.C. (3d) 97 (S.C.C.).

the defence to those incapable of appreciating the emotional or penal consequences of their actions, even if this lack of appreciation was caused by a mental disorder. In 1990, the Supreme Court expanded the mental disorder defence by holding that people should not be convicted if a mental disorder rendered them incapable of knowing that their acts were morally and not just legally wrong.[43] The courts are still working out the exact parameters of this holding and are not likely to apply the defence to psychopaths who, although aware that society would regard their actions as wrong, decide to substitute their own moral code for that of society. The accused still bears the burden of establishing the mental disorder defence on a balance of probabilities. The Court has recently suggested that those who have a valid mental disorder defence act in a morally involuntarily manner and this would suggest that Parliament could not repeal or significantly restrict the defence without violating the s.7 principle of fundamental justice that people should not be convicted for morally involuntary behaviour.[44]

The defence of non-mental disorder automatism is less stable. The Supreme Court expanded the defence in R. v. Parks[45] by holding that it applied to an accused who killed while sleepwalking. Like the Daviault defence, the automatism defence would lead to a complete acquittal. The Court has, however, continued to restrict non-insane automatism produced by emotional blows to extraordinary cases that would cause an ordinary person to go into a disassociative state.[46] Moreover, the Court's decision in Stone requires the accused to establish the non-mental disorder automatism defence on a balance of probabilities in part because of scepticism about claims of automatism. It also suggests that more cases of automatism will be classified as caused by mental disorders in an attempt to maximize the protection of the public. Cases such as Parks in which the accused receives an outright acquittal may be increasingly rare.

When considering defences that apply even though the accused may have committed a crime with the necessary fault element, the Supreme Court has been concerned with the fair administration of standards that require reasonable responses to external pressures. In Thibert,[47] the Court indicated that the ordinary person considered for the purpose of the provocation defence should be the same age and sex as the

---

43   R. v. Chaulk (1990), 62 C.C.C. (3d) 193 (S.C.C.).
44   Bouchard-Lebrun, above note 41 at para. 74.
45   (1992), 75 C.C.C. (3d) 287 (S.C.C.) [Parks].
46   R. v. Rabey (1980), 54 C.C.C. (2d) 1 (S.C.C.); R. v. Stone (1999), 134 C.C.C. (3d) 353 (S.C.C.).
47   Thibert, above note 33.

accused and have any other characteristic or experience that would give the act or insult special significance. The Court has clarified this approach in the subsequent provocation case of *R. v. Tran*[48] by stressing that the personal characteristics of the accused are only relevant in placing a provocative act or insult in context but that they do not change the reasonable standard of restraint required from all individuals. In *R. v. Lavallee*[49] and *R. v. Pétel*[50] the Court stressed that when determining whether self-defence was reasonable, the trier of fact should consider the accused's past experience, including the fact that she had been battered by the man she killed. A similar modified objective standard will be used when administering the common law defences of duress and necessity.[51] The courts will tailor objective standards in defences to the experiences and frailties of a particular accused. In *R. v. Latimer*,[52] the Court affirmed that a modified objective standard would be applied in determining whether the accused faced an imminent harm and had no safe avenue of escape or legal way out. At the same time, however, the Court indicated that the requirement of proportionality between the harm avoided and the harm inflicted should be determined on a purely objective standard and one that did not devalue the life of a victim who was severely disabled.

In *Lavallee*, the Supreme Court rejected the idea that self-defence was only justified in response to an immediate threat of harm. At the same time, the more recent case of *R. v. Cinous*[53] suggests that in other contexts self-defence may not even be put to the jury in a case in which an accused has alternatives other than killing the person who he believes threatens him. Parliament's recent reforms of self-defence and defence of property demonstrate a salutary Parliament interest in simplifying the criminal law, but they may also make these defences somewhat less predictable. The new section 34 imposes only general requirements that accused believe on reasonable grounds that force or threat of force is being used and that they act reasonably in the circumstances. Similarly, the new section 35 only requires a reasonable belief of a threat to property held in peaceable possession and reasonable actions in the circumstances. Proportionality in particular is only a factor that should be considered under section 34(2) and one that is not even specifically mentioned in section 35 with respect to defence of property.

---

48   *R. v. Tran*, [2010] 3 S.C.R. 350.
49   Above note 33.
50   *Ibid.*
51   *Hibbert*, above note 33.
52   *R. v. Latimer* (2001), 150 C.C.C. (3d) 129 (S.C.C.) [*Latimer*].
53   *R. v. Cinous* (2002), 162 C.C.C. (3d) 129 (S.C.C.).

The requirement in section 17 of the *Code* that an accused only has a duress defence if he or she faced immediate death or bodily harm from a person who is present when the crime is committed has been found to violate section 7 of the *Charter* because it could result in the punishment of a person who responded reasonably and in a morally involuntary fashion to threats from which there was no safe avenue of escape.[54] Little, except a long and constitutionally suspect list of excluded offences, would be lost and the law would be simplified and clarified if Parliament simply repealed section 17 and allowed the common law defence to apply in all cases without artificial distinctions between principals who commit the offence (to whom section 17 still applies) and parties to the offence who have long been subject to a common law defence of duress that is now informed by the constitutional principle that people should not be convicted for morally involuntary conduct. The courts have been reluctant categorically to exclude any offence from the ambit of the common law duress defence.

CONCLUSION

Canadian criminal law is constantly evolving. Parliament adds more offences and increasingly more mandatory sentences each year. It has recently simplified self-defence and defence of property. The courts continue to interpret offences and statutory and common law defences and the *Charter*. On occasion, courts recognize new common law defences such as entrapment and officially induced error. Fault requirements are designed to ensure that the morally innocent, such as those who are unaware that they possess drugs, are not punished. Although objective standards of fault are constitutionally sufficient for most criminal offences other than murder, attempted murder, and war crimes, the Supreme Court has emphasized that objective fault must be based on a marked departure from the reasonableness standard to distinguish it from mere civil negligence. The Court has also expanded some defences such as duress in recognition of the principle that people should not be punished for morally involuntary conduct that they could not realistically be expected to avoid. Most defences require that the accused respond reasonably to threats or circumstances, but some, such as intoxication and mental disorder, recognize that accused are not mentally responsible for their actions. Parliament can respond to the extension of defences and has done so with respect to the Court's con-

---

54   *R. v. Ruzic* (2001), 153 C.C.C. (3d) 1 (S.C.C.).

troversial recognition of a defence of extreme intoxication. Even when the Court applies *Charter* rights, Parliament retains the options of justifying reasonable limits on such rights or temporally overriding such rights. Canadian criminal law emerges from a dialogue between courts and Parliament that is conducted by means of development of the common law, interpretation of the *Criminal Code* and other statutes, and the interpretation of the *Charter*.

FURTHER READINGS

BOYLE, C., *et al.*, *A Feminist Approach to Criminal Law* (Ottawa: Status of Women Canada, 1986)

CAIRNS-WAY, R., *Dimensions of Criminal Law*, 3d ed. (Toronto: Emond Montgomery, 2002)

CAMERON, J., *The Charter's Impact on the Criminal Justice System* (Toronto: Carswell, 1996)

————, & J. STRIBOPOULOS, eds., *The Charter and Criminal Justice Twenty-Five Years Later* (Markham, ON: LexisNexis, 2008)

ERICSON, R., & P. BARANEK, *The Ordering of Justice: The Study of Accused Persons As Dependants in the Criminal Process* (Toronto: University of Toronto Press, 1982)

FRIEDLAND, M.L., "Criminal Justice in Canada Revisited" (2004) 48 Crim. L.Q. 419

MANDEL, M., *The Charter of Rights and the Legalization of Politics in Canada*, rev. ed. (Toronto: Wall & Thompson, 1994)

MANITOBA PUBLIC INQUIRY INTO THE ADMINISTRATION OF JUSTICE AND ABORIGINAL PEOPLE, *Report of the Aboriginal Justice Inquiry of Manitoba* (Winnipeg: The Inquiry, 1991)

MARTIN, D., "Retribution Reconsidered: A Reconsideration of Feminist Criminal Law Strategies" (1998) 36 Osgoode Hall L.J. 151

MORAN, M., *Rethinking the Reasonable Person* (Oxford: Oxford University Press, 2003)

PACIOCCO, D., *Getting Away with Murder* (Toronto: Irwin Law, 2000)

PACKER, H., *The Limits of the Criminal Sanction* (Stanford: Stanford University Press, 1968)

ROACH, K., *Due Process and Victims' Rights: The New Law and Politics of Criminal Justice* (Toronto: University of Toronto Press, 1999)

————, "A Charter Reality Check: How Relevant Is the *Charter* to the Justness of Our Criminal Justice System?" (2008) 40 S.C.L.R. (2d) 717

SIMON, J., *Governing Through Crime* (New York: Oxford University Press, 2007)

GLOSSARY

Absolute discharge: a disposition in which no conviction is recorded. It is available if there is no minimum penalty, the offence is not punishable by life or fourteen years' imprisonment, and the judge determines that it is in the accused's best interests and not contrary to the public interest.

Absolute liability: an offence for which the accused is guilty once it is proven that the prohibited act, or *actus reus*, was committed and regardless of the existence of any fault, including negligence.

Actus reus: the prohibited act in a criminal or regulatory offence. Proof of the *actus reus* may also include the requirement that the prohibited act be voluntarily and consciously committed by the accused.

Aiding or abetting: intentionally assisting or encouraging a crime and, by doing so, becoming a party to the crime.

Appellate court: a court that reviews the accused's conviction or acquittal at trial. In summary conviction matters, appeals are usually heard by superior courts, while in indictable matters, appeals are heard by the provincial courts of appeal. Courts, such as the Supreme Court of Canada, which hear subsequent appeals are also called appellate courts.

Attempt: an attempted crime occurs when the accused does something beyond mere preparation for the purpose of committing a crime. It is a separate crime of attempting the specific offence and is usually subject to less punishment than the completed crime.

Attorney General: the elected official ultimately accountable for prosecutions. For *Criminal Code* offences, this is normally the Attorney General of the province, while for other federal offences it is the Attorney General of Canada.

Automatism: a state in which the accused acts in an involuntary manner. It is known as mental disorder automatism if it is caused by a mental disorder, and non-mental disorder automatism if it is caused by some other factor such as a blow to the head.

Bail: also known as judicial interim release. It refers to the release of an accused person pending trial on the grounds that he or she is likely to appear for trial, not likely to commit offences in the meantime, and release will not undermine public confidence in the administration of justice.

Causation: an issue in determining whether the accused has committed the *actus reus* or prohibited act by causing the prohibited consequences, usually death.

Common law: judge-made law as opposed to legislation passed by the legislature.

Conditional discharge: a disposition in which no conviction is recorded so long as the accused successfully satisfies prescribed conditions. This disposition is available only if there is no minimum penalty and the offence is not subject to life or fourteen years' imprisonment.

Conditional sentence: a disposition in which the accused is found guilty and sentenced to imprisonment but serves the sentence in the community so long as he or she successfully fulfills conditions.

Counselling: procuring, soliciting, or inciting a person to commit a crime. A person who does this counselling can become guilty as a party to an offence that is committed by the person counselled or can be convicted of a separate crime of counselling if the offence is not committed.

Defence of property: A justification to a crime under section 35 of the *Criminal Code* generally available when persons reasonably apprehend threats to their property and respond in a reasonable manner.

Disease of the mind: a condition necessary for an accused to be found not criminally responsible on account of mental disorder. Diseases of the mind are now defined as mental disorders. They can include any mental disorder but not transitory or self-induced states.

Division of powers: the constitutional allocation of authority between the federal and provincial governments to enact legislation.

Due diligence: a defence available in strict liability offences that allows the accused to prove on a balance of probabilities that it was not negligent.

Duress: a defence available to those who commit crimes because they are threatened with serious harm. A codified defence of duress is found in section 17 of the *Criminal Code* and applies to principal offenders. The requirements of immediacy and presence in section 17 of the *Code* have been severed from the defence as unconstitutional. A common law defence of duress applies to parties to offences. In some rare circumstances, duress may also be relevant to the proof of the fault element.

Entrapment: objectionable police conduct such as offering a suspect an opportunity to commit a crime without a reasonable suspicion that he or she is involved with crime or when the police are not pursuing a *bona fide* inquiry in a high-crime area. It also includes disreputable police conduct that goes beyond providing a suspect an opportunity to commit a crime and actually induces the commission of the crime. The remedy for entrapment is a stay of proceedings.

Exclusion of evidence: the situation when evidence that would otherwise be relevant to determining the accused's guilt or innocence is kept out of a criminal trial because it was obtained in a manner that violated the *Charter* and its admission would bring the administration of justice into disrepute. Unconstitutionally obtained evidence is excluded if its admission would affect the fairness of the trial or if the seriousness of the *Charter* violation outweighs the harmful effects of excluding the evidence.

Fault element: the culpable state of mind that must be proven by the state. Fault elements can require proof of a subjective state of mind of the accused such as wilfulness, knowledge, or recklessness or can be based on objective fault such as negligence.

General intent: an offence in which the fault element relates only to the performance of the act in question, with no further ulterior intent or purpose. Intoxication has traditionally not been a defence to general as opposed to specific intent offences. Subject to section 33.1 of the *Criminal Code*, extreme intoxication producing involuntary behaviour may be a defence to a general intent offence.

Indictable offences: the most serious category of criminal offences. In most cases, the accused has the option to be tried before a provincial court without a preliminary inquiry or a jury, or tried in a superior court with a preliminary inquiry and/or a jury.

Intoxication: evidence of intoxication by alcohol or drugs that prevents the Crown from proving beyond a reasonable doubt that the accused had the *mens rea*, or fault element, required for the particular crime.

Judicial interim release: *see* bail.

Mens rea: the prohibited mental or fault element for the commission of a criminal offence. It may include intent, purpose, wilfulness, knowledge, recklessness, wilful blindness, criminal negligence, or negligence depending on the offence.

Mental disorder: *see* disease of the mind.

Mental disorder or insanity defence: a defence put forth when a person commits a crime while suffering from a mental disorder that renders him or her incapable of appreciating the nature and quality of the act or knowing that it is wrong. An accused found not criminally responsible by reason of mental disorder will be released unless a court or review board concludes that he or she is a significant threat to the public.

Mental element: *see mens rea*; fault element.

Moral innocence: The quality of a person who commits a prohibited act with no fault such as negligence or subjective *mens rea*. A morally innocent person cannot be imprisoned under section 7 of the *Charter*.

Moral voluntariness: The quality of a person who commits a crime but who because of emergency circumstances has no realistic choice but to commit the crime. A person who commits a crime in a morally involuntary manner cannot be convicted under section 7 of the *Charter*.

Necessity: a common law defence available as an excuse when an accused acts in response to an urgent and immediate peril that cannot be avoided by obeying the law.

Omission: the *actus reus* when a person is found guilty for failing to perform a specific legal duty, such as providing the necessities of life to a child.

Parole: discretionary release of an accused serving a term of imprisonment granted by a parole board.

Preliminary inquiry: a hearing to determine whether the prosecution has introduced enough evidence that, if believed at trial, would support a conviction.

Presumption of innocence: requirement in section 11(d) of the *Charter* that the Crown prove the accused's guilt beyond a reasonable doubt. The Crown must prove not only the elements of the offence but all matters essential for conviction, including the non-availability of relevant defences.

Probation: a court order that allows an accused to be supervised in the community. The breach of a probation order is a crime.

Prohibited act: The act or omission that is prohibited in the offence. *See also actus reus.*

Provincial courts: the court where most criminal cases are resolved. The judges are appointed by the provincial government and cannot sit with a jury.

Provocation: a partial defence that reduces murder to manslaughter. It is available when the accused is faced with a sudden act or insult that would make an ordinary person lose self-control, and which caused the accused to act suddenly and before his or her passions had cooled.

Public welfare offences: *see* regulatory offences.

Regulatory offences: offences enacted by federal, provincial, or municipal governments that are used primarily to regulate risky behaviour that may cause harm. They are presumed to require strict liability.

Search and seizure: any state activity that invades a reasonable expectation of privacy.

Self-defence: a justification to a crime under section 34 of the *Criminal Code* generally available when a person reasonably apprehends a threat and responds in a reasonable manner.

Specific intent: an offence that requires the Crown to prove not only a fault or mental element that relates to the performance of the act in question, but also some ulterior intent or purpose. Evidence of intoxication is always relevant when the accused is charged with a specific intent offence and operates as a defence if it raises a reasonable doubt about the existence of the mental element.

Stay of proceedings: a disposition where the court does not allow a prosecution to proceed because of objectionable police or prosecutorial conduct and/or a violation of the accused's rights. This remedy is not the moral equivalent of an acquittal because it does not reach the merits but has the same practical effects.

Strict liability: an offence for which the Crown must prove the commission of the prohibited act beyond a reasonable doubt. The existence of negligence is then presumed unless the accused establishes a defence of due diligence on a balance of probabilities.

Summary conviction offences: the least serious offences in the *Criminal Code*. They are subject to a maximum penalty of six months and/or a fine of not more than $5,000.

Superior courts: the highest level of trial court in a criminal case that hears all jury trials and the first level of appeal in summary conviction offences.

Suspended sentence: a disposition after conviction where the judge suspends passing sentence, while imposing conditions on the accused's release by means of probation orders. If the conditions are breached, the court may sentence the accused for the original offence.

Unfit to stand trial: a determination that an accused, on account of a mental disorder, cannot be tried because he or she cannot understand the nature or possible consequences of the proceedings or communicate with counsel.

TABLE OF CASES

"Reward" (The) (1818), 2 Dods. 265, 165 E.R. 1482 90
"Rhone" (The) v. "Peter A.B. Widner" (The), [1993]
   1 S.C.R. 497, 101 D.L.R. (4th) 188, 148 N.R. 349 .... 232, 235

A (Children) (Conjoined Twins: Surgical Separation),
   [2000] 4 All E.R. 961 (C.A.) 355
Adgey v. R. (1973), [1975] 2 S.C.R. 426, 13 C.C.C. (2d) 177,
   23 C.R.N.S. 298 473
Anderton v. Ryan, [1985] A.C. 560, [1985] 2 All E.R. 355,
   [1985] 2 W.L.R. 968 (H.L.) 135
Atlantic Sugar Refineries Co. v. Canada (A.G.), [1980]
   2 S.C.R. 644, 54 C.C.C. (2d) 373, 16 C.R. (3d) 128 137

B.(N.) v. Hôtel-Dieu de Québec (1992), 69 C.C.C. (3d) 450,
   86 D.L.R. (4th) 385 (Que. S.C.) 352
Baril v. Obnecki (2007), 214 Man. R. (2d) 7, 279 D.L.R.
   (4th) 304, 2007 MBCA 40 27
Beckford v. R. (1987), [1988] A.C. 130, [1987] 3 All
   E.R. 425, [1987] 3 W.L.R. 611 (P.C.) 325
Bedard v. Dawson, [1923] S.C.R. 681, 40 C.C.C. 404,
   [1923] S.C.J. No. 30 27
Bedder v. D.P.P., [1954] 2 All E.R. 801, [1954] 1 W.L.R. 1119,
   98 Sol. J. 556 (H.L.) 413
Bell Express Vu v. Canada, [2002] 2 S.C.R. 559, 212 D.L.R. (4th) 1 87
Bhatnager v. Canada (Minister of Employment and Immigration),
   [1990] 2 S.C.R. 217 229

Bratty v. A.G. for Northern Ireland (1961), [1963] A.C. 386,
[1961] 3 All E.R. 523, [1961] 3 W.L.R. 965 (H.L.)....................................290
Brosseau v. R., [1969] S.C.R. 181, [1969] 3 C.C.C. 129,
5 C.R.N.S. 331.. 472

Canada (Attorney General) v. Bedford, 2012 ONCA 186...........................66, 500
Canada (Attorney General) v. Dupond, [1978] 2 S.C.R. 770,
84 D.L.R. (3d) 420, [1978] S.C.J. No. 33... 27
Canada (Attorney General) v. PHS Community Services,
2011 SCC 44, [2011] 3 S.C.R. 134 ....65, 500, 504
Canada (Director of Investigation & Research, Combines
Investigation Branch) v. Southam Inc., [1984] 2 S.C.R.
145, 14 C.C.C. (3d) 97, 41 C.R. (3d) 97..35, 86
Canada v. Campbell (2000), 35 C.R. (5th) 314,
[2000] O.J. No. 2261 (S.C.J.)... 308, 313
Canadian Dredge & Dock Co. v. R., [1985] 1 S.C.R. 662,
19 C.C.C. (3d) 1, 45 C.R. (3d) 289...221, 227, 231
Canadian Federation of Agriculture v. Quebec (A.G.)
(1950), [1951] A.C. 179, [1950] 4 D.L.R. 689 (P.C.) 26
Canadian Foundation for Children, Youth and the Law
v. Canada (A.G.), [2004] 1 S.C.R. 76, 180 C.C.C.
(3d) 353, 2004 SCC 4 .... 63, 76, 90,
92, 262, 275, 351, 503
CanadianOxy Chemical v. Canada, [1999] 1 S.C.R. 743,
133 C.C.C. (3d) 426.. 87
Carter v. Canada (Attorney General), 2012 BCSC 886.............................. 63, 434
Chatterjee v. Ontario (A.G.), [2009] 1 S.C.R. 624, aff'g (2007),
86 O.R. (3d) 168, 221 C.C.C. (3d) 350, 2007 ONCA 406 27
Chow Bew v. The Queen (1955), [1956] S.C.R. 124,
113 C.C.C. 337, [1955] S.C.J. No. 71 .... 148, 400
Cloutier v. Langlois, [1990] 1 S.C.R. 158, 46 C.R.R. 37,
30 Q.A.C. 241.. 35
Corp. professionelles des médecins (Québec) v. Thibault,
[1988] 1 S.C.R. 1033, 42 C.C.C. (3d) 1, 63 C.R. (3d) 273............................ 78

D.P.P. v. Beard, [1920] A.C. 479, [1920] All E.R. Rep. 21,
14 Cr. App. Rep. 159 (H.L.) 247–48,
250–51, 262, 293
D.P.P. v. Camplin, [1978] A.C. 705, [1978] 2 All E.R. 168,
[1978] 2 W.L.R. 679 (H.L.) 413, 422
D.P.P. v. Morgan (1975), [1976] A.C. 182, [1975] 1 All E.R. 8 (H.L.) 203
Dagenais v. Canadian Broadcasting Corp., [1994] 3 S.C.R.
835, 94 C.C.C. (3d) 289, 120 D.L.R. (4th) 12 48
Dunbar v. R. (1936), 67 C.C.C. 20,
[1936] 4 D.L.R. 737 (S.C.C.) 155, 185, 376

Dunlop v. R., [1979] 2 S.C.R. 881, 47 C.C.C. (2d) 93,
    99 D.L.R. (3d) 301 148–149
Dusky v. United States, 362 U.S. 402 (1960) 281

Fagan v. Metropolitan Police Commissioner (1968),
    [1969] 1 Q.B. 439, [1968] 3 All E.R. 442, [1968] 3 W.L.R. 1120 106
Fain v. Commonwealth of Kentucky, 78 Ky. Rptr. 183 (C.A. 1879) 307
Fowler v. Padget (1798), 101 E.R. 1103 (K.B.) 106
Frey v. Fedoruk, [1950] S.C.R. 517, 97 C.C.C. 1, 10 C.R. 26 83

Henry Birks & Sons (Montreal) Ltd. v. Montreal (City),
    [1955] S.C.R. 799, 113 C.C.C. 135, [1955] 5 D.L.R. 321 32

Iorfida v. MacIntyre (1994), 21 O.R. (3d) 186, 93 C.C.C.
    (3d) 395, 24 C.R.R. (2d) 293 (Gen. Div.) 142
Irwin Toy Ltd. v. Quebec (A.G.), [1989] 1 S.C.R. 927,
    58 D.L.R. (4th) 577, 39 C.R.R. 193 .... 62, 221

Kilbride v. Lake, [1962] N.Z.L.R. 590 (S.C.) 118
Kindler v. Canada (Minister of Justice), [1991] 2 S.C.R. 779,
    67 C.C.C. (3d) 1, 8 C.R. (4th) 1 78

Labatt Breweries of Canada Ltd. v. Canada (A.G.) (1979),
    [1980] 1 S.C.R. 914, 9 B.L.R. 181, 30 N.R. 497 26
Lafrance v. The Queen (1973), [1975] 2 S.C.R. 201,
    13 C.C.C. (2d) 289, [1973] S.C.J. No. 156 456
Lennard's Carrying Co. Ltd. v. Asiatic Petroleum Co. Ltd., [1915]
    A.C. 705, 84 L.J.K.B. 1281, [1914–1915] All E.R. Rep. 280 (H.L.) 231
Lévis (City) v. Tétreault, [2006] 1 S.C.R. 420,
    207 C.C.C. (3d) 1, 2006 SCC 12 .... 95, 99, 121,
    218, 225, 243, 508–9
Lim Chin Aik v. R., [1963] A.C. 160, [1963] 1 All E.R. 223,
    [1963] 2 W.L.R. 42 (P.C.) 97

M'Naghten's Case (1843), 8 E.R. 718, 10 Cl. & Fin. 200 (H.L.) 287
Marcotte v. Canada (Deputy A.G.), [1976] 1 S.C.R. 108,
    19 C.C.C. (2d) 257, 51 D.L.R. (3d) 259 84
Mazzei v. British Columbia (Director of Adult Forensic Psychiatric
    Services), [2006] 1 S.C.R. 326, 206 C.C.C. (3d) 161, 2006 SCC 7 286
McNeil v. Nova Scotia (Board of Censors), [1978] 2 S.C.R. 662,
    25 N.S.R. (2d) 128, 44 C.C.C. (2d) 316 27
Meli v. The Queen, [1954] 1 W.L.R. 228 (P.C.) 396
Metropolitan Police Commissioner v. Caldwell (1981),
    [1982] A.C. 341, [1981] All E.R. 961, [1981] 2 W.L.R. 509 (H.L.) 171
Miller v. The Queen, [1977] 2 S.C.R. 680 152
More v. R., [1963] S.C.R. 522, [1963] 3 C.C.C. 289, 41 C.R. 98 301

Mugesera v. Canada (Minister of Citizenship and Immigration),
[2005] 2 S.C.R. 100, 197 C.C.C. (3d) 233, 2005 SCC 40 72–73,
142, 144, 506

New Brunswick v. G.(J.), [1999] 3 S.C.R. 46, 26 C.R. (5th) 203 178

O'Grady v. Sparling, [1960] S.C.R. 804, 128 C.C.C. 1, 33 C.R. 293 .... 27, 191
Ontario (A.G.) v. Hamilton Street Railway Co., [1903] A.C. 524,
72 L.J.P.C. 105, 7 C.C.C. 326 (P.C.) 32
Ontario v. Canadian Pacific, [1995] 2 S.C.R. 1031, 125 D.L.R.
(4th) 385, 99 C.C.C. (3d) 97 90

Parnerkar v. The Queen (1973), [1974] S.C.R. 449, [1973] 4 W.W.R. 298 413–14
Penetanguishene Mental Health Centre v. Ontario (A.G.) (2003),
2004 SCC 20, [2003] S.C.J. No. 67 286
People v. Goetz, 497 N.E.2d 41 (1986) 325
People v. Lewis, 57 P. 470 (S.C. Cal. 1899) 390
Perka v. R., [1984] 2 S.C.R. 232, 14 C.C.C.
(3d) 385, 42 C.R. (3d) 113 ....319–20, 328, 353–58, 360, 369

R. v. 1260448 Ontario Inc., [2003] O.J. No. 4306,
68 O.R. (3d) 51, 180 C.C.C. (3d) 254 (C.A.) 220
R. v. 974649 Ontario Inc., [2001] 3 S.C.R. 575,
159 C.C.C. (3d) 321 46
R. v. A.M. (2008), 293 D.L.R. (4th) 187, 230 C.C.C. (3d) 377,
2008 SCC 19 34
R. v. Abbey, [1982] 2 S.C.R. 24, 29 C.R. (3d) 193,
68 C.C.C. (2d) 394 ....297, 300
R. v. Ahmad (2009), 257 C.C.C. (3d) 199 (Ont. S.C.J.) 461
R. v. Allard (1990), 57 C.C.C. (3d) 397, 78 C.R. (3d) 228
(sub nom. Allard v. R.) [1990] R.J.Q. 1847 (C.A.) 301
R. v. Amato, [1982] 2 S.C.R. 418, 69 C.C.C. (2d) 31, 29 C.R. (3d) 1 42
R. v. Amway Corp., [1989] 1 S.C.R. 21, 56 D.L.R. (4th) 309,
37 C.R.R. 235 59
R. v. Ancio, [1984] 1 S.C.R. 225, 10 C.C.C. (3d) 385,
[1984] S.C.J. No. 12 ....72, 128–31, 161
R. v. Angelillo, [2006] 2 S.C.R. 728, 214 C.C.C. (3d) 309,
2006 SCC 55 474
R. v. Antley, [1964] 1 O.R. 545, [1964] 2 C.C.C. 142 (C.A.) 337, 338
R. v. Arkell, [1990] 2 S.C.R. 695, 59 C.C.C. (3d) 65,
[1990] S.C.J. No. 86 404
R. v. Arradi, [2003] 1 S.C.R 280, 173 C.C.C. (3d) 1 84
R. v. Ashlee (2006), 391 A.R. 62, 212 C.C.C. (3d) 477, 2006 ABCA 244 102
R. v. Askov, [1990] 2 S.C.R. 1199, 59 C.C.C. (3d) 449,
79 C.R. (3d) 273 47
R. v. B.(G.D.), [2000] 1 S.C.R. 520, 143 C.C.C. (3d) 289 50

R. v. B.(T.B.) (1994), 124 Nfld. & P.E.I.R. 328,
93 C.C.C. (3d) 191, 34 C.R. (4th) 241 (P.E.I.C.A.) 105

R. v. B.J.T. (2000), [2001] 4 W.W.R. 741, 200 Sask. R. 42,
2000 SKQB 572 270

R. v. Bagri, [2004] 2 S.C.R. 248, 184 C.C.C. (3d) 449, 2004 SCC 42 461

R. v. Bailey (1800), 168 E.R. 651, Russ. & Ry. 1 (C.C.R.) 94

R. v. Bain (1992), 69 C.C.C. (3d) 481 (S.C.C.) 49

R. v. Baker, 2010 SCC 9, [2010] 1 S.C.R. 329 299

R. v. Baltzer (1974), 10 N.S.R. (2d) 561, 27 C.C.C. (2d) 118 (C.A.) 301

R. v. Banks (2007), 84 O.R. (3d) 1, 216 C.C.C. (3d) 19, 2007 ONCA 19 27

R. v. Banwait, 2011 SCC 55, [2011] 3 S.C.R. 533,
rev'g 2010 ONCA 869, 272 O.A.C. 130, 265 C.C.C. (3d) 201 402

R. v. Barnes, [1991] 1 S.C.R. 449, 63 C.C.C. (3d) 1, 3 C.R. (4th) 1 43

R. v. Barrett, [1995] 1 S.C.R. 752, 96 C.C.C. (3d) 319, 38 C.R. (4th) 1 40

R. v. Barron (1985), 12 O.A.C. 335, 23 C.C.C. (3d) 544,
[1985] O.J. No. 231 (C.A.) 431

R. v. Baxter (1975), 27 C.C.C. (2d) 86, 33 C.R.N.S. 22 (Ont. C.A.) 348

R. v. Beatty, [2008] 1 S.C.R. 49, 228 C.C.C.
(3d) 225, 2008 SCC 5 .... 70, 89, 118, 120, 168–69,
176–77, 195–97, 199–201, 210–11, 236, 238, 429–30, 451, 497, 507, 508

R. v. Beaver, [1957] S.C.R. 531, 118 C.C.C. 129, 26 C.R. 193 .... 94, 169–70,
187–88, 203, 204, 216

R. v. Beierl, 2007 ONCJ 267 100

R. v. Belnavis, [1997] 3 S.C.R. 341, 10 C.R. (5th) 65,
118 C.C.C. (3d) 405 34

R. v. Bergeron, [1995] R.J.Q. 2054, 101 C.C.C. (3d) 69,
[1995] J.Q. no 600 (C.A.) 228

R. v. Bernard, [1988] 2 S.C.R. 833, 45 C.C.C. (3d) 1,
[1988] S.C.J. No. 96 .... 249, 251, 255–56,
258, 276, 452

R. v. Berriman (1987), 62 Nfld. & P.E.I.R. 239,
45 M.V.R. 165, 190 A.P.R. 239 (Nfld. C.A.) 359

R. v. Berryman (1990), 48 B.C.L.R. (2d) 105,
57 C.C.C. (3d) 375, 78 C.R. (3d) 376 (C.A.) 150

R. v. Big M Drug Mart Ltd., [1985] 1 S.C.R. 295,
18 C.C.C. (3d) 385, 60 A.R. 161 32

R. v. Billy (2004), 191 C.C.C. (3d) 410, 26 C.R. (6th) 119,
2004 BCSC 1474 99

R. v. Biniaris, [2000] 1 S.C.R. 381, 143 C.C.C. (3d) 1 .... 148, 400

R. v. Black, [1970] 4 C.C.C. 251, 10 C.R.N.S. 17 (B.C.C.A.) 149

R. v. Black, [1989] 2 S.C.R. 138, 50 C.C.C. (3d) 1, 70 C.R. (3d) 97 41

R. v. Blaue, [1975] 3 All E.R. 446, [1975] 1 W.L.R. 1411,
139 J.P. 841 (C.A.) 384

R. v. Bleta (1964), [1964] S.C.R. 561, 44 C.R. 193,
[1965] 1 C.C.C. 1 .... 303, 310

R. v. Borden, [1994] 3 S.C.R. 145, 92 C.C.C. (3d) 404, 33 C.R.
(4th) 147... 41
R. v. Born With A Tooth (1992), 131 A.R. 193, 4 Alta. L.R.
(3d) 289, 76 C.C.C. (3d) 169 (C.A.) 345
R. v. Boss (1988), 46 C.C.C. (3d) 523, 68 C.R. (3d) 123,
42 C.R.R. 166 (S.C.C.) 59
R. v. Bouchard-Lebrun, [2011] 3 S.C.R. 575, 2011 SCC 58 .... 262, 264,
289, 293, 300, 312–13, 510–11
R. v. Boucher, 2006 QCCA 1079, 215 C.C.C. (3d) 97,
42 C.R. (6th) 117 403
R. v. Boudreau (2005), 231 N.S.R. (2d) 81,
193 C.C.C. (3d) 449, 2005 NSCA 40 133
R. v. Boudreau, [1949] S.C.R. 262, 94 C.C.C. 1, 7 C.R. 427 33
R. v. Boulanger, [2006] 2 S.C.R. 49, 210 C.C.C. (3d) 1,
2006 SCC 32 .... 89, 120
R. v. Brant, 2011 ONCA 362 473
R. v. Brenton (1999), 28 C.R. (5th) 308, [1999] N.W.T.J.
No. 113 (S.C.), rev'd on other grounds, [2001]
N.W.T.J. No. 14, 2001 NWTCA 1.. 268–69, 271, 273
R. v. Bridges (1990), 54 B.C.L.R. (2d) 273, 62 C.C.C.
(3d) 455, 78 D.L.R. (4th) 529 (C.A.)... 354
R. v. Briscoe, [2010] 1 S.C.R. 411, 2010 SCC 13 .... 148, 151, 152,
189, 190, 400, 445
R. v. Brown (1983), 4 C.C.C. (3d) 571 (Ont. H.C.).................................. 192, 396
R. v. Brown (1992), 125 A.R. 150, 73 C.C.C. (3d) 242,
13 C.R. (4th) 346 (C.A.) 479
R. v. Brown, [1991] 2 S.C.R. 518, 66 C.C.C. (3d) 1, 6 C.R. (4th) 353 474
R. v. Brown, [1994] 3 S.C.R. 749, 97 Man. R. (2d) 169,
93 C.C.C. (3d) 97.. 487
R. v. Browne (1997), 33 O.R. (3d) 775, 116 C.C.C. (3d) 183 (C.A.),
leave to appeal to S.C.C. refused, [1997] S.C.C.A. No. 398 116
R. v. Broyles, [1991] 3 S.C.R. 595, 9 C.R. (4th) 1, 68 C.C.C. (3d) 308................ 42
R. v. Brydges, [1990] 1 S.C.R. 190, 74 C.R. (3d) 129,
53 C.C.C. (3d) 330 .... 40, 41
R. v. Budget Car Rentals (Toronto) Ltd. (1981),
31 O.R. (2d) 161, 57 C.C.C. (2d) 201, 20 C.R. (3d) 66 (C.A.) 229
R. v. Budreo (2000), 46 O.R. (3d) 481, 142 C.C.C. (3d) 225,
[2000] O.J. No. 72 (C.A.)... 93
R. v. Burgess, [1970] 2 O.R. 216, [1970] 3 C.C.C. 268 (C.A.)............................ 204
R. v. Burgess, [1991] 2 Q.B. 92 (C.A.) 307
R. v. Burlingham, [1995] 2 S.C.R. 206, 38 C.R. (4th) 265,
97 C.C.C. (3d) 385 41
R. v. Burt (1987), 38 C.C.C. (3d) 299, 60 C.R. (3d) 372,
60 Sask. R. 100 (C.A.).. 219, 230

R. v. Butler, [1992] 1 S.C.R. 452, 70 C.C.C. (3d) 129,
11 C.R. (4th) 137 .... 60, 502

R. v. Buzzanga (1979), 25 O.R. (2d) 705, 49 C.C.C.
(2d) 369, 101 D.L.R. (3d) 488 (C.A.) 167, 182, 184, 192

R. v. C.F., 2010 ONCA 691 473

R. v. C.M., 2010 ONCA 690 473

R. v. C.P.F. (2006), 262 Nfld. & P.E.I.R. 165,
[2006] N.J. No. 354, 2006 NLCA 70 292

R. v. Cameron (1992), 71 C.C.C. (3d) 272, 12 C.R.
(4th) 396, 7 O.R. (3d) 545 (C.A.) 423

R. v. Campbell (1972), 10 C.C.C. (2d) 26, 21 C.R.N.S. 273,
[1973] 2 W.W.R. 246 (Alta. Dist. Ct.) 94

R. v. Campbell (1977), 17 O.R. (2d) 673, 38 C.C.C. (2d) 6,
1 C.R. (3d) 309 (C.A.) 425

R. v. Campbell (1999), 133 C.C.C. (3d) 257,
24 C.R. (5th) 365, 171 D.L.R. (4th) 193 (S.C.C.) 44

R. v. Canadian Pacific Ltd., [1995] 2 S.C.R. 1031,
99 C.C.C. (3d) 97, 41 C.R. (4th) 147 92

R. v. Carker (No. 2) (1966), [1967] S.C.R. 114,
[1967] 2 C.C.C. 190, 2 C.R.N.S. 16 .... 183, 364, 375–76

R. v. Carosella, [1997] 1 S.C.R. 80, 112 C.C.C.
(3d) 289, 4 C.R. (5th) 139 46

R. v. Carpenter (1993), 14 O.R. (3d) 641, 83 C.C.C.
(3d) 193, 65 O.A.C. 220 (C.A.) 422

R. v. Caslake, [1998] 1 S.C.R. 51, 13 C.R. (5th) 1,
121 C.C.C. (3d) 97 35

R. v. Catholique (1980), 20 A.R. 126, 49 C.C.C. (2d) 65,
104 D.L.R. (3d) 161 (N.W.T.S.C.) 97

R. v. Cedono (2005), 195 C.C.C. (3d) 468, 27 C.R.
(6th) 251, 2005 ONCJ 91 270

R. v. Chan (2003), 66 O.R. (3d) 577, 178 C.C.C.
(3d)) 269, [2003] O.J. No. 3233 (C.A.) 135, 138, 153

R. v. Chapin, [1979] 2 S.C.R. 121, 45 C.C.C. (2d) 333,
7 C.R. (3d) 225 217

R. v. Charles (2005), 262 Sask. R. 239, 197 C.C.C. (3d) 42,
2005 SKCA 59 100

R. v. Chartrand, [1994] 2 S.C.R. 864, 91 C.C.C. (3d) 396,
31 C.R. (4th) 1 .... 181, 182

R. v. Chase, [1987] 2 S.C.R. 293, 37 C.C.C. (3d) 97,
[1987] S.C.J. No. 57 436

R. v. Chaulk (2007), 257 N.S.R. (2d) 99, 223 C.C.C.
(3d) 174, 2007 NSCA 84 .... 269, 274

R. v. Chaulk, [1990] 3 S.C.R. 1303, 62 C.C.C.
(3d) 193, 2 C.R. (4th) 1 .... 54, 280, 284,
298–300, 315, 511

R. v. Cheddesingh, [2004] 1 S.C.R. 433, 182 C.C.C.
(3d) 37, 2004 SCC 16..475, 478
R. v. Chenier (2006), 207 O.A.C. 104, 205 C.C.C.
(3d) 333, [2006] O.J. No. 489 (C.A.) 146
R. v. Cinous, [2002] 2 S.C.R. 3, 162 C.C.C. (3d) 129........................324, 332, 339,
350, 512
R. v. Clark (1983), 44 A.R. 141, 25 Alta. L.R. (2d) 218,
5 C.C.C. (3d) 264 (C.A.) 347
R. v. Clark, [2005] 1 S.C.R. 6, 193 C.C.C. (3d) 289, 2005 SCC 2...................... 88
R. v. Clarkson, [1986] 1 S.C.R. 383, (sub nom. Clarkson
v. R.) 50 C.R. (3d) 289, 25 C.C.C. (3d) 207 41
R. v. Clay, [2003] 3 S.C.R. 735, 179 C.C.C. (3d) 540 .... 63, 93
R. v. Clayton, [2007] 2 S.C.R. 725, 220 C.C.C. (3d) 449,
2007 SCC 32 37
R. v. Cline (1956), 115 C.C.C. 18, 24 C.R. 58,
[1956] O.R. 539 (C.A.) 128, 132
R. v. Colburne (1991), 66 C.C.C. (3d) 235,
[1991] R.J.Q. 1199 (C.A.) 130
R. v. Collins (1989), 32 O.A.C. 296, 48 C.C.C. (3d) 343,
[1989] O.J. No. 488 (C.A.) 403
R. v. Collins, [1987] 1 S.C.R. 265, 56 C.R. (3d) 193,
33 C.C.C. (3d) 1 35
R. v. Colucci, [1965] 2 O.R. 665, [1965] 4 C.C.C. 56,
4 C.R. 256 (C.A.) 117
R. v. Commander Business Furniture (1992), 9 C.E.L.R.
(N.S.) 185 (Ont. Prov. Div.), aff'd [1994] O.J. No. 313 (Gen. Div.).............. 225
R. v. Comtois Barbeau (1996), 110 C.C.C. (3d) 69, 50 C.R.
(4th) 357, [1996] R.J.P. 1127 (Que. C.A.)... 190
R. v. Cooper (1979), [1980] 1 S.C.R. 1149,
51 C.C.C. (2d) 149, 13 C.R. (3d) 97 .... 262, 292–94, 296
R. v. Cooper, [1993] 1 S.C.R. 146, 78 C.C.C.
(3d) 289, 18 C.R. (4th) 1 395–96
R. v. Cornejo (2003), 68 O.R. (3d) 117,
[2003] O.J. No. 4517 (C.A.) 448–49
R. v. Cotroni, [1979] 2 S.C.R. 256, 45 C.C.C. (2d) 1,
7 C.R. (3d) 185 137–38
R. v. Cracknell, [1931] O.R. 634, 56 C.C.C. 190,
[1931] 4 D.L.R. 657 (C.A.) 288
R. v. Creighton, [1993] 3 S.C.R. 3, 83 C.C.C.
(3d) 346, [1993] S.C.J. No. 91...318, 378, 399,
427, 429–31, 433, 451, 501, 507
R. v. Cribbin (1994), 17 O.R. (3d) 548, 89 C.C.C.
(3d) 67, 28 C.R. (4th) 137 (C.A.)... 110, 385–86
R. v. Cuerrier, [1998] 2 S.C.R. 371, 127 C.C.C.
(3d) 1, [1998] S.C.J. No. 64 ....103, 120, 439

R. v. Currie (2002), 159 O.A.C. 290, 166 C.C.C. (3d) 190,
[2002] O.J. No. 2191 (C.A.) 330
R. v. Czibulka (2004), 190 O.A.C. 1, 189 C.C.C. (3d) 199,
[2004] O.J. No. 3723 (C.A.) 395
R. v. D.B. (2008), 231 C.C.C. (3d) 338, 56 C.R.
(6th) 203, 2008 SCC 25 ....29, 63, 64,
100, 172, 474
R. v. D.S. (2004), 72 O.R. (3d) 223, 188 C.C.C. (3d) 514,
[2004] O.J. No. 3440 (C.A.), aff'd [2005] 1 S.C.R. 914,
201 C.C.C. (3d) 319, 2005 SCC 36 ....102, 437
R. v. Daley, [2007] 3 S.C.R. 523, 226 C.C.C. (3d) 1, 2007 SCC 53 .... 252, 275
R. v. Daoust, [2004] 1 S.C.R. 217, 180 C.C.C. (3d) 449 87
R. v. Darrach (1998), 13 C.R. (4th) 283 (Ont. C.A.),
aff'd [2000] 2 S.C.R. 443, 148 C.C.C. (3d) 97 450–51
R. v. Daviault, [1994] 3 S.C.R. 63, 33 C.R. (4th) 165,
93 C.C.C. (3d) 21 ....55, 57, 75,
108, 118, 176, 179, 222, 250, 253, 255–65, 267–73, 275–76, 280, 304, 312–13,
319, 446, 452, 497, 502, 510–11
R. v. Dawond (1975), [1976] 1 W.W.R. 262,
27 C.C.C. (2d) 300, [1975] A.J. No. 429 (C.A.) 453
R. v. Deakin (1974), 16 C.C.C. (2d) 1, 26 C.R.N.S. 236,
[1974] 3 W.W.R. 435 (Man. C.A.) 193
R. v. Decaire, [1998] O.J. No. 6339 (Gen. Div.) 268
R. v. Deegan (1979), 17 A.R. 187, 49 C.C.C. (2d) 417,
[1979] 6 W.W.R. 97 (C.A.) 337–38
R. v. DeMarco (1973), 13 C.C.C. (2d) 369,
22 C.R.N.S. 258 (Ont. C.A.) 454
R. v. Demers, [2004] 2 S.C.R. 489, 2004 SCC 46,
[2004] S.C.J. No. 43 .... 26, 93, 282
R. v. Déry, [2006] 2 S.C.R. 669, 213 C.C.C. (3d)
289, 2006 SCC 53 ....127, 138–39, 462
R. v. DeSousa, [1992] 2 S.C.R. 944, 76 C.C.C. (3d)
124, [1992] S.C.J. No. 77 ....68, 165, 172, 429
R. v. Detering, [1982] 2 S.C.R. 583, 70 C.C.C. (2d)
321, 31 C.R. (3d) 354 134–35
R. v. Deutsch, [1986] 2 S.C.R. 2, 27 C.C.C. (3d) 385,
52 C.R. (3d) 305 ....132–33, 161, 505
R. v. Docherty, [1989] 2 S.C.R. 941, 51 C.C.C. (3d) 1,
72 C.R. (3d) 1 .... 98, 183
R. v. Dorosh (2003), 241 Sask. R. 180, 183 C.C.C. (3d)
224, 2003 SKCA 134 .... 99, 186
R. v. Douglas, [1991] 1 S.C.R. 301, 63 C.C.C. (3d) 29,
3 C.R. (4th) 246 137
R. v. Dow, 2010 QCCS 4276 270

R. v. Downey, [1992] 2 S.C.R. 10, 13 C.R. (4th) 129,
72 C.C.C. (3d) 1 .... 56, 226

R. v. Drabinsky, 2011 ONCA 582 454

R. v. Droste (1981), 34 O.R. (2d) 588, 63 C.C.C. (3d) 418,
[1981] O.J. No. 3163 (C.A.), aff'd on other grounds
(sub nom. R. v. Droste (No. 2)) [1984] 1 S.C.R. 208,
10 C.C.C. (3d) 404, [1984] S.C.J. No. 11 .... 192, 396, 402, 411

R. v. Duarte, [1990] 1 S.C.R. 30, 71 O.R. (3d) 575,
53 C.C.C. (3d) 1 .... 33, 36

R. v. Dudley (1884), 14 Q.B.D. 273, 54 L.J.M.C. 32,
[1881–85] All E.R. Rep. 61 (C.C.R.) 353

R. v. Dumont (1921), 37 C.C.C. 166, 64 D.L.R. 128,
49 O.L.R. 222 (C.A.) 158

R. v. Dungey (1979), 51 C.C.C. (2d) 86 (Ont. C.A.) 138

R. v. Dunn (1999), 28 C.R. (5th) 295,
[1999] O.J. No. 5452 (S.C.J.) 266, 270, 271

R. v. Duong (1998), 39 O.R. (3d) 161,
124 C.C.C. (3d) 392 (C.A.) 159, 191

R. v. Dyck (2008), 90 O.R. (3d) 409, 232 C.C.C. (3d) 450,
2008 ONCA 309 27

R. v. Edwards Books & Art Ltd., [1986] 2 S.C.R. 713,
30 C.C.C. (3d) 385, 55 C.R. (3d) 193 32

R. v. Edwards, [1996] 1 S.C.R. 128, 104 C.C.C. (3d) 136,
45 C.R. (4th) 307 34

R. v. Effert, 2011 ABCA 134 427–28

R. v. Eizenga, 2011 ONCA 113, 270 C.C.C. (3d) 168 456

R. v. Ellis-Don Ltd., [1992] 1 S.C.R. 840, 7 O.R. (3d) 320,
71 C.C.C. (3d) 63 .... 55, 227

R. v. Elshaw, [1991] 3 S.C.R. 24, 7 C.R. (4th) 333,
67 C.C.C. (3d) 97 39

R. v. Esau, [1997] 2 S.C.R. 777, 116 C.C.C. (3d) 289,
7 C.R. (5th) 357 .... 103, 443

R. v. Esop (1836), 173 E.R. 203 94

R. v. Eurosport Auto Co. (2002), 11 C.R. (6th) 27,
173 C.C.C. (3d) 449 (B.C.C.A.) 224

R. v. Evans, [1991] 1 S.C.R. 869, 4 C.R. (4th) 144,
63 C.C.C. (3d) 289 41

R. v. Ewanchuk, [1999] 1 S.C.R. 330, 131 C.C.C.
(3d) 481, [1999] S.C.J. No. 10 .... 102–4, 120,
436–39, 444, 447–50, 506

R. v. Ewart (1989), 100 A.R. 118, 53 C.C.C. (3d) 153,
18 M.V.R. (2d) 55 (C.A.) 114

R. v. F.(D.L.) (1989), 100 A.R. 122, 52 C.C.C. (3d) 357,
73 C.R. (3d) 391 (C.A.) 110

R. v. F.W. Woolworth Co. (1974), 3 O.R. (2d) 629,
18 C.C.C. (2d) 23, 46 D.L.R. (3d) 345 (C.A.) 152, 222

R. v. Faid, [1983] 1 S.C.R. 265, 2 C.C.C. (3d) 513, 33 C.R. (3d) 1 340

R. v. Fallofield (1973), 13 C.C.C. (2d) 450,
22 C.R.N.S. 342, [1973] 6 W.W.R. 472 (B.C.C.A.) 489

R. v. Feeney, [1997] 2 S.C.R. 13, 7 C.R. (5th) 101,
115 C.C.C. (3d) 129 36

R. v. Ferguson, [2008] 1 S.C.R. 96, 228 C.C.C.
(3d) 385, 2008 SCC 6 .... 77, 487, 501

R. v. Fice, [2005] 1 S.C.R. 742, 196 C.C.C. (3d) 97,
2005 SCC 32 491

R. v. Find, [2001] 1 S.C.R. 863, 2001 SCC 32 49

R. v. Finlay, [1993] 3 S.C.R. 103, 83 C.C.C.
(3d) 513, [1993] S.C.J. No. 89 .... 69–70, 173,
177, 196–97, 238, 429

R. v. Finta, [1994] 1 S.C.R. 701, 88 C.C.C. (3d) 417,
28 C.R. (4th) 265 .... 59, 72–73,
172–73, 175, 262, 275, 506

R. v. Fisher (1992), 13 C.R. (4th) 222, 36 M.V.R. (2d) 6,
7 B.C.A.C. 264 (C.A.) 114

R. v. Fitzgibbon, [1990] 1 S.C.R. 1005, 55 C.C.C. (3d) 449 493

R. v. Fontaine (2002), 166 Man. R. (2d) 214, 168 C.C.C.
(3d) 263, 2002 MBCA 107 .... 192, 396

R. v. Fontaine, 2004 SCC 27, [2004] S.C.J. No. 23,
183 C.C.C. (3d) 1 .... 57, 253, 305–6

R. v. Forde, 2011 ONCA 592 338

R. v. Forster, [1992] 1 S.C.R. 339, 70 C.C.C. (3d) 59,
88 D.L.R. (4th) 169 95

R. v. Fortier (1998), 127 C.C.C. (3d) 217, 41 M.V.R. (3d) 221,
[1998] J.Q. no 2449 (C.A.) 197

R. v. Fraser (1980), 26 A.R. 33, 55 C.C.C. (2d) 503,
19 C.R. (3d) 193 (C.A.) 418

R. v. Fraser (2002), 3 C.R. (6th) 308, [2002] N.S.J. No. 400 (Prov. Ct.) 368

R. v. Free (1990), 110 A.R. 241, 77 Alta. L.R. (2d) 79,
25 M.V.R. (2d) 30 (Q.B.) 230

R. v. Friesen (1995), 110 A.R. 241, 77 Alta. L.R. (2d) 79,
101 C.C.C. (3d) 167 (C.A.) 427

R. v. G.(R.) (1994), 53 B.C.A.C. 254, 38 C.R. (4th) 123,
[1994] B.C.J. No. 3094 (C.A.) 449

R. v. Galgay, [1972] 2 O.R. 630, 6 C.C.C. (2d) 539 (C.A.) 408–9

R. v. Gardiner, [1982] 2 S.C.R. 368, 68 C.C.C. (2d) 477,
30 C.R. (3d) 289 .... 469, 473

R. v. Gee, [1982] 2 S.C.R. 286, 68 C.C.C. (2d) 516,
29 C.R. (3d) 347 347

R. v. George (2000), 49 O.R. (3d) 144, 145 C.C.C.
(3d) 405 (C.A.) 345, 347

R. v. George, [1960] S.C.R. 871, 128 C.C.C. 289, 34 C.R. 1 .... 248–49, 251

R. v. Geraghty (1990), 55 C.C.C. (3d) 460,
22 M.V.R. (2d) 57 (B.C.C.A.) 230

R. v. Gibson (2001), 153 C.C.C. (3d) 465, 41 C.R.
(5th) 213 (B.C.C.A.) 410

R. v. Gladstone, [1996] 2 S.C.R. 723, 109 C.C.C.
(3d) 193, [1996] S.C.J. No. 79 133

R. v. Gladue, [1999] 1 S.C.R. 688, 133 C.C.C.
(3d) 385, [1999] S.C.J. No. 19 .... 471, 483–84, 503

R. v. Glubisz (No. 2) (1979), 47 C.C.C. (2d) 232,
9 C.R. (3d) 300 (B.C.C.A.) 141

R. v. Godin, [2009] 2 S.C.R. 3, 2009 SCC 26 47

R. v. Golden, [2001] 3 S.C.R. 679, 159 C.C.C. (3d) 44 35

R. v. Goltz, [1991] 3 S.C.R. 485, 67 C.C.C. (3d) 481,
8 C.R. (4th) 82 487

R. v. Gomboc, [2010] 3 S.C.R. 211, 2010 SCC 55 34

R. v. Gonzague (1983), 4 C.C.C. (3d) 505,
34 C.R. (3d) 169 (Ont. C.A.) 142

R. v. Gosset, [1993] 3 S.C.R. 76, 83 C.C.C. (3d) 494,
[1993] S.C.J. No. 88 .... 69, 173, 194,
196–97, 429

R. v. Goulis (1981), 60 C.C.C. (2d) 347, 20 C.R.
(3d) 360, 37 C.B.R.N.S. 290 (Ont. C.A.) 85

R. v. Gralewicz, [1980] 2 S.C.R. 593, 54 C.C.C.
(2d) 289, 116 D.L.R. (3d) 276 .... 83, 136

R. v. Grant, [1993] 3 S.C.R. 223, 84 C.C.C. (3d) 173,
24 C.R. (4th) 1 35

R. v. Grant, [2009] 2 S.C.R. 353, 2009 SCC 32 .... 36–38, 41

R. v. Graveline, [2006] 1 S.C.R. 609, 207 C.C.C. (3d) 481,
2006 SCC 16, rev'g [2005] R.J.Q. 1662, 200 C.C.C.
(3d) 247, 2005 QCCA 574 313

R. v. Gray (1988), 54 Man. R. (2d) 240, 44 C.C.C. (3d) 222,
66 C.R. (3d) 378 (C.A.) 230

R. v. Greyeyes, [1997] 2 S.C.R. 825, 116 C.C.C. (3d) 334,
8 C.R. (5th) 308 .... 148, 151–53

R. v. Gunning, [2005] 1 S.C.R. 627, 196 C.C.C. (3d) 123,
2005 SCC 27 .... 89, 196, 347, 349

R. v. H.(L.I.) (2003), 177 Man. R. (2d) 178, 17 C.R.
(6th) 338, [2003] M.J. No. 232 (C.A.) 148, 400

R. v. H.A. (2005), 206 C.C.C. (3d) 233, 202 O.A.C. 54,
[2005] O.J. No. 3777 (C.A.) 137

R. v. Hall, [2002] 3 S.C.R. 309, 167 C.C.C. (3d) 449 39

R. v. Halmo, [1941] O.R. 99, 76 C.C.C. 116, [1941] 3 D.L.R. 6 (C.A.) 149

R. v. Hamilton (2003), 178 C.C.C. (3d) 434,
[2003] A.J. No. 1080 (C.A.), var'd [2005]
2 S.C.R. 432, 198 C.C.C. (3d) 1, 2005 SCC 47 142
R. v. Hannemaayer, 2008 ONCA 580, 234 C.C.C.
(3d) 3, 239 O.A.C. 241 473
R. v. Hansford (1987), 75 A.R. 86, 33 C.C.C. (3d) 74,
55 C.R. (3d) 347 (C.A.)..411
R. v. Harbottle, [1993] 3 S.C.R. 306, 84 C.C.C. (3d) 1,
[1993] S.C.J. No. 58 .... 109, 388–89, 405
R. v. Hasselwander, [1993] 2 S.C.R. 398, 81 C.C.C.
(3d) 471, 20 C.R. (4th) 277 .... 85, 86
R. v. Hauser, [1979] 1 S.C.R. 984, 46 C.C.C. (2d) 481,
8 C.R. (3d) 89 28
R. v. Hébert (1986), 68 N.B.R. (2d) 379, 51 C.R.
(3d) 264, 175 A.P.R. 379 (C.A.) 155
R. v. Hébert, [1989] 1 S.C.R. 233, 49 C.C.C. (3d) 59, 22 Q.A.C. 101................364
R. v. Hebert, [1990] 2 S.C.R. 151, 77 C.R. (3d) 145,
57 C.C.C. (3d) 1 .... 40, 42
R. v. Hebert, [1996] 2 S.C.R. 272, 107 C.C.C. (3d) 42,
48 C.R. (4th) 204..332, 376
R. v. Helsdon, 2007 ONCA 54, 84 O.R. (3d) 544,
275 D.L.R. (4th) 209 ....151, 433
R. v. Hennessey, 2010 ABCA 274..148
R. v. Hennessy, [1989] 2 All E.R. 9, [1989] 1 W.L.R. 287,
133 Sol. J. 263 (C.A.) 295, 311
R. v. Hess, [1990] 2 S.C.R. 906, 59 C.C.C. (3d) 161,
[1990] S.C.J. No. 91 ....68, 76, 165,
215, 220, 435
R. v. Heywood, [1994] 3 S.C.R. 761, 94 C.C.C. (3d) 481,
34 C.R. (4th) 133 .... 93, 119, 178
R. v. Hibbert, [1995] 2 S.C.R. 973, 99 C.C.C.
(3d) 193, [1995] S.C.J. No. 63............................... 150–51, 155–56,
161, 182, 185, 195, 210, 318, 321, 361, 370, 372–74, 376, 405, 456, 508, 512
R. v. Hickey (1976), 13 O.R. (2d) 228, 30 C.C.C.
(2d) 416, 70 D.L.R. (3d) 689 (C.A.).. 222
R. v. Hill, [1986] 1 S.C.R. 313, 25 C.C.C.
(3d) 322, 51 C.R. (3d) 97 .... 322, 405, 411–19, 423
R. v. Hinchey, [1996] 3 S.C.R. 1128, 111 C.C.C.
(3d) 353, 3 C.R. (5th) 187 .... 90, 208
R. v. Hoeppner (1999), 134 Man. R. (2d) 163,
25 C.R. (5th) 91, [1999] M.J. No. 113 (C.A.)............................... 287
R. v. Honish (1991), 120 A.R. 223, 85 Alta. L.R.
(2dd) 129, 68 C.C.C. (3d) 329 (C.A.)... 273
R. v. Horton (2003), [2004] 10 W.W.R. 762, 20 C.R.
(6th) 161, 2003 SKQB 510 113

R. v. Howson, [1966] 2 O.R. 63, [1966] 3 C.C.C. 348,
47 C.R. 322 (C.A.).. 98, 186, 454
R. v. Hufsky, [1988] 1 S.C.R. 621, 40 C.C.C. (3d) 398,
63 C.R. (3d) 14 .... 34, 37
R. v. Humaid (2006), 81 O.R. (3d) 456, 37 C.R. (6th) 347,
[2006] O.J. No. 1507 (C.A.), leave to appeal to S.C.C.
refused, 2006 SCCA No. 232 420–21
R. v. Humphrey (2001), 143 O.A.C. 151, 43 C.R. (5th) 258,
[2001] O.J. No. 1263 (C.A.) 102
R. v. Hundal, [1993] 1 S.C.R. 867, 79 C.C.C. (3d) 97, 19 C.R.
(4th) 169 ....69–70, 118,
168, 172–73, 177, 194, 196, 199, 238
R. v. Hutchinson, 2010 NSCA 3.. 439
R. v. Hydro-Québec, [1997] 3 S.C.R 213, 118 C.C.C. (3d) 97,
9 C.R. (5th) 157 26
R. v. I.L.W.U., Local 500, [1994] 1 S.C.R. 150, 111 D.L.R.
(4th) 383, 20 C.R.R. (2d) 383..217
R. v. Imoro, 2010 ONCA 122, aff'd [2010] 3 S.C.R. 62,
2010 SCC 50 43–44
R. v. Inwood (1989), 48 C.C.C. (3d) 173, 69 C.R. (3d) 181,
32 O.A.C. 287 (C.A.).. 479
R. v. Ipeelee, 2012 SCC 13 ....477, 484, 504
R. v. Issac, [1984] 1 S.C.R. 74, 9 C.C.C. (3d) 289,
[1984] S.C.J. No. 5 .... 148, 400
R. v. J.A., [2011] 2 S.C.R. 440, 2011 SCC 28........................ 90, 102, 444, 450, 506
R. v. J.F., [2008] S.C.J. No. 62, 2008 SCC 60..197, 432
R. v. J.F.D. (2005), 211 B.C.A.C. 235, 196 C.C.C. (3d) 316,
2005 BCCA 202 .... 148, 400
R. v. J.S.R., 2008 ONCA 544, 237 C.C.C. (3d) 305,
239 O.A.C. 42 ....387, 396, 398
R. v. Jackson (1991), 9 C.R. (4th) 57, 68 C.C.C. (3d) 385,
51 O.A.C. 92 (C.A.), aff'd on other grounds [1993]
4 S.C.R. 573, 86 C.C.C. (3d) 385, 26 C.R. (4th) 178........................ 147, 154,
160–61, 414, 433
R. v. Jackson, [2007] 3 S.C.R. 514, 226 C.C.C. (3d) 97,
2007 SCC 52 149
R. v. Jacquard, [1997] 1 S.C.R. 314, 113 C.C.C. (3d) 1,
4 C.R. (5th) 280.. 301
R. v. Jacques, [1996] 3 S.C.R. 312, 110 C.C.C. (3d) 1,
1 C.R. (5th) 229 34
R. v. James, [1971] 1 O.R. 661, 2 C.C.C. (2d) 141 (C.A.).. 133
R. v. Janeteas (2003), 172 C.C.C. (3d) 97, [2003] O.J. No. 348 (C.A.) 142
R. v. Jarvis, [2002] 3 S.C.R. 757 169 C.C.C. (3d) 1 .... 34, 42
R. v. Jaw, 2008 NUCA 2, aff'd [2009] 3 S.C.R. 26, 2009 SCC 42........................ 403

R. v. Jensen, [2000] O.J. No. 4870 (S.C.J.), aff'd (2005), 74 O.R.
(3d) 561, 195 C.C.C. (3d) 14, [2005] O.J. No. 1052 (C.A.) 271
R. v. Jobb (2008), 2008 SKCA 156, [2009] 1 W.W.R. 193,
239 C.C.C. (3d) 29 281
R. v. Jobidon, [1991] 2 S.C.R. 714, 66 C.C.C.
(3d) 454, 7 C.R. (4th) 233 ....104–5, 120, 441, 506
R. v. Joe (1993), 92 Man. R. (2d) 8, 87 C.C.C.
(3d) 234, 27 C.R. (4th) 79 (C.A.) 492
R. v. John Doe (R. v. Nelson) (2007), 228 C.C.C.
(3d) 302, 54 C.R. (6th) 393, 2007 BCCA 490 359
R. v. *Johnson (1994 S.C.C.). See R. v. Laba*
R. v. Johnson, [2003] 2 S.C.R. 357, 177 C.C.C. (3d) 97,
2003 SCC 46 476
R. v. Johnston, [1970] 2 O.R. 780, [1970] 4 C.C.C. 64 (C.A.) 472
R. v. Jones, [1991] 3 S.C.R. 110, 66 C.C.C. (3d) 512,
8 C.R. (4th) 137 .... 95, 96, 99, 186
R. v. Jordan (1956), 40 Cr. App. Rep. 152 (C.C.A.) 384
R. v. Jorgensen, [1995] 4 S.C.R. 55, 102 C.C.C.
(3d) 97, 43 C.R. (4th) 137 ....95, 99–100, 121, 190
R. v. K. (1970), [1971] 2 O.R. 401, 3 C.C.C. (3d) 84 (H.C.J.) 283
R. v. K.(B.), [1995] 4 S.C.R. 186, 102 C.C.C. (3d) 18,
43 C.R. (4th) 123 84
R. v. Kagan (2004), 224 N.S.R. (2d) 118, 185 C.C.C.
(3d) 417, 2004 NSCA 77 335
R. v. Kamipeli, [1975] 2 N.Z.L.R. 610 (C.A.) 254
R. v. Kanda, 2008 ONCA 22, 88 O.R. (3d) 732, 289 D.L.R. (4th) 304 219
R. v. Kang-Brown, [2008] 1 S.C.R. 456,
230 C.C.C. (3d) 289, 2008 SCC 18 34
R. v. Keegstra, [1990] 3 S.C.R. 697, 61 C.C.C.
(3d) 1, 1 C.R. (4th) 129 ....53, 61, 502
R. v. Keller (1999), 228 A.R. 24, 131 C.C.C. (3d) 59,
188 W.A.C. 24 (C.A.) 372
R. v. Kemp (1956), [1957] 1 Q.B. 399,
[1956] 3 All E.R. 249, [1956] 3 W.L.R. 724 295
R. v. Kennedy (1972), 7 C.C.C. (2d) 42, 18 C.R.N.S. 80 (N.S. Co. Ct.) 222
R. v. Kerr, [2004] 2 S.C.R. 371, 185 C.C.C. (3d) 1,
2004 SCC 44 .... 183, 359–60
R. v. Kerster (2003), 175 C.C.C. (3d) 29,
[2003] B.C.J. No. 999 (C.A.) 135
R. v. Khawaja (2006), 214 C.C.C. (3d) 399, 42 C.R.
(6th) 348, aff'd 2010 ONCA 862 .... 461, 463, 465,
R. v. Khawaja, [2008] O.J. No. 4244,
238 C.C.C. (3d) 114 (S.C.J.) 464
R. v. Khawaja, 2010 ONCA 862 ....187, 461–62, 507

R. v. Kienapple (1974), [1975] 1 S.C.R. 729,
15 C.C.C. (2d) 524, 26 C.R.N.S. 1 78
R. v. King, [1962] S.C.R. 746, 133 C.C.C. 1, 38 C.R. 52 .... 118, 261, 269,
272–74, 275, 277, 312–13
R. v. Kingsley (1995), 105 C.C.C. (3d) 85,
45 C.R. (4th) 381, [1995] J.Q. no 1325 (C.A.) 404
R. v. Kingston, [1994] 3 All E.R. 353, [1994] 3 W.L.R. 519,
158 J.P. 717 (H.L.) 118, 272
R. v. Kirkby (1985), 10 O.A.C. 356, 21 C.C.C.
(3d) 31, [1985] O.J. No. 166 (C.A.) 402
R. v. Kirkness, [1990] 3 S.C.R. 74, 60 C.C.C.
(3d) 97, 1 C.R. (4th) 91 .... 149, 151–52, 160, 400
R. v. Kitching (1976), 32 C.C.C. (2d) 159,
[1976] 6 W.W.R. 697 (Man. C.A.) 111, 389
R. v. Klundert (2004), 242 D.L.R. (4th) 644,
187 C.C.C. (3d) 417, [2004] O.J. No. 3515 (C.A.) 98
R. v. Knight [2003] 1 S.C.R. 156, [2003] S.C.J. No. 13 .... 111, 387
R. v. Knoblauch, [2000] 2 S.C.R. 780, 149 C.C.C. (3d) 1 491
R. v. Kong (2005), 371 A.R. 90, 200 C.C.C. (3d) 19,
2005 ABCA 255, rev'd [2006] 2 S.C.R. 347,
211 C.C.C. (3d) 1, 2006 SCC 40 338
R. v. Kopyto (1987), 62 O.R. (2d) 449, 39 C.C.C.
(3d) 1, 61 C.R. (3d) 209 (C.A.) 84
R. v. Kosh (1964), 49 W.W.R. 248, [1965] 1 C.C.C. 230,
[1964] S.J. No. 181 (C.A.) 134
R. v. Krieger, [2006] 2 S.C.R. 501, 213 C.C.C. (3d) 303,
2006 SCC 47 49
R. v. Krivicic, 2011 ONCA 703 281
R. v. Krug, [1985] 2 S.C.R. 55, 21 C.C.C. (3d) 193, 48 C.R. (3d) 97 78
R. v. Kubassek (2004), 188 C.C.C. (3d) 307,
25 C.R. (6th) 340, 189 O.A.C. 339 (C.A.) 90
R. v. Kulbacki, [1966] 1 C.C.C. 167, 47 C.R. 233,
52 D.L.R. (2d) 283 (Man. C.A.) 149
R. v. Kumar, 2011 ONCA 120 473
R. v. Kundeus (1975), [1976] 2 S.C.R. 272,
24 C.C.C. (2d) 276, 32 C.R.N.S. 129 .... 135, 204
R. v. L. (2003), 172 C.C.C. (3d) 44, [2003] B.C.J. No. 131 (C.A.) 151
R. v. L.(J.) (2006), 206 O.A.C. 205,
204 C.C.C. (3d) 324, [2006] O.J. No. 131 (C.A.) 197
R. v. L.(W.K.), [1991] 1 S.C.R. 1091, 64 C.C.C. (3d) 321, 6 C.R. (4th) 1 47
R. v. L.B., 2011 ONCA 153 427
R. v. L.M. (2008), 293 D.L.R. (4th) 1,
231 C.C.C. (3d) 310, 2008 SCC 31 .... 475–76, 478

R. v. Laba (1994), 34 C.R. (4th) 360 (sub nom.
    R. v. Johnson), [1994] 3 S.C.R. 965, 94 C.C.C.
    (3d) 385, 120 D.L.R. (4th) 175 .... 54, 56, 226
R. v. Labaye, [2005] 3 S.C.R. 728, 203 C.C.C. (3d) 170,
    2005 SCC 80 88
R. v. Ladouceur, [1990] 1 S.C.R. 1257, 56 C.C.C.
    (3d) 27, 77 C.R. (3d) 110 37
R. v. Lagace (2003), 178 O.A.C. 391, 181 C.C.C.
    (3d) 12, [2003] O.J. No. 4328 (C.A.) 190
R. v. Lajoie, [1974] S.C.R. 399, 10 C.C.C. (2d) 313, 20 C.R.N.S. 360 128
R. v. Laliberty (1997), 117 C.C.C. (3d) 97,
    102 O.A.C. 51, [1997] O.J. No. 2808 (C.A.) 157, 401
R. v. Lalonde (1995), 37 C.R. (4th) 97, 22 O.R. (3d) 275 (Gen. Div.) 357
R. v. Lamy, [2002] 1 S.C.R. 860, 162 C.C.C. (3d) 353 87
R. v. Landry, [1991] 1 S.C.R. 99, 62 C.C.C. (3d) 117,
    2 C.R. (4th) 268 .... 288, 297, 300, 315
R. v. Lapierre (1998), 123 C.C.C. (3d) 332, 15 C.R.
    (5th) 283, [1998] R.J.Q. 677 (C.A.) 487
R. v. Laprise (1996), 113 C.C.C. (3d) 87 (Que. C.A.) 114
R. v. Larsonneur (1933), 149 L.T. 542, 77 Sol. J. 486,
    24 Cr. App. Rep. 74 (C.C.A.) 118
R. v. Latimer, [2001] 1 S.C.R. 3, 150 C.C.C. (3d) 129 .... 77, 356–62,
    373–75, 488, 512
R. v. Latoski (2005), 77 O.R. (3d) 505, 200 C.C.C.
    (3d) 361, [2005] O.J. No. 3565 (C.A.) 130
R. v. Lavallee, [1990] 1 S.C.R. 852, 76 C.R. (3d) 329,
    55 C.C.C. (3d) 97 .... 318, 322,
    329–31, 334–40, 351, 357, 359, 374, 378, 508, 512
R. v. Lavigne, [2006] 1 S.C.R. 392, 206 C.C.C. (3d) 449,
    2006 SCC 10 492
R. v. Leary (1977), [1978] 1 S.C.R. 29,
    33 C.C.C. (2d) 473, 37 C.R.N.S. 60 .... 107, 251, 253–58,
    260, 263–64, 267–68, 271–72, 276, 446
R. v. Lee, [1989] 2 S.C.R. 1384, 52 C.C.C. (3d) 289,
    73 C.R. (3d) 257 48
R. v. Lees (2001), 156 C.C.C. (3d) 421, [2001] B.C.J. No. 249 (C.A.) 405
R. v. Legare, 2009 SCC 56, [2009] 3 S.C.R. 551 126–27
R. v. Lemire (1964), [1965] S.C.R. 174,
    [1965] 4 C.C.C. 11, [1964] S.C.J. No. 59 456
R. v. Lemky, [1996] 1 S.C.R. 757, 105 C.C.C. (3d) 137,
    46 C.R. (4th) 55 253
R. v. Lewis, [1979] 2 S.C.R. 821, 47 C.C.C. (2d) 24, 12 C.R. (3d) 315 184
R. v. Li (2002), 162 C.C.C. (3d) 360, 3 C.R. (6th) 173 (Ont. C.A.) 369
R. v. Liew (1999), 137 C.C.C. (3d) 353 (S.C.C.) 42
R. v. Lifchus, [1997] 3 S.C.R. 320, 9 C.R. (5th) 1, 118 C.C.C. (3d) 1 50

R. v. Lilly, [1983] 1 S.C.R. 794, 5 C.C.C. (3d) 1,
[1983] S.C.J. No. 57 ....98–99, 156, 454
R. v. Lindsay (2004), 70 O.R. (3d) 131, 182 C.C.C. (3d) 301,
[2004] O.J. No. 845 (S.C.J.) 457
R. v. Lines, [1993] O.J. No. 3248 (Gen. Div.) 352
R. v. Lobreau (1988), 90 A.R. 399, 62 Alta. L.R. (2d) 32,
67 C.R. (3d) 74 (C.A.) 133
R. v. Logan, [1990] 2 S.C.R. 731, 58 C.C.C. (3d) 391,
79 C.R. (3d) 169 ....72, 129, 144,
146, 156–57, 160, 172–74, 241, 374, 401, 505–6
R. v. Lohnes, [1992] 1 S.C.R. 167, 69 C.C.C. (3d) 289,
10 C.R. (4th) 125 ....85, 208
R. v. Louison (1975), 26 C.C.C. (2d) 266 (Sask. C.A.),
aff'd (1978), 51 C.C.C. (2d) 479 (S.C.C.) 410
R. v. Lucas, [1998] 1 S.C.R. 439, 123 C.C.C. (3d) 97,
14 C.R. (5th) 237 .... 61, 188
R. v. Luedecke, [2008] O.J. No. 4049, 2008 ONCA 716,
rev'g (2005), 35 C.R. (6th) 205, 2005 ONCJ 294 .... 295, 308, 313
R. v. Lutoslawski, 2010 SCC 49, [2010] 3 S.C.R. 60 436
R. v. Luxton, [1990] 2 S.C.R. 711, 58 C.C.C. (3d) 449,
[1990] S.C.J. No. 87 .... 401, 488
R. v. Ly (1987), 33 C.C.C. (3d) 31 (B.C.C.A.) 419–21
R. v. Lyons (1987), 37 C.C.C. (3d) 1 (S.C.C.) 481, 488
R. v. Lyttle, [2004] 1 S.C.R. 193, 180 C.C.C. (3d) 476, 2004 SCC 5 47
R. v. M.(C.A.), [1996] 1 S.C.R. 500, 105 C.C.C.
(3d) 327, 46 C.R. (4th) 269 .... 475, 477–79
R. v. M.(C.B.) (1992), 99 Nfld. & P.E.I.R. 280,
315 A.P.R. 280 (P.E.I.C.A.) 472
R. v. M.(M.R.) (1998), 129 C.C.C. (3d) 361,
20 C.R. (5th) 197, 166 D.L.R. (4th) 261 (S.C.C.) 34
R. v. M.(S.) (1995), 22 O.R. (3d) 605, 97 C.C.C. (3d) 281,
39 C.R. (4th) 60 (C.A.) 105
R. v. M.(T.E.), [1997] 1 S.C.R. 948, 114 C.C.C. (3d) 436,
6 C.R. (5th) 231 475
R. v. Mac, [2002] 1 S.C.R. 856, 163 C.C.C. (3d) 1 87
R. v. MacAskill, [1931] S.C.R. 330, 55 C.C.C. 81,
[1931] 3 D.L.R. 166 251
R. v. MacDonnell, [1997] 1 S.C.R. 305, 158 N.S.R. (2d) 1,
114 C.C.C. (3d) 145 47
R. v. MacDougall, [1982] 2 S.C.R. 605, 1 C.C.C. (3d) 65,
31 C.R. (3d) 1 96
R. v. MacIntyre (1983), 24 M.V.R. 67 (Ont. C.A.) 94
R. v. Mack, [1988] 2 S.C.R. 903, 44 C.C.C. (3d) 513,
67 C.R. (3d) 1 42–44

R. v. MacKay, [2005] 3 S.C.R. 725, 203 C.C.C. (3d) 289,
2005 SCC 79 436
R. v. MacMillan Bloedel Ltd., 2002 BCCA 510,
[2002] B.C.J. No. 2083 223
R. v. Mailloux (1985), 25 C.C.C. (3d) 171 (Ont. C.A.),
aff'd [1988] 2 S.C.R. 1029, 45 C.C.C. (3d) 193,
67 C.R. (3d) 75 292
R. v. Majewski (1976), [1977] A.C. 443,
[1976] 2 All E.R. 142, [1976] 2 W.L.R. 623 (H.L.) 107, 253, 257, 263
R. v. Malcolm (1989), 58 Man. R. (2d) 286,
50 C.C.C. (3d) 172, 71 C.R. (3d) 238 (C.A.) 292
R. v. Malcolm (2000), 148 Man. R. (2d) 143,
147 C.C.C. (3d) 34, 2000 MBCA 77, leave to appeal
to S.C.C. refused (2000), 156 Man. R. (2d) 320,
150 C.C.C. (3d) vi, [2000] S.C.C.A. No. 473 449
R. v. Malmo-Levine, [2003] 3 S.C.R. 571,
179 C.C.C. (3d) 417, 2003 SCC 74 .... 26, 63–64, 90, 175
R. v. Malott, [1998] 1 S.C.R. 123, 121 C.C.C. (3d) 457,
[1998] S.C.J. No. 12, aff'g (1996), 30 O.R. (3d) 609,
110 C.C.C. (3d) 499, [1996] O.J. No. 3511 (C.A.) 322–23, 330–31,
336, 410, 412
R. v. Manchuk (1937), [1938] S.C.R. 18, 69 C.C.C. 172,
[1937] 4 D.L.R. 737 .... 406, 411
R. v. Mann, [2004] 3 S.C.R. 59, 185 C.C.C. (3d) 308,
2004 SCC 52 37
R. v. Manninen, [1987] 1 S.C.R. 1233, 58 C.R. (3d) 97,
34 C.C.C. (3d) 385 40–41
R. v. Marshall, 2005 QCCA 852 473
R. v. Martin (1984), 51 A.L.R. 540 (H.C.) 260
R. v. Martin (1985), 19 C.C.C. (3d) 248, 15 C.R.R. 231,
8 O.A.C. 25 (C.A.) 84
R. v. Martin, [1992] 1 S.C.R. 838, 7 O.R. (3d) 319,
71 C.C.C. (3d) 572 227
R. v. Martineau, [1990] 2 S.C.R. 633, 58 C.C.C. (3d)
353, [1990] S.C.J. No. 84 .... 71–72, 74–75,
129, 146, 166, 172–74, 177–78, 187, 210, 248, 374, 392–93, 397, 506
R. v. Maybin, 2012 SCC 24 .... 109, 111, 385, 390–91
R. v. Mayuran, 2012 SCC 31 422
R. v. McBurney (1975), 24 C.C.C. (2d) 44 (B.C.C.A.) 91
R. v. McConnell, [1996] 1 S.C.R. 1075, 48 C.R. (4th) 199,
42 Alta. L.R. (3d) 225 .... 335, 360
R. v. McCrimmon, [2010] 2 S.C.R. 402, 2010 SCC 36 40
R. v. McDonald (1998), 127 C.C.C. (3d) 57, 17 C.R. (5th) 1,
111 O.A.C. 25 (C.A.) 487

R. v. McIlwaine (1996), 111 C.C.C. (3d) 426,
3 C.R. (5th) 76 (Que. C.A.) 105
R. v. McIntosh, [1995] 1 S.C.R. 686, 95 C.C.C. (3d) 481,
36 C.R. (4th) 171 ....85, 324, 378
R. v. McKay, 2009 MBCA 53.. 347
R. v. McKay, [2007] 1 S.C.R. 793, 217 C.C.C. (3d) 481,
2007 SCC 16 347–48
R. v. McKinlay Transport Ltd., [1990] 1 S.C.R. 627,
55 C.C.C. (3d) 530, 76 C.R. (3d) 283.. 34
R. v. McLeod (1970), 1 C.C.C. (2d) 5, 12 C.R.N.S. 193,
75 W.W.R. 161 (B.C.C.A.) 142
R. v. McMartin (1964), [1964] S.C.R. 484,
[1965] 1 C.C.C. 142, 43 C.R. 403 301
R. v. McMaster, [1996] 1 S.C.R. 740, 105 C.C.C. (3d) 193,
46 C.R. (4th) 41 .... 148, 252, 400
R. v. McNamara (No. 1) (1981), 56 C.C.C. (2d) 193 (Ont. C.A.) 138
R. v. McNeil, [2009] 1 S.C.R. 66, 2009 SCC 3...45
R. v. McQuaid, [1998] 1 S.C.R. 244, 122 C.C.C. (3d) 1 .... 148, 400
R. v. McRae (2005), 77 O.R. (3d) 1, 199 C.C.C. (3d) 536,
[2005] O.J. No. 3200 (C.A.)... 365
R. v. McVay (1982), 66 C.C.C. (2d) 512 (Ont. C.A.).......................................159
R. v. Meiler (1999), 120 O.A.C. 227, 136 C.C.C. (3d) 11,
[1999] O.J. No. 1506 (C.A.) 397
R. v. Meli, [1954] All E.R. 373, [1954] 1 W.L.R. 228,
98 Sol. J. 77 (P.C.).. 107
R. v. Mena (1987), 34 C.C.C. (3d) 304, 20 O.A.C. 50,
[1987] O.J. No. 392 (C.A.) 364, 367
R. v. Mentuck, [2001] 3 S.C.R. 442, 158 C.C.C. (3d) 449,
2001 SCC 76 48
R. v. Menzies (2002), 50 C.R. (5th) 343 (Ont. S.C.J.)...................................... 112
R. v. Merasty (2000), 30 C.R. (5th) 274, [1999] S.J. No. 899 (C.A.)...................410
R. v. Meston (1975), 28 C.C.C. (2d) 497, 34 C.R.N.S. 323 (Ont. C.A.)............. 152
R. v. Metro News Ltd. (1986), 56 O.R. (2d) 321,
29 C.C.C. (3d) 35, 53 C.R. (3d) 289 (C.A.)..95
R. v. Miller, [1982] 2 All E.R. 386 (C.A.), aff'd [1983] 2 A.C.
161, [1983] 1 All E.R. 978, [1983] 2 W.L.R. 539 (H.L.)...................... 107, 117
R. v. Mills, [1999] 3 S.C.R. 668, 139 C.C.C. (3d) 321 ....46, 266
R. v. Milne, [1992] 1 S.C.R. 697, 70 C.C.C. (3d) 481,
[1992] S.C.J. No. 28 453
R. v. Molis, [1980] 2 S.C.R. 356, (sub nom. Molis v. R.)
55 C.C.C. (2d) 558, 116 D.L.R. (3d) 291 94
R. v. Moore (1978), [1979] 1 S.C.R. 195, 43 C.C.C. (2d) 83,
5 C.R. (3d) 289 117
R. v. Moore (1984), 15 C.C.C. (3d) 541, 5 O.A.C. 51 (C.A.) 154

R. v. Morales, [1992] 3 S.C.R. 711, 77 C.C.C. (3d) 91,
 17 C.R. (4th) 74 .... 38, 92
R. v. More, [1963] S.C.R. 522, [1963] 3 C.C.C. 289,
 [1963] S.C.J. No. 52 401
R. v. Morgan (1993), 80 C.C.C. (3d) 16 (Ont. C.A.) 150
R. v. Morgentaler (1985), 52 O.R. (2d) 353, 22 C.C.C.
 (3d) 353, 48 C.R. (3d) 1 (C.A.) 355, 359
R. v. Morgentaler (No. 2), [1988] 1 S.C.R. 30, 37 C.C.C.
 (3d) 449, 62 C.R. (3d) 1 .... 62, 78, 355
R. v. Morgentaler (No. 5) (1975), [1976] 1 S.C.R. 616,
 20 C.C.C. (2d) 449, 30 C.R.N.S. 209 .... 353, 359
R. v. Morgentaler, [1993] 3 S.C.R. 463, 85 C.C.C. (3d) 118,
 25 C.R. (4th) 119 .... 26, 63
R. v. Morin, [1992] 1 S.C.R. 771, 71 C.C.C. (3d) 1, 12 C.R. (4th) 1 47
R. v. Morris, [1979] 2 S.C.R. 1041, 47 C.C.C. (2d) 257,
 10 C.R. (3d) 259 159
R. v. Morrisey, [2000] 2 S.C.R. 90, 148 C.C.C. (3d) 1 .... 175, 487
R. v. Morrissette (1970), 1 C.C.C. (2d) 307,
 12 C.R.N.S. 392, 75 W.W.R. 664 (Sask. C.A.) 481
R. v. Morrissey (2002), 8 C.R. (6th) 18, 169 C.C.C.
 (3d) 256 (Ont. S.C.J.), aff'd 2007 ONCA 770,
 87 O.R. (3d) 481, 227 C.C.C. (3d) 1 281
R. v. Moses (1992), 71 C.C.C. (3d) 347 (Y. Terr. Ct.) 474
R. v. Muchikekwanape (2002), 166 C.C.C. (3d) 144, 2002 MBCA 78 404
R. v. Munro (1983), 8 C.C.C. (3d) 260, 36 C.R. (3d) 193,
 [1983] O.J. No. 144 (C.A.) 403
R. v. Murdoch (2003), 11 C.R. (6th) 43, [2003] O.J. No. 2470 (C.A.) 65
R. v. Murphy (1981), 60 C.C.C. (2d) 1 (Alta. C.A.) 137
R. v. Naglik, [1993] 3 S.C.R. 122, 83 C.C.C.
 (3d) 526, [1993] S.C.J. No. 9264 .... 69, 115, 173, 194, 429
R. v. Nahar (2004), 23 B.C.L.R. (4th) 269,
 181 C.C.C. (3d) 449, 2004 BCCA 77 420–21
R. v. Nasogaluak, [2010] 1 S.C.R. 206, 2010 SCC 6 .... 38, 352, 470, 477, 486
R. v. Nealy (1986), 30 C.C.C. (3d) 460,
 54 C.R. (3d) 158, 17 O.A.C. 164 (C.A.) 425, 427
R. v. Nelson (1992), 8 O.R. (3d) 364, 71 C.C.C. (3d) 449,
 13 C.R. (4th) 359 (C.A.) 335
R. v. Nelson (2007 B.C.C.A.). See R. v. John Doe
R. v. Nette, [2001] 3 S.C.R. 488, 158 C.C.C. (3d) 486 .... 110, 113, 121,
 385–89, 391
R. v. Ng (2006), 397 A.R. 176, 212 C.C.C. (3d) 277, 2006 ABCA 230 301
R. v. Nickel City Transport (Sudbury) Ltd. (1993), 14 O.R.
 (3d) 115, 82 C.C.C. (3d) 541, 22 C.R. (4th) 155 (C.A.) 217, 219
R. v. Nixon (1990), 47 B.C.L.R. (2d) 222,
 57 C.C.C. (3d) 97, 78 C.R. (3d) 349 (C.A.) 150

R. v. Nolet, [2010] 1 S.C.R. 851, 2010 SCC 24 34

R. v. Nova Scotia Pharmaceutical Society, [1992] 2 S.C.R. 606,
74 C.C.C. (3d) 289, 15 C.R. (4th) 1 .... 91, 140

R. v. Nygaard, [1989] 2 S.C.R. 1074, 51 C.C.C. (3d) 417,
[1989] S.C.J. No. 110 .... 395, 402

R. v. O'Brien, [1954] S.C.R. 666, 110 C.C.C. 1, 19 C.R. 371 140

R. v. O'Brien, [1966] 3 C.C.C. 288, 56 D.L.R. (2d) 65 (N.B.C.A.) 295, 311

R. v. O'Connor, [1995] 4 S.C.R. 411, 44 C.R. (4th) 1,
103 C.C.C. (3d) 1 .... 45, 266

R. v. Oakes, [1986] 1 S.C.R. 103, 24 C.C.C. (3d) 321,
50 C.R. (3d) 1 50–52

R. v. Ogg-Moss, [1984] 2 S.C.R. 173, 14 C.C.C. (3d) 116,
41 C.R. (3d) 297 351

R. v. Oickle (1984), 11 C.C.C. (3d) 180, [1984] N.S.J. No. 291 (C.A.) 425

R. v. Olan, [1978] 2 S.C.R. 1175, 41 C.C.C. (2d) 145,
[1978] S.C.J. No. 57 454

R. v. Oommen, [1994] 2 S.C.R. 507, 91 C.C.C. (3d) 81,
30 C.R. (4th) 195 .... 288, 299–300, 315

R. v. Orbanski, [2005] 2 S.C.R. 3, 196 C.C.C.
(3d) 481, 2005 SCC 37 39

R. v. Osolin, [1993] 4 S.C.R. 595, 26 C.R. (4th) 1,
86 C.C.C. (3d) 481 .... 205, 443

R. v. Paice, [2005] 1 S.C.R. 339, 195 C.C.C. (3d) 97, 2005 SCC 22 105

R. v. Palin (1999), 135 C.C.C. (3d) 119, 41 M.V.R. (3d) 11,
[1999] J.Q. no 33 (C.A.) 197

R. v. Pangowish (2003), 177 B.C.A.C. 219, 171 C.C.C. (3d) 506,
2003 BCCA 62, leave to appeal to S.C.C. refused (2003),
176 C.C.C. (3d) vi, [2003] S.C.C.A. No. 126 .... 111, 387

R. v. Pappajohn, [1980] 2 S.C.R. 120, 52 C.C.C. (2d) 481,
[1980] S.C.J. No. 51 .... 204–8, 442–43,
445–47, 498

R. v. Paquette (1976), [1977] 2 S.C.R. 189,
30 C.C.C. (2d) 417, 39 C.R.N.S. 257 .... 155–56, 181–83,
185, 370, 373, 376–77

R. v. Paré, [1987] 2 S.C.R. 618, 38 C.C.C. (3d) 97,
60 C.R. (3d) 346 .... 85–87, 404

R. v. Parent, [2001] 1 S.C.R. 761, 154 C.C.C. (3d) 1 .... 303, 405, 425

R. v. Park, [1995] 2 S.C.R. 836, 99 C.C.C. (3d) 1,
39 C.R. (4th) 287 443

R. v. Parks, [1992] 2 S.C.R. 871, 75 C.C.C. (3d) 287,
15 C.R. (4th) 289 .... 118, 290, 293,
295, 303–4, 307–10, 314–15, 511

R. v. Parnerkar (1972), 5 C.C.C. (2d) 11, 16 C.R.N.S. 347,
[1972] 1 W.W.R. 161 (Sask. C.A.), aff'd (1973), [1974]
S.C.R. 449, 10 C.C.C. (2d) 253, 21 C.R.N.S. 129 413–14

R. v. Patrick, [2009] 1 S.C.R. 579, 2009 SCC 17 34

R. v. Patterson (2006), 79 O.R. (3d) 257, 205 C.C.C. (3d) 171,
    [2006] O.J. No. 361 (C.A.) 395

R. v. Pawliuk (2001), 40 C.R. (5th) 28, 151 C.C.C. (3d) 155 (B.C.C.A.) 410

R. v. Pearson, [1992] 3 S.C.R. 665, 77 C.C.C. (3d) 124, 17 C.R. (4th) 1 38

R. v. Pellerin (1989), 47 C.C.C. (3d) 35, 67 C.R. (3d) 305,
    10 M.V.R. (2d) 165 (Ont. C.A.) 230

R. v. Penno, [1990] 2 S.C.R. 865, 59 C.C.C. (3d) 344,
    80 C.R. (3d) 97 ....75, 261–62, 275

R. v. Pétel, [1994] 1 S.C.R. 3, 87 C.C.C. (3d) 97,
    26 C.R. (4th) 145 ....323, 330–31,
    336, 340, 508, 512

R. v. Pickton, 2010 SCC 32, [2010] 2 S.C.R. 198 .... 115, 147, 399

R. v. Pierce Fisheries Ltd. (1970), [1971] S.C.R. 5,
    [1970] 5 C.C.C. 193, 12 C.R.N.S. 272 ....203, 216

R. v. Pintar (1996), 30 O.R. (3d) 483, 110 C.C.C. (3d) 402,
    2 C.R. (5th) 151 (C.A.) 331

R. v. Plant, [1993] 3 S.C.R. 281, 24 C.R. (4th) 47, 84 C.C.C. (3d) 203 34

R. v. Poitras (1973), [1974] S.C.R. 649, 12 C.C.C. (3d) 337,
    24 C.R.N.S. 159 152

R. v. Polewsky (2005), 202 C.C.C. (3d) 257, 138 C.R.R. (2d) 208,
    [2005] O.J. No. 4500 (C.A.) 217

R. v. Pontes, [1995] 3 S.C.R. 44, 100 C.C.C. (3d) 353,
    41 C.R. (4th) 201 ....67, 96–97,
    121, 218–20, 243, 487, 509

R. v. Portillo (2003), 17 C.R. (6th) 362,
    176 C.C.C. (3d) 467 (Ont. C.A.) 148, 157, 400, 401

R. v. Potash (1994), 91 C.C.C. (3d) 315 (S.C.C.) 34

R. v. Powell (1989), 81 Sask. R. 301, 52 C.C.C. (3d) 403,
    19 M.V.R. (2d) 36 (C.A.) 114

R. v. Preston (1990), 47 B.C.L.R. (2d) 273, 79 C.R. (3d) 61 (C.A.) 482, 490

R. v. Prevost (1988), 28 O.A.C. 50, 42 C.C.C. (3d) 314,
    [1988] O.J. No. 707 (C.A.) 86, 403

R. v. Prince (1875), L.R. 2 C.C.R., [1874–80] All E.R.
    Rep. 881, 44 L.J.M.C. 122 202–3

R. v. Pritchard, [2008] 3 S.C.R. 195, 2008 SCC 59,
    299 D.L.R. (4th) 81 404

R. v. Prosper, [1994] 3 S.C.R. 236, 33 C.R. (4th) 85,
    92 C.C.C. (3d) 353 40

R. v. Proulx (1998), 110 B.C.A.C. 62, 127 C.C.C. (3d) 511,
    1998 CanLII 6317 (C.A.) 338

R. v. Proulx, [2000] 1 S.C.R. 61, 140 C.C.C.
    (3d) 449, 2000 SCC 5 .... 476, 483–84, 491, 503

R. v. Prue, [1979] 2 S.C.R. 547, 46 C.C.C. (2d) 257,
    8 C.R. (3d) 68 .... 96, 169

R. v. Quick, [1973] Q.B. 910, [1973] 3 All E.R. 347,
[1973] 3 W.L.R. 26 (C.A.) 290, 295
R. v. Quigley (1954), 111 C.C.C. 81 (Alta. C.A.) 90
R. v. Quin, [1988] 2 S.C.R. 825, 44 C.C.C. (3d) 570, 67 C.R. (3d) 162 249
R. v. R.(M.S.) (1996), 112 C.C.C. (3d) 406 (Ont. Ct. Gen. Div.) 292
R. v. R.H.L., 2008 NSCA 100, 270 N.S.R. (2d) 123 90
R. v. Rabey, [1980] 2 S.C.R. 513, 54 C.C.C. (2d) 1,
15 C.R. (3d) 225 (C.A.) 283, 290, 292,
294, 302, 309–11, 314, 426, 511
R. v. Raham, 2010 ONCA 206, [2010] O.J. No. 1091 219
R. v. Ratti (1991), 62 C.C.C. (3d) 105 (S.C.C.) 299
R. v. Rees, [1956] S.C.R. 640, 115 C.C.C. 1, 24 C.R. 1 .... 169, 203
R. v. Reid and Stratton (2003), 218 N.S.R. (2d) 23,
180 C.C.C. (3d) 151, 2003 NSCA 104 .... 113, 387, 391
R. v. Reilly, [1984] 2 S.C.R. 396, 15 C.C.C. (3d) 1,
13 D.L.R. (4th) 161 .... 329, 337
R. v. Rémillard (1921), 62 S.C.R. 21, 35 C.C.C. 227,
[1921] S.C.J. No. 15 155
R. v. Revelle (1979), 48 C.C.C. (2d) 267, 21 C.R. (3d) 161,
39 N.R. 486 (Ont. C.A.), aff'd [1981] 1 S.C.R. 576,
61 C.C.C. (2d) 575, 21 C.R. (3d) 161 .... 292, 312
R. v. Richard (1986), 43 Man. R. (2d) 160,
30 C.C.C. (3d) 127 (C.A.) 144–45
R. v. Richer (1993), 141 A.R. 116, 82 C.C.C. (3d) 385,
46 W.A.C. 116 (C.A.) 86, 404
R. v. Roach (2004), 192 C.C.C. (3d) 557, [2004] O.J. No. 2566 (C.A.) 151
R. v. Roberts, [2005] 1 S.C.R. 22, 191 C.C.C. (3d) 466, 2005 SCC 3 419
R. v. Robinson (2001), 53 O.R. (3d) 448, 153 C.C.C. (3d) 398,
[2001] O.J. No. 1072 (C.A.) 441
R. v. Robinson, [1951] S.C.R. 522, 100 C.C.C. 1, 12 C.R. 101 85
R. v. Robinson, [1996] 1 S.C.R. 683, 105 C.C.C.
(3d) 97, 46 C.R. (4th) 1 .... 76, 179, 251–53, 275, 510
R. v. Rodney, [1990] 2 S.C.R. 687, 58 C.C.C.
(3d) 408, 79 C.R. (3d) 187, ... 157, 401
R. v. Rojos (2006), 225 B.C.A.C. 32, 208 C.C.C.
(3d) 13, 2006 BCCA 193 .... 148, 400
R. v. Roks, 2011 ONCA 526 397–98
R. v. Ross (1944), 84 C.C.C. 107, [1945] 3 D.L.R. 574,
[1945] 1 W.W.R. 590 (B.C. Co. Ct.) 97
R. v. Ross (1989), 46 C.C.C. (3d) 129 (S.C.C.) 41
R. v. Roy, 2012 SCC 26 .... 169, 201, 236,
238, 430, 497, 507
R. v. Rube (1992), [1992] 3 S.C.R. 159, 75 C.C.C. (3d) 575,
[1993] 1 W.W.R. 385 217
R. v. Rubenstein (1987), 41 C.C.C. (3d) 91, 24 O.A.C. 309 (C.A.) 472

R. v. Ruptash (1982), 36 A.R. 346, 68 C.C.C. (2d) 182,
[1982] A.J. No. 424 (C.A.) 401
R. v. Rushton (1963), [1964] 1 C.C.C. 382, 48 M.P.R. 271 (N.S.C.A.) 273
R. v. Russell, [2001] 2 S.C.R. 804, 157 C.C.C. (3d) 1 .... 87, 404
R. v. Ruzic, 2001 SCC 24, [2001] 1 S.C.R. 687,
153 C.C.C. (3d) 1, aff'g (1998), 128 C.C.C. (3d) 97,
18 C.R. (5th) 58, 164 D.L.R. (4th) 358 (Ont. C.A.) 76–77, 119,
178, 262, 265, 267, 275, 318–20, 322, 328, 354, 357, 362, 364–65, 367–69,
371–73, 375, 380, 424, 513
R. v. Ryan, 2011 NSCA 30 .... 320, 329, 366
R. v. S.(F.J.) (1997), 115 C.C.C. (3d) 450 (N.S.C.A.)
aff'd [1998] 1 S.C.R. 88, 165 N.S.R. (2d) 160,
121 C.C.C. (3d) 223 158
R. v. S.(J.) (2001), 152 C.C.C. (3d) 317, [2001] O.J. No. 104 (C.A.) 44
R. v. S.A.B., [2003] 2 S.C.R. 678, 178 C.C.C. (3d) 193 35
R. v. S.N., 2012 NUCJ 2 269
R. v. Safety Kleen Canada Inc. (1997), 16 O.R. (5th) 90,
114 C.C.C. (3d) 214, 145 D.L.R. (4th) 276 (C.A.) 232, 235
R. v. Salajko, [1970] 1 O.R. 824, [1970] 1 C.C.C. 352,
9 C.R.N.S. 145 (C.A.) 149
R. v. Sandham, 2009 CanLII 58605 (Ont. S.C.J.) 374
R. v. Sansregret, [1985] 1 S.C.R. 570, 18 C.C.C.
(3d) 223, 45 C.R. (3d) 193 .... 171, 189–91,
206–7, 442, 444, 446–47
R. v. Sarrazin, 2011 SCC 54, [2011] 3 S.C.R. 505 .... 113, 390
R. v. Sault Ste. Marie (City), [1978] 2 S.C.R. 1299,
40 C.C.C. (2d) 353, 3 C.R. (3d) 30 .... 55, 95, 169–71,
192, 204, 210, 215, 217–19, 222–24, 226–28, 243, 508
R. v. Schneider, [1982] 2 S.C.R. 112, 39 B.C.L.R. 273,
68 C.C.C. (2d) 449 27
R. v. Schwartz, [1977] 1 S.C.R. 673, 29 C.C.C. (2d) 1,
34 C.R.N.S. 138 298–99
R. v. Scott (1963), [1964] 2 C.C.C. 257, 45 W.W.R. 479 (Alta. C.A.) 134
R. v. Seaboyer, [1991] 2 S.C.R. 577, 7 C.R. (4th) 117,
(sub nom. R. v. S.) 66 C.C.C. (3d) 321 .... 46, 206, 445–46, 502
R. v. Shand, 2011 ONCA 5 398
R. v. Shanks (1996), 95 O.A.C. 348, 4 C.R. (5th) 79,
[1996] O.J. No. 4386 (C.A.) 385
R. v. Sharpe, [2001] 1 S.C.R. 45, 150 C.C.C. (3d) 321 61
R. v. Sheppard, [2002] 1 S.C.R. 869, 162 C.C.C. (3d) 298,
2002 SCC 26 30
R. v. Sheratt Robinson, 2009 ONCA 886 473
R. v. Sheridan, [1991] 2 S.C.R. 205, 65 C.C.C. (3d) 319,
rev'g (1990), 105 A.R. 122, 55 C.C.C. (3d) 313 (C.A.) 412
R. v. Shivpuri, [1986] 2 All E.R. 334, [1986] 2 W.L.R. 988 (H.L.) 135

R. v. Shoker, [2006] 2 S.C.R. 399, 212 C.C.C. (3d) 417, 2006 SCC 44.............. 490

R. v. Showman, [1988] 2 S.C.R. 893, 45 C.C.C. (3d) 289,
   67 C.R. (3d) 61 44

R. v. Shropshire, [1995] 4 S.C.R. 227, 102 C.C.C. (3d) 193,
   43 C.R. (4th) 269 475

R. v. Shubley, [1990] 1 S.C.R. 3, 52 C.C.C. (3d) 481, 74 C.R. (3d) 1 78

R. v. Shymkowich, [1954] S.C.R. 606, 110 C.C.C. 97, 19 C.R. 401..................... 98

R. v. Simmons (1988), 45 C.C.C. (3d) 296 (S.C.C.).. 34

R. v. Simpson (1977), 16 O.R. (2d) 129, 35 C.C.C. (2d) 337,
   77 D.L.R. (3d) 507 (C.A.) 292, 296

R. v. Simpson (1981), 58 C.C.C. (2d) 122, 20 C.R. (3d) 36,
   [1981] O.J. No. 23 (C.A.).. 395

R. v. Simpson, [1988] 1 S.C.R. 3, 62 C.R. (3d) 137,
   38 C.C.C. (3d) 481 154

R. v. Sinclair, [2010] 2 S.C.R. 310, 2010 SCC 35.. 41

R. v. Singh, [2007] 3 S.C.R. 405, 225 C.C.C. (3d) 103, 2007 SCC 48................. 42

R. v. Sit, [1991] 3 S.C.R. 124, 66 C.C.C. (3d) 449,
   9 C.R. (4th) 126 ....74, 178, 394

R. v. Smith (1989), 14 M.V.R. (2d) 166, 44 C.R.R. 18 (Y.C.A.) 230

R. v. Smith (1989), 50 C.C.C. (3d) 308 (S.C.C.).. 40

R. v. Smith, [1959] 2 Q.B. 35, [1959] 2 All E.R. 193,
   43 Cr. App. Rep. 121 (C.A.).. 384

R. v. Smith, [1987] 1 S.C.R. 1045, 34 C.C.C. (3d) 97,
   58 C.R. (3d) 193 .... 77, 486, 488

R. v. Smithers (1977), [1978] 1 S.C.R. 506,
   34 C.C.C. (2d) 427, 40 C.R.N.S. 79 .... 109–10, 385–86, 388

R. v. Sokoloski, [1977] 2 S.C.R. 523, 33 C.C.C. (2d) 496,
   74 D.L.R. (3d) 126 140

R. v. Solowan, [2008] 3 S.C.R. 309, 2008 SCC 62.. 475

R. v. Sorrell (1978), 41 C.C.C. (2d) 9 (Ont. C.A.).. 132–34

R. v. Spence, [2005] 3 S.C.R. 458, 202 C.C.C. (3d) 1, 2005 SCC 71.................... 49

R. v. Spot Supermarket Inc. (1979), 50 C.C.C. (2d) 239 (Que. C.A.).................. 98

R. v. Squire, [1977] 2 S.C.R. 13, 29 C.C.C. (2d) 497,
   69 D.L.R. (3d) 312 408

R. v. Starr, [2000] 2 S.C.R. 144, 147 C.C.C. (3d) 449 51

R. v. Steane, [1947] K.B. 997, [1947] 1 All E.R. 813,
   [1947] L.J.R. 969 (C.C.A.).. 181–83

R. v. Steele (1991), 63 C.C.C. (3d) 149, 1991 CanLII 3882 (Que. C.A.) 281

R. v. Stephens (1991), 27 M.V.R. (2d) 24 (Ont. C.A.) 114

R. v. Stevanovich (1983), 43 O.R. (2d) 266,
   7 C.C.C. (3d) 307, 36 C.R. (3d) 174 (C.A.) 229

R. v. Stevenson (1984), 62 N.S.R. (2d) 193,
   11 C.C.C. (3d) 443, 136 A.P.R. 193 (C.A.) 149

R. v. Stewart, [1988] 1 S.C.R. 963, 41 C.C.C. (3d) 481,
   [1988] S.C.J. No. 45 .... 106, 453

R. v. Stillman, [1997] 1 S.C.R. 607, 5 C.R. (5th) 1, 113 C.C.C. (3d) 321 35
R. v. Stinchcombe, [1991] 3 S.C.R. 326, 68 C.C.C. (3d) 1,
    8 C.R. (4th) 277 45
R. v. Stone (1999), 134 C.C.C. (3d) 353, 24 C.R. (5th) 1,
    173 D.L.R. (4th) 66 (S.C.C.) 55, 57, 119,
    265, 280, 283, 290–91, 293, 295, 302–11, 313–15, 423, 426, 485, 511
R. v. Storrey, [1990] 1 S.C.R. 241, 53 C.C.C. (3d) 316, 75 C.R. (3d) 1 37
R. v. Strong (1990), 111 A.R. 12, 60 C.C.C. (3d) 516,
    [1990] A.J. No. 974 (C.A.) 404
R. v. Sullivan (1983), [1984] A.C. 156, [1983] 2 All E.R. 673,
    [1983] 3 W.L.R. 123 (H.L.) 290, 295, 311
R. v. Sutherland (1990), 96 N.S.R. (2d) 271, 55 C.C.C.
    (3d) 265, 22 M.V.R. (2d) 35 (C.A.) 230
R. v. Suzack (2000), 141 C.C.C. (3d) 449 (Ont. C.A.) 148, 400
R. v. Swain, [1991] 1 S.C.R. 933, 63 C.C.C. (3d) 481,
    5 C.R. (4th) 253 .... 26, 267, 283, 285
R. v. Sweeney (1992), 71 C.C.C. (3d) 82,
    11 C.R. (4th) 1, 33 M.V.R. (2d) 1 (B.C.C.A.) 480
R. v. Szczerbaniwicz, [2010] 1 S.C.R. 455, 2010 SCC 15 347–48
R. v. Taillefer, [2003] 3 S.C.R. 307, 179 C.C.C. (3d) 353,
    2003 CSCC 70 46
R. v. Talbot (2007), 220 O.A.C. 167, 217 C.C.C. (3d) 415,
    2007 ONCA 81 .... 111, 387
R. v. Taylor, (1992), 77 C.C.C. (3d) 551 (Ont. C.A.) 281
R. v. Tennant (1975), 7 O.R. (2d) 687, 23 C.C.C. (2d) 80,
    31 C.R.N.S. 1 (C.A.) 167
R. v. Terezakis (2007), 245 B.C.A.C. 74, 223 C.C.C. (3d) 344,
    2007 BCCA 384 457
R. v. Terrence, [1983] 1 S.C.R. 357, 4 C.C.C. (3d) 193,
    33 C.R. (3d) 193 105
R. v. Tessling, [2004] 3 S.C.R. 432, 189 C.C.C. (3d) 129, 2004 SCC 67 34
R. v. Thatcher, [1987] 1 S.C.R. 652, 32 C.C.C. (3d) 481,
    57 C.R. (3d) 97 .... 147, 399
R. v. Therens, [1985] 1 S.C.R. 613, 45 C.R. (3d) 97,
    18 C.C.C. (3d) 481 40
R. v. Théroux, [1993] 2 S.C.R. 579, 79 C.C.C. (3d) 449,
    [1993] S.C.J. No. 42 .... 118, 165, 167,
    455–56, 509
R. v. Thibert, [1996] 1 S.C.R. 37, 104 C.C.C. (3d) 1,
    45 C.R. (4th) 1 .... 324, 406–12,
    414, 416–21, 424, 508, 511
R. v. Thomsen, [1988] 1 S.C.R. 640, 40 C.C.C. (3d) 411,
    63 C.R. (3d) 1 39
R. v. Thornton, [1993] 2 S.C.R. 445, 82 C.C.C. (3d) 530,
    21 C.R. (4th) 215 .... 116, 120

R. v. Timminco Ltd. (2001), 42 C.R. (5th) 279, 54 O.R. (3d) 21 (C.A.) 223

R. v. Tolson (1889), 23 Q.B.D. 168, 58 L.J.M.C. 97,
   60 L.T. 899 (C.C.R.) 163, 203

R. v. Tramble (1983), 33 C.R. (3d) 264 (Ont. Co. Ct.) 273

R. v. Tran, [1994] 2 S.C.R. 951, 92 C.C.C. (3d) 218,
   32 C.R. (4th) 34 58

R. v. Tran, [2010] 3 S.C.R. 350, 2010 SCC 58 ....211, 322–23,
   405–11, 413, 415, 417–22, 512

R. v. Tripodi, [1955] S.C.R. 438, 112 C.C.C. 66, 21 C.R. 192 410

R. v. Tse, 2012 SCC 16 35–36

R. v. Tutton, [1989] 1 S.C.R. 1392, 48 C.C.C. (3d) 129,
   [1989] S.C.J. No. 60 ....168, 193, 196–98, 431

R. v. Ubhi (1994), 40 B.C.A.C. 248, 27 C.R. (4th) 332,
   [1994] B.C.J. No. 255 (C.A.) 431

R. v. V.(K.B.), [1993] 2 S.C.R. 857, 82 C.C.C. (3d) 382,
   [1993] S.C.J. No. 78 436

R. v. Vaillancourt, [1987] 2 S.C.R. 636, 39 C.C.C. (3d) 118,
   [1987] S.C.J. No. 83 .... 52, 71–72,
   74, 172, 178, 224, 248, 394

R. v. Vasil, [1981] 1 S.C.R. 469, 58 C.C.C. (2d) 97,
   [1981] S.C.J. No. 43 .... 198, 397

R. v. Vickberg (1998), 16 C.R. (5th) 164,
   54 C.R.R. (2d) 83 (B.S.S.C.) 268–69, 273, 277

R. v. Vucetic (1998), 129 C.C.C. (3d) 178 (Ont. C.A.) 138

R. v. W.(G.) (1994), 18 O.R. (3d) 321, 90 C.C.C. (3d) 139,
   30 C.R. (4th) 393 (C.A.) 105

R. v. W.(J.M.) (1998), 51 B.C.L.R. (3d) 377, 123 C.C.C. (3d) 245,
   [1999] 1 W.W.R. 172 (C.A.) 299

R. v. Waite, [1989] 1 S.C.R. 1436, 48 C.C.C. (3d) 1,
   [1989] S.C.J. No. 61 196–97

R. v. Walker (1979), 48 C.C.C. (2d) 126 (Ont. Co. Ct.) 222

R. v. Walker (2008), 310 Sask. R. 305, 231 C.C.C. (3d) 289,
   2008 SCC 34 30

R. v. Walle (2007), 417 A.R. 338, 230 C.C.C. (3d) 181, 2007 ABCA 333 426

R. v. Wallen, [1990] 1 S.C.R. 827, 54 C.C.C. (3d) 383, [
   1990] S.C.J. No. 35 402

R. v. Waterloo Mercury Sales Ltd. (1974), 18 C.C.C. (2d) 248,
   27 C.R.N.S. 55, [1974] 4 W.W.R. 516 (Alta. Dist. Ct.) 231–32

R. v. Watson (1999), 176 Nfld. & P.E.I.R. 263,
   137 C.C.C. (3d) 422, [1999] N.J. No. 212 (C.A.) 98

R. v. Watts (1953), 105 C.C.C. 193 (S.C.C.) 169

R. v. Welch (1995), 25 O.R. (3d) 665, 101 C.C.C. (3d) 216,
   [1995] O.J. No. 2859 (C.A.) 441

R. v. Wells, [2000] 1 S.C.R. 207, 141 C.C.C. (3d) 368, 2000 SCC 10 484

R. v. Westendorp, [1983] 1 S.C.R. 43, 41 A.R. 306, 2 C.C.C. (3d) 330 26

R. v. Whittle, [1994] 2 S.C.R. 914, 32 C.R. (4th) 1, 92 C.C.C. (3d) 11 281

R. v. Wholesale Travel Group Inc., [1991] 3 S.C.R. 154,
  67 C.C.C. (3d) 193, [1991] S.C.J. No. 79 .... 54–55, 62,
  67–69, 168, 221, 224, 226–28, 243, 508

R. v. Whynot (1983), 61 N.S.R. (2d) 33, 9 C.C.C. (3d) 449,
  37 C.R. (3d) 198 (C.A.) 329, 331

R. v. Whyte, [1988] 2 S.C.R. 3, 42 C.C.C. (3d) 97,
  [1988] S.C.J. No. 63 .... 53, 177

R. v. Wigglesworth, [1987] 2 S.C.R. 541, 37 C.C.C. (3d) 385,
  [1987] S.C.J. No. 71 78

R. v. Wiles, [2005] 3 S.C.R. 895, 203 C.C.C. (3d) 161, 2005 SCC 84 487

R. v. Willaert, [1953] O.R. 282, 105 C.C.C. 172, 16 C.R. 138 (C.A.) 475

R. v. Williams (2002), 171 B.C.A.C. 308, 168 C.C.C. (3d) 67,
  2002 BCCA 453 367

R. v. Williams, [1998] 1 S.C.R. 1128, 124 C.C.C. (3d) 481,
  15 C.R. (5th) 227 49

R. v. Williams, 2003 SCC 41, [2003] 2 S.C.R. 134,
  176 C.C.C. (3d) 449 .... 114–15, 120,
  131, 134–35, 153, 161

R. v. Willier, [2010] 2 S.C.R. 429, 2010 SCC 37 40

R. v. Wilson, 2011 ONSC 3385 366

R. v. Winning (1973), 12 C.C.C. (3d) 449 (Ont. C.A.) 113

R. v. Wobbes, 2008 ONCA 567, 242 O.A.C. 7, 235 C.C.C. (3d) 561 148

R. v. Wong, [1990] 3 S.C.R. 36, 1 C.R. (4th) 1, 60 C.C.C. (3d) 460 .... 33, 36

R. v. Woods, [2005] 2 S.C.R. 205, 197 C.C.C. (3d) 353,
  2005 SCC 42 40

R. v. Wray (1970), [1971] S.C.R. 272, [1970] 4 C.C.C. 1,
  11 C.R.N.S. 235 33

R. v. Wright, [1969] S.C.R. 335, [1969] 3 C.C.C. 258,
  2 D.L.R. (3d) 529 413–14

R. v. Wu, [2003] 3 S.C.R. 530, 180 C.C.C. (3d) 97 492

R. v. Wust (1998), 125 C.C.C. (3d) 43 (B.C.C.A.) 487

R. v. Yanover (1985), 20 C.C.C. (3d) 300, 9 O.A.C. 93 (C.A.) 152

R. v. Young (1993), 117 N.S.R. (2d) 166, 78 C.C.C. (3d) 538,
  [1993] N.S.J. No. 14 (C.A.), leave to appeal to S.C.C. refused,
  [1993] 2 S.C.R. xii, 81 C.C.C. (3d) vi, [1993] S.C.C.A. No. 120 410

R. v. Younger (2004), 187 Man. R. (2d) 121,
  186 C.C.C. (3d) 454, 2004 MBCA 113 .... 109, 384

R. v. Zelensky, [1978] 2 S.C.R. 940, 41 C.C.C. (2d) 97,
  2 C.R. (3d) 107 .... 26, 493

R. v. Zlatic, [1993] 2 S.C.R. 29, 79 C.C.C. (3d) 466,
  [1993] S.C.J. No. 43 .... 454, 456

R. v. Zundel, [1992] 2 S.C.R. 731, 75 C.C.C. (3d) 449,
  16 C.R. (4th) 1 61

Re Section 83.28 of the Criminal Code, [2004] 2 S.C.R. 248,
184 C.C.C. (3d) 449, 2004 SCC 42 42
Reference re Motor Vehicle Act (British Columbia) S. 94(2),
[1985] 2 S.C.R. 486, 23 C.C.C. (3d) 289, [1985] S.C.J.
No. 73 ....64, 67, 76,
172, 178, 218–21, 243, 477
Reference re Section 293 of the Criminal Code of Canada,
2011 BCSC 1588 66
Reference re ss. 193 & 195.1(1)(c) of the Criminal Code
(Canada), [1990] 1 S.C.R. 1123, 56 C.C.C. (3d) 65,
77 C.R. (3d) 1 ....60, 91, 502
Reniger v. Fogossa (1548), 75 E.R. 1 (Ex.) 246
RJR-MacDonald Inc. v. Canada (A.G.), [1995] 3 S.C.R. 199,
100 C.C.C. (3d) 449, 127 D.L.R. (4th) 1 26
Rodriguez v. British Columbia (A.G.), [1993] 3 S.C.R.
519, 85 C.C.C. (3d) 15, [1993] S.C.J. No. 94 .... 63, 433–34, 502, 506

Salamon v. R., [1959] S.C.R. 404, 123 C.C.C. 1, 30 C.R. 1 ....410, 412
Semayne's Case (1604), 77 E.R. 194, 5 Co. Rep. 91a (K.B.) 337
Shaw v. D.P.P. (1961), [1962] A.C. 220, [1961] 2 All E.R. 446,
[1961] 2 W.L.R. 897 (H.L.) 83
Steele v. Mountain Institution, [1990] 2 S.C.R. 1385,
60 C.C.C. (3d) 1, 80 C.R. (3d) 257 488
Strasser v. Roberge, [1979] 2 S.C.R. 953, 50 C.C.C. (2d) 129,
[1979] S.C.J. No. 79.. 228–29
Switzman v. Elbling, [1957] S.C.R. 285, 117 C.C.C. 129,
7 D.L.R. (2d) 337 26

Taylor v. The King, [1947] S.C.R. 462 407
Tesco Supermarkets Ltd. v. Nattrass (1971), [1972] A.C. 153,
[1971] 2 All E.R. 127, [1971] 2 W.L.R. 1166 (H.L.) 229
Thomson Newspapers Ltd. v. Canada (Director of
Investigation & Research), [1990] 1 S.C.R. 425,
76 C.R. (3d) 129, 54 C.C.C. (3d) 417 34
Toronto Star Newspapers Ltd. v. Canada, [2010] 1 S.C.R. 721,
2010 SCC 21.. 48

U.N.A. v. Alberta (A.G.), [1992] 1 S.C.R. 901,
71 C.C.C. (3d) 225, 13 C.R. (4th) 1 84
United States of America v. Burns and Rafay, [2001] 1 S.C.R. 283,
151 C.C.C. (3d) 97.. 78
United States of America v. Dynar, [1997] 2 S.C.R. 462,
115 C.C.C. (3d) 481, [1997] S.C.J. No. 64 .... 131, 135–37,
141, 153, 185, 188, 505
United States of America v. Nadarajah, 2010 ONCA 859 .... 459, 462

Weatherall v. Canada (A.G.), [1993] 2 S.C.R. 872,
    83 C.C.C. (3d) 1, 23 C.R. (4th) 1 34
Winko v. British Columbia (Forensic Psychiatric Institute)
    (1999), 135 C.C.C. (3d) 129 (S.C.C.) 92, 285–87
Woolmington v. D.P.P., [1935] A.C. 462, 104 L.J.K.B. 433,
    [1935] All E.R. Rep. 1, 153 L.T. 232 (H.L.) 50

Young v. R. (1950), 98 C.C.C. 195, 10 C.R. 142 (Que. C.A.) 158

INDEX

Aboriginal people, 2–3, 38, 95–96, 99, 286, 344–45, 471, 472, 474, 482, 483–85, 504

Absolute liability, 15–16, 67–68, 97, 215–22, 242–43, 496, 497, 507, 509, 515

Accessories. *See* Parties

Accessory after the fact, 12, 158–59

Actus reus, 9–11, 81–122, 130–34, 137– 39, 141–42, 146, 148–50, 154–55, 158, 228, 260, 304, 313, 383–91, 400, 428, 435–41, 453–59, 464, 506, 507, 509, 515

Aiding and abetting, 12–13, 147–53, 240, 370, 399–401, 433, 502, 515

Anti-terrorism Act, 461, 501

Appeals, 30–31, 474–75, 515

Arbitrary detention and imprisonment, 36–39

Attempts, 10–11, 115, 127–36, 138–39, 433, 505, 515

Automatism, 19, 55, 118, 255–61, 279– 80, 302–14, 426, 510, 511, 516

Bail, 38–39, 498, 499, 500, 516

Burden of proof. *See also* Presumption of innocence
   Automatism defence, 304–7

Intoxication defence, 250–61, 272–74, 249–52

Mental disorder defence, 283–85

Provocation, 405–6

Self-defence, necessity, and duress, 323–24

Strict liability and due diligence defence, 222, 224–25

Canadian Charter of Rights and Freedoms
   s. 1, 7, 9, 16, 31–33, 39–40, 54–55, 58, 60, 61, 64, 74–75, 172, 178, 218, 220–21, 226, 251–52, 256, 258, 262, 264–72, 284, 365–66, 393, 397, 486, 497, 499, 505
   s. 2, 32–33, 60–62, 142, 462
   s. 7, 7–8, 15–16, 20, 42, 45–47, 62–80, 82–84, 91, 93, 100, 107–8, 110, 119, 129–30, 139, 146, 156–57, 166, 169, 171–79, 187, 196, 213–14, 217–18, 219–21, 223–24, 229–30, 232–33, 234, 251–52, 255–58, 262, 264–72, 282–83, 285, 286, 287, 289, 297, 310, 320, 351, 352, 354, 355, 357, 362–71, 387, 392–94, 397–98, 404, 423–24, 429, 443, 450–51, 458–59, 461, 462, 463, 474, 497, 500, 503, 504, 507, 513

s. 8, 8, 33–37

s. 9, 8, 33, 37–39, 285

s. 10, 8, 33, 37, 38–42

s. 11, 7–9, 38–39, 45, 47–60, 74–75, 78, 83, 107–8, 172, 178, 214, 225–26, 251–52, 255–58, 262, 264–72, 275–76, 280, 282, 284, 310, 392–94, 397, 443, 501

s. 12, 75–76, 77–78, 175, 351, 478, 486–88, 492

s. 13, 59

s. 14, 58

s. 15, 75–76, 266, 286, 351, 362, 418, 5021, 503

s. 24, 31, 33–42, 79, 499, 500

s. 28, 266, 501

s. 33, 172, 178

Causation, 108–15, 121, 383–91, 516

Charter. See Canadian Charter of Rights and Freedoms

Common intent, 12–13, 154–57, 180–84

Common unlawful purpose. *See* Common intent

Consent, 21, 46–47, 57, 76, 81, 90, 101–6, 120, 130, 163, 189–92, 201–10, 249, 351, 433, 434–52, 466–67, 498, 506

Conspiracy, 1–12, 101, 136–41, 369

Controlled Drugs and Substances Act, 26

Corporate crime. *See* Corporate liability

Corporate liability, 15–17, 214–15, 221–22, 227, 230–44, 501, 508–10

Counselling, 11, 141–47, 240–41, 402, 433, 460, 516

Courts, 28–31

Crime control model, 500–2

Crime in Canada, 1–3

Criminal Code

s. 2, 234–36, 239, 288, 427

s. 4, 105

s. 6, 100–1

s. 9, 82–83, 117

s. 13, 101

s. 14, 104, 433–34

s. 16, 279–80, 283–85, 288, 293, 296–302, 304, 306, 315

s. 17, 76–77, 319–20, 362–71, 375–77, 380, 513

s. 19, 97, 121, 185, 509

s. 21, 12–13, 125–26, 147–57, 159–61, 181–82, 185, 240–41, 321, 370, 376–77, 399–401, 463, 506

s. 22, 12, 141, 145–47, 159–61, 240–41

s. 22.1, 215, 235–38, 241, 507, 509

s. 22.2, 209, 210, 215, 239–42, 509

s. 23, 158–59

s. 23.1, 145, 146, 155, 158

s. 24, 11, 125, 127–36

s. 25, 352

s. 26, 340

s. 33.1, 19, 261–74, 294, 312–13, 452, 498, 502, 510

s. 34, 19, 325–41, 350–51, 378–79, 512–13

s. 35, 325, 328–29, 342–50, 379, 513

s. 43, 75–76, 92, 351–52, 503

s. 45, 352

s. 83.01, 73, 139, 186–87, 458–63

s. 83.05, 459

s. 83.18, 126, 458–65

s. 83.19, 73, 126, 174, 458, 463–65, 507

s. 83.21, 126, 463–65

s. 129, 117

s. 150.1, 68, 104, 220, 242, 435

s. 161, 93

s. 163, 60–61

s. 172, 126

s. 179, 93

s. 215, 115–16

s. 217, 116

s. 219, 115, 197, 431

s. 220, 431–32

s. 222, 108–9, 384, 428–32

s. 224, 109, 384, 387

s. 225, 109, 384, 387

s. 226, 109, 384, 387

s. 229, 72, 74, 129, 180, 187–88, 192–93, 198, 391–99, 401–4, 411, 466, 506

s. 230, 74, 178, 392–94, 404, 506

s. 231, 86–87, 109, 383, 388–89, 394, 401–5, 466

s. 232, 383, 405–27, 466

s. 233, 427

s. 234, 383

s. 241, 63, 433–34

s. 264.1, 105

s. 265, 105, 128, 205, 435, 438, 443
s. 271, 434, 446
s. 272, 434, 446
s. 273, 165, 201–2, 434, 446
s. 273.1, 102, 434, 436–37, 439–40,
   444, 450, 498
s. 273.2, 130, 201–2, 206–7, 208, 210,
   242, 259, 445–51, 498
s. 276, 47
s. 277, 46–47
s. 286, 104
s. 319, 54
s. 322, 10–11, 105–6, 186, 453–54
s. 380, 454–57
s. 463, 127, 158
s. 464, 138, 141–45, 147
s. 465, 101, 136–41
s. 467, 457
s. 515, 39
s. 553, 49
s. 606, 473
s. 634, 49
s. 649, 49
s. 663, 427–28
s. 672.23, 280–82
s. 672.54, 286–87
s. 717, 489
s. 718, 469–71, 476–86, 490–91
s. 718.1, 469, 476–77
s. 718.2, 470–71, 476, 480, 482, 484–
   85, 490–91
s. 718.21, 471
s. 732.1, 490
s. 734, 492–93
s. 738, 493
s. 742.1, 490–91
s. 752, 491
Criminal process, 3–4, 498–505

Defences. See Due diligence; Duress;
   Entrapment; Intoxication;
   Mental disorder defence; Neces-
   sity; Provocation; Self-defence
Directing mind of a corporation, 17, 214,
   227, 230–32, 508–10. See also Se-
   nior officer of an organization
Disclosure, 45–46
Disease of the mind, 289–95, 302–4, 516
Division of powers, 5–7, 25–33, 516

Due diligence, 16–17, 55, 67–68, 94,
   216–19, 222, 224–27, 260–61, 497,
   509, 517
Due process model, 6–7, 33–45, 498–
   500
Duress, 18–20, 76–77, 181–84, 362–77,
   512, 513, 517

Emotional blows, 289–90, 309–11
Entrapment, 42–44, 496, 517
Evidential burdens, 55, 56–58, 252–53,
   304–7, 323–24, 443–44
Excuse, 319–21, 354–56, 406

Fault element. See Mens rea
Federal jurisdiction. See Division of
   powers
Fetal alcohol spectrum disorder, 292
Fines, 219, 233, 492–93, 436
Fitness to stand trial, 280–82
Fraud, 454–57, 509

General intent, 18–19, 20, 75, 248–50,
   253–72, 510, 517
Guilty plea, 472–73, 485, 500

Ignorance of the law, 94–100, 185, 218,
   449–50, 509
Impossibility, 134–36, 140–41, 144–45
Infanticide, 427–28
Insanity. See Mental disorder defence
Intent. See Mens rea
Interpretation Act, 85–86
Intoxication, 17–20, 75, 107–8, 118–19,
   179–80, 198, 206, 246–77, 293–94,
   312–13, 337, 426, 451–52, 498,
   510–13, 518
Involuntary intoxication, 118, 272–74,
   313
Irresistible impulse, 300-1

Judicial interim release. See Bail
Juries, 28–30, 48–50
Justification, 319–21, 328–29, 343–44,
   354–56, 406

Knowledge, 71–75, 129, 182–84, 187–88,
   395, 397–99, 442, 445, 446–47,
   463–65

Mens rea, 9, 10–11, 13–15, 66–75, 98–99, 102, 106–8, 128–31, 139–40, 142–44, 146–47, 150–53, 155–57, 158–59, 163–212, 228–29, 230–32, 251–64, 300–2, 321, 365, 375–77, 392–97, 424, 425–27, 441–52, 453–54, 455–57, 458, 496, 509, 518

Mental disorder defence, 19, 119, 262, 279–304, 308–9, 313, 426, 498, 510–13, 518

Mental element. See Mens rea

Mistake of fact, 17–18, 95–97, 164, 179–80, 202–7, 224, 443–52, 498, 509

Mistake of law. See Ignorance of the law

Moral involuntariness, 76–77, 117–19, 255–61, 302–14, 362–75, 508, 511, 513, 518

Motive, 184–87, 462–63

Necessity, 18, 353–62, 512, 518

Negligence, 13–17, 68–71, 166–69, 176–77, 193–201, 223–29, 236–39, 429–32, 497, 506–8, 509

Not criminally responsible by reason of mental disorder. See Mental disorder defence

Objective approach to defences, 17–20, 75–77, 321–23, 334–38, 344, 361–62, 374–75, 412–22, 512

Objective mens rea. See Negligence

Omissions, 9–10, 82, 115–17, 506, 518

Organizational liability. See Corporate liability

Ordinary person. See Reasonable person

Parole, 44, 22, 28, 98, 183, 383, 401, 481, 484, 488

Participation in crimes. See Accessory after the fact; Aiding and abetting; Common intent; Counselling; Parties

Parties, 11–13, 145–59, 233, 236–38, 399–401, 402, 433, 513

Persuasive burdens, 51–52, 57–58, 226, 228, 304–7, 310, 324

Presumption of innocence, 9, 16, 50–58, 74, 79, 182, 200, 214, 225, 228–29, 243, 252, 256, 258–59, 270–71, 276, 280, 282, 284, 310, 394, 426, 496, 497, 499, 501, 502, 510, 518

Prisons, 28, 500

Probation, 28, 98, 183, 219, 233, 234, 470, 489–93, 510, 519

Prohibited act. See Actus reus

Provincial jurisdiction. See Division of powers

Provocation, 21, 323–24, 405–27, 512, 519

Public welfare offences. See Regulatory offences

Purposive construction, 84–88

Quantum of proof, 9, 50–51, 76–77, 225–26, 275–77, 283–85, 323–24

Reasonable person, 19–20, 68–71, 166–69, 193–201, 207, 208, 223, 263–64, 321–23, 335, 337, 362–63, 372, 374–75, 406, 412–25, 430–32, 447, 454, 497, 501, 508, 512–13

Recklessness, 14, 73, 142–44, 151, 152, 170–71, 183–84, 191–92, 206, 254, 395, 403, 425, 442, 446, 455, 507

Regulatory offences, 6, 15–17, 27, 108, 116, 173, 213–29, 234, 507, 508–10, 519

Restitution, 493, 503–5

Right to counsel, 33, 39–42, 50, 499

Search and seizure, 33–37, 519

Self-defence, 18–19, 319–21, 324–51, 512, 519

Senior officer of an organization 17, 214–15, 227, 230, 233–43, 507, 509

Sentencing, 21–22, 30–31, 401, 403, 469–94, 500, 501, 503

Sexual assault, 20, 57, 101–4, 107, 130, 204–7, 259–61, 275–76, 404, 498, 502–3, 506, 510

Sleepwalking, 292–93, 295, 307–9, 313, 511

Specific intent, 18, 248–53, 275, 510–11

State of mind. See Mens rea

Strict construction, 84–88, 505

Strict liability, 16, 222–29, 260, 519

Subjective component of defences, 321–23, 329, 357–60, 367

Subjective mens rea
    as constitutional requirement, 71–75, 171–79

common law presumptions, 169–71, 442, 497
corporations, 230–32, 239–42, 509–10
distinguished from objective fault, 166–69, 506–8 *See also* Transferred *mens rea*

Terrorism, 5, 11, 73, 101, 126, 139, 174, 186–87, 404, 457–65, 501, 504, 505, 507
Transferred *mens rea*, 192–93, 396–97. *See also* Subjective *mens rea*

Unfitness to stand trial, 280–82, 520
Unfulfilled crimes. *See* Attempts; Conspiracy

Vagueness, 10, 64, 91–93, 460–61, 505
Vicarious liability, 229–30, 221
Victimization, 1–3
Victims' rights, 407–10, 483–84, 500, 502–5
Voluntariness, 10–11, 75–77, 117–19, 255–61, 272–74, 302–4, 369–70, 508, 510

War crimes, 14–15, 59–60, 72–73, 79, 101, 171–74, 506–7
Wilful blindness, 143, 152, 189–91, 206, 400–1, 442, 444–46, 507

Youth Criminal Justice Act, 26, 29, 101, 473, 489

ABOUT THE AUTHOR

Kent Roach is a professor of law and the Prichard-Wilson Chair of Law and Public Policy at the University of Toronto Faculty of Law. He is a graduate of the University of Toronto and of Yale University, and a former law clerk to Justice Bertha Wilson of the Supreme Court of Canada. Professor Roach has been editor-in-chief of the *Criminal Law Quarterly* since 1998. In 2002, he was elected a Fellow of the Royal Society of Canada. He is the author of twelve books, including *Constitutional Remedies in Canada* (winner of the Walter Owen Prize); *Due Process and Victims' Rights* (shortlisted for the Donner Prize); *The Supreme Court on Trial* (shortlisted for the Donner Prize); *Brian Dickson: A Judge's Journey* (winner of the Dafoe Prize; co-authored with Robert J. Sharpe); and *The 9/11 Effect: Comparative Counter-Terrorism* (winner of the David Mundell Medal). He is the co-editor of several collections of essays and published casebooks and is also co-author of the *Charter of Rights and Freedoms* volume in Irwin Law's Essentials of Canadian Law series. He has also written over 160 articles and chapters published in Australia, China, Hong Kong, India, Israel, Italy, Singapore, South Africa, the United Kingdom, and the United States, as well as in Canada. Professor Roach has served as research director for the Inquiry into Pediatric Forensic Pathology in Ontario (the Goudge Inquiry) and for the Commission of Inquiry into the Investigation of the Bombing of Air India Flight 182. In both capacities, he edited multiple volumes of research studies. He served on the research advisory committee for the inquiry into the rendition of Maher Arar and the Ipperwash Inquiry into the killing of Dudley George. He is presently an advisor to the Truth and Reconciliation Commission on Residential Schools. Professor Roach has represented Aboriginal and civil liberties groups in many interventions before the courts, including *Gladue*, *Wells*, and *Ipeelee* on sentencing Aboriginal offenders, *Latimer* on mandatory minimum sentences, *Stillman*, *Dunedin Construction*, and *Ward* on *Charter* remedies, *Golden* on strip searches, *Khawaja* on the definition of terrorism and *Corbiere* and *Sauvé* on voting rights. He is involved with the Asper Centre for Constitutional Rights.